IN THE RING

WITH

JACK DEMPSEY

Part III: The Championship and Beyond

ADAM J. POLLACK

WIN BY
KO

Win By KO Publications

IOWA CITY

In the Ring With Jack Dempsey
Part III: The Championship and Beyond

Adam J. Pollack

(ISBN-13): 978-1-949783-10-0

(hardcover: 50# acid-free alkaline paper)

Includes footnotes and index.

Cover design by Adam J. Pollack and Gwyn Flowers ©

Cover photo colorizations by Gwyn Flowers (front cover) and Gregory Speciale (back cover) ©

Manufactured in the United States of America.

Win By KO Publications
Iowa City, Iowa
winbykopublications.com

Contents

CHAPTER 1

Resting on Laurels While Others Fight

Following Jack Dempsey's exciting 2nd round knockout of Luis Firpo on September 14, 1923, which many called the greatest fight ever, the champion was more popular than ever. In late September 1923, the *New York Evening Telegram's* George Underwood wrote that Jack Dempsey was the greatest heavyweight champion of all time. John L. Sullivan perhaps could hit harder with his right and was stronger and more combative. Bob Fitzsimmons perhaps could hit as hard with his left, was wilier and craftier, and just as courageous. Jim Jeffries had a more powerful straight left, and perhaps was a trifle more rugged and enduring. Jim Corbett was faster, more skillful, and scientific. Jack Johnson was a better defensive fighter and could uppercut with both hands better.

> But none of the former heavyweight champions can compare with Dempsey in all-round ring brilliance. None of them boasted to such a remarkable degree the many essentials which go to make up a great fighter. None of them had a fistic chain so uniformly solid, with each and every link so strong and well molded. There is no heavyweight in ring history who combines bulk, strength, stamina, speed, skill, science, accurate and forceful hitting with both hands, courage, wiliness, and ring generalship in such proportion as does Dempsey.

Although certain fighters could boast stronger separate links than him, never was there one whose whole makeup was so uniformly strong and solid. "As an all-around fighter boxing never has seen Dempsey's equal as a heavyweight." In some ways, he had yet to be tested by an equal foeman, a high-class all-round good heavyweight.

> Jack has beaten mere bulk and strength in Willard; he beat speed, skill and science in Gibbons; he beat wonderful defensive ability in Battling Levinsky; he beat rugged strength and an untrained wallop in Firpo; courage, skill and a lightning fast and forceful right hand in Carpentier, and speed and a lightning fast left hand in Fred Fulton. He beat fairly good all-around ability in Billy Miske ... He beat mere courage and ruggedness in Billy Brennan.

Underwood said there was but one man who truly could test him.

> The one heavyweight of the present generation who, like Dempsey, combines most of the important ring essentials – bulk, strength, speed, skill, two-handed hitting power, courage and ring generalship – Dempsey persistently has avoided. Harry Wills is the man. Wills possesses, or at least did possess, almost as many rare ring

4

qualifications as Dempsey. He was stronger than Jack in some things and weaker in others.

But overall, Wills was almost as solid and uniform as Dempsey.

Wills had been inactive for a year. He had been handicapped by a lack of matches for a few years. He was avoided. If he was anywhere near what he was a year ago, he and the Manassa Mauler "would furnish the greatest ring duel in history, and for the first time in his entire career Dempsey would be put to the acid test." It would be a ring classic.

Underwood called Dempsey a Dr. Jekyll and Mr. Hyde, for he never fought two fights alike. He was at his best against Willard, showing his footwork, head movement, and fast combinations. He was a superb boxer, a savage fighter, and a wonderful, forceful, accurate, two-handed hitter. He showed at his best in the 4th round against Carpentier, but laid back and boxed prior to that. He was more of a boxer against Gibbons, refraining from slugging. Against Firpo, he was only a hitter, slugging away and beating him at his own game, but without the lightning footwork, gliding in, out, and around, or bobbing, weaving, and shifting, or use of bewildering feints. "Dempsey just stood up and slugged Firpo into submission." He left everything else in the dressing room.

> Jack now seems to have the habit of boxing against a boxer and fighting against a fighter. If he ever meets Harry Wills, however, Dempsey will have to flash forth in all his wonderful all-around brilliance. Against Wills, Dempsey cannot hope to win by mere boxing or by mere rough house slugging. The champion will have to play every card in the pugilistic deck to win. Wills can match skill with skill, punch with punch, strength with strength and cunning with cunning. If Wills is Wills and Dempsey is Dempsey when they meet, if they ever do meet, you will witness a contest unprecedented in ring history. No two heavyweights of such all-around ring brilliance ever met in the roped square.[1]

Writer "Uppercut" asked whether Harry Wills ever would get a chance at the title. A review of Dempsey's career showed that he had been knocked out only once. "He candidly admits that he permitted that alleged knockout for a purpose – to get a few hundred dollars when he was direfully in need of funds." Since he became champion, it appeared that he had cautiously and thoughtfully side-stepped Wills. Otherwise, he had fought the division's best. Dempsey-Wills had been in demand for more than three years, but no definite arrangements ever had been made. Once Wills attempted a court injunction to stop Dempsey-Firpo, Dempsey made it clear that the clash was even more remote.[2]

Frank Menke predicted that Wills never would get a crack at the title. He believed that Dempsey intended to fight Gibbons and Firpo again in 1924. Yet, "Dempsey's failure to meet Wills cannot be construed as the

[1] *New York Evening Telegram*, September 30, 1923.
[2] *New York Daily News*, September 30, 1923.

champion's fault." He was neither afraid nor unwilling to fight Wills. He had his price, and realized such a fight would yield a huge gate and profit for a promoter, so he wanted his fair share.

> But every promoter knows that somewhere in the high political circles of the state they frown upon the idea of a white man mingling with a negro, especially in championship endeavors. The political powers are afraid that the tussle might arouse race feeling and do a lot of other things which might destroy the politicians, who now dominate in the Empire State.

There was little assurance that politicians in other states wouldn't take the same view of matters. No promoter would want to shell out big money in forfeit deposits, advance payments, and pre-fight expenses, only to have the contest thwarted by the politicians at the last minute. Very few states could generate the big revenue required for Dempsey-Wills.[3]

In other news, as of September 15, 1923, Oklahoma Governor Jack C. Walton, who had been elected earlier that year, in an effort to crack down on the Ku Klux Klan's "reign of terror," which included violence, torture, mutilation, and lynching, and its assertion of control over the state, including via prosecuting attorneys and juries, making it impossible for citizens to be protected, declared a state of insurrection and rebellion against the state's laws and constitution by the "invisible empire." He declared martial law, requesting the state's military to occupy various places, and suspending the writ of habeas corpus. As a result, Governor Walton was impeached, and on November 19, 1923, convicted and removed from office.[4]

Writer "Fair Play" said a Harry Greb bout against Jack Dempsey was quietly cooking. "Greb, in the opinion of many fans, has a better chance than any one of outpointing the champion. … Jack does not care particularly for any fighter who presents a moving target." Regardless, "There is now an almost unanimous opinion that [Dempsey] is probably the greatest heavyweight who ever held the title."

Fair Play further said,

> A great deal of Harry Wills' prestige comes from the fact that he is a negro. Men of color in the ring impress the fans chiefly because they do not show the bruises and other results of blows as clearly as white men. The impression is they are harder to hurt than a white man. … Ring experience shows that they are hurt as easily by a wallop as men of any other color.[5]

Local Los Angeles boxing expert George Hussey said Dempsey could be hit, but it "seems that when Dempsey is hit and stung he fights all the harder." He proved that against Carpentier and Firpo, coming back from big blows and plastering his foes all over. Firpo was big, with tremendous

---

[3] *Rochester Evening Journal and the Post Express*, October 1, 1923.
[4] *Tulsa Tribune, Lawton Constitution*, September 16, 1923; *Tulsa World*, November 20, 1923.
[5] *Evening Star*, September 26, 1923.

strength, but Dempsey's strength could not be overlooked. "Jack doesn't put 'em away in a punch, but after he gets through they are not the same fighters." The question was what impact the beating that Firpo took would have on him.[6]

A Chicago paper claimed that while in Los Angeles, Dempsey allegedly privately said, "I'll never give Wills a chance to make a dollar. Not if I can help it. He tried every way to stop my fight with Firpo – and I'm off him for life. Furthermore, the way I feel about it right now, I don't think I'll ever give any colored fighter a chance at my title." Jack was inclined to give Gibbons a return match.[7]

On October 11, 1923 at Queensboro Stadium in Long Island City, New York, before a crowd of 7,000 or 8,000, in his first fight in over a year, 211-pound Harry Wills (79-7-7) knocked out 190-pound white Homer Smith (47-24-7) in the 2nd round. Smith went down five times in the 1st round, all from body punches. Wills decked him a few more times in the 2nd, the final blow being a right uppercut to the chin.

Smith had lasted 10 rounds with Firpo by utilizing survival tactics, running, grabbing, and going down 15 - 20 times, but the relative performances helped boost Wills, who was both clever and hard-hitting. Of course, both Dempsey and Miske had stopped Smith in the 1st round.

The *Brooklyn Standard Union* said Wills dispelled a lot of uncertainty as to whether he was a logical contender for Dempsey. It was an impressive showing. Edward Tranter said Wills demonstrated his suitability as a Dempsey opponent. The *Brooklyn Daily Eagle* said Smith had offered up no resistance at all, but just took punishment.[8]

Interestingly, Homer Smith was the first white opponent to take on Harry Wills since Gunboat Smith in 1921 (in Havana). It was the first time that a white man fought Wills in the United States since Fred Fulton in July 1920.

The *Buffalo Commercial's* Charles Murray said, "Wills looms up as an infinitely better fighter than Firpo. … Dempsey has made up his mind never to fight Wills. … When Wills tried to stop the Dempsey-Firpo fight, Wills cooked his own goose."

Even if Dempsey changed his mind and once again agreed to fight Wills, "what state in the union would stand for it? Somebody else will have to give you the answer." There simply was no place to host the fight.

The *New York Age's* William Clark said there was evidence that New York was discriminating against the colored athlete, and "this is particularly noticeable in boxing." Harry Wills could fight, but not for the title.[9]

George Underwood said New Orleans Panther Wills showed championship form against Smith and was as good as ever. He was in great physical shape, strong, and tremendously powerful, with good

[6] *Los Angeles Times*, October 3, 1923.
[7] *Collyer's Eye*, October 6, 1923.
[8] *Brooklyn Standard Union, Brooklyn Daily Eagle, New York Daily News, Buffalo Enquirer*, October 12, 1923.
[9] *Buffalo Commercial, New York Age*, October 13, 1923.

judgment of timing and distance. Wills was a seasoned, experienced veteran who could punch fast, sharp, and accurately with both hands; a ring general with every trick of the trade at his disposal. He was Dempsey's only real rival, but likely never would get a chance at the title.

> To beat Wills, Dempsey would have to call on every bit of ring strategy, skill, speed, heart, and punch he possesses. No one knows that any better than do Manager Jack Kearns and Promoter Rickard. Dempsey would be taking a desperate chance with Wills. … That is why Harry Wills never has been given the championship opportunity to which he is clearly entitled, and why he never will be given that opportunity as long as Tex Rickard and Jack Kearns hold the boxing game in the hollow of their hands.

Underwood believed that Rickard/Kearns would not want to risk the potential of their cash-cow losing; so Wills never would get a title fight.[10]

That same day, October 11, 1923, in Boston, before 6,000 fans, 166-pound Tommy Loughran (39-9-4) won an official 10-round points decision over 168-pound Harry Greb (210-11-18). According to the *Boston Globe's* Lawrence Sweeney, although Greb was aggressive and active as ever, Loughran stepped back and countered effectively with the cleaner, sharper blows while cleverly slipping and blocking punches, making Greb miss more than he landed. Greb "completely ignored the rules," grasping the neck with one arm and ripping punches to the body and face while he held the head, and also hit with open gloves.[11]

Sam Langford said, "Dempsey is no doubt a great fighter and a real mixer in the ring. He had to be a fighter to take what Firpo handed him and then turn around and beat him at his own game. … Jack, in my opinion, will beat Harry Wills if they ever meet."[12]

Jack Dempsey wrote that three times since he became champion, foes had come within a few punches of putting him down or out but could not do it, either because his chin was a little too tough, or they could not figure out how to do it, or Jack was smart enough to get himself out of trouble. In 1920, Bill Brennan hit him on the chin with everything he had back of the punch. "It rattled me from head to foot." Two or three more shots possibly might have dropped him. "I just grabbed Bill and kept in too close for him to hit me, until such time as the fog had cleared and I had steadied and was able to fight my way out of trouble." In the 2nd round with Carpentier, a right drove him back, though the follow-up blows did not have the same steam, for he was too far away.

> Then there was Firpo. I can say Luis certainly smacked me a beaut within five seconds after the fight began. That was a punch that hurt me more than any that was landed in the fight. It shook me from top to bottom and hurt me quite a bit. The fact is that the

[10] *New York Evening Telegram*, October 14, 1923; *Pittsburgh Courier*, October 20, 1923.
[11] *Boston Globe*, October 12, 1923.
[12] *Brooklyn Daily Eagle*, October 14, 1923.

punch hurt me so much and set me into such a wild rage that I haven't any clear or connected idea of everything that happened from that time on until the first round was over.

After I got to my corner in the second and got a little dash of water, everything cleared up nicely and I was completely myself again. I knew that I had gone though a rather tempestuous round and that Firpo, even though I had knocked him to the floor on quite a few occasions, was still tough and dangerous.

So I went out for that second, a little more carefully and with a little more caution, found the opening I wanted, hit Firpo without too much danger to myself- and the fight came to a speedy end.[13]

Harry Wills' manager Paddy Mullins turned down a Tex Rickard offer for another fight between Wills and Bill Tate.[14]

On October 19, 1923, American League Baseball President Ban Johnson persuaded owners to ban (temporarily, at least) professional boxing from taking place in any American League baseball parks.[15]

On October 22, 1923 in Newark, New Jersey, 166-pound Harry Greb fought a very close and competitive 12-round no decision against 163-pound Lou Bogash (87-11-19). Several newspapers reported a Greb victory, but several also reported that Bogash won. Some reported a close victory for one or the other, while others reported a very clear victory for either fighter. Opinions differed greatly.

Georg Underwood said Greb fought foully, including wrestling and holding and hitting, but still was beaten badly, 9-1-2 in rounds.

Nine-tenths of Harry's blows were delivered while he was holding Bogash with one hand and hitting him with the other. The champion butted often, heeled continually, repeatedly thrust out his open hand in an endeavor to stick his thumb in one of his opponent's eyes and his fingers in the other.

Referee Henry Lewis allowed Greb to get away with it all.

Yet all the rough house tactics Greb called into play couldn't prevent his receiving the beating of his gay young life.

Utterly unable to solve Bogash's puzzling style, Harry was forced to take all of his opponent's thumbs and get in mighty few in return. Bogash won so clearly and convincingly that even Greb realized what a sorry showing he was making and tried to turn it all off with a sickly smile.

Two things alone prevented Bogash from being crowned champion. One was that the bout was a twelve-round, no-decision affair which went the limit. The other was that both men were over

[13] *Pittsburgh Press*, October 14, 1923.
[14] *Brooklyn Daily Times*, October 18, 1923.
[15] *New York Times, Brooklyn Daily Eagle, Brooklyn Daily Times*, October 20, 1923. Clearly, the ban did not last, for fights were held in Yankee Stadium the following year.

the middleweight limit of 160 pounds, the champion scaling 166 pounds and the challenger tipping the beam at 163. ...

If Referee Lewis rightly had performed his duties he would have disqualified Greb long before the end of the bout, and if the men had been at weight that would have meant the crowning of a new champion despite the fact it was a no-decision bout. But the referee was delinquent and allowed Greb to commit everything short of murder. ... Greb was allowed to violate almost every rule of the Marquis of Queensberry code.

One round was about the same as the other.

Bogash, in his peculiar low crouch, bobbing, shifting head thrust out like a fighting cock's, would wait his chance and then suddenly leap inside Greb's guard like Don Quixote charging the windmill. Lou would lash his left to the body, whip it up to the head and then rip and slash away at Greb's midsection with rapid fire body blows.

When Greb wasn't heeling, gouging and butting he was trying to hold Bogash with his left and wallop him with the right or vice versa.

Bogash quickly solved Greb's style, while Harry found Lou a puzzling enigma.

Greb only won one round, the ninth. The first and sixth was even. Bogash took all the others, some of them by a margin which made the champion look like a tyro.

If Bogash holds his present form and gets Greb in a decision contest here in New York there would be a new champion as sure as you're born.

Fair Play reported that many of Bogash's friends got to the wire first to report that he won over the champion on points.

Yes, he did - not. Harry fought his usual type of battle, in close with his arms doing the piston act up and down and then suddenly changing to the sidewise windmill idea. The crowd had their chance as usual to hoot Greb for the way he used his head in clinches ... Greb's head action seemed more designed to avoid the hard impact of blows than to injure his opponent. ...

As the battle went Lou put up a surprisingly good fight. He took the third and fourth rounds by virtue of smashing clips to Greb's face and in the tenth and eleventh he gave a little better than he received.

But in the main Greb plastered his man good and proper with those stinging wallops that do not knock out but do cut a man up.

Writer Lev, in the *Paterson Morning Call*, wrote,

From our way of looking at it, Bogash came out on top. The Bridgeport boy smacked the Smokytowner plenty, and had him missing like a newly overhauled Ford engine. Greb, outside of a flurry here and there, confined his offense to rough tactics, which made him a target for more booes than Heinz has beans. Greb was razzed to a nice brown, and not until he confined himself to the dressing room did the shower of berries stop falling upon his ears. Bogash, on the other hand, was cheered to the rafters.

Bogash had a style which bothered Greb at all times. He crouched low and Greb could not reach him, try as he would. Lew would fly at Greb when he attacked, starting with a left to the belly, a left to the face, and then biff, bang, bang with both hands. He outfought Greb in this fashion the greater part of the way.

Regis Welsh for the *Pittsburgh Post* said Greb decisively outpointed Bogash but had a fight on his hands all the way. Bogash was tough, willing, rugged, and game, had an almost perfect left hook, and a two-fisted body attack. Bogash could dish it and take it. Still, Greb won 7-3-2. The sustained virility of Greb's irresistible attack, eager to go in and mix, for the most part proved to be too much. "Greb was Greb, that's all there was to it."

Ray Coll for the *Pittsburgh Gazette Times* said Greb won with ease. He moved, danced, ducked, jabbed the face, drawing blood from cuts, and hit the body, landing 3 to 1. What few the willing mixer Bogash did land, Greb took with a smile.

As a matter of fact, strange as it may seem, it was perhaps the cleanest fight that the champion has ever fought. Those who have seen the Pittsburgher in action more than often were unanimous that Harry was fighting at top form tonight. There were boos from the crowd, but they were few and far between. In fact, the boos were drowned out by the "yes" men in the audience, as our friends the English would say.

In breaking clean, fighting clean, the champion showed one of the best fights of his career. That's not a compliment. It's a fact.

From the very first gong the champion stuck his left hand out and worked a right hook to the body and then to the head. The combination proved to be the charm, because it won him the fight. Harry seldom changed his program. ...

In conclusion, let us all say that Greb won. Don't let anybody kid you into saying that he didn't.

Tom Dugan for the *Passaic Daily Herald* said Greb did not make an impressive showing, persistently holding with one hand and punching with the other. Because it was a no decision bout, Greb did not lose his title. "The reception he got last night for his unsportsmanlike tactics followed him from the ring to his dressing room."

Ed Van Every, scoring it 7-1-4 for Bogash, wrote,

> Lou Bogash outpointed Harry Greb. … Greb and Bogash fought hard the twelve rounds, with the champion taking a good pummeling in most of them. Bogash had an advantage in seven rounds, only one went to Greb, the other[s] being even.

> Greb was guilty of his usual foul tactics and came in for hissing. Practically all of the 6000 present were with the Providence boxer. Greb butted with his head, hit with the heel of his glove, shoved his thumbs into his opponent's eyes – in fact, displayed his well-known foul tricks, and got away with it. But he took a good pummeling from the rough Bogash and but for his remarkable endurance would have been in trouble several times.

The *Newark Evening News* said Greb behaved like a champion and established himself firmly by his splendid work. He did well enough to convince the club that he would be a safe investment against Battling Siki. He was willing to mix, and although at times he did foul, his offenses were not gross enough to warrant anything more than a mild censuring. It was a great fight. Greb certainly did not have an easy time of it with the rugged Bogash, who impressed as well. "It was necessary for Greb to fight his hardest and on some occasions Greb was plastered hard and plenty by Bogash."

Papers such as the *Brooklyn Standard Union*, *New York Daily News*, *New York Times*, and *Pittsburgh Press* via dispatches reported a Bogash victory, 6-5-1. The *Brooklyn Daily Times* reported that Bogash won 4-3-5.

The *Brooklyn Daily Eagle*, *Jersey Journal*, and several others via dispatches reported a close Greb victory, 5-4-3.[16]

Although he no longer trained him, Jimmy De Forest said Jack Dempsey was the greatest champion of all time. In his opinion, Jack Johnson vs. Jack Dempsey would have furnished the greatest heavyweight fight of all time. Both were supermen, and next to Dempsey, Johnson was the greatest champion. Both had everything. They could hit hard, take it, had endurance, speed, accuracy, force, ability to strike from any angle, and a tireless, nimble pair of legs.

Dempsey was a rough, tough, strong slugger, but he also was a master of the art of boxing and its finest points. He had speed equal to any.

If Johnson and Dempsey met, De Forest was not certain who would win, but was inclined to give Dempsey a shade, for two reasons. "The first is, other things being equal between a white and a black man, I have noticed that invariably the white man could exercise a psychological superiority over his brother of lesser civilization. Somewhat the white man always has managed to assume and maintain the mastery." The other reason was that Dempsey had shown a grimmer, more determined will to

[16] *Brooklyn Daily Eagle, Jersey Journal, Asbury Park Press, Paterson Morning Call, Newark Ledger, Buffalo Commercial, Buffalo Express, Elmira Star-Gazette, Buffalo Courier, Pittsburgh Post, Pittsburgh Gazette Times, Pittsburgh Press, Paterson News, Brooklyn Standard Union, New York Daily News, New York Telegram, New York Times, Brooklyn Daily Times, Courant, Paterson Morning Call, Passaic Daily Herald, Newark Evening News,* October 23, 1923. See also *Paterson Morning Call,* October 24, 1923: *Lewiston Evening Journal,* October 25, 1923.

win than Johnson. Johnson was more amiable, whereas Dempsey had a greater desire to defeat his foe decisively. Dempsey was more aggressive and active offensively; his goal to knock out his foe. Johnson was more cautious. However, Johnson was the greatest defensive fighter ever. He had a perfect sense of distance. He had great recuperative powers and could hide when he was in distress. He was great at feinting. Yet, De Forest believed that Dempsey was wiser and better, and also did not allow himself to dissipate as much as Johnson did.[17]

De Forest subsequently said the pro-Willard crowd's claims that Dempsey's gloves were loaded were false. Dempsey did to Willard what he had done to most top men before Jess and after, including Firpo, for he had natural speed and power. Speed was most important against a guy like Willard, and to load the wraps would have weighted them and slowed him down, which would have been counterproductive. "All I put on them when he went into the ring was seven wraps of soft gauze and two wraps of adhesive tape."[18]

With the profits from the Firpo fight, Dempsey and Kearns obtained full title to a large apartment house they had bought in Los Angeles.[19]

The *Brooklyn Citizen* reported,

> Wills insists emphatically that he will never fight for Rickard, and unless he changes his mind he will never get a shot at Dempsey, because the champion does not care to work for any promoter but Rickard. Dempsey has made money when Rickard was running the show, and he found out in Montana last summer that Rickard is the lone promoter in the country who can make big money for him.[20]

Jack Thompson left, and Harry Wills, right

On November 5, 1923 in Newark, New Jersey, before a crowd of 12,000, 209-pound Harry Wills stopped 200-pound black Jack Thompson in the 4th round. Thompson had taken a terrific bombardment of hooks and uppercuts in a rough-and-tumble fight before going down in the 4th round for a nine-count. He took more punishment before going down again, at which point his seconds tossed in the towel.

In his previous fight, in May 1923 in Cuba, Thompson had lost a very dull 12-round newspaper decision to 45-year-old former champion Jack Johnson.

[17] *San Francisco Examiner*, October 21, 1923; *New York Age*, October 27, 1923.
[18] *Philadelphia Inquirer*, November 3, 1923.
[19] *Glens Falls Post-Star*, October 31, 1923.
[20] *Brooklyn Citizen*, November 1, 1923.

Many reporters said Wills was fighting soft touches who could not compete with him, so it was unclear how he might do against a puncher who took it to him like Dempsey would. Some even questioned Harry's punch. The *Paterson News* said Wills showed little class in victory. The *Passaic Daily Herald* said Harry had gone back and had better wait until Dempsey was an old man.

The *Newark Evening News* said Wills failed to impress. "Matching Wills singlehanded with Dempsey would leave the promoters open to a charge of manslaughter, judging from Wills's work against Thompson last night." It took Wills "a thousand blows," with "more than half of them illegitimate punches such as the rabbit and kidney blows and hit on the break away," before finally putting the slow punching-bag Thompson down. Still, Thompson "managed to land with his left alarmingly often to Wills's face." Thompson could not punch, and Wills, with his brute strength, simply squeezed him in the clinches, held with his right around the neck and punched with his left. That won him the fight, not superior speed or boxing ability. He showed no footwork. "His showing was null and void, and when Dempsey gets through with him, if Wills doesn't queer his own chances of such a match before the time comes ripe, Dempsey will perhaps queer him for the remainder of his fistic career." This writer said there was little question that Wills first needed to meet and dispose of Firpo or Gibbons before he could go clamoring for a chance at the champion.

The *Brooklyn Daily Eagle* said Wills would gain nothing by toppling more setups like Thompson. Still, Harry showed that he could punch, and did what was expected of him.

The *Buffalo Commercial's* Charles Murray said Thompson used to be Dempsey's sparring partner (in 1922). Even with big gloves in practice bouts in which Dempsey was holding back, the champ still managed to knock Thompson out cold with a right to the chin in the 2nd round. Hence, by comparison, Wills doing his best in a real fight with small gloves but requiring 4 rounds to stop Thompson did not add to his credit.

The *Daily News'* James Crusinberry noted that after the 3rd round, a white spectator hollered at Wills, "You're a bum. Dempsey would finish you with one punch." Paddy Mullins responded by noting that no one had criticized Firpo for taking on lesser men.[21]

On that same date, November 5, 1923, in Pittsburgh, 164-pound Harry Greb came from behind to win a 10-round no decision over 176-pound Soldier Jones. Despite having been decked twice and badly hurt in the 1st round, and hurt again in the 2nd, Greb showed his ability to recuperate well, winning clearly from the 3rd round on, despite the early knockdowns he suffered.[22]

---

[21] *Brooklyn Daily Eagle, Brooklyn Standard Union, Paterson News, Passaic Daily Herald, Newark Evening News, Buffalo Commercial,* November 6, 1923; *Buffalo Commercial,* November 7, 1923.

[22] *Pittsburgh Post, Press, Gazette-Times, Sun,* November 6, 1923. In 1921, Gene Tunney had stopped Soldier Jones in the 7th round. Greb previously had stopped Jones in the 4th round in 1921 (though dropped by a body shot) and in the 5th round in 1919.

On November 7, 1923 in Omaha, Nebraska, before a crowd of about 5,000, 189-pound Billy Miske scored a KO4 over 206-pound Bill Brennan, who seemed to be out of shape and slow, and put up such a poor effort/performance that the commission suspended him. In the 3rd round, Miske decked Brennan with a right, and the bell saved him. In the 4th round, a short right to the jaw floored Brennan for the count.

The Firpo fight apparently had drained everything that was left of Brennan, who had claimed to be retired after that contest. Some argued that Bill never was the same again after the Dempsey championship fight. Brennan said he was through with the game for good. "Brennan...was no more like his former self than daylight is like darkness."

Miske had just recovered from a trip to the hospital, and the local press said he did not seem to be the same man either. "Miske hadn't fought since he beat Foley here many months ago because of sickness, and from his work it seems that he hasn't recovered."

However, Tommy Gibbons, who was on a theatrical tour and had attended the contest, said, "Miske surprised me by his punching ability. He seemed to be hitting with all his old-time skill. You know, Bill has been sick, and was reported to have gone back considerably. Brennan is about through. He has taken so much punishment that it has probably affected him." Gibbons also said, "There was no fake about the knockout! Brennan was hurt. ... I have fought Miske five times and I've always had a lot of respect for his punching ability. Billy can sock!"

Miske earned $2,100. It would turn out to be Billy Miske's final fight, as well as Bill Brennan's. Both men would die in 1924, though for much different reasons.[23]

On November 15, 1923 in Grand Rapids, Michigan, 166-pound Harry Greb clearly won a 10-round no decision over 177-pound Chuck Wiggins (58-29-14).[24]

On November 20, 1923 at Madison Square Garden in New York, before a crowd of 12,180 which generated $56,889.30 (net), $59,894, or $65,883.40 (gross), 174-pound Kid Norfolk won a clear 15-round decision over 172-pound Battling Siki.[25] Harry Wills already had defeated Norfolk in 2 rounds.

Jim Coffroth, who wanted to promote a Dempsey–Wills fight at his arena in Tijuana, Mexico, said Kearns told him that they would take the fight if paid one million dollars. Coffroth was satisfied that neither Kearns nor Dempsey wanted any part of Wills, and instead of admitting it, simply asked for an exorbitant sum that no promoter would pay.[26]

One fan wrote to Harry Newman, saying his constant criticism of Dempsey was bringing his sports page into disfavor, and did not decrease the champion's popularity.[27]

[23] *Omaha Evening Bee, Omaha Daily News, Omaha World Herald,* November 8, 1923.
[24] *Grand Rapids Press,* November 16, 1923.
[25] *New York Daily News, Brooklyn Daily Times, Brooklyn Standard Union, Brooklyn Daily Eagle,* November 21, 1923. Siki earned 30% and Norfolk 20%.
[26] *New York Daily News,* November 23, 1923.
[27] *New York Daily News,* November 29, 1923.

JUST RESTING.—Far from the madding crowd, William Harrison Dempsey, otherwise Jack, famed as a pugilist, takes life easy at Venice, Cal., with trainer Jerry.

Tex Rickard said he was trying to get Wills to sign for a bout with Luis Firpo, who wanted to fight him. Tex added, "Another thing, if Wills will agree to fight Firpo, I will sign him to a contract to fight Jack Dempsey in the event that he defeats Firpo. Also, I will guarantee him that Dempsey will take him on. That ought to be fair enough for Wills."[28]

Paddy Mullins told Henry Farrell that his man Wills was not going to be argued out of a chance at the championship. He said Firpo had no right to challenge Wills and should step back to the end of the line. Gibbons had been beaten by Dempsey already as well and was too light to stand a chance. "Wills is the only contender." "We've been promised a chance with Dempsey and we are still holding that promise. It has never been shown that a mixed bout will not be permitted and our failure to get Dempsey into the ring with Wills can mean only one thing. Dempsey does not want the match." Mullins held Tex Rickard to blame for putting Wills aside several times when he had a chance to promote the fight. Mullins said the "stories about [Wills'] glass jaw and weak heart are a part of the campaign to discredit him."[29]

On December 3, 1923, in Pittsburgh, before a crowd of over 5,000, or 7,000, dubbed "the greatest crowd which ever jammed into Motor Square Garden," which generated $11,678, 161-pound middleweight champion Harry

Harry Greb and Bryan Downey photographed in the ring at Motor Square Garden last night before their 10-round fight for the world's middleweight championship, which was retained easily by Greb. This was the first decision fight in this city and attracted a record crowd to the East End arena. Left to right—Greb's manager, Red Mason; Greb, Tom Dolan, one of Greb's seconds; Downey, Referee Eddie Kennedy, Jimmy Dunn, Downey's manager.

Greb clearly won a 10-round decision over 158 ½-pound Bryan Downey (81-25-16). Formal decisions recently had been legalized in Pennsylvania.[30]

---

[28] New York Daily News, December 2, 1923.
[29] Pittsburgh Sun, December 8, 1923.
[30] Pittsburgh Post, Gazette Times, Press, December 4, 1923.

James Sinnott said Jack Dempsey now occupied the same position as Jim Jeffries nearly 20 years ago after he twice defeated Fitzsimmons, Corbett, and Sharkey, and had no white man left to fight. Jack Johnson was around, but Jeff would not fight him. Historically, other than Fitzsimmons, who was a freak of nature, a man of youth and ambition defeated the reigning champion rather than a veteran. "Now they are looking for any sizeable man who is fast, can take a punch and give one." The three men Dempsey might fight again were Firpo, Gibbons, or Miske (who beat Fulton, Renault, and Brennan).

Harry Wills occupied the Jack Johnson role, but was not exactly similar, for Wills was three or four years older than Dempsey, not younger. Johnson was younger than Jeffries and "a far greater fighting man in those days than Harry Wills is now." "It is ridiculous to believe that any of the men now in the public eye as challengers for Dempsey's title will ever win it." Dempsey could knock out Firpo, Gibbons, and Miske. "It is doubtful whether a Dempsey-Wills match is ever made. If it is made, Wills will be soundly beaten." Some lesser-known youngster would have to be found to beat Dempsey, who "says he will retire soon." While that man was being developed, Dempsey would have to "lay off, and he will lose his zest for training," which would aid in his downfall. "And unless he is a greater fighter by one hundred per cent than any other man who ever donned a glove, Dempsey will emerge from seclusion to defeat."[31]

The big upcoming New York fight on the horizon was Greb vs. Tunney III, for the American light heavyweight crown, set to be held just one week after Greb's victory over Downey. Tunney was "being proclaimed as the successor to Jack Dempsey's throne." Former fighter Billy Myer, who had witnessed Sullivan-Corbett, said Tunney would conquer Dempsey, and could beat Siki with one hand tied behind his back. "Tunney, to my mind, has one of the best right hand crosses I have ever seen a big man use, and I'm willing to admit about the very best left jab and hook, a combination hard to beat." Tunney's hands were good now, and he had been improving.[32]

Harry Greb said,

> I expect to win from Tunney again as I did before, although the judges failed to put up my number the last time. I will make it sure this time, and then the 175 pound boys can have a crack at it. I have always had an easier time with the big fellows than with the 160 pounders, and hope to keep both titles until I have earned that $100,000. Where does Gibbons figure to get a crack at Dempsey when I made a show of him in the Garden. And I hope the fans will remember what I did to Jack the only day he allowed me to box with him.

---

[31] *New York Morning Telegraph*, December 5, 1923.
[32] *New York Sun and Globe*, December 6, 1923. Tunney was trained by George Engel and sparring with Jock Malone.

He Throws 'Em Fast

Alfred Dayton said Greb-Tunney promised to be as close as their two prior contests, which were extremely close, for each found many persons disagreeing with the official verdict. Picking a winner was not easy, but he gave a slight edge to Tunney.[33]

W. C. Vreeland said, "Unless he should score a triumph there is little or no hope for Harry meeting Dempsey. Of course any one who has the slightest knowledge of fistiana knows that Greb hasn't any chance of winning over the champion."[34]

Fred Keats said most of the betting had been at even money, with Tunney a slight favorite in some quarters. According to Keats, in their first contest, Greb's head butts broke Tunney's nose and cut him over the eyes, and the blood blinded him and made him sick in the stomach.

> Despite these handicaps Tunney made a remarkably good showing. In every mixup Greb was the one to back away or to clinch. He could not stand Tunney's harder, cleaner hitting, and twice he was badly hurt with solid shots to the body. But for the most part, Tunney was confused by Greb's trick of jumping in with a left or right swing and clinching to avoid the counter.

In their next fight, Tunney "outboxed him in a bout in which neither man did much damage." The referee forced Greb to observe the rules, and would not allow him to hold and hit, his best trick. "Greb was unable to do as well as usual because his whole style of fighting is based on illegal methods."

Since then, Greb had won the world middleweight crown, but recently had mixed success. In nontitle catchweight fights, he lost a decision to Loughran, whom Harry had defeated "easily" on other occasions. He "made a poor showing" against Lou Bogash, a smaller opponent, despite using tactics which, had he used in a New York ring, would have gotten him "disqualified before the first round was over." He got decked twice by Soldier Jones en route to a 10-round no decision win. He "ducked a match with Jeff Smith, who always did have something on him." Still, he clearly beat Wiggins and Downey. Greb fought often and was fit.

Tunney was a fine student of the game, and knew how to hit, but had bad hands, which had kept him from developing into a great fighter. Still, he was a sharp-shooter, landing to vital spots with short, snappy blows that jar and daze. Some thought he was too much of a gentleman in the ring and needed to be rougher to cope with Greb. "Boxing science is of little use against Greb because he does not fight according to the book. When he gets his opponent's head in chancery and proceeds to pummel him with his right, science is of no avail." Tunney sought to land clean blows, whereas Greb "is content to claw and scratch."[35]

[33] *New York Sun and Globe*, December 7, 8, 1923.
[34] *Brooklyn Daily Eagle*, December 10, 1923.
[35] *New York Sun and Globe*, December 10, 1923.

James Long, the *Pittsburgh Sun's* editor, said unless Greb's margin was wide, it was doubtful if New York judges would take the title away from a native son. There was a good chance for a draw. Greb's manager, James Mason, said there was a rumor afloat that Greb would be disqualified, for a lot had been printed regarding his purported foul tactics. Cognizant of this, Greb would give them no chance to disqualify him.

Henry Farrell reported, "Greb's established knack of making the best look bad has prevented the offering of any fat odds against him." In their first contest (May 1922), Greb had done "a lot of work" that "was regarded as foul by the experts." In their second meeting (Feb. 1923), Greb was "too careful" and lost the decision, "although loud cries went up that Tunney won on a funny decision."

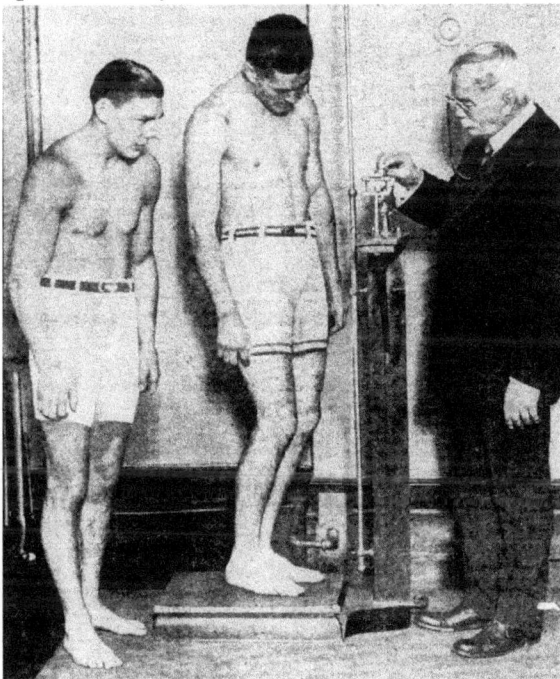

This time, Billy Gibson cleverly tried to get Greb's goat by having George Engel, Greb's former manager, work Tunney's corner. Tunney was a good fighter, but handicapped by his disposition and hand troubles, though his hands were said to be in good shape now. "If Tunney goes after Greb and carries a real offense he should win..." Georges Carpentier had asked Tex Rickard to match him with the winner of Greb-Tunney III.[36]

[36] *Pittsburgh Sun*, December 10, 1923.

On December 10, 1923 at Madison Square Garden in New York, before 11,079 paying customers who generated $43,016, in their third contest, 26-year-old 175-pound Gene Tunney (58-1-3) successfully defended his American light heavyweight title with a unanimous 15-round decision over 29-year-old 171 ½-pound Harry Greb (214-12-18). Their weights were taken at 2 p.m. on the day of the fight. The referee was Louis Magnolia, with Charles Mathison and Frankie Madden serving as judges. The vast majority of on-scene reporters agreed with the official decision, but there were some dissenters.

Harry Newman of the *New York Daily News* said Tunney punished Greb in close. Greb missed many wild sweeps for the head, while Tunney was ripping fierce punches to the heart and ribs. Greb was in bad shape in the 10th round from a left hook to the chin. In the 12th, while they were clinched, Tunney went through the ropes, but it was not from a punch, but a push, and Gene carried Harry with him. Tunney tired badly near the end though. The general feeling was that Greb got going too late. Newman said, "There was the usual booing and jeering at the verdict, but in our opinion Tunney was clearly entitled to the decision, although Greb finished strong."

Newman scored it 11-4 for Tunney, giving only the 2nd, 5th, 14th, and 15th rounds to Greb. Ultimately though, Newman concluded, "Tunney showed much improvement, but he lacks plenty to make a real champion. There isn't enough of the rough about Gene."

The *Brooklyn Daily Eagle's* W. C. Vreeland said no serious damage was done. The judges said Tunney won by a wide margin. However, many of the fans booed and catcalled for quite some time afterwards. One belligerent man started an impromptu bout with four police officers and had to accept the decision against him without any pay for his wounds.

Vreeland scored it 8-5-2 for Tunney. Gene's well-directed body work was effective, pounding Greb's body from start to finish. There was plenty of action throughout, and the aggressive Greb tried mightily and strenuously, but was a bit too wild in his head attack. Tunney met his onslaughts with right and left to the body, and an occasional uppercut. Those punches, largely not seen by the gallery gods, gave him the decision. Neither one was a big puncher, or ever hurt or rocked. Many of the rounds were close, but Tunney took them by a hair. It was the third and best bout between the two, with plenty of action.

Both were rough and foul, Greb by pushing and smothering after throwing, and Tunney by grabbing around the neck, but Greb was the greater offender. Tunney butted him in the 8th. Greb pushed him back through the ropes in the 12th.

Neither was damaged much, though there was a slight cut under Tunney's left eye. Both were bleeding slightly from the nose at the end of the 6th round.

The *Brooklyn Citizen's* Charles Segar said Greb gave Tunney a harder fight than most had anticipated, but he missed too frequently, and his continual holding hurt him with the judges. Tunney's showing was not impressive, but he did enough to earn the verdict. He fought back at Greb despite the latter's attempts to sock him with everything he had.

The crowd thought Greb was entitled to a draw. However, Tunney's body blows earned him the majority of the rounds. There were no knockdowns. In the 6th round, Greb caused a cut under Gene's left eye, but it was not serious and did not hamper him.

The *Brooklyn Standard Union* scored it 10-4-1 for Tunney.

The *Brooklyn Daily Times'* James Wood said Tunney put Greb out of the running so far as light heavyweight honors were concerned. Despite the booing, "the verdict was just," for Tunney proved his "superiority." His consistent body punching won him the fight without question. Greb fought in spurts, in and out. Wood scored it 7-4-4 for Tunney.

Jack Lawrence of the *New York Tribune* said it was a just verdict, despite what the fans thought. "It was Tunney who landed the harder blows and dealt out the greater punishment."

W. O. McGeehan in the *New York Herald* said Tunney won 7-4-4.

The *New York Times* (likely James Dawson) said Tunney won 10-4-1. Greb won only the 5th, 13th, 14th, and 15th rounds, while the 12th was even. "The decision did not meet with the unanimous approval of the huge crowd. Judging by the demonstration in favor of the verdict, however, the majority of those who witnessed the battle concurred in the decision of the bout officials. A majority of the ringside critics also approve the verdict."

This time, Tunney was not timid, but more confident, and his punching strength seemed to have improved, as well as his timing and accuracy, particularly his body punching. He punished Greb's body severely and almost exclusively. At times, Greb's face wore an expression of pain, though he recovered quickly. Tunney coolly hammered his way to victory in a convincing manner.

Although Greb did the forcing, Tunney waited and then ripped in accurate, effective body shots. Greb was wild and inaccurate, missing repeatedly.

Neither showed any great marks. Tunney was cut under the left eye and bled from the nose. Greb's nose was bleeding, and his body and sides showed large red spots. To Greb's credit, he fought one of his cleanest battles, which gained him admirers.

The *New York Evening Telegram's* George Underwood said Tunney "decisively defeated" Greb, for his body blows won the hectic encounter. Greb's unquenchable fighting spirit, stamina, vitality, and endurance enabled him to withstand the most merciless, withering, and ceaseless body bombardment the writer ever saw and yet remain on his feet. Gene landed both hands all over the body - heart, midsection, pit of stomach, ribs, liver, kidneys - and yet the iron man Greb kept blazing away. Tunney only occasionally landed left jabs and left hooks to the head. The terrific body barrage would have brought down most others. "There is no need of telling of the fight by rounds for one round was about the same as the other, with Tunney either boring in himself or meeting the rushing Greb coming in with a withering fire of lefts and rights to the body, accompanied occasionally with left-hand jabs and hooks to the head."

Early in the fight, Greb's mouth was open, and there were blue welts on his body. Until well into the fight, Tunney did just as much forcing as Greb. Late in the fight, realizing he was far behind, Greb constantly flung himself at Tunney, desperate to avoid defeat. Still, he missed often, and the ones that did land did not carry enough power to slow up Tunney, who tired at the end only because he grew arm-weary from punching Greb. Harry's return smashes did nothing to slow up or even temporarily stay Tunney's assault. Greb slowed up under the agony of punishment, yet he still had enough left to outwork Tunney in the final rounds.

> There was absolutely no question of Tunney being entitled to the decision. He won by so great a margin on points that there was no doubt of his worthiness to the award. He landed five clean punches to Harry's one, did his share of the leading, had much the better defense and excelled Greb in everything except aggressiveness and endurance.

Still, many fans booed. Many were biased, for some had wagered on Greb. Others failed to appreciate body punching. Some sat so far away that they could not see the body blows landing. However, those near the ring, including the judges, could see Tunney's blows slipping inside of Greb's guard and landing. Conversely, Harry's windmill flails could be seen from far away, but often they landed on the neck or shoulder or grazed by harmlessly. For every punch Greb that landed to the head, Tunney drove in five clean body jolts.

Underwood complimented Greb on fighting fairly and not fouling. Tunney often put his head on Harry's chest, and his head frequently came in contact with Harry's chin, but he did not do it with force or an intention to butt. Gene sometimes landed low, though many were borderline or brushed down by Greb. Harry never complained. Greb's sportsmanship, bulldog courage, flaming aggressiveness, and fair fighting all combined to gain him sympathy from the spectators, and contributed to the boos mixed with cheers at the decision.

Underwood was impressed by Tunney's ability to go 15 rounds at a dazzling pace, and "in fact...his best years may be ahead of him." He was improving, and he needed more fights. His brittle hands were the only thing that might be holding him back from fighting more often.

Fred Keats of the *New York Sun and Globe* agreed that the steady body pounding enabled Tunney to retain his title. The judges, Charles F. Mathison and Frankie Madden, together with referee Louis Magnolia, agreed. But many rabid Greb fans disagreed. One boisterous fan was dragged away by four policemen. The average spectator paid no attention to body blows, but "Tunney won by hammering Greb's body. In that way he outscored the Pittsburgher in a large majority of the rounds, but a portion of the crowd that did not understand boxing could see only Greb's spectacular swings for the head."

Keats scored it 11-4 for Tunney, but his margin was not as great as it sounded, for "he only had a shade in most of the rounds." He outlanded Greb 2 to 1, but this was offset by the fact that Greb did most of the leading and deserved credit for making the fight. But every time Greb led, Tunney countered with both hands to the body. Yet, he did not do much real damage, beyond causing Greb to hold on for a few seconds, for Greb was strong enough at the finish to take the last 2 rounds. He had to be in great shape to stand up under the body punishment. Harry's final rally also had a great deal to do with influencing the crowd. Ring fans soon forget the early rounds and remember only the final sessions.

Keats said it was a remarkably clean bout, free from fouls and protests. Even when Greb put his chin on the top of Tunney's head in the clinches, it was just a play for sympathy, for Tunney had no intent to butt him. "Greb showed that he can fight fairly when he knows that the referee will not allow him to transgress the rules."

Neither man ever was in serious trouble at any time. Both bled from the nose a trifle and Tunney received a small scratch under the left eye. "Gene was a better boxer and harder hitter, but he lacks the pugnacious disposition of Greb. If it were not for that, Tunney would have won so far off that no one could have doubted the justice of the decision."

Just before the end of the twelfth round Tunney was forced to the ropes and fell half way through, carrying Greb with him. Bell rang as they got untangled.

Tunney, Greb   Greb, Tunney   Greb, Tunney

The *New York World*'s Hype Igoe said Tunney "fought remarkably well," "clearly outpointing" Greb. "Tunney fought one of his best fights, if not the best. He pressed in always and, making Greb's body his target, didn't vary the plan of battle. That's what won for him."

> [A]lthough the usual boohooing arose from the disgruntled losers there wasn't any question that Tunney won and won fairly. He whipped Greb by lashing the very devil out of the middleweight champion's body and though Greb made gallant rallies he could not offset the Greenwich Village pride's hard, true punching. Few big men have taken a worse rib-roasting than Greb suffered last night. He weakened under it too, tired and clinched incessantly to avoid Tunney's hard rib smashes.

Greb could not escape Tunney's body punches, and Gene dug them deeper and deeper.

To his credit, overall, Greb fought cleanly, resorting to "none of his usual rough tactics, though toward the end, when weak and winded considerably," he held around the neck with one hand and hit with the other. But after referee Louis Magnolia cautioned him, Harry returned to fairer methods.

Writer "Fair Play" was a bit ambiguous. He said Tunney earned the decision over Greb, who proved to be too cautious. Greb was so anxious to fight cleanly that he held himself in reserve until the final 2 rounds, and then pummeled Tunney. The three judges, "good and true," awarded the fight to Tunney. However, the writer's tone implied some question regarding the decision.

Greb came into the ring to fight for the "cruiser-weight title" knowing that his conduct would be severely scrutinized. He wanted to show that he was not a foul fighter or even an unduly rough one. "As a consequence, for the first seven rounds there was little of an exciting nature doing." Tunney did not look much like a champion, but Greb dubbed along with him, doing most of the leading, but not acting up much to draw anyone's ire, seemingly holding back a great deal.

In the middle of the fight, Tunney began sending in straight right and left body blows that eventually left Greb reddened.

In the 14th and 15th rounds, Greb cut loose and fired away, lambasting him with everything. "But all of no avail. Tunney had won the fight in the opinion of the judges, and anything Greb could do would not avail to change their minds. Some of the spectators, quite a lot of them, booed the decision, and, as for Greb, he smiled faintly. He is getting used to it." Ultimately, Fair Play concluded that likely sometime in the future we would be favored with the fourth installment of the annual comedy entitled, "Handing the Decision to Tunney."

Westbrook Pegler, United News Staff Correspondent, questioned the decision. He said Greb swarmed all over Tunney from start to finish, but when it was over, the referee announced, "The winner – Tunney." "By what obscure process the judges of the bout arrived at their decision it was not possible to see, for the Pittsburgh fighter brought the quarrel to Tunney almost without cessation from the first jangle to the last."

Greb fought his customary aimless, impetuous campaign, leading off with his right hand to the body, and pelting Tunney with blows so fast it was almost impossible to follow them. "Greb was too bewilderingly swift for Tunney," who decided his best chance lay in a counter assault to the body. "Greb forsook the foul tactics which had set him apart as the master of all the roughest brawlers...and if there was foul work...it must have been scored against Tunney, who was guilty of butting on a few occasions." Pegler called the decision "stupefying."

Seabury Lawrence in the *New York Evening Post* said a large number of the 11,000 fans booed the decision. "A majority of the boxing writers, seated at the ringside, however, agreed that the decision was the correct one." Explaining the boos, "Greb is a very spectacular fighter and one who appeals to the crowd. To those sitting in the galleries or at any considerable distance from the ring it must have seemed that he did the most leading and landed the greater number of telling blows. This was not the case." Often, Greb's blows were wild, going around the neck, and if they did land, they did not land squarely or with damaging effect.

Conversely, Tunney kept up a steady bombardment with both hands to the body which visibly slowed up Greb and sometimes had him hurt. "It was Tunney's steady drumfire of body punches, especially during the last eight rounds, that won him the fight and won it fairly." Lawrence said it was the same old acrobatic, bouncing, clawing Greb who fired a shower of blows, but a different Tunney. This time, Tunney was rough too, hitting and mauling from bell to bell, infighting as well, which took Harry by surprise.

Regis Welsh of the *Pittsburgh Post* said as long as Tunney fought in his home zone of New York, he would not lose. Yet, in his round-by-round scoring, Welsh scored it a draw, 6-6-3: 1-T, 2-G, 3-T, 4-E, 5-G, 6-G, 7-G, 8-E, 9-T, 10-E, 11-T, 12-T, 13-G, 14-T, 15-G.

Ray Coll of the *Pittsburgh Gazette Times* said Greb clearly won, it was an absolute robbery, and the crowd practically was riotous over the decision. He claimed that even Tunney manager Billy Gibson agreed that Greb was entitled to a draw. Coll scored it 10-2-3 for Greb.

However, Jim Jab for the *Pittsburgh Press* said the decision was fair. "No man ever doubled Harry's tricks, snares and ruses as did Gene Tunney. Greb's best bets – his jumping attacks, his aviating assaults, his twisting tussles and other freak stunts – were not only frequently eluded, but often countered by the New Yorker." Tunney actually copied many of Greb's tactics. Gene's body work did damage and caused Harry to hold. Both men wrestled a lot.

Ultimately, "Greb hadn't registered sufficient points of supremacy to entitle him to dethrone the king. Tunney had a margin. Slim as it was, with all fairness, he was deserving of retention of his rank." Short-enders who took 8 to 5 odds on Greb booed.

Still, "Gene Tunney, mind you, lacks a lot. He cannot be labeled a first class fighter." The fight also proved, "Neither Tunney or Greb can hit hard."

Henry Farrell, United Press Staff Correspondent, said the decision was "just and meritorious." Farrell scored it 10-4-1 for Tunney.

> If points were awarded for holding and slapping on the back and shoulders, Greb won by a mile, but points are not scored that way. From the third round on when Tunney began to punish Greb with punches to the body, Greb did nothing but hold for his life. He led with wild swings that generally bounded off Tunney's shoulders. Then he would embrace Tunney, and the referee would almost have to blast him loose.

Tunney's body attack took away most of Greb's "circus gymnastics." However, Tunney's work was spotty.

Warned in advance of the fight that the referee would not stand for various illegal tactics, holding and hitting, elbowing, kicking, shouldering, heeling, and gouging, Greb fought fairly most of the time, but "could not entirely get away from his naturally foul style. Many times during the bout he led with the thumb protruding on his left hand. He held with his left hand and hit several times. Once he was warned by the referee for trying to choke Tunney."

The Associated Press reported that Tunney "decisively whipped" Greb, his triumph "due solely to a withering body attack, a relentless jolting drive to the ribs that gradually wore down Greb's resistance." Greb rallied spectacularly at times, bewildering Tunney with a leaping, swinging onslaught, but Greb's blows seldom landed squarely. His most sensational flurry occurred in the last round, battering Tunney about the ring, but the comeback could not offset Tunney's "wide margin" on points.

The *Newark Evening News* said Greb's typhoon and avalanche of gloves hurled at Tunney failed to impress the officials. The decision was booed and hissed. New Jersey fans were dumbfounded by the decision, for they considered Greb to be superior, and had no idea how or why the officials arrived at their verdict. "Greb fought his usual spectacular battle, always leading, landing, in his usual cyclonic fashion, and above all things, fighting absolutely clean, something the crowd did not give Tunney credit for doing at times."

The *Newark Star-Eagle*'s Bert Dodge said Tunney fought Greb instead of boxing him, and his aggressiveness earned him the decision. Tunney's plan to fight aggressively "succeeded admirably." "Tunney carried the fight to Greb...[and] kept sending in drives to the body that carried with them a lot of steam." He had learned to punch more powerfully, not box as much, and mixed it more. "There could be no question as to the fairness of the decision that was given in Tunney's favor by the judges last night." Some who believed that Greb had won were affected by his fierce

15th round rally, but "they forgot all about the clean-cut, consistent hitting that earned at least ten out of the fifteen rounds for the titleholder."

Tunney was an improved fighter. Greb proved that he could fight fairly. Tunney fired straight punches at the body, for Harry was easier to hit there than the jaw. "Gene did reach the body, and his blows plainly hurt Harry, though there never was a let-up in Greb's attack. Greb was hurt enough to give signs of pain, and he was willing to hang on once or twice until his head cleared." Both bled from the nose, and Greb's body was red.

That same day, in Philadelphia, the Pennsylvania State Athletic Commission announced that mixed-race boxing bouts would not be sanctioned in that state. William Rocap, chairman, said, "It was not deemed prudent nor for the best interest of the sport at this time to have Negroes and whites meet in ring combat." Any club that ignored the edict would have its license revoked. Hence, no Dempsey-Wills bout could be held in Pennsylvania.[37]

A couple days after the contest, Alfred Dayton said, "While there was a slight bit of discord when the decision was announced in the Tunney-Greb fight, it was but a momentary bluster and yesterday found the majority of fight fans and those mixed up in the old fistic racket entirely satisfied that Tunney had fought the best fight and was clearly entitled to the verdict."

The *New York Sun and Globe*'s Fred Keats said Tunney now was in line for fights with McTigue, Carpentier, and Gibbons.

Some alleged that Greb claimed his defeat was the result of a plot against him, but his allegation of collusion "was taken lightly in boxing circles yesterday by officials and followers of the sport alike." Either way, "Greb unequivocally denied the statements attributed to him in print." He further said that he would defend his middleweight title in Madison Square Garden. The chairman of the license committee said he spoke with Greb after the bout, and Harry never expressed any objection to the decision or the treatment he received.

The *New York Times* noted that the decision was unanimous, for judges Charles Mathison and Frankie Madden, as well as Referee Lou Magnolia, all voted for Tunney. Mathison and Madden both had voted for Greb when he won the middleweight title from Johnny Wilson.

The *New York American* said Greb denied that he said the judges were fixed. "There is no doubt that Harry talked out of his turn after the fight, and undoubtedly said a lot of things he didn't mean."

The *New York World* said Greb denied saying he was jobbed, robbed, or the fight was fixed, or that he never would fight in New York again. "Harry probably said it, but he didn't mean what he said."

---

[37] *New York Daily News, Brooklyn Daily Eagle, Brooklyn Standard Union, Brooklyn Citizen, Brooklyn Daily Times, New York Herald, New York Tribune, New York Times, New York Evening Telegram, New York Sun and Globe, New York World, New York Evening Post, Evening Star, Los Angeles Illustrated Daily News, Pittsburgh Post, Pittsburgh Gazette Times, Pittsburgh Press, Pittsburgh Sun, Newark Evening News, Newark Star-Eagle,* December 11, 1923.

The *World* said Greb was "thoroughly whipped" by Tunney. "Few men have received a harder, more relentless body beating than he got. He was wild and his punches, when they did land, didn't halt Tunney in his march to victory." The gamblers let out a yelp. "Any man who tells you that it should have been a DRAW is a man who BET on Greb. Ask him. Tunney deserved the victory without any question in the world. The best that we could possibly give Greb was three out of the fifteen rounds."

What had held up Tunney's career thus far were his bad hands, but now his career was progressing. "Personally, we'd rather see Gene pitted against a hitter than a jumping Jack like Greb."

In a special telegram to the *Pittsburgh Gazette Times*, New York scribes declared the Tunney-Greb decision to be fair. Writers explained the mob psychology which booed and jeered the decision. Greb's style always gave a "slant of victory" to the crowd. "A symposium of the beliefs of the boxing writers, however, indicates almost unanimity of judgment that Tunney, fighting Greb the only way Greb can be beaten, concentrating his fire on the body, defeated the Pittsburgh man in good measure."

Dan Lyons in the *Evening Mail* was positive that Tunney won. "It wasn't even close."

Ed Hughes of the same paper said, "Tunney now has Greb's number. He'll beat him any time they meet now."

Ed Van Every regretted "that Greb should be a poor loser. There was no other decision to be given."

George Underwood and Seabury Lawrence were quoted in support of the decision as well.

Ford Frick in the *Evening Journal* thought the battle looked like a "pretty good draw." Although the crowd hissed the decision, Tunney had more punch in his jabs, and in the closing rounds, Gene worked a tattoo on Greb's stomach, the blows sounding like a snare drum solo.

All of the writers expressed wonder at Greb's stamina and admired the clean way he fought the contest.[38]

Four days after the fight, Alfred Dayton of the *Sun and Globe* reported that Greb said he still could make 160 pounds on the afternoon of a fight and defend his world middleweight crown. Speaking of the recent Tunney contest, Greb said,

> I'm sorry all that misunderstanding came up over the fight, and I want to make it clear that I never accused the judges of being crooked or ever said that I would not fight again in New York. The Boxing Commission treated me very squarely and I have absolutely no complaint to make. … The fight with Tunney was very close, and I thought I won. But then a fighter can't judge a contest as well as those outside of the ring, and if the judges and referee thought I lost why I'm ready to abide by their decisions.

---

[38] *New York Sun and Globe, New York Times, New York American, New York World, Pittsburgh Gazette Times*, December 12, 1923.

And don't fool yourself about this fellow Tunney. He's a class boxer, and has improved more than anybody in the fight game during the last few months. He's punching twice as hard as he did a few months ago, and very shortly I think that he'll be able to lick any of them outside of Jack Dempsey. Tom Gibbons, with all his cleverness, would be outpointed by Tunney, in my opinion, for if Tunney ever hit Gibbons in the stomach like he hit me the other night Tom would forget all about his science.

I don't see where Carpentier figures to beat Tunney at all. If Gene can hold the same form he displayed against me on Monday night, he ought to knock out Carpentier inside of five rounds. Tunney handed me some terrible body punishment and it was only my fine physical condition which enabled me to stand up under the punches.

With all this praise I'd like to meet Gene once more. We've met three times and every time the fight has been very close. He has the edge on me now, having won two fights while I have only received the decision in one, but I feel certain that if we meet again I'd even up the score between us. Gene is a great fighter and a fine fellow and I'm very sorry that the trouble came up after the fight last Monday.[39]

Subsequently discussing the Greb-Tunney fight in the February 1924 edition of *The Ring*, Nat Fleischer wrote,

Only two sports writers out of thirty-six gave the bout to Greb…yet the supporters of Greb emitted a howl that could be heard for blocks around the Garden when it was announced by Joe Humphries that Tunney won.

So long as boxing exists, mob rule among the supporters of popular fighters will exist and so long as biased opinions are voiced, will there be a condemnation of the proceedings by which one boxer receives the decision over another. Our sporting experience has taught us that at no time can one satisfy every person. It is differences of opinion that make sport so interesting and fascinating. We expect to have the patrons of the sport voice their opinion on fights, but we trust that some of the rabid fans will learn to argue from an unbiased point of view.

Recently enacted Pennsylvania boxing rules held that the ring had to extend at least three feet beyond the ropes, there should be no less than three ropes, the ring had to be covered with felt or other flexible material no less than one-inch in thickness, and the posts were to be no less than two feet from the ropes. The gloves were to be no less than 5 ounces for lightweights, and 6 ounces for all weights greater than lightweight. Three

[39] *New York Sun and Globe*, December 14, 1923.

coaches were permitted, and they were not allowed to coach during the round. No one less than the age of 18 could compete as a pro. All boxers were to be weighed in on the day of the fight. Only soft bandages were allowed on the hands. Kidney punches were barred. A physician had to examine the fighters before the fight and be present at ringside. Smoking was prohibited at indoor events. No boxer could wear a white costume. Greasing of boxers was prohibited, as well as the wringing or breaking of the gloves. The gloves were to be put on in the ring. Gambling at the show was prohibited, as well as the sale of tickets to known speculators. An accounting was required. Two judges would render a decision, but if they disagreed, the referee would render the final verdict.

On December 11, 1923, in St. Louis, Missouri, as part of a show at the Coliseum, attended by over 6,000, Jack Dempsey boxed 2 two-minute rounds with local Jack Pendleton (a.k.a. Kid Whitey) and 3 of the same with his regular partner, welter/middleweight Alex Trambitas. Pleasing the crowd, Jack danced around the ring with the agility of a bantamweight, and mixed in some comedy, intentionally missing, grabbing the referee and punching him, and feigning grogginess with Trambitas and intentionally taking a 9-count.

Local writer Joseph Holland said Dempsey had changed tremendously since there five years ago, becoming a proper speaker with the verb tenses and adverbs all in line.

Dempsey said that wanting to please the crowd, he made a tactical blunder by going right at Firpo and meeting him at his own game instead of boxing him, setting up his attack, and driving home when he saw an opening. The first punch he absorbed from Firpo within the first few seconds shook and dazed him, and thereafter he was fighting on instinct alone. The first thing he remembered was in the corner after the round when Kearns put a bottle of smelling salts at his nose and he pulled away from it. The round was a blank to him until he saw the films.[40]

While in St. Louis, Dempsey also said, "Any matches for me are with the approval of promoters and the public. I'll fight whomever they bring out. The way things look at present there are only three topnotchers around. In order of importance I arrange them with Harry Wills first, Tom Gibbons second, and Luis Firpo third." Dempsey said he would like to fight those three in 1924.

> I was considerably peeved at Wills' attempt to interfere with the Firpo affair last summer and told Kearns to call off all negotiations for a future bout with Wills. I've cooled down since then because I understand there are some people who believe Harry has a chance with me. I believe I could lick Wills quicker than either Gibbons or Firpo. Wills is getting pretty old. I don't think he could stand up under a lacing, and take it from me, if we ever get together I'll give it to him good and plenty.

[40] *St. Louis Post-Dispatch, St. Louis Star,* December 12, 1923.

Regarding Gibbons, Dempsey said Tom was very tough, and their fight spoke for itself. "He kept so close to me that I couldn't get a full swing and flatten him. He was censured by some for doing a lot of clinching and holding. It must not be forgotten that Tommy was looking out for himself and realized what it meant for him to go the full distance with me." Many insisted that Gibbons was not a dangerous challenger and Dempsey did not show all his stuff at Shelby.[41]

Fred Keats said the three prospective opponents for Dempsey were Gibbons, Firpo, and Wills. "Harry [Wills] seems to be no nearer a championship battle than he was three years ago… He has had plenty of promises and once he was allowed to sign an agreement, but the boxing solons promptly repudiated that document." Gibbons, since losing to Dempsey, had been inactive.[42]

Dempsey gives reporter Imogene Stanley a rose

Imogene Stanley of the *Daily News* said love had failed to thrill the cynical Dempsey, who mourned the fickleness of men and women. He preferred being a bachelor. "Now, this most perfect specimen of the physical male has had a great deal of experience with the fair sex. He admits it." Further, Jack said, "And I'm woman-proof. The public wants me to get married. And to please the public I'm going to get married – some day. But love?" Jack, who the sportswriters liked to call a big, overgrown boy, had some experience with love, too. "Men are fickle. I'm honest. They see a beautiful woman and get infatuated with her; then another beautiful woman comes along and they fall for her. And women. Are they true to men? I've yet to see the first one." Jack said he wanted a "sweet, good woman with brains. A woman who's intelligent. When I really fall in love, I'll marry her. And I won't care who she is or what she is. But I've yet to meet her." He was not a woman hater, just woman-proof. Women were lovely. "Especially between sixteen and twenty." "A woman ought to marry when she is sixteen or seventeen. She knows all she will ever know then. A man ought not to marry before he's forty-five – he's just old enough then to know what he wants." Jack said he might not be champion at that age, and therefore, ambitious, beautiful ladies might not pursue him with so much gusto.

Jack also indicated that he was bored with being heavyweight champion. "It's not such an easy job. You have to keep fighting and

[41] *Pittsburgh Sun*, December 12, 1923.
[42] *New York Sun and Globe*, December 13, 1923.

training to keep in trim, and that's hard work." The public was fickle. "Up today and down tomorrow. That's what a champion gets." One could not please everybody. "I'd rather have fifty enemies and fifty friends – even it up." He planned to go before the footlights on the vaudeville circuit, do a step or two, perhaps a monologue. Several offers were under consideration.[43]

DEMPSEY FIRPO
Fight Pictures NOW
Showing at the
ROSE THEATRE
Madison near Dearborn

First Exclusive Showing in Chicago

See Dempsey Knocked Out of the Ring

See Him Knock Out the "Wild Pampas Bull"

"The motion pictures give us the same close-up as if we had our heads where the movie camera stood." —Carl Sandburg in Chicago Daily News.

NOT a boxing match—
NOT a pugilistic show—
BUT A FIGHT from the first tap of the gong.
SLOW MOTION makes the critical moments of the fight unusually clear and vivid.
CONTINUOUS
Every Day, 8 a. m. to 2 a. m.
Admission 50 Cents
Including Tax
Ladies Especially Invited

Readers subsequently were asked whether Dempsey was correct when he said a woman knows all she ever will know or need to know at age 17. Some agreed and some disagreed. One man replied, "No, I don't think he is right. Women keep on learning every day they live. ... Day by day they think up more schemes to get what they want than you would believe possible." Another said, "Yes, most women certainly know everything they ever will know at seventeen. ... Of course they get a little more sensible as they grow older but without actually learning more." Others said that Dempsey's statement was foolish, absurd, libelous, and wrong.[44]

As had been the case with Dempsey-Carpentier and Dempsey-Gibbons, demand to see the Dempsey-Firpo fight films was so high that copies were smuggled out of New York state and projected onto theater screens throughout the country, including Chicago.

Back on November 28, 1923 in Chicago, Superior Court Judge Charles Foell restrained the police and city authorities from interfering with the projection of the Dempsey-Firpo pictures, saying there was nothing indecent or immoral about them, for it had been a lawful contest in New York, and there was no reason why sports fans should be deprived of seeing the pictures in Chicago. They would be shown at the Rose theater in downtown Chicago, Madison at Dearborn, and the showings of the "Greatest Battle of the Age" were advertised regularly in the *Chicago Tribune*.[45]

An exhibition of the Dempsey-Gibbons fight at the Rose theater several months ago resulted in a federal investigation, for it remained against federal law to transport fight pictures in interstate commerce. However, it was not unlawful to project them. It was a "murky" area of the law.[46]

---

[43] *New York Daily News*, December 14, 1923. Dempsey planned do stage work, as most heavyweight champions did between fights.
[44] *New York Daily News*, December 25, 1923.
[45] *Chicago Tribune*, November 29, 1923.
[46] *Boxing Blade*, December 15, 1923.

Despite the federal law, there was so much money to be made from exhibiting Dempsey's championship fight films that the promoters were copying and transporting the films, exhibitors were projecting them, and patrons were paying to see them. Newspapers were making money from weekly advertisements for the showings. Everyone was making money.

Chicago was an important city, because as of 1920, after New York City, which had 5,620,048 people, Chicago was the next most populous city in the nation, at 2,701,705. Philadelphia was third, at 1,823,779. More people meant more ticket sales, both for fight gates and theatrical fight film showings.

The promoters/filmmakers/exhibitors might not have gotten away with the film transportation and exhibitions with the same wink and sometimes fine if the contests had been black vs. white bouts. Potential huge fight-film revenues likely impacted what fights promoters did or did not want to make. Politicians, police, and judges were less likely to crack down on fight films that were less likely to induce riots and cause political unrest. Such concerns and hysteria gradually had been diminishing in the era after Jack Johnson's reign, for neither Willard nor Dempsey had defended against a black man.

Harry Wills and Paddy Mullins were peeved by stories and claims that Dempsey would dispose of Wills with ease. Mullins said making claims and actually doing those things were two different things. Paddy asked, if Wills was such an easy fight, why then wasn't the fight being made with the acknowledged most formidable and deserving contender? They had been waiting for four years for their chance at the title.[47]

Harry Newman said politicians were the biggest impediment to the sport of boxing. They blocked big matches. "It is public property that there would have been a Wills and Dempsey fight here last summer if it hadn't been for the political interference. Certain Tammany powers wanted that million-dollar fuss themselves." Incompetent officials also posed roadblocks. The New York Boxing Commission soon would be re-organized. William Muldoon (allegedly) was retiring as chairman of the board. Another deputy commissioner had served his tenure. Governor Al Smith would have to fill the vacancies. It was hoped that political interference with the sport would end.

On December 25, 1923, in Pittsburgh, Pennsylvania, before a crowd of more than 5,000, 168-pound Harry Greb clearly won an official 10-round decision over 168 ½-pound Tommy Loughran (42-10-3). Ray Coll said Greb never was any better, showing all his speed and generalship. Tommy did not win a round, with two perhaps being even: 8 0 2. Regis Welsh scored it closer, at 5-3-2 for Greb, who at times reverted back to his holding and hitting style. Unlike Coll, Welsh said Greb was not the fighter he was 2 years ago. Jim Jab agreed that "Harry pulled everything

[47] *Brooklyn Standard Union,* December 26, 1923.

for which he is famous," including holding and hitting, "a trick some referees will not stand for. Others do, and there you are."[48]

Tex Rickard tried to make a match between Harry Wills and white Bartley Madden at Madison Square Garden, but "was informed not to try it, as mixed bouts of importance are still under an unofficial ban."[49]

On January 1, 1924, at only age 29, Billy Miske died of Bright's disease, a disease characterized by inflammation of the kidneys. Since his knockout loss to Dempsey in their 1920 championship contest, his only knockout loss in over 100 fights, Miske had gone 21-1-1. Even after the Dempsey fight, Miske had beaten Bill Brennan, Willie Meehan, and Fred Fulton, amongst others, only losing a decision to Tom Gibbons.

Jack Dempsey said, "It was with the deepest sorrow that I learned of the death of my friend, Billy Miske. He was a great fighter and did much to elevate boxing by his splendid sportsmanship. He was a gentleman, both in and out of the ring."

Miske's manager Jack Reddy said, "There were times when I was tempted to inform the public and newspapers of Miske's true condition in order that they might pay proper tribute to a real fighter."

Tom Gibbons said they had fought five times. "Although I usually won from Miske, he gave me more trouble than any other boxer I ever met – and that includes Jack Dempsey."

Mike Gibbons said, "Billy Miske was one of the greatest heavyweights I ever saw. If his health had not failed him I am sure he would have won the championship."

George Barton said Miske had suffered from Bright's disease since early 1920, but at various times showed such improvement in his health that it was believed he would recover. Apparently, it went into remission at times. He had been ailing for the past six months of 1923, but it was not until he collapsed completely the week prior that his family and friends realized his condition was so serious. He had been unconscious since Saturday, December 29. He left behind a wife and three children.

Despite physicians' advice that he should retire from boxing, Miske had remained in the ring to earn money for his family, because he lost his savings in an auto business in 1920. However, he never complained of his illness.[50]

George Underwood wrote, "There is only one real opponent for Jack Dempsey in a sporting match. Every one knows that is Harry Wills. ... A Dempsey-Wills match would draw a record gate even in the Arctic zone." Yet, Underwood heard that Tex Rickard was looking to make a Dempsey vs. Gibbons rematch.

Rickard offered to sign Wills for bouts with Firpo and Dempsey if the Black Panther first met George Godfrey at Madison Square Garden. Such offers were "very tempting bait."[51]

---

[48] New York Daily News, Pittsburgh Gazette Times, Pittsburgh Post, Pittsburgh Press, Pittsburgh Sun, December 26, 1923.
[49] New York Daily News, January 1, 1924.
[50] Minneapolis Morning Tribune, January 2, 1924.
[51] New York Telegram and Evening Mail, January 8, 9, 11, 1924.

Jack Dempsey was vacationing in Miami, enjoying the beach and the ocean, as well as acquaintances.

Two Jacks, Both Champs—Jack Dempsey and Jack Ott on beach at Miami. Little Jack is champion child athlete and is called the "world's perfect baby." (P. & A. photo.)

Dempsey in the water at Miami Beach, FL, with expert swimmer Wanda Ellwood

On January 15, 1924 at the Coliseum in Grand Rapids, Michigan, 178-pound Gene Tunney won a 10-round no decision over 189 ½-pound Harry Foley (16-6-1). Newsmen, via dispatches, said Gene won 7-2-1.

For the *Grand Rapids Press*, Roscoe Bennett said Tunney beat Foley decisively. Tunney was very methodical and stylish in subduing his foe, impressing the public. "Tunney could not or would not knock out his opponent but he outboxed him so badly as to leave no doubt...that it's going to take quite a battler to take his title from him." Gene had an earnest, businesslike style, with piston-like snappy punches, clever footwork, and finesse on defense. "Gene in action reminds one of Benny Leonard." He was careful, making no foolish moves with hands or feet, while always pressing in and keeping his foe on his heels. Foley could not solve his style. Tunney clearly had improved since last seen there.

The *St. Joseph Herald-Press*, critical of Tunney's failure to stop Foley, said Gene was a most likeable chap, but would not be a great champion, because he was not made to be one. "Tunney is too nice and has too little of the primitive in him to be a savage fighter, and the element of the savage is a big factor in the equipment of a champion."[52]

Harry Wills had an injured right hand, an x-ray confirming a split metacarpal bone. The hand would need to be in a cast for several weeks.[53]

Tex Rickard donated the use of Madison Square Garden for the 1924 Democratic National Convention, which would start in late June. Underwood called the move a masterful, shrewd, brilliant coup. "Already reported 'in good' with Republicans, he now worms his way into the

---

[52] *Grand Rapids Press, Benton Harbor News-Palladium, Kansas City Star, St. Joseph Herald-Press,* January 16, 1924.
[53] *New York Telegram and Evening Mail,* January 16, 1924.

Democratic party and puts himself into a position of stilling the troubled seas of boxing and drawing fire away from himself."[54]

On January 18, 1924 at Madison Square Garden in New York, 11,093 paid $50,737 to see 158 ½-pound Harry Greb successfully defend his world middleweight championship with a clear 15-round unanimous decision over southpaw former champ 159 ½-pound Johnny Wilson (58-22-8). There were no knockdowns.[55]

The Ring's Nat Fleischer reported that competent ringside critics said Greb never fought a better battle in his life, ending talk regarding whether he was lucky to have defeated Wilson previously.

> Harry Greb is a peculiar person. He can fight some very poor fights, as he often has done, but it truly can be said that when he wants to fight he can and with a vengeance. ...
>
> It has been said, and not without justification, that Greb is not a great middleweight champion. He does not, for instance, rank with Fitzsimmons or Ketchel, but we seriously doubt if the ring will turn out another Ketchel or another Fitz in a long, long while. But it would be interesting, mightily so, to discover a middleweight who can whip Greb right now.[56]

The *Binghamton Press* said it had learned "from a source that is absolutely authentic and reliable" that Dempsey and Wills would not be allowed to fight in 1924, and "it is doubtful that they ever will be allowed to fight in this country." New York would not allow Dempsey-Wills or Firpo-Wills. The authorities were willing to sanction Dempsey rematches with either Gibbons or Firpo. Connecticut might consider a mixed heavyweight fight, but "Pennsylvania and New York will never permit one."[57]

In February 1924, word was that William Muldoon was going to return as a member, and possibly back to the throne of the New York Boxing Commission. New York Governor Al Smith had reappointed him.[58]

Ultimately, George Brower was elected to serve as chairman of the New York boxing commission, with William Muldoon and James Farley acting as the other two commission members.

The *New York Age* noted that the re-appointment of Muldoon to the athletic commission was not rejoiced by colored boxing fans. "For it was while Muldoon was in charge that the efforts to match Dempsey and Wills were squelched. No reason was ever given by this official as to why he changed his mind and discouraged this contest after having accepted Wills' challenge and forfeit of $2,500." Likely, behind-the-scenes politics were involved. Muldoon had done the bidding of the higher-up politicians, which got him reappointed to the commission.

[54] *New York Telegram and Evening Mail*, January 17, 1924.
[55] *New York Daily News, Brooklyn Daily Eagle*, January 19, 1924.
[56] *The Ring*, March 1924.
[57] *Binghamton Press*, February 2, 1924.
[58] *Binghamton Press*, February 7, 1924.

James Farley, William Muldoon, George Brower

Tex Rickard, who promoted Jeffries-Johnson and Gans-Nelson, when speaking about his life, "spoiled it all for his colored readers by continually referring to Gans as a 'darkey.'"[59]

During mid to late January, at the Miami Beach Casino, 202-pound Jack Dempsey did some sparring with Walter Monaghan, Willard's former sparring partner, Chuck Wiggins (58-30-14)(who in early February was sent to prison for contributing to the delinquency of a minor and escape), Chief Metoquah, and others.[60]

Subsequently, Dempsey went on a barnstorming tour giving boxing exhibitions, primarily in the South, including places like Raleigh, NC (Jan. 30), Savannah, GA (Feb. 1), Shreveport, LA (4th), Eldorado, AR (6th), Arkansas City (7th), and Helena, AR (8th). Wearing large 16-ounce gloves, he usually sparred 1 or 2 rounds each with locals, and also boxed with regular sparring partner Dan O'Dowd, who toured with the champ. The Dempsey-Firpo fight films often were shown as part of the show, or just before or after it. Jack Kearns and Teddy Hayes were with him.

On Saturday February 9, 1924 in Memphis, Tennessee, before 2,000 fans, an alleged 190-pound Dempsey boxed a scheduled 4-round exhibition with 4-ounce gloves against "Dutch" Seifert, a 225-pound Arkansas fighter who purportedly never had been knocked off his feet before and had a 21-bout career, with 15 won by knockout.

At the gong, Seifert rushed at Dempsey and attacked. Big mistake. Dempsey responded with a series of short right and left jolts, mostly to the head, and 45 seconds later, Seifert was out cold. After being revived and given some rest, Seifert boxed another round with Dempsey, but soon was helpless again.

The champ also boxed a few rounds with Dan O'Dowd.[61]

---

[59] *Brooklyn Daily Eagle*, February 8, 1924; *New York Age*, February 9, 1924.

[60] *Buffalo Express*, January 30, 1924.

[61] Dan O'Dowd's record included: 1919 LND8 Bill Brennan and LND8 Gene Tunney; 1920 W10 Eddie McGoorty and TKO12 Clay Turner; 1921 W12 Turner, L12 Battling Levinsky, WND8 Leo Houck, W15 Bob Roper, L12 Bartley Madden, LTKOby3 and LTKOby6 Tommy Gibbons, and L12 Brennan; 1922 L12 Roper and L10 Jack Renault; 1923 LND12 Jeff Smith, LTKOby6 Roper, TKO8 Al Reich, L12 Tunney, WND8 Jack Burke, and D12 Young Bob Fitzsimmons.

Kearns had arranged the barnstorming tour to make some easy money and keep the champ sharp. Still, it was said that Dempsey did not like barnstorming. He had been enjoying himself at a Florida resort when Kearns called on him to go back to work.[62]

On February 11, 1924 at the Coliseum in New Orleans, Louisiana, Dempsey boxed 6 rounds, 2 each with Martin Burke, who was scheduled to meet Gene Tunney there in four days, local Tommy Marvin or Martin, and Dan O'Dowd, his regular sparring partner.

When asked about his knockout of Dutch Seifert, Dempsey declared that he "hated to do it, but the big fellow was getting a bit too rough."[63]

New Orleans Prohibition agents invaded Dempsey's temporary residence, where a party was being held, seeking to enforce the Volstead Act. Dempsey was eating dinner at the time. The agents quickly grabbed all of the glasses and sniffed them. They decided that Jack was not violating the 18th Amendment. It was just ginger ale. However, agents claimed to have found a pitcher of liquor in the kitchen, so Pete Herman, former world bantam champ, who was hosting the gathering, had to face charges.[64]

Dempsey subsequently exhibited in Charlotte, NC (14th), Richmond, VA (15th), Roanoke, VA (18th), and Asheville, NC (20th).

On February 15, 1924 at the Coliseum in New Orleans, a very large or capacity house of 4,000 or 5,000, which generated $11,500, saw 177 ½-pound Gene Tunney win a clear 15-round decision over 182 ¾-pound Martin Burke (33-17-6), winning every round, battering Burke's ribs. Burke held quite often. Referee Al Wambsgans rendered the decision.

For the *New Orleans Item*, Fred Digby said Tunney beat and outclassed Burke, who made a sorry fight. "Tunney's ability to punch fast and counter, his infighting and superior generalship, brought about his victory. Gene likes to make an opponent carry the fighting to him while he depends on counters to the body." He was defensively skilled. He always outhit Burke on the inside. Nevertheless, "his performance wasn't anything to brag about." Most believed that Gibbons would beat him. Many wondered how Tunney beat Greb.

For the *New Orleans States*, Col. Cluke said Tunney outclassed, outpunched, and outfought Burke, who made the poorest showing of his career, hooted for holding excessively. Burke lost every round.

The *New Orleans Times-Picayune's* William Keefe said Tunney was speedy, shifty, two-fisted, hard-punching, and clever, and probably would have scored a knockout had Burke ever opened up with a serious attempt to fight back instead of constantly rushing and falling into clinches. "Tunney proved beyond doubt he has plenty of class." His footwork and

[62] *Nashville Tennessean*, February 11, 1924; *El Paso Times*, February 10, 1924. At Eldorado, ringside seats were $10, and in Memphis, the best seats were $3.
[63] *Alexandria Town Talk*, February 11, 12, 1924; *St. Joseph News-Press, Pittsburgh Gazette Times*, February 12, 1924. Burke was insured for $10,000 against injury in the set-to. The crowd, which paid $5, $3, and $2 to witness the exhibition, thought it was too tame. They wanted to see a knockout. The champ was headed to Charlotte to exhibit there on the 14th, and/or Raleigh, North Carolina.
[64] *Shreveport Times*, February 12, 1924.

counters were spectacular and effective. "Quick thinking and with a quick eye, Tunney fights well either tearing into his opponent or waiting for him to tear in. His speed and shiftiness bewildered Burke." He smothered Burke's attempts at infighting. He took well what few blows Burke landed.

> At long range Tunney made his man look amateurish. Tunney would feint him into knots, then either flash in with a left to the body or head, followed by a right uppercut to the stomach, or if Burke fell for this feint and attacked, Tunney would glide back like a phantom, set himself in a flash and meet Burke with a terrific right uppercut which usually landed clean to Burke's body.[65]

George Underwood said there was talk of another Dempsey-Gibbons contest, but the New York State Athletic Commission might force Dempsey to fight Wills first, which Underwood hoped they would do.[66]

During February, Jack Kearns said he and Dempsey were willing to fight Wills, "but it looks as though they won't let us fight."

Harry Newman said Wills-Dempsey was a guaranteed million-dollar gate. Hence, some promoter likely (or hopefully) would come along with an offer.

Kearns said Dempsey would fight Wills if guaranteed $500,000. Given that Dempsey had made nearly that amount to fight Firpo, such a demand did not seem preposterous or unreasonable, particularly since Dempsey's gates against Carpentier and Firpo had exceeded one million dollars.[67]

Tom O'Rourke claimed that Tex Rickard was getting around New York's ticket-price law by colluding with a prominent ticket speculator. Rickard denied the accusation. However, if Tex was doing so, such would make sense. He could charge the face value limit the regulators allowed, have the speculators greatly mark up the tickets on the open market, then revenue-share with them. Or he could secretly charge them a marked-up rate, and the speculators could sell the tickets for whatever they could make above and beyond that amount. That way, Rickard would inoculate himself from loss, but still make more than face value.

The board of aldermen and the mayor of Newport, Rhode Island said a Dempsey-Wills bout would *not* be allowed there, nor would a Wills-Firpo contest.[68]

Jack Kearns claimed that he intended to sign for bouts against Gibbons, Firpo, and Wills. He would meet with Rickard to discuss.

George Underwood opined that a main bout referee should be paid 2 or 2.5% of the gate, with the judges and alternate referee receiving 1 1/3% each. "Well paid referees and judges means better officiating. Putting referees on a pittance encourages sharp practice."[69]

---

[65] *New Orleans Item, New Orleans States, New Orleans Times-Picayune, Shreveport Journal*, February 16, 1924. The *Item* said Tunney was 177 to Burke's 183 ¾ pounds, while the *Times-Picayune* said Tunney was 177 ½ to Burke's 182 ¾-pounds.
[66] *New York Telegram and Evening Mail*, February 18, 1924.
[67] *New York Daily News*, February 17, 18, 20, 1924.
[68] *New York Daily News*, February 21, 22, 1924.
[69] *New York Telegram and Evening Mail*, February 22, 1924.

On February 22, 1924 in Washington, D.C., Dempsey and Kearns met Republican U.S. President Calvin Coolidge, who was running for re-election. Democrat New York Governor Al Smith also was running for President, attempting to secure his party's nomination.

President Coolidge greeted Dempsey as "one who has been before the public longer than I have." Kearns told the president that Dempsey could knock out a man with a 2-inch punch. President Coolidge replied, "Well, that is two inches more of a punch than I would like to get from you." When asked if he had any engagements in sight, Dempsey said he expected to box two or three times in the spring and summer.

Dempsey exhibited that evening in Washington D.C. at the Central Coliseum, but just shadow boxed, for the police were present to ensure that no blows were exchanged.

Dempsey told Nat Fleischer, "I told the President I expected to have three [fights] this summer, with Wills, Firpo, and Gibbons, and when I do, I hope he will accept a complimentary and come and see them." He also said, "There is one man above all I want to get a crack at. Harry Wills. If I ever get him into the ring I'll flatten him in less than three rounds."

Kearns said they were not under contract to Rickard, but preferred doing business with him because he never failed to carry out a contract properly, and he paid in full, which was more than could be said about 90% of promoters. Any others needed to put up the forfeit money first.

Regarding a Wills fight for any other promoter, Kearns said, "We'll sign for a guarantee of $500,000 and will demand that $300,000 be placed in a bank to our credit to guarantee good faith and act as an assurance that political or other influence will not be used to stop the bout." Fight preparation required expenses, time, and effort, and they had to forgo other opportunities, which they did not want to do for a fight unless it was guaranteed to be allowed, and such promise was backed by real coin.

Kearns said that cities visited in Dempsey's southern exhibition tour included Raleigh, New Orleans, Savannah, Key West, Miami, Shreveport, Palm Beach, Eldorado, Arkansas City, Helena (Ark.), Memphis, Charlotte, Richmond, Roanoke, Nashville, and Washington, D.C.

Kearns noted the greeting that Dempsey received from thousands throughout the South spoke highly of the regard the public had for him. "I've been all over the world, but never have I seen such wild enthusiasm for a boxer as exhibited in the case of Dempsey throughout the South. Why, only yesterday he shook the hands of more than 3,000 persons in

Washington." The champion visited Woodrow Wilson's grave and laid a wreath upon it.[70]

In subsequent days, Dempsey said he did not care who his next opponent was, for they all could have a fight, so far as he was concerned. "What difference does it make? Tommy Gibbons, Firpo, or Harry Wills – any one - I think that I can beat them all." He knew that he would not last forever, for everyone was knocked off eventually. "However, while I am in the racket I am going to try and get all I can out of it." He wanted to earn as much as he could. Jack said he had been out of the ring too long to be at his best against Gibbons. If the public wanted a Wills fight, he would fight him. "Honestly, I believe that Wills will prove easy and I would like to have it over with."

Paddy Mullins was convinced that Dempsey did not want any part of the Black Panther's game. Nevertheless, they would keep right at his heels until he was forced into a match.[71]

On February 24, 1924, in Buenos Aires, Argentina, Luis Firpo knocked out Farmer Lodge in the 5th round.

On February 27, 1924, in New York, Jack Dempsey underwent an operation for fistula, or hemorrhoids. He did not leave the hospital until March 4.[72]

Davis Walsh reported that a man who rubbed political elbows with New York Governor Al Smith told him that the Dempsey-Wills issue had received a thorough burial, beyond hope of excavation. Wills was aware of that fact and knew he never would meet Dempsey. Harry made that declaration not as a matter of opinion, but a statement of fact. "Through the underground passages known only to the politically informed the word has been passed, this man says, that the bars are up against Dempsey and Wills from one end of the country to the other." Wills knew that talk about fighting Dempsey was "useless." That made him willing to talk about fighting Firpo, whereas a year ago, it was Dempsey or nobody. "Harry Wills and Jack Dempsey will never meet in the ring."

> Meanwhile, Dempsey never neglects to mention Wills when discussing prospective opponents. This is all part of the game, of course, the great game of political camouflage. Wills is not to be barred openly. It is merely a case of tacit understanding that such is the case.
>
> With a presidential campaign impending, it is not good business to bar anyone... At the same time it would be more than equally dangerous for any governor or any party to sanction or tolerate a mixed bout for the heavyweight championship. The safest course, naturally, is to say nothing for publication.

---

[70] *Brooklyn Daily Times*, February 22, 1924; *New York Daily News, New York Telegram and Evening Mail, Allentown Morning Call, Lexington Herald, Atlantic City Daily Press, Evening Star*, February 23, 1924.
[71] *New York Daily News*, February 24, 25, 1924.
[72] *New York Daily News*, February 28, 1924, March 5, 1924.

After the campaign is over it might be imagined that political vigilance on the Wills matter might be relaxed, but we are reliably informed that such will not be the case. There are other campaigns to come and neither Democratic nor Republican is willing to pile up trouble for his future years.

There had been some talk of the fight taking place in Tijuana, the one place where it might be tolerated, but the locality seemed to have lost interest. Coffroth talked it up for a while, but nothing came of it.[73]

On March 7, 1924, in Buenos Aires, Argentina, before a crowd of 30,000, 216 ½-pound Luis Firpo knocked out Italy's 184 ½-pound Erminio Spalla (34-4-2) in the 14th round, with a right to the jaw.[74]

Jack Dempsey was set to leave New York to head back to Los Angeles to work for the motion pictures.[75]

The United Press' Henry Farrell wrote, "Dempsey has done more to earn the respect of the public for the heavyweight champion than any other title holder. ... Dempsey has become an asset to the whole fight business. Jack Johnson nearly ruined it, and Jess Willard made no effort to get it back in the respect of the public."[76]

Some Providence, Rhode Island businessmen, represented by John Griffin and James J. McGinnity, claimed to have offered Kearns $500,000 for Dempsey's end for a Wills contest to be held on July 4, offering $250,000 up front as a good faith guarantee. The Rhode Islanders said Kearns had promised to fight for them if they could show some money and guarantee that they could hold the fight. They insisted that they had a check for the money, had obtained a license, and could guarantee they would be able to hold the bout. Nevertheless, they claimed that Kearns turned them down, saying Dempsey would not fight Wills in 1924 and was not likely to fight anyone at all until September.

Kearns believed the public was most interested in a Firpo rematch. Furthermore, he said,

> That syndicate from Providence did a lot of talking, but they weren't flashing much coin. Dempsey has several good offers to make pictures on the coast, which will probably take about ten weeks, and then we will be ready to fight again. I'd rather not have anything further to say about the offer for a Wills bout.[77]

Kearns claimed that the Rhode Islanders didn't actually have the cash up front to be paid when the contract was signed. "They have been doing a lot of talking, but I have not yet seen any money either from them or from any other promoter... [T]o date all I've heard is talk. I've seen no action. ... The trouble is with the promoters. They talk a lot, but do nothing."

[73] *Buffalo Enquirer*, March 7, 1924.
[74] *Binghamton Press*, March 8, 1924.
[75] *Olean Evening Times*, March 8, 1924.
[76] *Binghamton Press*, *Chickasha Daily Express*, March 8, 1924.
[77] *New York Daily News*, March 11, 1924.

Paddy Mullins believed Kearns had no intentions of allowing Dempsey to meet Wills.[78]

U.S. Attorney General Harry Daugherty revealed the existence of a nationwide conspiracy to exhibit the Dempsey-Carpentier fight pictures, in violation of federal law. He informed a Senate committee that F. C. Quinby (or Quimby), one of the owners of the films, admitted that the films were exhibited in more than 20 states, the buyers being supplied with names of lawyers in their respective states who would "see that everything was all right." In many instances, the exhibitors paid $1,000 fines, but thereafter reaped huge profits. Quinby said, "Jack Kearns, Rickard, and I owned the pictures, and the contract for showing the pictures over the country was signed by all three." Kearns told Quinby that a plan was submitted to him whereby the pictures could be sold all over the U.S. The idea was to show the pictures before a veteran's organization first, they would be taken before a federal judge and fined, and then they would be at liberty to show the pictures thereafter. Quinby said he had been fined $1,000 and was told to wait to show the pictures until things subsided. That same plan was followed in all the states. When asked how much he got in New York from showing the films, Quinby answered, "$75,000." They started showing the films again 30 days later.[79]

Kearns allegedly told Rickard that Dempsey could not fight until the fall because he just had an operation. Kearns did not want to take any kind of a chance with him and would lay him off for a while. Jack then would need time to get back into shape again.[80]

Yet, Kearns kept saying they were willing to fight Wills. He said Wills' backers were expecting *him* to come up with a promoter, which was not his job. As soon as a reputable, reliable promoter laid something real on the table, the fight would be signed. Kearns insisted that they wanted the fight. "You don't suppose that Jack and I want to toss off a Dempsey and Wills purse do you? We'd be fine muckle-heads if we did chuck it, now wouldn't we? Let me see the dough. That's plain enough, isn't it? Money – Money!" He was not going to work with dreamers who talked and promised big but could not prove they had the actual financial backing to pay *in full*. He did not want another Shelby situation. "No more shooting at the moon with the dreamers. … I'm cured, I tell you."

Kearns said Wills was his own worst enemy by laying idle instead of continuing to fight and creating big demand for the fight. Kearns said Wills should knock out men like Gibbons, Firpo, Godfrey, and Renault, which would make a Dempsey fight more valuable.[81]

On March 17, 1924 at the Auditorium in St. Paul, Minnesota, before a crowd of nearly 9,000 (8,127 paid admissions) which generated $20,352, in a rematch, 176 ½-pound Gene Tunney won a 10-round no decision over 171-pound Jimmy Delaney (38-3-6).

[78] *New York Telegram and Evening Mail, Yonkers Herald, New York Daily News*, March 11, 1924.
[79] *Brooklyn Standard Union*, March 15, 1924.
[80] *Brooklyn Daily Times*, March 16, 1924.
[81] *Buffalo Commercial*, March 20, 1924.

George Barton scored it 8-0-2 for Tunney, saying he won decisively. "Performing like the real champion that he is, Tunney won by a clear margin, being Delaney's master at every department of the game. He outboxed Jimmie at long range work, outfought him in the clinches, outpunched and outgeneraled him." Tunney was too strong and fast for him. "Tunney is a master of his craft." He had a great left jab, snappy left hook, and powerful right to the heart. He had Delaney's left eye puffy and cut, and his nose and mouth bloody.

John Getchell agreed, "Tunney was the master of the entire bout last night. … Tunney pecked and pecked away at Delaney and tied the St. Paul boy up in knots." He had him cut and bloody.

Edward Walker said Tunney was too rugged for Delaney, outgeneraling and outpunching him, winning 8-1-1. Delaney only shaded the 1st and got a draw in the 8th. Gene was effective at countering leads with left hooks. He fired his right only at intervals, but when he did, it landed. "Tunney proved that he is one of the best 175 pounders in the country and why he can defeat Harry Greb. … He is cool, a great counter puncher and a real champion."

There was talk of matching Tunney with Tommy Gibbons, but Tom's manager Eddie Kane said he would not be interested in such a match unless and until he was certain that a Dempsey rematch was not happening.[82]

Harry Wills had undergone a hand surgery a couple months ago, in order to cure the hand troubles he had endured for years, and his hand still was healing.[83]

An attempt in the New York assembly to repeal the boxing law and make boxing illegal again was defeated in committee by a 13 to 2 vote.

In late March 1924, Jack Farrell for the *Daily News* reported that he had it on good authority that Dempsey would be out of the ring for a year with the movies, for which he would be paid a fortune. A lucrative year-long movie contract would keep him tied up with the cinema.

Apparently, the Universal Film Corporation had offered Dempsey a million dollars. That was too much money for anyone to turn down. No fight could earn him that type of money.

However, Kearns said he would insist that Dempsey be allowed to fight after the pictures were made in June. He thought Jack's next fight likely would be a rematch against Firpo, around Labor Day.[84]

---

[82] *Minneapolis Morning Tribune, Minnesota Daily Star, Minneapolis Journal*, March 18, 1924. Their weights were taken at 3 p.m. Curley Ulrich refereed. Since losing a 1923 10-round no decision to Tunney, Delaney had won a 10-round decision over Chuck Wiggins, fought Tommy Loughran to a 12-round draw, and won 4-round decisions over Willie Meehan and Martin Burke.

[83] *New York Telegram and Evening Mail*, March 19, 20, 1924.

[84] *New York Daily News*, March 21, 25, 26, 1924; *Buffalo Courier*, March 25, 1924.

Jim Coffroth was discussing a potential Dempsey-Wills fight to be held in "Tia Juana." George Underwood said there was little or no chance of that fight happening in any place other than New York, or possibly New Jersey.[85]

Subsequently, Kearns allegedly said that Dempsey would fight Wills in Tijuana on Labor Day, and they were going to sign articles with promoter Jim Coffroth. Dempsey would complete his three-month movie contract first. The *Daily News'* Harry Newman doubted the genuineness of the promotion. A similar claim had been made a year ago and nothing came of it. It likely was a propaganda campaign to keep folks interested in the champ so the new picture arrangement would not look so bad. Paddy Mullins said he had not heard a thing about a proposed Dempsey-Wills bout in Mexico.[86]

Such reports often either were used as negotiating ploys, marketing, or just plain false news. California promoter Coffroth had not promoted any boxing card since early 1919 (4 rounders only, per California law), and no major heavyweight contest since 1909, with Jack Johnson vs. Al Kaufman. The odds of a major heavyweight championship fight taking place in Mexico, far away from a large U.S. population base, was low.

Tex Rickard announced that he had signed Wills to fight opponents of his choosing in the summer, with a possible go with Dempsey in September.[87]

No one was quite sure exactly what Kearns/Dempsey would be doing, fighting Firpo, Gibbons, or Wills, or not fighting at all in 1924 and just working in the movies.

On March 31, 1924, Jack Dempsey signed a contract with Carl Laemmle, president of the Universal Motion Picture Company, for a series of ten pictures, for a total of $1,000,000. No fight could compare.

Rickard had offered Dempsey $500,000 to fight in New York or New Jersey on Labor Day. Kearns said they might accept that offer as well.[88]

The *New York Age's* William Clark said that previously in sporting circles, it generally was asserted that the real reason Rickard did not offer to promote Dempsey-Wills sooner was that he was not certain Dempsey could beat Wills, and he did not care to promote a heavyweight championship in which the title passed to a colored man. There were too many problems and too much fallout associated with his promotion of Jeffries-Johnson. However, recent reports that Wills had hand problems

---

[85] *New York Telegram and Evening Mail*, March 25, 1924.
[86] *New York Daily News*, March 28, 29, 1924.
[87] *New York Daily News*, March 30, 1924.
[88] *New York Daily News*, April 1, 1924.

and was slipping had led Rickard to feel more comfortable that Dempsey could beat him; and hence his willingness to promote the fight.[89]

On April 5, 1924, in Buenos Aires, Argentina, 220-pound Luis Firpo knocked out 213 ½-pound Al Reich (30-16-1) in the 1st round.

A man who allegedly was close to the champion and his manager told writer Jack Lawrence that Dempsey had fought his last battle and would abandon the ring. So certain was he of his claim; he was willing to wager $500. Dempsey had more money than he ever could spend, and he wanted to retire undefeated as champion. He was making plenty of money in the motion picture game, too, and did not need to fight. He also was earning money from the real estate market in California. Another claim was that Dempsey was going to get married, and his future wife did not want him to fight anymore.

This source said Dempsey did not want to meet Wills, and nothing but need for money would make him take that fight. It was not that Dempsey was afraid, for he wasn't afraid of any living man, and believed the overrated Wills would be easier than Firpo. Jack did not think Wills could take the punishment he would hand out. "The truth is that Dempsey is averse to boxing a colored man. He told me that he would do it if such a thing became absolutely necessary in order to keep the title in the hands of the white race. But he admitted at the same time that he would rather retire from the ring than box Wills or any other colored fighter."[90]

On April 7, Harry Wills signed to meet Bartley Madden, known for his durability. Neither Bill Brennan, Fred Fulton, Jim Coffey, Tom Gibbons, Battling Levinsky, nor Joe Jeannette could stop him. Underwood, who did not like the matchup for Wills, said, "Madden is one of those rough, rugged, awkward maulers who make a first-class fighter 'look bad.'" He had a hit and clinch style. "Many will blame Wills for the holding and the criticism will not do the proposed Dempsey-Wills match any good."[91]

On April 18, 1924, in Los Angeles, Jack Kearns was arrested on a drunk and disorderly charge, being found with a quart of whiskey inside an automobile, where he and five friends were diverting themselves. Kearns made light of it, saying to the press, "You know how it is boys. We all have been on parties like this." Leaving the jail after five hours in the drunk tank, Kearns said, "I've been in better jails than this. So has everybody." Kearns was eager to ensure that Jack Dempsey's name not be mentioned in the ensuing publicity. "He's a nice, clean boy. Don't drag his name into this. As for me, I don't care what you say, but spell my name right." Kearns plead guilty to the charge and paid a $25 fine.[92]

On April 19, 1924, in Boston, before a crowd of 9,000, 172 ¾-pound Kid Norfolk won his rematch with 172 ¾-pound Harry Greb, when at the end of the 6th round (of a scheduled 10), Greb was disqualified. The *Boston Globe's* Lawrence Sweeney reported that Referee Jack Sheehan had

[89] *New York Age*, April 5, 1924.
[90] *Los Angeles Times*, April 6, 1924.
[91] *New York Telegram and Evening Mail*, April 7, 1924.
[92] *Los Angeles Record*, April 18, 1924; *New York Daily News*, April 19, 1924.

warned Greb repeatedly, but he continually resorted to foul tactics. "Throughout the fight, Greb displayed a tendency to wrestle, holding his opponent's head in chancery while he himself inflicted unfair punishment." Harry was losing. "For the first five rounds Greb was outclassed." As the bell clanged to end the 6th round, Norfolk landed a body blow. In response, clearly after the bell, Greb struck Norfolk four times, leading to the disqualification.[93]

During April 1924, Grantland Rice reported that 57-year-old Jim Corbett, who looked about 38 or 39, who had won and lost the heavyweight championship before Tunney was born, went through a workout with Gene Tunney for the Pathe Sportlight motion picture series (perhaps on the 19th), demonstrating various moves and punches on one another, playfully sparring. Portions of the films still exist.

Rice said Corbett still was as fast as a lightweight, a whirl of motion with both feet and hands, and quick and active as a man of 24. His flashes of dizzy speed told of a great past. Gene Tunney remarked, "If he was much faster then than he is now, what a wonder he must have been." Corbett showed no signs of his profession's alleged brutality.[94]

Just to see how good he was, Jack Dempsey had a try-out with the local Los Angeles professional baseball team, fielding and hitting. Apparently, he did not do well enough to join the team. However, Dempsey said, "Wait. My ring percentage wasn't so good at first. I didn't start as champion. You never can tell."[95]

The Universal Theatre in Hanford, California was advertising that the Dempsey vs. Firpo fight films were being shown there.[96]

New York's *Daily News* kept pushing for Wills to get his chance at the title, for he was the one man who could test Dempsey:

After Jack Dempsey's Diamond Try-Out, Verdict Is That as a Ball Player He's a Good Fighter

> Wills has size, cleverness, and a hard clout when his hands are right. Then again he has had the necessary experience. He wouldn't have to spot Dempsey anything in the weight or height line, but he might have to concede something to Dempsey in the hitting department. The fight fans will never be satisfied until Wills gets his chance.

[93] *Boston Globe*, April 20, 1924.
[94] *Muncie Morning Star*, April 22, 1924.
[95] *Long Beach Telegram*, April 25, 1924.
[96] *Hanford Morning Journal*, April 27, 1924. The fight was being shown in conjunction with a lecture by Col. Macks Willard, who would lecture on 1,000 feet of moving pictures and show 20 views from ringside.

Many said Wills would be easy for Dempsey, while others said Wills had a swell chance of beating him. Harry already was getting older for a fighter, yet still was formidable.[97]

Dempsey and Kearns told Robert Edgren that it was news to them that he was not going to fight for a year. They did not know anything about it. Kearns said it was not their fault that they were not matched for a fight. Everybody talked, but when Kearns tried to pin the promoters down, it was just talk and no action. Hence, he accepted the moving picture offer. "Dempsey is one of the best business assets in the world, and it's foolish to let him wait around doing nothing while everybody talks." Kearns also said,

> Nobody knows the complications connected with matching Jack up with Wills. When the New York Boxing Commission put it up to us to sign for Wills a couple of years ago they never thought we'd do it. We surprised them… We wanted that fight. But the moment it was known Jack was willing, politics stepped in and the match-making was blocked. It's been blocked ever since – always something the promoters couldn't get over.

Kearns said he never had been worried about Wills. "It would be pie for Jack. Wills can't fight without holding and if he tried to hold Dempsey he'd be torn to pieces."

Kearns said Dempsey was in the same position that Jeffries was after he beat Munroe. There was no one in sight to give him a real battle. "Jeffries dropped out and made the mistake of waiting too long before coming back into the game." Jack would remain in shape and be ready for anything that turned up. Dempsey echoed, "No, I'm not tied up with an agreement not to fight this year. If I have to go through the year without a bout it won't be my fault."[98]

Tex Rickard said Dempsey likely would meet Wills on September 6 in a 12-round bout at Boyle's Thirty Acres, Jersey City. He had Wills under contract, and believed he would have little trouble in signing the champion. Of course, he had to negotiate with Kearns.

Kearns said he would agree to Dempsey-Wills if there was a sizable purse guarantee for Dempsey, such as $750,000, with a privilege of a percentage if such would be greater.

Immediately after Rickard and Kearns publicly indicated that there was a possibility of Dempsey-Wills taking place, it was announced that New Jersey's clergymen would organize to stop a Wills-Dempsey bout and apply political pressure to ensure it would not be allowed.[99]

Skeptical George Underwood believed that Kearns, despite his public utterances, would try to find a way for Dempsey to escape a meeting with Wills. Underwood felt that Kearns did not want Dempsey to take a chance with a truly dangerous foeman. "Dempsey never has defended his

[97] *New York Daily News*, April 29, 1924.
[98] *San Bernadino Daily Sun*, April 30, 1924.
[99] *Long Beach Telegram*, May 1, 3, 4, 1924; *New York Daily News*, May 2, 1924.

title against a boxer of Wills' bulk, strength, speed, skill, ring generalship and punching power." Kearns was very careful with his meal ticket. Yet, Underwood granted that if there were no other viable options, Dempsey might fight Wills. "It will be Dempsey's first real fight since winning the title. It will be the fastest, fiercest heavyweight duel in the annals of boxing, the real 'battle of the century.'"

Wills had an upcoming bout scheduled with Bartley Madden, and Harry had to be careful, for Madden was rough, tough, awkward, and durable, never having been down and always finishing the fight on his feet, even against Fulton and Brennan, and he had a knockout victory over Jim Coffey. He knew how to clinch and maul. "No matter how you view the Madden match it is a bad one for Wills. He can gain nothing, but can lose a whole lot."[100]

Jim Corbett said the man who beat Dempsey had to be a clever boxer who could hit and take it, but above all he had to be fast and clever, ideally with the ability to move or hold.

> I could punch when I was young. But I decided to pick the clever route, not the slugging one. I decided to put speed of foot and speed of head above the wallop. And one of the hardest things ever known is to work for cleverness, to be on the jump, in and out, always in motion, and at the same time to develop a killing punch. You have to be set for a killing punch. And it's hard to get set against a fast man who knows how to keep away. Any one who tries to slug with Dempsey will get outslugged. First, because Jack is a terrific hitter with either hand. Second, because he is exceptionally fast. Third, because he is game and can take it. Some fast boxer who can tie Jack up or keep away from him will have the better chance. This is why Tom Gibbons the boxer lasted fifteen rounds where Firpo the slugger couldn't last two.[101]

[100] *New York Telegram and Evening Mail*, May 2, 1924.
[101] *Asheville Citizen*, May 7, 1924.

CHAPTER 2

Continuing Good Life and Estelle Taylor as Challengers Try to Justify a Big Fight

In early May 1924, Jack Dempsey started his film work at Universal City. His mother and sister visited him.[102]

(By Pacific & Atlantic)
Dempsey is visited on movie lot by his mother (left) and sister. Probably first picture taken together.

On May 4, 1924, in the Los Angeles area, among those in attendance to watch the auto races at the Ascot Park Speedway were Hollywood's Jack Dempsey and Estelle Taylor.[103]

A married woman, who was a movie extra who lived in Hollywood, California, charged Jack Kearns with having attacked her. She allegedly fought off his advances, but either she was struck in the head or fell unconscious as a result of a drug which may have been put in the water he gave her. She woke up in a house in a bedroom, unclothed.

Kearns replied, "I deny all of the allegations made against me. ... I would not know the woman if she were to walk into the room now." The district attorney was investigating.[104]

There were rumors circulating that linked Dempsey with film actress Estelle Taylor for a possible marriage. Dempsey hosted a birthday party at the Barbara Hotel café in Los Angeles, which Dempsey and Kearns owned, in honor of Estelle and Helen Taylor. The sisters were born a year apart, on May 19 for Estelle and May 20 for Helen.

Dempsey admitted that he was very fond of Estelle and liked her a lot, but denied that they were engaged. He said he knew her back East when she was "a little girl" in a dramatic school and he was fighting. (30-year-

---

102 *Los Angeles Illustrated Daily News*, May 4, 1924.
103 *Los Angeles Times*, May 5, 1924.
104 *Pomona Bulletin*, May 14, 1924; *New York Daily News*, May 14, 15, 1924.

old Taylor was nearly one year older than Dempsey, having been born on May 20, 1894.) Taylor said, "I've known him for eight years, and we have been very good friends. I first met him in Wilmington, Del., and then later when I was attending a dramatic school in New York." They had not discussed marriage, and she was focused on her acting career. She admitted that Jack called almost every evening, and she was very fond of him too.[105]

That Birthday Cake
On the left Teddy Hayes, who is Dempsey's trainer, Dorothy Hayes, Harry Gillis, Mary Harlan and Mervin Leroy. At the end of the table are Dr. and Mrs. Wilson. On the right are Estelle Taylor, Jack Dempsey, Jack Sullivan, Florence Lee and Helen Taylor.

BEHOLD THE SHEIK!—"If you knew what I know about this woman" (Esther Ralston), says the villain, and our hero, yes, Jack Dempsey (center), gets ready to sock the traducer, in scene in movie Jack's in. Wonder if his hair'll be mussed in scrap.

George Underwood said he had information from an informant that Dempsey would not fight Wills on September 6 as claimed, but instead meet Tom Gibbons again. Kearns expected a Gibbons victory over Carpentier in their upcoming bout, which would set up another Dempsey match. The informant said, "Rickard never had any intentions of staging a Dempsey-Wills match. He signed up Wills in a last desperate attempt to club Firpo into signing a contract. ... Kearns is stringing along with Rickard but is keeping other irons in the fire in case things break wrong with Tex."

---

[105] *Los Angeles Times*, May 20, 21, 1924.

Underwood believed it practically was certain that Dempsey would not meet Wills, regardless of what was said in public. In order to sidestep Wills, Kearns and Rickard would ballyhoo others. "Should the winner of the Gibbons-Carpentier match meet and be beaten by Gene Tunney, Tunney will be the man who will be tossed into the ring against Dempsey."[106]

Collar ad Jack with Jack Kearns's son

The Los Angeles District Attorney's office found the Kearns accuser's story not to be substantiated and declined to charge him with anything. "A check on the past record of the woman shows that she made a similar charge against another man and settled the case for a cash consideration. Also, we found evidence contradicting a number of her statements." She sued Kearns anyway, for $200,000.[107]

On May 24, 1924, 30,000 spectators were in the Los Angeles Coliseum for the Olympic Trials. Jack Dempsey boxed 6 short exhibition rounds with big gloves, 2 rounds each with Jack Duran (or Doran), Jack Moore, and Mick Newman, toying with them, but also pummeling them a bit. The multitude loudly and vociferously cheered the champ.[108]

Dempsey and Jack Duran   Jack Moore and Dempsey

In late May, it was reported that Jack Dempsey and Estelle Taylor had been seen together continually for a whole month.[109]

On May 26, 1924, U.S. President Calvin Coolidge signed into law the Immigration Act of 1924, further limiting immigration into the United States based on a national origins quota system.

Tex Rickard was negotiating a Luis Firpo vs. Harry Wills match for August or September, allegedly as a way of deciding the next opponent for Dempsey.[110]

[106] New York Telegram and Evening Mail, May 22, 1924.
[107] Los Angeles Times, May 24, 1924.
[108] Los Angeles Evening Express, May 24, 1924; Los Angeles Times, May 25, 1924. Bull Montana acted as Dempsey's chief second, and Teddy Hayes refereed.
[109] New York Daily News, May 25, 1924.
[110] Los Angeles Evening Express, May 29, 1924.

The next big fight was Georges Carpentier vs. Tommy Gibbons. Since his 1923 decision loss to Dempsey, Gibbons had scored four knockouts, all within 3 rounds, including KO1 205-pound Joe Downey. Since losing to Battling Siki in 1922, Carpentier had won three fights by knockout.

GIBBONS

CARPENTIER

On May 31, 1924 at Floyd Fitzsimmons' arena in Michigan City, Indiana, before a packed crowd of an estimated 24,000 (some said 35,000), 177-pound Tommy Gibbons (89-4-4) clearly won a 10-round no decision bout against 174-pound Georges Carpentier (87-13-5). There were no knockdowns, but the sportswriters believed Gibbons won every round, or no worse than 7-0-3 or 7-1-2. Harry Newman had it 10-0 for Gibbons.

Gibbons feinted and landed nearly at will, while Carpentier could not, hurting Tom with only one effective right during the entire fight, in the 4th round. Georges often retreated and held on, groggy from the blows, bleeding from his mouth, and blood dripping from a cut over his right eye. Gibbons was quicker, stronger, more aggressive, and had a nearly perfect defense.

Robert Edgren said Gibbons thrashed Carpentier all the way, keeping him on the retreat. He was too clever for Carpentier, who could not land his big right. At close quarters, Georges could not defend himself from Tommy's tearing body attack. Even at long range, Tom landed two or three to one. Gibbons' punches had plenty of snap and power, but Georges was in great shape and moved about, clinching when he could. "Tom Gibbons never fought a better fight."

Carpentier said, "Monsieur Gibbons is the best boxer I ever faced. I know now how he managed to stay fifteen rounds with Dempsey. He hits with terrific force."

Gibbons said, "I think I have convinced the public that I am entitled to another crack at Jack Dempsey."

The receipts were $227,397.50,

GIBBONS

excellent for a non-title fight. Carpentier earned $70,000, and Gibbons $61,781. Total paid attendance was 16,586, but officials estimated that 7,000 – 8,000 crashed the gate.[111]

On June 2, 1924 in Newark, in federal court, Tex Rickard, matchmaker Frank Flournoy, and Fred Quimby, the movie man who made the Dempsey-Carpentier fight films, all plead not guilty to charges of conspiring to transport fight films illegally. They posted $2,500 bonds.[112]

On June 3, 1924 at Jack Doyle's Vernon Arena, in the Los Angeles area, for a children's charity Milk Fund benefit, before a crowd of more than 9,000, Jack Dempsey exhibited against three men for a scheduled 2 rounds each. $35,000 was raised.

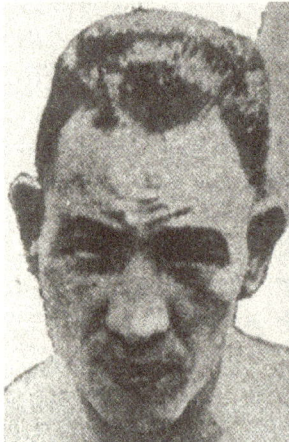

Rocco Stramaglia   Dempsey and Rocco Stramaglia

Dempsey decked and knocked out in 50 seconds Rocco Stramaglia, who cut Jack while training for the Gibbons fight. After Rocco recovered, in their 2nd round, Dempsey clouted Rocco relentlessly, had him groggy, and stopped him with a solar plexus punch in 1 minute 45 seconds. It took several minutes to revive him with smelling salts. Rocco had a black eye, and the left side of his face was puffy.

[111] *Battle Creek Enquirer, Richmond Item, Indianapolis Star, Chicago Tribune, New York Daily News, Dayton Daily News*, June 1, 1924.
[112] *New York Daily News*, June 3, 1924.

Local heavy Joe Ryan was tall and strapping, but soon after the bell, Dempsey vigorously smote him with a left hook and he went down to the canvas. Jack lifted him to his feet, but later flattened him with a short right cross. Jack again lifted him up. The bell was rung after 1 minute 20 seconds. Bleeding from the nose, Ryan refused to continue further.

Eli Stanton danced about the ring, jabbing. Dempsey measured him carefully, then landed a precise, smashing left hook on the chin, knocking him down. Jack picked him up. Another left hook to the chin sent him down for keeps. He sat there, blood trickling from the bridge of his nose. He had lasted 45 seconds.[113]

Indications were that neither Dempsey-Wills nor Dempsey-Firpo II were likely to take place in 1924, even if the former fight was possible. Firpo would not be ready for Wills any sooner than late August, which would put off a follow-up bout for the winner with Dempsey, given that there was not enough time between bouts prior to the weather change. Rickard said Dempsey was willing to fight someone as late as September 15, which would have worked if Wills-Firpo could have been staged in early August as Tex had hoped, with the winner to fight Jack a month and a half later.[114]

Bartley Madden   Harry Wills

Up next for Wills was a bout with Bartley Madden. Harry said, "I'll knock out Madden as quickly as I can. I try to stop all my opponents, and Madden will be no exception. I feel great, my hands are in good shape and I'm going to give the public a run for its money." Madden said no one had stopped him, and Wills would not either.[115]

On June 9, 1924 at the Queensboro Stadium, Long Island City, Queens, New York, 16,500 people paid $80,000 (one said $63,783) to see 213-pound Harry Wills (81-7-7) clearly win a 15-round decision against 185-pound white Bartley Madden (34-20-7).

However, many said Wills' failure to stop Madden was a negative. Even staunch supporter Harry Newman said, "Wills won, to be sure, but his prestige received an awful jolt." He "suffered a setback that will make it difficult for him to sustain his claim to a sock at the champion." It was a

113 *Los Angeles Evening Express, Bakersfield Californian*, June 4, 1924.
114 *New York Telegram and Evening Mail*, June 4, 1924; *New York Daily News*, June 5, 1924.
115 *New York Telegram and Evening Mail*, June 9, 1924.

clumsy affair. Wills hit Madden's body and cut his left eye open with a sharp right, but Madden was there at the end, still fighting hard.

There was nothing to it but Wills until the 10th round, when Madden spurted and did well, a right chop to the chin sending Harry back on his heels. Bartley also won the 11th, though Wills won the remaining rounds.

Newman scored it 12-2-1 for Wills.

This was the closest Madden came to being knocked down when in the tenth round he slipped to knee after Wills jarred him with left hook after rushing him to ropes.

Madden ducked to get away from shower of rights and lefts to body and face in fifth round. Photo shows Wills shooting left under arm to the jaw.

They fought like a brace of longshoremen, said our fight expert, Harry Newman, and this photo seems to bear out that statement. It shows Madden hanging on and apparently butting his colored opponent with his head in tenth round.

In the fifteenth and last round Wills tried desperately to put his game but smaller foe away, but without avail. He shot right to stomach as bell sounded.

The tenth and eleventh rounds were only ones credited to Madden. He's shown here planting left to Wills's stomach in the tenth. He followed up with left hook to Harry's chin.

WINNING EVERY ROUND but two, Harry Wills, giant colored challenger of Jack Dempsey, last night received verdict over Bartley Madden after fifteen-round bout in Queensboro stadium, Long Island City. —Story on page 27

James Wood said at no time was Bartley near a knockout, or even a knockdown. Wills mauled, shoved, stung, and cut him, but could not drop him. Yet, there was no question about the decision.

In Wills' defense, Madden had not been stopped since 1914, when he was green. Men like Brennan, Miske, Fulton, and Gibbons had not stopped him either.

Regardless, many said Wills was disappointing, not showing the master boxing, devastating punch, or speed claimed for him. Wood said Wills would be no match for Dempsey. His ability to stand up for any length of time would depend on how much he could take, not something brought out by Madden. Harry was wide open at times, and Dempsey's short hooks would have found a ready target, particularly to the body. Wood thought Wills would look better against Firpo, for he would outsmart him in the clinches and outbox him at long range.

Wood granted, "Wills can hit. He may have lost his speed and may be on the downward path but his blows are still terrific, destructive punches that hurt no matter where they land. Madden, of course, is a glutton for punishment and he knows how to offset the hard wallops by rolling his head and twisting his body." "But as for Dempsey, the Brown Panther showed that he is not in the same class. He may have been at one time but that time has past."

Thomas Rice was even harsher. "On what Wills showed last night a bout between him and Dempsey would be a reproach to the boxing game and a fraud on the public." Wills fought like an old man, one who had lost his fire, spring, and confidence of youth. Some even thought he might be holding back.

Damon Runyon said Wills looked bad at times, and he tired. He won clearly, but all the plaudits were for Madden in gamely lasting. Runyon granted that no one had been able to stop Madden.

> But Wills tonight displayed little of the prowess popularly credited to him. He seemed absolutely helpless when it came to trying to box at long range. He was impressive only when he could drag Madden to him as a grizzly bear might drag in a lamb, and while clutching him, beat him about the body with his right.

Furthermore, Madden landed fairly often. "But Madden is a light puncher. He does not hurt when he hits. It is conceivable that against a man who could put some power behind his punches Wills tonight would soon have been in dire trouble."

Still, Wills won with relative ease, in a "good workout."

The *Brooklyn Standard Union* said Harry's speed and punch were missing, and age and inactivity were turning him into a plodding, deliberate-swinging, ordinary fighter, different from the formerly fast-stepping, quick-thinking, and hard-landing one he used to be. He no longer was agile. "No longer can he step around and poke and jab lefts and rights with the speed and precision" of yesteryear. He won, but never had his foe in any distress.

Luis Firpo said Wills probably had an off day. Every boxer had one. He had an off day with Spalla. Plus, Madden had been a tough out for many others.

George Underwood said Wills won the official decision, but Madden won the moral victory. Though belted, flayed, and battered unmercifully, Madden's courage was undimmed, and he gave Wills a stubborn battle throughout, never going down. The opinion expressed by fans as they left was, "Dempsey will murder him." However, "Cooler minds saw things differently." Regardless, "the fact remains that Wills has slowed up, does not punch half as snappily or as fast as of yore, and the burden of the years has affected his wind and stamina not a little. Wills undoubtedly has gone back." However, Dempsey had gone back too, even against Firpo, and with more idleness was not going to get any better. Wills still could "give and take more than any man Dempsey has yet faced ... Wills still remains Dempsey's only real rival."

> Despite Harry's failure to put Madden away you will find Jack Kearns, Dempsey's manager, just as coy as ever about allowing Dempsey to risk his title against Wills, although Kearns will be just as blatant as ever, perhaps more so now, in shouting Dempsey's willingness to meet Wills.

What limited films still exist primarily show Wills and Madden punching, clinching, and firing some inside blows in the clinches. Wills would stalk, jab or hook, and then uppercut on the inside or dig body blows. Madden was game and would fire back, but he was more defensive and cautious than Wills, moving around a bit as Harry gradually but cautiously and calmly slid towards him.

Jack Kearns turned down an offer of $150,000 for Dempsey vs. Madden in July, for he declared that Dempsey's motion picture work would prevent him from fighting in July, and furthermore, the champion would not risk his crown except against an outstanding contender, such as Wills or Firpo.

Tex Rickard said he was greatly disappointed by Wills' poor showing, which indicated that Harry had gone back. Tex even said he was debating whether to put on a Wills vs. Firpo contest, concerned that it would not be as big a draw as previously believed. When asked what Wills' chances were with Dempsey, Tex said, "I never like to make predictions, but I will say that Wills convinced me as he did 16,000 other fight fans last night that he is no match for Dempsey."[116]

Geoge Underwood said if Wills was the easy mark that many declared he now was, the best way to prove it would be to fight him. The "white heavyweights should be tumbling over themselves to get a crack at him." He predicted that most would continue to avoid Wills. Underwood argued that Wills' failure to stop Madden was no worse than Dempsey's failure to stop Gibbons, for both foes were nearly impossible to stop.[117]

On June 15, 1924, in the Tia Juana restaurant at Broadway and 171st street in New York, which he owned and managed, Bill Brennan was shot and killed. He was only 30 years old.

Two men with lengthy criminal records were arrested and charged with murder. Bill's sister witnessed the shooting, screamed, and then the assailant fired at her, barely missing, but striking James Cullen below the neck. He was in critical condition in the hospital. It was unclear why they

---

[116] *New York Daily News, Brooklyn Daily Times, Brooklyn Daily Eagle, Buffalo Courier, Brooklyn Standard Union, New York Telegram and Evening Mail,* June 10, 1924.
[117] *New York Telegram and Evening Mail,* June 12, 20, 1924.

shot Brennan. A police lieutenant was hit with the butt-end of a gun as the assailants were escaping. Police gave chase until they surrendered.

Upon hearing of Brennan's death, Jack Dempsey said, "He gave me more trouble than any fighter in the world. There's the gamest man I ever met. Poor old Bill! What a pity!"[118]

Dempsey's film series, "Fight and Win," would be released in early July. The first of the series would be "Winning His Way."

On June 24, Jack Dempsey celebrated his 29th birthday at his Wilshire home in Los Angeles.

In accordance with the law that all fighters must undergo an examination before entering the ring. Estridge, Greb, Loughran, Stribling, Moore, Tunney, Spalla and Gans (in boxing togs, l. to r.) were examined by doctors.

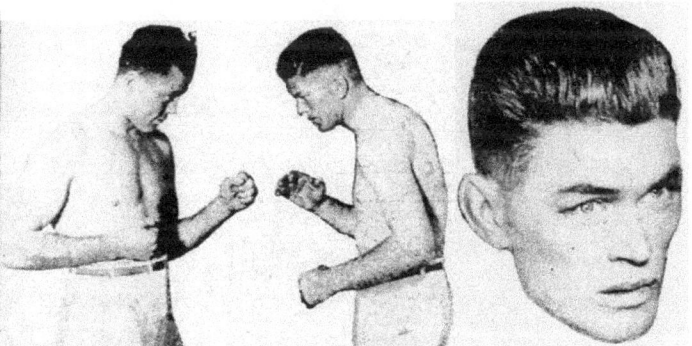

Spalla faces off with Tunney

On June 26, 1924, as part of a Milk Fund show at Yankee Stadium, in the Bronx, before about 45,000 to 50,000 people who generated a gate of about $185,000 to $200,000, 183-pound Gene Tunney stopped 191-pound Erminio Spalla (35-5-2) in the 7th round, winning every round until the referee stopped it when Spalla was helpless in a corner. In March that year, Firpo had stopped Spalla in the 14th round.

The *Buffalo Evening News* commented that Tunney undoubtedly would be one of Dempsey's most formidable opponents in the next two years.

---

[118] *New York Daily News, Los Angeles Record,* June 16, 1924.

In the main event, 159 ½-pound Harry Greb defended his world middleweight championship with a 15-round unanimous decision over 160-pound English champ Ted Moore (52-8-2).[119]

Dempsey kept filming his ten movies for Universal. During July, Dempsey's serial, "A Society Knockout," began showing.[120]

On July 20, 1924, at 10 p.m. in Galivan, just north of San Juan Capistrano, California, Jack Dempsey was injured badly in an automobile accident, which also badly damaged his $15,000 auto. Jack had a wrenched back, sprained ligaments and muscles in his neck, several cuts on his hands, face, and body, a bloody nose, and numerous scratches and bruises. Internal injuries were feared. An X-ray would be performed.

Dempsey Auto After Collision

[P. & A. Photos]

Expensive car of Premier Pugilist was badly damaged and the owner may be seriously injured as a result of crash near San Juan Capistrano. Inset—Jack Dempsey.

Dempsey, trainer Teddy Hayes, and Hayes' film star wife Florence Lee (with whom Dempsey co-starred in one of his films), were headed to a film location in Dempsey's auto, a Rolls-Royce limousine, with the fighter's "negro" chauffeur at the wheel. The chauffeur claimed that another vehicle came at them, careening from one side of the road to the other. In trying to avoid a head-on collision, he dodged away, but was sideswiped nevertheless. Dempsey's car was hurtled across the road and turned over completely, landing in a ditch on its side. Florence Lee was knocked unconscious.

—C-V Service Photo

AND WHO MAY THIS BE? HEH! HEH! HEH!—Pipe the moustachios and the bit of spinach on the chin, and, too, the American "Beauty" on the right lapel. It's too good to keep. The young lady is Florence Lee, motion picture actress. The other—haw! haw! haw!—is none but Jack Dempsey doing his stuff for a two-reel thriller on the S. S. Ruth Alexander.

When Lee awoke, she blamed Dempsey's chauffeur for driving too fast, and Hayes and he started fighting, until Dempsey broke it up. Dempsey said they were lucky to be alive.

---

[119] *New York Daily News, Brooklyn Daily Times, Buffalo Evening News,* June 27, 1924. Also, Young Stribling won a 6-round decision over Tommy Loughran.

[120] *Los Angeles Times,* July 19, 30, 1924. Dempsey also was starring in "West of the Water Bucket" during late July.

The driver who struck them continued and did not stop. He only later reported the accident to the police in Santa Ana. He blamed it on Dempsey's driver.

A witness said the front wheel of the Dempsey machine hit the rear wheel of a sedan and then turned over completely, facing the opposite direction. Dempsey scrambled out, seeming dazed, and appeared to be more worried about Florence Lee's condition than his own. The witness said Dempsey was lucky to escape with his life.[121]

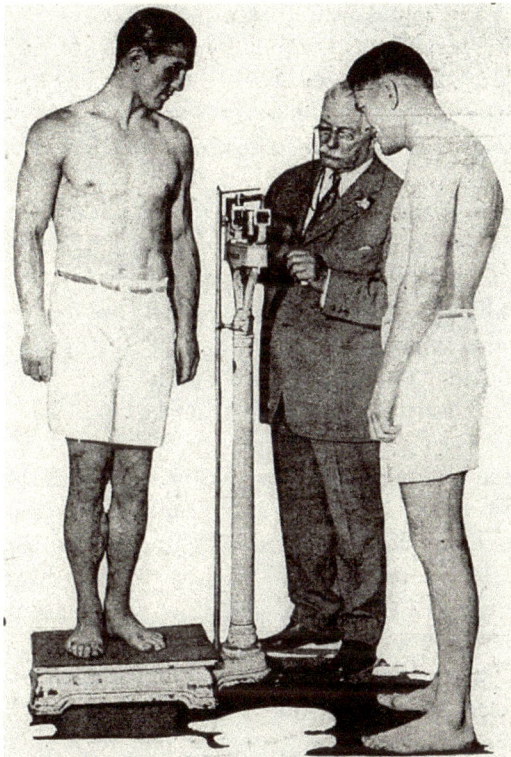

Carpentier and Tunney weighed in by Muldoon.

On July 24, 1924 at the Polo Grounds in New York, before 30,000 (or 40,000 or 50,000) fans who generated $125,000, 173 ¼-pound Gene Tunney dominated, but scored a controversial 15th round technical knockout over 173-pound Georges Carpentier. Although Tunney clearly was winning up until the end, scoring several knockdowns in the 10th round, the finish came with some debate, for many argued that Tunney had hit Carpentier low at the conclusion of the 14th round.

According to Harry Newman, Tunney had controlled the fight, winning 10-3-1 up to the end. Carpentier only won rounds 4, 8, and 9, with the 12th even.

In the 10th round, Tunney decked Carpentier for a 9-count with a left hook to the chin followed by a right uppercut. Carp was decked again for a 2-count. Georges was staggering, yet made a magnificent stand. He released a furious attack that drove Tunney back. Still, Carpentier went down twice more, four times in all in the 10th. The referee tried to stop the contest, but Carp refused to stop, and just kept on fighting, swinging away.

Others said Carp was down three times in the 10th, and took a bad beating, primarily from hooks and right uppercuts to the head. Throughout the bout, Tunney hit him with an assortment of blows.

[121] *Los Angeles Times, Long Beach Telegram*, July 22, 1924; *Los Angeles Evening Express, Long Beach Telegram, Los Angeles Record*, July 21, 1924.

Just as the bell rang to end the 14th round, there was a flurry on the ropes, and Carpentier dropped to his knees. He claimed foul – a low blow. He appeared to be in pain. Referee Andy Griffin did not see a foul. Saved by the bell, Carp's seconds dragged him to his corner and worked over him. Carp was bent over, spitting blood. Descamps cried "Foul!" over and over. Carp had the minute rest to recover and continue.

When the bell rang to start the 15th round, Carpentier still was not ready to fight, even though he was wearing an aluminum foul protector. Hence, Tunney was awarded a 15th round technical knockout victory.

Newman wrote, "There was a variance of opinion among the 50,000 spectators, but for the most part they appeared satisfied that Tunney had struck a fair blow, and even if there had been a low blow it was unintentional and in no way affected the result." There was "nothing to it but Tunney."

Thomas Rice said Carpentier had figured in yet another bout that ended in a sensational claim of foul. He was known for such claims earlier in his career. This time though, he lost, for his claim was not allowed. He was declared technically out when he was not in shape to continue for the 15th round. Had he not had the reputation for being famous for making such claims, and being as good an actor as he was a boxer, he might have won on a foul. He was losing clearly, so he or his manager might have seen this as his way of snatching victory out of the jaws of defeat.

Carp had been decked three times in the 10th round, but kept fighting. In the 14th round, he had been tamed somewhat by two lefts to the chin and several body punches. He then rallied and fired left and right, driving Tunney back against the ropes. The referee was somewhat behind them when Tunney fired the controversial blow. Rice could not see where it landed, nor did he think the referee could either.

However, Rice heard a sound as if the blow had landed on Carpentier's aluminum foul cup. Bill Farnsworth of the *American* agreed, feeling it was low. Some, including Jack Curley, thought Tunney's knee struck him low. Yet, some asserted there was no foul at all, that the blow landed above the belt with a water-soaked glove, and that caused the peculiar sound.

Referee Griffin claimed that Carpentier caused the foul. Carp jumped upward as he stepped in, causing Tunney's blow to land low.

Most thought the referee was behind the fighters, so he could not see the punch. Carp certainly acted as if he had been fouled. However, Carpentier was so theatrical that some thought he was faking or exaggerating, particularly since he was wearing a foul cup. The feeling was that he should have been able to continue after the minute rest.

When the bell rang to start the 15th round, Carp's seconds still were in the ring, and Carp was bent over until his gloves almost touched the canvas. Griffin stopped it on the ground that Carpentier was not able to defend himself.

The *Brooklyn Standard Union's* writer believed it was low, for it made the distinct sound made when a punch lands on the protective cup.

The *Brooklyn Daily Times'* James Wood said he could not see it.

The *Brooklyn Citizen's* William Granger said Tunney soundly beat Carpentier, who claimed a foul when a body wallop hurt him. Tunney handed him a beating, and the final blow was not low, but a paralyzing left to the stomach.

The *New York Evening Post's* Harry Cross said the blow appeared to shoot into the pit of the stomach. Referee Griffin insisted the blow was not a foul. Cross also noted that in the 10th, Carpentier was in such bad shape that Griffin stepped in and tried to stop the bout, but Georges refused to give up. "In ten out of the fourteen rounds Tunney had a decided advantage." Carp was game, but mostly missed, and the times he did land his famous right, Tunney never appeared hurt. Some were disappointed by the fact that Tunney took so long to finish him, but the "body blows of Tunney and Dempsey are quite different." Despite the victory, "Tunney did not appear brilliant."

For the International News Service, Jack Lait said no one saw the blow about which Carpentier complained. "Maybe the hit was low, and maybe it wasn't. Georges had struck Tunney below the belt several times in earlier rounds and had been forgiven." "As for Tunney, he is young, strong and willing but has no class. Neither is he murderous enough to ever become a great card." Gene should have finished the game Carpentier in the 10th round, but instead allowed him to recuperate.

Frank Getty, United Press staff correspondent, said Tunney unintentionally hit Carpentier in the groin. When Georges went down, Tunney smirked and said, "Faker." Regardless, Tunney was well ahead on points, and it likely would be Carp's last big fight. Getty also said Tunney lacked the killer instinct that makes a "real ring champion."

W. O. McGeehan said, "Tunney is too much of a human being ever to make a heavyweight champion."

Donald Cameron said Carpentier was beaten badly, and his charge of foul was not given too much credulity. Tunney's steady fusillade of blows, particularly to the body, wore him down.

On the limited remaining films in existence, Carpentier appeared to be a bit more of the aggressor, but the patient, lightly bouncing Tunney was very good at firing very fast well-timed counterpunches, often in combination, and he snuck in short body punches on the inside. Both men clinched a fair amount.

In the 10th round, after Carpentier stepped in with a jab, a Tunney left hook followed by a right uppercut decked Carpentier. Carp went down again from a short right and perhaps slight push with the left, but rose quickly, seemingly without a count. Tunney lambasted him with well-placed blows, including a head-jarring right uppercut, even as Carp tried to move in and clinch. Gene simply moved back and kept firing. Tunney landed jabs, uppercuts, hooks, straight rights, and even some body blows.

Carpentier bent over, seeming defenseless, partially leaning sideways into the ropes, and the referee stepped in as if to stop it, pushing Gene back, not allowing him to finish his man, but then Carp stood up, moved in aggressively, and appeared to push the referee back, insisting on continuing. The referee stepped away and allowed it to continue.

Carpentier fired away gamely, but Tunney kept countering him effectively, particularly with his right uppercut. There seems to be an edit, and the referee wiped Carp's gloves briefly, so it is possible that it was after rising from either a slip or a knockdown. A lead left hook dropped Carpentier again. He rose, and Tunney kept pummeling his head and body, but Carpentier fired back valiantly.

Carp, shown floored for count of nine in the tenth, rose from this to be at Tunney again. Floored four times this round, each time he gamely went back to battle.

Regarding the 14th round, the official pictures are not clear or definitive, but it does appear that Tunney's left hook may have strayed a bit low. Carpentier leapt/stepped in quickly and somewhat extended his legs upward and squared up, and as he did so, his left arm went over the top and onto Gene's right shoulder and neck area at the same time that Gene was dipping and leaning left for a left hook/uppercut to the body, so the leg extension, squaring and lifting up, and the pressure of Carpentier's own arm and body weight pushing down on Tunney contributed to the blow possibly straying a bit low. Carpentier immediately responded to the punch as if it was low, grabbing at his groin area. At first, he remained standing, but then took a knee. Probably, had Carp not put weight onto Tunney and pulled/pushed down on his head/neck, the blow would not have gone low at all, if in fact it went low, which isn't clear, owing to the film's poor quality plus Tunney's back obscuring the view of the blow.

Some who saw the films insisted that the movies did not verify a low blow, and that it was legal. Others said Tunney fouled him with his knee, not a punch. Tunney insisted it was an uppercut to the stomach.[122]

[122] New York Daily News, Brooklyn Daily Eagle, Brooklyn Standard Union, Brooklyn Daily Times, Brooklyn Citizen, New York Evening Post, Buffalo Courier, Buffalo Enquirer, Buffalo Evening News, Glens Falls Post-Star, Yonkers Herald, Yonkers Statesman, July 25, 1924.

Regardless of the manner of finish, because Tunney had dominated the fight, beating a respected big name, ultimately the result greatly increased his prestige. Still, Carpentier was coming off the loss to Gibbons a couple months prior.

AGE MEETS YOUTH.—Hiram Dempsey, 67, father of champ, married Lottie D. Blasingame, 26 (both above), at Salt Lake City. She's now Jack's stepmother.

On August 1, 1924 in Farmington, Utah, Jack Dempsey's father, 67-year-old Hiram or Hyrum Dempsey, married 26-year-old Lottie Dexter Blasingame of Idaho. Apparently, the romance began when Hyrum met her during the Dempsey-Gibbons fight. Four years earlier, on July 9, 1920, just under a month after Jack Dempsey's acquittal on draft-dodging charges, Mary Dempsey, Jack's mother, had been granted a divorce from Hyrum on grounds of nonsupport. She claimed that her son Jack had supported her for years.[123]

On August 9, 1924, in London, England, at Wembley Stadium, 178 ½-pound Tommy Gibbons knocked out 178-pound British Cruiser-weight champion Jack Bloomfield (28-5-2) in the 3rd round. The fight was filmed. In the 2nd round, Gibbons decked Bloomfield with a combination left hook to the body, left hook to the head, right uppercut, and left hook to the head. After rising and taking several blows, a final left hook dropped Bloomfield a second time, laying on his back. He barely beat the count. A left hook, right uppercut, and left hook sent him down and out cold under

[123] *Los Angeles Times, New York Daily News*, August 23, 1924. *Oregon Daily Journal*, July 10, 1920.

the ropes. Apparently, the bell saved him, and his cornermen picked him up. In the 3rd round, a left hook and right hook wobbled Jack back to the ropes, and a set-up jab and right sent Bloomfield down through the ropes onto his back out cold again, to be counted out.

Luis Firpo and Harry Wills were scheduled to fight one another on September 11 at Boyle's Thirty Acres in New Jersey.[124]

Tex Rickard said he received a telegram from Dempsey saying that he would be ready on short notice to meet the winner of the Wills-Firpo fight. Hence, Tex was considering hosting the match in October. He had not expected Dempsey to be ready to fight before 1925.

Kearns said Dempsey might accept an offer to fight Gibbons in London in October. The champ was tired of picture work. "Dempsey wants action."[125]

Yet, on August 19, 1924, in Los Angeles, one month after his auto accident, Dempsey had plastic surgery on his nose to have it straightened. Many believed it was cosmetic, done for the movies, and signaled the end of his boxing career. Kearns said it was not cosmetic, but rather because Jack was bothered in his breathing by an obstruction which needed to be removed. Some wondered whether his new nose could handle a punch.

A surgeon re-made Dempsey's nose by using a piece of his left ear. It corrected his outstanding ear, and the strip of cartilage was used on the bridge of his nose. Jack now would be able to breathe easier. His nose would be in a cast for one week.[126]

It wasn't clear how Dempsey was going to fight or spar, given that he just had nose surgery. It was looking much less likely that he would fight any time soon, and his lack of activity from 1921 to 1923 was about to repeat itself.

On August 21, 1924, in Fremont, Ohio, 166- or 167-pound Harry Greb won a very close 10-round no decision bout against black southpaw 161 ½-pound Theodore "Tiger" Flowers (69-8-4). Most reported that Greb won, though some called it a draw or even gave it to Flowers. The local *Fremont News-Messenger*, in scoring it a 4-3-3 shade win for Greb, said,

> Although the major number of newspaper men about the arena, including Associated Press representatives, Regis Walsh [sic – Welsh] and Ray Cull [sic - Coll], of Pittsburgh; H. B. Ante of the Cleveland Press; Larry Grill of the Toledo Times, the Messenger representative gave Greb the edge, the dusky Flowers was no boxer to be toyed with. He, perhaps, made the celebrated 'Pittsburgh Windmill' step the fastest ten rounds that he has ever stepped in his life and extend himself all the way to win the bout on ring generalship and number of clean wallops landed.

> Flowers was great, even if he was shaded...

[124] *Los Angeles Times*, August 10, 1924.
[125] *New York Daily News*, August 11, 1924.
[126] *Los Angeles Times*, *Los Angeles Evening Express*, August 20, 1924; *Brooklyn Daily Eagle*, August 22, 1924; *New York Daily News*, August 22, 1924.

Others had it: *Cincinnati Enquirer* (Greb won 8 rounds), *Lima Republican-Gazette* (Greb, 4-1-5), *Dayton Herald* (Greb, 4-2-4), *Pittsburgh Post* (Regis Welsh, Greb, 6-3-1), *Pittsburgh Gazette Times* (Ray Coll, Greb 8-0-2).

Harry Bradbury of the *Lima News* said, "It would be unfair, unreasonable and unjust to give a decision otherwise than a draw."

J. M. Glatz for the *Port Huron Times-Herald* said Flowers won, 6-2-2.

At no time was the rangy colored fighter, whose style of fighting is that of a whirling dervish, in danger. He rocked the champion continually with rights and lefts to head and body. Greb, labelled 'hold and hit Harry' and the 'Pittsburgh Windmill' couldn't cope with Flowers' defense. He had a difficult time dodging his offense.

This writer claimed that the majority of newspapermen at ringside gave Flowers the decision.[127]

Well Known Actor Leaves For Trip. William Harrison Dempsey and his party, as they went away yesterday. Left to right, Mrs. Helen Carter, Estelle Taylor, the champion and his sister, Elsie. (Times photo.)

On August 26, a week after his nose surgery, Jack Dempsey left Los Angeles via train to visit Salt Lake City. Accompanying him were his sister Elsie, trainer Teddy Hayes, Estelle Taylor, her sister Mrs. Helen Carter, and 7-year-old niece Frances.[128]

After visiting family in Utah, Dempsey headed to the East Coast to see Wills vs. Firpo. Jack believed it was an even fight in its inception. He said, "I am anxious to fight. I am tired of making pictures and if Rickard or any of the other promoters can show me some money I will meet any man indoors this winter."[129]

However, given the financial demands and requirements of a Dempsey fight, a large outdoor arena would be required, which also meant it could not be too cold for such a fight, which is why promoters typically liked to host big fights in the summer or no later than the fall.

Another article quoted Jack as saying that he would quit the ring

---

[127] *Fremont News-Messenger, Cincinnati Enquirer, Binghamton Press, Lima News, Lima Republican-Gazette, Dayton Herald, Port Huron Times-Herald, Pittsburgh Post, Pittsburgh Gazette Times*, August 22, 1924. On May 8, 1923, Kid Norfolk had knocked out Tiger Flowers in the 1st round.

[128] *Los Angeles Times*, August 27, 1924. Many believed that Jack's new nose actually was done for motion picture purposes.

[129] *New York Daily News*, August 29, September 1, 1924.

for good when he married Estelle Taylor. He would retire, settle down in the country, and be a family man for the rest of his life. No wedding date had been set, but he anticipated it would take place in a year or two. He wanted to have a couple more fights first. After that, both would retire from their respective professions.

One of Dempsey's problems was convincing Taylor that beneath it all, he was gentle. Estelle said, "He's always telling me how harmless he is. You know he is always trying to get the fighting idea out of my head. Well, I watched him while he was making one episode in his picture out in Hollywood, and maybe he didn't have to lay on the cave man stuff!" Word was that Dempsey was pretty rough with his fellow actors in the fight scenes and didn't play at it as much as they would have liked.[130]

According to the press, both Dempsey and Taylor had some interesting histories. He had been married to Maxine Dempsey, a prostitute who accused him of throwing the Flynn fight, using snuff, cocaine, and strychnine, and of draft dodging.

Estelle Taylor previously had been dating a married man, George Walsh, whose wife Seena Owen accused her of many things. Taylor sued for slander, but later dropped it. Owen got her divorce from Walsh, and child custody. Taylor had announced her engagement to Walsh before the divorce.

Another alleged Taylor affair included George E. Barnes, a Hollywood cameraman, whose wife insisted that Taylor and her husband were far too friendly.

The *Daily News* further claimed and announced that Taylor still was married to a man named Kenneth Malcolm Peacock, and she had not yet obtained a divorce from him.

When Dempsey had arrived in Hollywood, he set every female heart fluttering. The very sight of him seemed to be enough to turn women's heads away from their husbands.

Albert Siegal had sued Jack in 1921 for the alienation of the affections of his wife, "shimmy girl" Bee Palmer. Jack denied it, and after a while, Al and Bee made up.

When Jack was at the Belmont hotel in July 1921, folks were talking about his friendship with Sylvia Jocelyn of the movies, who curiously enough stopped at the same hotel. Some even claimed they were engaged.

Jack and Sylvia were introduced by Bebe Daniels, who also had not been averse to basking in the limelight of the pugilistic king's presence.

[130] *New York Daily News*, September 3, 1924.

Another "girl" Dempsey infatuated was Mae Devereaux, a dancer of the musical comedy stage, who had a gift for boxing herself.[131]

Subsequent to such reports about Estelle Taylor's personal life, when Dempsey was informed that Estelle Taylor was married and had thrown down her husband after he trained her for the stage and she achieved film fame, he allegedly became upset, and denied an intention to marry her. Jack grumbled, "I can't walk the street with any girl nowadays, but some blank paper comes out and says I'm engaged to the dame. Now get this right. I'm not engaged. And as for getting married right away – that's the bunk." He also said, "She's already married – how can I marry her, or anybody else?" He declined to talk further – for publication. "What he said otherwise can't be printed."

Taylor declined to comment. Estelle's sister Helen admitted that Estelle still was married. "He simply won't give her a divorce. You know he says he paid all the expenses of training her for the stage and that then she threw him down. Of course, that isn't true. Mr. Peacock didn't appreciate Estelle's love for her art." He tried to get her to give up her film career. "He's only a bank clerk, though he rides around in a car nowadays."

Taylor was 30 years old, one year older than Dempsey. She had gotten married in December 1911, when she was 17 years old, to then 22-year-old Kenneth Peacock, a bank clerk. He was contemplating

Estelle Taylor looking pensive. Wonder why?

Meet the future Mrs. Jack Dempsey, known to screen fans as Estelle Taylor. She's shown here in what her press agent was pleased to call gypsy attire.

a suit against Dempsey for alienation of affections.

Peacock alleged that Taylor had betrayed him multiple times. In 1919, after he had taken her to New York and paid for her attendance in dramatic school, he filed a suit against Gasper Sharpless, a rich dairyman, for alienation of affections, which settled for $2,500. Allegedly, Sharpless introduced Dempsey to Estelle.

Ultimately, Peacock decided not to sue Dempsey, but to sue for divorce. He said he intended to name a prominent motion picture man in

131 New York Daily News, September 3, 1924.

the divorce proceedings, but ultimately declined to name his name. Apparently, Peacock had not lived with his wife for several years.[132]

The *Daily News'* Jack Farrell was not impressed with Luis Firpo's appearance in training for the upcoming Wills fight, saying that he was far from the same man who faced Dempsey. "He lacks spirit; he is absolutely devoid of any pep or aggressiveness. What's more, his wind is bad." He needed more than just strength to beat Wills. Some wondered whether the Dempsey fight and the good life had taken something away from Firpo.

The confident Wills said if he was beaten, he probably would retire. If he won, he would press his claims for a Dempsey bout. He was dead-set on whipping Firpo. Harry allegedly said,

> There will be the first line to really compare us on this bout. If I keep out of harm's way and am not dropped and on the verge of a knockout as was the champ and then score a knockout there will be any number of people who will rate me better than the champion. ... [I] have trained like I never did before for this match. If I were a champion, defending my crown, I couldn't have done any better, and if I ever do get a crack at the title it will be impossible for me to round into any better form than now.
>
> I see Dempsey will be on deck for the fight. I hope he'll be near enough so I can spill Firpo into his lap, but I hope he won't toss him back in the ring as reporters tossed Jack when Firpo sent him through the ropes. ...
>
> My wind and legs are perfect. I'm as strong as a bull. My hands are perfect, so what more could I want?[133]

Luis Firpo, George Underwood, Young Stribling   Underwood and Wills

On September 5, the Pennsylvania State Athletic Commission granted Jack Dempsey a referee's license.

On September 8, 1924, in Philadelphia, Jack Dempsey refereed the Joe Lynch vs. Pete Sarmiento featherweight bout, the latter winning a 10-

[132] *New York Daily News,* September 4, 7, 9, 1924.
[133] *New York Daily News, New York Telegram and Evening Mail,* September 3, 1924.

round unanimous decision. On that same card, 200-pound white Jack Renault won a unanimous 10-round judge's decision over 215-pound black George Godfrey.

George Underwood said 90% of experienced students of boxing believed Wills would triumph over Firpo, but when two powerful men got together, anything could happen. "From a viewpoint of boxing technique, hitting power, speed, strength, stamina, condition, experience, Wills should win. But should win and will win are horses of a different color." Wills was "one of the fastest, most clever and scientific, sharpest hitting heavyweights we ever have seen" and was just as big and strong as Firpo, who had far less speed and skill on offense or defense. But Firpo was powerful, with a bone-smashing cuff and the heart of a lion.

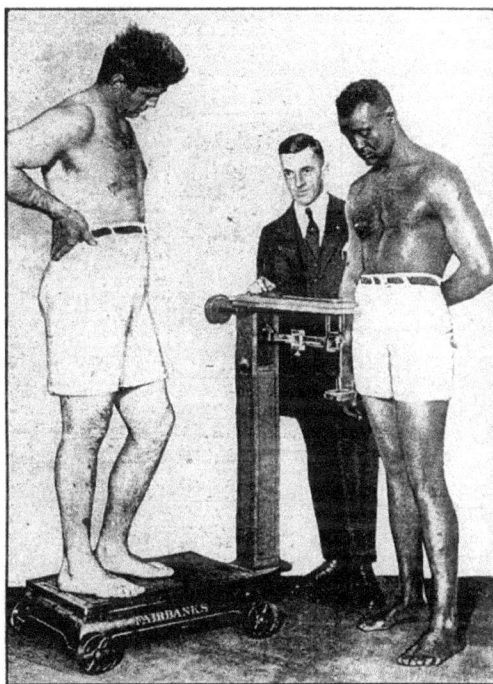

Firpo (on scales) weighed 224¼; Wills 217. C.C. Walter did the honors

Dempsey fought Firpo at his own game. Had he boxed more, it would have taken him one or two rounds more to stop him, but Jack would not have been floored. Wills most likely would avoid a slugging match.

The vast majority of boxing experts and fighters interviewed believed that Wills would win by knockout relatively early on, being too classy for Firpo, but some, including Benny Leonard and Gene Tunney, picked Firpo. Manager Lou Brix said Wills was too old. Jack Dempsey said he now thought it was a toss-up, though much earlier he thought Firpo would win by knockout. Jimmy De Forest picked Wills to win by knockout in 5 rounds.[134]

On September 11, 1924 at Boyle's Thirty Acres in Jersey City, New Jersey, in the year's biggest fight, before an alleged 60,000 or 75,000 fans, 217-pound Harry Wills won a 12-round no decision over 224 ¼- or ½-pound Luis Firpo. The fight mostly was a dull and uninteresting clinching and wrestling match, but Wills won it as it was fought.

In the 2nd round, on a referee break, Wills scored a knockdown with a right to the jaw, for a 4-count, the only knockdown. Firpo claimed it was the only punch that hurt him, which was foul. Afterward, Firpo had a swollen right jaw, split lip, and a bruised left side.

134 New York Telegram and Evening Mail, September 10, 11, 1924.

Firpo alleged that Wills used unfair tactics, including holding too much, holding and hitting, and hitting on breaks, which led to his knockdown. Luis admitted that Harry was strong and clever.

The fight was filmed, and the films backed Firpo's claim that Wills hit him with a right as Referee Dan Sullivan was pushing them apart from a break. Actually, with the referee's hands on both of their arms, in the process of calling for a break and breaking them, Wills first hit Firpo with a right uppercut, and then, as Firpo turned to look at the referee as if in complaint, with the referee's hands still on both of them, Wills hit him with a straight right, which decked Firpo. Throughout the bout, both men held, held and hit, and threw rabbit punches.

Wills claimed that he would have won by knockout had Firpo opened up more and not fought continually at close range and hugged tightly and persistently. Wills said he was not hurt at any time. He was cautious, for his experience had taught him to respect his foes.

Many believed that Wills did most of the holding, while others blamed Firpo. Each fighter insisted the other was the chief offender. Perhaps they mutually held, and then blamed the other. Yet, Firpo's fights were not known for having a great deal of clinching, while Wills was known for clinching and hitting in the clinches.

W. C. Vreeland said the two hugged, mauled, and wrestled, and did little else. Wills waited for the Firpo charges, and time and again found his defense open, landing straight rights to the jaw and lefts to the stomach. At close quarters it was all Wills. He was the stronger man and handled Firpo like a rag doll. He twisted, bent, and shoved Firpo.

Often, Firpo would advance with a lead right, Wills either would duck or smother the blow, and they would clinch, rabbit punch, and fire rights to the body while holding with their lefts. Wills often was cautioned for holding and hitting. But he landed more often than Firpo, in a poor fight.

Most observers said Wills won every round, with two rounds possibly even or for Firpo if one was being generous. Wills gave him a boxing lesson and outclassed, outfought, and outgeneraled him throughout. He blocked and smothered Firpo's blows and rarely was hit hard. Wills fought defensively and tied up Firpo's arms very well. There was little action; with a lot of wrestling, but Wills outlanded him.

Some said it did not appear that either one was trying very hard to win by knockout. Many said Firpo did not fight with his usual style, vim, and fervor. He seemed weak and lacking his former power. Others said Wills' defensive tactics threw him off his game. Conversely, Wills was taking no chances with him, and rarely pressed his advantage. Ultimately, Vreeland called it a "bum fight."

Thomas Rice, while admitting that Wills won every round, primarily by hitting the body, nevertheless said he gave a "wretched exhibition." It was the "sorriest contest" for top prices ever staged. "If what they did last night was their very best, both should be deported after today from the sporting pages of the newspapers, for they are no longer worth while as pugilists." Throughout, they simply rushed together and clinched, with Wills hammering the body. The referee broke them, and they repeated, in monotonous, uninteresting manner. "If it proved anything it proved that Wills is a complete has-been. .... It also proved...that Firpo in 12 months has entirely lost a punch that would have jarred a battleship."

The *Brooklyn Standard Union's* William Rafter said Wills won clearly, outclassing Firpo. "It was Wills' extreme overcautiousness that kept him from putting Firpo to sleep."

Referee Danny Sullivan said Wills was the stronger of the two, decidedly the cleverest and coolest, and toyed with him throughout.

Jack Dempsey, who was in the arena as a spectator, left after the 8th round.

Most said the bout was unsatisfactory, and Wills should have stopped Firpo. Jim Corbett called it the sorriest fight he ever had seen in his life. There was little science, the men were clumsy, and clean hitting was absent. The fight simply was swing, clinch, slap, break, and repeat.

Others said Wills lacked power and polish. Wills claimed he hurt his hand in the 4th round.

Firpo hit and hurt Wills less often than he did Dempsey, but Wills hit and hurt Firpo less often in 12 rounds total than Dempsey did in 2 rounds. Few telling punches were landed, though Wills did punish his body. Firpo's lasting the distance with Wills highlighted what a tremendous puncher, finisher, and risk-taker Jack Dempsey was.

Davis Walsh said, "Wills won, but was unimpressive. Firpo lost. Neither, therefore, can or will occasion a serious misgiving on the part of the champion. Both, in fact, were made the target of no inconsiderable abuse from gentlemen of the press this morning." Dempsey was so bored and uninterested by the fight that he left well before it concluded.

Eddie Tranter called the fight unsatisfactory. Firpo was through.

Wills has just landed an uppercut on the heavyweight pretender that rocked him from heels to head. It was this blow that broke Harry's right hand.

Fans were treated to this picture in every round. Wills ducking inside of Firpo's lead and trying him in a knot. Poor Luis looked worried in this—the third stanza.

Snacko! Wills drove punch to ribs that could be heard in Harlem.

Firpo wincing under punishment in clinch in third.

In eleventh round Firpo's shown dropping right to chin, but steam was lacking.

At close of third round Wills backed against ropes, making Firpo fan air.

THE CRAFTY Brown Panther from Harlem turned the so-called Wild Bull of the Pampas in twelve rounds at Jersey City last night. Wills dropped Firpo with smack to chin in second. After that he kept Firpo's right tied up and beat a tattoo on ribs and kidneys. It was a tattoo that spelled finis for the pugilistic ambitions of Dead Pan Louie. Injury to Wills's hand prevented kayo. *Story on page 2. Other photo, page 7.*

Happy as a couple of kids were the Brown Panther and his wife yesterday after the victory. The big battler read newspaper accounts of the scrap while Mrs. Wills looked on admiringly and listened to the tale of Firpo's defeat.

HARRY WILLS

James Wood said Wills stood first in line for a shot at the crown by soundly trouncing Firpo and clearly proving his superiority, even though it was a very slow bout. 80,000 booed at the end, but it was not Harry's fault. Firpo was not the same fighter that went against Dempsey, Willard, or Brennan, but was content to hit and grab. Wills won all the way, for he was too strong, his defense too good, and his rights to the body bothered Luis. The bout "probably broke all modern records for clinching."

The fight allegedly generated around $800,000, huge for a non-title fight. Others estimated about $700,000. Those numbers later were disputed. Ticket prices ranged from $2 up to $25.

The Associated Press report said that as convincing as Wills' triumph over Firpo was, "his performance did not, in the opinion of most critics, brighten whatever prospect he has of dethroning Dempsey. To those who watched the giant Negro pound and wrestle his ponderous opponent into subjection, there remained a conviction that, for the present at least, Dempsey has little to fear."

Firpo often complained about Wills' holding, and holding and hitting, which Harry did often, liking to grab with his left and hit with his right. However, they had agreed to fight in the clinches if one hand was free, so Referee Danny Sullivan stayed out of it.

Referee Sullivan said the blow that floored Firpo was perfectly legitimate. "It landed simply because Firpo was too careless in breaking away to hold up his hands and protect himself. He came out of the clinch with his hands down, and Wills simply popped him." This statement gave the impression that it was a straight Queensberry rules fight in which combatants were expected to protect themselves at all times, rather than break away clean at the referee's command.

Sullivan further said, "The better man won on his form in my opinion. Firpo was a big disappointment, and Wills showed that he is ready for anything." Yet, Harry was overcautious throughout. When Firpo hit the floor for a 4-count, Wills might have tried to win by knockout, but did not press his advantage.

Firpo did not make his usual slam-bang, crushing, vicious attack. He either would not or could not fight. His hard right to the body did no damage. Wills had a good defense, and took the fight out of him. "Wills, as I saw it, was far too clever for Firpo." Firpo could not land his right cleanly, and yet, it was Wills' fear of that blow that kept Luis from being knocked out, for Harry was taking no chances. "Wills, to me, seemed too careful." Firpo was aggressive, but too slow for Wills, who was stronger and in better condition. Harry was able to throw him around the ring.

George Underwood said Firpo was outclassed, but Wills' caution permitted Luis to last. "Wills pounded out a victory that left no doubt about his superiority over Firpo, but did so in a manner that also left no doubt in the minds of many of the vast army of onlookers of Wills' inferiority to Champion Jack Dempsey." Wills did not show his usual lightning speed or catlike agility. He stood flat footed and exchanged, or came to close quarters and pulled, tugged, and wrestled. He did not demonstrate his usual array of blows, nor any footwork, but just stood there and waited on Firpo's advance. "In short, Harry was slower than cold molasses and showed scarcely more aggressiveness than a jackrabbit."

William Brady said, "On what Wills showed against Firpo tonight, Dempsey's advisers probably will consent to the champion defending his title against the colored man." However, Brady believed that Wills was intentionally hiding his true form in order to get a Dempsey fight.

> If Wills had shown his true form the clever and astute Mr. Kearns, who so long and adroitly has steered Mr. Dempsey out of the Brown Panther's path, would not be prevailed upon to change his course and run the risk of having his meal ticket punched full of holes by the black man.

> And I doubt even now, as careful as Wills was to cover up his hand, that Mr. Kearns will allow Mr. Dempsey to enter into the ring with him, for try as Harry might he could not hide his herculean strength, powerful punch and ability to take the same socks on the chin that twice had Mr. Dempsey on the canvas.

In a post-fight interview, Wills was quoted as saying, "Why didn't I knock him out? Because the big foreigner who has a heart the size of a pea wouldn't open up and fight! ... I'd knock him deader than a mackerel if he had fought me." When asked about Dempsey, Wills said, "Paddy's the boss, any time he wants me to fight the champion I'll be ready." Harry said Firpo landed a terrific right to his jaw in one of the early rounds, "and the blow didn't even feaze me. Yet he landed the same kind of a punch and knocked Dempsey through the ropes." In this interview, Wills denied hurting his hand. "I didn't hurt it at all." Concluding, "I had that guy's number from the very start. ... Of course, I had to be careful..." Harry said his body blows clearly had a big effect on Firpo, while Luis's blows had no effect on him. "I chopped his kidneys so that he won't be able to walk straight for a few days. How that guy hollered for mercy when I smashed to the midsection! I thought once or twice he was going to quit. ... No siree, he didn't hurt me at all in the fight. I ducked most of his wild lunges." Harry also said he often laughed at Firpo's efforts. "Now that I have a chance to think it all over I laughed myself out of a knockout." Wills admitted, "I agree with you that my long layoffs haven't done me any good, but hereafter I'll fight oftener and against anybody Paddy selects."

Firpo admitted that "Wills beat me," and "got all the best of it," but he also said, "He used the kidney punch which I understand was barred, and he held and held continually. He wouldn't fight. ... He was afraid and feared my right. That's why he was so cautious."[135]

Harry Newman, a big Wills supporter, said the bout disappointed, in part, because Harry was too careful. However, the fact remained that Wills won clearly, and stood out as the logical fellow to challenge for Dempsey's crown.

[135] *Brooklyn Daily Eagle, Buffalo Enquirer, Buffalo Courier, Brooklyn Standard Union, Brooklyn Daily Times, New York Daily News, Rochester Democrat and Chronicle, Pittsburgh Sun, New York Evening Telegram and Evening Mail*, September 12, 1924.

Yet, there was nowhere to host a Dempsey-Wills fight in 1924. With the outdoor season about to close, and limited time for preparing the usual details, and indoor arenas being too small, it could not happen until 1925, even assuming it would or could be allowed to take place.

Most *Daily News* readers believed Dempsey would beat Wills (many saying with ease) but agreed that he deserved a title shot.[136]

Many, including Fair Play, said Wills' showing against Firpo indicated that Dempsey had little to fear. Wills would not see Dempsey's punches coming as easily as he did Firpo's, for "Dempsey doesn't telegraph. His punches come from a short distance and behind them lurks oblivion. Wills' punches have not the deadly snap of Dempsey's and the snap is what spells knockouts." Furthermore, unfortunately, Wills was so risk-averse in style, taking so few chances, such that "it would be difficult to draw a respectable crowd to see the [Dempsey-Wills] fight."

Wills said, "Now that I decisively defeated Firpo, the world will agree that I am entitled to a fight with Jack Dempsey for the world title. There is no question of my victory. Many folks criticized the bout, but Firpo made me do all the fighting. He is a good tough man, and his blows carry force."

Firpo said, "How can a man fight one who persists in holding and clubbing with his right hand? In every round Wills violated all rules of hitting and holding. It was impossible for me to show my ability under those conditions. …. That blow that felled me was a hit coming out of a clinch."

Jack Dempsey said, "Boys, I was bunked – like the rest of the 80,000 cash customers. I was given to understand that there was going to be a spine-tickling slugging match, but all I saw was a nice, refined wrestling match. Wills just handcuffed Firpo. He went into the ring with that purpose and he succeeded." Luis landed very few, and did plenty of clinching himself, as well as complaining to the referee. "I'd give the fight to Wills. … In my opinion he won because he was stronger than Firpo; then, too, he is four years older, and therefore has a little edge in knowledge of wrestling holds."

A couple days after the fight, reports were that the attendance actually was 48,500, and gross receipts $471,000, still very good, but far less than previously reported.

Most agreed that Wills had fouled Firpo by hitting on the break when he decked him, which caused Firpo's second, Bill Tate, to protest, but the referee chose to take no notice of it.

Tex Rickard said he was not impressed by Wills' showing, and hence was making no plans to match him with Dempsey. Even if he was so inclined to put on the fight, it would be at least a year before such a bout could be staged. In the meantime, he was considering staging several additional elimination contests before finally picking the champion's next challenger, depending on public sentiment.

---

[136] *New York Daily News*, September 13, 18, 1924.

Furthermore, Rickard said only 48,500 paid to attend the bout, generating $424,000 in net receipts. Firpo received a guaranteed 37 ½%, or $159,000; and Wills a flat $100,000 sum. Both made the most they ever had for any fight. However, Tex had a lot of expenses. $60,000 was for renovation of the giant bowl arena, $18,000 in insurance premiums, and $6,000 for five preliminary bouts. General and other incidental expenses wiped out most of the remaining money, such that he allegedly only broke even or made very little.

George Underwood insisted that the result of a bout between Dempsey and Wills was a toss-up, in part because Dempsey was sitting on the shelf allowing rust to gather. Underwood said his belief "is shared privately if not publicly by the majority of the trained, experienced, understanding followers of fisticuffs, whose judgment is not warped by racial personal prejudice."

Underwood made some interesting observations. "The tendency among some of us as we get along into life is to become blasé and cynical. With all of us time throws a halo over the past and we consciously or unconsciously heap glory and grandeur on 'them good old days.'" The reality was that if one went back in time, most heavyweight fights contained the same holding, pulling, hauling, mauling, shoving, and wrestling that Wills-Firpo contained. The Dempsey vs. Firpo thriller was the anomaly, not the rule. "In all your years in the ring, old timer, have you ever seen one single, solitary heavyweight encounter in which there was such a world of thrills and sensations as were crowded into the Dempsey-Firpo blizzard of blows one year ago?" Not every fight could or would live up to that. Furthermore, Firpo did more of the clinching than Wills.[137]

Damon Runyon said if Wills had knocked out Firpo in impressive fashion, the demand for a Dempsey fight would have been huge, and the fight would have been made. "But Wills, failing to make the most of his many opportunities, can scarcely expect more consideration than any other aspirant." Runyon's view was that the "indifferent" victory hurt Wills more than it helped him. "It seems to the writer that more excuses are offered for Harry Wills than for any other fighter in recent years." Runyon said one need not feel sorry for Wills, for he had made more money than any other colored fighter ever, with the possible exception of Jack Johnson.

Billy Kelly said the Firpo-Wills wrestling bout was so unpleasant that "the prospect of Wills meeting Dempsey is most distant or non-existent. There wasn't a man, woman or child in the crowd of 48,000 that would pay a $2 note to see such a bout." Yet, nevertheless, "Wills has proved beyond a doubt his right to be considered the next best man to the champion," and had a right to demand his chance at the title.[138]

[137] *Yonkers Herald*, September 12, 1924; *Daily Home News, Morning Call, Paterson Evening News, Buffalo Courier, Rochester Democrat and Chronicle, New York Telegram and Evening Mail*, September 13, 1924.
[138] *Buffalo Courier*, September 14, 15, 1924.

Less than a week later, Gene Tunney and Harry Greb would fight for the fourth time. Tunney was up 2-1 in their series. Greb had won their first fight clearly, Tunney won the second controversially, while most agreed with the official decision for Tunney in their third contest. Their fourth contest would be another one difficult to score.

On September 17, 1924, before a crowd of 8,000 - 9,000, or 10,999, at the Olympic arena in Cleveland, Ohio (134 miles northwest from Pittsburgh), 175-pound Gene Tunney and 166-pound Harry Greb fought a 10-round no decision bout. Several said the contest was a draw, too even to give it to either one, slightly more said it was a shade or clear for Greb, while others said it was a shade for Tunney. The aggregate of reports/votes (3 for a draw, 2 for Tunney, 4 for Greb) led most to view the contest as a draw. It was 1-1-1 even in Pittsburgh, Greb's hometown. There was no official decision.

The Associated Press scored it a draw, but said a shade, if any, could be given to Tunney. The referee said he would have called it a draw. The *Pittsburgh Gazette Times'* Ray Coll called it a draw.

The *Cleveland News'* Ray Campbell said Tunney won, 5-3-2. The *Pittsburgh Post's* Regis Welsh also said Tunney won 5-3-2.

However, the *Cleveland Plain Dealer's* Stuart Bell and the *Cleveland Times'* Dan Taylor had it the same; a 5-4-1 close shade win for Greb. The *Cleveland Press'* Russell Needham and *Pittsburgh Press'* Jim Jab said Greb won clearly, scoring it 8-1-1 and 7-3 respectively.

For the *Cleveland Plain Dealer*, Stuart Bell said Greb won close, 5-4-1, though Tunney made a spirited finish after a slow start and won the 4th, 7th, 8th, and 10th rounds, with the 6th even. Tunney had Greb bleeding from the mouth in the 8th round. "While Greb pulled his copyrighted holding act, grabbing Tunney around the neck with his left arm while he punched Tunney with his right, the middleweight title holder did most of the leading in the early rounds and this offset much of his questionable holding." Afterward, Tunney complained that Greb butted, held, and wrestled. Bell scored it: 1-G, 2-G, 3-G, 4-T, 5-G, 6-E, 7-T, 8-T, 9-G, 10-T.[139]

Dan Taylor for the *Cleveland Times* had it exactly the same as Stuart Bell: Greb, 5-4-1. Even his round-by-round scoring was the same. It was a vicious 10-round battle. The Pittsburgh Windmill never let up in carrying the fight to the Greenwich Village lad. "Tunney scored many telling wallops, but always found Greb coming back for more. Greb did the leading all the way, Tunney never once taking the initiative."

Greb started out like a whirlwind and piled up a big lead on points in the first three rounds. "Harry danced around his bigger foe and flailed

---

[139] *Cleveland Plain Dealer,* September 18, 1924. Bell's description of the 6th round (which he scored even) actually sounds more pro-Tunney than Greb, noting more Tunney connections than Greb connections (4 to 2). If that round went to Tunney, it would have been a draw. Regardless, this writer ultimately believed that Greb had a slight edge overall. Both entered the ring wearing bathrobes. Red Mason, Greb's manager, was in his corner, while Billy Gibson, Tunney's manager, was in the light heavy champ's corner. Matt Hinkel was announced as the referee despite Mason's pre-fight protest that he would not stand for the Clevelander.

away at both body and chin with both hands. He was always on top of Tunney and the only blows Gene landed in these periods were when the men were clinched." Tunney spurted in the 4th, landing a flock of straight lefts to the jaw, and scoring heavily in the clinches, landing two to one. Greb won the 5th by returning to his jumping-jack tactics. Tunney started to pile up a lead in the 6th, but Harry closed with enough speed to earn a draw in that round. Tunney won the 7th and 8th principally because of his work in the clinches, landing telling body wallops. The 9th found Greb again tearing into Tunney with tiger-like ferociousness, winning the round by a wide margin, rushing in and landing left and right to the body. Early in the 10th, Greb fought like a demon and piled up a big lead, chasing Tunney across the ring. However, in the midst of one of Harry's kangaroo-like leaps, Tunney caught him with a straight left that had Greb in distress. Tunney followed up by clouting him with vicious rights and lefts. Greb wanted to hold but could not find Tunney. Greb rallied with body blows, but Tunney again slowed him up with a murderous right cross to the chin. A left sent Greb back on his heels again, but he spurted once more. "Tunney won the round by a big margin but his advantage in this round could not offset the early lead compiled by Greb." "Greb had a slight shade in the bout."

The crowd of 10,000 was the largest that ever turned out for a fight at the Olympic arena.

Russell Needham of the *Cleveland Press* said Greb won clearly, but neither fighter got overheated, as the rounds went by and the crowd yawned. Greb windmilled his way to a characteristic points victory in a no-decision. Needham said the victory did not mean much, because the way Tunney fought, most anyone could have licked him, and a fighter with a punch would have laid him horizontal. "Tunney's showing was pitifully sorry. Laughable, even. Tunney would last as long with Dempsey as it would take the heavy champ to get across the ring and swing once."

Referee Matt Hinkel "had the double duty of keeping out of the way of Greb's wild swings and separating the two when Greb swung away and then clinched."

All Tunney did during the first 7 rounds was back away and swing softly to the paunch and ear when Greb dove in and hung on. The first 7 rounds were alike. Greb would dance around, and then wade in, swinging right and left. After landing several smacks, he would hang on with his left and punch with his right. Tunney would use his right a couple times and they would break. They did this with endless monotony. Greb did all of the leading, landing three or four to one, and what Tunney did land "wouldn't have broken a pane of glass." Tunney seemed listless, like a man who had just been woken up from a sleep.

However, in the 8th, Tunney seemed to wake up. He held Greb even in that round, lost the 9th, and finally started to fight in the 10th. "It was the only round in which he did fight and he won it. It showed that had he wished, he could have beaten Greb, maybe knocked him out." Ultimately though, based on his descriptions, Needham had it 8-1-1 for Greb.

Jim Jab for the *Pittsburgh Press* said Greb won 7-3, for Tunney was not eager to mix it. This writer noted that on the strength of Gene's strong finish, many gave Tunney the fight. But Jab disagreed, saying Greb alone made the set-to worth looking at.

Conversely, Ray Campbell for the *Cleveland News* said Tunney was the easy winner, having the middleweight king all but out in the final round, earning a decisive victory by using hard body punches. Greb whirled on his nimble legs with all of his old abandon for 3 rounds, taking an early lead. However, beginning with the 4th round, Tunney stopped the windmill with vicious jolts to the short ribs, pit of the stomach, and occasionally to the head. Greb's prancing became less pronounced. "Tunney belted him and flayed him with vicious short uppercuts to the jaw and to the body which brought the crimson foam from Greb's lips and caused him to vomit when he returned to his corner at the end of the seventh and eighth rounds." It was not until the 10th round that Gene punched consistently to the jaw, and he had Greb badly hurt.

Overall, the match was clean, with little fouling, though Greb held and hit, despite the referee doing all he could to prevent it, "but, after all, that is the fellow's style and he probably grasped Tunney around the neck instinctively." Also, "Greb did an astonishing amount of clinching. He led quite a bit, it is true, but he always fell into a clinch after leading. Then up went his left arm around Tunney's neck while he punched spasmodically with his right." However, Tunney "punished" him "severely in these clinches," and after the 6th, Greb devoted more attention to holding Tunney's right than to holding his neck.

Campbell scored it 5-3-2 for Tunney, saying, "Tunney won clearly and decisively." 1–G, 2–E, 3–G, 4–T, 5–T, 6–T, 7–E, 8–T, 9–G, 10–T.

> By splitting hairs one of those even rounds could have been awarded to Gene. Tunney won by even a wider margin than the count of the rounds would make it appear, for the sessions he carried were taken by terrific punching, while Greb's margin of victory in his three periods was captured by ineffective rushing. At the end of the tenth round Greb was dizzier than I've ever seen him and I've been watching this wonder man for many years. A left hook to the jaw delivered after about one minute of fighting in the tenth all but knocked Greb unconscious. His knees buckled, his hands flopped to his sides. There he was – a perfect target for a knockout punch. But Tunney hesitated for a fraction of a second and Greb's marvelous recuperative powers saved him. Up went his hands, down went his jaw and Harry dove into a clinch. Tunney battered his ribs with right uppercuts then and after they had been separated by Matt Hinkel he hooked his left to the jaw again. It lacked some of the potency of the first blow, but Greb nevertheless staggered. Spectators screamed for Tunney to finish his man, but

the time in which to do it was lacking. Greb ran into another clinch and had his body sorely pelted for his pains but he didn't go down. … I am positive [Greb] would have been knocked out in fifteen rounds.

Tunney took the first few rounds to get his bearings. Greb won the 1st easily, dashing in with rights to the head and body, as well as some wild, harmless swings. The 2nd was rather even. Greb won the 3rd with several left hooks to the jaw and body. Tunney countered one hook with a scorching right cross to the jaw which sent Greb back on his heels, but Harry came back immediately and rushed Tunney to the ropes. Tunney won the 4th, between the innumerable clinches punishing Greb severely with body blows. One right uppercut to the body was one of the best punches landed in the contest. Tunney won the 5th and 6th as well. Greb held him fairly even in the 7th. Harry was spitting blood, though, and vomited when he returned to his corner as a result of all the hard body blows that he took. Greb was wild in the 8th, and Tunney took the round. Greb won the 9th. There was not much effective work, but Harry forced Gene about the ring and landed the majority of blows. In the 10th, Greb rallied and threw a score of punches at Gene. However, Tunney landed the left hook that nearly knocked him out, and Greb was battered.

Afterwards, Greb had a puffed eye, while Tunney suffered a slight cut on the forehead when their heads came together in the 8th. Matt Hinkel did a good job as referee.

Regis Welsh, who was ringside for the *Pittsburgh Post*, said Tunney won close, outpointing Greb by a slight shade. This time, Harry did not tie him up in close, and Tunney hit his body. The battling demons mauled each other throughout 10 vicious rounds, fighting like bantamweights. Both were bleeding, Tunney from a cut above his right eye, and Greb from his mouth, where several hard lefts had nailed him. Tunney fought more aggressively than ever before.

In scoring it 5-3-2 for Tunney, Welsh said Tunney won rounds 2, 4, 6, 8, and 10, while Greb won 1, 3, and 9, with the 5th and 7th being even.

Ray Coll, for the *Pittsburgh Gazette Times,* called it a draw. Greb piled up an early lead, forcing the fighting throughout, but Tunney made a strong finish with his body punches, earning an even break. At the end of the 10 slashing rounds, the "majority of ringside critics were of the opinion that it was a dead heat. In this the writer concurs." It was a see-saw affair. Greb was the aggressor, but Tunney landed more cleanly, particularly to the body. Coll said the fans were content with the draw opinion. "Greb said after the bout he thought he was entitled to a shade over his antagonist because of his aggressiveness, and this he would have been entitled to had he not run afoul of that hard right hook in the middle of the final round. Such are the breaks of the game."

Coll said the weights were not announced from the ring. He believed Tunney was close to 180 and Greb around 163.[140]

The Associated Press report said they fought a draw, with perhaps a slight shade, if any, to Tunney, according to newspapermen.

> Gene Tunney, American light-heavyweight champion and Harry Greb, world's middleweight champion, fought ten rounds on fairly even terms last night, according to a majority of the newspaper experts at the ringside. Tunney, punching more accurately and effectively, possibly was entitled to the shade in the opinion of the experts. Greb fought his characteristic battle, bounding around the ring like a rubber ball and throwing punches from every angle.
>
> Tunney centered his attack on the middle weight champion's body, punishing him with ripping right and left hooks at close quarters. He made Greb break ground half a dozen times with right smashes under the heart, robbing the Pittsburger of his speed.
>
> Although they fought at a furious pace, neither was damaged. Tunney left the ring with only a slight cut on the forehead as a result of coming in contact with Greb's head in the clinches.[141]

According to the *Dayton Daily News*, "Matt Hinkle, referee of the contest, said that if he had been permitted to give a decision, he would have declared the contest a draw. The newspaper experts, however, even those from Pittsburgh, were of the opinion that Tunney had the shade." They fought at the pace of bantamweights.

Tunney did most of his fighting at close range, battering the body, while Greb swung from all angles, missing frequently. The 10th round was the most ferocious. Greb sailed in swinging away, but Tunney returned with a furious attack, catching Greb with a left hook that nearly knocked him down.

The *Pittsburgh Sun*'s account was based on the Associated press story. It too reported that Referee Hinkel/Hinkle said if he had been permitted to give a decision, he would have declared it a draw. Tunney "today holds a draw with a possible shade, if any, over Harry Greb."

Yet, a "special" out of Cleveland in the *Pittsburgh Gazette Times* scored it 5-3-2 for Greb. 1-G, 2–T, 3–G, 4–T, 5–G, 6–E, 7–G, 8–E, 9–G, 10–T. In this account, "Matt Hinkel after the bout told the correspondent he thought Greb was winner by a shade." Hinkel not only was a referee, but a "well known Cleveland promoter."[142]

---

[140] *Pittsburgh Gazette Times, Cleveland Plain Dealer, Cleveland Times, Cleveland Press, Pittsburgh Press, Cleveland News, Pittsburgh Post, Fremont Messenger,* September 18, 1924. The fight was broadcast on radio from KDKA, East Pittsburgh, but not live from ringside, but only after being relayed to it via telegraph.

[141] *Lafayette Journal and Courier, Brooklyn Citizen, Chillicothe Gazette, Dayton Daily News, Lima News, Cincinnati Enquirer, Buffalo Evening News,* September 18, 1924. Ohio's *Portsmouth Daily Times* reported that the majority of newspaper experts at ringside said it was a draw. *Portsmouth Daily Times,* September 18, 1924. Also reporting a draw were - *Hamilton Evening Journal* and *Times Recorder* – Ohio papers.

[142] *Dayton Daily News, Pittsburgh Sun, Akron Beacon Journal,* September 18, 1924. The United Press and International News Service reports matched the reports of Stuart Bell and Dan Taylor, likely relying on them.

In the *Akron Beacon Journal,* Chick Maglione, former Ohio lightweight, said Greb won and proved he was the better man. They punched each other all over the ring with stinging blows.

Another report had it 4-3-3 close for Tunney. 1–E, 2–T, 3–G, 4–T, 5–G, 6–T, 7–E, 8–T, 9–G, 10–E.

Once again with a Greb-Tunney contest, there was a great diversity of opinion, and it was a matter of what one liked. It seems that overall, if one liked aggressiveness and punch volume, Greb was favored, but if one appreciated cleaner, harder connections, even if counterpunches, and counted body punches, one leaned towards Tunney. Their fights simply were difficult to judge.

Tex Rickard claimed that he lost $9,000 on Firpo-Wills. As a result, he declared, "Fighters will have to gamble on the gate with me hereafter. There will be no more guarantees. Their day is over."

Davis Walsh said word was that Dempsey did not want to fight for the sake of fighting and getting exercise. He had to train hard for any bout, and training had become somewhat of a tedious grind for him. "He would be a fathead to lose his title for a comparatively small purse." Hence, he only wanted to fight if a lot of money was on the line.[143]

George Underwood believed that Kearns was wily and astute and knew Wills would be a tough match for Dempsey, which is why for four long years, by every conceivable method, he had steered Dempsey clear of a meeting with him, despite his public proclamations otherwise.

Underwood noted that Wills had not stood over Firpo to hit him before he arose fully, as Dempsey did. He evaded, blocked, or took Firpo's blows without going down, whereas Dempsey was floored three times. None of the men whom Dempsey had met compared physically or pugilistically with Wills.[144]

Underwood reported that a close friend of Dempsey's told him that there was no chance of Dempsey boxing until next summer, although there was talk of him possibly fighting either Gibbons or Jack Renault before then. Kearns said he had not been shown the color of the money and would not make the Wills or any other fight until he got what he thought Dempsey's services were worth.[145]

Just 10 days after fighting Greb, on September 27, 1924 in Ebensburg, Pennsylvania, east of Pittsburgh, Gene Tunney won a clear 10-round decision over Ray Neuman/Newman, but was so cautious that the crowd loudly booed and hissed throughout. As a result of the tame, listless performance, many suspecting that he carried Neuman, the Pennsylvania State Athletic Commission fined Tunney $200 and suspended him for 90 days.[146]

Jim Coffroth was discussing the possibility of promoting Dempsey vs. Wills in Tia Juana. However, Underwood questioned the economic

[143] *Pittsburgh Sun,* September 19, 1924.
[144] *New York Telegram and Evening Mail,* September 19, 1924.
[145] *New York Telegram and Evening Mail,* September 22, 1924.
[146] *Pittsburgh Post,* September 29, 1924; *Pittsburgh Gazette Times,* September 30, 1924.

feasibility of such a promotion, feeling that there was nothing to it. A match at such a remote location would not draw half the seating capacity of the large arenas in New York or New Jersey, i.e., Yankee Stadium and Boyle's Thirty Acres, with 10 million people at their doors and nearly as many people within a day's ride. Furthermore, as big as the Eastern arenas were, even they could not fit all those who wanted to see the fight.

Regardless, Underwood questioned whether Kearns intended to put Dempsey back into the ring ever again. Still, Dempsey was doing some training at Stillman's gym. On September 29, he worked the pulleys, did calisthenics, punched the big and little bags, shadow boxed, and sparred bantam Eddie Cox and former bantam Jackie Sharkey, who nearly had grown into a middleweight.[147]

BREAKING RECORDS
LOEW'S STATE
ALL THIS WEEK
THE KING OF CHAMPIONS
JACK DEMPSEY
(HIMSELF)
IN PERSON
—AND—
IN ACTION
A REAL TREAT
FOR
EVERYONE
DEMPSEY
APPEARS
ABOUT
3 P.M. 6 P.M.
9 P.M.
DAILY
SUBJECT TO CHANGE
GET IN
EARLY
PHOTOPLAY FEATURE
'SIDE SHOW OF LIFE'
AND ALL REGULAR
PROGRAM NUMBERS

Kearns/Dempsey signed with Marcus Loew for a vaudeville tour. Jack would tour Loew's theaters throughout the East, starting in Buffalo on October 20. The unnamed figure allegedly was the largest amount ever paid to any single vaudeville performer. Dempsey would spar several rounds in one of the acts. Kearns might appear in the show with him.

A subsequent report said Dempsey would earn $5,500 per week for six weeks of work ($33,000). His "Fight and Win" movie series also would be exhibited at the Loew's theater houses.[148]

On October 13, 1924, before a crowd of 7,000 in Philadelphia, Harry Greb and Tommy Loughran (46-12-5) fought to a split 10-round draw. The two judges disagreed. Jack Kelly scored it for Loughran, while Harry McGrath said Greb won. Referee Frank McCracken had the tiebreaking vote and ruled it a draw. Both weighed 168 pounds.[149]

Jack Kearns said he hoped the winter months would produce a marketable foe for Dempsey, for no formidable opponent was in sight. Kearns said the vaudeville game would last at least five months, and then be followed by a possible European tour. If a promoter showed enough coin, Jack would fight in Europe, though it was not likely.

Kearns did not anticipate any fight occurring until at least spring 1925. "I am of the personal opinion the public is not keen for a match between Wills and Dempsey at present, or another go with Firpo at this time." Neither man had been impressive in their recent contest. Perhaps one of them would do something soon which would entitle them to further consideration.

---

[147] *New York Telegram and Evening Mail*, September 30, 1924.
[148] *New York Daily News*, October 2, 5, 8, 1924.
[149] *Philadelphia Inquirer*, October 14, 1924. Perry Lewis said Greb had "cream puff punches." "Harry was lucky to escape disqualification," for he butted, as well as held and hit.

Walter Kelly said Dempsey was the best fighter in history, and the only pair that would have a chance with him at all were John L. Sullivan and James J. Jeffries when they were in their primes.

Dempsey discussed some of his biggest fights. He had seen Willard box and was confident that he could lick him. Kearns did not want to rush him into the fight, but "the fact that he was the heavyweight champion of the world did not feaze me at all. In fact, it made me all the more anxious to box him. I saw a championship to gain and with it a fortune." Jack decked Willard seven times in the 1st round, going at him with all of his strength and speed. "I knew I had to do it quickly or he might get me." Everyone thought Willard had been counted out, for there was such a din that the bell was not heard. When Willard's seconds rushed into the ring to assist him, Jack started to leave, thinking the bout was over. But he was called back in, and two rounds later, Willard retired.

Jack said Carpentier was game and took a nasty lacing until he fell. He never saw such a crowd in his life. Georges was fast in the 1st round, and Jack was boxing cautiously, looking out for Carpentier's famous right cross. Still, "I gave him severe body punishment in the opening stanza and I knew it was only a matter of a few rounds before I would get him." Jack boxed on his toes, with his jaw well protected. In the clinches, he could tell that he was much stronger than Georges and was going to get him. However, "Don't let anybody get the idea that Carpentier could not hit at that time. …. He let fly that right in the second round and the punch landed. It shook me to my knees, but I never lost my head. I began to wreak severe body punishment upon the Frenchman and finally he wilted and I won the fight. I always like to praise an opponent even though I do beat him." Georges gave him a good battle while it lasted, and the 91,000 in attendance agreed, satisfied by the contest, but convinced that Dempsey was his master.

Gibbons was a scientific master, very skillful. "He is one of the cleverest big fellows I ever met and is a marvel at defense. I wasn't quite myself in that bout, for I had laid down my tools for quite a spell. … The smart defensive methods of Tom Gibbons enabled him to stay the limit. They call him the St. Paul wizard and he is aptly named." Yet, the bout was good preparation for the one with Firpo.

Jack believed the best plan for Firpo was to attack him right away, to tear in and give him all he had from the start. It was a tough fight. "That fellow can hit, but I found I could hit just as hard and more effectively." When he went out of the ring, it was from a partial punch and partial push. Firpo's ponderous weight bore down upon him, and with the lower rope being near his legs/knees, he went hurtling backwards out of the ring. "There has been considerable discussion ever since then as to whether there was some infraction of ring ethics by my being pushed back into the ring. I would have got back, all right, whether anybody tried to help me or not, for I wasn't a bit dazed. Everybody knows I dropped Firpo plenty and finally he was counted out."[150]

On October 20, 1924, in Chicago, the Kansas City Monarchs (from Missouri) won the first Negro League World series of baseball, 5 games to 4, with one even, against Pennsylvania's Hilldale Club.

The *Buffalo Commercial* said at present, Jack Dempsey was much different than the one who fought there seven years ago. He was suave, polished, sure of himself, and at ease in any company. Back then he was an awkward, bashful, ill-at-ease, rather uncouth rube, which showed in his speech and unfamiliarity with the most ordinary of city customs. "Today he is a thorough man of the world." He gave his dialogue on the stage with his manager, and there was not the slightest trace of self-consciousness.

The *Buffalo Courier* said Dempsey's vaudeville act was nifty, and he was a good actor. He also demonstrated, with sparring partners Marty Cutler, Andy Palmer, and Jackie Sharkey, highlights and sequences of his bouts.

Dempsey said some folks incorrectly had the impression that he did not want to fight Wills. There weren't any promoters wanting to sign him for a Wills match. "I'd fight him tomorrow, and, honestly, I think he'd be easier for me than Firpo was."[151]

On October 24, 1924, in New Orleans, Tommy Gibbons knocked out Ted Jamieson in the 1st round. There was occasional talk of Dempsey possibly fighting Gibbons again.

Dempsey and Estelle Taylor skip rope

Reports were that Jack's on-again off-again relationship with Estelle Taylor allegedly was off again. Initially, the two had been seen everywhere together, and all Jack talked about was her. But then they started quarrelling. Apparently, there were reports of Jack possibly dating a dancer named Ann Pennington, and Taylor showing interest in fellow actor Lawford Davidson, with whom she was starring in a film.

On October 27, Dempsey was in Newark, New Jersey for a week's vaudeville engagement. Jack said, "The newspapers have had me engaged a half dozen times. As a matter of fact, I have never been engaged. Ann Pennington? Nothing to it." Jack said he was friendly with both, meaning Ann and Estelle.[152]

Also on October 27, 1924, in Memphis, Tennessee, in a rematch, 2,220 watched 175-pound Gene Tunney score a 1st round knockout over

[150] *Buffalo Enquirer*, October 21, 1924.
[151] *Buffalo Commercial*, October 21, 22, 1924; *Buffalo Courier*, October 21, 1924. They were in Buffalo from October 20 – 25, Newark, NJ from October 27 – November 1, New York City from November 3 – 8, and Brooklyn from November 10 – 15.
[152] *New York Daily News*, October 27, 28, 1924.

170-pound Harry Foley (17-9-1). An overhand right decked Foley, who rose at 4. Soon thereafter, a left hook to the jaw knocked him out cold. In January that year, Tunney had won a 10-round no decision over Foley. Tunney was "one of the few fighters of the day who is conceded a chance to eventually dethrone Jack Dempsey."[153]

Dempsey endured some criticism for defending his title so infrequently. He and Kearns apparently only wanted to risk the title in big fights for big money. And unless such was guaranteed, the champ and/or his manager seemed to prefer acting and the vaudeville stage rather than fighting and remaining active in the ring.

Writer Sparrow McGann, opined, "Jack Dempsey probably will never fight again." His new nose was a tip-off regarding his intentions. Some said he wanted to retire as undefeated champ. Others said he wanted to make as much money as possible, so that no one ever would have to host a benefit for him.

> The man who will probably force Dempsey into retirement will be Harry Wills. The inside dope is that Dempsey's backers believe that the negro is big and strong enough and clever enough to tie up the champion and perhaps win a decision over him. It is as sure as anything in the freakish prize ring game can be, that Dempsey will never step into the ring with Wills.[154]

On November 4, 1924, by a close final vote of 518,631 yes to 498,217 no, California voters passed a boxing law legalizing 12-round no decision or 10-round decision contests. In 1914 (while Jack Johnson still was champion), the state had made boxing illegal except for 4-round bouts or "amateur affairs."[155]

Jack Dempsey was sparring in New York with Marty Cutler as part of his act, but it was more of a comedy show than anything. He also talked with Kearns on the stage.[156]

Davis Walsh reported that according to sources close to the champ, Dempsey was seriously considering retirement from the ring, for boxing no longer intrigued him. "His retirement, they say, will not be a public one, merely a tacit withdrawal while he continues to hold the title and reap the benefits, financial and otherwise, accruing therefrom." He had enough money that he did not need to fight. Furthermore, Dempsey no longer considered himself to be the perfect physical specimen that he once was, for he no longer enjoyed training, but found it to be dull.[157]

On November 12, 1924, in Newark, New Jersey, before a crowd of 7,000, 184-pound Charley Weinert clearly won a 12-round no decision over 222-pound Luis Firpo. Writers said Weinert beat Firpo even more badly and clearly than did Wills. Weinert gave him a boxing lesson. Firpo could not block Weinert's jabs, and was bruised, cut, and bleeding from

[153] *Memphis Commercial Appeal, Chicago Tribune,* October 28, 1924.
[154] *New Brunswick Daily Home News,* October 28, 1924.
[155] *San Francisco Bulletin, Los Angeles Record, Riverside Daily Press,* November 5, 1924. **Ballotpedia.org. pages (uclawsf.edu).**
[156] *New York Daily News,* November 1, 4, 1924. From November 17 – 22, they were in Boston.
[157] *Dayton Herald,* November 11, 1924.

his face, nose, and mouth. Some said Weinert won every round, while others said he won 10-2.

Most said the bout showed how far back Firpo had gone, for in 1923, Luis had stopped Weinert in a mere 2 rounds. Gene Tunney had stopped Weinert in 4 rounds in 1922. Others said Weinert had improved.

Damon Runyon called Firpo the "Wild Bull that was."

Davis Walsh said Weinert was supposed to be an easy win, a setup, so to speak, and therefore Firpo did not train properly, and as a result took a beating, losing every round.

Thomas Holmes said Firpo had not been the same since losing to Dempsey. He was sluggish and fat.

Paul Gallico said, "Mr. Weinert further proved that Mr. Harry Wills is not a very good nor a very dangerous prizefighter any more either." Even a good "second-rate" fighter had done as well with Firpo as had Wills. The question though was how much Jack Dempsey would be going back from inactivity.[158]

William Keefe said Jeff Smith of Bayonne, N.J. had been on the trail of champions for 14 years, wanting to step into the ring with a titleholder. For some reason, no champion would defend their titles against him, including Harry Greb (for Smith gave Greb some of his toughest bouts). He finally was getting his chance against Tunney.

Gets His Chance After Long Wait

JEFF SMITH.

> If Gene Tunney decisively defeats Jeff Smith, then Tunney can set himself up as a real great champion notwithstanding the fact the general boxing public believes Tommy Gibbons is his superior. Because no other man, over a period of fourteen years, ever has been able to decisively defeat Jeff Smith.

Smith had met the best, and more than held his own, including against Carpentier, Clabby, Darcy, Mike Gibbons, McGoorty, Chip, Greb, Panama Joe Gans, Jamaica Kid, Mike O'Dowd, and Mike McTigue. Nevertheless, Tunney was the 8 to 5 odds favorite.

Smith was 33 years old. His manager said the way Jeff had taken care of himself, and with his good defense, he was like a 25-year-old. He said Smith was the greatest fighter Tunney ever had met, and he had forgotten more about boxing than Tunney knew. The *New Orleans Times-Picayune* reported that Smith had over 600 fights.[159]

---

[158] *Buffalo Courier, Buffalo Enquirer, Brooklyn Daily Eagle, New York Daily News,* November 13, 1924.
[159] *New Orleans Times-Picayune,* December 7, 8, 1924.
Jeff Smith's record included: 1911 WND10 Jimmy Clabby and WND10 Willie Lewis; 1912 W15 George Chip and LND10 Mike Gibbons; 1913 L20 Georges Carpentier; 1914 W20 Eddie McGoorty and W20 Clabby; 1916 LND10 Mike Gibbons; 1917 LND10 (twice) Harry Greb and WND10 Mike McTigue; 1919 W12 George Chip, WND10 Mike Gibbons, L/DND8 Panama Joe Gans, LND12 Greb, WND8 and DND10 Jamaica Kid; 1920 W15 Mike McTigue, WND12 Jamaica Kid, L15 Mike O'Dowd, and LND10 Greb; 1921 L10 and D15 Greb, LND12 Mike Gibbons, W15 Jimmy Darcy, and L15 Mike McTigue; 1922 D/LND10 Greb (Smith landed the harder, more damaging, effective blows, but Greb landed many more), W15 Bob Roper, W15 Martin Burke, and KO2 Clay Turner; 1923 W12 Fay Keiser, WND12 and W10 Jamaica Kid, WND12 Jimmy Darcy, LND10 and WND8 Tommy Loughran, WND12 Roper, WND12 Jamaica Kid, and W15 Chuck Wiggins; and 1924 W12 Jamaica Kid.

In August 1924, fighter Eddie McGoorty, a "wonder in his day," said of Jeff Smith, "I can't get away from the ever increasing thought that there is only one man in the world that Smith can't whip. And that man is Jack Dempsey."[160]

On December 8, 1924, in New Orleans, Louisiana, at the Coliseum Arena, before 5,000 fans, 179-pound Gene Tunney clearly won a 15-round no decision contest against 166 ½-pound veteran Jeff Smith (135-27-5). Tunney twice decked the durable Smith in the 12th round with wicked lefts to the ribs, the first time anyone had decked Smith since he was a beginner (1912 W15 George Chip, who floored him), though the local paper said it was the first knockdown suffered in his career.

JEFF SMITH

The *New Orleans Times-Picayune*'s William Keefe said "old master" Smith caved in before Tunney's liver punch.

> Smith found himself unable to cope with the speed of Gene Tunney, American light heavyweight champion, and Tunney decisively beat the Bayonne veteran in their fifteen-round no-decision fight. More than that, Tunney did what none of the best middleweight and light-heavyweights in the world had ever been able to do through a period of Smith's fourteen-year career in the ring, a career of nearly seven hundred battles. For the first time in Smith's life, Smith was knocked to the mat in a ring contest. Not only once, but twice. Following a nasty right uppercut to the chin, wicked 'liver punches' of Tunney…cut Smith down in the twelfth round. … A couple more half hooks, half uppercuts, landed with the left to Smith's right side, dropped Smith again in a heap. He cuddled up, his face twisting in agony.

Smith rose at nine. He weathered the round, and the final few rounds. "But he was a beaten man. Tunney won nearly all the way, notwithstanding Tunney's extremely cautious and displeasing fighting and the fact Smith every now and then ripped out with spectacular punches, many of which appeared to almost frighten Tunney into fits."

Tunney won 11-3-1. Smith won the 1st, 9th, and 11th, and was even in the 10th round, but those were the only rounds in which he showed to any advantage. Tunney was wary and unwilling to mix, and disliked the clinches, holding tightly or jumping away nervously, which brought jeers. Between the 11th and 12th rounds, Referee Al Wambsgans had to warn them to fight more. Still, Tunney was outboxing Smith. And he decked Smith twice in the very next round after the warning, when both got going more.

Smith said, "I know my ribs aren't broken. I don't know what was the matter. Several rounds before that I started to get dizzy and my whole

[160] *New York Evening Tribune-Times*, August 30, 1924.

body felt dead in that round. I did my best, but just couldn't get to him as I wanted." About midway in, he lost sight out of his right eye, and his left was blurring considerably toward the end, which explained why he was missing so many punches.[161]

Keefe subsequently said that Tunney "looked bad" against Smith to some degree because never before had he fought someone with such great defensive ability. As a result, Tunney was only "half-hearted in all his blows" except for his left hook to the right side. He felt that he could not land anything else but his left. "That's why his punches looked weak at times." "There must be quite a lot to that left hook of Tunney's, however. No light puncher could have caused Jeff Smith to cave in like that." Tunney was a cautious boxer, and at times "actually seemed frightened," but any time Smith landed an occasional vicious punch, Gene "steamed up with the lust of battle and came right back into the fray, unhurt and unafraid." The Smith fight gave Tunney great experience against a first-class man. "He is a clear-headed, cool lad, and is as fast and shifty as a lightweight, and as soon as he learns how to meet all sorts of obstacles, will be a great fighter." Yet, Keefe thought Tunney still needed more experience to beat Gibbons.[162]

On December 9, 1924 at Madison Square Garden, New York, before a crowd of 13,000 - 14,000, 174 ¾-pound Tommy Gibbons impressively stopped 171-pound Kid Norfolk (113-23-8) in the 6th round, decking him both in the 5th (with a right uppercut to the chin) and 6th rounds (series of rights and lefts to the head), forcing the referee to stop it, for Norfolk was helpless. Tom showed more aggressive offense than usual.[163]

The *Brooklyn Citizen* wrote, "Gibbons not only established himself as the most perfect fighter of his weight, but he earned a return bout with Jack Dempsey for the heavyweight championship."

---

[161] *Times-Picayune*, December 9, 1924. Others reported that Tunney won 11-2-2. *Shreveport Times, Alexandria Daily Town Talk*, December 9, 1924. Smith later revealed that he had persistent "double vision" from an eye injury suffered as a result of being laced by Martin Burke in 1922. He also came into the Tunney fight suffering from a sprained neck as a result of wrestling with his sparring partner. *Camden Post-Telegram*, December 12, 1924; *Bayonne Times*, August 18, 1925.
[162] *Times-Picayune*, December 10, 1924.
[163] On that same card, Tiger Flowers stopped Johnny Wilson in the 3rd round.
   Kid Norfolk had victories over Tiger Flowers (1923 KO1), Battling Siki (1923 W15), and Harry Greb (April 19, 1924 WDQ6 – Greb held and hit, and hit after the bell; Norfolk ahead on points at the time; and a 1921 DND10 Greb).

Tex Rickard said he wanted to make a Dempsey-Gibbons rematch.[164]

There also was talk of a potential Gibbons vs. Wills fight. Gibbons said he was willing to fight Wills.

The *Daily News* said the fight that the fans most wanted to see in 1925 was Dempsey vs. Wills.[165]

Yet, no top promoter with the finances to guarantee big purses seemed willing or all that interested in making Dempsey-Wills. The reason did not appear to be economic, because likely, if not certainly, such a fight would yield a huge gate. Some thought Kearns and Dempsey were too greedy, and would price themselves out of the market, but the feeling also was that everyone had their price, and from an economic standpoint, the fight probably could be made. Ultimately, it was understood by almost everyone that the main reason it might not be made was race and politics.

On January 8, 1925, in Grand Rapids, Michigan, 179-pound Tommy Gibbons stopped 178 ½-pound Jack Burke (16-9-3) in the 6th round. When Burke was helpless against the ropes, taking blows flush to the jaw, his manager Joe Woodman threw a towel into the ring at the same time that Referee E. W. Dickerson stopped it. "Tommy was as accurate as ever."[166]

Harry Newman picked Gibbons to beat Dempsey should they meet again. He said Tom had a better chance of beating Dempsey than anyone.

In early January 1925, Estelle Taylor was granted a divorce from her husband. She had filed the suit for divorce, citing cruel and barbarous treatment. Her husband chose not to contest the divorce. Jack Dempsey had signed a contract to act as her business manager, an indication that the two were growing closer.[167]

On January 16, 1925, Jack Dempsey and Estelle Taylor announced that they were engaged to be married.[168]

HONEST:—No fooling, Jack Dempsey really signed contract in Los Angeles to become business manager of Estelle Taylor, film star, to whom he was once reported engaged. The question is: Who would be the manager if they wed. Ask your wife.

The *Los Angeles Times* reported that Dempsey would get married and then retire from boxing. Jack said, "The fact is that when I marry it will mean the end of my career in the ring. The two don't go together." He said there would have to be a tournament to determine a new champion.

[164] *New York Daily News, Brooklyn Citizen,* December 10, 1924; *Boston Globe,* April 20, 1924. Some might notice that when Harry Wills stopped Norfolk in 2 rounds in 1922, several newsmen said he should fight stiffer opposition, failing to give him proper credit, at least not the kind that Gibbons received. Regardless, Tom's victories over Georges Carpentier and Kid Norfolk helped garner momentum for him. Still, some reporters could not get over the fact that Gibbons already had his chance against Dempsey, had lost nearly every round, and did not put up a particularly exciting contest other than the drama of his lasting the distance.
[165] *New York Daily News,* December 12, 1924, January 4, 1925; *Buffalo Enquirer,* December 13, 1924.
[166] *Grand Rapids Press, Escanaba Daily Press,* January 9, 1925.
[167] *New York Daily News,* January 10, 11, 1925.
[168] *New York Daily News,* January 17, 1925.

There was no one whom he would rather see win the championship than Tommy Gibbons. "He's a good clean fellow and he's white."[169]

Harry Wills had an injured left thumb, which was slow to heal. He claimed it had been injured before the Firpo fight.[170]

On January 27, 1925, in Los Angeles, federal authorities arrested Dempsey's trainer Teddy Hayes on a New York warrant charging him with being a fugitive from justice in connection with an alleged conspiracy to transport films of the Dempsey-Carpentier fight. A federal grand jury had indicted Hayes.[171]

On January 30, 1925, in Detroit, 179 ½-pound Tommy Gibbons knocked out 225-pound "Tiny" Jim Herman (37-8-9) in the 3rd round.[172]

Jack Kearns denied rumors of strained relations with the champ. He said Dempsey's matrimonial voyage would not end their boxing pact. They had a fruitful 8-year business relationship and Dempsey never once questioned his bidding. "When I said fight, Dempsey fought." Kearns said Jack had talked about retiring for a while. He was tired of fighting, and also felt that no one in the game could give him a fight. "But Dempsey is too young to retire." He was only 29 years old and still had some good fights left in him. Kearns said he had no contract with Dempsey other than his word. "It's been good enough for both of us for eight years."

Kearns said it would be bad for boxing if Dempsey retired, for black fighters like Harry Wills and George Godfrey could beat Gibbons, and that would result in another black champion, "a return to the tempestuous days of Jack Johnson's reign and the black eye boxing received as a result of his escapades." Most thought that Dempsey eventually would fight again.[173]

Tex Rickard allegedly signed Tom Gibbons for a bout with Dempsey to be held on June 1.

Kearns said, "Don't believe dispatches announcing the champ's retirement. It's a lotta bunk. Jack ain't going to quit until I tell him; I'm the boss." Kearns said Jack would fight again even if he got married.[174]

In early February 1925, Tex Rickard announced that he had received a wire from Jack Kearns saying that Tex's offers for Dempsey-Gibbons and Dempsey-Wills fights were agreeable, and that Kearns would be in New York in a couple weeks to talk business.

Some said an appeal would be made to New York Governor Al Smith and possibly even the legislature to prohibit another Gibbons match until Dempsey fought Wills first, or Gibbons beat Wills. Alderman George Harris said,

> Harry Wills must be Jack Dempsey's first opponent in this state. There will be no Dempsey-Gibbons farce. Tex Rickard's announcement that Dempsey will meet Gibbons, winner to meet

[169] *Los Angeles Times*, January 17, 1925.
[170] *New York Telegram and Evening Mail*, January 22, 1925.
[171] *New York Times*, January 28, 1925.
[172] *Detroit Free Press*, January 31, 1925.
[173] *Los Angeles Times*, January 31, 1925.
[174] *New York Telegram and Evening Mail*, February 2, 1925.

Wills, is an insult to the intelligence of the public. Did not Rickard announce in every New York newspaper, in fact in almost every newspaper throughout the country, that the winner of the Wills-Firpo fight would meet Dempsey?

Every one knows that the plan now is to let Dempsey and the man he already has soundly beaten come into New York, grab a ton of money and then for Dempsey to officially retire and once more and for all leave Wills stranded on the reef of broken promises.

Harris said Wills had been the only logical rival for 5 years, only to be shoved aside. "The public three times by voting contests in two big New York papers, one of them the evening Telegram and Mail, and by another contest in a boxing magazine of national circulation, registered overwhelmingly in favor of Wills as the one and only contender for Dempsey." Harris wanted the commission to stop any other bout.

> This latest attempt to defraud Wills of his justly earned rights is the last straw, and I repeat I will go to the highest authority in this State to get him a square deal. I will have the support of every fair minded and unbiased sportsman in this State. Already several Harlem societies boasting memberships of several thousand have urged me to act.[175]

In an article written by Dempsey about his life, as told to W. B. Seabrook, Dempsey said he was mostly Irish and Scotch, but he also had some ancestry that included Cherokee Indian, Jewish, and Mormon. Dempsey did not realize he had any Jewish ancestry, until,

> Two or three years ago, out seeing my mother in Salt Lake City, I told her about that story Bat Masterson printed about my being Jewish, and she said, 'Well, William Harrison, maybe you don't know it, but you have got a little bit of Jewish in you, and I reckon somebody was smart enough to see it.'

> I said, 'How?' And she said, 'Well, according to what I've been told, there was a great grandfather on my side of the family by the name of Jacob Levy, who was full-blooded Hebrew – a good man that the family was well proud of in his time.' She told me, too, that there was supposed to be a streak of Cherokee blood in the family somewhere a long time back, but she didn't know whether that was true, or just a story.

> So I guess that makes me part Irish, part Scotch, part Jewish, part Cherokee Indian, and part Mormon – if you want to look at it that way.[176]

[175] *New York Telegram and Evening Mail*, February 4, 1925.
[176] *Buffalo Courier*, February 1, 1925; *Winnipeg Evening Tribune*, February 4, 1925; *New York Daily News*, February 19, 20, 1920; *Albany Times-Union*, November 8, 1924; *Buffalo Evening Times*, April 23, 1918; *Sioux City Journal*, April 29, 1918; *Beckley Post-Herald*, September 29, 1960.

Back in 1918, Masterson and others had claimed, falsely, that Dempsey's real name was Julius Shinsky, and that he was a Polish or Russian Levantine Jew, and suggested that Kearns had him change his name. His sister had debunked that claim. The question is whether Dempsey was just teasing and kidding around in response to those who for years claimed he was part Jewish. However, lineage records indicate that Jack Dempsey's great-great grandmother, Rachel Solomon, who married John Dempsey in 1788, may have been Jewish. There also have been allusions to ancestry from England, Ireland, Scotland, Sweden, France, and Holland.

Answering the question regarding why so many women fell so hard for and chased after Dempsey, W. B. Seabrook said a psychologist told him that the fundamental attraction of man is physical strength, for a woman instinctively wanted a man who would be a strong and healthy father for her children, who could protect them if attacked. These were instincts that civilization could not change. Paradoxically, women also liked Jack's boyish quality, which catered to their mothering instincts. Also, Dempsey was "rather handsome," had big black eyes, thick wavy hair, fine white teeth, a charming smile, was a good dancer, and had a way of surprising or amusing people "by saying naive and simple things that have a real sparkle of wit in them."

Almost 50 girls had been rumored to be engaged to Dempsey over the years, including Estelle Taylor, Peggy Joyce, Sylvia Jocelyn, Bebe Daniels, Jennie Dolly of the Dolly Sisters; Mary Lewis, Ann Pennington, and Doris Keane.

Dempsey had been divorced for years, and they say a burnt child fears the fire. "No one has ever heard him say anything against the woman who was once his wife. He neither hates nor blames her. They were simply unhappy and it is a closed chapter that he will not talk about."

Dempsey said if he had married one of the Dolly sisters, he would need to marry them both, for "I think they like each other better than they will ever like any man. They'd have to marry a couple of brothers or another pair of twins and all live together in the same house to be happy." He had met them before, but got to be real friends with them on the trip over to Europe on the *Aquitania* in 1922, and "we had a lot of fun." However, they were just friends, and laughed and kidded about the rumors that he was to be engaged to one of them.

The only marriage rumor that upset him was Winifred Hart, the motion picture actress, because she was married already, and Jack was friends with her husband Bill. The rumor was totally false.

A lot of odd things had happened to Dempsey. One girl from New England told her mother that she was going to New York to marry him, and her mother later found a photo of Dempsey in the girl's bureau with some writing saying, "To My Darling Wife." Her father got on a train to New York, and "I had a tough time making him understand that I'd never even heard of his daughter and that I hadn't written what was on the picture. It wasn't even like my handwriting. The girl had written it herself." "Women are a queer lot." Some women liked him simply because he was the heavyweight champion, not because they actually liked him. "Some of them are plum crazy. They want me to beat 'em up – or at least that's the way their letters sound."[177]

The champ said he and film actress Doris Deane never were engaged, and just were friends. There was a photo of them kissing, but it was a stage kiss. "I never really kissed her in my life."

The Dolly sisters   Ann Pennington   with Winifred Westover Hart

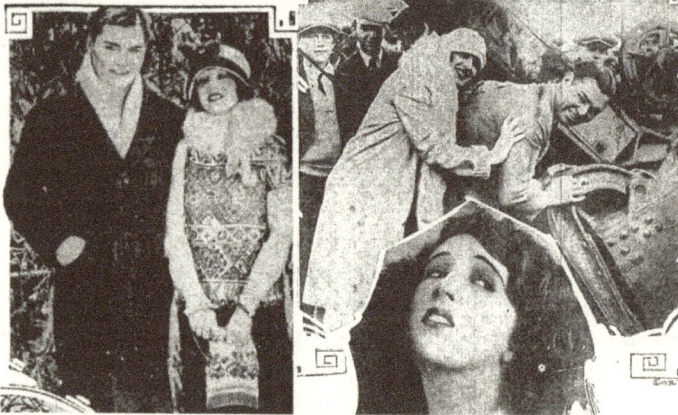

Dempsey and Estelle Taylor

Jack said life had been rough for him from age 17 on.

It's no easy life working with a shovel in a mine, and hoboing it from town to town. And it wasn't much easier when I first came east with Jack Price, poor, on the edge of ragged, and no prospect of being anything else – or at least that was the way we sometimes thought. Believe me, no girl would look at me then.

In New York (1916), Price left him in a dump of a bedroom in a cheap rooming house on Sixth Avenue with a cot and a chair. Restless Jack went to the park and sat there, sore and miserable. He was poor and hungry, sticking paste-board inside the soles of his shoes to cover the holes.

A nifty roadster stopped, and a couple got out and sat on a bench together. "They didn't pay any more notice to me than if I'd been an ash-barrel, but I noticed them. You could look at them and tell they had had

[177] *Buffalo Courier*, February 4, 1925.

everything." She was beautiful, with nice clothes, gloves, and jewels, and it was obvious they were rich.

> And you could tell from the way the man acted that she belonged to him and that he was proud of her. And you could tell from the way she acted…that she was glad she belonged to him.
>
> That fellow didn't know it – but it's the one time in my life I wanted to commit murder. I wanted to throw him in the lake. … I hated and envied him. It seemed like he had something I would never have as long as I lived. …
>
> Now I've got it. And sometimes it makes me happy, and sometimes I'm just as restless as I ever was when I was broke…and sometimes it seems like a sort of a dream that has happened to somebody else who is not me at all. But in the long run I think I get a lot more out of it than the guys who have had it all their lives.[178]

Dempsey was in love with Estelle Taylor, saying she was both good and beautiful. There had been rumors of their engagement before they actually were engaged. They did not want to make any final decision or announcement until she secured her divorce from Kenneth Peacock.

> Estelle and I plan eventually to get married – this coming summer, I hope – but when I do marry, I want my chief concern to be staying at home and looking after my wife and family. … She has some pictures to make, and I want very much to get one more good fight off my chest before I retire and settle down.

Taylor was even more attractive in person than on the screen, and she was equally at home in the ballroom as on a ranch. They had met when Dempsey was making a series of pictures in Los Angeles. He travelled East with her from Los Angeles, just before the Firpo fight, but she was properly chaperoned by her grandmother.

Estelle's family subsequently invited Jack to their home in Wilmington, Delaware. "It was just after I had my nose fixed, and everybody was saying that I had it fixed up to please Miss Taylor. The chief reason I had it fixed was that it made it easier for me to breathe." In his early boxing days, he had his nose smashed up from the awful beatings he used to take before he really learned to box. "I breathe a lot easier now, and I'm not troubled as much with little colds in the head as I used to be. Of course the new nose looks better, too, and I'm glad of it. Who wouldn't be?" And if he ever worked in the movies again, they wouldn't have to fix it up with wax every time like they did for the other pictures.

Dempsey claimed that it was no news to him that Taylor had married Peacock 10 years ago, but it came as a surprise to the public. They had separated long before he and Taylor ever met. He had nothing to do with their separation. Despite rumors of a lawsuit for alienation of affection,

---

[178] *Buffalo Courier,* February 8, 1925.

Peacock did not sue, and let the divorce proceedings go through without trouble. "Estelle's not the kind of girl who would let anybody put something over on her. If Mr. Peacock had started anything, she was ready to fight back in the courts. But Mr. Peacock acted square enough, and as you know, she got her divorce without scandal of any sort."[179]

Rumors were that Dempsey would marry Taylor sooner rather than later. He reportedly had purchased a $5,000 ring.

Indeed, on February 7, 1925, in San Diego, California, in a small, private ceremony, Jack Dempsey married Estelle Taylor. The only people present at the First Presbyterian Church were the reverend, lightweight Joe Benjamin - the champ's friend, Eddie Connors - Benjamin's manager, Helen Taylor - Estelle's sister, and Jack's mother Celia Dempsey.

Jack spiked rumors of his retirement. He said he was not yet ready to retire, and he knew Estelle would not object too hard.[180]

Jack Kearns claimed that Dempsey likely would fight Gibbons and Wills in 1925. He believed that the champ would earn $1.5 million from those bouts and then retire undefeated as champion.

However, a well-known moving picture man told George Underwood,

> Dempsey is through with the ring for good and for all. He is under contract with the Metro people for thirty weeks at $2,000 per week. Now that Estelle Taylor is Mrs. Jack Dempsey she also will be more in demand. Mr. and Mrs. Dempsey will make more out of the pictures than Dempsey can get in the ring.
>
> The most Dempsey can command now is $500,000 for a fight. Forty per cent of that would be taken out in taxes. Half the remainder would have to be split equally with Kearns. That leaves Dempsey $150,000 without deducting expenses.
>
> Dempsey will do all of his fighting hereafter at home and in the pictures. Future events will prove my contention.[181]

The Fistic Cross Word Puzzle: Will He Take Off His Coat or Put on the Trousers? -:- By Ed Hughes

[179] *Buffalo Courier*, February 6, 1925.
[180] *Los Angeles Times*, February 8, 1925.
[181] *New York Telegram and Evening Mail*, February 9, 1925.

CHAPTER 3

The Split, Edicts, and
Making the Next Title Defense

Discussing the next prospective Dempsey foe, Robert Edgren wrote,

> [Gene Tunney] is a great boxer and an aggressive, hard hitting fighter. Tunney showed his real class last year when he knocked out Spalla, the rugged Italian heavyweight champion and Carpentier. ... Tunney ignored Carpentier's right, crowded Carpentier round after round, was hit hard and shook the punches off, and knocked Carpentier out.

Edgren ranked Tunney above Gibbons, who beat Carpentier and Kid Norfolk. A Gibbons-Tunney fight "should be the biggest drawing card of the coming outdoor season."[182]

On February 17, 1925, Paddy Mullins, Harry Wills' manager, posted an official challenge to Dempsey and a forfeit check for $2,500 with the New York State Athletic Commission.[183]

Wills and Mullins asked the New York Commission to stop any Gibbons-Dempsey fight, should it be signed, urging that they were first entitled to a contest.

It was understood that two of the three members of the commission were inclined to vote that Gibbons and Wills should meet to decide whom Dempsey should fight next. Tom's manager Eddie Kane was agreeable to that proposition, but doubted whether Wills would agree. "When Wills was offered a contest with Gibbons last December...he turned it down because of bad hands. We think his hands are still bad."

Paddy Mullins said, "Wills is willing to meet Gibbons, but we do not feel that he should be required to prove his right for a fight against Dempsey. Gibbons has been beaten once by Dempsey, and Wills never has been given a chance." Another newsman quoted Mullins as saying, "I have not signed, agreed to or listened to any proposition that Harry Wills meet Tom Gibbons. Until I find there is absolutely no chance of a Dempsey-Wills bout this year I will listen to no other offers."

Billy Gibson, Gene Tunney's manager, said there was an offer for a Gibbons-Tunney match, which would be an even bigger draw and payday than Gibbons-Wills.[184]

On February 24, 1925, newly married 205-pound Jack Dempsey surprised folks by working out for 12 rounds at a Los Angeles gym on

---

[182] *Buffalo Times*, February 15, 1925.
[183] *New York Telegram and Evening Mail*, February 18, 1925.
[184] *New York Telegram and Evening Mail*, February 23, 1925; *Brooklyn Citizen*, February 24, 1925.

Spring-street, including boxing 3 rounds with featherweight Tod Morgan and wrestling with Jerry the Greek (Luvadis).[185]

A jury took just 30 minutes to exonerate Jack Kearns and find him not liable in the civil suit brought by Mrs. Mary C. Tenny, who alleged that he had attacked her.[186]

George Underwood predicted, "By September 1926, neither Dempsey nor Wills will be world's heavyweight champion. Either Gene Tunney...or Jim Maloney, the young Boston Irishman, will be cock o' the walk among the heavies one year and a half from now. Laugh now. You may not get the chance later."[187]

Behind the scenes, the New York commissioners disagreed about how to handle the title challenges of Gibbons and Wills. Supposedly, current chairman George Brower and former chair William Muldoon were in favor of a Gibbons-Wills elimination bout, while Commissioner Jim Farley supported a Dempsey-Wills fight on the grounds that Wills had been waiting for his chance for five years, while Gibbons had his chance already.

> Farley is regarded as the personal representative of Gov. Smith on the commission and if he should let it be known that he favors a Dempsey-Wills fight it would signify that the Governor hasn't anything against a mixed bout. On the other hand, politicians point out that the Governor does not want a Dempsey-Wills fight and he figures that the two Republican members of the board will vote against it and thereby assume the political responsibility.[188]

On March 6, 1925, James Farley was elected chairman of the New York State Athletic Commission, supplanting acting chairman George Brower. A Democrat, Farley was a former New York State Assemblyman.

Farley's first act as chairman was to telegraph Jack Dempsey to inform him of the challenges of Harry Wills and Tom Gibbons, filed in late February, and notifying the champ that he had to answer Wills' challenge first, within 24 hours. Farley alerted Dempsey that the commission's rules required a champion to defend his title at least once every six months, and that time period had passed long ago.

Jack Kearns said he would pay no attention to the New York commission, for Dempsey's New York license had expired.

> We are not under the jurisdiction of the New York Commission, and we will take no orders about any matches. I am the only one to decide Dempsey's opponents. The New York Commission didn't give Dempsey the heavyweight title and the commission can't take it away. Dempsey is willing to fight any one and any time provided a suitable purse is offered by a competent promoter.

[185] *Los Angeles Times*, February 25, 1925; *New York Daily News*, February 26, 1925.
[186] *Los Angeles Times*, February 27, 1925. The District Attorney had declined to pursue criminal charges.
[187] *New York Telegram and Evening Mail*, February 28, 1925.
[188] *Brooklyn Standard Union*, March 1, 1925.

Kearns said if the commission would run through its files, it would see that Dempsey had been ordered to fight Wills once before, and he had accepted, only to have the same commission later declare that the fight could not be held. "I will listen to the commission if it is acting as a promoter and will put up a purse and find a place for the fight. But I'm not going to accept any opponents until I see the money and am assured that the fight can be held."

Kearns said he was not worried about a report that the commission might stage a Gibbons-Wills fight and declare the winner the champion. "There is only one way to take the heavyweight title away from Jack Dempsey and that is by winning it from him in the ring." Such statements set up a potential tussle between Kearns/Dempsey and the commission.

Dempsey said, "I have said a thousand times that I would fight Wills and no one has called me on it. The commission, if it wants to force me to fight Wills, ought to get a promoter to make an offer and then see what I would do." He also said, "I'll fight either Wills or Gibbons just as soon as they accompany their challenges with a suitable purse."

Tex Rickard said he intended to promote a Wills vs. Gibbons fight in the summer at Yankee Stadium, and a Dempsey bout in September.[189]

Rickard subsequently said Kearns wanted $750,000 for Dempsey's next fight, which Tex said was crazy. But was it?

Rickard was not particularly interested in a Wills-Dempsey fight, because he did not want to deal with the potential obstacles to it. "In these days you have to lay $100,000 on the line before you can make a move to stage a heavyweight championship and you've got to be pretty certain that you're safe when you put that amount down." If he had sufficient assurances, he might consider making Dempsey-Wills.[190]

Charles Henderson announced that he was willing to post a certified check for $500,000 in Kearns' hands for a Dempsey-Wills fight, to act as a forfeit if he failed to bring off the fight. Jimmy De Forest, Polo Grounds matchmaker, also telegrammed Kearns, offering Dempsey more money than he ever received before, for a September bout with Wills. Underwood said it all was ballyhoo at the moment, and what the promoters *said* needed to match what they *did*. "Wait till they DO something."

Commissioner James Farley strongly suggested that it would be in Rickard's best interests to stage a Wills-Dempsey bout in New York, given that Tex had vast interests in New York, and hence "it would be sound business sense for him to assist the commission to carry out its mandate" for Dempsey to fight Wills before anyone else. The commissioner was more than subtly hinting that the commission would come down hard on Rickard if he did not make that fight, for doing otherwise would indicate that he held the commission in contempt.[191]

[189] *Brooklyn Standard Union, New York Telegram and Evening Mail*, March 7, 1925; *New York Daily News*, March 8, 1925.
[190] *Brooklyn Standard Union*, March 9, 1925.
[191] *New York Telegram and Evening Mail*, March 13, 1925.

George Underwood said the next big heavyweight fight was Jack Kearns vs. the New York State Athletic Commission, given that he had flaunted its authority. Kearns said the commission had better follow up its matchmaking by acting as a promoter and posting a forfeit. He questioned its authority over Dempsey.

Kearns wrote a letter to the commission, noting that three years ago, Mr. Muldoon, then chair of the commission, ordered Dempsey to defend the title against Wills, which challenge was accepted, and expenditures of time and money were made.

> Then Mr. Muldoon specifically forbid the meeting between Dempsey and Wills in New York State and informed me personally that it would not be permitted.
>
> Dempsey might now in all fairness ask what assurance he can have from the New York State Athletic Commission, which still has Mr. Muldoon as a member, that he will be treated any differently if he should again accept a challenge from Harry Wills.
>
> Does the New York State Athletic Commission intend promoting the match for which it is attempting to serve as matchmaker? Or will it produce a promoter who will guarantee the champion the rights and privileges of a champion in defending his title?
>
> When it became obvious that Dempsey would not be permitted to meet Wills in New York State and when no offer was presented for the match elsewhere, Dempsey accepted a challenge from Tom Gibbons…and gave him such a thorough drubbing in fifteen rounds…that no one who saw it has since doubted the champion's superiority.

Kearns said Dempsey already had accepted Wills' challenge, so he saw no reason why he needed to accept it again. He asked the commission to follow up on its matchmaking by acting as the promoter and giving Dempsey a financial guarantee in the form of a cash deposit, along with "the absolute official assurance of the ability to carry out the match."

Underwood suspected the result of Kearns' letter might be that the board would refuse Dempsey and Kearns licenses to participate in contests in New York. He believed that Kearns feared Wills; and feared losing his meal ticket.

Paddy Mullins said he had not agreed to put Wills in with Gibbons. "I have told no one I would let Wills fight Gibbons. … The match I want for Wills is with Dempsey."[192]

Harry Newman predicted that Dempsey probably never would fight again. He had signed a $250,000 movie contract with the Associated Exhibitors, which allegedly prohibited him from fighting until October. Estelle Taylor would be his co-star. This was further evidence that she was determined to have him quit fighting.

---

[192] *New York Telegram and Evening Mail*, March 16, 17, 1925.

Before his marriage, there was a rumor that Dempsey and Kearns had a violent quarrel, and the breach could not be healed. Rumor was that Taylor was responsible for Dempsey's determination to quit the game, and that she and Kearns were not friends.[193]

Kearns said Dempsey could fight whenever he wanted.

George Underwood reported that several factors would prevent Dempsey from boxing at all in 1925 – his moving picture contracts, the hard feelings between Dempsey and Kearns, particularly regarding the trouble between Kearns and the new Mrs. Dempsey, and the fact that she would not permit her husband to re-enter the ring.

Underwood noted that Kearns wanted a guaranteed purse. However, "Guarantees are not permitted in this State. No one knows that better than Kearns." He had to work on percentage in New York. "In championship bouts in this State a champion gets 37 ½% and a challenger 12 ½%." If they had worked on such a percentage basis for the Carpentier fight, they would have made $609,967.50, over $300,000 more, or double what they received, given that the receipts were $1,626,580. Underwood said Kearns had cost Dempsey a lot of money. Hence, Underwood argued that Kearns should be willing to fight Wills with no guaranteed purse, because such a fight would garner them more than any fighter ever was paid.[194]

According to the *New York Daily News*, Dempsey said the upcoming motion picture would take only four weeks to film, and he might fight in the summer (of 1925). He said Kearns was not in on the picture deal at all. "If I do fight I will fight under Kearns, but there will have to be an adjustment about our percentage. There will be no more 50% splits with Kearns." This confirmed that there was tension between Dempsey and Kearns. Dempsey no longer was willing to give his manager 50% of his purses.[195]

Tex Rickard's matchmaker was trying to make a Gibbons vs. Wills fight for late May at Yankee Stadium.[196]

On March 19, 1925, in Trenton, New Jersey, after deliberating for 10 hours, a federal jury found Tex Rickard, Fred C. Quimby (movie producer), Teddy Hayes (secretary to Jack Kearns), and Jasper Muma (newspaperman) guilty of conspiracy and illegal transportation of the Dempsey-Carpentier films. Frank Flournoy (MSG matchmaker) was found guilty of conspiracy but acquitted of the transportation charge. Philadelphia fight manager Jimmy Dougherty was acquitted on all charges.

For the conspiracy charge, they faced a penalty of a fine of $10,000 or imprisonment in a federal penitentiary for 2 years, or both. The penalty for illegal transportation of the films was a $1,000 fine.

When asked if he had anything to say, Rickard replied, "Nothing, I guess, but it is a bit tough when the Government collects $500,000 in

[193] *New York Daily News*, March 18, 1925.
[194] *New York Telegram and Evening Mail*, March 18, 1925.
[195] *New York Daily News*, March 20, 1925.
[196] *Plainfield Courier-News*, March 17, 1925.

taxes and then hands out this." Rickard's attorney said, "Why wasn't the Government indicted? The Government collected its tax from every showing of these pictures. Now the Government asks conviction of Rickard and Flournoy because they got a little money out of the exhibitions."[197]

On March 24, 1925, the New York Commission (Farley and Muldoon voting, with Brower not present) held that Dempsey's refusal to answer the challenges directed at him rendered him ineligible to box in New York. Kearns was deemed ineligible to manage fighters in New York as well. Furthermore, the commission warned all licensed promoters, managers, and boxers that their entering into any kind of boxing business with Dempsey or Kearns would result in suspension or revocation of their licenses. George Underwood wrote, "That pretty effectually bars Dempsey from boxing any one, not only in any of the twenty-seven States having a working agreement with the New York State Athletic Commission, but shuts out Dempsey from New Jersey, which split with the New York board." Dempsey/Kearns would have almost no other options. "The big money practically only is obtained in New York and New Jersey. It is only the big money Kearns and Dempsey are after."

Kearns replied, "Dempsey has never refused to fight Wills. ... We will fight Wills any time a responsible promoter will assure us that the fight can be held and will put enough on the line to guarantee his part of the contract."

Kearns also was quoted as saying, "This is too small and too ridiculous for me to pay any further attention to the matter. Dempsey has no license in New York. We have violated no laws that I know of." Kearns also noted that Dempsey had accepted Wills' challenge years ago, but the New York commission ultimately had refused to sanction the bout. Kearns had accepted the Gibbons challenge as well, but likewise, a promoter with backing was needed.

Dempsey said, "I am ready to meet Wills or any fighter as soon as I am promised enough dough for the match. I don't even hold a license in New York, and I fail to see where the boxing commission can take such action and keep a straight face. I wish they would stop kidding me and start talking business."

Tex Rickard confirmed that he was endeavoring to match Wills with Gibbons in May, with the winner to meet Dempsey in September.[198]

Gene Tunney and Harry Greb had fought four times. Each had won clearly once, with two fights being about even, when weighing everything in the balance, although officially Tunney had 2 wins, Greb 1, and the third being a no decision generally perceived as a draw. They were scheduled to fight for a fifth time, in St. Paul, Minnesota, on neutral territory, as somewhat of a tiebreaker.

---

[197] New York Times, March 20, 1925. If the government had received $500,000 in taxes, just imagine how much revenue was generated by the film exhibitions.
[198] New York Daily News, Minneapolis Tribune, New York Telegram and Evening Mail, March 25, 1925.

The local *Minneapolis Tribune* said Tunney seemed to be stronger, heavier, and more rugged than when he fought there a year ago.

On March 23, four days before the fight, Tunney sparred 6 rounds, 2 each with Kid Muskie, Carl Augustine, and Rusty Jones. Gene shot snappy left jabs to the head and short rights to the heart with a sharpshooter's skill. His footwork was fast and shifty, whether on the attack or defense. He could dodge and sidestep, and fire from any angle, bewildering his foes. Kid Augustine said Gene was stronger and hitting harder than he did a year ago when he sparred with him.

Tunney met and shook Tommy Gibbons' hand, which some took as a sign that Gibbons was considering fighting him.

On March 24, Greb appeared to be in excellent condition in his 6 rounds of sparring with Mark Moore and Harry Roberts. Greb said,

> I have trained harder for this fight than any bout I have been in since I won the middleweight championship from Johnny Wilson. … Honestly, training to me is harder than fighting. I am anxious to whip Tunney and prove to boxing fans throughout the country that I was robbed both times the judges gave the decision against me in my last two fights with Gene in New York. … I am always in pretty fair condition because I often fight three or four times a month. Fact is, I believe in keeping in shape by fighting. However, I decided to pass up all other bouts and concentrate my efforts in getting into perfect condition for Tunney. I am ready in every sense of the expression and if I lose Friday night I will have no alibis to offer.[199]

Promoters were attempting to make a Tunney vs. Gibbons fight. Jimmy De Forest, matchmaker for the Polo Grounds Athletic Club in New York, was ready to guarantee the boxers a $100,000 purse, to be divided however they saw fit, for a 15-round bout to a decision. Jack Reddy was offering Gibbons $50,000 for the fight, to be held in St. Paul. Others were trying to make a Wills vs. Gibbons bout.

Billy Gibson, Tunney's manager, was eager for a Gibbons contest. "I am sure Gene would whip Tommy and that would place him in a position to demand a fight with Dempsey."

Those who saw Tunney in training noted his improvement.

> He was the personification of grace as he glided and pranced around the ring, easily evading his sparring partners' leads and smacking with left hooks and short straight rights to the body and face. He is far more aggressive and now takes the fighting to the other fellow instead of laying back and permitting his opponent to bring the milling to him. … Tunney's accuracy and snappy punching caused much favorable comment among close students of boxing.[200]

[199] *Minneapolis Tribune*, March 23, 24, 25, 1925.
[200] *Minneapolis Morning Tribune*, March 26, 1925.

The day of the fight, George Barton, who would referee the contest, said both Greb and Tunney had trained faithfully, for the result meant so much to both. The winner would be in line to fight Tommy Gibbons for a lot of money. Billy Gibson believed that De Forest would go as high as $150,000 for a Tunney-Gibbons fight. Greb was hoping to be the one who earned that fight instead.

Manager Jimmie "Red" Mason and Greb

Barton also believed the upcoming fight would be furious because of the bad blood engendered by their prior fights, and because of warring factions. Mason had been Greb's original manager, then Engel, but Greb went back to Mason, and Engel now was in the Tunney camp.

Fans were excited to see the scrap. "The men appear to be so well matched that betters are offering even money on the result." Those who favored Greb liked his speed and ability to shower in blows. Tunney was more methodical than the flashy Greb, "who does everything opposite to the generally adopted style of boxing. We'll say this much; any boxer, regardless of weight and class, who beats Greb over the 10-round route, must step his fastest from the tap of the gong in the first round until the final second of the last round." Tunney had the size advantages, being taller, longer, and 10+ pounds heavier.[201]

---

[201] *Minneapolis Tribune*, March 27, 1925. Locals had seen Greb win a January 30, 1925 10-round no decision over 171-pound Jimmy Delaney. They had seen Tunney beat Delaney the same way back in March 1924.

In their fifth contest, on March 27, 1925, in Saint Paul, Minnesota, reporters unanimously agreed that 181 ½-pound Gene Tunney (71-1-3) clearly won a 10-round no decision against 167 ½-pound Harry Greb (235-14-20) in dominant fashion. Weights were taken at 3 p.m. that day.

The local *St. Paul Pioneer Press* said Tunney won a decisive victory over Greb with a punishing body attack. Tunney gave Greb as "thorough a beating" as he ever had received. Starting in the 4th round, Greb was "outclassed and outfought" so completely that he began holding and stalling, resorting to defensive tactics, rarely flashing offense, which quickly terminated when Tunney launched a devastating counterattack to the body, which landed with deadly accuracy and telling effect. Greb rarely landed.

Tunney landed the harder and more accurate blows, but also was superior in his clever boxing, which enabled him to parry every attack and then counter with damaging blows. Greb was discouraged by his inability to land, and he was surprised by the power and persistence of the slashing attack into his stomach and heart. "It is doubtful that the bounding Greb, counted the most elusive fighter in the ring, has ever taken so many solid blows in any given 10 rounds." Few other fighters could have stood up to the blows he took, which showed Harry's durability.

Greb's best connections were the result of pulling Tunney's head with his left into a right hook, for which he was warned for holding and hitting. So, he hit less and held more.

Tunney fought a clever, vicious, and intense fight. Tunney not only outhit Greb, but accepted all of Harry's characteristic rough work and outroughed him. Greb tried every trick known – butting, thumbing, holding, pulling, and holding and hitting, but Tunney kept plugging away.

Tunney won 8-2, with Greb only wining the 2nd and 3rd rounds.

The *St. Paul Daily News'* Ed Shave said Tunney handed Greb a neat lacing, winning decisively, 7-1-2. Tunney stood as one of the leading challengers for Dempsey's title. He administered one of the worst defeats that Greb ever sustained in his long and brilliant career. Greb started fast, won the 1st round, while the 2nd and 3rd were even, but thereafter it was all Tunney.

Although defeated, Greb gave Tunney plenty of trouble. Just when it appeared that Harry was in a bad way, he would flash his old bounding, leaping game and hurl blows at Tunney from every direction. However, Tunney's body blows had their effect, and slowed him down greatly after the 5th round. Greb had to call upon all of his ability, experience, and legs to carry him away or in close. The bout was marred considerably by Greb's clinching, which brought forth boos. At one point, Tunney twice talked to Greb, telling him to keep his thumb out of his eye.

The *St. Paul Dispatch* said Greb could not be criticized too severely for not wanting to take too many chances with his stronger opponent, given that he was 14 pounds smaller. "Tunney fought a masterful battle, launching a terrific body attack at the outset and continuing it for the 10 rounds. It was surprising that Greb stood up under such punishment."

Afterwards, Greb said he had fought his last battle with Tunney, and would not fight him again. He told Gene, "You are getting too big and too strong for me. You are hitting better and harder than ever. If you fight Tommy Gibbons my money will go down on you."

Jimmy De Forest called it a remarkable fight. Tunney was an improved fighter. Jimmy never saw anyone force Greb to hold on as much as he did. He believed Gene would give Gibbons a hard battle. De Forest thought he soon would sign them for a fight.

De Forest did not want Gibbons to fight Wills, because he said it would be a bad fight that would hurt Tom's drawing power, because even if Gibbons won, it would be an ugly contest, with Wills holding and mauling a lot, so Tom would not be able to make a good showing. De Forest was offering Gibbons 30% of the receipts for a fight with Tunney.

Tommy Gibbons, who was in attendance, said, "Tunney is a big, strong fellow and ought to give me a good hard fight. I like the way he boxes. He hits hard and accurately." Mike Gibbons, his brother, considered Tunney to be one of the craftiest ring generals he had seen in years.

The *Minneapolis Daily Star's* John Getchell said Tunney won clearly, administering a "decisive beating." Nevertheless, the fans still believed he did not have enough class to beat Gibbons, whom Tunney was scheduled to fight in June.

Greb did a great deal of holding, which affected Tunney's performance. For the first two rounds, Tunney was the aggressor, and Greb was cautious. In the 3rd, Greb charged in swinging, landing several hard blows. However, thereafter, Tunney proved to be as good or better in retaliation. Tunney was the aggressor at the start of the 4th, landing a shower of body blows and a stiff left to the head that hurt Greb.

From then on, Harry started holding on, while Tunney piled up the points, which continued until the end. Tunney won every round after the 3rd, in part because Greb did not care to make a fight of it, but instead held too much, which caused the fans to boo him.

Writing for the *Minneapolis Morning Tribune*, George Barton, who refereed the contest, said Tunney outpointed Greb in a disappointing fight, because Harry held continually to save himself. The fight started off viciously, with Greb setting his usual fast pace, winning the first few rounds, but from the 4th round on, Greb tired perceptibly under the heavy punches that Tunney directed at his body, and he held on in order to go the 10 rounds. In flashes, Greb would open up with an overhand right and sweeping left hook to the jaw, as well as short right uppercut to the jaw, but as soon as Tunney began bombarding his body at close quarters, Harry held. The spectators booed his clinching tactics.

Tunney fought cleanly and placed his punches more accurately and effectively than Greb. Furthermore, "Greb resorted to many of the tricks for which he is noted, such as holding around the neck and punching with his free hand, butting and wrestling."

> To Tunney's credit it must be said that he did his best to make a fight of it. He was always willing to trade punches, but Greb continually tied up his arms in the clinches and for the most part prevented Tunney from dealing out the punishment of which he is capable. Despite Greb's defense the middleweight champion was forced to take more punishment at close quarters than it was apparent to the majority of spectators. Tunney is largely a body-fighter and he gets terrific power into short punches. ... Tunney won because of his superior boxing and condition.

Barton scored it 6-3-1 for Tunney, awarding the 1st, 2nd, and 3rd rounds to Greb, the 4th, 5th, 6th, 7th, and 8th rounds to Tunney, the 9th even, and the 10th to Tunney.

The fight drew $22,125, and each fighter received a $6,500 guarantee.

For the *Minneapolis Journal*, Edward Walker said Tunney's body attack paved the way to his victory over Greb in a contest marred by holding. Walker scored it 5-3-2 for Tunney. 1-E, 2-G, 3-G, 4-T, 5-T, 6-T, 7-E (Greb's nose bleeding), 8-T (though a Greb right opened an old cut over Tunney's left eye), 9-G, 10-T.

Outweighed by 14 pounds, Greb elected to fight a defensive battle, making the contest uninteresting. Greb was outpunched and outgeneraled, facing a two-fisted fighter who continually bored in and scored so often that after the 3rd round, Greb was slowed up and unable to keep up his offense. Harry's punches had no effect. He tried, but found his master, so he decided to last the route if possible. Tunney was dangerous, particularly on the inside, and slugged Greb out of his many "deathlike grips."

> The referee would have been fully justified in leaving the ring as early as the fifth round, or in disqualifying Greb. Tunney was Greb's master all the way and it is my belief that in a 15 round battle Tunney will come mighty close to scoring a knockout. Greb took plenty of punishment and he is one of the hardest men in the ring to box. He is always on the move, hits from any angle and resorts to tactics unbecoming to a world's champion. Greb proved conclusively that he cannot hit a lick.

Tunney's best attack was a body barrage. In close, Greb hung on. "Tunney's best punch is a short right to the heart, and he also packs a vicious left hook. He is very adept at placing either of these punches to the head or heart." He was much improved from the version that fought Jimmy Delaney. "He is more rugged, weighs more and has improved his footwork greatly."

Tommy Gibbons said, "Tunney was handicapped by Greb's peculiar style. Greb is absolutely unorthodox in his fighting and every fighter who meets him is up against a different proposition than with other boxers.

Greb should not be criticized for holding." Their size disparity excused such tactics.

Gibbons seemed amenable to De Forest's offer of 30% of the gate receipts to fight Tunney. De Forest said, "It looks like the match is as good as made. I found Gibbons to be very agreeable to my terms. He made no unreasonable demands whatever."[202]

A couple months later, Henry Farrell called Harry Greb a "physical marvel."

> Greb's greatest asset perhaps is his stout heart and his absolute confidence. He is not a great fighter, because he has no punch, but he is one of the most effective fighters in the ring. His tactics are sometimes open to question, but a fighter can get no sympathy by crying to the referee – "He's stickin' his finger in my eye."

In their first fight, Gene Tunney tried to be gentlemanly with Greb but got fouled and injured. Tunney said, "That'll never happen again. The next time I'll rough it with him and he'll quit." In future bouts, when Greb started roughing, Gene responded in kind, which caused Greb to stop using such tactics and fight according to the rules.[203]

Tommy Gibbons said his main objective was to fight Dempsey, and if beating Wills would get him that fight, he preferred to fight Wills. He said he was not dodging Tunney, but had promised promoters in New York to box Wills in late May. "I would much prefer to fight Wills before Tunney as such a match would give me a chance to prove my right to a return contest with Jack Dempsey, the one fight I really want."

Tunney signed to fight Gibbons for 20% of the gate, but Jimmy De Forest needed to work to get Gibbons to sign.

Prospects for Tunney-Gibbons looked brighter when it appeared that the Milk Fund folks had not actually signed Wills to fight Gibbons. There was a question as to whether Wills was willing to fight Gibbons. Eddie Kane, Tom's manager, asked them to produce the alleged signed contract. If they could not produce an agreement signed by Wills or his manager to fight Gibbons, then they were going to go ahead and fight Tunney. There even was a question as to whether the New York commission would sanction a Wills-Gibbons bout. Kane said he was satisfied with the current De Forest offer of 35% of the gate receipts to fight Tunney.

Jack Dempsey said the toughest job for him was finding helpful sparring partners who would allow him to open up. Very few could take his punches or were willing to do so. He had to hold back so much on the few men he could get that he really was not getting the right kind of work.[204]

World welterweight champ Mickey Walker said he had trained in the gym with Dempsey for a few weeks. Walker had taken tips and advice

---

[202] *St. Paul Pioneer Press, St. Paul Daily News, St. Paul Dispatch, Minneapolis Daily Star, Minneapolis Morning Tribune, Minneapolis Journal, Daily News,* March 28, 1925. The *Minneapolis Daily Star* said Greb was 176 ½ pounds, but all of the other local papers and those throughout the nation reported 167 ½.
[203] St. Joseph Herald-Press, May 19, 1925.
[204] *Minneapolis Tribune,* March 29-31, 1925.

from Jack, and also watched him train, looking quite well. They did not spar. "No, sir-e-e-e. Say, I wouldn't even play tag with him with the gloves on. Ugh, how he hits. I'll box or fight any man in the world save Dempsey. That's one chap I bar." He said Dempsey was not slipping.[205]

On March 30, 1925, in Newark, New Jersey, Tex Rickard was fined $7,000 for his conspiracy and film transportation convictions. Fred Quimby and Jasper Muma were fined $7,000 as well. Frank Flournoy and Teddy Hayes were fined $1,000 each. William Rudolph, who pled guilty before trial and cooperated with the government, was fined $500.

When issuing his sentence of only fines, Judge Bodine stated,

> In this case, who can say how the Government was injured? The statutes were flouted, but who of the citizens of the several States were hurt? Boxing bouts can be shown in the States where these pictures were taken. Accounts of boxing matters can be and are broadcast over the radio. Newspapers and periodicals carry the information and show pictures of the ringside and the contestants. Many people who regard themselves as high-minded persons look at the pictures and go to the encounters.
>
> Still, a law has been violated and punishment must be imposed.

Apparently, the Dempsey-Carpentier films had been copied and transported to 22 different states. "In every district where the pictures were taken and shown, the Federal Courts imposed fines ranging from $200 to $1,000."

The government's lawyers announced that they were preparing to start prosecutions regarding the transportation of the Dempsey-Firpo pictures as well.[206]

Tex Rickard revealed that Dempsey and Kearns had signed an agreement the prior winter to fight for him. "You will find Dempsey and Kearns will not do any business with any syndicates. They got enough of syndicates at Shelby. ... When he fights Harry Wills it will be under my auspices." Tex said Dempsey would not again be fooled by alleged syndicates which could not actually come up with the money they claimed to have. Dempsey knew Tex always paid in full.

However, another promoter, Charles Henderson, insisted that Dempsey would fight for him in September. Yet, many believed that Dempsey would not fight at all.[207]

On April 1, it was announced that Tom Gibbons and Gene Tunney were matched to fight at the Polo Grounds in New York in June. Gibbons opened as an 8-5 betting favorite to beat Tunney.

> Harry Wills, the negro heavyweight challenger, finds himself back in his familiar place on the shelf for the season and perhaps for the rest of his career. Following the helpless hunch that he would get a

---

[205] *New York Telegram and Evening Mail*, March 28, 1925.
[206] *Brooklyn Standard Union*, March 30, 1925; *New York Times*, March 31, 1925.
[207] *New York Telegram and Evening Mail*, April 1, 1925.

match with Jack Dempsey, the big colored boy would not consider an offer to meet Gibbons.

Wills never had signed to meet Gibbons. Wills intimated that he might consider a Gibbons fight if offered $300,000, but that amount ensured he would not get the fight. As a result, Wills would have to go back to fighting "the second-raters that he has been using for years."[208]

W. S. Farnsworth, Universal Service Staff Correspondent, said, "Either Harry Wills is afraid of Tom Gibbons or the negro's manager, Paddy Mullins, has pulled the prize boner move in the history of pugilism." It seemed that Mullins was holding out for one fight – Dempsey, which may or may not happen. Fighting and beating Gibbons would have created more momentum for a Dempsey-Wills fight. "His refusal to let Wills fight Gibbons has absolutely killed whatever chance Harry might have had to meet the champion." Plus, beating Gibbons would have removed one more potential lucrative option for Dempsey.[209]

Dempsey wrestles with Bull Montana

Also on April 1, 1925, at the Los Angeles Coliseum, before a crowd of close to 10,000, as part of a series of athletic events, Jack Dempsey boxed 3 rounds with lightweight Lee Moore, exhibiting his defense and fast footwork, pulling his punches. He then wrestled with Bull Montana for ten minutes.[210]

Tex Rickard said, "When Jack Dempsey fights, if he ever does fight again, he will fight for me." Rickard wasn't sure when Dempsey would fight again. "Personally, I don't think the champion will fight again until next September. He has some valuable movie contracts to fulfill and it may be that he will not fight until next year. But it will be for me when he does re-enter the ring."[211]

Kearns claimed that Dempsey would be ready to fight on Labor Day 1925. He wanted to match Dempsey with the winner of the upcoming Tunney vs. Gibbons fight. However, Walter Eckersall said the prevailing opinion was that Dempsey would not fight again.[212]

Speaking of his past challenge to Dempsey in New York, Harry Wills said, "My challenge created many debates behind locked doors in the office of the commission. A political campaign was coming on and it would not do to offend colored voters. At the same time the commission was determined not to permit a Dempsey-Wills fight." So, the commission accepted his challenge and $2,500 forfeit, and Dempsey was

[208] *Buffalo Evening Times*, *New York Daily News*, April 1, 1925.
[209] *Buffalo Courier*, April 2, 1925.
[210] *Los Angeles Times*, April 2, 1925.
[211] *New York Daily News*, April 4, 1925. Dempsey previously claimed that he was not himself after two years of inactivity.
[212] *Los Angeles Times*, April 5, 1925.

notified that he had to fight Wills in six months or lose his license. "But William Muldoon, who ruled the commission with an iron hand and was the one opposed to the bout, issued a new ruling that was a masterpiece of logic." Muldoon said the fight could not be held in New York, and "added that the commission never would permit the match in New York." The farcical articles of agreement that were drawn up were full of loopholes and unenforceable.

Wills further said that the only top white who had been willing to fight him was Fred Fulton. "For the most part, the other white heavyweights have frankly admitted that they do not want any part of my game. Only Dempsey has the gall to pretend he can beat me easily and at the same time refuse to try to prove it in the only way to settle such matters."

W. S. Farnsworth reported that there was no doubt that Dempsey and Jack Kearns had split forever. "Letters were received today from the champion's attorney in Los Angeles to business connections in [New York] asking that henceforth all financial statements be made direct to Dempsey instead of to Kearns, who in the past has supervised the affairs of the firm."

Since his marriage to Estelle Taylor, Dempsey had changed his mind about splitting 50-50 with Kearns, and he also believed that the one match that would net him real money, with Harry Wills, never could be held. A close friend of Dempsey's said, "The champion does not believe California, New York or New Jersey authorities would stand for a fight with Wills." Therefore, Dempsey had signed with a moving picture concern, and he and his wife both had become partners in the concern.

Speaking of a potential Dempsey-Wills fight, Tex Rickard said, "I doubt if that fight ever could be staged, and I hope it never will be. Even should it be held, and I did the promoting and made a lot of money out of it, that match undoubtedly would kill boxing all over the country. Mixed matches between heavyweights are not good for the game."

Rickard also said the most attractive bouts could not be made. "It begins to look like Dempsey is through. Wills doesn't want to fight any of the top-notchers. The Gibbons-Tunney match, which has been made by Jimmy De Forest, is a good match and is one of the few naturals available."[213]

The next day, Dempsey denied rumors that he had a break with Kearns. He denied reports that his wife was attempting to control his ring affairs. Jack said Kearns always did the negotiating, but Doc consulted with him before signing him up for a fight. He said his wife had not given him any advice regarding his business affairs. However, Jack also said that Kearns was his fight manager, but did not manage anything else.[214]

By that logic, Dempsey would earn more with his film career than his boxing career, because he did not need to split the money with Kearns. That made it even less likely that he would fight.

213 *Buffalo Courier, New York Telegram and Evening Mail*, April 8, 1925.
214 *Los Angeles Times*, April 9, 1925. On April 8, Dempsey injured his right hand in a fight scene at the Selig Studios, which required several stitches. He missed a villain and hit a door, causing a deep gash.

Interestingly, on April 10, the *Los Angeles Times* reported that Dempsey had retired, something which allegedly he told only his closest friends. His reasons for retiring were that he hated the training grind, believed that moving pictures would make him as much or more than fighting, and he could capitalize on his crown to that end, and furthermore, he was well off financially and no longer needed to fight. He co-owned with Kearns the Wilshire apartments and the Barbara Hotel in Los Angeles, two properties worth $1,000,000 combined. He also had a trust-fund established with a New York bank in which he would receive $10,000 annually for the rest of his life.

Dempsey allegedly said,

> The title is worth something so long as I keep it. Jim Jeffries held it for six years and retired undefeated. He was an idol until coaxed out of retirement and into the ring with black Jack Johnson. I've held the title for six years. I can retire and still be heavyweight champion of the world. I won't give the title away. I'll keep it.

Inside information was that Dempsey thought it unfair to be splitting his boxing earnings 50-50 with Kearns. His wife, family, and he thought their division should be more along the lines of a 70-30 split, but Kearns balked and laughed. Word was that there was a real rift between the two for the first time in their relationship.[215]

Harry Wills was scheduled to fight Charlie Weinert, who recently held victories over Quintin Romero Rojas, Luis Firpo, and newcomer Jack Sharkey (twice), but in the past had been stopped by Firpo and Tunney.[216]

Some said that Wills should fight George Godfrey, Dempsey's former sparring partner and the next best black man. Godfrey's challenges to Wills had not been accepted.[217]

Having arranged a European vacation, in mid-April 1925, Jack Dempsey and his wife Estelle headed east to New York, arriving there on April 23. Gene Tunney was among those welcoming the Dempseys at the train station. Jack and Gene shook hands.

215 *Los Angeles Times*, April 10, 1925.
216 *New York Telegram and Evening Mail*, April 9, 1925.
217 *Los Angeles Times*, April 12, 1925.

On April 17, 1925, in Boston, 168 ½-pound Harry Greb won a 10-round decision over 164 ½-pound Johnny Wilson (60-26-8).[218]

On May 1, 1925, in Detroit, 169-pound Harry Greb won a 10-round decision over 195-pound Quintin Romero Rojas (22-9-3).[219]

The *Daily News* asked whether Dempsey was afraid of Wills. Opinion was mixed. Mostly the feeling was that Dempsey was not afraid physically, but did not want to risk losing his title and all the money that came with it, and wanted a lot of money to fight again. Neither he nor his manager or promoter wanted to risk in any way the title going to a black man if they could help it and there were other ways to make a lot of money, nor did they want to have to deal with the political or legal fallout of a mixed-race heavyweight championship contest, given what had happened in the wake of Jack Johnson. Johnson being champion had caused politicians to crack down on the sport, and they even had limited the sport's economic success with the fight-film-ban. Even if they all thought Dempsey would beat Wills, nothing ever was guaranteed in sports. So, the feeling was that one way or the other, Wills' skin color was going to bar him from getting a title shot.

One promoter said Dempsey might be killed if hit on his new nose, and furthermore, his long layoff would prevent him from being half the man that he was, which is why this promoter hoped he would retire permanently.[220]

On May 6, 1925, Jack Dempsey and Estelle Taylor departed for Europe on the *Berengaria*. They were honeymooning. Jack said he had no plans for a fistic engagement before returning, but he did not rule it out. He denied that he had retired.[221]

Jack and Estelle arrived in England on May 12, 1925. While in London, Dempsey said he was there for a honeymoon, and had no intention of boxing at that time. Others reported that Dempsey allegedly said he would like to fight, "but my wife won't let me." Then he explained that he was ill in crossing and did not feel well enough to enter the ring. His wife was ill as well. Jack's film, *Fight and Win*, was showing in England.[222]

While in London, Dempsey was measured and fitted for a new suit by former two-time title challenger Frank Moran, who, in his retirement, had opened a fashionable tailor shop in Seville Row, London.

[218] *Boston Globe*, April 18, 1925.
[219] *Detroit Free Press*, May 2, 1925. Rojas had a 1924 TKO9 over a young 188-pound Jack Sharkey (then 8-1).
[220] *New York Daily News*, May 4, 1925.
[221] *New York Daily News*, May 7, 1925.
[222] *Olean Times, Western Daily Press*, May 13, 1925; *Brooklyn Times Union*, May 15, 1925; *Daily Mail*, May 11, 1925.

Jack and Estelle arrived in Paris on May 19, 1925. They were greeted by Georges Carpentier, and dined with him. That evening, at the Gaumont Palace in Paris, Jack refereed a bout between Arthur Debeve and Rene Kelly, won by Kelly in the 5th round by technical knockout.[223]

JACK DEMPSEY & FRANK MORAN

Carpentier greets Dempsey and wife Estelle

Dempsey chagrined the French by announcing that he would not fight while in Europe. It was just a pleasure trip. Most said if Dempsey fought, it would be after cool deliberation, a big, guaranteed purse, and months of training.[224]

Gene Tunney believed he would be the next heavyweight champion.

I am as tall as Jack Dempsey and only a few pounds lighter. I consider myself every bit as good a defensive boxer as Tom Gibbons, who held Jack off for fifteen rounds. Dempsey can be hit, and he can be hurt! Carpentier proved this. So did Firpo. If I whip Gibbons on June 5, and I feel downright positive that I will, then I'll be ready for Dempsey and the world's heavyweight title.[225]

On June 2, 1925, the Dempseys arrived in Berlin, Germany. Jack was scheduled to appear at Berlin's Luna Park in exhibition bouts for $15,000 per week, plus something of the gate receipts.[226]

Dempsey cabled Billy Gibson, Gene Tunney's manager, saying that he would meet the winner of the Tunney-Gibbons match "if proper inducements are offered."[227]

[223] *Ithaca Journal*, May 19, 1925. *Buffalo Courier*, May 20, 1925.
[224] *Rochester Democrat and Chronicle*, May 21, 1925; *New York Daily News*, May 28, 1925.
[225] *New York Daily News*, May 24, 1925.
[226] *Buffalo Courier*, *Rochester Democrat and Chronicle*, June 2, 1925; *New York Daily News*, June 3, 1925. Dempsey also exhibited in Hamburg at HSV Platz, Cologne at Luna Park, and Hanborn's Apollotheatre, through at least June 21, 1925.

Gene Tunney said, "Somebody has to succeed Jack Dempsey as the heavyweight champion of the world, and I might just as well be the one. I feel confident that I am going to be the next champion. … I believe I can beat Dempsey if he ever fights again."

Tunney was confident that he would beat Gibbons. He said,

> I am bigger than he is, am stronger and, although he is ten years older than I am, I know that I have had enough experience in the ring not to be a sucker for anyone. Gibbons went fifteen rounds with Dempsey when the champion was rusty from idleness, and he lasted the route because he remained entirely on the defensive. If he fights that way against me I know that I can outpoint him because no decision can be given justly for a defensive fight. If he opens up and fights I'm sure I'll knock him out. I know Gibbons never has been knocked out or knocked off his feet. Neither have I.[228]

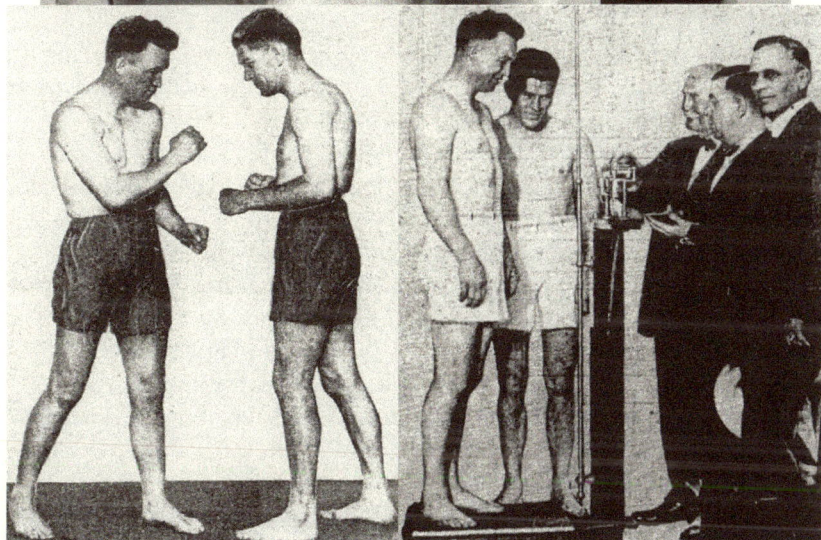

On June 5, 1925 at the Polo Grounds in New York, before an estimated 33,000 (others said 40,000) fans who generated $161,166.50, 181 ½-pound Gene Tunney of Greenwich Village, New York scored a 12th round knockout over 179-pound Tommy Gibbons (96-4-4). It was

[227] *Olean Times Herald*, June 4, 1925.
[228] *Brooklyn Standard Union*, June 4, 1925.

the first time that anyone ever had stopped Gibbons. In doing so, according to much of the white press, Tunney made himself the logical contender for Dempsey's heavyweight crown. However, others said he and Wills should fight for the right to fight Dempsey.

The fight was filmed, and large portions still exist. Tunney had very fast hands, and smooth, gliding or dancing footwork. He could step in quickly or step or lean back away quite adeptly. He knew how to clinch and smother on the inside, or fight when there if he chose. He had a very sharp, quick jab and fast right, and put his punches together rapidly. He gauged distance and timed his blows very well. He used his height, reach, and speed from the outside, but also could fire quick uppercuts, hooks, and body blows when closer. He seemed to rely a bit more on speed than strength, both with leads and counters, but he had snap on his blows. He had cautious instincts, but was sufficiently active with his punches, keeping a good pace. Although a bit more of an outside fighter, standing tall with his hands down, Tunney knew how to slightly roll his head away or angle subtly off to the side from punches, or he could dip and come under with body blows. He was very calm, loose, and relaxed, but at the same time, quite alert, reactive, and peppy. Based on the limited footage, he appeared to be in control throughout.

As the fight progressed, Tunney grew more aggressive, particularly in the 7th round, walking or sliding in, pumping his jab in metronome fashion, and following with quick, flowing combinations. Gene still could step back away quickly from blows, or elude and counter, as the mood suited him.

Tunney paced himself well, picking it up in certain rounds, backing off in others, moving forward a bit more in some, or being a bit more cautious in others.

At times, Gibbons tried to counter or time Tunney, or step in aggressively, but overall, Tunney was too fast and clever, and his ring generalship, defense, and countering much too good. What few blows that Gibbons did land, Tunney took very well.

In the 12th round, a Tunney jab followed by a straight right caused Gibbons to stagger off to the side, and then drop down to the canvas on the seat of his pants for the first time in the fight, and in his life.

A 1-2 and 1-2 sequence put Gibbons down for the second time. Gibbons used the ropes to try lift himself back up, but barely missed beating the count. It seemed that he had been worn down from the accumulation of blows throughout the course of the contest.

118

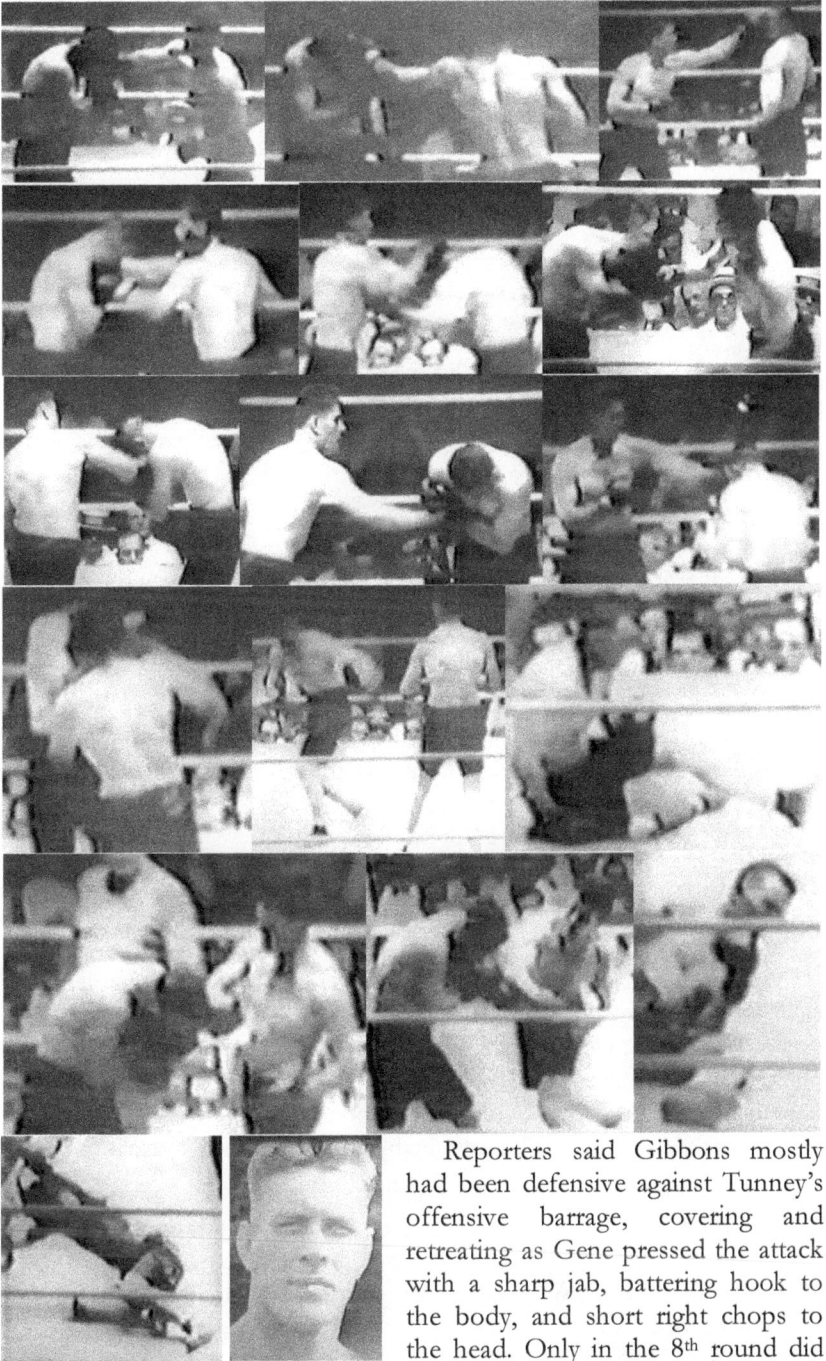

Reporters said Gibbons mostly had been defensive against Tunney's offensive barrage, covering and retreating as Gene pressed the attack with a sharp jab, battering hook to the body, and short right chops to the head. Only in the 8th round did Gibbons rally and land two terrific rights which jarred Tunney. However, it was only a flash. Gene dropped him twice in the 12th with rights to the chin. The first time he went down for a seven-count. He was trying to rise from the second knockdown when he was declared out, rising just after the count of 10.

Harry Newman said Tunney fought a cautious and careful battle but was Gibbons' master from the start, outboxing him. Gene grew more aggressive, and eventually had Tom running away.

The *Brooklyn Standard Union* said Gibbons was outboxed and outpunched. His eye was closed and discolored. Tom's offense was not there, and even his defense was not what it once was. Tunney outboxed him in all but one round. "Tunney kept him away with a long, sneaky left hand and pounded him on the head and body with a right hand that had Gibbons on the point of exhaustion."

It was intensely hot, particularly under the movie lights, but both had to suffer.

The bout was broadcast on the radio via WNYC.

The *Brooklyn Daily Times'* James Wood was very high on Tunney's performance, saying he had vastly improved.

> Tunney was at the peak of his form. He touched the heights and deserves all the credit available for his work. He boxed splendidly, made no mistakes and actually was aggressive when the occasion demanded. He completed the knockout in masterful style. He scored the first knockdown with a short left and driving right to the head and leaped in as soon as Gibbons regained his feet to shoot over another left and right which closed out the performance.
>
> It was quick and efficient work, worthy of a champion. No lost motion nor wasted effort was noticeable in Tunney's work throughout the battle. He is a new boxer, a remade ringman who will give Harry Wills the tussle of his career if the Black Panther wins from Charley Weinert as expected and meets Gene for the right to smoke out Dempsey for a titular test.
>
> Gene has shortened his punches and quickened his pace. He travels faster, seems to think faster and is less cautious in his movements.
> …

Of course, Gene was not facing the Gibbons who met Dempsey. … However, this should not detract from the credit due Tunney. Gibbons is the smartest boxer in the ring today, despite his knockout by Tunney. He is ringwise and experienced, conservative and careful. And it took genuine ability to knock him out.

The *Brooklyn Citizen* confirmed it was the first time that Gibbons ever had been sent to the canvas. "Tunney's accurate left hand had Gibbons all at sea from the start to the finish. Gene seldom, if ever, missed with his left. Outside of the knockdown and knockout punches, Tunney's most telling blows were short right-hand uppercuts under the heart. These punches seemed to sap all of Gibbons' strength."

Thomas Rice of the *Brooklyn Daily Eagle* said Tunney had won every round. True, Gibbons no longer was the same, and he seemed to get old overnight. But Tunney had shown surprising improvement.

> Tunney last night put up far and away the best bout he has ever shown. His boxing was beautiful, he was aggressive, he used his brains, feet and hands. Never before have we seen Tunney so successfully engage at sharpshooting, and carry the battle as he did against Gibbons. He had full command of both hands, and his judgment of distance in the last eight rounds was excellent. … In his form last night Tunney was almost as much a master of boxing as was his opponent when Gibbons was in his heyday.

Alan Gould in the *New York Evening Post* said, "Gene Tunney is no longer 'Genial Gene,' the soft-mannered and non-destructive light-heavyweight champion of America. The Tunney who battered and slashed Tom Gibbons last night at the Polo Grounds, then knocked out the pride of St. Paul in the twelfth round, is a two-fisted he-fighter." Tunney had "smashed the Gibbons myth – the myth of impenetrable defense – and lifted himself to a firm and full-fledged place in the heavyweight ranks." It was the greatest performance of his career, doing what neither Dempsey nor any other fighter had been able to do – drop and stop Gibbons. Tom's eye was gashed and nearly closed, his mouth puffed and bleeding, a red stream trickled from his nose, and he was battered badly. His occasional flash of offense did not bother Tunney, who landed four to one. In an astonishingly effective, one-sided performance, Gene "outsmarted and outgeneraled one of the smartest men who ever donned the gloves."

Some folks wondered whether Tunney really was that good, had improved vastly, and made Gibbons look bad, or if Gibbons had gone that far back and got old at age 36 (actual age 34), or a combination of both. Gibbons recently had defeated both Carpentier and Norfolk in 1924, was on an 11-0, 10 KOs win streak since losing to Dempsey in 1923, and was being considered for another title fight with Dempsey. So, perhaps it was great Tunney rather than or more so than bad Gibbons. Most said it was a little of both. Either way, Tunney looked very good, in a dominant performance. He had done to Gibbons what everyone else, including Dempsey, had failed to do in over 100 fights.

Gibbons said, "I just couldn't get started. I was tired and weary all through the fight. Tunney is a greatly improved fighter. I have no kick coming. I've had my chances, and I'm fixed so that I can retire." Indeed, Tom Gibbons never fought again.

Henry Farrell reported that Tunney said he was going to demand a fight with Dempsey, and also expressed his willingness to fight Harry Wills. Tex Rickard was figuring on a Tunney-Wills fight for late summer.

Most of the local New York newspaper writers agreed that the performance put Tunney at the front of the line to fight Dempsey. He had soundly beaten Carpentier, Greb, and Gibbons. The *New York Daily News* announced, "Tunney-Dempsey Fight Looms." The *Brooklyn Citizen* said the victory made Tunney the logical contender for the championship, and it would be an act of poetic justice if military champ Tunney, of the A.E.F, would knock out Dempsey the "Slacker." The *Brooklyn Daily Eagle* called Gene "Dempsey's Next Opponent." Others hoped for a Tunney-Wills elimination match.[229]

The *Brooklyn Daily Eagle* wondered how far diminished Dempsey would be as a result of his inactivity. In a few months, it would be two years since he had been in the ring. If he did not fight for another year, it would be three years, and no champion ever had taken off that amount of time and won. Dempsey was the type of fighter who only was at his best when he was active. He said that himself after the Gibbons fight, blaming his inactivity on his inability to stop him. Yet, now he was even more inactive. Conversely, Tunney was fighting regularly, and clearly was improving.[230]

TODAY and All Next Week
Exclusive Showing

GIBBONS VS. TUNNEY
FIGHT PICTURES

NEW PARK THEATRE
TODAY AND TOMORROW
Complete Pictures of The
GENE   TOM
Tunney vs. Gibbons
FIGHT
Every Blow including the Knockout Punch shown. 4,000 feet of Action.

On June 7, and continuing thereafter, the Broadway theater on 41st street in New York City started showing the Tunney-Gibbons fight films. Other theaters soon would follow, throughout New York state.[231]

It subsequently was reported that the Tunney-Gibbons fight drew a gate of $163,583. Gibbons received 30%, which brought his end to close to $50,000, while Tunney got 20%, about $33,000.[232]

[229] *Brooklyn Citizen, Brooklyn Daily Eagle, New York Daily News, Brooklyn Standard Union, Brooklyn Daily Times, New York Evening Post, Binghamton Press, Elmira Star-Gazette*, June 6, 1925.
[230] *Brooklyn Daily Eagle*, June 7, 1925.
[231] *New York Daily News*, June 7, 1925.
[232] *Yonkers Herald*, June 9, 1925.

On or about June 17, 1925, at Lunapark, in Cologne, Germany, Jack Dempsey sparred a couple rounds with a young 172-pound light-heavyweight Max Schmeling, then 14-2-2, as well as Harry Drake and Marty Cutler, his regular sparring partners. Having begun his pro career the year prior in 1924, on May 9, 1925 in Cologne, future champion Schmeling had lost a 10-round decision to a black fighter named Jack Taylor, a former Dempsey sparring partner.

According to the local *Deutsche Reichs-Zeitung*, Dempsey, as nimble as a flyweight, landed on Schmeling several times, but Schmeling, just as fast, came in on Dempsey so often that one hardly could tell them apart. Schmeling was a second Dempsey in terms of facial features and build. Several German boxers, as well as Dempsey, thought very highly of Schmeling, and considered him to be the coming man in the light heavyweight division.

Dempsey next sparred Harry Drake, who donned a headguard, but Jack twice knocked him to the floor. Marty Cutler wore both head and body protection, and therefore Dempsey showed his punching power more. The local German writer called Dempsey a phenomenon of all boxers, who would not be beaten so easily.[233]

One report said Dempsey worked for two weeks in Berlin/Germany and was paid $28,000. However, he had to pay $6,000 in income tax plus a special tax under the Dawes plan.[234]

Harry Wills said he did not think he ever would get a fight with Dempsey. He did not believe Jack ever would fight again. His new nose was not meant to be hit. At that time, Harry said he was willing to fight Tunney, or anyone else. But what would his manager do?[235]

In late June, Dempsey received $5,000 for a one-day appearance in Hamburg, Germany.[236]

On July 1, the New York Athletic Commission refused to grant Jack Kearns' request for a second's license. Kearns was handling Mickey Walker, who was fighting Harry Greb. Kearns would be refused admittance to New York fights in any capacity. The commission was trying to force him to answer the challenges flung at Dempsey by Wills.[237]

On July 2, 1925, in New York, at the Polo Grounds, before a crowd of about 50,000, 213-pound Harry Wills knocked out 184 ½-pound Charley Weinert in the 2nd round. In the 1st round, Wills sent Weinert down through the ropes, the result of a flock of head and body blows. In the 2nd, Harry decked him with a right to the chin for the full count.

It was the Black Panther's first fight in nine months, since his September 1924 sloppy-looking victory over Firpo. Weinert was coming off several good wins, including: 1924 WND12 Quintin Romero Rojas, WND12 Luis Firpo, and WND12 Jack Sharkey; and 1925 W10 Sharkey.[238]

---

[233] *Deutsche Reichs-Zeitung*, June 19, 1925.
[234] *Buffalo Courier*, June 25, 1925.
[235] *New York Daily News*, June 26, 1925.
[236] *New York Daily News*, July 5, 1925.
[237] *Glens Falls Post-Star*, July 2, 1925.
[238] Tunney had stopped Weinert in 4 rounds in 1922. Firpo had stopped Weinert in 2 rounds in 1923.

Paul Gallico said Dempsey's challenger slaughtered the Newark Adonis. Wills, who had kept Dempsey from donning the mitts and stepping into the squared circle, appeared to be the logical contender for the crown.

Yet, the *Brooklyn Daily Times* said the victory did not mean Wills was the outstanding contender.

The *Brooklyn Standard Union* wrote, "By no process of reasoning can the victory of Wills over Weinert be construed as meaning that Wills is the outstanding contender in the heavyweight class."

Len Wooster said Wills blew out a past-it shell in Weinert. Regardless, "Dempsey will not give him a crack at the championship, that is about as certain as anything can be in the boxing game."

Weinert and Wills

The *Brooklyn Daily Eagle* also called Weinert a has-been and hollow shell, saying the victory meant nothing. "Wills is neither more nor less logical than he was before he socked Weinert on the chin and other places." This writer said Weinert could not take it and could not punch. Wills outclassed him in strength, speed, and stamina, and could take anything Weinert could hand out. "The answer to the question as to how much of a chance Wills would have against Dempsey remains just as mysterious as it ever was."

William Granger for the *Brooklyn Citizen* said Wills performed like a real champion, in dominant fashion.

The fact is that when Wills fought Firpo, many writers and promoters were hoping that Firpo would win, though suspecting he would not. Those who wanted Wills-Dempsey had hoped that Wills would win impressively. Neither happened. Then, when Weinert beat Firpo, it was used to argue that Wills' victory over Firpo did not mean much, for Firpo had stopped Weinert prior to the Dempsey fight, Firpo clearly had slipped badly, and Wills' victory over Firpo meant even less in hindsight. When Wills dominated the man who beat Firpo in Weinert, once again some writers were ho-hum, feeling it did not prove much. Tunney had stopped Weinert too. Still, Wills was winning his fights, and justifiably demanding a Dempsey fight, like a thorn in the side of boxing. Many agreed that Wills deserved a title shot, or they urged that he should fight Tunney in a final elimination match.

On that same card, 159-pound Harry Greb (243-15-18) successfully defended his world middleweight championship, winning a 15-round unanimous decision over 152-pound former world welterweight champion Mickey Walker (70-13-2). Greb had Walker on the verge of a knockout in the 14th round, but the smaller Mickey made it to the end.

Both fights had been filmed, and the motion pictures were exhibited in local theaters, though sadly the films appear to have been amongst the many lost to history.

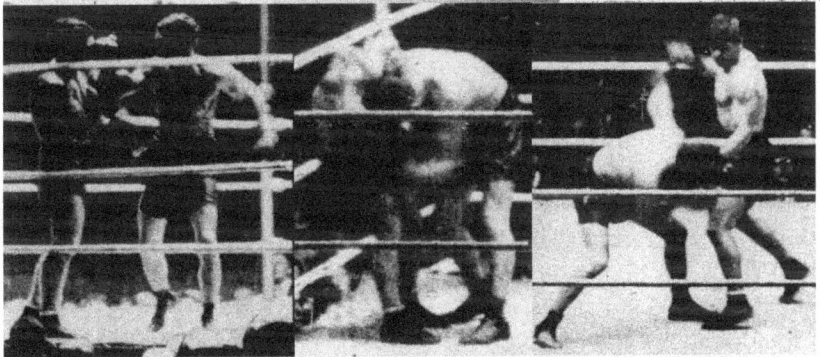

Eddie Purdy, the referee, had a most unhappy time of it in the Greb-Walker mix-up. Three times the milling fighters knocked him down—but he kept on fighting just the same.

The *Brooklyn Standard Union* said Gene Tunney was the only fighter who had Greb's number. "Greb is free to admit it, acknowledging that the recent conqueror of Tom Gibbons is the greatest in the ring to-day."[239]

On July 3, 1925, in Kansas City, Missouri, 186-pound Gene Tunney knocked out 188-pound Italian Jack Herman in the 2nd round.[240]

In England, Dempsey said, "I am unemployed because there are so few fighters who would give the public a good show for their money if we met. Nobody is more anxious to get into the ring than I am." The *Brooklyn*

[239] *New York Daily News, Brooklyn Daily Times, Brooklyn Standard Union, Brooklyn Daily Eagle, Brooklyn Citizen, Binghamton Press,* July 3, 1925. Also on that card, Dave Shade stopped Jimmy Slattery in the 3rd round.
[240] *Kansas City Times, Joplin Globe,* July 4, 1925.

Daily Eagle said, "The champion sees little prospect of any work before July of next year, when he is to meet Gene Tunney."[241]

On July 4, 1925 in Brighton, England, in a charity exhibition to support the local Royal Sussex hospital, Dempsey sparred 4 rounds, 1 each with emerging English heavyweight Phil Scott, Oxford Rhodes scholar and former 1920 Olympic light heavyweight gold medalist Eddie Eagan (who lost at heavyweight in the 1924 Olympics), and former amateur heavyweight titleholder Captain Ernest Chandler.[242]

Dempsey received a cable saying that Kearns was ready to "make up," and had a match arranged for him. Dempsey allegedly had claimed that he wanted to fight before the year was through; the likely opponent being Tunney. Apparently, Dempsey was frustrated either by his lack of activity, and/or because Kearns was refusing to alter his percentage.[243]

The *Daily News* noted, "Wills is still the logical contender, but the promoters do not appear to be stumbling over each other in an effort to get the match." They were "not willing to gamble with a Wills and Dempsey go because it may never be allowed to go on."

Jimmy De Forest said he represented financial interests who were willing to make a Dempsey-Wills match at the Polo Grounds on September 18. But he wanted the New York commission to pass favorably upon the fight in advance.[244]

Jack Kearns subsequently said it would be impossible for the champ to defend his title against Wills or Tunney in 1925, for he would need at least four months of hard training, and possibly several preliminary bouts, to be prepared properly, given how long he had been idle. He suggested Bartley Madden as a suitable interim tune-up bout.[245]

On July 8, Dempsey and his wife left Paris for Cherbourg, where they would sail home on the liner *Homeric*.[246]

William Muldoon said no promoter would be allowed to dicker for a Wills-Dempsey match in New York until Dempsey stepped in front of the commission and agreed to the contest. Muldoon claimed that there never had been any political opposition to a mixed-race contest between the two, but also said the commissioners were not so sanguine or optimistic about the bout ever taking place.[247]

Senator Jimmy Walker, father of the New York boxing law, said Dempsey ought to fight or retire. He claimed,

> There has never been any political opposition to a match between Jack Dempsey and Harry Wills that I know of and I think I would have heard something about it. It is mere conjecture on the part of some folks who think that the political leaders are afraid of such a

[241] *Brooklyn Daily Eagle, Binghamton Press*, July 3, 1925.
[242] *Brooklyn Daily Eagle, Buffalo Courier*, July 5, 1925. Dempsey spoke well of Phil Scott, whom he said had a future once he obtained more experience with better men than available in England. Scott, whose career began in 1919, held a 1924 W20 Tom Heeney, W15 Soldier Jones, and 1925 W12 Paul Samson Koerner.
[243] *Buffalo Courier*, July 6, 1925.
[244] *New York Daily News, Olean Times*, July 7, 1925.
[245] *Buffalo Courier*, July 8, 1925.
[246] *Brooklyn Daily Eagle*, July 9, 1925.
[247] *New York Daily News*, July 8, 1925.

match because one of the principals happens to be a colored man.[248]

Of course, it was not exactly conjecture to think there was or would be political opposition to a mixed-race heavyweight championship fight. New York was the state that absolutely barred Jack Johnson from fighting anyone there, and for years overtly barred *any* mixed-race black-white fight. Rickard once before had heard politicians tell him that a mixed-race heavyweight championship fight was authorized, only to invest a great deal of money, and then to have the politicians do an about-face. That happened with the Johnson-Jeffries fight, when California's governor booted it out of the state after previously telling Rickard that the fight was welcome there. After that fight, boxing never endured such hardship and attack from politicians, both state and federal. The New York commission had played games with the Dempsey-Wills fight before.

Yet, Paul Gallico said,

> I am convinced that far too much stress is being laid on the shade of Harry Wills's skin as far as Dempsey's willingness is concerned. I am by this time convinced that could Wills by some magic become a member of the Aryan race, and still remain Wills in size, skill and punching power, the champion would be just as reluctant to face him in the ring. The fact remains that Dempsey has never in his later ring career met as formidable a foeman as Wills is today. And he doesn't want to.[249]

On July 13, 1925, Illinois made legalized boxing possible in the state, but the new law gave each local town/municipality the ultimate power to vote on whether to allow boxing, via local elections.[250]

On July 14, 1925, world flyweight champion Pancho Villa died during an operation on an abscess, the result of a jaw infection spreading from his gums to his throat, subsequent to recent tooth extractions.

On July 15, 1925, Jack Dempsey and his wife arrived back in the U.S.

James A. Farley, current chairman of the New York Boxing Commission, suggested that the champion make a final decision by July 21 regarding whether he would fight Wills or retire. "If he refuses to accept the challenge, the public will reach only one conclusion – that he is afraid."[251]

Some reported that Dempsey was insisting on a warm-up bout to shake off the ring rust before taking on a top contender. There were rumors that he would fight in Michigan City for Floyd

[248] *New York Daily News*, July 13, 1925.
[249] *New York Daily News*, July 14, 1925.
[250] *Belleville News-Democrat*, July 13, 1925.
[251] *New York Daily News*, July 15, 1925.

Fitzsimmons in September with a lesser man, such as Bartley Madden.

As for Wills, he would be taken on, if ever, just as soon as the champion cast off his manager in September 1926. Jack said his contract with Kearns would expire on September 1, 1926. "If I fight this year, which I really want to do, Kearns will have to get his cut." Dempsey also claimed that promoters told him that a Wills fight was impossible in 1925. "I would like to fight him a year from this September, and in New York." The clear indication/suggestion was that Dempsey could have all of the money from the big fight, and cut Kearns out, if he waited to take on Wills until the expiration of his contract with Kearns in September 1926.

Regardless, Jack wanted a tune-up. "Anyhow, my speed and boxing need sharpening up. I must have a warm-up bout before taking on Wills. Anybody knows that, and, if the New York Commission is fair, it will admit it." He thought that he and Madden would make a nice match, and allow folks to compare him with Wills, for Madden had gone the full 15 rounds with Wills. Jack said he would like to fight someone before the end of the summer. He also discussed possibly fighting Tunney before taking on Wills in 1926.

Dempsey said perhaps if he signed to fight Wills next year (1926), the commissioners would let him fight someone else this year (1925). "I really need a couple of fights before a Wills match."

Jack was not worried about his nose. He took care of his old nose as well. "No punch on a new or old nose ever stopped this fighter."[252]

Tex Rickard said he hoped to bring off a Dempsey-Wills fight by September 1926.[253]

On July 16, 1925, in Newburgh Heights, Ohio, just outside Cleveland, 166-pound Harry Greb won a 10-round no decision over 164-pound Maxie Rosenbloom (33-3-5).

Tex Rickard and Dempsey allegedly had agreed verbally to a two-fight deal, one in September 1925, the first choice being Tunney, and another contest in one year, against Wills, although nothing had been signed yet. Rickard said he wanted 6 to 8 months to whip the Wills bout into order.

However, there were those who said Dempsey was not keen on giving Kearns half of his earnings any longer, and might not fight again at all until the following year, when their contract expired.

Kearns said any contract between Dempsey and Rickard without his approval was invalid. "I won't recognize any contract Dempsey made with Tex Rickard in New York yesterday. Dempsey is not going to fight anybody without me having a say to the match, nor without my full approval of all the terms." Kearns said he was not going to sign Dempsey to fight any setup. "I hold an ironclad legal contract with Dempsey. It's written under the laws of New York. We always had fought under an agreement giving me 50 per cent."[254]

---

[252] Olean Times, Rochester Democrat and Chronicle, Buffalo Courier, July 16, 1925.
[253] Brooklyn Daily Eagle, July 16, 1925.
[254] New York Daily News, July 17, 1925.

On July 17, 1925, Jack Dempsey met with the New York Commission and squared himself with them by formally accepting Harry Wills' challenge. Therefore, the commission said Dempsey would be permitted to box in preliminary bouts before meeting Wills.

However, Paul Gallico said, "In my estimation, if Dempsey takes on Tunney as his first fight since his layoff, he runs as much, if not more, chance of being knocked off than if he were to step in with Wills tomorrow."[255]

l to r: Commissioners George Brower, William Muldoon, Dempsey, commission secretary Dan Skilling, and Commissioner Edward Curry.

In an interview with the *Glens Falls Post-Star*, 27-year-old Gene Tunney said, "I'm going to be the next heavyweight champion of the world! Dempsey will never fight Wills if he meets me first." Gene believed Dempsey planned to fight Madden at Michigan City on Labor Day as a warm-up, and then to meet him two weeks afterwards.

Tunney said Wills had sidestepped Gibbons. Instead, the confident Tunney took the chance against Tommy and won.[256]

On July 18, 1925, Adolph Hitler, a German World War I veteran, who subsequently had served only 9 months of a 5-year prison term for treason (for his unsuccessful 1923 attempt to forcefully overthrow the German government; 20 died in the attempt, including 4 police officers), published the first volume of his book, *Mein Kampf* (My Struggle). In it, he announced his hatred for communism, capitalism, Judaism, social democrats, Marxists, and the Weimar Republic's Parliament. He wanted war with France and Russia, the genocidal extermination/elimination (or at least removal) of what he deemed to be "impure" or inferior races, and absolute dictatorship. Gradually and increasingly over time, many Germans, economically devastated by the loss of the world war and the subsequent reparations, and wanting change, started to latch onto Hitler's brand of racism intertwined with nationalism and totalitarianism.

During the 1920s, there had been and would continue to be a rise in the popularity of Social Darwinism and eugenics throughout the world, including in the U.S. and Europe, fueling racism and anti-immigration theories, policies, and laws. In the U.S., famous automaker Henry Ford

[255] *New York Daily News*, July 18, 1925.
[256] *Glens Falls Post-Star*, July 18, 1925. Gene recently had an operation to remove his tonsils.

had very similar views to Hitler when it came to Jews, publishing such opinions in the early 1920s in the *Dearborn Independent*, which he owned. The Ku Klux Klan was on the rise again throughout the 1920s.

Robert Edgren humorously noted that one was taking a risk offering advice to or criticism of the New York Boxing Commission. When Kearns received an order to match Dempsey with Wills, Kearns thoughtlessly dashed off a letter asking the commission if it remembered having secured Dempsey's signature on such a contract two or three years ago; and he did not see any use in wasting more ink (given that the commission would not allow the fight). Not appreciating his regarding them with "well deserved levity," the commission then barred Kearns in every way.

Edgren said the commission had odd whims. "No mere outsider can understand the gyrations of the boxing commission." Still, even those usually thought to be "in the know" were just as puzzled.

The commission allowed Wills to fight Madden, something it never would have allowed Dempsey to do, and would have denounced as manslaughter. Yet, Wills was allowed to fight him. If Dempsey had fought Weinert, the commission would have roared like a lion against it and accused Dempsey of fighting a set-up. "While the commission is busy telling Dempsey who he must fight, why doesn't the commission tell Wills who he must fight? ... For several years Wills has been handled like a basket of eggs. He has been matched with second raters at that." Firpo was the closest thing to a risk, but Firpo had dropped back 50% since the Dempsey fight. "Even then Wills was allowed to foul Firpo continually, holding with one hand and mauling with the other."

Edgren said commissions should do more to stop fouling, for they were "inexcusably lax in enforcing the rules they write." It was a foul to hold with one hand and hit with the other.

> Yet many of our star boxers do this little thing and get away with it. Harry Greb nearly always manages to grab his man around the neck with his left and paste him with the right at frequent intervals. ... Harry Wills habitually fouls by holding and hitting. I've never seen Wills fight fairly more than a few seconds at a time. He has a habit of grabbing with one hand and hitting with the other, pulling his man into the punch.

Wills even did it when he did not need to do it. "Just why the boxing commission allows Wills to foul in fight after fight is a puzzle."

Charlie White once threw two prominent fighters out of the ring in the 1st round because they both kept holding and hitting and refused to stop. "There was almost a riot and White has refereed no more fights." Edgren said a referee like White was needed nowadays to end all of the dirty boxing.

Edgren listed those fighters whom he considered fair, including Gibbons, Tunney, Walker, Dempsey, and Leonard.[257]

Harry Newman said things might not turn out for Dempsey the way he anticipated, and Wills and Mullins were concerned about that too. "Gene Tunney is far from being a sucker for any fighter. Gene may let one fall on Dempsey and ruin him. That is exactly what Mullins and his fighter Wills fear." The concern was that Tunney might beat Dempsey, especially given that Jack had not fought in a couple of years, while Gene had been quite active, was sharp, and had shown real ability. They feared that their opportunity to fight Dempsey for the title and a lot of money would be gone.[258]

The *Daily News* reported that Harry Greb might be Dempsey's next opponent, in a bout promoted by Floyd Fitzsimmons at Michigan City, Indiana in September, if the public reaction to Greb's candidacy indicated a worthwhile gate.

Word was that Dempsey and Kearns indeed were parting ways. One or the other would sell his joint real estate holdings to the other.

Apparently, New York Commissioner James Farley favored forcing Dempsey to fight Wills first, and to do so in 1925. However, others on the commission got him to relent, at least temporarily.

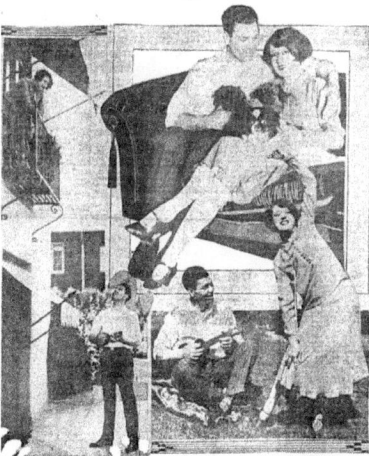

The *Binghamton Press* said the New York boxing writers were turning against Dempsey, charging him with running away from Wills. Further, they panned the state commission for failing to act against him and force him to fight Wills. They no longer were calling him a fighter, but an actor.[259]

Dempsey informed Floyd Fitzsimmons that he was agreeable to a bout with Harry Greb. Fitz said he would wire Greb's manager.

Tunney manager Billy Gibson said Dempsey and Tunney would meet in the fall. "You can write your own ticket that Dempsey and Wills won't meet this year, next year or any other year. I've talked it all over with Dempsey."[260]

At a meeting of Chicago sports writers with Promoter Floyd Fitzsimmons, Harry Greb was chosen as the best currently available opponent for Dempsey, given that Jack said he was not yet ready to fight Tunney or Wills in 1925. Fitz said he had received assurance from Dempsey that he would box Greb and post a forfeit as soon as the match was closed.[261]

[257] *Miami Herald*, July 19, 1925; *Fort Worth Star-Telegram*, *Buffalo Times*, July 26, 1925.
[258] *New York Daily News*, July 21, 1925.
[259] *New York Daily News*, *Binghamton Press*, July 22, 1925.
[260] *Brooklyn Daily Times*, *Binghamton Press*, July 23, 1925.
[261] *Brooklyn Daily Times*, July 24, 1925.

131

The New Jersey state athletic commissioner said Dempsey would not be allowed to fight any pushovers there. He added that only Wills or Tunney fit that bill.

Dempsey returned to Los Angeles, where he started training on July 25. At that time, the press said it appeared that Greb would be his opponent in Michigan City, Indiana on September 19 or 25.[262]

Dempsey said, "Harry Greb is one of the fastest men above the lightweight class in the ring today. I have not defended my title since I fought Firpo in 1923. That's a long lay-off, and if I meet Greb I'll expect plenty of trouble for twelve rounds."[263]

Harry Newman did not think Dempsey would be willing to enter the ring with Greb in a limited-rounds bout to a decision, because there was a chance that Harry could outpoint him. Hence, the shorter the contest, the more likely it would be a no decision, if Dempsey fought him at all.

Newman said all talk of Dempsey fighting in New York in 1925 was nonsense, for Dempsey had no intention of fighting there until 1926. It was clear that he wanted to fight Tunney next, in July 1926, and then, if he could win that fight, and it was no cinch that he would, to fight Wills in September. Those would be huge paydays, and then he would retire. He wanted a pusher or two before then to work off the ring rust, but such bouts would not be allowed in New York.

However, Dempsey's biggest fight was with Jack Kearns, whom he no longer wanted taking such a big share of his purses. "Dempsey indicated very strongly when he was here a few days ago that his break with Kearns is final, with no chance at all of any reconciliation." Hence, there was a chance he might not fight at all until the Kearns contract ended.[264]

Dempsey was training at the Manhattan Club gym in Los Angeles. On July 27, he knocked out Tex Meeks in less than a minute, sparred 2 more rounds with Frankie Grandetta, and then wrestled a round with famous heavyweight champion wrestler Joe Stecher.[265]

On July 28, 1925, in Los Angeles, Dempsey and Kearns met at the Barbara Hotel. Both had lawyers with them. Dempsey insisted that Kearns no longer was his active manager, that he would do his own matchmaking, but during the life of the contract, which spanned until September 1926, Doc would be paid 35% of his ring earnings, which was the maximum that the New York Commission allowed, and that was where the contract was filed. Kearns claimed that everything was all right, and matters soon would be adjusted satisfactorily for all concerned.[266]

Kearns and Dempsey split up their jointly owned Los Angeles properties. Kearns took over the Wilshire Apartments, while Dempsey

[262] *Rochester Democrat and Chronicle, Olean Times,* July 25, 1925; *Los Angeles Times,* July 26, 1925.
[263] *Lancaster New Era,* July 27, 1925.
[264] *New York Daily News,* July 26, 27, 1925.
[265] *Los Angeles Times,* July 28, 1925. Jack Curley was present and took a photo with Dempsey and Stecher.
[266] *Los Angeles Times,* July 29, 1925. On the 28th at the Manhattan gym in Los Angeles, Dempsey boxed a fast round with middleweight Jimmy Darrah, and wrestled and tugged with Curtis "Tex" Meeks.

got the Barbara Hotel on West 6th Street. The Wilshire hotel was worth about $300,000, while the Barbara was valued at $500,000, but had a $200,000 mortgage on it, which Dempsey assumed.

The New York commission said Dempsey could box in interim matches only if he *first* signed formal articles of agreement to fight Wills with a date certain, or neither he nor his opponents would be allowed to box in New York ever again. Some even discussed potentially stripping him of his title and no longer recognizing him as champion.

In response, to appease the commission, on July 30, Dempsey wired the New York Boxing Commission to say that he would fight Wills on July 4, 1926. He informed them that he had split with Kearns and would do his own matchmaking. Dempsey said Jimmy De Forest, acting as matchmaker for Charles Stoneham, had offered a $1,000,000 purse for him to fight Tunney at the Polo Grounds in New York in the fall. However, Dempsey said he had contracted for no match other than the Wills affair. Proposed battles with Tunney, Greb, Madden, and others had not been consummated. He had signed no contracts.[267]

Both Tex Rickard and Jimmy De Forest were trying to make a Tunney vs. Wills fight for September 1925. Billy Gibson, Tunney's manager, said he was willing to put Tunney in with Wills. "It's now up to Wills and his manager, Paddy Mullins."

However, Mullins said,

> The only fight we want right now is the Dempsey fight. Wills has been recognized by the commission as the foremost challenger for the title, and if Dempsey refuses to come to terms we expect the commission to declare Wills the champion. If this is done, Wills will be ready to defend his title against Tunney any time. But it must be understood that Wills enters the ring [as] the champion and Tunney [as] the challenger, in which case Wills would receive 37 ½% of the receipts and Tunney 12 ½%.

Jack Kearns admitted that there was a definite breach between he and Dempsey. Regardless, Kearns said, "I predict Dempsey will knock out Wills in the first round. I certainly wish Jack well. I want the public to know my side of things. But there will be no 'exposures.' There is nothing to expose."[268]

Billy Gibson said if Dempsey did not accept the very big Jimmy De Forest offer to fight Tunney at the Polo Grounds, then the champ was through forever. Dempsey's end would top anything he ever received in any prior ring engagement. Billy did not think Dempsey wanted to fight again if he declined to sign for a fight that lucrative.

Gibson said if Dempsey did not want to fight, Tunney would fight Wills instead. "Let them sanction a match between Tunney and Wills, the

[267] *Los Angeles Times*, July 30, 31, 1925.
[268] *New York Daily News, Yonkers Herald*, August 1, 1925.

winner to be known as the champion. Dempsey evidently wants no part of a Wills match. Tunney will fight either one of them."[269]

Allegedly, Dempsey refused $400,000 to meet Greb. Jack said he would meet Wills and no one else. Dempsey apparently did this to avoid the commission suspending him or declaring the title vacant.[270]

The New York Commission formally announced that it would ban any fighter who fought Dempsey before he signed articles and posted a forfeit to fight Wills. Others quoted Chairman Farley as saying no one could fight Dempsey until he fought Wills. The commission did not believe it had the authority to strip him of his title, but could prevent him from fighting anyone else, and prevent anyone else from fighting him, if those fighters ever wanted to fight in New York. Dempsey said he would fight Wills for any promoter who could induce Paddy Mullins to sign.

Tex Rickard said the Dempsey–Wills fight would take place on July 4, 1926 under his direction. "I have been in daily communication with the champion and have a definite understanding with him."

Jimmy De Forest kept trying to get Wills to fight Tunney, but Paddy Mullins said, "What's the use of talking about Tunney until we have disposed of Dempsey. We want a shot at Dempsey." His attitude was Dempsey or bust; no one else, or at least no one who posed a real threat.[271]

Billy Gibson said Wills feared the outcome of a match with Tunney, and that is why he did not want to fight him. The fight was a natural, with Dempsey seemingly retired.

James Wood said Dempsey either needed to retire or to meet Wills or Tunney. "Dempsey is about at the end of his rope as a moving picture attraction. The resentment against his vacillating pugilistic policy has already brought on a strong reaction of public opinion."

William Brady said he liked Wills' chances against Dempsey, unless age caught up with Harry, for Wills was a master craftsman. The crowd hissed and booed his fight with Firpo, but that was unjust. Wills was very crafty, and although he did not make a pretty fight or one good to look at, he was very experienced and knowledgeable of the finer points of the game.

According to Fair Play, Dempsey said, "I want to fight Wills, and fight him just as soon as I can get in condition." He would fight for any promoter who could make it happen. "I have agreed to fight for Floyd Fitzsimmons of Indiana, if Fitzsimmons can get Wills' signature. On the other hand, if Tex Rickard or any other responsible promoter can get the necessary signatures first, then he will land the bout."

Dempsey explained that he had an understanding with Kearns, that he would handle all of his own business, including his fight engagements, but Kearns still would get his cut for as long as their contract was in existence.

Tex Rickard said, "I am satisfied that Dempsey will fight Wills under my direction, in accordance with an agreement we entered into when I

[269] *Yonkers Herald; Los Angeles Times*, August 3, 1925.
[270] *Los Angeles Times* August 4, 1925.
[271] *Brooklyn Daily Times, Brooklyn Daily Eagle, Los Angeles Times*, August 5, 1925.

talked the matter over with Jack. This agreement was confirmed in a wire I received from Dempsey a few days ago and practically amounts to a contract, from my point of view."

Rickard also was trying to make Wills vs. Tunney.

Tex said claims of a Dempsey vs. Wills fight in the west [the Floyd Fitzsimmons promotion] were the purest bunk.

August 5, 1925 was the grand opening of the Olympic Auditorium in Los Angeles. 15,000 fans were present. On hand with wife Estelle, Jack Dempsey's introduction was greeted by "a mixture of cheers and jeers, but the applause ultimately drowned out the adverse howls. Which proves that the propagandists have not entirely succeeded in putting the great champion in a bad light."

Floyd Fitzsimmons said Dempsey wanted $1 million to defend his title against Wills. "He'll get it." Jack Curley agreed. Fitzsimmons believed that New York or New Jersey were the only places that could generate enough money to pay him that well.[272]

On August 6, 1925, from the Hotel Barbara, Dempsey sent Tex Rickard a Western Union Telegram that said,

> Wire received. Situation requires quick action. Under no circumstances will I fight under New York commissions jurisdiction. Boyles Acres o.k. All requires is Mullins signature and mine ready immediately under our mutually agreed conditions. Mullins dickering with other promoters, so I must end my continuance as martyr. I must get Wills. This is my official declaration despite adverse propoganda [sic]. Get Mullins, then you will have Dempsey immediately. Jack Dempsey.

However, on August 7, Floyd Fitzsimmons announced that Jack Dempsey had signed a contract with him for a 1926 fight with Wills, to be held between July and September. Paddy Mullins told Fitz that he would sign Wills if he saw Dempsey's signature on the contract.[273]

Some said Wills was being as careful with his top contender status as Dempsey was with his championship, for Harry did not seem inclined to fight Tunney. However, that decision might have been short-sighted, because knocking off Tunney would leave Dempsey with no viable alternatives for a big payday. Of course, if Wills lost to Tunney, that would ruin his chances at obtaining the title shot which Mullins/Wills correctly believed had been earned and was owed for quite a long time.[274]

On August 8, 1925, the nation's capital, Washington, D. C., saw a parade/march containing an estimated 30,000-35,000 (police estimate),

[272] *Brooklyn Standard Union, Brooklyn Daily Times, Buffalo Courier, Yonkers Herald, Daily News, Los Angeles Evening Express*, August 6, 1925.
[273] *Rochester Democrat and Chronicle, Binghamton Press, Kingston Daily Freeman*, August 7, 1925. The press reported that the fight would be held at Fitzsimmons' Michigan City, Indiana arena. Wasn't Indiana the same state that prevented Dempsey-Brennan? Also, Indiana had amongst the largest if not the largest Ku Klux Klan membership in the nation. The odds of that state authorizing Dempsey-Wills were low. It is more likely that the Fitz contract did not have a definite location in the terms.
[274] *Brooklyn Daily Eagle*, August 7, 1925.

50,000 or 85,000 (press estimates), or 100,000 (Klan estimate) unmasked members of the Knights of the Ku Klux Klan, wearing their white robes. The *Washington Post* said, "There were nearly as many women as men." "Klan officials estimated that they had more than 100,000 of the invisible empire in the city. Probably they did."

The *Washington Star* called it a "picturesque parade" and a "spectacular march," showing the strength of the order, for the "phantom army" and "invisible empire" had added a "vivid chapter" to the city's history. At least 20,000-25,000 were in the procession, while 100,000 watched. The acting grand dragon of the Pennsylvania KKK was present, as well as the grand kleagle of the District of Columbia Klan. The members sang, "Onward, Christian Soldiers." Klansman gave speeches, and urged that they were not motivated by hate, malice, or prejudice, but love toward all. "It was not to race prejudice that the Klan was appealing in its demand for white supremacy, the speaker declared, but to 'race purity.' The glory of the black man is in his black skin, the glory of the yellow man is in his yellow skin, and the glory of the white man is in his white skin." If and for as long as there was race purity, peace would reign. "It was mixed blood, he declared, which resulted in races of 'degenerates and mongrels,' and was responsible for most of the wars on earth. The Klan was determined that the 'races remain as God intended they should remain.'"

Initiates were asked to verify that they were native-born, white, Protestant American citizens, loyal to the U.S. and Christianity, who believed in white supremacy, and klannishness, or associating exclusively with members of one's own group. In the evening, a huge 80-foot fiery cross was erected. 75,000 massed on roads and hills. "We have no fight against the Catholics nor the Jews, but the Catholics want to control the politics of this country and the Jews the money." Klan leaders claimed that its membership had grown to millions.[275]

Some estimate that the Ku Klux Klan had between 3 million and 4 million members, possibly many more, and was more mainstream in the early- to mid-1920s than at any time in history.

[275] *Washington Post, Evening Star*, August 9, 10, 1925.

Both Tex Rickard and Jimmy De Forest kept trying to make a Tunney-Wills bout, given that a potential Dempsey-Wills fight was so far off.[276]

Jimmy De Forest, who saw him train in the gym, said Dempsey was in very bad condition and form, and if he fought in 1925, the title would change hands. Four heavyweights could stop him in his current condition. Jack needed at least six months of training. "He is slow on his feet and sluggish in his actions, his color is bad and there is no snap to his eyes. His heart doesn't seem to be in his work and I believe that is because of his business worries." A life of ease also had taken its toll on his abilities.

Dempsey and Taylor at their Hollywood home

Tex Rickard signed Gene Tunney to meet Harry Wills at Yankee Stadium in a fight to be held in late September 1925. Tex was trying to get Wills/Mullins to agree. "If Wills refuses to accept the Tunney match he will have to give his reasons and it will be difficult for him to find a plausible excuse." Rickard told Mullins that Dempsey would not fight in 1925, and therefore they could make real money by fighting Tunney, "five times as much" for fighting Tunney as Wills ever received for any fight before in his entire career. However, Mullins said, "I will not consider a Tunney match until I close with Dempsey."[277]

Mullins signed a preliminary agreement with Floyd Fitzsimmons for Wills to fight Dempsey in July 1926.[278]

Kearns and Rickard signed preliminary articles for a Dempsey-Wills fight to be held on July 4, 1926 in New York. Each posted $25,000 forfeit checks. As a result, the New York commission issued Kearns a manager's license and restored him to good standing.[279]

[276] Los Angeles Times, August 10, 1925.
[277] Pittston Gazette, August 11, 1925; Binghamton Press, Brooklyn Citizen, August 12, 1925.
[278] Los Angeles Times, August 15, 1925.
[279] Los Angeles Times, August 19, 20, 1925. Floyd Fitzsimmons claimed he would arrive in New York with $100,000, to assure Wills of his end of the purse.

On August 20, 1925, Johnny Dempsey, Jack's brother, who gave his age as 30, was locked up in the Los Angeles County jail for being intoxicated. At the Hotel Barbara, his wife Edna screamed for help, claiming she was being beaten. Johnny subsequently was removed to a psychopathic ward for observation and evaluation as to his sanity. It was alleged that he was addicted to the use of drugs and stimulants, had threatened his wife's life, and hurled their child to the floor.

From Paris, Harry Wills said he was ready to take on anyone with one month's notice. He was not sure the commission would allow him to fight Tunney, given their size disparity. Harry was anxious to earn a big purse against Dempsey. "I have been in the fighting game for eleven years and never got any money out of it until the past two years. I fought Sam Langford, one of the toughest babies that ever put on gloves, twenty-two times and received about $20,000 for the twenty-two fights."

Kearns did not believe the Fitzsimmons offer to be genuine. He heard that Fitz allegedly offered Dempsey $1,000,000 and Wills $300,000. "That is foolish money talk. Where does he get that stuff?"[280]

Wills gave multiple reasons why he believed that Dempsey would not fight him – he was afraid of spoiling his nose, his wife refused to let him fight, he was afraid of losing the championship, he was too proud to fight for anything less than a million dollars, and colored John Lester Johnson broke one of his ribs and put him in the hospital for a couple months, so he was superstitious of colored boys now. "Wills said if he was a white man he would insult Dempsey and make him fight, but, being colored, such a procedure would not be tactful."[281]

Jim Coffroth got in on the act and offered to stage Dempsey-Wills on Thanksgiving Day, 1926, in "Tia Juana." He offered Dempsey $500,000, and Wills $250,000.

Reports were that articles of agreement would be signed in Chicago for a Floyd Fitzsimmons promotion of Wills-Dempsey.[282]

Harry Wills again said Dempsey was just kidding about fighting him, and it all was just a bluff. "I don't ever expect to meet Dempsey in the ring. He has been dodging me for many years, and now I am convinced that he has been kidding all along." If that was what he truly believed, why then would Wills/Mullins not want to fight Tunney for big money instead?[283]

On Labor Day afternoon, Monday September 7, 1925 at the San Francisco Baseball Park on Valencia street, before a crowd of 15,162 or 17,000, which paid from $1 to $5 each and generated $39,420.15, Jack Dempsey boxed Bill LaRue and Cowboy Ed Warner 2 rounds each, pleasing the spectators. When he entered the ring, the crowd gave Jack a big ovation.

---

[280] Los Angeles Times, August 21, 22, 1925.
[281] Los Angeles Times, August 29, 30, 1925. Dempsey was training at Venice, by the seashore. Binghamton Press, August 28, 1925.
[282] Los Angeles Times, Brooklyn Standard Union, September 2, 1925.
[283] New York Daily News, September 5, 1925.

Dempsey plastered 220-pound "Fat" LaRue with two hard left hooks to the midsection and the latter almost folded up, falling into a clinch. Jack whispered, "I won't hurt you." The 2nd round was much the same, with Jack allowing him to last the 2 rounds.

Dempsey socked Cowboy Ed Warner, the wrestler-fighter, with a short left hook to the chin

Dempsey decks Ed Warner

and Warner went down rather hard. Jack pulled him up and clinched, holding Ed until his head cleared. In the 2nd round, Dempsey landed a tap to the jaw and Warner dropped to the canvas again, in apparent pain. Referee Tom Laird picked him up, and Warner started swinging punches at the referee, but missing. Warner pulled Laird to the canvas and the crowd howled with glee.

The *San Francisco Examiner's* A. T. B. said to know Dempsey was to like him. "He is vicious in the ring only." Even with 16-ounce gloves, he still hit hard.

Frank P. Brown said Dempsey was the most impressive figure he ever saw. He could have ended matters whenever he felt inclined. He boxed with wonderful restraint. Many champions of the past might have hit Dempsey, but that did not mean they would beat him. He was a weaving-in attacker and did not mind taking a few to land his bombs.[284]

Paddy Mullins posted a $25,000 forfeit with the New York Commission for a Wills-Dempsey match – the one arranged by Kearns and Rickard. Such reflected a lack of confidence in the Fitzsimmons promotion.

However, Dempsey had told Wills to trust in the Fitz promotion, for he had nothing to do with the Kearns-Rickard deal, which he said Kearns had no right to authorize. Things definitely were in a muddle.[285]

Dempsey said he was fighting Wills on July 4 for Floyd Fitzsimmons, likely in Michigan City, Indiana. He was through with Kearns forever. Supposedly, a meeting would be held in Chicago, in which Dempsey, Mullins, and Wills would sign a contract.

Kearns said Dempsey would have to fight Tunney or Wills for Rickard, based on the contract that Kearns had signed with Rickard. Kearns possibly believed that although he had to alter his percentage, he

[284] *San Francisco Examiner*, September 7, 8, 1925. Dempsey was scheduled for some exhibitions in Texas, at Dallas on Sept. 22 and then San Antonio the following week. *Buffalo Courier*, September 11, 1925.
[285] *Los Angeles Times*, September 8, 1925.

still had managerial control. However, Dempsey's response was to refuse to fight pursuant to any contract which Kearns signed.

Billy Gibson, Tunney's manager, accused Wills of ducking Tunney.[286]

Wills said he was willing to fight Tunney, but Dempsey was the man he most wanted. "If I should knock him off I'll guarantee the fight fans of this country that I'll do everything in my power to be a creditable champion and that I won't dodge any opponent for five years, as I have been dodged." The *New York Age* believed that despite representations, Wills was as far away from a Dempsey fight as he was five years ago.[287]

Paddy Mullins wanted a contract with Kearns and Rickard that left no loopholes for Dempsey to wriggle out of the match. The New York Commission agreed and asked that the parties draft the contract accordingly.[288]

Allegedly, one million dollars had been raised by local South Bend, Indiana businessmen to finance Floyd Fitzsimmons' promotion of Dempsey-Wills. The plan was for Dempsey and Wills to sign articles of agreement in late September.[289]

Billy Gibson said Tex Rickard had offered $150,000 to Harry Wills for a match with Tunney in New Jersey, which Wills had not accepted.[290]

On September 25, 1925 in San Antonio, Texas, at the local baseball park, 5,000 saw Dempsey box 6 rounds, 2 each with sparring partners Ray Newman (real name Neuman – 1924 L10 Tunney), Marty Cutler, and Curtis 'Tex' Meeks. The *Austin Statesman's* Sam Pace said that whatever may be his slacker record in the ring, Dempsey still was one of the greatest heavyweights ever. He glided in and out and all about, jabbing and parrying with the quickness of a cat toying with a kitten. Jack's hardest work was in avoiding the crowds constantly at his heels. As a result, he mostly remained in his hotel.[291]

Also on September 25, 1925, in Minneapolis, 186-pound Gene Tunney knocked out 189-pound Bartley Madden in the 3rd round, a quick left jab followed by a crushing right to the jaw decking him for the first time. Madden rose at nine, and then a left hook put him down and out.

This was significant, given that Madden went the full 15-round distance with Harry Wills the year

Tunney shakes hands with Bartley Madden

[286] *San Francisco Examiner*, September 9, 10, 1925.
[287] *New York Age*, September 12, 1925.
[288] *Rochester Democrat and Chronicle, Daily News*, September 12, 1925.
[289] *Chicago Tribune*, September 20, 1925.
[290] *Yonkers Herald*, September 23, 1925.
[291] *Marshall Messenger*, September 24, 1925; *Austin Statesman*, September 25, 26, 1925.

before. Billy Gibson said Tunney had done in 3 rounds what Wills was unable to do in 15. Tunney wanted to fight either Dempsey or Wills.

Charles Johnson of the *Minneapolis Daily Star* said Tunney was the real title contender. "Gene Tunney stood out as a heavyweight fighter that both Harry Wills and Jack Dempsey had better think twice before agreeing to meet in the ring." In stopping Madden, the man that so many had failed to stop, including Wills, "He installed himself as the logical gent to exchange punches with the elusive champion of the heavyweight ranks – Jack Dempsey."

Gibson said Tunney was the coming champion of the world. "The negro will never consent to a match with Tunney now and I doubt whether Jack Dempsey will ever don the gloves again to battle my man." Johnson replied, "What Gibson says is true. Tunney looked every inch a champion."[292]

Jack Kearns said that despite the attempts to go through with a Michigan City, Indiana Dempsey-Wills match, "the money is not there and it will not be put up."

Rob Roy Benton, Dempsey's personal representative, claimed that Mullins would post a $50,000 forfeit, Dempsey $75,000, and the financial backers $200,000 for the Fitzsimmons promotion of Dempsey-Wills.[293]

Mullins wanted assurances that the money actually was there. "I have been bunked so many times that they will have to show me money before I'll get excited. Dempsey will have to fight Wills sooner or later. He can't fool the public much longer about his intentions."[294]

On September 29, 1925 in Niles, Michigan, just 4 miles north of the state line, just north of South Bend, Indiana, Jack Dempsey, Harry Wills, Floyd Fitzsimmons, and Paddy Mullins all met, along with several other parties, and signed articles of agreement in the presence of a notary public, for Jack Dempsey to defend his world heavyweight title against Harry Wills sometime in September 1926, at a location to be determined. The articles called for a 10-round no decision contest (or whatever the laws of the state where it took place allowed). Forfeits aggregating to something over $300,000 allegedly had been (or purportedly would be) deposited by the principals and promoter with the First National Bank of South Bend, Indiana as evidence of good faith. Allegedly, Dempsey posted a forfeit of $100,000, Wills $50,000, and the syndicate $200,000. The fighters were or would be advanced $25,000 each for expenses.

Some reported that the bout was being delayed intentionally until September 1926; after Dempsey's contract with Kearns expired, purportedly on August 3, 1926. This way, he would not have to pay him anything. The parties agreed that should Kearns press forward with his legal claims, they would re-sign new, more definite, specific articles only once his contract was over.

[292] *Minneapolis Daily Star, El Paso Herald*, September 26, 1925.
[293] *San Francisco Examiner*, September 27, 1925.
[294] *Los Angeles Times*, September 28, 1925.

The fighters would work on a percentage basis, and not guarantees, which was preferable to Dempsey, who believed that the battle, no matter where it was held, would exceed a $1.3 million gate. The percentage figures were not revealed.

Above: Dempsey and Wills sign a contract at Niles, Mich., for a title bout. Left to right, seated: Dempsey, Floyd Fitzsimmons, Wills. Rear, standing: Rob Roy Benton, Babe Culnan, John A. Sweeney, Lou Raymond, and Paddy Mullins.

Tex Rickard said he was entitled to promote the Dempsey-Wills fight, and his lawyers had informed him that the contracts signed with Kearns would withstand any kind of test. However, he was not prepared to say whether he would press his claims.

> I feel as if I'd like to wash my hands of the whole matter, and yet I can't believe that Dempsey has made such a fool of himself until I get more facts on the matter. Dempsey has told me repeatedly he would fight the Wills bout under my direction. ... His last word to me was to straighten out things with Kearns and get Wills lined up.[295]

[295] *San Francisco Examiner, Chicago Tribune, South Bend Tribune,* September 30, 1925.

Some suspected that Dempsey was the real promoter behind the contest, or at least had a promotional interest, and was determined to cut Kearns out as much as possible.[296]

The Fitz contract lacked a specific date or location, but set it for September 1926, after any potential Kearns contract expired. The major issue was finding a jurisdiction that would allow the contest, have an arena large enough to hold a lot of people, and be close enough to a major population hub, with easy railroad access, lodging, etc.

The *Dayton Daily News'* Carl Finke said Dempsey wanted to fight Wills, but was leery about doing it in New York, for fear that Kearns would outwit him and get his 35% share of the purse. He also did not care for the way the commission there had treated him.

During the past couple of years, Dempsey had done little boxing, except for what his vaudeville contracts required. Jack was on another exhibition tour. He was receiving between $5,000 and $10,000 for each ring appearance. His wife was with him.

Finke said one should not rush into making reservations for Michigan City, Indiana (Fitz's arena location), for the fight was not certain. Both fighters would get plenty of publicity as a result of the signing, and make good money in exhibitions, which would draw more than usual, but,

> I'm not looking for them to enter the ring against each other. There will be too much opposition in Indiana, Dempsey and Wills know it. Tex Rickard and Jack Kearns have already stated they will not interfere with the proposed Fitzsimmons show. They know that interference will come from other sources so why should they bother.

Rickard and Kearns also strongly doubted that the financing really was there in Indiana. Finke did not believe the fighters ultimately would sign final articles on a percentage basis, but instead would demand guarantees. There was little chance that they would gamble on a promotion in Indiana. Of course, technically, the contract did not mention a location.[297]

The *East Liverpool Review-Tribune* said a heavyweight title bout in Indiana was impossible. It was well known that the governor would not sanction Dempsey-Wills. Therefore, it would have to take place elsewhere. The mere fact that they signed the contract in Michigan and not Indiana was proof that they knew it. The state attorney general was on record that the fight could not happen in Indiana. Three years ago, Dempsey was matched to fight Bill Brennan there, and the governor prohibited even a sparring exhibition between the two; and that was a proposed bout between two white men. "It is a foregone conclusion that a championship encounter between a white and a colored man cannot take place in Indiana." It was foolish to think otherwise.[298]

[296] *New York Daily News*, October 1, 1925.
[297] *Dayton Daily News*, September 30, 1925.
[298] *East Liverpool Review-Tribune*, September 30, 1925.

As a result of their belief that economic, political, and legal factors would prevent the Fitzsimmons promotion, Rickard and Kearns did not think they necessarily needed to take any steps to prevent the Fitzsimmons-sponsored Dempsey-Wills promotion, although both alluded to the possibility of bringing a lawsuit.[299]

On September 30, 1925 in Cleveland, Ohio, at a sold-out Olympic arena, Jack Dempsey sparred 6 rounds, 2 each with Cleveland's Nick Newman and regular sparring partners Ray Neuman and Marty Cutler.

Gene Tunney did not understand why Dempsey would turn down $500,000 guaranteed to meet him in New York, instead signing to fight Wills on a percentage basis. Dempsey and Wills had agreed not to fight anyone else until they fought each other. Gene did not think Dempsey-Wills would occur, and believed or hoped it just was a "dance." "Time and time again Dempsey has promised both Billy Gibson and myself that whenever the time arose he would give me the first opportunity at the big purse. But now that he has heard about my fights with Gibbons and Madden he back-fires."

Bartley Madden, who had gone the 15-round distance with Wills but was knocked out in 3 by Tunney, compared the two. "People don't know how hard Tunney hits. I know because I felt his punches." Gene decked him with a right, and once again with a left. Bartley was badly dazed.

> Anybody who tells you Tunney can't hit doesn't know Tunney and the improvement he has undergone. I think he has a good chance of knocking out Wills if they ever meet. I tasted the punches of each man and I think Tunney hits more effectively. That doesn't necessarily mean that he is a stronger puncher than Wills. But Tunney hits cleaner and shoots straighter, and altogether gets better results with his blows than does Wills.

The management contract between Dempsey and Kearns was for the scheduling and arranging of public exhibitions, theatrical engagements, and athletic entertainments for three years, and went from August 3, 1923 to August 3, 1926. It was signed before the Firpo fight. It called for Kearns to receive 33 1/3% of the proceeds earned, after deducting all expenses (not 50%). It also said that in the event of the refusal or failure of Dempsey to render services contracted for by Kearns, the latter would be entitled to 33 1/3% in damages.[300]

While in Dayton, Ohio, Dempsey said, "Gene Tunney is a better all-around boxer than Harry Wills, but Wills has been up there for so many years that the public has demanded a bout between myself and Wills. I actually believe that Tunney would give me a

[299] *Minneapolis Daily Star, Wilkes-Barre Times-Leader*, September 30, 1925.
[300] *Dayton Daily News*, October 1, 1925.

tougher bout than Harry Wills, but it is a financial proposition with me. Wills will draw more than Tunney." Jack wanted to fight whoever would make him the most money; which would be the fight the public most wanted to see. He had been hearing about Wills for several years, but Tunney more recently.

Some questioned why the Dempsey-Wills bout was scheduled for only 10 rounds, when most championships were decided in at least 15-round contests. The suggestion was that Dempsey was not necessarily that confident in his condition anymore.

Dempsey said most of his fights ended quickly, within 10 rounds anyhow, and most states only allowed 10-round contests. The Wills fight "will be held in September 1926, and I'll win in a couple of rounds."

Dempsey noted that the fight agreement with Wills said nothing about where the fight would be held. That was up to the promoter, who needed to secure a location. He said there was not a no-decision clause, but rather it would be held under the rules of the state in which the bout was staged.

Dempsey also said the management contract filed with the New York Commission between he and Kearns was made to fool the commission. Although New York only allowed a manager to take 33 1/3%, Kearns was expecting and had received 50%.

Jack was with his new business manager, Ralph J. Cannon, also known as Ray Cannon, a Milwaukee lawyer. Cannon was the attorney who helped Dempsey beat John 'the Barber' Reisler's contract claims.

GENE TUNNEY PLAYS AT POLO

Grantland Rice said Gene Tunney would be the most popular champion since John L. Sullivan. He was an exception to the usual type of top boxer. He was a soldier, boxer, student, philosopher, and sportsman. He did not drink or smoke, and he read literature. He was good-looking, over six feet tall, a "pleasant-faced blond with an attractive smile and more than his share of magnetism." He had a friendly, pleasant manner. He could talk about topics usually reserved for the higher brows, including science and art.

Rice and other reporters claimed that Tunney was born on May 25, 1898. However, official military, marriage, and census records all say he was born in 1897, making him just 2 years younger than Dempsey.

Tunney was a boxer for a couple years, then enlisted in the marines. He resumed his boxing career thereafter. Over time, he gained weight, though his brittle hands had hampered him.

Tunney lacked the killer instinct, the yearning to tear a rival apart, but he could take it, and had courage. He took on the sport's hardest man to beat in Greb, and though he lost the first time, he kept learning and improving, and was willing to fight him multiple times, usually winning, but doing no worse than fighting evenly. He developed sufficient speed and skill to outpoint Greb, one of the world's fastest and most elusive boxers. His increased strength and power enabled him to win their last bout clearly.

Some accused Tunney of lacking aggressiveness, fighting with too much caution, paying too much attention to defense. But he had a keen brain, stout heart, and lived cleanly. His punch had improved, getting his weight behind his punches better, as shown by his victories over Carpentier, Gibbons, and others. He stopped Gibbons, a man who never before had been stopped, including by Dempsey, and Gibbons had been the favorite to beat Tunney. Gene had a brilliant left hand, and could cut through with a right when the opportunity presented itself. He had improved 100% over the past year or so. He was bigger, faster, and stronger. He appeared to be a better boxer than either Wills or Dempsey, though they were stronger, more aggressive, and harder-hitting than he was. Regardless, "we must never forget that a marine is no opponent to take lightly in any form of warfare."[301]

On October 1, 1925, at Memorial Hall in Dayton, Ohio, with about 2,000 in attendance, generating just over $5,000, Dempsey sparred 4 2-minute rounds, 2 rounds each with big gloves against Ray Neuman and Marty Cutler. A left hook decked the 225-pound Cutler in the 1st round. In the 2nd, a right to the body sent him through the ropes, and Cutler refused to continue.

Gene Tunney attended the show, likely scouting the champ, and he and Jack shook hands before the exhibition. Gene received great applause.

Tunney Greets Dempsey In Ring at Memorial Hall

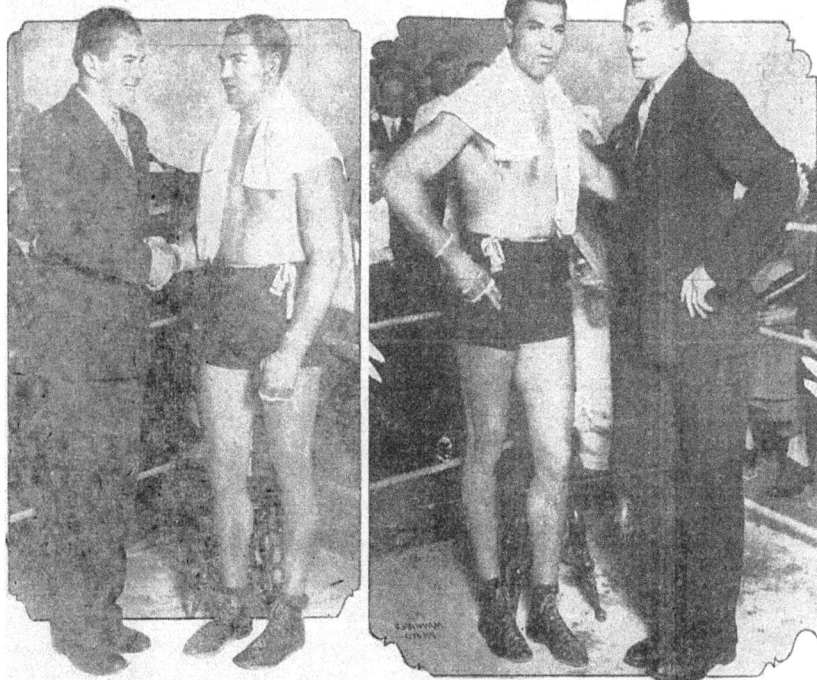

[301] *Dayton Daily News*, October 1, 1925.

Gene said Jack was cordial, congratulated him on his recent victories over Gibbons and Madden, and wished him luck in the future. The champion's appearance impressed him. Nevertheless, "I am confident that I can take the championship away from Dempsey."

The *Dayton Daily News'* Carl Finke was not impressed, saying Dempsey was more cautious and defensive than ever before, less active and aggressive, and his long layoff had slowed him up considerably, "and when an athlete's legs go back on him it usually means curtains."

Finke said Tunney received an even bigger ovation than did Dempsey.

Fans saw that in terms of height, reach, and weight, Dempsey and Tunney appeared to be evenly matched.[302]

On October 3, 1925, in Ashland, Kentucky, accompanied by Floyd Fitzsimmons, for 3,000 fans, Jack Dempsey boxed three 2-round exhibitions, with local welterweight Jimmy Perdue, Marty Cutler, and Nick Newman.[303]

Sparrow McGann said Dempsey's funds were dwindling. Not that he was broke, but he wanted and needed more money to support his many business ventures.

McGann said Estelle Taylor and Kearns had not liked one another, and that facilitated the break between the two Jacks. It was personal, not just business. Regardless, McGann believed that at the moment, Dempsey needed a shrewd manager/adviser like Kearns.

Dempsey never had any faith that New York could or would host the Wills contest, ever since the commission ordered him to sign to meet Wills, and then, when Dempsey complied, Muldoon informed him that the bout would not be permitted. Hence, he did not trust New York.

A fight with Wills would generate him the most money, so he signed up with Floyd Fitzsimmons. Many believed the fight would not come off, either for political or financial reasons, and that the only places which might allow it on the continent were Mexico or Canada, which venues would not be as lucrative. Fitzsimmons claimed to have financial backing, but if so, it was more than he had when he last was in New York, when all he had were papers with signatures, but not any actual proof of financial backing.[304]

Dempsey was the world's wealthiest athlete. He could make hundreds of thousands of dollars for one fight. Babe Ruth only earned $52,000 for playing baseball for seven months out of the year.[305]

Dempsey's attorney, Ray Cannon, had represented baseball players like Happy Felsch and Shoeless Joe Jackson when they were thrown out of baseball for laying down against the Cincinnati Reds in the 1919 world series. He also helped to organize a baseball players union. He was only 31

---

[302] *Dayton Herald*, September 30, October 2, 1925; *Dayton Daily News*, October 2, 1925. The promoters likely took a loss, for Dempsey was guaranteed $7,500, the largest amount ever paid for any bout in that town, let alone an exhibition. Estelle Taylor was not with Dempsey in Dayton. She had to return to Hollywood to re-act part of her latest film.

[303] *Owensboro Messenger, Helena Independent*, October 4, 1925. Dempsey left for Los Angeles after the exhibition. In his party were Ray Newman, Gus Wilson, Marty Cutler, Ray Cameron, and friend Don Chalfin, the famous Logan County, West Virginia sheriff.

[304] *Dayton Daily News*, October 4, 1925.

[305] *Los Angeles Times, Elmira Star-Gazette*, October 5, 1925.

years old, and was the product of an orphanage, having lost his parents when he was 4 years old.

Cannon said the Kearns contract was invalid. They could prove many violations of the contract, and furthermore, it was by mutual agreement terminated when Dempsey and Kearns split their real-estate holdings in Los Angeles. Cannon said he was Dempsey's lawyer, not manager, and simply his advisor. Dempsey made all final decisions.[306]

Upon his return to Los Angeles on October 7, Dempsey denied that he was kidding, and reaffirmed his intention to fight Wills. He believed the fight would take place somewhere in the Midwest, near Chicago.[307]

On Saturday October 10, 1925, at Dick Donald's Ascot arena in Los Angeles, 33 Arcade Building, Dempsey exhibited as part of a larger boxing show. 20,000 people showed up, paying prices of $1 up to $7.50, plus tax.

Referee Benny Whitman mercifully halted Dempsey's exhibition with Sailor Jack Stafford of the U.S.S. West Virginia, runner-up for the fleet boxing championship in its last tournament, in the 2nd round. Stafford's eyes were cut, and he was "pretty sick" when it was stopped. After Joe Bond had been smacked down a couple of times, he was too weak to continue. Ray Neuman or Newman, the best of Jack's three foes, completed his 2 rounds with only a nosebleed.[308]

Dempsey's lawyer Ray Cannon was fined $15 for being drunk and disorderly. The patrolman testified that he found it necessary to use force with the attorney, Cannon struck him on the jaw, and he retaliated. "I think I broke his nose," the patrolman said.

At the Barbara Inn, which he owned, Dempsey said, "No more pictures for me." He was done with the movies. He had fun, and made a lot of money, but realized it took years to become a real actor.[309]

The New York Evening World conducted a poll, asking fans whether they thought Dempsey had any intention of fighting Harry Wills. The results were - Yes: 129, No: 2,371. Asked whether he intended to fight Tunney or any other serious contender – Yes: 141, No, 2,539. When asked whether boxing commissions should declare the title forfeited if Dempsey did not defend it within the next six months – Yes, 2,351, No, 149.[310]

[306] Los Angeles Times, October 6, 1925.
[307] Los Angeles Times, October 8, 1925.
[308] Los Angeles Times, October 4, 11, 1925.
[309] Los Angeles Times, October 16, 17, 1925.
[310] Los Angeles Times, October 25, 1925.

On October 26, 1925, at the armory in Newark, New Jersey, before a crowd of 13,000, 215-pound Harry Wills stopped 203-pound Floyd Johnson (39-11-11) of Iowa in the 1st round. Johnson once had lasted into the 11th round with Jess Willard (1923). He offered up zero opposition to Wills, who ripped and tore at him, primarily to the body, but landing some solid head blows as well, with little in return, until Floyd's seconds threw in the towel after only two minutes of fighting, with Johnson on the ropes covering up, but not yet down.

The upset fans called it a fake, for Johnson had not even been down and did not appear to be out on his feet either. Still, it was a mismatch.

Harry Newman said the fight was a blow to boxing, for Johnson had nothing, and the fight never should have been permitted. "Wills gains little in prestige as a result of the barney."[311]

Interestingly enough, several days before the Wills-Johnson bout, Jack Dempsey had telegrammed Paddy Mullins, stating that his lawyer Ray Cannon and he thought it advisable for Mullins/Wills to cancel the match, feeling that Johnson might be tough and was risky for Wills.

> You could have picked some one easier and none could blame you for protecting yourself. It is poor policy to risk tossing away chance on next year's match. Wills surely will be panned if he does not stop Johnson and it will not do our match much good. I will stand half expense and repay promoters for advance advertising if you cancel Johnson match. Cannon will go to New York to assist you if you desire his legal services in cancellation.[312]

---

[311] *New York Daily News, Camden Courier, Bergen Evening Record*, October 27, 1925.
[312] *Chicago Defender*, October 24, 1925.

CHAPTER 4

Trouble

In late October 1925, the *Los Angeles Times* reported that if Jack Dempsey fought Harry Wills, it likely would be in New York or New Jersey. Supposedly, despite claims otherwise, Floyd Fitzsimmons had been unable to obtain the proper financial or political backing, and therefore he and Dempsey were willing to talk with Eastern promoters, trying to peddle the fight to them. Tex Rickard, Charles Stoneham, and a New Jersey syndicate allegedly were after the match.[313]

Dempsey said he did not care if his wife resumed her film career if the pay was good enough.

On October 31, 1925, in Mexico City, Mexico, for 25,000 Mexican fans, Dempsey boxed 4 rounds, 2 each with Jack Lee (who endured a severe battering) and Jack League, who was knocked out in 2 rounds.[314]

Rob Roy Benton quit as the champ's adviser. Benton said he had information that Ray Cannon was representing both Kearns and Dempsey in a move to throw the Fitzsimmons contract overboard.

Ray Cannon had reason to suspect that Fitzsimmons was not able to fulfill the contract. "We are not doing business on promissory notes." He said Dempsey would not be cajoled into anything else. Fitz would have to fulfill the contract as it dictated, or he would be in breach. Cannon was inferring that Fitz was having difficulties financing the bout, and apparently was trying to get Dempsey to agree to a delay in the funding of it. It seemed that Fitzsimmons, like the Shelby promoters, had made claims that he could not back up financially.

From San Antonio, Texas, on November 4, Dempsey declared that the Fitz promotion was on, he was not reconciling with Kearns, and the Wills bout would not be staged in New York.[315]

Customs agents kept a black pug dog that Estelle Taylor purchased in England and had arrived on November 10 in New York. She valued it at $58, but dog experts said it was of a nearly extinct breed and was worth $10,000. Hence, a greater tax was owed. Years prior, Jack Johnson and his wife had their own issues with customs agents as well.[316]

Indiana's Attorney General gave Governor Ed Jackson an opinion which said that an exhibition of boxing skill was legal, but the exchange of blows to determine superiority was illegal. Essentially, he concluded that a real title fight in Indiana would violate the law. Dempsey-Wills was not wanted there.[317]

---

[313] *Los Angeles Times*, October 27, 1925.
[314] *Los Angeles Times*, November 1, 2, 1925. The champ was scheduled to exhibit in Monterey and Tampico but canceled the latter.
[315] *Los Angeles Times*, November 4-6, 1925.
[316] *Los Angeles Times*, November 12, 1925.
[317] *Los Angeles Times*, November 19, 1925.

On November 18, 1925, in Cleveland's Public Hall, 188-pound Gene Tunney clearly won a 12-round decision against local 192-pound Johnny Risko (20-7-1). The local *Cleveland Plain Dealer*'s James Doyle said referee Matt Hinkel awarded Tunney the decision over Risko in a classy bout. Although the young Clevelander staged a game fight and made a splendid showing, the ex-marine clearly outboxed him. Tunney started slowly, spurted midway, eased up again in the 8th through 10th rounds, but then finished strongly in the last two. Gene, handicapped by a hurt, tender, and fragile left hand, did not use it as often as his hard right to the jaw, which made the bout more competitive than it otherwise might have been. Risko put up the best performance of his career, and shook-up Tunney on several occasions, but at no time was Tunney in serious trouble.

One report said Tunney won 6-2-4. Gene's margin in the rounds he won was so great that there could be no question about the decision.

The *Akron Beacon Journal* said Tunney was not likely to beat Dempsey, for he was not ferocious enough and not enough of a puncher. Sure, he beat Risko badly, but he never scored a knockdown. This writer believed if Dempsey was anything near what he was a few years ago, he would give Gene a beating and stop him. Still, Tunney was cool, deliberate, and skillful.[318]

On November 30, 1925, Tex Rickard's wife died.

It was anticipated that Floyd Fitzsimmons would be selling his interest in the Dempsey-Wills promotion. The South Bend, Indiana syndicate likely would withdraw. They had been unable (or unwilling) to post the required substantial forfeits. Kearns and Rickard had been proven correct – Fitzsimmons did not have the financial backing he claimed.[319]

Dempsey said Firpo was a striking example of what easy living did to an athlete. When he was broke, Luis worked hard and lived and slept properly. He was at peak form against Dempsey. But then he started living a life of luxury and got fat, flabby, and slow, and lost his accuracy and effectiveness, rusty from his layoff. He made a miserable showing against Wills, and was just a punching bag against Weinert, whom he stopped previously in a couple rounds. Now, he was a has-been.[320]

The *Pittsburgh Gazette Times'* Harry Keck reported that Gene Tunney said if he beat Dempsey for the championship, he would not fight Wills, and would draw the color line. Tunney was not in favor of mixed bouts, although he once wanted to meet Wills in an elimination bout, but Wills refused. Tunney said Wills had refused all offers to fight him, including a $150,000 guarantee from Rickard. Wills said the only man he wanted to fight was Dempsey. Tunney believed that a Wills-

Draws the Color Line

---

[318] *Cleveland Plain Dealer, Akron Beacon Journal, Coshocton Tribune, Dayton Daily News, Cincinnati Enquirer*, November 19, 1925. Afterward, Tunney claimed hand injuries. Present to watch the fight was former champion Jim Corbett.
Johnny Risko's record included: 1924 WND10 Homer Smith and LND10 Martin Burke; 1925 L12 Quinton Romero Rojas, TKO7 Bert Kenny, L12 Jack Renault, LND10 Young Stribling, LDQ5 and WND10 Chuck Wiggins, and L10 Jack Sharkey. In subsequent years, Risko would be a top contender.
[319] *Los Angeles Times*, December 11, 1925.
[320] *Pittsburgh Press*, December 13, 1925.

Tunney fight would have created a stronger mandate for the winner to fight Dempsey. Gene said,

> As matters stand now, his balking has held us both back. I never have fought a Negro and do not approve of mixed bouts, but I was willing and anxious to make an exception in the Wills case. He has seen fit to do the dictating, however, and, as a result, has lost whatever chance he ever had of getting a match with me if I become champion. Harry has made the mistake of toting all of his eggs in one basket, has centered his campaign for a championship bout on Dempsey and has lost out in his quest. Unless I am sadly mistaken, Dempsey has no intention of fighting him, and neither have I, now.

Dempsey had been offered $500,000 to fight Tunney in New York on July 4. Tunney did not think Dempsey-Wills ever would happen. "Money talks, and we are in a position to give Dempsey what he has asked, a cool half million dollars to fight me." Gene believed that a fight between he and Dempsey would be made.[321]

In mid-December, Ray Cannon said the Floyd Fitzsimmons contract was null and void because the terms had not been fulfilled. Therefore, Fitz could not sell his interest. If Fitzsimmons could not contract with Dempsey again, and fulfill his contractual obligations, then Dempsey would seek other promoters until a bout could be arranged.[322]

Dempsey said Fitzsimmons had failed to make payments due on November 1, and the money was not paid even after extensions were granted. Formal notice that the contract was voided was served on the promoter on November 27, 1925.[323]

Michigan Governor Alexander J. Groesbeck said a Dempsey-Wills fight would not be countenanced in his state.[324]

The *Scranton Republican* said the sturdy ex-marine Tunney, who figured to beat Dempsey with his straight lefts to the jaw, either was the weirdest pug ever or the greatest kidder ever. He was not like a fighter outside the ring. He used words with more than one syllable. He was well groomed. He adored poetry, philosophy, history, opera, and theater. He read Emerson. "It's so erudite and yet so fascinating," Gene commented. Tunney said the type of women who liked prizefighters did not interest him. "Such girls could give me nothing, either spiritually or mentally." The writer responded, "This from the gent who is either the best or the second best prize fighter in America."

Tunney said that after fighting in the war, he was offered $60 a fight, which was good money, so he pursued his boxing career. He might have taken a nice secretary's job at $35 a week, had it been offered.[325]

[321] *Pittsburgh Gazette Times, Lancaster Daily Eagle*, December 14, 1925.
[322] *Los Angeles Times*, December 15, 1925.
[323] *Los Angeles Times*, December 20, 1925.
[324] *Pittsburgh Gazette Times*, December 23, 1925.
[325] *Scranton Republican*, December 26, 1925.

Billy Gibson and Gene Tunney

Billy Gibson was pushing for a Tunney title shot. He said Wills refused to meet Tunney, only wanting to fight Dempsey, but a mixed-race heavyweight championship match was almost impossible to stage, and demand for Dempsey-Tunney was greater.

Gibson said he would endeavor to keep their respective war records out of it. He was not a mud slinger, and Tunney asked that none be slung. "Gene has always objected to capitalizing upon the fact that he was a marine. He sees no reason why his war record should be injected into ring affairs." Still, the fact was that many would be pulling for Tunney because he had enlisted, while Dempsey had not. The fact that Gene was from New York did not hurt either, given that it was the most populous state in the nation. A greater population generally translated into greater ticket sales, and at higher prices.

Jack Kearns insisted that attorneys had informed him that no matter when Dempsey met Wills or Tunney, he still would share in the receipts at his usual 50%. "He can go ahead and act as his own manager in all other affairs after August 15 and I would not have a share. But if he meets Wills or Tunney, the outstanding challengers, then I would share."[326]

On December 29, 1925 in Saint Petersburg, Florida, just outside Tampa, at the Waterfront arena, before a crowd of 8,000, 185-pound Gene Tunney knocked out St. Paul's 182-pound Dan O'Dowd in the 2nd round, with a right to the jaw. A prior 1923 fight between them had gone the 12-round distance, with a points victory for Tunney. O'Dowd had been a former Dempsey sparring partner.[327]

In January 1926, the Pennsylvania State Athletic Commission sent Jack Dempsey a letter stating that it would welcome a Dempsey bout with either Tunney or Wills. "Responsible promoter assured. Big money return." This contradicted its prior edict forbidding Dempsey-Wills.[328]

A group of Los Angeles businessmen claimed that they would back a Dempsey-Wills fight at the Los Angeles Coliseum for $2 million.[329]

However, California Boxing Commissioner William Hanlon said he never would approve of a Dempsey-Wills bout in California and would do whatever he could to prevent it. He did not mention race, but instead said it was utterly absurd for boxers to be paid what they were (as if it was any of his business, rather than the result of economics). He said the fight was a publicity stunt anyhow.

[326] *Los Angeles Times*, December 27, 1925.
[327] *Tampa Daily Times*, *Tampa Tribune*, December 30, 1925.
[328] *Los Angeles Times*, January 7, 1926.
[329] *Philadelphia Inquirer*, January 12, 1926.

Lightweight Ace Hudkins, Dempsey, wrestler John Pesek

In mid-January 1926, Dempsey said he would give Floyd Fitzsimmons ten more days to come up with financial backing, or else the deal was off and he would consider other options.[330]

Dempsey had been training at the Manhattan Club in Los Angeles.

Paddy Mullins said Floyd Fitzsimmons was supposed to pay him $25,000 when he signed the contract, and a like amount to be paid at certain intervals. Mullins was looking for the second installment, which was long overdue. If Fitz could not come up with the money, Wills would make other matches. Mullins had approached Jack Renault and Jack Sharkey about potential fights with Wills.[331]

With wife Estelle, Dempsey arrived in Miami on January 19, 1926, set to exhibit there and throughout Florida. With him were sparring partners Gus Wilson, Jack League, and Ed Warner. Jack also planned a Florida real estate deal.

When asked about Wills, Dempsey said, "Name the time, the place and the amount. I'd like to get it all over with. I have four or five propositions which I am considering."

Jack had changed his tune about New York. "I think that a Wills bout could be best staged in either New York or New Jersey." After all, his biggest purses had been in New York and New Jersey. Plus, Wills primarily had boxed in the East, so he was most popular there.

When asked who was better, Tunney or Wills, Dempsey replied, "Tunney. He is younger, is coming up in the game, hits hard from all that I can learn and I consider him the better man of the two. Yes, I think Tunney is the best man in the world – next to me."[332]

Tex Rickard was noncommittal regarding reports of a potential Dempsey-Tunney clash. Rumors were that Rickard and Dempsey were in negotiations for a bout between the two in New Jersey.

Tom O'Rourke wired an offer of $500,000 to Dempsey to fight Wills for him. He allegedly was backed by a wealthy syndicate from Connecticut. Of course, everyone claimed they had backing; but proving it with actual cash often turned out to be another thing entirely.[333]

[330] Los Angeles Times, January 15, 1926.
[331] Miami News, January 18, 1926.
[332] Miami News, January 20, 1926.
[333] Los Angeles Times, January 21, 1926.

Tex Rickard confirmed that he was trying to make a Dempsey-Tunney match, preferably in September. When asked who he thought was the logical contender, Tunney or Wills, Rickard responded,

> Tunney, positively. Tunney has fought himself into a position which no other heavyweight occupies. Name a man he has refused to fight. He knocked out Georges Carpentier, Tommy Gibbons, Erminio Spalla and holds the only knockout against Bartley Madden. In addition he has defeated Martin Burke, Harry Greb, Jimmy Delaney and Charlie Weinert.
>
> Then Tunney signed a contract to meet Wills, with the winner being guaranteed a match with Dempsey. I offered Wills $150,000 to meet Tunney but he would not come near me. He elected to go over to Jersey City to get $7,000 for a knockout over Floyd Johnson.[334]

The *Los Angeles Record* said speedy Harry Greb had more endurance than any other living fighter. He could have fought in the old days for 20, 25, 40, or 50 rounds without slowing down.

> [Greb] is credited with being one of the hardest men to hit in the head the ring has had in years. His wonderful legs take his body away from trouble. If he could punch as well as his legs can dance he would be even greater. Greb handles punches like an explosion. His fists go in all directions. ... Some like Greb's style. Some don't. But still he is a wonder, just the same. ...
>
> Greb does everything wrong. He fights wide open, he leads with his right, he telegraphs his punches and he bounces around like a clown. Yet tremendous vitality, blinding speed and a rubber body that enables him to assimilate punishment that would destroy most men carry him to victory. He is the exception that proves the rule. He is a great fighter, and no foolin'.

Greb fought so often that he did not need to train much.[335]

On January 26, 1926, in Vernon, California, in the Los Angeles area, 163 ¾-pound Harry Greb won a 10-round decision over England's 166 ¼-pound Ted Moore (57-12-6). Referee Benny Whitman scored it 6-2-2 for Greb.[336]

Philadelphia promoters, with the approval of the Pennsylvania State Athletic Commission, allegedly offered Dempsey $500,000 to fight Harry Wills there, or $300,000 to fight Gene Tunney.[337]

[334] *Philadelphia Inquirer*, January 22, 1926.
[335] *Los Angeles Record*, January 22, 1926.
[336] The local *Los Angeles Record*'s Ed Frayne disagreed, saying Moore won 5-3-2. The *Los Angeles Illustrated Daily News'* R. A. Cronin scored it 9-1 for Greb. The *Los Angeles Evening Express* scored it 8-0-2 for Greb. January 27, 1926.
[337] *York Dispatch*, January 23, 1926.

Crowds showed up to Lido Villas in Miami to watch Dempsey work out each day while there.

Tom O'Rourke said he had offered Dempsey $500,000 plus a 40% privilege of the net gate (if more) to fight Harry Wills, but had received no response.

Dempsey allegedly said he was not interested in O'Rourke's offer because he already was signed up with Fitzsimmons, and still was trying to see things through with him.[338]

On January 28, Dempsey, his wife, and three sparring partners arrived in Havana, Cuba, scheduled to exhibit there on January 31.[339]

The *Chicago Defender* reported that James Farley said Dempsey had to fight Wills or no one, and the ban on him would be lifted only once he proved his willingness to fight Wills. Tex Rickard would not be allowed to promote Dempsey-Tunney in New York. "Dempsey is ineligible, and it is a rule that no matchmaker or promoter may do business with him at this time any more than he might do business with any other ineligible boxer." Rickard countered by saying he was not a promoter or matchmaker, but a director and employee of the Madison Square Garden corporation. Farley responded, "If Rickard said that…he spoke very foolishly."

Tom O'Rourke said, "If Dempsey wants to fight Wills I will give him more money than he ever received in his life, and will stage the bout in Long Island City." His backers were prepared to build a huge amphitheater in Queens. He said the fight would draw a $2 million gate. "Dempsey will get an awful roasting if he takes on Tunney instead of Wills, who deserves recognition and a square deal."

The *Defender* said, "It will be remembered that the veteran O'Rourke attempted to stage a Wills-Dempsey scrap two or three years ago and had the proper backers, but the bottom fell out because of the fake champion's attitude."

Philadelphia, Pennsylvania promoter Herman Taylor also wired Dempsey in Miami a $500,000 offer to meet Wills.[340]

Many writers were saying that it was looking more and more as if Dempsey would fight Tunney. Sparrow McGann said, "The silence of Harry Wills' manager, Mullins, is evidence of his conviction that his big dusky battler is to be shunted aside." Paddy's influential friends had worked to make a Wills-Dempsey fight, but "they have found themselves unable to hurdle the obstacles they have encountered. They were real obstacles. Those in the know, dare not divulge them. Politics plays an important part in boxing and it is hinted that politics is one of the barriers that the Wills adherents have found to be insurmountable."

---

[338] *Miami News*, January 28, 1926; *Zanesville Times Recorder, Allentown Morning Call*, January 30, 1926.
[339] *Los Angeles Times*, January 29, 1926. In Cuba, Dempsey sparred Marty Cutler, Jack League, and Cowboy Ed Warner.
[340] *Chicago Defender*, January 30, 1926.

McGann said the Dempsey who knocked out Levinsky, Fulton, Willard, and Firpo was one of the best fighters ever. "But the Jack of yesterday and today may be two different persons." The question was how much rust had gathered, and how much could be polished off with training. The feeling was that the old Dempsey would finish off Tunney, but a lesser version might not find it so easy.

Tunney's war record, good looks, pleasing personality, and excellent record over 8 years, having lost only once by decision, which was avenged, would make him a good drawing card. Dempsey was the biggest draw in the ring, for the fans knew they would see a real fight whenever he crawled through the ropes.[341]

A story was going around that Harry Greb had lost his eyesight in one eye as a result of pugilism. Those close to him said he had lost sight in his right eye. Ted Moore came back to his corner after the 2nd round of their recent fight and told his handlers that the champ could not see his lefts and was keeping his right up in a manner he had not done in their prior bouts. A few nights later, Buck Holley hit him with a left hook that was telegraphed, but Greb did not get away from it.

> Even with defective vision, Greb is still the best middleweight in the world, and one of the best in history. He has everything but a punch. He is the fastest middleweight champion that ever lived. He is one of the gamest fighters of all time. He has stamina and recuperative power such as few ringmen have had.
>
> No, it will take more than an eye to stop Harry Greb. He could even donate an arm and whip most of his challengers.[342]

While in Tampa, Florida, Dempsey said he had interests in coal mines, hotels, and restaurants. He was not trying to stop Estelle from having a career, for that would not be any fairer than her trying to stop him from boxing. Both professions were arts to their respective participants. Dempsey got paid very little up until the time he was champion, but he loved the sport. He was cashing in now, but it was not all about the money to him. "To do one's best, there has to be an intense love of the work and a desire to accomplish a goal."

Dempsey said Cuba was beautiful, but they did not have enough money to pay him to fight there. Florida was warmer than California and had the advantage of being closer to the East coast, but California had more beautiful scenery. He said he might weigh a little less than 200 since the boat trip, for both he and Estelle were rather seasick. He admitted that he was no sailor. He felt like a bird in a cage all the way from Havana.

According to the *Tampa Tribune's* writer, Dempsey's voice was soft and musical, unusually so for a big man. He dressed immaculately in the latest style, and his hair was slicked back.

[341] *Miami News*, January 31, 1926.
[342] *Los Angeles Record*, February 1, 1926. There had been claims that Greb had defective vision as early as 1921 or 1922, which he denied.

Jack said, "The public wants me to fight Wills, so I suppose I'll have to. It's not a question of race or color, likes or dislikes, but of ability against ability. If he's the best, then I want to meet him because I want to compete with the best." He said he planned to fight Wills somewhere in the U.S. on Labor Day. Hopefully, Floyd Fitzsimmons would promote it on a percentage proposition, although Floyd would have to put up $500,000 as a guarantee of his ability to go through with the bout. Jack did not want a duplication of the monumental bust at Shelby, Montana. Fitz was looking for a place where the promotion could be a success.

On the afternoon of February 3, 1926, in Tampa, Florida, at the North Side Country Club, a Hammer property, 10,000 people watched Dempsey spar four opponents 7 total rounds. "After skinning the red paint from a couple of his foes, torpedoing another and sending a fourth into wild S.O.S. signaling, he called it an afternoon." Dempsey decked heavyweight Joe Lavigne in their 2 rounds, decked 210-pound Jack League in their 2nd round with a blow to the chin, and worked speedily with Ed Warner for 2 rounds. Big Marty Cutler went 1 round. A right to the abdomen sent Cutler through the ropes into the crowd.

Tex Rickard said the champ must have been kidding when he claimed that arrangements were being made to fight Wills at Madison Square Garden or somewhere else on Labor Day. He characterized such talk as ridiculous.[343]

On February 8, 1926, in Memphis, Tennessee, in an exhibition, Dempsey knocked out four of six men who appeared against him, all in the 1st round. The victims were Jack League, Tony Catalina of Memphis, Cowboy Ed Warner, and Marty Cutler. Two others were badly trounced, but managed to last a round each. Tony Catalina was first. He was stowed away in 1 minute 14 seconds. Jack League suffered a broken nose from a right. League took his ten-count in less than two minutes. The champ eased up thereafter, going 2 rounds each with Jack Laverne and Shifty Logan. Cowboy Warner was unable to respond for the 2nd round. The champ then put Marty Cutler to sleep in the 1st round. Dempsey took the scales for the newspapermen, tipping the beam at 198 pounds.[344]

Dempsey said Philadelphia was a logical place to hold his proposed match with Wills. He was impressed with proposals made to him by promoters there, Robert Gunnis and Herman Taylor. Ultimately, he did not care where the Wills fight occurred, as long as there was a guarantee that there would be no political interference, it was sponsored and backed by the state's athletic commission, and they could ensure an arena that would seat 110,000 people.[345]

Unfortunately, a week later, Philadelphia Mayor W. Freeland Kendrick officially went on record "as opposing a fuss between Harry Wills and the champion." Hence, Philadelphia was out.[346]

---

[343] *Tampa Tribune*, February 4, 1926.
[344] *Chattanooga Daily Times, Kingsport Times, Scranton Times, Salt Lake Telegram*, February 9, 1926. Dempsey exhibited in Denver on Feb. 12.
[345] *Newport Daily Press*, February 9, 1926.
[346] *Philadelphia Inquirer*, February 17, 1926.

Jack and Estelle arrived in Wilmington, Delaware on February 16 to visit her mother.[347]

The champ was supposed to box in Richmond, Virginia on the 20th. However, Ralph Brooks, who was scheduled to box with Dempsey, committed suicide, allegedly the result of his disappointment over a love affair. Hence, Jack canceled the exhibition.[348]

Looking back over his 50 years of experience with boxing, De Witt Van Court ranked the heavyweights: 1. James J. Jeffries, who had everything that makes an invincible champion. 2. John L. Sullivan, the hardest puncher of them all. 3. James J. Corbett, who had the skill. 4. Peter Jackson. 5. Jack Johnson. 6. Bob Fitzsimmons. 7. Jack Dempsey. Fitzsimmons was the greatest middleweight and light heavyweight ever.

Australia's H. M. McAshan, who also followed boxing closely for more than a half century, said, "I agree with Van Court that Jeffries was the greatest of all heavyweights, but I think Dempsey should be placed much higher in the list." He'd add Sam Langford to the list as well.[349]

In a series of articles in February 1926, Dempsey explained his break with Kearns. He said his manager never gave him any sort of accounting, never kept books, nor showed him a record of earnings or expenses. No written contract existed between them from 1917 up to 1923. The late 1923 contract was forced upon them by the New York State Athletic Commission, despite both of their protests. Kearns began managing him in 1917 and had taken 50% of his earnings ever since.

Jack said he began his career in 1914 at age 18, when he only weighed around 150 pounds. He did most of his fighting in mining camps. He had a good punch even then, and soon the men in his own mining camp decided it was foolish to try conclusions with him. So, he started fighting men from other camps. He earned money in side-bets. He won his fights, and eventually quit his job as a miner in 1914 to pursue a real career in boxing. Back then, $50 was considered big money, and even $10 was considered to be a "whale of a purse."

The reason why he had so many managers during his first few years was that he wanted action, no matter how little he was paid, whereas his managers thought he ought to sit back and wait for weeks or months until they had secured a big shot for him for good money. Jack wanted to fight, and fight often. He loved the game. His greatest thrill was when the bell rang to start a fight. He would have fought every night if he could.

In 1916, Jack Price convinced him to go to New York with him. He had three fights and earned $174 total - $27, $47, and $100 purses. After Price was forced to leave town, John Reisler, known as John the Barber, painted glowing pictures of the money he could make for him. Reisler arranged the fight with black John Lester Johnson, who broke some of Jack's ribs and gave him a rather bitter lesson in body punching. After that

[347] *Los Angeles Times*, February 17, 1926. Trainer Gus Wilson was with them. Dempsey left Wilmington on Feb 19 for Richmond, VA.
[348] *Newport News Daily Press*, February 20, 1926; *Harrisburg Telegraph*, February 19, 1926; *New York Daily News*, February 18, 1926.
[349] *Dayton Daily News*, February 21, 1926.

fight, John the Barber decided that Dempsey was a wash and a waste of time. He made no efforts to get him more fights, and expressed doubts about him as a fighter. So, he jumped a train and went back West.

Jack drifted around, between Ogden and Salt Lake, then Seattle, and finally wound up in San Francisco, where eventually he met Jack Kearns.

Up to 1917, he had lost a couple fights, had a few draws, won about a dozen decisions, and acquired a reputation as a puncher by knocking out about 20 men. He was 21 years of age, rated as a rough, tough kid who had fought in the "sticks." He had boosted his purse earnings from $2.50 for his first real fight, all the way up to $1,400. That year, Kearns became his manager.

Like James J. Jeffries, Dempsey said he actually was left-handed, although he had knockout power in both hands. "It may be interesting to know that I am naturally left-handed and even in my earliest days, long before Kearns knew me, I did as much damage with my left hand as I did with my right hand." In 1916, his then-manager Fred Winsor said his left was twice as effective as his right. So, any claim from Kearns that he helped develop Dempsey's left was nonsense, according to Jack.

He learned body punching from John Lester Johnson, simply from their fight, which showed him how effective body punching was. Up until then, his main goal was to land on the chin, though he hit the body too when the opportunity presented itself. Johnson showed him the great worth of body punching, especially a right under the heart. "Johnson's whole attack against me was to the body. He gave me a sad beating there and I figured it out that if he could hurt me by hitting to the body, I could do damage to other fellows with the same attack." Thereafter, he began perfecting his body attack.

When Kearns began managing him, he had Jack train at his Oakland gym. Kearns gave him some tips, like shortening his left hook, but for the most part, he tutored himself, and Kearns made the matches.

Their initial deal was for Kearns to earn 25% of his purses, and Dempsey would pay the expenses out of his end. Their first real battle together was against Gunboat Smith. The 1st round was even. In the 2nd, Smith hit him on the jaw with a right, and Jack did not remember anything after that. He returned to complete consciousness in the dressing room, after the fight was over. He was broken-hearted, thinking that he had lost, and asking in what round he had been knocked out. Kearns told him that he won the decision after 4 terrific rounds of battling. That Smith right had lifted him about a foot off the floor, driving him back a couple feet, but he landed standing up and fought like a wild man. Kearns said, "You just ripped and tore into Smith in that round, in the third and fourth, and you did everything but knock him out. You were like a cageful of lions." Jack was proud of the fact that he took Smith's best punch, stood up, and still gave him a lacing. That fight also launched him into national prominence.

During 1917, Dempsey was sick for a while and unable to fight. Jack felt badly that Kearns was not making any money, and he offered to make it up to him by giving him 50% of the money, but Kearns had to pay the expenses. It was just a verbal agreement, but it remained in force throughout the years. There was no written agreement until August 1923.

Dempsey could have reduced his cut at any time, or fired him, given that there was no formal contract for any term of years. The only written contract was forced upon them. The New York commission insisted upon a written contract. They also fixed the maximum that Kearns could take at 33 1/3%. Despite the written contract, Dempsey still agreed to let Kearns take 50%, figuring that 16 2/3% was for the expenses. That contract was for three years and would expire on August 3, 1926.

Dempsey earned $470,000 from the Firpo fight. He gave Kearns $235,000, about $80,000 more than what the contract allowed.

Regardless of the financial rewards for his services, either in the ring, in vaudeville, or moving pictures, Kearns collected all of the money and then paid Dempsey his end. As the purses increased, the expenses remained relatively stable, particularly since the promoters often paid for travel expenses, so Kearns' relative end was increased over time. Jack never saw any books. Sometimes there was a general receipt, sometimes itemized, but only in a general way. He allowed Kearns to make all of the business and matchmaking decisions, and he did not interfere.

In answer to the question regarding who made whom, did Dempsey make Kearns or did Kearns make Dempsey, the champion responded that if it was not for his ability to hit harder than any man in the ring and stand up under punishment, he never would have been champion. Kearns got him the matches, but if he was not of championship timber, he would not have won them. He would have been unmade in a hurry if he could not win, and Kearns would have ditched him in a hurry if that were the case.

Kearns got him the matches, but Jack said it was not difficult to find bouts at that time, because a lot of heavyweights did not take him seriously, and figured they could beat what they thought was just a tough, rough, wild-swinging kid from Utah.

In answer to those who said Kearns helped secure him big purses, bigger than anyone before, Jack responded that his style of fighting, which provided fast and furious action which excited crowds, is what generated the interest and the income. Other than the Gibbons fight, his contests always made money for promoters, and that wasn't because fans came to see Kearns. Jack did not make real money until he became champion.

Dempsey faulted Kearns for some of his deals. He received a relatively small amount compared to what Willard got for their contest. Also, the champ was all for 50% of the receipts for the Carpentier fight, but Kearns accepted a $300,000 guarantee, which cost them a half million. Carpentier received nearly as much as him. The promoters made over a million dollars on the promotion. Jack believed the least a champ should earn was 37 ½% of the gate, and sometimes up to 50%. Kearns did not want to gamble on 50%, but wanted a sure thing, and that cost them. Dempsey had wanted them to gamble on the gate.

The Gibbons bout was a financial fiasco. He was to be paid $310,000 guaranteed, with a first payment of $110,000 immediately, the second $100,000 on June 15, and the final payment of $100,000 on July 2. The promoters barely made the second payment by securing a $50,000 loan from George Stanton, a banker, and the rest was realized by loans, which really were donations, by several men in the Great Falls and Shelby area.

When they failed to make the third payment, Kearns was opposed to Dempsey announcing that he would fight anyway, for then the promoters would not pay. "These fellows have the money, but they are trying to bluff us into fighting for $210,000 and they are not going to get away with it." Jack wanted Kearns to secure an interest in the first $100,000 of the gate and announce that he would fight no matter what, or else the insecurity might cause folks not to come. But Kearns did not like that idea, and announced that if the money was not paid, there would be no fight. That cut down on the attendance and hurt the promotion's ultimate success. Kearns finally backed down from his no-fight-stance and agreed to take the gate, but that was 36 hours before the fight, and by then it was too late for all those who would have taken trains from the East and elsewhere. That soured folks to Dempsey; for they thought he still might run out on the match, even though he had no intention of doing so. Fearing potential harm, Kearns hired 11 armed bodyguards.

Dempsey said he was nervous that someone in the Shelby crowd might do him harm, and that affected him. Some joshed him about trying to run out on the match, or they said Gibbons would beat him.

Jack said he was not right for the Gibbons fight. Despite good reports about his training, he could not get his muscles working right. He did not have his usual springiness in his legs and could not hit with his usual accuracy and power. That worried him. He was not eating or sleeping well. The crowd was not friendly towards him. All of that put his nerves on edge. Gibbons did not make things easier. He was moving and fighting defensively, and Jack was afraid to go all out and gas himself. He hoped to wear down Gibbons by punishing him in the clinches. But Jack wore down as well from all of his own work. There were boos and hisses when he mauled Tommy. Throughout, Jack did more work than Gibbons did, for Tommy was more concerned with running, twisting, and side-slapping. Gibbons nailed him with some good blows in the 11th round. Jack opened up with what he had, trying to slug it out. But Tommy resolved that although he could not win, he was not going to be knocked out. So, he fought strictly on the defensive, clinching as often as he could. After Jack won, he left the arena quickly, fearing harm from those who had wagered on Gibbons.

Dempsey said the popular opinion that he never was better than he was in the Willard fight was a myth, and incorrect. He was overtrained and not in good condition at all. He had very little reserve energy. He had not been allowed to lay off or taper properly, which would have made him even sharper. He had been trained as if he was overweight, but that was not necessary, for he was near peak condition when he started to train. Jack believed a fighter should have a little bit of extra fat for energy. He weighed 187 pounds for the Willard fight but thought he would have been better at 190. Kearns and De Forest drove him down further, and he came close to leaving his fight on the roadways or in the gym. His pleas for a letup were ignored. As a result, he had little zip and energy after his furious attack in the 1st round.

Dempsey believed that Jess had been counted out on the floor. "I jumped out of the ring and tried to fight my way through the crowd to my dressing room." But then they called him back. "I had to battle about twenty people to get a clear passage to the ring – and that exertion has since been set forth as an alibi for my failure to drop Willard again in the two final rounds." Jack admitted that when he got back into the ring, he was tired. He had not been hit or hurt, but the exertion winded him, along with the fact that he had trained too hard and often. He was tired, and unable to maintain his cyclonic attack. He was thankful when Willard's second threw in the towel. If Jess had not retired and had shown real signs of returning to life during the next several rounds, he might have retained his championship.

Dempsey said Kearns was not the great cornerman folks thought he was. He misled him into believing that he had won against Willard. Kearns ordered him out of his corner and to the dressing room before the result was official. His absence from the ring nearly lost him the fight.

In the 2nd round of his fight with Gibbons, with a stiff punch, Tom broke open an old cut over Jack's eye. In the corner, someone, in his efforts to put a liquid medicine into the cut to stop the flow of blood, accidentally poured most of it into Dempsey's eye, and he was blinded up until the 7th or 8th round.

The only time he ever really needed help from his corner was in the Firpo fight. That was the first time under Kearns' management that he ever was in any real trouble. He had gone a bit "goofy" in the 1st round of madhouse fighting. He needed someone to tell him what had happened, snap him back into physical condition, and give him advice.

Usually, he had insisted that unless he was groggy or goofy from punches, his seconds were not to give advice, for he believed that as long as he was in full possession of his faculties, he was best able to know what to do or not do. He did not like to go into fights with a game plan either, but rather preferred to take things as they came, to find an opening and punch through it. Therefore, Kearns refrained from giving advice. Dempsey just wanted his seconds to give him some water, rub some ice on his back if needed, to fix up a cut, give him smelling salts if warranted, and to advise him if he was punched so badly that he did not know what was going on.

Dempsey claimed that the only time he needed smelling salts and advice was in the Firpo fight. Jack said Firpo landed a right to his chin before the sound of the clang of the first bell to start the fight had died away, and that wallop did a lot of things, including ruining his disposition and knocking him loose from his reasoning powers. The round started with Jack swinging a vicious left hook that missed. Firpo then caught him with a right flush on the jaw. Things went blank and remained so until revived by his Greek trainer Jerry Luvadis, who threw a half bucket of water over him as he returned to his corner after the round.

When he returned to his corner, it was obvious that he needed smelling salts, for he was rather confused mentally, and he needed some calming advice. After the water was splashed in his face, his brain began to clear. Someone finally put smelling salts under his nose. He thought it was Jerry, who was rubbing ice on his back, pouring water on his head, and sponging him off. Kearns spoke, but Jack could not understand what he said. He heard Jerry say, "Keep in close, do not try only long distance slugging with him." He heeded the advice and stopped Firpo soon thereafter. It was the wildest fight ever, and the crowd had been transformed into the wildest mob that ever witnessed a ring battle.

Dempsey and Kearns were hooked up for eight years. It was a business relationship, not a friendship. Kearns often mingled freely in the night life, whereas the champ was the opposite. There was an invisible barrier between them. Not a dislike, but their temperaments, ways, and desires were different. They had little in common.

Eventually, when real estate in California was booming, they decided to purchase properties together in joint ventures – the Wilshire Apartments and the Hotel Barbara. They had a few other business holdings in common, but they did not amount to much.

Over the last year and a half, without any bouts, they drifted apart more and more. In their meetings, things which might have been settled harmoniously were not. Friction continued to build. Part of it was regarding the hotel, which became Dempsey's pet project. Kearns regarded the hotel as a sort of playground for himself and his friends, not taking it seriously as a business, even using the lobby for shadow boxing exhibitions for his boxing friends, which turned off many higher-class guests. For a while, Kearns refused to budge. Kearns irked Dempsey by claiming that he had made him, owing to his managerial greatness.

But the real blow-up came when Dempsey decided he would marry Estelle Taylor. More than a year ago, Jack became engaged to Taylor. He told Kearns about it. Kearns heartily opposed Dempsey's marriage, believing that married life was not a good thing for a fighter. Kearns told Dempsey that while he was champion under his management, he was not going to get married, and had to remain single. Dempsey thought that really crossed the line. Kearns hoped it was a passing infatuation and could talk him out of it with jokes or jeers, but that only further widened and deepened their rift.

Eventually, Dempsey told Kearns that he would marry Taylor regardless of whether Kearns liked it or not.

> And after that I'm going to handle my own affairs. But that won't lose you your cut. For, even though I'll do my own matchmaking and managing, I'm willing that you should have your cut of my earnings, under the original contract, while that contract exists (which is until August, 1926). After that I'll continue to cut you in, even though there's no contract and I'll give you a twenty-five per cent cut.

Kearns had the idea that Dempsey would submit to him in all matters, and became sarcastic and sneering, which did not help matters. He turned down the proposition. "I've got you hooked on that contract – and you'll stay hooked. I'm your manager – and I'll remain your manager. And I'm going ahead now and make matches for you." Dempsey responded, "Make as many as you want. After that you can do the fighting, too – and keep the whole purse for yourself. In the meantime I'll do my own managing – and I guess I won't make any more blunders than you've made." He again offered to give Kearns his cut, but he refused. The champ replied, "That's okay with me. My offer is withdrawn. I'll manage myself, do my own fighting – and I'll keep the purse."

When he became champion, Dempsey said he would be a fighting champion who took on all comers. He had not done that, but there were several reasons for it. He had fought five men in title defenses in six and a half years as champion – Miske, Brennan, Carpentier, Gibbons, and Firpo. It was about the same average or higher than other former champions. But it would have been greater if he had his own way.

His plan was to get into action as of the summer. "The first big shot is to be against Harry Wills. For three or four years he's been telling the world he can whip me. I don't think he'll ever come close to it. For I believe that Wills is made to order for my style of fighting and I think I can move that fellow out of my path without an awful lot of trouble."

After that, Tunney could have his chance, if he still wanted it. "And I'm not going to try to mace the promoters into big purses for those fights. They can have me for a fair purse – or I'll work with them on a decent percentage arrangement." He wanted to fight more often.

Dempsey said that back in his early years, before Kearns was his manager, he used to fight two and three times a week and loved it. "I'm never so happy as when the bell sends me into action and it's up to me to knock my man – or get knocked."

He was through with Kearns. It did not matter who made whom. They both had advanced their careers together. Their eight-year partnership was over. Kearns made at least an average of $125,000 a year in profit. Kearns was to get 33 1/3% of what Dempsey earned, but he had not earned anything for a while, so Kearns had not lost anything, and was entitled to no damages. Jack agreed that if he fought before August 3, 1926, then Kearns would be entitled to a cut.[350]

Frank Menke said Harry Wills had made very good money battling "just about the most mediocre collection of fisticuffers that the mind can conceive." Menke called Wills' foes "has-been set-ups and ring wrecks – and still this man, favored as has been no other warrior in ring history, sobbed about being denied a 'fair break.'" Menke claimed that Wills had dodged every good fighter for 3 to 4 years, and yet for some inexplicable reason, promoters permitted him to take on far inferior men. Since 1921, the only men Wills fought who had even a fair reputation were Bartley Madden, a human punching bag who couldn't hit and had no defense, and Luis Firpo, who was all washed up as a result of the Dempsey beating and fancy living. Firpo was fat, flabby, and crude, and yet, Wills still could not knock him out, nor could he knock out Madden. The tip-off regarding how little the Firpo victory meant was when less than 3 months later Charley Weinert rose from a "fistic graveyard" and beat Firpo with ease. Bill Tate got a draw and won on a foul against Wills. "After that, Wills refused to hearken to every defi that Tate slung at him." Gibbons agreed to spot Wills 40 pounds and 5 inches in height, but "Wills dodged him." Furthermore, "He has repeatedly ignored challenges from Gene Tunney – and refused huge offers for a match with George Godfrey, another of Dempsey's ex-sparring partners." Menke said it was Wills who was the most careful avoider the game has known. Yet, as long as promoters paid him big money to knock off "broken-down wrecks," he would be foolish to do otherwise.[351]

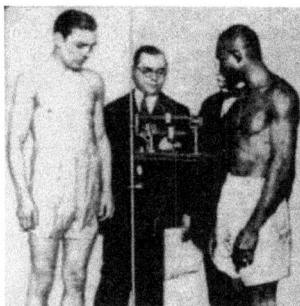

The New York Boxing Commission had ordered Harry Greb to meet Tiger Flowers or else have his name placed on the ineligibles list. Hence, he agreed.[352]

On February 26, 1926 in New York, at Madison Square Garden, before 16,311 paid admissions which drew a gate of $104,569.30 or $105,134.70, 30-year-old 158 ½-pound southpaw Theodore Tiger Flowers (110-14-5), a black man who previously had lost a close 1924 10-round no decision to Greb (though some said Flowers won or it was a draw), won the world middleweight championship with a close 15-round official split decision over 31-year-old 159 ½-pound Harry Greb. Judges Charles Mathison and Tom Flynn voted for Flowers, while referee Gunboat Smith voted for Greb. Flowers was the first black world champion since Battling Siki (who won his title in France), and the first black man ever to win the world middleweight championship.

The *Brooklyn Standard Union* said Greb's fouling and ineffective punching cost him the title. His every rally was nullified by a

[350] *Buffalo Courier*, February 14 – 25, 1926.
[351] *Sport* (Adelaide, Australia), February 26, 1926.
[352] *Binghamton Press*, December 30, 1925.

counterattack. There had been much clinching, with little effective clean punching. One of Greb's favorite fouls was to grab behind the neck and hit with the right. Referee Gunboat Smith's admonitions went unheeded. Greb also used his thumb to the nose or eyes, and he wrestled a great deal. "The decision was a just one."

The Associated Press had it 9-5-1 for Greb. Another A.P. report said the ringside newspapermen scored it 6-5-4 for Flowers.

Sam Hall said Flowers was lucky to catch Greb passed his best. Of the 1,500 punches thrown, 1,000 missed. Hall scored it 7-6-2 for Flowers.

Harry Newman said Greb was at his worst in a close, fumbling affair. Flowers edged it and won fairly, but it was surprising that it was not ruled a draw, which is how the spectators saw it. Yet, Newman's round-by-round scoring had it 6-5-4 for Greb.

William Granger said the long-expected happened. For two or three years, Greb had violated every training rule, but somehow kept winning. He was a ring freak, always fooling the wise ones, but it could not go on forever. This time, his old stamina was not there.

James Wood said Flowers won a listless fight, and Greb was a ghost of himself. The decision was not wholly popular, but Flowers won by a margin wide enough to justify it. Greb marred his good work by using rough and unfair tactics. Many believed a draw would have been fine too. Regardless, there was a new world middleweight champion.

Davis Walsh said, "Flowers got the decision and he earned it."

Jack Lawrence had it 8-6-1 for Greb.[353]

This bout was important and symbolic. Historically, black fighters receiving title-winning opportunities in the U.S. was rare. Other than 1917 Benny Leonard KO1 black Leo Johnson (68-17-12) in Harlem, New York to defend his world lightweight title, until Flowers W15 Greb in 1926, no black man had challenged for a world championship on U.S. soil after Jack Johnson lost his title in 1915. Of course, those bouts were at lightweight and middleweight. Heavyweights title fights had the greatest symbolic value, and as such, raised the most political eyebrows. Yet, even mixed-race title fights in the lower weight divisions were the rare exception rather than the norm. No black man ever before had fought to win the world heavyweight championship on U.S. soil. Jack Johnson had won his crown in Australia.[354]

[353] Brooklyn Standard Union, Binghamton Press, Buffalo Courier, Buffalo Morning Express, New York Daily News, Brooklyn Citizen, Brooklyn Daily Times, Yonkers Herald, February 27, 1926.
[354] In an over-the-weight nontitle bout, six days after his victory over Leo Johnson, 133-pound Benny Leonard also scored a 1917 KO2 over 138-pound black Eddie Dorsey in Buffalo, New York.

Harry Newman said being a Dempsey sparring partner was not good for one's career, for the champ had ruined many promising-looking heavyweights by beating on them too much. "Dempsey was unquestionably the cruelest man to work with during a training campaign that ever lived. He couldn't pull a punch on his mother once he climbed into the ring." He had a dual personality. In the ring, he was vicious and cruel, a veritable fiend. Outside, he was laughing, affable, and good natured. Even when he held back, or tried to do so, his lightest blows still were hard, and he pounded on his sparring partners, often knocking them dead. He ruined Larry Williams, knocking him out all the time when preparing for Carpentier. Leo Houck got it so rough that he had to leave. Jack Burke was a splendid-looking prospect, but he worked with Dempsey for Gibbons and Firpo and had a real fight with him every day. Burke still was fighting but had not reached the heights predicted for him. Dempsey even knocked stiff the tiny Midget Smith in Great Falls, Montana. "That bird, Dempsey, couldn't pull a punch on his life."

In late February, Dempsey and Floyd Fitzsimmons were in New York, apparently still trying to make the Wills fight happen. They were going to speak with Rickard.[355]

James Wood called Floyd Fitzsimmons "Mr. Flip-flop," for every other day he was in and then out of the Dempsey-Wills contest.

When speaking with newspapermen, Tex Rickard offered to wager that "Dempsey and Wills will not meet in 1926. I'll make another wager that Dempsey and Tunney will meet in 1926." Wood said,

> We'd rather toddle along with Mr. Rickard than string with Mr. Dempsey in the matter of future heavyweight activity. Mr. Rickard doesn't always call his shots. He is wide of the mark now and then. But he has not been issuing statements with his right hand and denials with his left at the same time the past three years.[356]

Floyd Fitzsimmons insisted that the Wills fight would occur on or about Labor Day. He claimed there were several big cities which could host it. They would make good money no matter where it was held.[357]

On Wednesday March 3, 1926, in Baltimore, Maryland, at the Fifth Regiment armory, before a crowd of 6,000, using 16-ounce gloves, Dempsey boxed five men 2 rounds each for 2 minutes per round. The local *Baltimore Sun* said Dempsey toyed with his five foes and clipped them at his pleasure. Against Navy champ George Davis, in the 1st round, a Dempsey right cross to the jaw sent the sailor to the floor. Jack picked him up. A right to the body sent Davis down again. In the 2nd round, a left sent Davis down once more.

235-pound Farmer Lodge was in the fourth match. A left clip on the jaw floored Lodge. Before the bell, a left and right floored him again,

[355] *New York Daily News, Brooklyn Standard Union,* February 28, 1926.
[356] *Brooklyn Daily Times,* March 1, 1926.
[357] *Baltimore Sun,* March 3, 1926.

between the ropes. In the 2nd round, Lodge went down yet again. Ringsiders could see him wince as he took a body beating.

Dempsey decks Farmer Lodge

The other boxers to appear were Third Corps heavy champ Benny Fundenburk, Jimmy Sullivan, and Jimmy Gold. Jack took it easy on them.

Harry Newman said, "We noticed particularly that Dempsey did not snort and gasp for wind which was so usual with him before they rebuilt that old beak." His nose surgery had done him some good. Jack's opposition was not good, so it was difficult to get a real line on him, but nevertheless, he stepped about in lively fashion and was very accurate.

Dempsey was heading to Chicago to discuss the possibility of the Wills bout taking place there.[358]

Tex Rickard was trying to make a Tunney-Dempsey fight. He believed that Dempsey-Wills simply could not be made or held. Tex also suggested that Wills had forfeited his standing as first-ranking challenger by refusing matches with any capable opponents, including Tunney. Some claimed that Tex already had signed Tunney, and "Dempsey has given him assurance he will accept terms on a percentage basis as soon as he is able to get square with the Commission."

Jack Lawrence reported that Dempsey-Tunney would take place in late August. Tunney/Gibson had signed, and Dempsey had given his word to Rickard, although no official announcement had been made. Floyd Fitzsimmons never could get financial backers, and those whom he did obtain had more talk than actual cash.[359]

However, starting on March 6, 1926 and continuing for several days, Dempsey and Fitzsimmons conferred with a Chicago group representing the Chicago Coliseum Athletic Club about a potential Dempsey-Wills fight in Chicago, where a bill to legalize boxing was under consideration. They met with B. E. Clements, the club's president. The press reported that the fight being held there, and legal papers being signed, hinged on the passage of the boxing bill in April. "The negotiations provide for merging of the South Bend, Ind., syndicate, which first posted the money binding the match, and the Coliseum A. C." Dempsey still was working with Fitzsimmons, trying to make the Wills fight happen.[360]

Lincoln Quarberg reported on March 12 that in Los Angeles, a Dempsey-Wills bout had been signed, and would take place on Labor Day, likely either in Chicago (if the pending law passed) or Michigan City.

[358] *Baltimore Sun, New York Daily News,* March 4, 1926.
[359] *Brooklyn Standard Union, Buffalo Evening News,* March 5, 1926.
[360] *Chicago Tribune,* March 7, 1926; *Los Angeles Evening Express,* March 8, 1926; *Yonkers Herald,* March 9, 1926. It later was claimed that the parties signed a contract on March 13, 1926.

"All that remains to bind the deal, they said, is the posting of guarantees and they promised that before nightfall $550,000 in cash will have been deposited in Los Angeles banks." The promoter claimed that Dempsey and Wills already had received $100,000 for training expenses (which Dempsey later disputed). Floyd Fitzsimmons said the match was being backed by Chicago and South Bend capitalists, primarily the Chicago Coliseum Club. Wills had signed in New York.

When asked if there was any chance that he would fight Gene Tunney, Dempsey replied, "No, the Wills articles forbid me to meet anyone else until after Labor day. I am glad that the fight is definitely fixed up, and my money will be in the banks today, thus proving to the public my good faith and intentions to defend my title."

International News Service Staff Correspondent Copeland Burg reported that the money would be deposited in a Los Angeles bank within 24 hours. Dempsey was to be paid $300,000 before the fight, plus he was to receive one-third of the gross receipts. He expected to collect $1,000,000, for he and Fitzsimmons anticipated the receipts would exceed $3,000,000. Wills was to receive 10%.[361]

Harry Newman said a Dempsey-Wills contest likely would have a $3-million gate, which certainly would be enough of an incentive to get Dempsey to fight Wills and get Rickard to bankroll it in New Jersey. Furthermore, "The old roar about mixed matches has simmered down to a whisper." There were not any undue squawks when colored fighter Tiger Flowers beat Harry Greb for the middleweight crown a couple weeks ago. That paved the way to a potential Dempsey-Wills go.[362]

Some claimed that Dempsey did not really want to fight Wills, quoting him as allegedly saying, "If I were to be defeated by Harry Wills or any other negro I would be eternally censured." Men like Burns and Jeffries had suffered such censure for losing to Jack Johnson.[363]

Harry Wills   Gene Tunney

Tex Rickard said, "Dempsey is more likely to meet Gene Tunney than Harry Wills. However, it is just as possible that he will not fight at all this year."[364]

Allegedly, Floyd Fitzsimmons posted $250,000 for Dempsey-Wills, furnished by the syndicate of Chicago and South Bend capitalists. Dempsey allegedly posted $250,000 as his guarantee as well, utilizing his Barbara Hotel as security with a bonding company.[365]

R. A. Cronin said, "Mr. Dempsey has said so often that he will fight Mr. Wills and has as often reneged or made subsequent denial that the Angelenos will not take him seriously until he actually steps into the prize ring."

[361] *Brooklyn Daily Times, Binghamton Press, Brooklyn Citizen, Olean Evening Times, Hollywood Daily Citizen*, March 12, 1926; *Los Angeles Illustrated Daily News*, March 13, 1926.
[362] *New York Daily News*, March 12, 1926.
[363] *New York Daily News*, March 13, 1926.
[364] *Olean Evening Times*, March 13, 1926.
[365] *Brooklyn Daily Times, Los Angeles Illustrated Daily News*, March 14, 1926.

Dempsey had agreed to train in Hendersonville, North Carolina for the Wills fight. However, the town's local churches and the Knights of the Ku Klux Klan were against his training there for a mixed-race contest. They did not approve of supporting in any way whatsoever a mixed-race contest. If he was going to fight a colored man, he was not wanted.[366]

Tex Rickard revealed why he would not and had not made the Dempsey-Wills fight. He said he feared the national race rioting of the kind that followed Johnson-Jeffries, which had not been good for the sport. Rickard was concerned that the rioting would approach near civil war; a certain result of the match. "The worst thing that could happen to the colored people of America would be to arrange a fight between Harry Wills and Jack Dempsey." He said his bitter experience in ignoring the color line had led him to the belief. True, he had promoted mixed-race bouts for Dixon, Johnson, and Flowers, and most had no incidents, but the heavyweight championship of the world was a different matter. The symbolism was much greater. He noted that 12 colored men died as a result of one of the mixed-race fights, and 7 after another. Still, Rickard had arranged a return match between Greb and Flowers.[367]

Paul Gallico said Rickard was being silly:

> Of course, Tex is a southerner, which may have something to do with it. I think that in the mind of a southerner the race riot is always a good deal more imminent, possibly, than in others who have lived in the north. These are no longer the days of Jeffries and Johnson. A Wills victory over Dempsey would cause a good deal of red fire to be burned in Harlem and nothing more.
>
> The colored man of today, I believe, is not the colored man of twenty, even ten years ago. He is less concerned with triumphs over the white man than he is with achieving a success that will redound to the credit of his own race. ...
>
> Much of the bitterness that gives Tex Rickard his viewpoint was caused by ignorant white numskulls in the days when they were mouthing frantic appeals for a white hope to bring the heavyweight championship back to the white race. I hope that our viewpoint has changed sufficiently that such tactless, insulting jingoism could never again occur. ...
>
> The well-earned victory of Tiger Flowers over Harry Greb caused no white men to be pushed off the sidewalk...and if politicians had any brains or any vision beyond their own interests they might take that as a significant sign. Flowers is the first colored man ever to hold the middleweight championship. Still, the legend persists that only the heavyweight championship will cause the Harlemite to become overexuberant. From flyweight to light heavyweight, the

[366] *Los Angeles Illustrated Daily News, Asheville Citizen*, March 15, 1926.
[367] *New York Daily News*, March 16, 1926.

dark-skinned fighters may be permitted to triumph without danger to the peace and quiet of the Lenox ave. asphalt. But let a colored heavyweight champion be crowned and pandemonium will reign. What utter rot![368]

On March 25, 1926, in Fresno, California, Jack Dempsey and his chauffeur Robert Gates were arrested for speeding and reckless driving at 68 miles per hour. Gates was driving the car.[369]

Paddy Mullins said he had heard nothing but talk, and the Wills-Dempsey fight seemed to be a phantom contest.

Rickard and Billy Gibson wanted to know if Dempsey was willing to fight Tunney, or else they would make other plans. Rickard said, "I can't understand this fellow Dempsey at all. One day he wants to fight and the next day he doesn't." Gibson said if Dempsey did not want to fight, they once again would try to arrange a fight between Tunney and Wills.[370]

Rickard signed the "comely ex-marine" Tunney to a one-year contract which gave Tex the power to select any opponent for him.

Dempsey was reported to have told newspapermen, "I have no intention of fighting Tunney until after I meet Wills. I have signed with Floyd Fitzsimmons to meet Wills on Labor Day in Chicago or Michigan City. I'm not dealing with Rickard, and I don't care to."

Rickard again confirmed that he would have nothing to do with a Dempsey-Wills contest, a fight which he believed could not happen.

> I don't want the fight. Never did want it. It will never be staged in Chicago for many reasons, the principal one being that legalized boxing out there hasn't advanced beyond the probationary stage. A Dempsey-Wills fight would kill the game in the Windy City and the gentlemen who worked so hard to legalize it aren't going to see their good work undone by anything so risky as a Dempsey-Wills fight.[371]

Jim Farley, current chairman of the New York commission, threatened to declare the championship vacant if Dempsey did not soon sign to fight someone, and they would recognize a fight between Tunney and Wills as a championship fight. However, he also said Wills was recognized as the ranking challenger, and the commission would not recognize a Dempsey-Tunney contest in New York. Hence, it really was an edict for Dempsey to fight Wills and no one else, or else.[372]

According to Jack Curley, Dempsey said he was willing to fight anywhere in the U.S. except New York. He feared a bad decision there. He noted that many bad decisions had been rendered there, yet the referees and judges who made them remained employed as such, which was a bad sign.[373]

[368] *New York Daily News*, March 19, 1926.
[369] *Los Angeles Times*, March 26, 27, 1926.
[370] *New York Daily News*, March 26, 28, 1926.
[371] *New York Daily News*, March 30, 1926.
[372] *New York Daily News*, March 31, 1926.
[373] *New York Daily News*, April 1, 1926. Dempsey likely also was concerned that Kearns might have a better legal argument in New York.

Dempsey clearly also had been irritated by the treatment he had received by the New York commission, which acted as if he was responsible for making the Wills fight happen, when the reality was much more complex, and not entirely within his control.

When asked whether Dempsey was afraid of Wills, Tex Rickard said, "Dempsey is afraid of nobody. He wanted to sign to fight Wills or any man I named right in my office last year, but when I heard of his trouble with Jack Kearns I wouldn't let him. Jack would do the same thing right now – if I asked him to." Rickard was planning a trip out west for a conference with Dempsey concerning a contest with Tunney.[374]

The *Brooklyn Daily Times* said a reliable source informed it that Dempsey would fight Tunney in August or September. The champion would meet Rickard in the West late in the month to sign an agreement, but terms allegedly had been accepted.[375]

Westbrook Pegler said politics were keeping the champion and Wills from fighting. Many believed that Dempsey was afraid of Wills. However, Pegler said he had discussed the matter with Rickard, Dempsey, Kearns, and Mullins at least 500 times in the last 6 years, and,

> [T]here never was a time in which Dempsey would have been allowed to fight Harry Wills in New York. As to New Jersey…this correspondent has no positive information, but there is rather persuasive evidence that New Jersey would not have permitted Tex Rickard to dump a fight there which had been barred on grounds of public policy or political expediency in New York. …

> [T]here never was a time when Tex Rickard, the only promoter in the country who could handle the production; wanted the match. For one reason, Rickard is the agent of a large corporation which makes great profits from the prize fight business and which therefore shuns any bout that would endanger the business. This is one of the few instances in which any one connected with the prize fight business looked out for the welfare of the business, which enjoys precarious health at best. …

> There is much debate as to whether a Dempsey-Wills fight, involving a white man and a negro, would endanger the peace of the city or the nation, or the prestige of the New York Democratic party, which is wooing the Southern Democracy. As to whether this danger is real or imaginary, you may draw your own conclusions again. But certainly the governing powers in New York have such fears.

A few years ago, Muldoon ordered Dempsey to fight Wills, apparently thinking that Dempsey would sidestep. But Dempsey called his bluff and agreed to the fight. "And then Muldoon turned about and, with the same gruff authority, forbade Dempsey to fight Wills." Subsequently, the

[374] *New York Daily News*, April 2, 5, 1926.
[375] *Brooklyn Daily Times*, April 9, 1926.

commission changed its mind again. "But, it is reasonable to suspect the commission is only bluffing again and is making Dempsey the goat."

The *Daily News* said the chances for Dempsey-Wills taking place were becoming more remote. Rickard did not want it. He wanted to promote Tunney-Dempsey.

Davis Walsh said regardless of all the edicts, decrees, and proclamations by the New York State Athletic Commission, there would be no Dempsey-Wills fight in New York state. There was no way that New York Governor Al Smith would allow it. Furthermore, no other state appeared to be willing to allow it either, for politics made the bout too hot for anyone to handle.

> The fight was never 'on' here and now it is absolutely off, probably for good.

> The political cat has jumped in Albany and from now until the presidential campaign of 1928 the Dempsey-Wills proposition is taboo. By that time, it will have died of malnutrition, anyhow.

> This is the reason Tex Rickard is proceeding serenely with plans to stage a meeting between Dempsey and Gene Tunney. He knows that if the commission ever went so far as to get out of its depth with the Wills-Dempsey issue, something would be allowed to happen that would postpone the business indefinitely, the first ninety-nine years being by far the hardest.

> The plot runs something like this: Governor Al Smith is one of the leading candidates for the Democratic nomination in 1928. He might even be considered a hot favorite for the honor if it wasn't for the fact that he has been unable to 'sell' his candidacy to the Southern States. Without this support, he can go no further than he did in 1924 and the fact that he realizes this was proved.

> Would the governor further his Southern interests by placing a white champion in a position where he may be beaten by a colored man under the Governor's patronage? ...

> As a matter of fact, the match is a load of dynamite, which no one wishes to carry around.

Chicago had been mentioned as a possible site, yet the local authorities knew fully well that Chicago had been the scene of race riots, and Rickard noted that riots had started in Chicago when the Johnson-Jeffries pictures had been shown there. Chicago was not likely to allow Wills-Dempsey.

Los Angeles also talked of the fight, but a few days later, the State Athletic Commission crushed the idea, though not explicitly referencing race, but the distaste for the enormous amount of money to be paid to the principals.

Philadelphia promoters discussed bringing the bout there, but the "city administration threw the proposition out the window on the car tracks, where it died in its own blood." The politicians did not want it.

Towns like Boston, Cleveland, and Detroit never showed any interest in the fight. In towns like St. Louis and Michigan City, the race issue would be a concern as well.

Walsh concluded that the country had been "pretty well canvassed. The thing is just a fistic waif without a home, parent or guardian. It is over such an implausible project that the New York Commission threatens to read Dempsey out of his title and may even go so far as to do it."[376]

Regardless of any obstacles, James Farley, chairman of the New York state athletic commission, said a Dempsey-Tunney bout would not be approved there, for Wills was the logical contender.[377]

On April 13, 1926, Chicago, Illinois voters passed the local boxing bill, allowing 10-round decision bouts in that city. Illinois legalized boxing in early July 1925, making it the 23rd state to legalize boxing out of 48 states (only 48%), but allowed each city to pass local referendums on the issue. The governor still needed to appoint a commission.[378]

The real question was whether, given boxing's always tenuous legal existence, the politicians and athletic commission, once organized, would risk hosting a mixed-race world heavyweight championship contest.

The Chicago Coliseum Club purportedly was supposed to post a guarantee for the Dempsey-Wills fight by April 15, but failed to do so. President B. E. Clements denied that any payment was due. Some claimed that Fitzsimmons had merged his contractual interests with Clements.[379]

According to Dempsey, neither Fitzsimmons nor the Chicago Coliseum Club ever had posted or gave him any cash to bind the Wills agreement. He clearly believed they were supposed to post money but had not done so. Nor had he heard about a definite location either.

Dempsey said he intended to defend his title in September, no matter what.

> Promoters have bobbed here and there who made a lot of talk about staging a fight for big money, but when it came to putting up the guarantee, none of them was able to deliver. I'm frank to state that I am disgusted with the situation. The first real fight that comes along, I don't care who it is with, I'll take it. I have been running around the country, seeing first one promoter and then another, without having any luck. ...
>
> Tex Rickard, I understand, is on his way to see me. ... I expect him to make me an offer for a Tunney fight, as I know that he is not interested in a Wills match. If he does so, I will probably sign. ... It makes no difference to me whether I fight Wills or Tunney first, so long as I get a fight.[380]

---

[376] *Chicago Tribune, Bayonne Evening News,* April 3, 1926; *Washington Post,* April 11, 1926. *New York Daily News,* April 11, 1926. Hence, unless or until assured that an approved location for Dempsey-Wills had been secured, investors did not want to provide funds that likely would be forfeited. Floyd Fitzsimmons had encountered these obstacles.
[377] *New York Daily News,* April 13, 1926.
[378] *Chicago Tribune,* April 14, 15, 1926; *San Bernardino County Sun, Rochester Democrat and Chronicle,* July 5, 1925.
[379] *Chicago Tribune,* April 14, 15, 1926.
[380] *El Paso Herald,* April 17, 1926.

CHAPTER 5

A New Plan and Its Obstacles

On April 18, 1926 in Juarez, Mexico, before a crowd of 7,000, at the opening of the new coliseum, wearing 10-ounce gloves, Dempsey exhibited against and knocked out Barney Farrow in the 1st round, mussed up and buckled Farmer Lodge with a left hook and uppercut in their 4 shortened rounds, knocked Ray Stevens down so many times in their 3 shortened rounds it was as if he was on roller skates, causing his seconds to retire him, and slammed Marty Cutler through the ropes into the laps of the customers in their 1st round. He gave all of them considerable punishment.[381]

Word was that Tex Rickard was headed to Texas to sign Dempsey to a contract to fight Tunney, and that Dempsey had agreed.[382]

Gene Tunney had support from the New York press because he was a fine, upstanding, veteran marine, a very good, experienced fighter, handsome, and from Greenwich Village, New York.

Nevertheless, Paul Gallico said, "[I]t's a shame that Harry Wills, a square, clean-living colored man, can't get a square deal and he ought to be given the fight with Dempsey, and it's an outrage upon the fair name of boxing."[383]

Billy Gibson and Tunney

Tex Rickard was not concerned by the New York commission's threat that no fight would be allowed other than Dempsey-Wills, or James Farley's threat that Rickard would lose his license if he promoted a different Dempsey fight, such as Dempsey-Tunney. "Gene Tunney is the logical opponent for Dempsey." Tex said Tunney was better than Wills. Dempsey, who wanted to fight Wills, agreed that Tunney was a more dangerous opponent. "Dempsey has shown a preference to fight Wills rather than Tunney in past dealings. Last year Wills refused $150,000 for a bout with Dempsey. Now I believe Tunney should be given a chance." Rickard said if necessary, Dempsey-Tunney could be held in New Jersey or elsewhere.[384]

B. E. Clements of the Chicago Coliseum Club asserted that he had Dempsey and Wills signed for a bout in Chicago for the late summer.

[381] *El Paso Herald, Los Angeles Times*, April 19, 1926.
[382] *Chicago Tribune*, April 19, 1926.
[383] *New York Daily News*, April 19, 1926.
[384] *New York Daily News, El Paso Herald*, April 21, 1926. Gene Normile allegedly said he was Dempsey's acting manager. *Chicago Tribune*, April 20, 1926. Normile later disputed this statement. *Memphis Commercial Appeal*, April 24, 1926.

There were plenty of witnesses when Jack Dempsey and Tex Rickard put their names on the dotted line shortly before noon Wednesday in The Star-Telegram building, to a contract that calls for a world's heavyweight championship fight next September. Seated is Jack Dempsey, on the left, and Tex Rickard, on the right. Standing, left to right, are Amon G. Carter, Capt. Tom Hickman of the Texas Rangers, Postmaster W. N. Moore, Dr. Webb Walker, Sheriff Carl Smith and Gene Normyjle.

On April 21, 1926 in Fort Worth, Texas, Jack Dempsey signed on the dotted line with Tex Rickard to fight in mid-September against any opponent Rickard selected. Rickard said the agreement did not name the opponent, but "Gene Tunney seems to me at the present time to be the best man for Dempsey to meet. In my estimation he is not only the best fighter among the challengers, but is the type of man who would make the most attractive match from other standpoints." Rickard further said, "[Tunney] is simply a better fighter than Wills." Tex said Wills was too old and would not last more than 3 rounds. He believed that at present, George Godfrey was better than Wills. Tunney would give Dempsey a real fight. Tex said Dempsey was afraid of no one. He had wanted to fight for a long time, but a force of intricate circumstances kept him idle.

Rickard admitted that a Dempsey-Wills match would be the greatest attraction pugilism ever had known. However, he said such a fight never could be held on account of politics, race feeling, and thousands of reformers. Jeffries vs. Johnson had caused him no end of trouble. "Never again." Rickard blamed that fight for the anti-boxing legislation throughout the country. "That fight was the reason why Texas today can not see moving pictures of boxing exhibitions. Legislation was secured shortly afterward which made the transportation of fight films from one state to another against the law."

Tex said Dempsey and Jim Jeffries, in their primes, were the greatest champions of all time. However, Dempsey was due to lose to a man like Tunney. He had lived far too easily for too long to retain the championship. "There is no question but what he has gone back."

Some reported that Dempsey would earn a guaranteed $450,000, with an option of taking a percentage of the gate, though exact details were not revealed. Tex said the division would be on a percentage basis. Others said Dempsey would receive 37 ½% of the gate.

Rickard noted that the contract did not say who Dempsey would fight or where, so no edict of the New York Commission had been violated. Besides, Tex noted that Jim Farley was only one of three commissioners.

Some said Rickard's actions likely would start an internal war within the New York State Athletic Commission.

The *Fort Worth Record-Telegram* noted, "The contract which Dempsey signed with Harry Wills, the negro fighter, last Fall, became void last Thursday when the promoters failed to bind the agreement with the prescribed amount of money." Once that happened, Dempsey finally decided to go with Rickard.

Dempsey said he was tired of wandering around the country talking with promoters who conversed volubly but lacked money. Clearly, at that point, Dempsey believed that Rickard was the only promoter who truly could make things happen and pay him well, without illusory promises, and bring off a big fight. Others made offers and claims, but Tex had the proven track record of always coming through with the coin and paying in full. Dempsey's two biggest money-making fights to that point, against Carpentier and Firpo, both had been successful Tex Rickard promotions.

Dempsey said, "I am ready to fight any man – Tunney or Wills. It makes not a particle of difference to me which one Tex picks. I think I can beat either of them."

Fistiana was satisfied that Dempsey really would defend his title in September 1926, for the public had confidence in Rickard. "He does not play around. There is a gilt-edge character about everything he takes part in."

Andy Weisberg, South Bend, Indiana hotel operator and head of a South Bend syndicate, declared that Dempsey's agreement with that syndicate to meet Wills in September was binding. Judge G. A. Farabaugh, the syndicate's legal adviser, would call Dempsey's attention to clauses in an iron-clad contract signed at Hendersonville, North Carolina.

However, Floyd Fitzsimmons declared that the syndicate had failed to meet certain financial requirements. "They failed to meet terms of their contract with me and for that reason I was unable to carry through my understanding with Dempsey. Consequently I couldn't stand in the way of Dempsey taking on another match at this time."[385]

81-year-old William Muldoon, one of the New York commissioners, fully supported Rickard's plan for a Dempsey-Tunney fight. Muldoon was "decidedly opposed" to a Wills bout and said a Tunney contest would be "far more interesting."[386]

Paul Gallico noted that George L. "Tex" Rickard appeared to be approaching a showdown with the commission, which had decreed that no promoter was to do business with Dempsey until the champ had agreed to fight Wills. Noted was the fact that once before, the commission had done the same thing – ordered Dempsey to fight Wills,

[385] *Fort Worth Record-Telegram, Fort Worth Star-Telegram, Chicago Daily Tribune,* April 20-22, 1926; *Los Angeles Times,* April 22, 1926; *Memphis Commercial Appeal,* April 24, 1926.
[386] *Los Angeles Times,* April 23, 1926.

and then that same commission, when Dempsey agreed, "forbade him to meet the colored man." So, no one knew exactly what direction they would go in at any moment.

Allegedly, Farley had support from George Brower, the other member of the three-member commission, and they were dead-set on a Wills contest. However, others said such might not be the case, that Brower had revised his opinion, feeling that it was not for the commission to mandate whom a fighter fought.

Muldoon noted that Dempsey and Wills had agreed to fight in Indiana or elsewhere, yet the financial backing did not appear to be there.

Harry Newman believed, "Muldoon probably never will agree to a fight between the colored fighter and Dempsey," and hence, likely there would be some lively debate amongst the commissioners.[387]

The *Los Angeles Times* reported that Tunney was the opponent, for Rickard did not want Wills.

Dempsey said, "I have signed to meet anybody in the world that Tex Rickard can find to fight me."[388]

Harry Newman also called out the New York commission on its hypocrisy. Despite allegedly pushing for a Dempsey-Wills fight at various times, it all was bluff and bluster, and the commission never really was in favor of such a fight. After Dempsey signed to fight Wills back in 1923, then-chairman Muldoon barred the scrap. Such was announced in a *Daily News* headline back on February 3, 1923, which was reproduced for readers.

Paul Gallico said Wills had been sidetracked again and would wind up like Peter Jackson, never getting a title fight. "White folks have once more displayed that genius for making inordinate fatheads of themselves." He said everyone knew Muldoon would not stand for a Dempsey-Wills fight. It never was denied. Most expected him to wait to announce it publicly until they were matched.

> Imagine if you will how that great body governs boxing functions. Papa Muldoon sits back and lets young Farley mouth fine phrases about giving Wills a square deal and recognizing him as foremost challenger, knowing that when the time came he would wreck the whole shooting match and Brower would help him. This is nice clean sportsmanship for you. Hooray for the grand old man. Well, there you have it anyhow. Muldoon with the one track mind bars Harry Wills, and George Brower in his statements indicates that he is going to string along with William.

Gallico said Muldoon was a menace to boxing. Governor Smith made a bad botch of it when he re-appointed him. Gallico called the commission "silly" and "utterly incompetent to deal with anything where breadth of vision or mature judgment was needed."

[387] *New York Daily News*, April 22, 23, 1926.
[388] *Los Angeles Times*, April 23, 24, 1926.

Of course there have been no official announcements or edicts or public bulls from the high commission as yet, but one hardly needs them. The farce is complete. A colored man cannot meet a white man for the heavyweight championship of boxing…in the land of the free and the home of the brave. …

And now, of course, you realize why Rickard could go ahead and dicker with Dempsey to fight Tunney in the face of Farley's warning. He knew all the time that Muldoon was waiting and ready with his trusty knife.

Gallico said it was unfair, unjust, petty, and narrow-minded, but so long as men of the caliber of Muldoon were in charge of boxing, Dempsey and Wills never would meet.[389]

Dempsey was in Hendersonville, North Carolina, starting to train and exhibit there daily on April 26 for a September fight. He said he would fight anyone in the world but preferred to get into a ring with Wills. Of course, he knew the odds of that were low, given that he just signed with Rickard, who previously had said he did not want to promote a Dempsey-Wills contest. With Dempsey were sparring partners Marty Farrell, Tillie Kid Herman, and Farmer Lodge.[390]

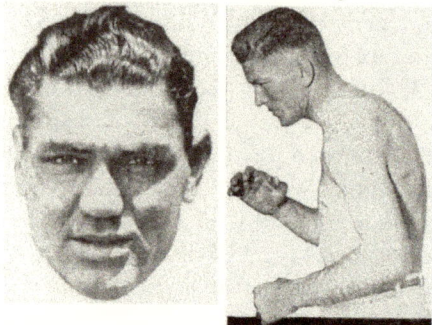

Rickard publicly said he did not know whether the opponent would be Wills or Tunney. "I don't know who it will be, but I'll tell you right now Dempsey would rather fight Wills than Tunney. He figures the negro will be an easier opponent." Tex said any talk of Dempsey being afraid of Wills was bunk. Rickard had both Tunney and Dempsey under contract to fight whomever he named, so newsmen believed they likely were going to fight one another.

Rickard said he had tried to make a Tunney-Wills bout several months ago, but Paddy Mullins, Wills' manager, declined a $150,000 offer.[391]

Dempsey said he would be in Hendersonville for 30 days or more. He would "much prefer Wills" as his opponent, because he thought Harry would draw a much larger gate, which would earn him more money.[392]

At that time, Gene Tunney was in California to make a motion picture.

Jim Farley could not see why there was any opposition to a Dempsey-Wills fight. He bitterly denounced the suggestion that the anti-boxing reformers would get up in arms the moment the fight was made. "I have been all over the state and have yet to hear any opposition to a fight between the white man and the colored challenger. In all my time as

[389] New York Daily News, April 24, 25, 1926.
[390] Los Angeles Times, April 26, 1926; Asheville Citizen, April 23-26, 1926.
[391] Asheville Citizen, April 28, 30, 1926; New York Daily News, April 28, 1926.
[392] New York Daily News, April 29, 1926.

chairman of the board I haven't received a single letter from any direction against the champion meeting Wills."

Regardless of Farley's prior threats, the full commission ruled that Dempsey was eligible to fight in New York, and it granted Rickard a promoter's license. Farley had thought Dempsey was ineligible as a result of his failure to sign articles of agreement for a Wills match, but George Brower and William Muldoon overruled him, stating that Dempsey's action of July 17, 1925 in coming before the board and verbally agreeing to meet Wills had lifted any bars against him.[393]

Harry Wills said, "I'll fight any one, if they will let me fight."[394]

Dempsey's Hendersonville sparring partners also included 185-pound Mike Arnold, middleweight Johnny Klesch, 182-pound Pete Angelos, lightweight Frankie Garcia, 147-pound Johnnie O'Neill, and 133-pound lightweight Solley Smith. Eventually, wrestler Jim Londos arrived, as well as the highly touted light heavyweight Young Stribling (141-8-16).[395]

In Hendersonville, Dempsey spars Farmer Lodge and wrestles Jim Londos

Robert Edgren said the public knew that Gene Tunney was entitled to a chance at the champ's crown. Wills was ferocious only against weak opponents and old-timers whom he knew he could defeat. "Tex Rickard has offered Wills $150,000 to fight Tunney. Tex says Wills' manager laughed at him." Tunney would be able to give Dempsey a good battle if he survived the first few rounds.

> Just why Harry Wills should be any commission's pet is a puzzle unless it's a matter of politics. If any ordinary white heavyweight made a business of challenging for a championship fight, and showed no more activity than Wills has, no boxing commission anywhere would pay any attention to him.
>
> Since 1923, when he boxed a couple of inconsequential heavies, Homer Smith and Jack Thompson, Wills has shown absolutely nothing that would entitle him to consideration as a challenger. He has dodged challenges from Renault, Tunney and Godfrey, who might be dangerous, and he has fought set-ups that the New York Boxing Commission certainly would not allow in a ring with Jack Dempsey.

---

[393] *Asheville Citizen*, May 1, 1926.
[394] *New York Daily News*, May 1, 1926.
[395] *Asheville Citizen*, May 6, 11, 17, 1926.

Wills boxed 15 slow rounds with little Bartley Madden in 1924, showing no aggressiveness or fighting ability at all. Madden forced the fighting nearly all the way – what fighting there was. Madden received a cut over the left eye in the eleventh round, but never was in the slightest danger of a knockout. Tunney showed Wills up by knocking Madden out afterward.

Edgren said Firpo was fat and out of shape, lacking his old spirit, and yet Wills was very careful throughout, only scoring a knockdown by hitting on the break. "It was a slow, clumsy, floundering fight on both sides." Old Charlie Weinert had no punch at all, and Wills held around his neck and hit with his right to finish him. Wills only showed great aggressiveness with a "human punching bag that can't punch back." Floyd Johnson was another safe foe, a "total wreck" after taking many beatings, and could not take a punch.

Edgren concluded, "Wills shows nothing at all that would justify putting him into the ring with a real fighter. The fight following public knows that a Dempsey-Wills fight would probably end in the first round, with Wills on the floor. Wills was a strong, fast, clever and dangerous fighter 10 years ago. He's still strong, and that's all."

Edgren said if Dempsey had slowed up as a result of his inactivity, there was a fair chance that Tunney might beat him, for he was a better boxer than Dempsey, more scientific, and could hit hard.

> Tunney improves as a fight goes along. … He is more of the old type of ringster. He boxes, gives and weathers blows, and takes his opening when it comes. … He never looks around for easy marks, like Wills. He takes matches as they're offered, preferring to take on the tough fellows. He keeps in firstclass condition at all times.
>
> If anyone has earned a chance with Dempsey it is Gene Tunney. Every follower of ring affairs knows it. The public knows it. And apparently the only people still in the dark about it are boxing commissioners.[396]

Knowing full well that Dempsey already had signed with Rickard, Tom O'Rourke offered $1 million for Dempsey to meet Wills. O'Rourke alleged he previously had offered Dempsey $800,000 to fight Wills, but his offer found no acceptance. O'Rourke declared that he would post $250,000 immediately, as soon as Dempsey signed articles, and that money would act as a forfeit. He also would guarantee Dempsey 50% of all gate receipts in excess of $2 million.

O'Rourke said, "Dempsey set his figure at $750,000 when I first asked him his terms for a match with Wills. He failed to give me a definite

[396] *Pittsburgh Post, Minneapolis Journal*, May 16, 1926.

answer on that and later when I raised it to $800,000 he again evaded me. Now I'm offering him the biggest purse ever proposed for a fight."[397]

On May 24, 1926, the U.S. Supreme Court decided *Corrigan v. Buckley*, 271 U.S. 323 (1926), holding that racially restrictive covenants, which barred the selling of a house to a black family, were legally binding agreements, and a sale in violation of the covenant was a void contract. Hence, racially restrictive covenants in land deeds were legally enforceable. Such covenants had fostered racial segregation in the North for many years, and would continue to do so. Hence, although many Northern states did not have de jure Jim Crow laws like the South, racial segregation was instituted by custom and by private contracts that were legally enforceable in the courts.

Young Stribling and family with Dempsey in Hendersonville

Dempsey ended his training and exhibiting in Hendersonville, North Carolina on the afternoon of May 25, 1926, giving an exhibition there. The month-long contract had ended.[398]

Harry Newman said a Dempsey-Tunney title bout in the fall seemed certain. Although Jim Farley wanted Wills, William Muldoon and George Brower would vote for Tunney.

A warrant was issued for Dempsey's arrest for failing to appear on his traffic charge in California. Dempsey said, "I wasn't even driving my car, and the chauffeur has been fined $50 for speeding."[399]

Johnny Klesch, who sparred with Dempsey in Hendersonville, said,

> There never was a man who could punch like Dempsey. ... Did he cut lose with me? No, he never tried to sock me on the jaw or chin, but he crashed me one on the shoulder last Saturday and knocked me clear out of the ring. Get that – the shoulder! ... Stribling visited the camp for a few days. I worked out a couple of rounds with him and it was like working out with a cream puff, as far as trying to compare him with Dempsey goes. Jack would take care of Stribling inside of two rounds.[400]

---

[397] *Asheville Citizen*, May 18, 1926. For whatever reason, neither Dempsey nor Kearns ever seemed to have any faith or real interest in any of O'Rourke's offers. O'Rourke primarily was known as a famous fight manager in the late 1800s and early 1900s, and later as an occasional promoter.
[398] *Asheville Citizen*, May 25, 1926.
[399] *New York Daily News*, May 26, 28, 1926.
[400] *Dayton Daily News*, May 25, 1926.

Dempsey was in Memphis on May 27, sparring five men in tame exhibitions: Canada's 190-pound Walter Ross for 2 rounds, with Ross going down in the 2nd seemingly without being hit; Louisiana's tall blonde 215-pound Mike Arnold for 2; "Pennsylvania Iron Man" Joe Kurp for 1; Knoxville's 190-pound Bill Clemons for 1; and pipe organist Albert Malotte for 1, Dempsey tottering him with a right and then catching him, and later hitting his nose and drawing some blood. Overall, Jack was careful not to hurt any of them.[401]

Joe Williams had observed Dempsey in Hendersonville. He noted that it had been nearly three years since the champion had an actual fight, and as a result, he had gone back. No athlete could be as inactive as he had been for so long and still be as good as he was when he was fighting regularly. "Were it necessary for Dempsey to step into the ring today against either Tunney or Wills I don't think he would be able to hold his title. He is not timing his punches as he used to and he is not getting around on his feet with his old-time certainty." Such things could bring about his defeat, for it was easier to counter-attack him now. Tunney had youth, superior stamina, and was a quick counterpuncher. Wills hit hard enough to drop him if he landed right. Regardless, Jack still had his punch. He had tremendous knockout force. "When he hits a man dynamite explodes."[402]

Dempsey said he never would need a benefit fund, for he never would be broke. He owned a Los Angeles hotel, the Barbara, valued at $600,000. He had other properties on the coast worth about $150,000. He lost money in some bad investments. Regardless, he had a trust fund of $200,000 that would pay him $1,000 a month for as long as he was alive. The champ said he would be able to write his first million-dollar check after the upcoming September fight, win or lose. He had a lot of expenses, though. He had $80,000 in expenses the prior year, including the deficit in his hotel operations. He also maintained separate homes for his father, mother, and some of his brothers.[403]

Joe Williams said Dempsey used pickle brine on his face to toughen up his skin. Jack said he had been brining his face for his entire career. He never had been cut by a blow, but always head butts. He had suffered cuts three times over his left eye from butts, underneath his eyebrow. The first time was back in his preliminary days. Jamaica Kid opened it at Toledo. Then Brennan. All were head butts.

Dempsey discussed his style. "I have never gone into the ring with the idea of winning on points. Always my uppermost thought and ambition was to win by a knockout and as speedily as possible. I like to win that way and I think the fans like to see you win that way." "It's a bad thing for a fighter to get the idea that he can win on points. This frequently makes a holder and a clincher of him, and nobody ever got anywhere by

---

[401] *Anniston Star*, May 27, 1926; *Memphis Commercial Appeal*, May 27, 28, 1926. Joe Kurp's real name was Kurapka.
[402] *Paducah News-Democrat*, May 28, 1926.
[403] *Wisconsin Rapids Daily Tribune*, May 28, 1926.

holding and clinching. I think every fighter ought to try to be a knockerout." Based on his record gate receipts, boxing fans agreed.[404]

While in Hot Springs, Arkansas on May 28, Dempsey grew ill, overcome with chills and a fever, so he did not exhibit there. He called off his exhibition bouts for the next few weeks and returned to Los Angeles.[405]

On May 31, 1926 in Juarez, Mexico, 48-year-old Jack Johnson, who was floored at the end of the 7th round, was unable to continue, and retired in the corner between rounds against Bob Lawson, a colored light heavy. Johnson's claim of foul was not recognized. It was his first loss since the Willard fight in 1915, 11 years prior. Johnson still had not been allowed to fight in the U.S. since his last fight there on July 4, 1912.[406]

In a surprise, on June 1, 1926, the New York commission announced that Jack Dempsey had to accept Harry Wills' challenge and enter into proper articles of agreement with him no later than June 22, 1926. Given that on July 17, 1925, Dempsey had accepted Wills' challenge, ample time had elapsed for the signing of formal articles of agreement with a definite date and location. Jim Farley, commission chair, and Colonel John Phelan, chairman of the license board, made the ruling.

Dempsey, having heard the edict, said, "I have already signed with Tex to defend my title on Sept. 16 against any opponent he selects. I don't care who I fight."[407]

Jim Farley said,

> I don't think that Dempsey wants to fight Wills anyhow. If Dempsey wants to fight Wills and thinks he would be so easy; why in thunder don't he get him out of the way? Why so much consideration for that fellow? He wants a handpicked opponent for which he expects to grab off something like a million dollars. You don't think he does the boxing game any good, do you? I am not in here holding a personal brief for Wills, but the commission is on record for a Dempsey and Wills fight and we are not interested in anything else, just now. I have nothing in the world against Gene Tunney, but you can go and bet plenty that if I have anything to say in the matter there never will be a Tunney and Dempsey fight here until Dempsey fights Wills first. This talk about a nation-wide opposition to a mixed match is all rot. If Harry Wills cannot fight Jack Dempsey in New York, the best thing to do is to wipe the Walker law right off the statute books. You cannot discriminate in the matter. Makes me tired when I have to listen to the silly prattle about race riots and what not if Dempsey and Wills were matched.[408]

[404] *Lancaster New Era*, May 28, 1926.
[405] *Nashville Tennessean*, May 29, 1926; *Cincinnati Enquirer*, May 30, 1926.
[406] *New York Daily News, Allentown Morning Call*, June 1, 1926.
[407] *New York Daily News*, June 2, 1926.
[408] *New York Daily News*, June 5, 1926.

On June 8, O. W. Huncke, chairman of the Illinois boxing commission, which recently had been organized and started meetings, said Illinois would join the national boxing association, and no bouts would be authorized in the state that month. This spiked rumors that the local body contemplated affiliation with the New York boxing commission, the only body of its kind in the country not a member of the national association.[409]

On June 14, 1926, in Chowchilla, Madera County, California, near Fresno, a jury of three women and nine men, six being farmers, found Jack Dempsey not guilty of speeding at 68 miles per hour. Dempsey testified that he was talking to his wife and did not know at what speed his car was going when his chauffeur Robert Gates was stopped by a motorcycle patrolman. The officer, the only prosecution witness, stated that "because they were courteous to me, I wrote the ticket for two miles less than they were going. Their actual speed was seventy miles an hour."[410]

Jim Farley said he would not change his position on the Dempsey-Wills matter. "The issue before us is not one of pugilism, but one of patriotism. I have planked myself firmly on the broad platform of fair play – equal opportunity for all." He said he would give everyone equal protection of law. Everyone should have an even chance, and the door of opportunity open to all.

> Merit has been the sole test. It is our country's proud boast that the chance to show one's worth shall be denied to no man. ... The great American, Theodore Roosevelt, with characteristic patriotism, received Booker T. Washington at the White House. Merit, regardless of race or color, was a passport to the nation's capital. I am confident it will earn no less recognition in the nation's greatest state – New York. We shall turn from petty politics in pugilism to the proud practice of pure patriotism and justify our American standards by truly American conduct.[411]

On June 17, 1926 in Philadelphia, before 25,000 to 30,000 fans at the Sesqui Stadium, 173 ½-pound Tommy Loughran (62-15-7) won a 10-round decision over 174 ½-pound Georges Carpentier (87-15-6). Loughran scored a knockdown in the 7th with an overhand right smash. Georges rose at 9 and had the generalship to last.[412]

On June 22, Tex Rickard filed an application with the New York boxing commission for permission to stage a fight between Jack Dempsey and Gene Tunney at Yankee Stadium on September 16. However, in a 2-1 vote, Rickard was turned down, when James Farley and George Brower voted no, while William Muldoon voted yes. Furthermore, they said Dempsey was on the ineligible list to fight, given the rule that said

[409] *Belvidere Daily Republican*, June 8, 1926. The Illinois commission was composed of Chairman O.W. Huncke, John Righeimer, and Paul Prehn. *Chicago Tribune*, June 19, 1926.
[410] *New York Daily News, Los Angeles Times*, June 15, 1926.
[411] *New York Daily News*, June 16, 1926.
[412] *Philadelphia Inquirer*, June 18, 1926.

champions had to defend their titles every six months. How then was he supposed to defend his title?

Rickard told the commission that he did not go after Tunney until Paddy Mullins, Wills' manager, turned down an offer to fight the champ for more money than he ever earned before. Tex further told the commission that he stood ready to post $50,000 to guarantee a match between Wills and the winner of the Tunney-Dempsey fight. He said under no circumstances would he desert Tunney. If he could not hold the fight in New York, he would take it somewhere else.

Paul Gallico predicted that Dempsey and Tunney would go the distance without a knockdown the entire way. Dempsey was a shopworn champ who had not been in the ring for a very long time, facing a young man of reasonable ability whose specialty was beating has-beens, but he was a good defensive fighter and boxer. "There is not much reason to believe that Dempsey will knock him out. Nor is there much more reason to think Tunney will knockout the champion."[413]

In early July, 205-pound Dempsey, along with trainer Jerry Luvadis, moved to Colorado Springs, Colorado, at an elevation of 9,000 feet, at the summit of Cheyenne Mountain, to engage in conditioning work.[414]

Tex Rickard said Chicago was bidding for the Dempsey-Tunney fight. There was uncertainty regarding where it would land.

On July 10, 1926, Dempsey telegrammed B. E. Clements (also called B. C. or William Clements) of the Chicago Coliseum Club to say that Clements had no contract and to stop kidding himself, essentially repudiating any agreement. Jack refused to be examined for insurance purposes as requested and allegedly required pursuant to their contract, saying he was too busy training for Tunney.

There had been a prior agreement for Dempsey to meet Wills, but allegedly the contract was deemed void because the champion had not been paid the $100,000 the agreement purportedly required.

Clements consistently disputed that there was any such requirement for an advance posting of money. He claimed to have contracts with Dempsey's and Wills' signatures, and was planning to put on the Dempsey-Wills fight during the first two weeks of September at Soldier's Field in Chicago.

Had there been a new contract, and did it require a substantial advance payment? If not, why not? It would be odd for Dempsey to sign a contract that did not require an up-front posting of a guarantee, as was the case with the Fitzsimmons contract. The entire reason Dempsey and his lawyer repudiated the Fitz contract was because of his inability to post the required payments. So why then would he sign a new contract that did not require the same, if he did? Furthermore, when the new agreement was first announced, the newspapers reported that large sums would be

[413] *New York Daily News*, June 23, 1926.
[414] *Grand Junction Daily Sentinel*, July 2, 1926, *Los Angeles Times*, July 7, 1926.

posted. Dempsey consistently claimed that a substantial guarantee was required to bind the contract and it had not been paid or deposited.

In late July, Gene Tunney started training at Madame Bey's training camp at Summit, New Jersey.

Members of the Illinois boxing commission declared that they had not approved either a Dempsey-Tunney or a Dempsey-Wills bout and "knew nothing about either." Clements of the Chicago Coliseum Club had been granted a license, but he had not discussed a Dempsey-Wills bout with them. The commission declined to state its views on whether either bout would be sanctioned.

Gene Normile, purported to be Dempsey's de facto acting manager, said Jack had signed with Clements on March 13, but,

> The local promoter failed to live up to the terms of his contract calling for delivery to the champion of $100,000 on March 25. On March 29, $35,000 was offered to the champion, Normile said, but this Dempsey refused to take and thereby believes he nullified the contract.

Normile said Dempsey had not received any money from Clements, and the only promoter to give him any money in the past year was Rickard.[415]

On July 23, 1926, B. E. Clements of the Chicago Coliseum Club announced that Dempsey and Wills would fight in Chicago between September 16 and 20, likely at Soldiers' Field. Clements had a contract that was drawn up on March 3 at the Morrison hotel in Chicago and allegedly signed by Dempsey and Clements in the Barbara hotel in Los Angeles on March 13, with their lawyers present – Harry Harper representing Dempsey and Ralph Rosen representing Clements.

Tex Rickard, who had seen a copy of the contract, claimed that the contract's terms were violated by the club's failure to post $100,000 in March. However, "This contract, or a copy of it shown by Clements, does not call for the payment of any moneys to Dempsey until August of this year." Were there different versions? Clements said he was ready to turn over to Dempsey the required sum on the required date in August.

According to the *Chicago Daily News*, Clements released excerpts of the contract, yet, oddly enough, would not release a copy of the contract for publication in its entirety. One has to wonder why he would refuse to release the entire contract. What were the additional terms? Was it the contract that Dempsey signed? Did it contain his signature?

Regardless, in one of its terms, Dempsey pledged not to fight anyone until he boxed Wills (paragraph 15, page 4).

Furthermore, the contract held nullified any other contracts that the champion may have had, notably the one with Floyd Fitzsimmons. In addition, Fitzsimmons sold and assigned to the club all of the contracts Fitzsimmons held, including all of the contracts with

[415] *New York Daily News, Chicago Tribune,* July 20, 21, 1926; *Minneapolis Star, St. Louis Post-Dispatch, Grand Junction Daily Sentinel,* July 21, 1926.

Wills/Mullins/Dempsey from September 29, 1925 at Niles, Michigan, and one with Dempsey in October 1925 signed in Huntington, West Virginia.

The contract called for an advance payment of only $10. Why would Dempsey agree to such a small advance payment/forfeit, if he did? Nevertheless, $800,000 total was to be paid to Dempsey, with $300,000 to be paid on August 5, and the remaining $500,000 before the fight.

The *Chicago Daily News* reported that the contract also had a clause (paragraph 7, page 2) that said if because of a contingency beyond the control of the promoter the fight did not take place, then any advance payments would be returned by Dempsey to the promoter. Why would Dempsey agree to such a term, if he did, given the uncertainty regarding whether the Wills bout would be authorized politically? Such made no sense. However, the Associated Press claimed that the contract called for the $300,000 to be forfeited to the champion if the fight did not occur.

Clements added that Rickard and his attorneys had seen a copy of the contract, which he claimed contained Dempsey's signature, and upon viewing it, Tex allegedly said, "Jack the penman."

Fitzsimmons claimed the Chicago Coliseum Club promised to pay him and Dempsey $150,000 for the assignment of his contract, to be paid in installments of $100,000 and $50,000 each. Fitz claimed the payments were not made, and "produced a draft several days ago he had drawn on the Chicago Coliseum Athletic Club for $100,000 which was returned to him unpaid, to prove his claim that this voided the contract."

Articles of agreement had been signed on March 13, along with the assignment of the Fitz contract calling for those monetary payments.

> These [contracts] were to have been placed in escrow with a Chicago bank until payment of that sum was made. When the draft was sent through and payment was not met, Fitzsimmons said he turned the papers over to Dempsey, and the latter asserts he destroyed them.
>
> Clements claims the contracts are still in escrow here. Fitzsimmons asserts that if Clements has a copy of the originals he holds them illegally.[416]

Why would Dempsey destroy what possibly could be evidence of the real contract and its terms, which could prove a breach of said terms? However, if Clements did not have an original with Dempsey's signature, could he prove a contract, or its terms, with an alleged unsigned copy? Did he actually have a signed copy?

Dempsey was peeved by Clements' attempts to thwart him from fighting Tunney in Chicago. Jack said, "Why, I fooled around with those fellows for eight months without anything happening. Then Rickard came through and Fitzsimmons, like the gentleman he is, got out of the way – and now comes Clements trying to get some money out of it." Bottom line is Dempsey had been willing to fight Wills if Fitzsimmons had come

[416] *Chicago Daily News, St. Louis Daily Globe-Democrat,* July 23, 1926.

up with the financial backing, but he never did; failing to make required payments in a timely fashion when required, even after extensions were granted. So, he argued, any side agreement or assignment Clements had with Fitzsimmons was null and void, because the Fitz contract had been breached. Dempsey claimed he never signed a contract with Clements, and furthermore, never was paid, even if there was a valid assignment, and Clements never came up with a firm date or location for the fight.[417]

Clements claimed that the Dempsey-Wills contract called for $300,000 to be posted by August 5, and he planned to do so, as required. Gene Normile, Dempsey's current acting manager, said Rickard was the only one with a binding contract for the champion's services.[418]

Promoters were trying to match Harry Wills with Jack Sharkey.[419]

Tex Rickard refused to enter into a partnership with Chicago promoter Clements. Rickard said his attorneys had advised him that the Clements contract was not binding. "I also told him I never would be a party to a Dempsey-Wills contest."[420]

Dempsey, scheduled to enter his training camp on August 6 at Saratoga Springs, New York, said he never underrated any opponent, and "Tunney is a fine fighter."[421]

Gene Tunney criticized Jim Farley, saying,

> He talks about the challenge of Harry Wills being on file with the commission for a long time and that is the only challenge he will recognize. ... The chairman carefully avoids mentioning that the challenge of Tommy Gibbons was posted and accepted by the commission at the same time Wills was notified to put in his challenge. And he probably does not want to recollect that Gibbons tried in vain to get Wills to accept a match with him. ... In defeating Tommy Gibbons, my natural ring inheritance should have been equal recognition in this contendership business. Just to prove my superiority over the celebrated and patriotic chairman's pampered panther, I endeavored in every manner possible to coax him into a ring. For positive evidence of what I claim, one can see the contract signed by Billy Gibson and myself at Tex Rickard's office. Or, step into the Polo Grounds A.C. office and question Jimmy De Forest.

Tunney claimed that Farley had political motives and did not know anything about boxing.[422]

On July 27, at commissioner George Brower's behest, Tex Rickard's representatives again asked the New York commission to allow the

[417] *Grand Junction Daily Sentinel,* July 24, 1926.
[418] *Memphis Commercial Appeal,* July 25, 1926.
[419] *New York Daily News,* July 24, 1926.
[420] *New York Daily News,* July 26, 1926; *Chicago Tribune,* July 27, 1926. Jack Kearns said the problem could be solved if Dempsey fought under the prior Kearns-Rickard contract, which superseded any contract with Clements. Things appeared to be in a bit of a contractual muddle.
[421] *Grand Junction Daily Sentinel,* July 28, 1926. Jack also said his nose was just as good as the original.
[422] *New York Daily News,* July 27, 1926. Tunney would train at Lake Pleasant in the Adirondacks, New York. In 1928, James Farley would become Franklin D. Roosevelt's campaign manager for the New York governorship, which he won. Farley later was named chairman of the New York State Democratic Committee.

upcoming Dempsey-Tunney fight. The commission took another vote. This time, Brower voted with Muldoon to authorize the fight in New York. Some said New York wanted the tax revenue, after all. Others said Wills had hurt himself by not fighting Tunney and by remaining idle for the past year. Brower insisted that the Wills fight simply could not be made, so there was no reason to punish Dempsey and Tunney. "No promoter ever came in here to say he would promote a fight between Dempsey and the colored champion and that is why I am for having a Dempsey-Tunney fight."[423]

Still, there was some concern regarding whether Colonel Phelan would grant Dempsey's application for a license. He had separate licensing authority. That question loomed. The commission also said it would not allow Rickard to charge more than $25 per seat. So, despite authorizing the promotion, there remained obstacles. Regardless, Rickard was planning for the fight to be held on September 16 at Yankee stadium.[424]

Also on July 27, at the Illinois Athletic Commission's meeting, in a masterful stroke of bizarre logic, despite boxing being legal, it was announced that *all* heavyweight boxing matches were barred. Chairman O. W. Huncke said,

> We do not intend to sanction any heavyweight contests in this state whether it involves a championship or not.
>
> Fights between heavyweights generally are brutal, and we do not interpret the law to call for a spectacle of that kind. ... We aim to regulate boxing so that it will be a sport at which ladies may attend.
>
> We have no information, officially, regarding the Dempsey-Tunney and Dempsey-Wills fights. All we know is what we read in the newspapers. Neither Rickard nor Clements thought of consulting this commission in the matter.

Huncke also was quoted as saying, "We are not ready for a heavyweight championship bout. We are not in a position to handle a contest which would involve a tremendous amount of money. In addition, the big fellows generally put up a clumsy, brutal bout which usually is distasteful even to the dyed in the wool fans."

The *Chicago Tribune's* Walter Eckersall noted, "The commission is unanimously against heavyweight contests, and judging from the remarks of Chairman Huncke, those who think there is a chance of putting on a Dempsey-Wills match in Chicago should look elsewhere for a battleground." Clements had not cleared or even attempted to clear a Dempsey-Wills fight with the commission, and given the edict, his claim that Dempsey Wills would or could take place in Chicago was false.[425]

Nevertheless, on July 30, 1926, the Chicago Coliseum Club/B. E. Clements filed in federal court in Denver, Colorado a request for an

[423] *New York Daily News*, July 28, 1926.
[424] *New York Daily News*, July 28, 31, August 4, 1926.
[425] *Belvidere Daily Republican, Chicago Tribune*, July 28, 1926.

injunction against Jack Dempsey fighting pursuant to any contract other than its own. Its lawyer filed an alleged copy of the contract for Dempsey to fight Wills, which contract stated that the Club had until August 5, 1926 to pay the champion $300,000, which the Club claimed it was ready, willing, and able to do, with another $500,000 to be paid 10 days prior to the fight. The contract allegedly was signed by Dempsey, but the copy filed with the court did not bear Dempsey's signature, but rather his typed name, as well as the typed names of B. E. Clements, club President, and Ralph Rosen, club secretary.

The bill alleged that on September 29, 1925, Floyd Fitzsimmons, Benton Harbor promoter, entered into a contract with Harry Wills for him to box Dempsey, and the bout would be held in either Michigan, Indiana, Illinois, Kansas, or Ohio, in September 1926. Fitz reserved the right to assign his rights to others, provided that both contestants agreed to the assignment, with the assignee to assume all obligations thereunder. Dempsey signed a contract with Fitzsimmons to box Wills, and Wills and Dempsey later signed a contract to meet each other. Dempsey was to be paid one million dollars. Dempsey signed an additional contract with Fitzsimmons shortly thereafter in early October 1925 at Huntington, West Virginia.

Continuing, the Club alleged that on March 6, 1926, said contracts were assigned by Fitzsimmons to Clements for $1, with all parties mutually agreeing to the assignment. However, the agreement subsequently also declared the Fitzsimmons contract to be null and void and of no force and effect.

Under this new contract, Dempsey agreed to box Wills for payment of a minimum of $800,000. The fight was to take place in any state except New York. Dempsey agreed to have his life and health insured with companies the promoter designated, with the premiums to be paid by the promoter, with any proceeds as a result of a claim going to the promoter's benefit. Dempsey also agreed not to have any other fight prior to said contest without the Club's consent and the consent of the manager of his opponent (meaning Paddy Mullins).

The agreement required the Club to deposit in escrow on or before August 5, 1926, $300,000 at the Hellman Bank at Los Angeles, California, to be paid to Dempsey on the 10th day prior to the date fixed for the contest, and also $500,000 to be deposited in said bank at least 10 days prior to the contest, to be paid to Dempsey (likely after the fight).

However, in the event of a contingency beyond the Club's control which prevented the fight from taking place, any money paid beforehand to Dempsey was to be returned to the promoter. Also, the parties agreed that in the event of a contingency that necessitated a postponement of the fight, the contestant agreed to perform at a later date.

In addition, if the total receipts from tickets exceeded $2 million, after deducting state and commission taxes, Dempsey would be paid 50% of whatever amount exceeded $2 million. Dempsey also would receive 50% of the net revenue derived from all moving picture royalties.

The contestants would have at least 30 days of notice prior to the date fixed for the contest, which would be during September 1926. Dempsey agreed to enter training at a designated location at least 30 days prior to the date fixed for the fight.

The contract also said Dempsey agreed that he received $10 at the time of the execution of the contract. These terms made no sense, particularly since Dempsey had been so insistent upon receiving a large forfeit to bind the highly uncertain match.

Five days later, on March 11, 1926, the parties modified the agreement regarding the financial terms and timing of the payments to state that the promoter agreed to pay Dempsey on or before August 5, 1926, $300,000 *cash*. The promoter agreed to pay Dempsey at least 10 days before the date fixed for the contest a further sum of $500,000 cash. Time of the payments was declared to be the essence of the contract.

Further, the contract was changed to give Dempsey a share of the "gross revenue" (of the film proceeds) as opposed to the "net revenue." Interestingly enough, the change referenced page 3, paragraph 2 of the original contract, but in the contract filed with the court, the phrase "net revenue" appears in paragraph 1, not 2. Was that a scrivener's error, or was the contract that was filed with the court somewhat different from the original?

Finally, the parties agreed that if all conditions of the contract were not carried out in full in every respect, the contract was null and void.

However, once again, the letter filed with the court, confirming said changes, was typed, but unsigned by either party.

Four months later, on July 10 (and 12), 1926, the Club mailed, registered, return receipt demanded, to Dempsey, in Colorado Springs, Colorado, notices requiring him to train for the contest no later than August 1, 1926 in Chicago, Illinois, and also to appear in Chicago on or before July 25, 1926 to meet the requirements of Illinois Boxing laws and to execute other papers or contracts which might be necessary under said laws. The letter also informed him that representatives of life and accident insurance companies would call him to arrange a time to examine him for insurance purposes according to the terms of the contract, asking him to cooperate accordingly.

The Club alleged that when post office authorities attempted to deliver said notice to Dempsey, he refused the attempt. The Club then sent Dempsey a telegram, to which Dempsey wired a refusal and total repudiation of the contract, stating that he was training for a match with Tunney (a fight to which the Club did not consent), declining to be examined by insurance representatives: "ENTIRELY TO [sic] BUSY TRAINING FOR MY COMING TUNNEY MATCH TO WASTE TIME ON INSURANCE REPRESENTATIVES   STOP AS YOU HAVE NO CONTRACT SUGGEST YOU STOP KIDDING YOURSELF AND ME ALSO. JACK DEMPSEY".

In its complaint, the Club claimed that it had been prepared to erect an arena in Chicago capable of seating 150,000 spectators.

The Club alleged that it had designated September 18, 1926 as the date of Dempsey vs. Wills, to be held in Chicago, informing Dempsey of such since July 12, 1926, although it did not include a copy of its July 12 letter as part of its exhibits in its filing. The July 10 letter which was filed did not reference a date for the contest. (The complaint failed to note that the Illinois Commission had not approved the fight and recently barred all heavyweight contests. The Club had not even requested approval.)

The Club believed that instead of honoring its contract, Dempsey intended to box Tunney on or about September 16 for Rickard in New York. The Club further alleged that ever since June 1, 1926, Dempsey had conspired with others to violate the contract's terms by publicly announcing that he would not carry out and perform its terms and conditions.[426]

The Club had similar or duplicate petitions for injunction drawn up, which it intended to file in Missouri, Illinois, Ohio, Indiana, and New York.

Unperturbed, Dempsey said the court action would not interfere with his training for the Tunney bout. "The whole thing is an effort to shake me down, and I am not going to fall for it. I am not in the least disturbed. My attorney here will handle the entire matter."[427]

On August 3, 1926, the Chicago Coliseum Club asked the superior court of Marion County, Indiana, to restrain and enjoin Jack Dempsey from engaging in the Tunney contest, which it believed was to be held on September 16, which would be in violation of the terms of an agreement entered into with Dempsey at Los Angeles on March 13, 1926 for him to fight Harry Wills for the Club.

Regarding his upcoming opponent, Dempsey allegedly said,

> I do not think much of Tunney's record. He went fourteen rounds with Carpentier and then didn't knock him out. Over in France that Italian boxer hit him so hard they stopped the fight to save Tunney. I know he stopped Gibbons, but Gibbons was an old man, about ready to quit, anyway. They tell me that the heat under those lights sapped him.[428]

Damon Runyon wondered whether Dempsey's old flame still was burning. Tunney was no easy mark, but a very patient man. The real question was not Tunney, but Dempsey. Jack would look good on the outside, but it was unclear what he still had on the inside.

The Dempsey that flattened Carpentier in a few well chosen punches in 1921 ought to be able to lick the Tunney that took

[426] Court filings from Chicago Coliseum Club vs. Jack Dempsey, In the District Court of the United States for the District of Colorado.
[427] Atlanta Constitution, July 31, 1926; Raleigh News and Observer, August 1, 1926.
[428] Harrisburg Evening News, August 4, 1926. Dempsey's alleged claims regarding Tunney over in France [likely a W10 KO Sullivan, who was Italian] appear to be unsupported.

fifteen rounds to stop the same Carpentier several years later. The Dempsey that swamped the giant Firpo in 1923 in two rounds ought to lick the Tunney that plodded fifteen rounds with Martin Burke and Jeff Smith in 1924, or even the Tunney that floundered through twelve rounds with John Risko, the human pogo stick as late as the fall of 1925. ... It isn't so much what Tunney is – it's what Dempsey is.

You will see Tunney the same methodical, patient, careful boxer that he has always been, painstakingly piling up points, and taking few chances. The pugilistic leopard doesn't change its spots.

It was unclear whether Dempsey still had that same old fierce, restless energy and ambition driving him relentlessly. Champions who were idle and out of the ring for so long had a way of blowing up once in a fight. If he was off, he would not be able to catch up with Tunney. Dempsey thought Tunney was timid, but in truth he was cautious and patient. He was not a great puncher, but he was a persistent puncher. Dempsey, on the other hand, always was impatient, eager to end matters as quickly as possible. Yet, he had become more placid in recent years, a sign that his flame was wavering. "It will never do for him to get in the ring and hope to out-patient the patient Tunney."[429]

Dempsey arrived in New York on August 4. With him were his wife, her mother, his personal representative Gene Normile, and trainer Jerry 'the Greek' Luvadis.

According to Harry Newman, when Dempsey entered Madison Square Garden on August 5 to watch the bouts, he was greeted with only half-hearted cheers, mingled with boos and catcalls, but when Harry Wills entered, he received a tremendous ovation, dwarfing the titleholder's reception. Davis Walsh said the crowd enthusiastically cheered Dempsey.

When Harry Wills walked over to Dempsey's seat, Jack arose, smiling, and they shook hands. Wills then walked over to his seat, accompanied by an ovation far greater than that which had been accorded to Dempsey.

To Tex Rickard's annoyance and chagrin, New York Boxing Chairman James Farley refused to allow Dempsey to be introduced from the ring. "Farley said in explanation that Dempsey did not have a license to box in New York and therefore was not eligible for an introduction." Some saw this as a harbinger of things to come.

Davis Walsh claimed that Dempsey told him that he was willing to fight Harry Wills if paid $1 million. "All I want is $1,000,000." Jack said sap promoters who didn't know what they were doing had approached him nearly every day. "Therefore, when B. C. Clements steps out with a contract on which he has failed to make his payments, I can do nothing else but laugh."

The next day, Dempsey said the Chicago syndicate never paid him a dollar for agreeing to fight Wills. He alleged that the contract called for

[429] *Harrisburg Evening News*, August 5, 1926.

two payments of $125,000 each to him. Never a dollar was paid, though they allegedly paid Wills $50,000. Dempsey was to receive another $300,000 the day before (August 5), but he never received a cent. A lot of folks talked big about making the Wills fight, but never actually came through with the money, a date, or an approved location.

Dempsey said Tunney was the logical contender. Jack had a lot of respect for the young Irishman:

> Gene is a strong, rough fellow and he may lick me, but I don't think he can. I realize that I have been away from the ring for some time, but I think I can whip myself in to shape again within three weeks. I'm working all the time, even when I haven't got a fight on. I'm on the road a lot and while a lay off affects every fighter to some extent, I really think I'll be all right when the time comes for Tunney.

Jack would start training at Saratoga Springs, New York, right away. He weighed 195 pounds, and likely would weigh 188 for the fight. He admitted that he lost 11 pounds during a three-day illness in Hot Springs, which might have accounted for some wild rumors about his health.

The champ and his board of strategy, the line-up being (l. to r.): Jerry (the Greek) Avardis, Gus Wilson, Jack Dempsey and Gene Normile.

The champ also said that as far as he was concerned, there was no chance to reconcile with Kearns. Any reports to the contrary were false.[430]

On August 5, 1926, B. E. Clements, president of the Chicago Coliseum Club, deposited a check for $300,000 with the Equitable Trust Company of Chicago, to be paid to Jack Dempsey for a Dempsey-Wills fight to be held in Chicago, which Clements insisted was timely, pursuant to their contract. (Payment to Dempsey was not in cash or deposited with the Hellman Bank in Los Angeles, as the purported contract required.)

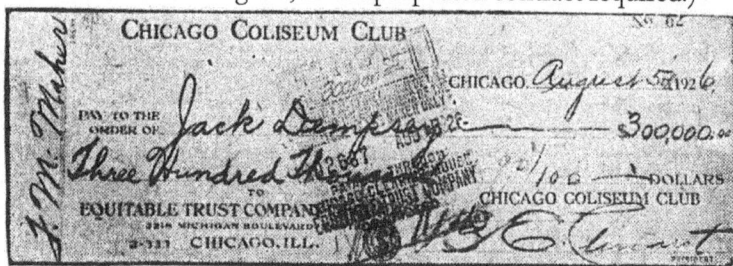

B. E. Clements displayed for the press the check he posted in Dempsey's favor with the Equitable Trust Co. of Chicago

---

[430] *New York Daily News*, August 5, 6, 1926; *Cedar Rapids Evening Gazette*, August 6, 1926.

Gene Normile, Dempsey's business representative, scoffed at Clements' claims, saying, "Our information is that it will not have to be delivered until 48 hours after the planned Dempsey-Wills fight." He said they had not received anything. (Furthermore, if the club was unable to bring off the fight for reasons beyond its control, any money given to Dempsey would have to be returned. They had no assurances that Chicago would allow the contest.)

More importantly, the Illinois "boxing commission stands firm on its ruling that heavyweight bouts are barred here. Chairman O. W. Huncke says there isn't a chance of rescinding the rule at the present time." Huncke said the commission did not intend to change its stance any time soon.

> Heavyweight fights are not to be permitted in this state, because the commission feels that there is enough good, clean, interesting and entertaining boxing to be had from other classes. It is our opinion that heavyweight fights too often become exhibitions of brutality, and for that reason we will not sanction such bouts.

> We were not called upon by any promoter qualified to appear before the commission to discuss Dempsey or Wills or Tunney. That is why the commission did not feel it necessary to make any statements or decisions in that controversy.

The blanket ban on heavyweight bouts enabled the Illinois boxing commissioner to avoid the race issue regarding a Dempsey-Wills contest, similar to how Muldoon dealt with it years ago by using a race-neutral justification.

Illinois was not going to allow the Dempsey-Wills fight, certainly not in September, the month called for in the Clements/Chicago Club contract. So, the contract's validity and financing did not matter anyhow, for the Chicago promoters had no location to host the fight. Rickard was right. He had told Dempsey that the Wills fight would not be allowed, to stop wasting his time on that contest.[431]

Gene Tunney trains and spars with Oskar Till

[431] Chicago Tribune, De Kalb Daily Chronicle, New York Daily News, August 6, 1926; Yonkers Statesman, August 9, 1926.

Gene Tunney said his training would focus on his legs and footwork first. "Most of the present generation of boxers neglect the most important part of their physical makeup – their legs."[432]

Tunney spends time with youngsters

On August 7, Dempsey worked out at Stillman's gym in New York, sparring 2 rounds with Johnny Dundee and 3 rounds with Canadian heavy Frankie McGowan.[433]

Interestingly, the black-owned *New York Age*'s William Pickens questioned Jim Farley's motives and challenged him, writing,

> Farley need not think he can fool anybody by pretending that he is all for Wills, but that the two other Commissioners are overruling him. Colored people are used to that sort of bunk, - especially from white men who, like Farley, are looking forward to being run for some elective political office and are anxious to make the "cullud brother" think that this particular white man, at least, was "for you." If Farley wants to prevent this injustice to Wills and this disgrace to the whole boxing business, Farley can do it.[434]

On the 8th at Speculator, New York, before a crowd of 3,000, Tunney sparred 4 rounds with middleweight Oskar Till. Gene's nifty boxing drew rounds of applause. He landed blows and deftly parried Till's attempts. Between rounds, Gene chatted and joked with youngsters. That day, he attended mass at St. Ann's Catholic church.

Dempsey arrives at the Flatiron building to apply for a New York boxing license

Tunney apologized to New York Boxing Chairman Jim Farley for panning the boxing commission. In his letter, Gene expressed regret for permitting his feelings to get the better of him.[435]

On August 9, both Tunney and Dempsey applied for boxing licenses with the New York commission. Although a huge crowd of fans greeted him outside the Flatiron building, inside, Dempsey received a

---

[432] *New York Daily News*, August 6, 7, 1926. Osk Till was Tunney's only sparring partner at present, but Jimmy Delaney might join him.
[433] *New York Daily News*, August 8, 1926. Jack was attempting to secure as sparring partners Bill Tate, Tommy Loughran, and Tiger Flowers.
[434] *New York Age*, August 7, 1926.
[435] *New York Daily News, Mount Vernon Daily Argus*, August 9, 1926.

frosty reception by the commission. The secretary of the board asked if he ever had a license before, which Jack replied that he had, but had lost it. He was told that he would have to make an affidavit to that effect, and his application for a renewal would have to contain a photograph, some references, and $5.

On the 9th, Dempsey boxed 2 rounds with Clinton-street sheik lightweight Sid Terris (76-4-3), 2 rounds with English middleweight Ted Moore (61-13-9), and 1 round each with Jerry Scott and Frankie Garcia.[436]

Dempsey spars Sid Terris

On August 10, Dempsey sparred in New York with claimant to the South American heavyweight championship, Alfredo Porzio, knocking him out, and Roberto Delfino, both Argentinians.

With Dempsey were wife Estelle Taylor and manager Gene Normile. He soon would set up camp at Saratoga Springs. Chicago detective sergeants Mike Trant and Fred Tapscott would act as bodyguards. Trant had been with the champ in all of his training camps.[437]

Also on August 10, the New York commission's Colonel Phelan turned down Dempsey's license application, purportedly owing to the fact that he had not defended his title once every six months. So, what did he expect Dempsey to do now? Noted in the champ's defense was the fact that Dempsey had signed a contract at Niles, Michigan to fight Wills, and the

---

436 *New York Daily News,* August 10, 1926.
437 *Knickerbocker Press,* August 13, 1926.

promoters to that contract had been unable to bring off the battle. The press hinted that Phelan was doing this in support of Jim Farley, the lone vote against Dempsey-Tunney. Phelan vehemently denied the accusation.

The commission had measured Dempsey and Tunney. Tunney scaled 197 ½ pounds and stood 6'2 ½" tall to Dempsey's 202 ½ and 6'1 ¾".

Muldoon intimated that a fight agreement needed to be filed, and the license would come along in due course.[438]

As a result, on the 10th, Dempsey signed a contract with the Rickard Sporting Club to box Gene Tunney 15 rounds at Yankee Stadium on September 16, 1926 for 37 ½% of the gross receipts of the house, less state tax and compensation for ring officials. Dempsey would post a $5,000 forfeit and Tunney $2,500.

Paul Gallico did not want the Dempsey-Tunney fight moved from New York to New Jersey, for only no decisions were allowed there. Hence, if they went through 12 rounds, the championship would remain in Dempsey's hands, and Wills would remain the logical contender. Regardless, even if Tunney beat Dempsey,

> [A Tunney-Wills fight] will be as impossible as is a Dempsey-Wills in this state. The reason for this is one of those hush hush things that nobody cares to discuss. Rickard, when you put it up to him, gets very mysterious, and talks of situations which he cannot reveal, and inside stuff, and reasons why he could not promote the battle. Rickard's favorite phrase is, "If you fellows only knew what I did about this thing, if you knew my position, and what I'm up against, you'd understand a lot of things."

On August 11, Dempsey walked back into the New York commission office with a flock of contracts that either he or his representatives had signed, agreeing to fight Wills, but out of which came nothing. It was his way of showing that he was willing to fight Wills, had tried to do so in good faith, but no promoter had been able to back the fight financially or bring it off politically/legally. One contract was signed at Niles, Michigan in September 1925, another at Huntington, West Virginia, and another with the Coliseum A. C. of Chicago, signed at Los Angeles on March 6 (or 13) last. Wills received some money for signing, but Dempsey said he never received a dime. George Brower called for another meeting.[439]

At the special commission meeting on August 12, an angry and upset Paddy Mullins verbally attacked Dempsey and said he wanted to fight him. Mullins said Dempsey had tricked him. "I thought you told me everything was all right. What do you mean by double crossing me like this?" Jack replied, "I didn't double cross you, Paddy." "You did, you know you did. That was a fine trick you pulled on me, you're a bit rat." "What do you mean by rat?" "Just what I say! You sent me a telegram saying that you would fight Wills, that everything was O.K. Now you run

[438] New York Daily News, August 11, 1926.
[439] New York Daily News, August 12, 1926. That day, Dempsey boxed with a few local boys at Stillman's.

out." Dempsey denied sending him any telegram. Mullins called him a liar. Paddy pulled the telegram from his pocket and snapped, "There it is." "I tell you I didn't send it." "You're a liar. I'll bet you $1,000 you sent it." "That is a bet." Mullins then plunked down the money, but Dempsey said he did not have that much with him. "I thought not. You're a cheap guy, a piker, and I've got a good notion to take a poke at you. If you will step in another room I'll fight you even if you won't go against any fighter." Jack replied, "It's a good thing you are an old man. If you weren't an old man I'd do something to you for that." Mullins replied, "Never mind my age. I'll take care of myself. You won't fight my fighter, but you'll fight me. Well, here I am. I never backed down in my life." Mullins drew back his arm and was going to punch, but Deputy commissioner Eddie Curry stepped in, along with Rickard and newspapermen, and prevented fisticuffs.

Mullins was referring to a March 16, 1926 telegram from Dempsey that read, "I signed contract in escrow in Equitable Trust company, Chicago. Everything satisfactory to Fitzsimmons and myself. Regards, Jack Dempsey."

Mullins also claimed that an agent of Rickard's offered him $50,000 to withdraw the Wills challenge.

Anyhow, the board – William Muldoon and George Brower, outvoted dissenter James Farley, and again voted to allow Dempsey to fight Tunney and to restore Dempsey to good standing, recommending that the license committee grant him his license.

However, the license board still might not grant Dempsey a license. They would meet separately to decide what they were going to do. The overall impression/vibe had not been good. There were hints that they would align with Farley and deny Dempsey a license.

George Brower asked the New York Attorney General for a legal opinion regarding whether the licensing board could deny Dempsey a license when the commission already had sanctioned him fighting.

Dempsey said he had been trying for five years to get a fight with Wills, but nothing ever came to fruition.

Tunney sparring partner Bud Gorman said Tunney was a certain winner over Dempsey. Gorman had trained with Dempsey, Gibbons, and others. Three years out of the ring would not do the champ any good. Gorman trained Gibbons for the Shelby fight, and he said Gene had what Gibbons lacked – a good, fast left jab and a snappy right cross, plus the speed, strength, and durability to carry and prolong an attack.

Dempsey's sparring staff included black/colored fighters Bill Tate, Jimmy Brown, and Ray Thompson, and whites/latinos Babe Herman, Alberto Progio, Roberto Delfino, Johnny Saxon, Jimmy Robert, Frankie Carpenter, Jack Clements, and Bill Weisberger.

On August 15, his first day of training in Saratoga Springs, 2,000 fans saw Dempsey work out, including 5 rounds of sparring, 1 round each with welterweight Johnny Saxon, colored Jimmy Brown of Panama, who threw and ran so much that Dempsey could not catch him, Jimmy Roberts, Ray Thompson, who had fought Tunney several times, whom Jack decked and knocked upside down with a blow to the chin, and Alberto Porcio, a clever Argentinian giant, who landed solid left jabs, but Jack hooked a left to the ear and the Argentinian went half through the ropes. "While the champion looked fast and worked with all the vigor of yore, we thought that his sense of judgment was bad. The long layoff had its effect on his accuracy and his shooting this afternoon was very wild at times."

Paddy Mullins threatened to file an injunction to prevent the Dempsey-Tunney fight if Dempsey was granted a license. Mullins said,

> Why does Brower change his mind so often? One time he admits that Wills is the logical contender for Dempsey's title and the next time he is in favor Tunney. Funny man. At the hearing for the application for an injunction on the Firpo fight, Brower said that Harry was the man for Dempsey, and look at him now.[440]

On August 16, after three hours of deliberation, the New York license board, Cols. James J. Phelan and D. Walker Wear, ruled against Dempsey and turned down his boxing license application until he had "complied with the resolutions and orders of the commission by fighting Harry Wills." The license officials utterly ignored New York Attorney General Albert Ottinger's formal legal opinion that they were without legal authority to withhold a license from a boxer for a bout that the commission had sanctioned, meaning Dempsey vs. Tunney. There was discussion of potentially taking the license board to court to seek a writ of mandamus to force them to issue Dempsey a license.

Dempsey said he had expected the board to "spoil the works."

That same day, August 16, Jack Kearns sued the champ for a third of a million dollars, his share of what he claimed Dempsey would be earning for his next fight. Kearns alleged that he and Dempsey entered into a contract on August 3, 1923, and he was to receive 33 1/3%. Kearns also charged that he had a contract with Rickard for Dempsey to fight Wills on July 4 last, and another agreement for a Tunney fight on August 15.

In his sparring on the 16th, Dempsey was especially vicious against Benny Fundenburk, Bill Tate, Roberto Delfino, welter Joe Kurp, and Bill Clemons or Clemens, 1 round each.

192-pound Tunney had a badly discolored right eye from his sparring with 200-pound heavyweight Bud Gorman (35-7-8) and middleweight Oskar Till (20-6-7). Gene anticipated fighting at 190, at which weight he would be as strong as a bull and as agile and graceful as a dancer.

William Brady offered Dempsey $500,000 to meet Wills on the same date that Rickard planned to stage the Tunney fight.

---

[440] *New York Daily News*, August 13-16, 1926; *Knickerbocker Press*, August 13, 1926. In 1929, New York Governor Franklin D. Roosevelt would appoint George Brower to be the Kings County District Attorney. In 1931, Brower would be appointed to one of five new New York Supreme Court judgeships in Kings County, becoming a trial court judge. He remained on the bench as a judge until mandatory retirement at age 70.

On August 17, Dempsey's attorneys moved to dismiss the Colorado injunction action for lack of personal jurisdiction, arguing that neither the Chicago Coliseum Club nor Dempsey were residents of Colorado. The Club was based in Chicago, Illinois, and Dempsey resided in California.

On the 17th, Dempsey decked Bill Weisberger, and then boxed colored welter Panamanian Jimmy Brown, Johnny Saxon, and rugged Argentinian Roberto Delfino.

On August 19, 1926 at Madison Square Garden in New York, before a crowd of 15,000 (14,034 or 14,125 paying $75,176, $74,748 or $82,222.80 with the tax included), world middleweight champion 159 ¼-pound Tiger Flowers once again defeated 159-pound Harry Greb via another close 15-round split decision, successfully defending his title. Judges Charles Mathison and Harold Barnes voted for Flowers, while referee Jimmy Crowley voted for Greb.[441]

Instead of taking the Dempsey license matter to court, fed up with all of the obstacles, Tex Rickard moved the Dempsey-Tunney fight to the Sesquicentennial Stadium in Philadelphia, which could hold 100,000 people. The fight was set to be held on September 23, one week later than previously scheduled. The longest bout allowed in Pennsylvania was a 10-round contest with a judges' decision, so no 15-rounder.

Seats for the fight would sell as low as $3 and as high as $27.50.

Dempsey was a 9 to 5, and then 8 to 5 favorite.

The champion said he would leave for Atlantic City to train there. His last day of training in Saratoga Springs was on August 22. He sparred Bill Tate and Jimmy Brown.

Tunney sparred 9 rounds on the 22nd with Bud Gorman, light heavy Billy Vidabeck (60-6-3), and Oskar Till. Lou Fink was training him. "Gene is developing a mean right hand."[442]

Joe Williams wrote that in 1918 and 1919 in France, Tunney was a soldier, seeing action at Belleau Wood. He also boxed in the military, fighting as a light heavyweight, defeating

Gene Tunney, who is to fight Jack Dempsey, training at Luther's Training Camp where he has entered a period of intensive work

heavyweight Bob Martin and light heavy Ted Jamieson, the latter in the

---

[441] Harry Newman scored it 7-4-4 for Flowers. The *Brooklyn Citizen* scored it 7-6-2 for Flowers. Vincent Clabby of the *Brooklyn Daily Times* scored it 6-4-5 for Flowers. Davis Walsh said Flowers won 10 of the 15 rounds. W. O. McGeehan scored it clear for Flowers. The *Brooklyn Daily Eagle's* George Nobbe said Greb lost to southpaw Flowers "just as decisively" as in their prior bout. "One round was like another. It was shove, slip, slap, miss, jump, dodge, run and hold from beginning to end. There was no punching to speak of. Neither of the contestants is a puncher. Both of them are hard to hit." The *Brooklyn Standard Union* said Greb won. *New York Daily News, Brooklyn Citizen Brooklyn Daily Times, Yonkers Statesman, Brooklyn Daily Eagle*, August 20, 1926.
[442] *New York Daily News*, August 17 - 23, 1926.

American Expeditionary Forces light-heavyweight championship. Martin later whipped Bill Brennan, though the records did not accord him the decision. When he returned to the U.S., veteran referee Billy Roche, who had seen him fight overseas, convinced Tunney to make boxing his career.[443]

Tunney would leave Speculator, NY, and head to Stroudsburg, PA. He said he had been working an average of 15 rounds daily.

Norman Brown said the Dempsey who would fight Tunney was older, heavier, and slower than the Dempsey who annihilated Willard. These facts were self-evident to this writer. Tunney had youth, speed, a keen brain, and courage, and Dempsey would need to be at his best to beat him. "He has quite a way to go."[444]

Tex Rickard explained why he never made a serious effort to put on a fight between Dempsey and Wills. He also defended Dempsey against the charge that he was afraid of Wills, which he said was not true.

> My experience with the Jeffries-Johnson bout long ago convinced me that a Dempsey-Wills match would not be a good thing for boxing. As I became better acquainted with the game and talked with persons of influence, I saw no reason to change this opinion. I have made more Negro champions and promoted more mixed bouts than any other man in the country, but I did not think it wise to hold this particular match.
>
> Nevertheless, in Sept. 1924, I prepared to hold it, with the ready consent of Dempsey and even went so far as to have tickets printed. ... That the bout was never held was no fault of the contestants or of mine.
>
> If I had needed anything beyond my own conviction that the holding of this match was not practicable, that experience would have settled the matter.
>
> Finally I decided to match Dempsey with Tunney, whom I considered and still consider his most dangerous opponent. In March of this year I wired Dempsey, saying I wanted him to box Tunney. His telegram in reply read: "Why not Wills?"

[443] *Elmira Star-Gazette*, August 24, 1926.
[444] *New York Daily News, Bridgewater Courier-News*, August 25, 1926.

When I went to Ft. Worth to meet him he asked me the same question but I told him that for business reasons I did not wish to promote a Wills bout, and that I did not believe it could be held.

Dempsey had given me solid power to represent him before the New York Boxing Commission. That meant that I was empowered to go before the commission and agree that Dempsey would box any opponent I named. I had already agreed to give Tunney the match, but, if I had switched to Wills, Dempsey not only would have been willing but would have been more pleased. I believed Tunney the tougher opponent, and thought he would make the better battle. ... To say that Dempsey fears Wills is a joke. He considers him a clean living, estimable citizen, but a second rate fighter.[445]

In 1957, in the book *The Magnificent Rube. The Life and Gaudy Times of Tex Rickard*, published by McGraw-Hill in New York, Charles Samuels wrote:

There was, for example the problem of the Negro heavyweight Harry Wills, the so-called Black Panther, Dempsey's most persistent challenger. The commission, being political appointees, were subject to orders from Albany. And the orders were to insist that Tex match Dempsey with Wills. That pleased thousands of Negro voters in New York.

But the orders were countermanded each time Tex and the two Jacks agreed to give Wills his title shot.

This was because the state authorities feared that another mixed heavyweight title match might be followed by race riots more extensive than in 1910, with the Democratic administration in Albany getting the blame. So the politicians, being politicians, played both ends against the middle - and Tex Rickard was the middle.

What infuriated him was that he had turned over the old Garden free of charge to the Democrats for their 1924 National Convention, even throwing in the concessions for an extra contribution. And that convention turned out to be the longest since the founding of the Republic.

"So why don't they take that into consideration," Tex would yell, "instead of making me the goat in this Harry Wills business? Them fellers in Albany are playing me for a sucker, all the way down the line. They're crucifying me in the eyes of the public."

What he said made sense. What the politicians had to do - play both ends alternatively to keep their voters deluded and happy - made just as much sense, from their point of view. And it seems now

[445] *Bridgewater Courier-News*, August 26, 1926.

quite likely that another mixed heavyweight title fight in the mid-twenties could have killed boxing in New York.

The dilemma was solved when Gene Tunney became a logical contender, following his knockouts of Tommy Gibbons, who had stood off Dempsey, and Bartley Madden, whom Wills had been unable to put away. Finally, Gene defeated Johnny Risko.

On August 25 in Atlantic City, Dempsey sparred Jimmy Brown, Mexican welter Tillie Kid Herman, and heavy Mike Arnold.

One observer of Gene Tunney's work said those who doubted his killer instinct were mistaken, for he had been throwing rights with the deadly precision of an expert marksman. His sparring partners, Bud Gorman, Osk Till, and Billy Vidabeck, all said his blows were no love taps. Tunney had been working on keeping out of the way of left swings. His footwork and general efficiency had improved vastly.[446]

On the 26th at the dog race track in Atlantic City, over 5 rounds, vicious Dempsey mauled seven men – lightweight Alex Hart; Hughie Adams - who did not last a round; Joe Kurp (sometimes called Karp); a colored deaf mute named Silent Puryear, who was out on his feet when Jimmy Brown came in to complete the round; Jimmy Roberts; and Bad Bill Tate.

Harry Greb was on hand to watch, and said although he was not predicting a winner, Tunney might not be aggressive enough to beat Dempsey.

Tunney and Osk Till

That day at Speculator, Tunney boxed Osk Till, Bud Gorman, Billy Vidabeck, and 190-pound Johnny Grosso (18-3).[447]

On the 27th, Dempsey sparred middleweight Frank Carpenter, Bill Tate, Jimmy Brown, Joe Kurp, and Johnny Saxon.

Harry Newman opined if Dempsey wanted to beat Tunney, he needed to use his right hand more often and get some better sparring partners. Jack had been knocking a lot of "eggs" dead with a left hook. His sparring mates, with few exceptions, had been too afraid to fight back, which did Dempsey no good. In the old days, Dempsey used his right quite often, but now, he primarily used his left hook.

Harry Greb agreed, saying,

[446] New York Daily News, August 26, 1926.
[447] New York Daily News, August 27, 1926.

Dempsey will have to use that right more. That is one punch that Tunney can't get away from. I never had any trouble hitting Gene with a straight right, and Dempsey must spruce up his. .... Dempsey should be farther advanced in his training now. That boy Jimmy Brown gives him plenty of speed, but he must have stronger men to hit and some that will fight back.[448]

That same day, August 27, in Marion County Superior Court, Indiana, Jack Dempsey via his attorneys entered his general appearance and answer to the Chicago Coliseum Club's request for an injunction of the Dempsey-Tunney contest. Oddly enough, they did not challenge jurisdiction, which might have been a mistake.[449]

3,000 people watched Dempsey train at the dog track on the afternoon of August 28. Dempsey sparred giant colored fighter Charley Anderson, who landed some corking good rights, Bill Tate, Mexican Tillie Kid Herman, clever middleweight Frankie Carpenter, and Joe Kurp. Newman said, "To be absolutely truthful I don't think the champ made much of a hit with the throng." He still was neglecting his right.[450]

On the 29th, Jack sparred 2 rounds with colored Charles Anderson, rapping him good and plenty, savagely pounding on him the clinches, 2 with Frankie Carpenter, and 1 each with Joe Nasser, welter Jimmy Brown, and welter Johnny Saxon. William Brady watched, and said he thought Jack was in great shape and ready to go.

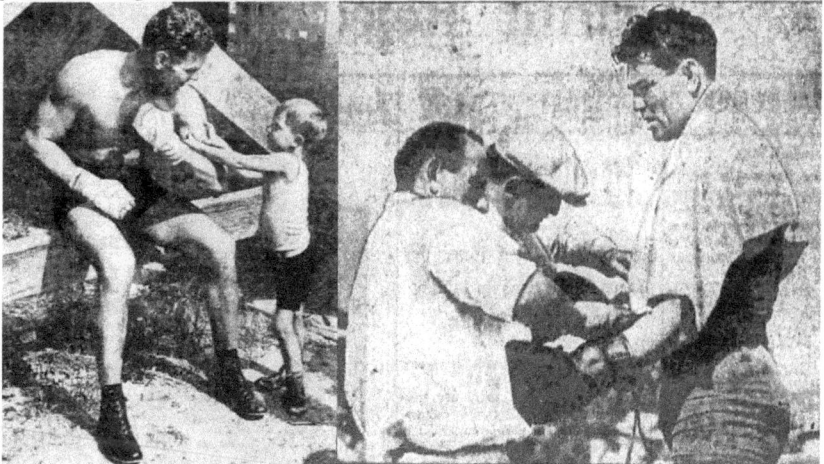

Turfman Tim Mara (more on him later) said Tunney was in the best shape of his career and would knock out Dempsey. "Tunney is hitting harder today than he ever has, and he carries more than enough dynamite in that right of his to put Dempsey away with the birdies."

Frank Wiener, chairman of the Pennsylvania Boxing Commission, issued an edict to Rickard that tickets were not to be given out to speculators, for they would resell the tickets at much higher prices, which

[448] *New York Daily News*, August 28, 1926.
[449] *Indianapolis News*, August 28, 1926.
[450] *New York Daily News*, August 29, 1926.

was not good for the public. "If you don't want to agree to this, then you take your fight back to New York again."

A furious Rickard replied, "You talk like that to me, and you won't be on the commission in two days!" Wiener responded, "I'll take a chance on that, and no threats of yours can budge me from my position. I'm not going to stand idly by and see you allow speculators to get the choicest seats, and that goes, or you'll promote no fight in Philadelphia or anywhere else in this state." Tex said, "I'll give you $10,000 in cash right now if you point to one ticket that I've given to any speculator. I never do business that way, and I'm not going to be treated in any such manner. I mean it, too." Wiener: "That's all right, too, but we owe something to our people. I might tell you that I've been informed by police officials that they are going to arrest any man seen on the street offering fight tickets at a premium." Rickard agreed and said he would do his utmost to fight off speculator ticket raids.[451]

The next day, Rickard agreed to set aside a block of 4,000 tickets that would be at Mr. Wiener's disposal, and that settled their differences.

Dempsey spars and trains with pulleys at Atlantic City

On the 30th, when a ringside spectator suggested to black Charley Anderson that the champ hurt him with a left hook to the head, Anderson replied that Jack hurts with every punch. Bill Tate barely lasted 1 round as well. Tillie Kid Herman was twice on the floor during his 1 round. Frankie Carpenter was down within the first minute but rose and finished the round. Colored Jimmy Brown engaged in lively hitting, running, and ducking to get away from the wallops.

Harry Newman said Dempsey was looking better and improving, hitting on every cylinder and tearing along at a fierce clip. Harry Greb predicted that Dempsey would have to chase Tunney.[452]

Dempsey trainer Gus Wilson said they needed more sparring partners. Few could last more than a round with Dempsey. Hence, Jack was not getting the kind of work he needed. Still, Wilson said the "Man Killer" did not need 10 rounds to knock out Tunney, for he could "sock so hard that concrete walls and granite monuments are not safe when he's around."[453]

Tunney wanted bigger sparring partners so he could get used to dealing with wild haymakers. He planned to pulverize Dempsey with

[451] *New York Daily News*, August 30, 1926.
[452] *New York Daily News*, August 31, 1926.
[453] *Camden Courier*, September 1, 1926.

short rights, as well as his half-hook half-uppercut submarine punch. Gene had studied Dempsey's style, his ducking and weaving, and thought Jack would be a mark for his punches.

Dempsey said he recognized that Tunney was as fast and shifty as anyone he ever had faced. "He's a speedy, tricky, moving fellow, and the only way I'll catch up with him is to move a little faster."

On August 31, 196-pound Dempsey knocked out welter Johnny Saxon/Saxton with a short left hook to the jaw. It took five minutes to revive him. Jack said he did not mean to hit him so hard, but Johnny ran into the punch. Lightweight Alex Hart finished the round. Bill Tate, Tillie Kid Herman, and Jimmy Brown each worked a round.

Harry Newman said Dempsey was moving around like a bantam and had his old sock going splendidly. Atlantic City Mayor Ed Bader's presence perhaps motivated him.

On September 1, Dempsey rested with a black left eye. Not one of his eight sparring partners would admit responsibility for the shiner, for if they did, they knew Jack would get revenge the next time they sparred.[454]

Gene Tunney arrived in Philadelphia on September 1. As many as 25,000 cheering fans greeted him. Police and marines gave him an escort. Gene met Philadelphia Mayor W. Freeland Kendrick.[455]

Marshall Hunt interviewed James Joseph Tunney, more commonly known as Gene. Tunney said, "I cannot see how I possibly can lose to Jack Dempsey. The champion certainly is not the fighter he was three years ago and he never can hope to be the same. Any fighter who has been out of the ring for three years cannot expect to return and be a conqueror." He said Dempsey essentially had retired, and his mental attitude had changed. He had lost his killer instinct and his love of fighting. Conversely, during the time that Dempsey was idle and doing no fighting, Tunney was hungry and active (with 19 fights from late 1923 through 1925). He was in superb physical condition.

[454] *Philadelphia Inquirer, New York Daily News, Asbury Park Press,* September 1, 1926.
[455] *Philadelphia Inquirer,* September 2, 1926. Mayor Kendrick had forbidden Dempsey-Wills to be held in Philadelphia.

On September 2, Dempsey decked Tillie Kid Herman with a left hook, though Herman rose and fought back gamely as he took his daily beating. Martin Burke (1921 L10 and 1924 L15 Tunney), Frank Carpenter, Charley Anderson, and Jimmy Brown all took turns absorbing blows. Harry Newman said, "Incidentally, Dempsey took quite a few smacks from his companions and it didn't look to me as though he could help being hit."

CHAMP CHEERS CRIPPLES. Jack Dempsey visited the Sea shore Home for Crippled Children at Atlantic City yesterday. He passed up and down the aisles at the hospital whispering cheery greetings to the unfortunate ones. Photo shows him with little Mabel Larbee.

Referee Jimmy Dougherty said 10 rounds was too short a time for Dempsey to beat Tunney.[456]

Dempsey heard that Tunney (allegedly) had said that Dempsey had never whipped a really good man. Dempsey replied that Tunney could not stop Risko, Greb, Renault, Delaney, Houck, Loughran, O'Dowd (actually, Tunney had a W12 and KO2 O'Dowd in 1923 and 1925), Sampson/Samson, Levinsky, Jeff Smith, Martin Burke, Foley (actually, 1924 WND10 and KO1), Keiser, or Weinert (actually, 1922 WND12 and KO4). Many were men with whom Jack had sparred and could knock out or had knocked out. Dempsey had stopped Levinsky four years before Levinsky went the distance with Tunney. Farmer Lodge, a former Dempsey sparring partner, stopped Paul Sampson in a few punches, but Tunney could not stop Sampson (1920 WND10). Marty Burke and Jack Renault had been Dempsey sparring partners. Tunney could not stop either of them. Tunney also fought Ray Neuman, another of Dempsey's former sparring partners, and did not get much the best of their 10-round bout (1924 W10). Dempsey said the record book was rougher on Tunney than it was on him.

Tunney said he was 195 pounds when he started training, but now was a trifle under 190, with two weeks to go. He was glad that he did not have to shed weight to make 175, for he felt stronger when bigger. He always kept in tip-top shape and was ready to go 50 rounds.[457]

Harry Newman said Dempsey did not look so good to him on the 3rd. He sparred with Martin Burke, Charley Anderson, Frankie Carpenter, and Frankie Bush. Jack shuffled though his work, and "wasn't there."

Jimmy De Forest said Dempsey was not punching with the same sharpness that he did before the Willard bout, and "his judgment in distance is faulty." He also was not stepping around as lively as he once did. His work overall lacked his past snappiness.

Harry Greb thought Tunney had a "swell chance" to win. Jack still could punch, but it would not be easy for him to land on a big, clever fellow like Tunney, particularly in his current diminished state.

[456] New York Daily News, September 3, 1926.
[457] Philadelphia Inquirer, September 3, 1926.

To my way of thinking, Tunney has a fine chance to win the title. I have watched Jack work out almost every day, and he is by no means the cinch some people think he is. He hasn't got the pep, and he looks to me like a man who is all dried out. Everything is an effort with him. He is missing too much ... Where is that great right hand that one time would have knocked these eggs all over the ring?

Another quoted Greb as saying, "Dempsey is not showing up to his previous good form. He is missing too much and he is being hit too often by sparring partners who are not particularly brilliant."

Dempsey sparring Frankie Bush

Dempsey said the key to success was getting into position to hit the other fellow. Sometimes he intentionally left openings for his opponents so that they would throw and leave themselves open to his attack. He set traps. If his foe happened to beat him to the punch it was not utterly by surprise, because he was ready to ride with any punch if hit. Once he hurt or decked a man, he knew how to finish him. Some did not stay down the first time they went down, but once down, eventually they were finished.

Tunney said, "I don't fear Dempsey's punch – wouldn't fear it if it were at its superlative best now instead of having lost much of its earlier snap and power. I know Dempsey can't hurt me, for I've taken wallops as hard as he can deal out – and never was off my feet in my life." Conversely, he did not think Dempsey would be able to defend against his blows.[458]

Frank McCracken of the *Philadelphia Public Ledger* called Tunney a firm-jawed, right handsome, poet pugilist who also was a soldier and knocker-out of men. "Tunney is different. He is different from any boxer I ever have met or talked with." He used words like "marvelous," unexpected from a challenger for the world heavyweight championship. "Yet that is the way Tunney talks, without the slightest show of affectation, sincerely, sure of himself and certain of his choice of words."

Gene played golf in the morning at the Glen Brook Country Club. One writer suggested that Gene should try to hit a ball at a passing motor car. Gene smiled and waited for it to pass. "I might have hit it and that possibly would have meant a lawsuit. I will leave them for Jack."

Tunney was training in seclusion in the Poconos mountains. Gene believed he was a "man of destiny," chosen to inherit the title. "I will fight

458 *New York Daily News, Philadelphia Inquirer, Brooklyn Standard Union*, September 4, 1926.

my best fight against Dempsey. I will knock him out." He did not fear Dempsey's punch. "Well, what is there about a punch to fear? I never was really hurt by a blow I received, with the exception of one. That was the time Knockout Sullivan of Shenandoah hit me with a wicked blow and sent me staggering. I nailed him coming off the ropes and knocked him out." He also said, "I've never been knocked off my feet in any of my fights. I know all about Dempsey, have watched him in several of his important battles, but I do not think he can hurt me enough to knock me unconscious." Gene would remain under control at all times in the ring, whereas, "I do not think that is possible with Dempsey. He is high-strung, allows his nervous energy to get the better of him." Tunney was absolutely convinced of victory, and yet there was nothing bombastic in his attitude. He was not a braggart.

After working out, Gene preferred seclusion, for he enjoyed reading books, including classics and plays, such as Shakespeare. "It is not a pose with Tunney. He likes to do these things, that's all." "Yes, Tunney is different. Decidedly different."

Tunney said golf helped him to relax, which helped him in boxing. "You know any of the pro golfers will tell you that the best way to play golf is to relax, not to be tense when you play your shots."

Tunney's manager Billy Gibson said, "Gene certainly can hit, and every one knows that Dempsey isn't the hardest person to wallop with a right on the jaw." He had fast, straight punches, which came out like a shot. Furthermore, "Gene will stand up under the best Dempsey has. If Tunney does go down he's going to get up again."

Tunney's trainer Lou Fink said no one could run on the road with Gene, for he was too fast, and had the best legs in the business.

Prevailing odds had Dempsey the 2 to 1 favorite, or slightly under that mark.[459]

On September 4, the champ sparred Frankie Carpenter 2 rounds, Frankie Bush/Busch 1 round, and Martin Burke 2 tame rounds. One observer said Dempsey missed quite often, his sense of distance being off. Another said he showed plenty of pep.

Dempsey felt he was getting down rather fine and did not want to go stale. Hence, he was thinking of cutting down on his boxing and taking more days off. Bill Tate said Dempsey was hitting better and harder than ever. However, Harry Newman countered, "It is not quite clear how Bill knows. Bill doesn't get hit often enough to qualify as an expert."[460]

After seeing Tunney spar on September 4, Frank McCracken opined that the challenger "WILL FIGHT." Gene said, "I always try to keep myself under control when I am boxing. If I find I am becoming unduly excited I strive to restrain myself – try to keep calm and collected because I think my boxing is more effective in this mood." Yet, he still showed plenty of flashes of real fighting fire. "He can be aroused to a real fighting

[459] *Philadelphia Public Ledger*, September 4, 1926.
[460] *New York Daily News*, September 5, 1926.

pitch." Brawny 200-pound Bud Gorman stung Gene with a left hook to the jaw. In response, Gene went after him and crashed a right to his jaw. The 1,500 on hand were impressed with his swift and sure smashes, which he repeated against light heavy Harold Mays of Bayonne and light heavy Billy Vidabeck. He sparred each man 2 rounds, for 6 rounds total. Tunney appeared to have the stamina, strength, and skill necessary to win.[461]

Dempsey said his training had puzzled a lot of folks, many saying he was all through and the old fighting spirit gone. "Maybe they are right, but I'd suggest that they wait until a few days before the fight to get a real line on my work." He said his training had differed from the past, because for the first time, he was directing his own training. He had gone into some fights in the past stale and overtrained. Not this time. He was not going to leave his fight and energy in the training camp. He had been going easy with his sparring partners. He still had his punch, showing it occasionally, but then worked on other things – side-stepping, blocking, and ducking. He was not trying to punch his sparring partners into drunkenness and neglect other aspects of his game. Still, several observers said his punch was about all he had left.

On the 5th, Dempsey sparred 2 rounds with Charlie Anderson, 1 with Mike Arnold, who was decked by a left hook to the jaw, 2 with Martin Burke, and 1 with Frankie Busch, for 6 rounds total.

Newman said Dempsey was all there, wading through his sparring partners, looking better than ever. He was murderously inclined, kicking the stuffing out of each of them. He was hitting freely and throwing his wicked right more.

Dempsey spars Mike Arnold, left, and Charlie Anderson, right

Tunney noted that Dempsey never had seen him box. Jack did not like to see his foes until he was in the ring with them. Gene's point of view was the opposite. He liked to know whatever he could about his opponents. He had watched Dempsey box many times. "I've studied his form and the flaws in it. I've noticed how he delivers his punches and just how open he is to counter blows. A careful analysis of his style has enabled me to determine just which punches to use on him and which to

461 *Philadelphia Public Ledger*, September 5, 1926.

avoid using." Watching Dempsey gave Tunney a line on him, so he knew what to expect, and enabled him to map out a battle plan. Dempsey fought differently than anyone he ever had boxed, so Gene would have a different game plan. He boxed no two men exactly alike, but tailored his style to suit what would work best against a particular foe.[462]

Billy Vidabeck said Tunney was hitting harder and faster than ever before. Billy had trained with Gene for Tunney's bout with Spalla. "One thing he can do is beat you to the punch. I have never seen a big fighter do that as well as Gene."

Bud Gorman said Tunney could fight aggressively or counterpunch. He was versatile.[463]

Wow! Some fighting face! Look at those intent eyes and that iron jaw — the champ looks like he's just in the mood to sock some one for the count. He was snapped after a furious sparring bout. But he seems to be ready for any comer any old time. This is a rare closeup of the champ at his best.

Several Dempsey critics said he was missing a lot of punches and doing all of his work at long range, which wasn't his natural style at all. His legs were slower, too. Dempsey could not catch Jimmy Brown, and if he could not catch up with Jimmy, how was he going to catch Tunney?

Philadelphia Jack O'Brien said, "If Dempsey is anywhere near as good as he was against Firpo he should win. But at the same time I look for Tunney to give him the greatest fight he has had since winning the title, and I wouldn't be surprised to see it go the limit, for Tunney is a shifty fellow."

O'Brien said he met Dempsey a few months ago in New York. The champ sat down next to him and playfully hit him on the knee with his open hand. "I tell you, he almost paralyzed me." O'Brien had boxed him 1 round when Dempsey was training for Carpentier, but would not do so now. "I will NOT. … That day I boxed with Dempsey, I hoofed it some and made him miss for a while. But he finally dug a left into my stomach, and I was through. NOT for ME again."

About 25,000 people total had seen Dempsey train daily over the last several weeks, paying $1.10 apiece, which included the 10-cent tax. The worst day netted 800 admissions, and the best over 4,000.

Tunney told a group of friends that he would mystify Dempsey with feints until Jack left openings for his powerful right. Both Carpentier and Firpo had hit him with rights. Carpentier was not big or strong enough, and Firpo did not know how to handle the situation. Gene had the power to knock out Gibbons, something Dempsey could not do. Tunney had a fast right hand, with uncanny accuracy in sharp-shooting. He knew how

---

[462] *Philadelphia Inquirer, Daily News,* September 6, 1926. Tunney said he was down to 189 pounds.
[463] *Philadelphia Public Ledger,* September 6, 1926. The rabbit punch was barred under the Pennsylvania State Athletic Commission rules.

to throw the right in corkscrew fashion, such that it was neither straight nor a plain hook. He had excellent judgment of distance and good timing.

Tunney fires a right at Howard Mays

On September 6 at Stroudsburg, Tunney boxed 2 rounds each with Billy Vidabeck, light heavy Harold Mays, and Bud Gorman. Gene feinted constantly, his punches were fast and snappy, his right like a flash of lightning, he stepped in and out quickly, he had keen judgment of timing and distance, and knew how to move his head to elude blows.

Gene was not using a head guard in sparring, feeling that he wanted his training to be like actual fighting. He told his sparring partners to cut loose with everything they had. His battered lips bore testimony to the fact that they had been trying their best.

Bud Gorman said Tunney was hitting harder than ever. Even with big gloves, his blows stung. Gene was sparring men who were big and husky enough to take it, so he did not need to hold back, which helped him prepare properly, unlike Dempsey, who was compelled to hold back.

Lou Fink said Tunney was one of those fighters who improved constantly and exponentially. Gene was even better now than he was against Gibbons or Carpentier.

Jack Renault, who had fought Tunney, said Gene was bigger and stronger than ever, and boxed a thousand times better than when he fought him.

Harry Newman said Tunney never looked better, scoring often with a counter-right and left to the body. He was hitting harder and more often.

Born on May 25, 1898 (actually, 1897), in Greenwich Village, New York, Irish American James Joseph Tunney was 28 years old (actually, 29). He had joined the Marine Corps in 1918. He had few marks of his profession. His nose was just as straight as ever, no cauliflower ears, and a full row of teeth. His father died several years ago, and since then, Gene had been supporting his mother, a brother, and three sisters, one of whom was a nun. In school, he had played baseball and basketball, and even became a long-distance runner. He first made his mark on the fistic world in 1922, when he won the American light heavyweight title from Battling Levinsky. He lost to Greb, but retrieved his crown in early 1923 and had not lost since.

Tunney's actual military records confirm that at age 21 (the eligibility age) he entered Parris Island, South Carolina on July 13, 1918. He next went to Quantico, Virginia on September 4, 1918. He joined Company D in the 11th Regiment on September 26, 1918. He arrived in France on October 13, 1918. One month later, on November 11, 1918, the armistice was signed. Nevertheless, Tunney remained in France until July 19, 1919. He returned to Quantico on July 29, 1919. He was discharged from service on August 18, 1919. "Character Excellent."

Dempsey confirmed that he had not seen Tunney box. People found it strange that he would not want to assess a man's style. He almost never watched any of his opponents prior to fighting them. He preferred to have no prior preconceived ideas, but to decide what to do when he was in the ring with them. Otherwise, the other fellow might do the unexpected and throw him off. He even adapted from round to round. "Every round that I fight in every fight is a new and completely different round with me, and not any continuance from the other round." If he was in top shape, with accurate, hard punches, and his legs were in good shape, his breathing good, and he did not tire, "well, I don't care much about what the other fellow's style is."[464]

Responding to the Chicago Coliseum Club, which filed for an injunction in Indianapolis to prevent Dempsey from fighting Tunney until he met Wills pursuant to the contract it had with him, Dempsey's attorneys denied the existence of such a contract. Pursuant to interrogatories propounded by Dempsey's attorneys, the Club admitted that it did not currently have in its possession a contract bearing the champion's signature. Hence, there was a real question regarding whether Dempsey ever had signed the contract, and if he did sign, what exactly did he sign. All that was filed was an unsigned copy of the purported contract. The question was whether that was the same contract Dempsey signed, if he did, and whether there were supplements to the agreement. The Club alleged that the original was held in escrow by the Equitable Trust Company. The Club allegedly had a letter from Dempsey in which he approved the contract with certain changes and agreed to accept it with the posting by the club of $300,000 with the trust company.

Even if an injunction was to be granted in Indiana, it was not clear what force and effect such an injunction would have in Pennsylvania.[465]

In support of Dempsey's motion to dismiss the request for injunction in federal court in Colorado for lack of personal jurisdiction, J. H. Dempsey swore an affidavit stating that he was 37 years old, 6 years older than his brother Jack, that Jack Dempsey was born on June 22, 1895 (yes, it said the 22nd) at Manassa, Colorado. Jack had lived in Colorado with his parents until age 12, when the family moved to Provo, Utah. For several years, his father operated a farm there. His father still was a Utah resident, and always was from that point on, except for 1.5 years in which he and Jack's mother lived in Los Angeles, California with their son Jack, where he resided, voted, and claimed as his legal residence.

In 1911, when Jack was about age 16, he went with his father and mother on a visit to their old home in West Virginia. Upon their return, he visited for a short period with his older brother Bernard Dempsey at

[464] *Philadelphia Inquirer, New York Daily News,* September 7, 1926.
[465] *Indianapolis Times,* September 7, 1926.

Cripple Creek, Colorado, but then returned to live in Salt Lake City, Utah, where the family had moved. Although he traveled for boxing purposes, his residence remained in Utah.

On July 4, 1922, Jack moved to Los Angeles with the intention of making that city and state his permanent home and residence. He already had purchased on January 4, 1922 a residence at 2415 South Western Avenue, Los Angeles [on the corner of 24th street], for himself and other members of his family. Since that time, he had been a permanent resident of Los Angeles. After that purchase, Jack lived there for approximately 1.5 years with his mother and father, who eventually returned to Salt Lake City. Jack continued to make that home his residence until December 1924, when he and his manager, Jack Kearns, purchased the Barbara Hotel in Los Angeles, and Dempsey lived there. In 1923, he and Kearns had purchased the Wilshire Apartments, also in Los Angeles. The two properties represented an investment of approximately $800,000. Dempsey lived in the Barbara until his marriage [February 7, 1925], when he and his wife moved to 2535 North Commonwealth Street, Los Angeles. In the spring of 1926, Dempsey moved to 5254 Los Feliz Boulevard, Los Angeles, which property he had leased with the option to purchase. At no time since age 12 had Dempsey resided in Colorado, and he had not visited except as a transient visitor. He only traveled to different parts of the country for work-related purposes, but always resided in Los Angeles and returned there as soon as his work permitted. Dempsey owned some property in Utah, a home for his mother and father, but owned no property in Colorado. His income tax statements were filed in Los Angeles.

After signing articles of agreement with Gene Tunney in April 1926, Dempsey returned to California in June 1926, remaining there for 4 weeks, leaving for a brief period to train in the Colorado mountains. It was well known that he was in California at Madera for a trial on a charge of a violation of the motor vehicle laws there.

Jack Dempsey swore out and signed an affidavit stating that he resided at 5254 Los Feliz Blvd., Los Angeles, and had not resided in Colorado at any time in the last 20 years. He still owned the Hotel Barbara [at the corner of 6th and Westlake streets, Los Angeles], and voted and filed tax returns in Los Angeles. He noted that in the action filed in Marion County, Indiana, the Chicago Coliseum Club verified upon oath of B. E. Clements on August 2, 1926, that Dempsey is, and at all times mentioned in its complaint was, a resident of California.

Attorney Kenneth E. Grant stated that Dempsey was a member of Los Angeles Lodge No. 99, Benevolent and Protective Order of Elks, formally becoming a member on April 7, 1926, after demitting from the Long Branch, New York [sic – New Jersey] Lodge on January 21, 1926.

Ultimately, it appeared that the federal case in Colorado was going nowhere, for lack of personal jurisdiction.

On September 7, 1926, in Indianapolis, Judge Clinton Givan admitted into evidence a purported carbon copy of the Dempsey-Coliseum Club contract alleged to have been signed by the champion.

The sensation of the hearing was created when from the witness stand, B. E. Clements, club president, declared that Dempsey told him that he had burned the original copies of the contract after Floyd Fitzsimmons gave them to him. Clements said, "I asked Dempsey if he didn't know he had destroyed property of the Chicago Coliseum Club." "Yes, but it's too late now to do anything about it." Clements alleged that when he asked Dempsey if he had signed anything with Tex Rickard which would interfere with his contract, Dempsey told him that Rickard had given him $40,000.

Clements asserted that a $300,000 check had been deposited for Dempsey in a Chicago bank, but Dempsey had not redeemed it. A photostatic copy of the check was introduced into evidence. Clements sent Dempsey two registered letters, but he refused to sign for them.

Clements testified that after Dempsey signed three copies of the contract, he signed two copies of a supplementary agreement. This agreement changed portions of the original contract to read that Dempsey was to get 50% of the gross receipts instead of the net, and that the money was to be paid directly to him instead of through a Los Angeles bank. Dempsey's attorney brought out the fact that the date on the post-agreement was March 11, but Clements testified the contract and supplement were signed on March 13, the March 11 date being an error on the part of a stenographer.[466]

The next day, Clements testified that Dempsey was offered a $10 binder in Los Angeles when the alleged contract was signed, but he refused it.

William Huffman testified that he went to Colorado Springs, Colorado to make arrangements for Dempsey's physical examination in compliance with the contract, but Dempsey refused the exam and said there was no contract. Huffman asserted that Dempsey told him that Floyd Fitzsimmons returned the contracts for the fight to him and that he (Dempsey) destroyed them.

There was a real question regarding whether Dempsey would show up in Indiana to testify and rebut Clements' claims. He was training in the East and might not be able or inclined to take time off to travel. The judge had refused to allow Dempsey to testify via affidavit. Ultimately, Dempsey did not show up, so anything he had to say regarding the matter was inadmissible.[467]

Harvard trainer Pooch Donovan, who had seen every champion since Sullivan, said Tunney seemed top-heavy, with his body a trifle large for his legs. He telegraphed his punches, especially his right, got in a bad position when he hit, and was very bad when against the ropes. He did not wrestle

---

[466] *Indianapolis Star, Times, News*, September 8, 1926. It appears that no signed copies of the original or supplementary agreements ever were put into evidence, the argument being that Dempsey had destroyed them.
[467] *Indianapolis Times, News*, September 9, 10, 1926.

very well either. However, he also said Tunney's condition was far superior to Dempsey's.

In describing Tunney's right, Harry Newman said it was a bit looping, but powerful. "Gene shoots the bang high, but as the punch nears his opponent it sort of drops with fearful speed on the target."

On September 7, Gene sparred 2 rounds each with Billy Vidabeck, Harold Mays, and Bud Gorman. Leo Houck, who fought Tunney twice, said Gene looked great.

Tunney said he was at Quantico Marine Corps Base in 1917. Many criticized him for not having the killer instinct or desire to hurt and knock out his foes. Gene said should the opportunity arise, he would try for a knockout, not because he derived any thrill from it, but because it would bring him the championship. He would do what he needed to do to win, because it was his business, just as he was trained to do what was necessary against the Germans in war.

Lou Fink said Tunney had courage, gameness, and heart, and could take it. When he fought Greb the first time, he was battered into a pulp. His nose was broken at the start of the contest, his eyes were split, an artery severed, and he scarcely could see. He gamely finished the fight on his feet, having fought hard all the way. Afterwards, he said, "I can lick that fellow." "Now, anybody who could take the beating Tunney took and talk like that is as game a guy that ever crept under the ropes."

Fink said Tunney had improved vastly. "Dempsey never fought as good a man as Tunney in his life." Gene refrained from bad habits. He had youth, strength, brains, boxing ability, and punching power, and Dempsey never met a man quite like him. At 188 pounds, he was big and strong enough to handle Dempsey.[468]

A confident Tunney said Firpo, a poor, clumsy fighter, without the slightest knowledge of boxing skill, managed to land and knock Dempsey out of the ring. When Jack came back, Firpo did not know what to do next. "I have never lost my head in a fight and I don't think I will if a crisis arises in this row."

Dempsey said he never weighed as much or as little as some speculated. He weighed 200 pounds at the start of training camp. His nose was holding up under blows just the same as it ever did. In fact, his nose was even better, because he could breathe through it now. He had it broken in his early years of fighting, and broken pieces of cartilage had interfered with his breathing.

Dempsey said he was not worrying. "It's true that I'm missing a few that I throw at sparring partners' heads and it's also true that I'm not getting out of the way of all the punches tossed at me. But my legs are all right." He could go 30 minutes on his toes without ever dropping his heels. His strong legs ensured he could take it, and with his punching power, he would find a way to land and win.[469]

[468] *Philadelphia Inquirer, New York Daily News*, September 8, 9, 1926.
[469] *Philadelphia Inquirer, New York Daily News*, September 9, 1926.

Early in his life, Gene worked for the Ocean Steamship company at a modest salary of $12 per week. Some claimed that Tunney did not start boxing until he entered the marines, but such was not true. He had five pro fights prior to enlisting in the marines (though some claim more).

Harry Newman said Tunney was fast with both of his hands, speedy of foot, and hitting like a trip-hammer.

On the 9th, Tunney sparred 2 rounds each with Bryan Downey, Billy Vidabeck, and Harold Mays.

Tunney wrote, "I am going to be heavyweight champion. This may smack of braggadocio, but it is merely a firm conviction on my part that I am a better pugilist than is Jack Dempsey."

Dempsey submitted a list of names of officials who would be acceptable to him. One of them was Tommy Reilly. Commission chairman Wiener informed the parties that the selection of officials would be made in advance, but the choices kept secret until a few moments before the contestants stepped into the ring. That method prevented any potential tampering.

Under Pennsylvania law, if the two judges agreed, the referee did not give a decision, but if there was a divide, then the referee would cast the deciding vote.

Paul Gallico said Tunney appeared to be bigger, stronger, and better than ever. Although Dempsey seemed to be rounding into form, no one really knew whether he ever could approach real condition or the form he had three years ago. And there was no way to know whether Tunney could take Dempsey's punch. Ultimately, Gallico picked Dempsey to retain his title by knockout.

Dempsey said he was going to fight, even if Tunney was going to try to box. His method was to step out and knock or get knocked out. "Stalling and posing and making motions – that's not my idea. I never was tossed out of any ring for not providing action in any bout in my career – and I'm not going to be. I figure the crowd pays its money to see plenty of terrific action; to see two men striving to the utmost to secure a knockout victory." Jack had been in the ring many times with men who figured they'd just step around and strut their cleverness, but none got away with it for long, for he made them fight. He did not want to lose while still on his feet.[470]

---

[470] *New York Daily News, Philadelphia Inquirer,* September 10, 1926. Jack again admitted that he never had seen Tunney in action.

Dempsey weighed about 200 pounds, having gained some weight during his respite. He said the extra poundage would prevent him from becoming too drawn. On September 10, he sparred Bill Tate, Charley Anderson, Frank Carpenter, and Martin Burke. He was particularly homicidal against his black sparring partners, for he knew they could take it.

Several said Dempsey seemed to have recaptured his old form. Many, including Leo Houck, Benny Leonard, Jim Londos, and Pooch Donovan, all said Tunney would be lucky to remain upright for 10 rounds. Doc Bagley, once Tunney's manager, said Dempsey would stop Tunney in less than 3 full rounds.

However, another local report said Dempsey was slow and boxing clumsily, missing often, and wild with his blows when trying to land to the head. He paid no attention to defense, being hit hard and often, apparently willing to do so in order to land body blows.

In an affidavit in the lawsuit Kearns filed against Dempsey for a third of a million dollars, which was transferred to federal court, Dan McKetrick quoted Dempsey as having admitted to him, "I have nothing against Doc, but Estelle cannot get along with him and we have reached the parting of the ways.. .... If I cannot get out of my contract with him I won't put on another glove during the life of that contract, and if I should fight, you may be sure Kearns will get his share of the purse." The affidavit further said that Dempsey commissioned Kearns to arrange bouts with Tunney and Wills, assuring Kearns that he could beat both.

Billy Gibson, on Tunney's behalf, and Gene Normile, acting for Dempsey, met with the commission to discuss the rules. Each corner would be limited to four seconds. Dempsey's seconds would be manager Gene Normile, Captain Charles Mabbutt, Gus Wilson, and trainer Jerry Luvadis (Jerry the Greek). Tunney's seconds would include manager Billy Gibson, trainer Louis Fink, and two others.

The rules governing the battle barred the rabbit, kidney, and pivot blows. Furthermore, when a man went down, his foe had to go to a neutral corner and remain there until the downed fighter rose again.

Dempsey said he had quality sparring partners. Bill Tate had Wills on the floor twice. Marty Burke twice went the distance with Tunney (10 and 15 rounds), giving a good account of himself. Tillie Kid Herman was one of the best in his division (middleweight). 212-pound Charlie Anderson was a comer, a hard hitter, fast, clever, and a wonder at taking it.[471]

Before Gene's workout on September 11 at Stroudsburg, before a big crowd of several thousand, General John A. Lejeune presented Tunney with a gorgeous blue lounging robe from the U.S. Marine Corps, a gift from the 18,000 marines, Gene's former buddies. It was made of doeskin, with the elaborate gold insignia of the marines stitched onto the back. Gene intended to wear it into his corner on fight night.

[471] *New York Daily News, Philadelphia Inquirer*, September 11, 1926.

According to Harry Newman, that day, Tunney looked like a million dollars as he whaled the life out of his sparring partners. He shook Billy Vidabeck repeatedly with straight rights during their 2 rounds. Gene showed a swell left hand, hooking ripping lefts to the stomach. Tunney wore a plaster over his sore lip, which started as a cold sore but spread all over his lower lip. The rugged Harold Mays, during his 2 rounds, rushed Gene to the ropes and missed a fierce left. Gene immediately responded in an instant with a right that nearly tore Harold's head off. A wild scrimmage followed, and a woman spectator fainted. Even though Mays was throwing all sorts of punches at him, Gene saw her and called for trainer Lou Fink to fetch her some water. Yet, Gene never stopped.

Frank McCracken said Tunney loomed as the best man Dempsey ever had to beat. He was not flashy, but had confidence, speed, good power, skill, and condition, was game, could take a punch, and had a good record, with plenty of experience. He knew how to fight. He was stronger than Carpentier. He also had youth on his side. He was not a lumbering giant like Firpo, but was quick on his feet. Three years had softened up Dempsey. Still, it was hard to conceive of the ruthless, hard-hitting champion being beaten.

Gordon MacKay for the *Philadelphia Inquirer* said Tunney had a splendid chance to win. He had youth, strength, skill, and confidence. Dempsey was the favorite, but it likely was going to be a great fight. Tunney was the best man Dempsey had met since he won the crown, for Gene "has a knowledge of boxing such as none of the foes of Dempsey in the alter days, not even Tom Gibbons, possessed." He did not fear Dempsey. He had proven ability to take it, too.

As champion, Dempsey always had come through to win. He had the ferocity and power of a lion. But three years absence from the ring made him an enigma. He even seemed to be training differently, not as hard or as often as in the past. He used to love training. Some said he was getting hit more than in the past, too.

Jimmy De Forest said Dempsey had not lost his jaw-jarring, body-bruising punch. He remained the hardest-hitting two-fisted fighter in the ring. "Why, this man Dempsey can punch three inches or less and knock an opponent into the next hour. He hits so hard that no man can stand up under a sock that lands on the button or around the heart. ... Say what you please about him – about his lay-off, his age, his lack of accuracy and so forth – Dempsey hasn't lost his punch."

Tommy Loughran   Bill Tate   Charley Anderson

On the 11th at Atlantic City, before a crowd of 3,000, Dempsey sparred 1 round with Bill Tate, 2 with Tommy Loughran, and 1 round each with Charles Anderson and Mike Arnold.

Tommy Loughran (65-15-7), known as the "uncrowned" light heavyweight champion of the world, who once fought Tunney (1922 LND8) and was coming off a recent W10 over Carpentier, went at it with Dempsey for 2 thrilling rounds. The champ landed several savage lefts and rights to the face and body, but Tommy responded in kind, several times sending Dempsey's head back. Loughran was a masterful boxer, and he carried Dempsey at a terrific pace, forcing him to extend himself to the limit to avoid being shown up. Tommy shot in straight lefts to Jack's reddened face and rights to the chin. Dempsey responded with several heavy blows.

When it was over, Loughran said, "What a hitter that man is! If Tunney ever steps back from him, as is his style, the champ will floor him with one punch. His short punches are so fast I didn't know where they were coming from. What snap and sting to those shorter blows!" Another quoted Loughran as saying, "Oh boy, how that man can sock. … He moves around fast, bobbing and weaving and makes a tough target, and he always comes tearing in, no matter how hard you hit him."[472]

Dempsey ducks Loughran right   Dempsey wallops Tommy Loughran

On September 12, 4,000 people watched Dempsey give Loughran a pasting over 2 strenuous rounds. In the 2nd round, a small trickle of blood was observed on Loughran's jaw. Dempsey also went 2 rounds with Martin Burke and 1 round with Frankie Carpenter.

Afterwards, Loughran said,

---

[472] New York Daily News, Philadelphia Inquirer, Philadelphia Public Ledger, September 12, 1926. Dempsey was the 2 to 1 odds favorite.

223

I was impressed by Dempsey yesterday, but today his timing and his idea of distance were much better. ... Dempsey will knock out Tunney in three rounds, possibly four. Tunney may outbox Jack for two rounds, but I think about the third round Jack will reach him, and it will be all over. This Dempsey is the most wonderful fighter in the world. He could be 50 per cent worse than he is now and lick all the heavyweights in the world, one by one, in a day.

Loughran said Tunney could be twice as good as when they fought in 1922 and still would lose to Dempsey.

Philadelphia Jack O'Brien said Dempsey was too powerful, and he made you fight him. He knew some tricks too. He feinted and then hit with the same hand. He knew how to double up the same hand to the body and head. He could time his foe and beat him to the punch. There were only two ways to fight him – one was to take a chance with everything you had, like Carpentier and Firpo, and the other was to cover up and do little fighting, like Gibbons.

When asked about Wills, Dempsey said, "You can tell the wide world that I never will fight Harry Wills. He or his manager, Paddy Mullins, never will make a cent out of me. They have hampered me in nearly every way possible. They even tried to stop me from meeting Tunney."

Dempsey said he enjoyed the adulation of the crowds, but it also grew tiresome at times. He had about as much privacy as a goldfish. In the morning, he ran from 6 to 8 miles. Mike Trant, Captain Tapscott, trainer Jerry Luvadis, and Miss Lubudda, his cook, were his companions. Trant had been with him since 1918, when he was in his corner for the Homer Smith fight, and he had been in his corner for every battle since then. Trant was a detective on the Chicago force, but always took time off to join him for training camps and the fight.

Jimmy De Forest said both fighters were training incorrectly, in charge of their own training. Still, he believed that Tunney was ahead of Dempsey in preparation. He thought Gene was the best man that Dempsey ever had faced, in fine condition, and it would be a great fight.

In his workout on the 12th, before 4,500 spectators at Stroudsburg, Gene the Marine looked both speedy and vicious against Vidabeck and Mays. He landed continual lefts, and his right was working to perfection.

Johnny Dundee said Tunney was a greatly improved fighter, and Dempsey would have to win by knockout, because if it went the distance, Tunney was liable to outpoint him.

The *Philadelphia Inquirer*'s Perry Lewis said Tunney was very popular in Pennsylvania. "The challenger's remarkable personality has captured this country, and the population is with him to a man." Gene was an intellectual, a reader, cultured, refined, and well-spoken. Dempsey had the image of a caveman, but in fact had a suavity that gave him an air of distinction.

In the ring, Dempsey was vicious, with a scowl, down to work, with intense focus and concentration. Tunney had a smile, a pleasant nod, and was more relaxed in demeanor. Both men could punch, but Tunney was hitting with greater sharpness, and his judgment of distance was superior.

The parallels to Sullivan-Corbett were unmistakable. Like Corbett, Tunney was a fast, skilled, slick, defensively-sound boxer with excellent footwork, fighting a hard-punching champ who had not fought in three years, a very long time for a fighter, particularly when competing at the highest levels. If Tunney won, he would be the third James J. to win the heavyweight crown. Tunney's real name was James Joseph, the same as James J. Corbett. James J. Jeffries also had been champion.[473]

On September 12, in court in Indiana, Floyd Fitzsimmons asserted on the witness stand that the Chicago Coliseum Club "had never paid a dime" to Dempsey to bind the Wills fight.

Fitzsimmons said Dempsey signed the contract on March 13 in Los Angeles and handed the documents back to him to be put in a bank and held in escrow. The contract never was sent to Clements. Some reported that later, Fitz placed the contracts in escrow in a Chicago bank.

Fitzsimmons said he and Clements left Chicago on March 11 with four copies of the contract and a check for $100,000 to be paid to Dempsey. After Dempsey signed three of the contracts and learned the $100,000 was deposited in a Los Angeles bank, Dempsey said, "I want my money in cash or there won't be no fight." Clements quieted Dempsey by a private agreement whereby the champion was to be paid in cash. Dempsey signed one copy of the private supplementary agreement.

Fitzsimmons testified that he attempted many times to persuade Clements to raise the $100,000 cash by the date specified in the contract to bind the contract. Fitz said he begged the Chicago officials to produce the $100,000 many times, even after the time limit designated in the contract had expired.

Fitzsimmons further said that when the club failed to pay the $100,000 to bind the agreement, Dempsey asked him for the contracts, which he gave him, and Jack destroyed them, given that he believed the club could not make payments. Fitz also said Dempsey objected when he learned that he was to get only $800,000, for he wanted $1 million. Furthermore, Fitz was not aware of any term that prevented Dempsey from boxing Tunney as an interim contest.[474]

Unfortunately, no one produced that supplementary agreement, if it existed, but clearly, based on his multiple interviews, and Fitz's testimony, Dempsey believed he was owed money well before the August 5 date, and felt that since he never received it, he was entitled to repudiate the contract and move on with Rickard, who always paid him very well, gave him money up front, always pulled off the fights, and had warned him that no jurisdiction would allow the Wills fight. Clements never cited a jurisdiction in which the Dempsey-Wills fight would be allowed (Chicago

[473] New York Daily News, Philadelphia Inquirer, September 13, 1926.
[474] Indianapolis News, Times, September 13, 1926. The real question is whether Dempsey ever signed the version of the contract that Clements had filed with the court, for neither Dempsey nor Fitzsimmons appeared to be aware of several of its terms, and, given Jack's prior and subsequent positions, likely would not have signed such a contract.

forbade it), so Rickard had a point. Anyhow, if a supplementary agreement ever existed in which he was to be paid $100,000 by a certain date, Dempsey possibly foolishly destroyed it.

Even though prize fighting purportedly was illegal under Indiana law, on September 13, 1926, Indiana Superior Court Judge Clinton Givan enjoined the Dempsey-Tunney fight, holding that Dempsey must fight Wills before Tunney, for the Chicago Coliseum Club's contract entered into on March 13, 1926 in Los Angeles with Dempsey was an enforceable contract (at least under other state's laws), and Dempsey had breached it. The judge also enjoined Dempsey from training or preparing for or making contracts concerning any other fight.

It was unclear what cognizance, if any, Pennsylvania courts would take of the injunction.

The judge held that Dempsey had breached the contract first by refusing to fight pursuant to it, insisting that he was preparing to fight Tunney, a fight he took without the Club's consent, repudiating and declaring the contract nonexistent, and also by refusing to be examined for insurance purposes as the contract required.

The press reported that on September 25, 1925, Dempsey signed at Niles, Michigan a contract with Floyd Fitzsimmons to fight Harry Wills in either Michigan, Indiana, Ohio, Illinois, or Missouri. Fitz sold the contract to William E. Clements, president of the Chicago Coliseum Club. Dempsey signed a new contract with the club to meet Wills in any state except New York. He was to receive $300,000 before the fight, and another $500,000 after the fight, the money to be held in escrow in Chicago banks. The judge noted that the Club was ready, willing, and able to pay Dempsey the $300,000 on August 5, as required by the contract.

According to the press, showing bias, the judge noted, perhaps orally, or perhaps an invention of the press, "I believe the court in this case would have to take notice that while Mr. Dempsey was very peaceable when America's best youth was fighting for $30 a month he is a formidable fighter when a million dollars is at stake for one night's work..." However, the judge's actual written ruling did not say that.

The press reported that the judge recognized that although the carrying out of the contract would be illegal in Indiana, he acknowledged that a property right had been accrued in other states where it had been legal both to make and carry out the contract. But then the question is, why wasn't jurisdiction in Illinois or one of those other states? Why was the case brought and heard in Indiana? The contract was made in Illinois and California. In fact, this judge never mentioned in his written ruling the legal status of boxing in Indiana. Regardless, one has to question why the case was not brought and heard in Illinois. Also not mentioned in the ruling was the fact that the plaintiff proffered no definite date or location for the fight. Illinois, where the Chicago Club claimed the fight would be held, was out of the question, given that the state athletic commission said heavyweight fights were barred for the foreseeable future.

Dempsey's lawyers had argued, unsuccessfully, that he never was paid any money, and hence the agreements were invalidated by the default on the installment payments due; a great deal of time had elapsed since the contract was signed, and nothing happened; and by the time they tried to pay him in August, he already had signed with Rickard to fight Tunney.

Tex Rickard was confident that any attempt to stop the Dempsey-Tunney fight in Pennsylvania would be unsuccessful. He had received Pennsylvania Governor Pinchot's approval, as well as officials of the Sesquicentennial. "Before signing Dempsey, I went thoroughly into the claim of the Chicago Coliseum Club and was convinced it was without merit. The club promised Dempsey a million dollar purse, but did not put up a nickel."

Tex claimed he guaranteed Dempsey $450,000, plus 10% of all receipts above $1,000,000, while Tunney would earn a flat fee of $150,000. Tex anticipated that the receipts would reach at least $1.7 million, for $1,368.377.14 already had been deposited from ticket sales. Rickard retained the motion picture and broadcasting rights.

Pennsylvania athletic commission chairman Frank Wiener said, "We will go right ahead and plan for the bout and let the legal end take care of itself. Just how far-reaching that injunction is, and whether it can stop the fight in Pennsylvania will have to be determined later. But I hardly see how it can stop the fight."[475]

In Dempsey's sparring on the 13th, it was Tommy Loughran for 2, Martin Burke for 2, and then 1 round each with Mike Arnold and welter Herman Auerbach, son of his first manager.

Dempsey floors Herman Auerbach   Loughran on left and Dempsey on right

Gordan MacKay's take on Dempsey's training was that Loughran was faster, stepping all around him, peppering him plentifully at long range, working his jab well, holding the champ at bay, completely outboxing Dempsey, not giving him many opportunities to wade in and land a big one, though not hurting him in their 2 rounds. Jack's judgment of distance was poor, though his sock was stronger and his blows hurt when they did land. Loughran landed some hard, solid blows, but Dempsey took them like an elephant being slapped with a feather duster.

[475] *New York Daily News, Richmond Palladium and Sun-Telegram, Indianapolis Star, Indianapolis Times, Indianapolis News, Elmira Star-Gazette, Buffalo Times,* September 14, 1926; Chicago Coliseum Club v. Jack Dempsey, A 36542, Marion County, Indiana.

MacKay quoted Loughran as saying that Jack's judgment of distance was not so good, but "don't make any mistake about his punching, he was hitting harder than ever." Dempsey's punches hurt all the time, and one could not keep away forever. Jack could take a punch, knew how to ride them, and never stepped back.

Another quoted Loughran as saying, "I don't see how anybody can beat this guy. How are you going to fight him when you got to think about hitting him at the same time that you are trying to keep away from him. It can't be done."

One observer said that overall, Dempsey eased up a bit, letting loose only against Marty Burke. Jack threw a fast flock of punches, a right uppercut drawing blood from Burke's nose and mouth, and he was a gory, bleeding spectacle.

Pooch Donovan said Dempsey was not right at first mentally in his training, but he was right now. Donovan said Tunney was cocky and would be tough to beat.

Ike O'Neill said stories about Dempsey and his bad legs, poor boxing, and general rundown condition were baloney. "Look at him. On his toes all the time. He hooks from any angle. He is unlike anybody who ever lived as a fighter."

Gus Wilson, one of the champ's trainers, said nothing could daunt Dempsey, and he had an overwhelming will.

Benny Leonard said, "He is a remarkable fighter. He looks as good to me as he ever did."

Dempsey said that early in his training camp, he was experimenting with a different style, but he was through with that. He would fight with his usual slam-bang aggressiveness, as always. Some advisers wanted him to try out counterpunching, allowing partners to take the offensive. He tried it, but such was not for him. It was not his nature to wait for the other fellow. He simply could not wait patiently. Attacking and punching all the time was his way. It was what he knew, and what brought him to where he was.

> Countering is Tunney's game. I hear he is good at it. He'll need to be if he thinks he's going to do any successful countering with me. No man ever did it yet for the simple reason that I tear into a man so fast when I'm in action and shoot so many punches at him that he's usually too busy getting out of the way to be spending much time trying to nail me with a counter punch. I might point out that even with the use of my old weaving, shifting, bobbing style I'm pretty good at countering myself.

Jack preferred to counter while on the attack, should a foe throw back at him.

The press noted that Tunney had fought Soldier Jones in a preliminary to the Dempsey-Carpentier fight. He won a technical knockout, but it was "a terrible fight." He made a mistake in fighting Greb, who gave him the worst beating of his career. But he won rematches. Gene's knees buckled and sagged against KO Sullivan in the 1st round of their contest, but he did not go down, and Tunney knocked him out (though he badly broke his right hand in the process). Gene never had been down in his entire career. In 1924, he and Jack Renault both were fined for stalling. Tunney had some dull, lackluster performances mixed in.

On the 13th, Tunney was looking formidable, sparring with Oskar Till and Harold Mays. A Till jab in the 2nd round managed to bring blood from Gene's bruised lip. Mays went at Tunney hard, and Gene countered with tantalizing left jabs and counter rights.

Perry Lewis said Tunney cut loose against his sparring partners and was quite vicious. He was very impressive as he shot punches with splendid precision to the jaw and body. He could counter better than any man in the ring. His boxing was perfect.

Tunney backed into corner   Tunney strikes Osk Till

Tunney said Billy Gibson was the best manager in the business. In three years, he had taken him to the American light heavyweight championship, and then to a duel for the world heavyweight championship, making more money for him than he ever expected to see in his life.[476]

Rickard anticipated a sellout, which would eclipse the record of $1,626,580 set by Dempsey-Carpentier by at least $100,000. The initial seating capacity was 72,000, but with the temporary stands being built, the capacity would be increased to 125,635, which would be the largest crowd ever to see a fight.

Dempsey said comparisons between he and John L. Sullivan were not fair. Sullivan abused himself badly, indulged in food and drink, and was some 45 pounds overweight, rarely putting on a glove during the time he did not fight. Conversely, Jack rarely was more than eight pounds overweight, had trained and exhibited, and for the last year had been active. He noted that he had no fewer fights as champion than most former champions.

Jimmy De Forest said Dempsey was fit. "Tunney may be a better man and may win the fight – that remains to be seen – but it will be the old

[476] New York Daily News, September 14, 15, 1926; Philadelphia Inquirer, September 14, 1926.

Dempsey in the ring. I'll tell you something: Once a puncher, always a puncher. Jack hits harder now than ever."

Tommy Gibbons made somewhat contradictory statements. He claimed that Dempsey's long layoff had not hurt him, and he looked even better than when they fought at Shelby. Jack was 10-15 pounds bigger. Still, Tommy admitted that Dempsey was a bit flatfooted.

Gibbons said Loughran, who had fought Tunney, had given Dempsey some snappy workouts, mixing boxing skill and speed to counteract Dempsey's boring-in style. "Though Loughran fought well, Jack was on top of him every minute and saw to it Loughran was on the receiving end of all the important wallops." Loughran was a lot like Tunney, but Dempsey broke through his guard, and even occasionally outboxed him. "Dempsey, although loggy at times, proved he could step out when the occasion demanded."

Dempsey's training system for this fight included resting frequently so as not to overtrain. Still, Gibbons said, "I do think the Manassa mauler should do a little more mauling. Before all of his previous battles Dempsey did more intensive training than he is staging here." At Shelby, he pounded on his sparring partners. In this instance, "Jack drifts along pretty easily." Tom thought Jack should be training harder. Dempsey was using a "slow and easy training system."

> He's good, awfully good just now, but he's liable to need everything before Gene gets through whanging at him. I speak from experience. When Mr. Tunney starts his scientific countering and slams home a few wicked lefts to the liver Jack will have to step lively. Gene caught me with one of those liver hammers last year and I won't forget it for some little while.

Regardless of Dempsey's training, Tunney's counter timing had to be perfect, for if it was not, the birds would start singing early. "I remember at Shelby he was all over the ring, on top of me every minute and a mighty hard lad to avoid." Conversely, "Tunney is a different style fighter. He does more jabbing, is faster and more deceptive with his feet and is constantly watching for an opening for that deadly left. ... I remember he used it effectively against Greb, Jimmy Delaney and me."

Tom said Tunney had to be careful defensively against both of Dempsey's fists. Dempsey had a vaunted left, and in their fight, he especially watched out for it. But in the 1st round, Tom ran into a very fast right. "It mighty near finished me up right then and there."

Tunney was good at using his left, both offensively and defensively. "He uses this arm like a ramrod that knocks and keeps opponents out of range." He would use his left to keep Dempsey off of him.

Concluding, Gibbons said, "Summed up, I believe Dempsey is still a great fighter, with a terrific wallop. He is fast on his feet, when necessary, has a cobra weaving motion that works him through a defense to slam home important blows and he can take wallops on the chin that would knock the ordinary fistic gent out of the ring." Still, Tom said Jack needed to speed up and lose some weight.

Dempsey was not worried about any injunction. He said he did not receive a cent from the Chicago folks. Given that they had not put anything on the line, he considered the contract void. His lawyer said an appeal would be taken against the injunction, and by the time that was decided, the fight would be over. Furthermore, Philadelphia authorities declared that the order had no force or effect in Pennsylvania whatsoever. Local Mayor W. Freeland Kendrick promised to support the fight. The Attorney General said Pennsylvania was not bound to enforce the Indianapolis injunction, for it had no legal force there. Pennsylvania Governor Gifford Pinchot believed that at least ten state governors would attend the fight.

Dempsey thought the attempts to stop the fight were laughable. He said the contract with the Indiana folks was not worth the paper it was written upon since last November 1925.

> When Fitzsimmons told me he had plenty of promised backing I agreed to wait for my first payment so that he could advance Wills $55,000 and tie Wills up. I got that $55,000 for Wills and never got a nickel for myself. The contract provided that on a certain date I was to get a first payment of $125,000, with other payments following at stated intervals. When the time came for that first payment that was to tie me up to the contract there was no money.

Dempsey graciously gave Fitz a time extension.

> Another date was fixed. When that came there was no money. I don't blame Fitzsimmons. He's a nice fellow. But the people with the money wouldn't put up until Fitz had a sure-fire place to hold the fight, and everywhere he tried the opposition to Wills killed it. It just went flat after a while, and I notified Fitzsimmons that the contract was void because the payments called for hadn't been made. Then I went ahead with Rickard. I waited as long as I could for Fitz to make good and put the fight on, and he couldn't do it.

The champ said it cost $30,000 to train for a championship fight.

> It cost a lot more than that with Kearns on the job, but that's what it costs me. There are hundreds of things to pay for in a big camp. I have made just about enough out of the gate money [charged to watch him train] to pay my training expenses. I did it [charged folks to watch him train] because when I started I wasn't as sure of winning as I might have been if I'd been fighting oftener. I didn't know just what shape I could get into. Thirty thousand isn't much money to a winner, but it might be pretty important to a loser, and you have to think of everything in this business.

Retired lightweight champ Benny Leonard said he sparred Dempsey on the 14th (for the motion picture camera), and asked Jack to let himself out more. "I wanted a sample of the real Dempsey." Leonard jabbed him often, and said, "Listen, Jack, no one has a right to get you with a left jab like that, and they will as long as you try this boxing. Fall into your stuff." In the 2nd round, Jack came after him. Benny decided to move in too and take a chance. "I moved in with a left feint and planted a hard right on the champion's nose. Jack himself says I am no light hitter." Jack hit him with stiff jolts to the wind, and a sock from his right raised a bump on his left cheek. "I tried my best to box but you can't keep Dempsey off with any kind of punch once he sets in with that great tidal wave rush of his."

In conclusion, Leonard said, "When Dempsey is fresh, you cannot box him. You can't fight his style, your style or any style. He forces you to fight. ... You are carried along helpless, unable to do the things you ordinarily can do. ... [A]nd all you try to do is grab or swing or shoot punches wildly at a rapidly moving target." Leonard said even when Dempsey landed lightly, his blows carried weight and force. "They feel a good deal like a heavy log that is being propelled on a wagon. ... Oh, mamma, when he lets go they just numb you." Leonard said Dempsey was faster than he seemed, for he kept Benny stepping at top speed.[477]

Regarding the sparring on the 15th, Harry Newman said Loughran and Burke smacked Dempsey with many blows. "They cuffed him around plenty, ripped right hand uppercuts through his guard and smacked him good and hard with straight left hand smacks to the kisser." Dempsey was hittable. Loughran especially rapped him with some corking short right uppercuts, and varied it with a left jab to the face. Still, there were times when Tommy had a tough time holding the champ off, and he took many socks to the ribs. The furious body bombardment hurt Loughran.

Burke, also a light heavy, went 2 more rounds, and Marty kept pegging in left jabs, rights, and right uppercuts. It seemed as though the champ did not care whether he was hit or not. He kept boring in, and he never tried to weave away from anything fired at him. Nevertheless, Dempsey beat Burke's face and body badly.

Robert Edgren said Dempsey took hard socks from Loughran that might have annoyed a lot of people, but Dempsey ignored them. He also boxed with Burke and Benny Kruger, German middleweight champ.

Various notables offered their opinions regarding the upcoming fight:

Tommy Loughran: "I don't figure that Tunney can stand up under any more than three or four rounds of Dempsey's terrific battering."

Benny Leonard: "Dempsey's condition is remarkable. He's a marvel at taking punishment and I don't think a man lives who can survive in a ring very long after Dempsey crashes that fearful left hook to the chin or his right hand to the body."

Philadelphia Jack O'Brien: "When I first saw Dempsey I thought he was slow and not so good. But today he looks like a million dollars... I can't see anything now but Dempsey – and maybe in about five rounds."

477 *Philadelphia Inquirer, New York Daily News, Philadelphia Evening Bulletin*, September 15, 1926.

Featherweight champ Johnny Dundee: "This bird Dempsey will be champion until a long set of whiskers interferes with his marksmanship."

Al Auerbach: "It will hardly be a workout for Jack." However, another quoted him as saying, "Tunney is big and strong, is young and can box. To me, Tunney figures to be the best man Dempsey has ever fought."

Jack Curley: "Dempsey's a cinch to win – and in a hurry."

Jack Renault (who fought Tunney and previously had been a Dempsey sparring partner): "Dempsey is in great shape and those who call him the greatest champion aren't far wrong."

George Godfrey: "Nobody can beat this Jack – and that includes Tunney. This man Jack, well, he is a fighter."

Martin Burke, Dempsey's sparring partner, who twice fought Tunney: "Jack can't lose this fight. Tunney isn't in his class."

On Tunney's behalf, Ray Campbell submitted Gene's boxing license application. Campbell was the *Cleveland News* writer who in September 1925 said Tunney clearly won the fourth fight with Greb. Apparently, Campbell recently had been hired as a Tunney publicity/press agent.[478]

Tommy Loughran said it was no good boxing Dempsey, for he crowded in all the time and there was no escape. Punches had no effect on him. "I don't think he even knew that I hit him." Tunney could not afford to fool with the champion for a minute. "God help Tunney." Jack was boxing and timing his punches better, and his blows stung worse. The champ thought quickly and immediately seized upon openings.

Jack McAuliffe, former lightweight champ, was not impressed with Dempsey. He said he was being hit too often. Still, Dempsey did everything by instinct, whereas Tunney had to study out everything.

Spencer Penrose said Dempsey was in good condition. He had been in Colorado Springs for a time, running every morning for 5-6 miles.

Jack said, "Never felt better in my life. I'm in great shape, and I can walk right into the ring now. … I tip round 195 pounds now."

Gus Wilson said Jack was as good as ever, as fast as ever, stronger, boxing better, slipping punches off his shoulder that he once took, and blocking better too.[479]

On September 16, with the fight one week away, a Loughran right drew blood from Dempsey's nose, but it was just a slight trickle. Dempsey laughed and said his nose was fine, taking punches well. Still, even before the workout, Jack had a bit of a black eye.

The champ opened the sparring by shellacking Frankie Carpenter for 1 round. For the first minute of his sparring with Loughran, it looked like he was determined to knock him out, but then Jack slowed down, and Tommy held his own. "Dempsey appears to be getting better as he nears the end of his training campaign." Burke also boxed 2 rounds.

[478] *Pittsburgh Daily Post*, September 16, 1926.
[479] *New York Daily News, Philadelphia Inquirer, Philadelphia Evening Bulletin*, September 16, 1926.

Dempsey said he was better than before the Firpo fight. Even if he did not knock out Tunney, he would win on points, just as he did against Gibbons, who then was rated as the cleverest, shiftiest heavy in the game. Tom was elusive and hard to hit cleanly. Nevertheless, Jack clearly outpointed him, and proved his condition, finishing stronger at the end than the start, disproving claims that he was not much on long distances.

Loughran said he did not think he could last more than 4 or 5 rounds with Dempsey in a real fight. He was shaken up several times even with big gloves.

Harry Newman said a reliable source had informed him that Dempsey was doing secret training every morning with Bill Tate, which is why Tate was not seen in the afternoons. In those secret bouts, supposedly Dempsey cut loose with everything, which explained why he appeared so indifferent during his afternoon sparring for the newspapermen.

Fair Play said Dempsey's workouts with Loughran had helped his timing. "Jack cornered the lighter and faster Loughran repeatedly, smashing terrific blows to the body. ... You have heard stories that his timing is bad. The writer does not agree with this at all. When he can catch the fleeting Loughran at will and hang a glove on him, it is stretching matters pretty far to say that his timing is poor." Jack was vicious and fast, with very powerful short blows that were mighty hard to block or ward off. Loughran imitated Tunney, and "Loughran is not showing up Dempsey at all. Jack easily reaches his clever partner's face and body at will."

Tunney's first pro bout earned him $200, and he gave one-third to his manager Billy Roche. Eventually his purses rose to $1,000 or $1,200. The newspapermen started talking about him. Never did he foresee that he would be earning the type of money he was earning now.

On September 16, Benny Leonard got his first look at Gene Tunney in this camp. Benny said Tunney was towering and in marvelous physical condition. Gene said, "I'm no pygmy, Benny. I'm bigger than I was in the old days [when they sparred before]." Leonard said when it came to health, excellent condition, and general physical excellence, "Tunney is ahead of Dempsey right now."

Leonard, who once seconded Jimmy Delaney against Tunney, saw Delaney (51-10-8) spar with Tunney that day, giving him a great workout. He soon had Gene's lip bleeding from a right in the 1st of their 2 rounds. Gene also boxed Vidabeck 2 rounds.

Some thought Gene might be going stale, for he took more than usual, and did not have the same zip. However, others said Gene never was a great gym fighter. Regardless, Leonard admitted that Delaney might give Dempsey a tough scuffle too. Tunney said he was a little slow because he already ran 4 miles that morning.

Tom Gibbons believed that Tunney would make a defensive stand early, trying to evade Jack's crushing blows for a few rounds before opening up.

Benny Leonard, retired lightweight champion of the world, and Tom Gibbons, who hasn't fought since Tunney licked him, visiteed the challenger in his camp. Tunney is telling Gibbons something that makes Tom Smile broadly, Benny draws away in a gesture of disbelief, as though he thinks Gene spoofing.
—International Newsreel, photo.

Tunney in white shirt and dark shorts spars Jimmy Delaney

Tunney spars Billy Vidabeck

Jack Kearns wrote that a heavyweight champion has but a few short years to be at his best. Dempsey was at his best against Willard.

He was and always will be just a fair fighter. I mean that. All that he ever was in the ring I made him through sheer ballyhoo. There never was a time in his whole career that he fooled me. He fooled the experts into believing that he was the greatest heavyweight of all time. He didn't fool them. I fooled them.

Kearns also said "every move that Jack Dempsey ever made in the ring was Jack Kearns' move, Jack Kearns' ideas." To Dempsey's credit, he followed orders well. Kearns believed that Tunney would beat Dempsey. "He hasn't anything left."

Gene Tunney reported that Jack Kearns had given him advice regarding how to fight Dempsey, and he was taking his advice seriously. "Kearns, better than anyone, can and has told me of Dempsey's weaknesses. Personal observation has taught me the few glaring faults in his style as well as the best features of his attack." He also received advice from Benny Leonard, Jim Corbett, and Jim Jeffries.[480]

Kearns advised Tunney to take the play away from Dempsey by going to him and keep going, taking it to him and crowding him. "Dempsey is essentially a front runner." Jack could not wait, always loving to play the aggressor, crowd in, and give his man no rest. Making Jack break ground with fast fighting was the way to beat him. Tunney could not just stand around and outthink Dempsey, but needed to keep a fast pace, which would expose the fact that Dempsey was past-it. "He's an old man as fighters go now and when he tires this time, he won't come back. They never do. … It's nature. They can't go on forever. Once the divine fighting spirit has been curbed, they don't respond." The heart and brain might still be there, but the legs and arms would not respond when necessary. In his prime, Jim Jeffries never tired, but after years of inactivity, despite his form in training, he tired in the Johnson fight. The same would happen to Dempsey. Kearns predicted that he would tire after about 3 rounds.[481]

Tex Rickard had to appear in court to defend a taxpayer's suit to prevent him from paying any prize money until after the fight. Present were Paddy Mullins and Chicago promoter B. Clements, representing the Windy City's Coliseum Club, who claimed Dempsey ran out of a

DEMPSEY - TUNNEY
Choice Ringside Seats on Sale
Capitol Ticket Office
1348 Sansom St. Locust 7977
$5, $7, $10, $15, $20, $25
Open Daily 9 A. M. to 11 P. M.

Wills fight. Clements also was trying to enjoin the Tunney-Dempsey fight in Pennsylvania.

On September 17 in Stroudsburg, at the Glenbrook Country club, before 1,500 fans, Tunney pasted Jim Delaney plenty in a fast affair. Delaney again drew blood from Tunney's lips. But Tunney caught him with some hard cracks and drew blood from Delaney's nose. He showed a 100% improvement over his form from the previous day. Tunney was a

[480] New York Daily News, Philadelphia Inquirer, Philadelphia Public Ledger, Philadelphia Evening Bulletin, Buffalo Times, September 17, 1926.
[481] Buffalo Times, September 18, 1926.

vicious, high-geared, fighting machine, timing his every move and countering with accurate blows. Vidabeck went 2 rounds and fared worse.

Delaney said Tunney was hard to hit in vulnerable spots, because he had fast feet and knew how to twist and turn so fast it was almost impossible to land effectively. "He's dynamite."

Rickard believed 130,000 people would see the bout in person and generate $1.7 million, which would exceed the records set by Dempsey-Carpentier. "It will be the biggest gate ever taken at any sporting event," even though the top ringside seat prices were limited to only $27.50. It also would break the attendance record. Seats practically were sold out already. The fight also would eclipse Dempsey-Firpo, in which 80,000 paid $1.2 million.

Robert Edgren said, "The fact is that this will be a fight between well matched men, each of whom has points of superiority. The result depends upon how far Dempsey has gone back and Tunney come up since their last appearances in the ring. And that only the fight can tell."

Tommy Loughran said although Tunney was making really good money,

> [W]hen I think about what Dempsey deals out when he's just fooling around with big gloves, I get to wondering if Gene's getting any sort of bargain. ... That man [Dempsey] is a murderous puncher, and the greatest ring general I ever met. He's tricky and really remarkable on defense without even getting credit for it. He seems to be taking punches, yet the real truth is that he slips them over his head, without the slightest damage to himself. It's discouraging to fight Dempsey. Any ordinary boxer who is hit solidly usually backs away. .... But hit Dempsey and he fights only harder and faster. I can't see a chance for Tunney. He will surprise me if he gets as far as four full rounds. I know that Tunney is good on defense, he is no cheap opponent, no soft mark for anybody, but when he meets Dempsey he is tackling a superman, he can't beat Dempsey in a slugging match. His only chance would seem to be in using his legs and clinching, and Dempsey is murderous in clinches.

Fair Play was firmly convinced that Tunney, who was bigger and stronger than ever before, would be the next champion.

Billy McCarney was picking Tunney too. He said,

> On the surface, Dempsey may appear to be the same, but, after all, he has been idle for three years, and has grown older and softer. Tunney, on the other hand, is a strong young fellow, fired with an ambition, whereas Dempsey is burdened with concern. Tunney, the challenger, is striving for a title, while Dempsey, the champion, is worrying about keeping it. There is a tremendous strain attached to this alone. Besides, he is giving at least a little worry to the

injunctions, attachments, etc. no matter if he does talk about them with a grin.

McCarney also said Dempsey had held the championship for 7 years, longer than anyone other than Sullivan. He was under mental strain from his legal troubles and lack of fighting for three years. Yes, he appeared to be nearly as strong and aggressive as ever, in training. But, "Every champion I ever saw looked great when he was training to go to defeat. Jeffries looked good at Reno. The world knows he fooled everybody."

Dempsey said he always gave the crowd its money's worth. "It is up to Tunney to furnish his share of the battle. I'm going in there to win as quickly as possible. I imagine Tunney will attempt to drag the contest out, but if he is willing to come in and trade punches, he will be out of luck."[482]

Harry Newman said Dempsey denied the secret workout rumors. His recent work had the experts guessing. "There are those who think that the champ is not right and that if he doesn't perk up he is on for the licking of his life."

Former Tunney manager George Engel said Dempsey would win in a few rounds. However, Babe Cullen said Dempsey was not right and would lose. Dempsey remained a 5 to 2 betting favorite.

Jack Farrell said Wills had an opportunity to derail any Dempsey-Tunney bout and prove his right to a Dempsey match, but had refused a bout with Tunney. In August 1925, Rickard offered Mullins a flat guarantee of $150,000 for Wills-Tunney. By failing to accept the offer, Wills/Mullins allowed a viable alternative option for Dempsey.

On the 17th, Dempsey went to the movie theater, where he saw his wife in her latest picture.

Dempsey noted that Kearns called him a boob. He agreed, for he had to be one to keep Kearns with him for so long. He said Rickard was the one who paid him well. In five fights under Kearns, he earned $1,185,000, and Kearns got half, or just under $600,000. In his first fight under his own management, he would earn more than what Kearns got him in five fights.[483]

The general feeling was that Tunney was 50% better than a couple years ago, while it was natural that Dempsey had retrograded over the past three years. But Jack still was a tough bird with a punch and a lot of experience, and always had come through as champion. Many wise men noted that champions did not find success in coming back after long layoffs. Sullivan, Jeffries, and Willard were in part beaten by long layoffs.[484]

Challenger Gene Tunney

[482] *Philadelphia Evening Bulletin, New York Daily News, Philadelphia Public Ledger*, September 18, 1926.
[483] *New York Daily News, Philadelphia Inquirer*, September 18, 1926. Tunney boxed a couple private rounds on the 17th with Benny Leonard.
[484] *New York Daily News*, September 19, 26.

On the 18th, 2,500 watched Tunney slug with Delaney for 2 rounds, uncorking a whirlwind attack which had Delaney bewildered and jarred. Gene smothered every attack. His judgment of distance was accurate, and punches right to the mark. He then went 2 rounds with Harold Mays. Both Delaney and Mays said Tunney was hitting harder than ever.

George Engel said Dempsey might knock Tunney down, but he would get up. "Make no mistake about that. Tunney is the greatest foe that Dempsey has ever met, and yet I think that Jack will beat him and retain his title."

Some said Tunney was an in-and-out fighter, and he would have to be "on" to beat Dempsey. Of course, some were saying that about Dempsey's training performances as well – one day looking good and the next looking bad.

On the 18th, Dempsey boxed 1 round with German light-heavy champ Young Ernie or Benny Kruger, 2 rounds with Tommy Loughran, tearing in, hooking and sending him back on his heels, followed by a whirlwind attack that broke down Loughran's defense, before easing up in the 2nd round, and 2 more with Martin Burke. Jack said he anticipated an early knockout. Some said that Dempsey had Loughran dizzy and his legs shaky from a hook to the jaw.

Loughran said, "I probably could stand off Dempsey for four rounds – maybe five. But Tunney won't be able to go that far."

Cleveland promoter Matt Hinkel, who refereed Tunney-Greb IV, picked Dempsey to win, though he noted that all champions eventually got beaten. However, "In this battle, any one with half an eye can see that Dempsey is a long way from being through. … I will be greatly surprised if Tunney goes the limit."

Tunney said, "I never have been knocked down. I do not think Dempsey will punch me off my feet. But if Jack does knock me down, I'll get up. … He'll not put me down for keeps."

Carpentier, who had fought both, picked Dempsey. "Tunney hasn't got a chance. Of course, you never can tell. Tunney may have improved since I met him in 1924, and Dempsey may be slower than he was when he knocked me out in 1921."

In his lawsuit, which was pending in New York, Kearns alleged that Dempsey could have earned $500,000 for fighting Wills. Kearns signed articles of agreement with Rickard on August 18, 1925 for Dempsey to fight Wills on or before July 4, 1926 for a $500,000 guarantee. What Kearns overlooked was that even if the fight could be brought off, according to Kearns' own argument, Dempsey would earn only half of that amount, or no better than 66.66%, if Kearns took 1/3.

Dempsey said if Kearns was such a great manager, why then had he not had success with all of the other fighters he had managed. He bungled his management of Mickey Walker and got him beaten up by Greb. Dempsey never claimed to be great. He was not a bragger. That was Kearns. Now that he wasn't managing him, Kearns had changed his tune and claimed that Dempsey never was a great fighter.[485]

Harry Newman said Dempsey still was a rip-tearing, vicious fighter, even if some of the sting was removed from his best punches. It would take a lot of fighting to wrest the title away from him. Yet, despite outward appearances, he likely was not what he once was.

Personality-wise, there were two Dempseys, the vicious one in the ring and the "rollicking, laughing lad who just oozes good nature when not annoyed." He was powerful, fast for a big man, and clever at eluding blows, though that was not acceded generally, making him one of the greatest champions ever. His best punch was his left hook, which was deadly accurate. His right was powerful too, though. "There is a suspicion that Dempsey is not a long distance performer, and that if he doesn't get his man in the first four or five rounds, he is likely to blow up." Still, he went 15 with Gibbons and 12 with Brennan, finishing strong in both contests. He fought his best when stung. He was a bulldog who tenaciously attacked, caring little for his opponent's blows.

On September 19, four days before the fight, Tunney did his final training in Stroudsburg, Pennsylvania. 7,000 fans saw Tunney go 2 rounds each with Delaney and Mays. The *Inquirer* said Tunney showed spectacular form, battering his mates. He had plenty of speed, power, and stamina.

Harry Ertle believed the Manassa Mauler's bull strength and deadly sock would predominate over whatever Tunney had.

Tom Gibbons said, "Dempsey looks good, no matter if others think he has slowed up since his battle with Firpo. Of course, he is older and perhaps not as fast, but he is in good physical shape." He also said,

> And yet, of course, he hasn't uncorked his knockout wallop so it is still a mysterious quality. Before he trained for me at Shelby and for Firpo he displayed in training much more than he has in getting ready for the Tunney fight but he has shown enough for me to know that he must be holding something in reserve.

Gibbons said Jack was an aggressive rusher, whereas Tunney was a calm counterpuncher, more defensive. "I fought Dempsey much like Tunney will." Dempsey was the better infighter. Gene got foes to lead so he could counter and clinch.

Dempsey was irritated, annoyed, and angered by the Kearns lawsuit, as well as all of the legal assaults against him and the fight. Gus Wilson said of Dempsey, "He's sore as a pup. All this trouble, tying up his money and getting out injunctions and so forth, have him on edge, and he'll bite anybody's head off who goes near him."

---

[485] *New York Daily News, Philadelphia Inquirer, Philadelphia Public Ledger*, September 19, 1926.

Yet, when Dempsey saw Benny Leonard, he greeted him cordially. "How do I look to you? Let me see the black eye Tunney gave you." Benny told him he looked wonderful. Jack said he was not worried. "Let the other fellows do the worrying, champ. I'm going to fight."

Leonard admired Dempsey's double left hook, which was fast. Jack shot it for the body and immediately followed it up with lightning rapidity to the jaw. It was a "lallapaloosa," very hard to avoid. Tunney stood straight up, and the only way he could avoid it was by blocking and moving his head back at the same time in a very quick fashion.

Tunney was working on perfecting his right uppercut. "He had it down pretty well when I boxed him [in private on the 17th]," though it still needed some more polishing. "Tunney's right to the heart is a good punch, too."

Leonard said he ran into his Philly friend Maxey Hoff, also known as "Boo Boo." Hoff claimed to have a distinct leaning towards Dempsey. (More on Max "Boo Boo" Hoff later, but suffice to say for now that he reputedly was a gambler/bootlegger/gangster.) However, former New York commissioner Frank O'Neill was sure that Tunney would win. Leonard said, "They're both good judges."

Dempsey told Robert Edgren,

> I'll be happy when I get into the ring. This has been a long grind, but I always train a long time. This trip I had to make sure of getting into condition. I had a little fat on me, all over, and I wanted to make sure there was none inside, because I know Tunney is going to give me a real fight. I expect to win, but I don't think it's going to be as easy as fighting those big fellows who stand still and take a socking. It's easy to put everything in a punch when you know it's going to land. It was harder to fight Tommy Gibbons than to fight Morris or Willard. I had a lot of trouble hitting Tommy on the right spot and I may have just as much trouble finding Tunney. ...
>
> Get this straight. I'm going to do my best to stop Tunney.... But if Tunney can knock me out I hope that my head will be clear enough when I get up to walk right over and shake hands and congratulate him. Tunney's all right. A fine fellow. He'd be a good champion. ... Perhaps I'm not exactly what I was at Toledo, but I'm in good shape. I don't feel any difference. I know more about boxing. If Tunney beats me there'll be no alibi.

Financially, Dempsey stood to earn more money from the upcoming fight than any prior fight in his career, and he did not have to split it with Kearns.

Tunney said, "I think Dempsey has been a great fighter, but I think the time has come for him to be beaten, and I think I've developed to the point where I can beat him. I admire Dempsey. I think he's been misunderstood and given an unfair deal in many ways, and he hasn't been credited with his really fine qualities."

COMING AT YOU, BIG BOY!— Bill Tate is some giant, but giants are Mons. Dempsey's specialty. The champ doesn't look timid in this pose with big Bill. He fights Tate like any one else. Jack is worried a bit by legal fight over impending bout. Story on page 16.

Dempsey and Tate

Both men had shut down their public training. Tunney was bothered by a cut lip, as well as adverse remarks when he took a few in sparring. Dempsey was annoyed by remarks and jeers from a few spectators, bothered by Kearns' attempts to annoy him, and the attempted injunction to stop the fight. "Kearns is a desperate character who won't stop at anything to get revenge." Dempsey said the only thing that Kearns had done which did not give him a laugh was the seizing of Mrs. Dempsey's car at Saratoga. That got him mad.[486]

Dempsey refused to take the scales for Gibbons, saying he was at the proper poundage. Gene Normile said Jack was 191. Tom thought he was larger than that. Jack previously said he was 193.

Two-thirds of the country would hear about the fight live via radio broadcasts, by the joining of the WEAF and WJZ chains with the studios of the General Electric and Westinghouse Electric companies. Rumors were that $35,000 had been paid to Rickard for the privilege. The *Daily News* said fight broadcasting rights were sold for between $15,000 and $20,000.

The official 6-ounce gloves had arrived, made by Sol Levinson of San Francisco. Levinson and his father had been manufacturing gloves for almost every important championship fight for the past 30 years. They were the same kind that Dempsey used for his other championship fights, from Willard on. They cost $14.50 a pair, with postage at $1.46. Tunney requested gloves that were an inch longer and a trifle wider than Dempsey's.

Benny Leonard said if floored, both men would get up and continue. They were very evenly matched physically. If necessary, Tunney could take it and stand punishment, though he fought to avoid such.

Tunney told Leonard,

> They say that I back up too much, that I run away from a furious onslaught. That's true, Benny, I do. But there is no question of gameness or grit involved here. I run to avoid punishment. Any fool can stand and take them. I think I'm a better boxer than Dempsey. Therefore, why should I not make use of this superior skill to win the fight? … If I can make Dempsey miss by backing up and can hit him after he misses, I'll win the title.

[486] *New York Daily News, Philadelphia Inquirer, Philadelphia Evening Bulletin*, September 20, 1926.

From this, Leonard deduced that Tunney intended to box Dempsey, not fight him. Tunney had been working on his speed, defending himself against rushing attacks, and escaping punches.

Leonard said that a week ago, "Jack was slow, sluggish and he tired quickly," and he had a worn, worried look. Yet, Leonard still was on record as picking Dempsey to win within 6 rounds.

Edgren said there had been $1.7 million in ticket sales already, and the gate likely would be around $2 million.

Edgren further said Dempsey had been ridden, threatened, and pestered by Kearns, the New York boxing authorities, the Chicago promoter with his discarded Fitzsimmons contract, and by Wills' manager. They were attempting to obtain injunctions, suing, seizing assets, and trying to seize his purse. Kearns also was seeking his share of the 1924 and 1925 Dempsey exhibition bouts in Europe, including Germany, as well as Mexico and other places. His contract went from August 3, 1923 to August 3, 1926.

Dempsey blamed Kearns for a great deal of his lack of popularity. He knew the crowd would be against him. He felt like his back was to the wall. Still, Dempsey was the 2 to 1 odds favorite.

Luis Firpo picked Dempsey, who was just as strong as ever, though Luis gave Tunney a chance. He said,

> Tunney must be very cautious during the first rounds when the champion is most terrible and dangerous and if the battle goes more than four rounds the chances of Tunney will be increased. I have seen Tunney in action. He has much energy and stamina and fights with the same vigor from the first to the eighth round and is particularly aggressive in the final rounds.

Harry Newman said it was Tunney's jab against Dempsey's hook. Gene also had a very good right uppercut.

Tunney's last real workout was on the 20th, three days before the fight. He sparred 2 rounds with Delaney and 2 with Mays. His manager declared him to be at his peak and right on edge.

Tunney's brother, Thomas Tunney, was a New York motorcycle patrolman, hailing many into traffic court.

Dempsey said his training was done. He was in great shape and had not allowed himself to overtrain or go stale. He trained for speed, durability, and power. "I don't really think that Tunney is going to slug it with me, as he says he will. I think he'll do a lot of backing and twisting and turning. If that's the case I will have to do some fast stepping to catch up with him, and when one keeps stepping like that one needs not merely speed but plenty of endurance." He knew Gene had a good right, but Jack was used to hard punches. He never clinched, held, or got out of the way of combat. "I guess he'll hit me. They all have. But hitting me and knocking me out with such a hit − that's different." Meanwhile, Jack would be punching too.

Tunney said he was in perfect condition at 186 pounds, and mentally serene, well satisfied with his boxing and hitting. "I am in the finest condition of my entire ring career." He was confident that he would win. He boxed Benny Leonard in private the other day, and Leonard was greatly pleased with his work. The heavyweight championship had been his ambition for the last five years. He would have no excuses if defeated. "I am certain that Thursday's fight will justify the enormous amount of interest evinced in it by not only the boxing-loving public but by the entire Nation, and, I suppose, a great part of the entire world."

The *Philadelphia Public Ledger* said Dempsey now was a 13 to 5 favorite. Many, including Tunney, believed Jack's legal troubles and worries would affect him. Dempsey said such would have no impact.

Gene gave the Stroudsburg mayor a pair of red leather boxing gloves with an inscription from him. The mayor prevented the service of court papers on Tunney.[487]

Davis Walsh said Dempsey lacked brainy seconds, just like the overconfident Willard. Dempsey wanted to fight his own way, with no interference from his corner. Jerry Luvadis, Gene Normile, Gus Wilson, and Captain Mabbutt were "yes" men, not knowledgeable boxing men. "I can't think of a more inept combination, neither can Dempsey, according to reports." He was considering hiring Philadelphia Jack O'Brien, but "Philadelphia Jack was right the last time they used nail files for tooth brushes." Also under consideration was Doc Bagley, Tunney's former manager.

Dempsey's sparring partner, Bill Tate, who had fought Harry Wills six times, said, "Jack Dempsey is the hardest hitting champion we've ever had. Jack hits harder than any man I've ever fought, and I've stood up against them all - Willard, Firpo, Gunboat Smith, but Jack hits harder, and I ought to know. ... I guess I know Jack about as well as anybody knows him...and...I've yet to find out what Jack can't do." Tate said one had to move against Dempsey, because if you stood still in one spot, he would knock you off that spot quickly. "[T]he only way I know that a feller can stand up against Jack − just keep jumpin' where he ain't. And he's everywhere." Tate said Dempsey didn't need seconds. "Jack knows what he's in that ring for, and he don't need anybody else to tell him. ... Say Missy, maybe you don't know how a feller like Dempsey loves to fight! ...

[487] *Philadelphia Evening Bulletin, New York Daily News, Philadelphia Inquirer, Philadelphia Public Ledger*, September 21, 1926.

Tunney don't love to fight." When Gene felt Dempsey's punch, he'd be lucky to remember anything. Plus, Dempsey could take a punch. "Even if Gene does give Jack a sock that makes him feel giddy, Jack won't know he did it. ... He's a fighter by instinct, not by practice, like Gene."[488]

Motion pictures of the fight would be taken and shown at theaters throughout Pennsylvania, and possibly elsewhere if smuggled out of state.

Some said Tunney would receive a flat fee of $200,000.

Harry Newman said Dempsey's style was just what Tunney liked. He liked foes to come to him so he could step away and "bang" them as he did it. He was a natural counter puncher. But the question was whether Tunney could weather the champ's punches. He would be foolish to stand there and slug. If he ran for several rounds, folks would get a chance to see how good Dempsey still was.

In his court pleadings, in answer to the Kearns lawsuit, Dempsey claimed that "scoundrel" Kearns was dishonest and guilty of moral irregularities, an ex-convict who had been in the Washington State penitentiary for a considerable period of time for a statutory crime, and had defrauded him out of hundreds of thousands of dollars, appropriating to himself money which did not belong to him. Kearns had filed litigation against Dempsey on August 16, 1926.

In his final workout on Tuesday September 21, just two days before the fight, wearing 6-ounce gloves, the same as he would wear for the fight on Thursday, Tunney allowed Delaney, Vidabeck, and Mays to whale away at him. He beautifully defended himself against the rushes and picked off their punches. "It was the most remarkable exhibition of defensive work this writer has ever witnessed in a training camp." Another observer said, "Showing impressive fleetness of foot, he ducked out of range almost at will or brushed the blows aside."

Tunney did not expect Dempsey to reopen his cut lip, for Jack was not a jabber. Gene was "Absolutely satisfied." He was in great shape, having trained for three solid months: at White Sulphur Springs, then Speculator, and then Stroudsburg. He had worked harder than ever and was in perfect condition.

Although Tommy Gibbons picked Dempsey to finish Tunney in 5 rounds, he admitted that Tunney was a great fighter, one of the greatest heavyweights of the age. Nevertheless, Dempsey would be too much, with his harder punches and fighting instincts. Tunney was fighting "the greatest mauler alive today." Gene was fast, but Tom did not think he could avoid Jack's furious onslaught.

Regarding Gibbons-Tunney, Gibbons felt that if he was in the same condition as he was against Dempsey back in 1923, he could beat Tunney right now, but Tunney had fought an older and diminished version of himself. Tom believed that Dempsey would have stopped in 3 rounds that same version of himself that fought Gene. Tunney was fond of clinching and backing up to the ropes, which would prove disastrous against

[488] *Philadelphia Evening Bulletin*, September 21, 1926.

Dempsey. However, Gibbons granted that Tunney was no set-up. "In fact he is one of the toughest customers Jack has ever faced."

John Dugan said Dempsey was the puncher, which was why most thought he would win. Yet, Tunney had power, a really good right, had flattened numerous rivals, and had shown ruggedness and boxing ability. Favorites had lost before. "Few champions have retained the winning punch and speed after three-year layoffs. Dempsey himself had his troubles in 1923 when he fought Tom Gibbons and Luis Firpo after two years of idleness." Jack now was past age 31, and youth mattered in all sports. "The former marine may not have the fighting instinct that always has been Dempsey's guiding star but he has determination, condition, youth and no little battling equipment in his favor."

Regarding the decision methodology, "Pennsylvania has its own style for rendering decisions. When a fight is over the announcer enters the ring and first obtains the referee's slip. He puts this away before collecting the slips from the judges. He reads them aloud and if there is a disagreement then the referee's verdict is read."

Dempsey said he felt like a two-year-old horse and would knock out Tunney as soon as he could. "Tunney will have to be a good catcher to go over five rounds the way I feel today."

Fair Play believed that Dempsey's punch, courage, and indomitable will would carry him to victory. He was a man who fought hard without let-up and had the punch to end a fight at any time.

Pennsylvania Governor Gifford Pinchot said he would be ringside at the fight, rooting for Tunney. He had no intention of doing anything to prevent the fight. The governor praised the manly art, which was supported by the armed forces, and defended it as a lawful, legitimate form of professional sport. He claimed to have boxed with Roosevelt himself.

> I call your attention particularly to the fact that the nations in which boys and men are in the habit of doing their fighting with their fists are precisely those in which they are not in the habit of using the knife or the bullet for that purpose. On the basis of some personal experience, I regard boxing as a sport admirably fitted for physical development and also to foster the qualities of initiative, steadiness, courage and endurance which are so necessary in the battle of life.

Robert Edgren picked Dempsey but gave Tunney a fair chance to win. Jack was the greatest and most sensational "knocker-out ever seen in a ring." He dropped big men as if they were lightweights. But anything could happen in a fight. Tunney was cool and confident. He had the spirit of a marine. Gene believed Dempsey could not put him down or keep him down. "I fight better and faster when I'm hurt." He knew how to beat a rushing fighter. The harder puncher did not always win. Dempsey was a natural fighter, but Tunney had studied and learned his craft over many years. He had developed a fine physique and was as strong as Dempsey. They were well-matched physically. Tunney had a really good, whipping right hand that came out as suddenly and savagely as a rattlesnake strike. "If Tunney can hit Dempsey like that, on the chin, Dempsey is going to be pretty well shaken, and he may go down." Gene also had a good left to the body.

The former Devil Dog would be the crowd's sentimental favorite, and likely would have an edge in any decision. "If the fight goes ten rounds Tunney certainly won't be given the worst of the decision. It would be a bold official who'd decide against him if it is even close."

Dempsey had a greater love for the sport. "Tunney wants to make a fortune fighting and then get away from the game and go higher. He doesn't care for fighting. Dempsey likes to fight. He says the greatest thrill in the world is his when the bell rings and he leaps from his corner." And yet, Tunney had fought more often than Dempsey, although much of that difference had to do with economics and other issues once Dempsey became champion. Dempsey's determination made him the most dangerous of all heavyweights. He did not mind taking chances, even reckless ones. He was a savage rusher, could hit fast, and on the inside dig in short, tearing blows that were hard to block. Tunney liked to stand off and box deliberately, looking for chances to whip in blows.

Dempsey's condition after years of idleness from formal fights could have an impact. In training, Dempsey had not been shaken up by Loughran's hard blows, and he kept coming in for more. However, what a fighter showed in training could differ from their true form in a real fight. Although he looked good on the surface, he might have "inside fat," and might not dish or take them like he once did.

One thing that might count heavily against Dempsey was the constant strain of all the legal charges by his enemies, and the "contemptible tricks" by those who wanted him beaten and would stop at nothing to injure him. "He says he isn't worried, but if this is so he's more than human. In one way the attacks on Dempsey have backfired, for they have made sympathizers out of thousands who were against him before." The public liked fair play; and was not in favor of the unfair hounding to which Dempsey had been subjected.

Dempsey would be weighed in by a commission representative at his cottage at 203 Florence avenue, West Atlantic City, New Jersey, at 1 p.m. Thursday afternoon, the day of the fight. Tunney would weigh in at the commission office at 2 p.m. Preliminary fighters would weigh in at the Arcadia Gym. Frank L. Wiener, chairman of the Pennsylvania State Athletic Commission, said there was not enough room to have both combatants weigh in at their offices, given the more than 300 out-of-town newspapermen wanting to be present.

The referee would not be named until both men were in the ring getting their hands bandaged. The officials would not know their assignments until they were told right before the fight. Eventually, eight referees were called upon to be at ringside.

Dempsey sent for a copy of the commission's rule book, an indication that he intended to abide by their rules. Boxers were allowed only two-inch gauze, as much as they liked, but it could not be bunched or knotted. One yard of one-inch adhesive tape was allowed for each hand as well. Previously, boxers had been allowed to use heavy tire tape. The commission would supervise the bandaging.

If there was any disagreement between the judges, the referee's verdict was final. Such was the case even if one judge had it for one fighter, the other had it a draw, and the referee had it for a different fighter than the judge who named a winner. The referee's verdict still would stand.

The gloves would be 6 ounces, 10 ounces lighter than their training mitts. The referee could consult with the ringside physician regarding low blows. A cornerman could not stop the fight. Only the referee or a fighter's unwillingness or inability to continue could end the contest. The kidney, rabbit, and pivot blows all were illegal.

Although he picked Dempsey to win by knockout, Jack McAuliffe also said, "Dempsey doesn't look as good to me as when he fought Firpo three years ago. His legs don't 'stand up' like they used to. He has gone back, but he hasn't gone back that much that he isn't good enough to knock out Tunney. Despite the fact that Dempsey has gone back he has strength and a real fighting heart."

On the 21st, Dempsey said, "I am ready. I felt great today. I hope I feel as well when I go into the ring." He always carried nerves into the ring, but when the gong sounded, they were gone. He was 31 years old. He had been inactive for three years, but not idle.

Ed Pollock said if the Dempsey of 1923 were pitted against the Tunney of 1926, the odds would be even wider. However, concerns about how diminished Dempsey was after three years made the odds much closer. "No man can retire from competition for three years and be as good as he was when last he faced a foe. This applies not only to boxing, but to any sport you mention. It is particularly true of personal-contact sports." Dempsey claimed he had remained in good physical condition. However, "The ring requires a great deal more than good physical condition. It demands quick thinking, fine timing and good judgment of distance." Such things were maintained through actual competition. "It is not practice, but competition, which makes perfect." Yet, ultimately, he concluded, "Dempsey has lost something, but it is still very doubtful if he has fallen below Tunney's level. ... The outcome of the fight depends on how much Dempsey has lost in his three years of idleness and also on how much Tunney has improved."

Leon Britton had secured the motion picture rights. Two dozen cameramen on special platforms located sixty feet from the ring would shoot every detail from every possible angle.

Philadelphia was packed with a million visitors. Hotels were at capacity.[489]

[489] *Philadelphia Inquirer, Philadelphia Evening Bulletin, Philadelphia Public Ledger, New York Daily News*, September 22, 1926.

On Wednesday September 21, 1926, in Boston, 187-pound Jack Sharkey (22-6) won a clear 10-round decision over 220-pound George Godfrey (30-10-1). The victory was significant, because some writers had said Godfrey was as good as or better than Wills. Godfrey once had been a Dempsey sparring partner. The *Boston Globe* said Sharkey won 7-2-1. Godfrey only won the 3rd and 8th, with the 2nd round even. Godfrey wrestled most of the time, showing no inclination to mix, despite his 33-pound weight advantage, rarely landing effectively, causing the crowd to boo him. Sharkey tried to make a fight of it throughout.

> Sharkey's best work was with a straight left jab, after which he would invariably work inside and play a tattoo on Godfrey's body. In the closing rounds, he brought his right hand into effective play. At times, it seemed as if the negro would have been content to quit had he been given the opportunity.[490]

About nine out of ten men picked Dempsey in the upcoming fight.

However, the *Philadelphia Inquirer's* Perry Lewis favored Tunney, believing that all of the legal issues had undermined Dempsey's nervous system and sapped him of his reserve energy. Dempsey had been harassed, embarrassed, annoyed, and prodded with injunctions, which had to wear on him psychologically. Physically, both looked great. Dempsey hit as hard as ever, but not as accurately or as sharply, and his judgment of distance was not perfect, though he had improved through training. Tunney was three years (sic) younger, serene, and confident. He could hit hard too, and few could take his right on the jaw for long. Gene also could take it. His manager said he absorbed punishment like a sponge.

Dempsey wanted to wait to travel to Philadelphia, in part to avoid the crowds, but also because he wanted to wait until after the courthouse closed so there could be no last-minute legal actions taken against him.

It was estimated that $1.5 million had been wagered. Around $1.8 million was expected to be collected at the gate. Nearly 140,000 people were expected to be in attendance.[491]

Fair Play said, "Dempsey is a fighter and Tunney a boxer and a fighter can always beat a boxer. Tunney is hardly in Dempsey's class."

---

[490] *Boston Globe*, September 22, 1926. The judges were John Glackin and W. T. McDermott, and referee John Brassil for the main event.
[491] *Philadelphia Inquirer*, September 23, 1926.

Gunboat Smith said Dempsey was only 60% of what he once was, but still was good enough to whip Tunney.

Robert Edgren said, "Dempsey ought to defeat Tunney but anything can happen when one of the men fighting is as cool and confident as Tunney." Edgren said there was an undercurrent of betting on Tunney.

Tex Rickard told Edgren that the event would make history. Philadelphia was packed with people from all over the world who had come to see the fight. The demand for tickets was extremely high. He believed the attendance would be around 130,000. Tex said,

> This is going past anything I ever dreamed of. It is going to outclass any championship fight I ever held – make them all look small. ... Dempsey and Tunney have caught the world's fancy. I knew they would. I knew this was far better than any Dempsey-Wills match, and my judgment has turned out O.K. ...
>
> There's never been anything like this before in the world. I think it will stand as a record. My imagination can't picture a championship fight that will ever draw more people. There may never be anything like it again. This is history you're going to see, boy.

Tex said the Chicago promoters had no contract with Dempsey, and never paid Fitzsimmons for his contract, just loaned him a few hundred dollars. "Fitzsimmons never paid Dempsey a cent of the payments provided for in the contract. It has been nothing but a piece of paper for months." Hence, Rickard was not worried.

William Muldoon said, "I expect to see a fine contest. Tunney was the man to meet Dempsey. He will give the champion a real contest."

Tennis champion Suzanne Lenglen of France said she would be rooting for Dempsey. "I do hope Mr. Dempsey is victorious over Mr. Tunney. He is such a refined gentleman. I really don't know where people get that man-eating idea about him. While Mr. and Mrs. Dempsey were in Paris I had luncheon with them, and if Mr. Dempsey's ring manners are as nice as his table manners he is sure to win."

Estelle Taylor was en route from Los Angeles but planned to remain in seclusion until after the fight.

The *Philadelphia Public Ledger's* Frank McCracken said the champion ruled as the favorite, but Tunney was his best foe since 1919. Tunney had condition, experience, boxing knowledge, a hard right, and brains. Dempsey was the favorite because he had crushed 4 out of his 5 challengers, and clearly defeated the one who lasted the distance. Despite three years of inactivity, Dempsey had been training quietly during those years, and worked to get himself on edge in camp. McCracken believed Jack was back, and keen, though he had been distracted by lawsuits and writs. "Dempsey worked hard, much harder than Tunney." Tunney, already in good shape, did not want to overtrain and go stale. He was ready on September 16, the original date. Outside the ring, both men regarded the other highly.

McCracken predicted that Tunney would mix up his style, starting off more defensively, but then shifting to offense, and back and forth. He had fighting spirit and would not just be defensive. "In the seven years that Dempsey held the title, Tunney has fought sixty-one fights, while the champion has taken part in only five contests." True, most of the men Tunney fought were not top men. Still, several were rough, rugged foes, and in his entire fistic career, Gene never had been knocked off his feet.

McCracken believed that Tunney was better all-around than any prior Dempsey foe. Tunney was in better shape than Brennan, bigger, stronger, and tougher than Carpentier (though less spectacular), a harder hitter than Gibbons, and better skilled than Firpo.

Yet, "Those who favor Tunney to win the championship are few and far between." They expected Dempsey to rush as ferociously as always and unleash his terrible punches. However, "In training, I did not like his leg movement." Jack's footwork did not seem the same as it did when he prepared for Carpentier and Firpo. Still, Dempsey's punch had enough power that it could lift men into the air.

Tunney believed his defense would rob Dempsey of his effectiveness. Gene never had to stand the shock of the Dempsey brand of power, but had endured the blows of all others. He showed heart against Greb in their first bout in 1922, when he had cuts opened over both eyes and his nose broken due to Greb's "headwork." Yet, he never weakened, and finished the fight. He had grown since then in height, weight, and reach.

> So, summing up the entire situation, Tunney looms as the best man Dempsey has fought since he won the title. Carpentier had a chance - for he rocked Dempsey with a right to the jaw. Firpo had a chance because he knocked the champion to one knee with the first blow struck and later knocked him out of the ring with a punch to the jaw. Why not Tunney?

Tunney stood 6'1 ½" and allegedly was 28 years old (actually 29). Other than being three (sic – two) years younger, physically they were about the same.

Dempsey's share of the estimated $1.8 million in receipts would be about $710,000.

Dempsey		Tunney
31	Age	28
191	Weight	185
77 in.	Reach	76½ in.
6 ft., 1 in.	Height	6 ft., 1½ in.
9 in.	Wrist	8 in.
13 in.	Forearm	13½ in.
14½ in.	Biceps	13½ in.
40½ in.	Chest (normal)	41 in.
44¾ in.	Chest (expanded)	44 in.
33 in.	Waist	23 in.
16½ in.	Neck	17 in.
22 in.	Thigh	23 in.
15½ in.	Calf	16 in.
9 in.	Ankle	9 in.

The championship fight was scheduled for 10 rounds, the longest allowed in Pennsylvania. Seven fights would comprise the card, including five prelims and one walk-out - all scheduled for 6 rounds, starting at 8 p.m. The State would earn $90,000, the Sesqui-Centennial $180,000, and the U.S. tax would be about $180,000. Dempsey was the 3 to 1 favorite.

The day before the fight, Dempsey said he would tear after Tunney from the start and try to make the fight as short as possible. "I do not like to predict what round the fight will end for it really is foolish to say so. Tunney is a great fighter and underestimated by many. Gene has a pair of dangerous fists and no one can tell what he might do." Jack said he was in excellent condition, ready for the battle of his life. "I've never felt any better at any time since I won the title." When he started training, he was fearful that he had gone back, but after several weeks of hard work, "I can't figure out how I've slipped any. ... I'm punching as hard as I ever did. I'm seeing openings and making the best of them. In fact, my eyes and muscles are coordinating perfectly." He said Gene was a "nice boy," and there was no grudge between them. "I wish the fight was tonight instead of tomorrow, so I could have it over with."

Tunney said he was in perfect condition. "I am confident that I will win." If defeated, he would have no alibi. The day before the fight, he played 18 holes of golf, and it was his best score in a year, proving that his nerves were good. "A man whose nerves are not all right can't play golf."

Billy Gibson said Tunney would be called upon to fight his hardest to resist the champ's aggressive attacks, but he would survive the test, and as the bout progressed, he would become stronger and stronger.

The *Daily News* said Tunney had engaged in 62 fights (at least) over seven years, losing but once. 30 fights were won by knockout, including his most important fights against Carpentier, Gibbons, and Madden.

In fact, Tunney had about 81 career fights to that point, some saying he was 77-1-3. He actually had slightly more official fights than Dempsey, who was about 57-4-9.

Harry Newman picked Dempsey to win in about 5 rounds. Paul Gallico picked Dempsey in 6.

Marshall Hunt said Dempsey was a killer, a natural born fighter. He might not be the same killer who ripped Willard to shreds, but still was good enough to stop Tunney, in about 5 rounds. He was more versatile, punched with murderous instinct, harder than Tunney, was quicker on his feet, and excelled at infighting.

Jack Farrell picked Tunney to win a 10-round decision, saying unless Jack got him early, he probably would not get him at all, and would be outpointed. Farrell did not think Dempsey was the same dynamic force he once was. No man ever had come back from a three-year layoff with success. Tunney likely would fight on the defensive early, and then pick up the offense as the fight progressed and Dempsey slowed down.

More than 20 million people would hear about the "Battle of a Century and a Half" on the radio. Two great chains of at least 32 stations, headed by WEAF and WJZ, would air the fight.[492]

[492] *Philadelphia Evening Bulletin, Philadelphia Public Ledger, New York Daily News,* September 23, 1926.

CHAPTER 6

Gene Tunney

On Thursday, September 23, 1926, in Philadelphia, Pennsylvania, at the Sesquicentennial Stadium, the Jack Dempsey vs. Gene Tunney championship fight took place.[493]

On the morning of the fight, the local Philadelphia Common Pleas Court No. 1 refused to grant the Chicago Coliseum Club's request for a preliminary injunction to prevent the contest as a result of an alleged breach of its contract with Dempsey to fight Harry Wills. B. Clements, for the Club, was unable to produce a signed copy of the original contract. Regardless, the Court held that the alleged contract was vague and uncertain, instead of clear and specific, as required. There was no proof that the Club had a specific date or location to host the fight, and none was mentioned in the contract. Also, Clements admitted that Dempsey never had received a cent of the $300,000 advance payment due him under the alleged agreement. The Court's ruling in part stated,

> No proof was offered by plaintiff that it was prepared to carry out the contemplated exhibition in so far as the said Wills was concerned; nor did the plaintiff establish, by sufficient proof, it had complied with the terms of its alleged contract by the payments of $300,000 to Dempsey, and it seeks to restrain a breach of a conjectural, rather than a proven, contract.

The Court refused to recognize the injunction against Dempsey by an Indiana court as having any force or effect against Rickard and Tunney, who were not parties to the suit in that state. Also, neither Dempsey nor Tunney were served with the suit in Pennsylvania. Hence, the final remaining potential obstacle to the fight was resolved.

At 12 noon, in the garage attached to the cottage where Dempsey resided in Atlantic City, representatives of the Pennsylvania Boxing Commission weighed in Dempsey. Perry Lewis said he tipped the scales at 194 pounds. Most others reported he weighed 190. To Gus Wilson's dismay, Dempsey chose Philadelphia Jack O'Brien to be his chief second.

Showing his courage (or perhaps foolishness), Tunney arrived in Philadelphia via airplane with a stunt flier, coming from the Shawnee Country Club near Stroudsburg, touching down at the Navy Yard Naval Aviation Station at 1:13 p.m. Rickard did not like him flying, and was extremely vexed by it, but Gene did it anyway. He was smiling, and shook hands with several marines. He took an auto to the boxing commission offices in the Drexel Building, arriving at 1:45 p.m. Huge crowds lined the

---

[493] The following account is from *Philadelphia Inquirer, Philadelphia Public Ledger, Philadelphia Evening Bulletin, Pittsburgh Press, New York Daily News, Yonkers Herald, Buffalo Times, Brooklyn Daily Times, Brooklyn Daily Eagle, Glens Falls Post-Star, Chicago Tribune*, September 24, 1926.

streets and showed Tunney great adulation as he traveled to the commission offices. Special guards of mounted police protected him from the curious. The cut on his lip still could be seen.

Frank Wiener, commission chair, weighed Tunney in at 185 ½ pounds, as Gene expected. Dr. Baron said Tunney was in excellent condition. "He is the most astonishing subject I ever examined." Tunney was optimistic and confident.

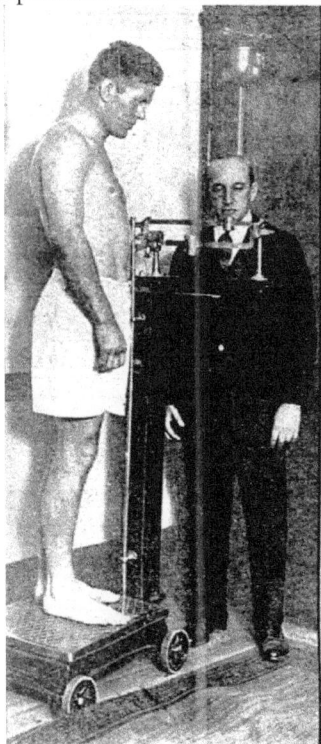

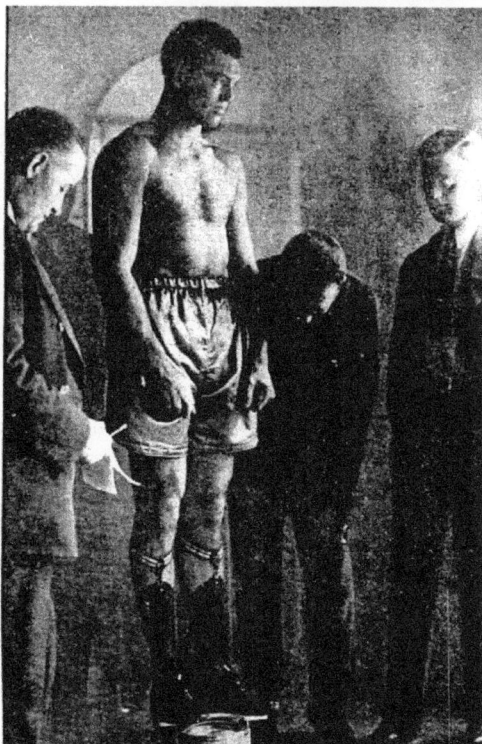

Tunney 185 ½ pounds, Dempsey 190 (though some reported 194)

A pair of Dempsey training mitts were auctioned off for $100, the money to be given to the Red Cross fund for the relief of Florida storm sufferers. A tobacco company officer purchased the gloves.

59 special trains took folks from New York to the fight. Rail officials said they never before were called upon to handle such large crowds, not even for football games or the World Series.

The Sesqui stadium gates were opened at 3 p.m.

At 3:30 p.m., a sticky haze hung over the massive stadium. The dark sky threatened to open up with rain all day and throughout the early evening, but held off during the preliminary battles.

CHOSEN AS SCENE OF DEMPSEY-TUNNEY FIGHT

Some paid $5.50 to sit at the rim of the bowl. Others paid from $50 to $200 each to sit at ringside. Scalpers were busy. Many were arrested and fined. However, ticket scalping simply could not be prevented entirely. There was too much money to be made, given the great demand.

College boys served as ushers, wearing vari-colored freshman caps and their arm bands. Red-and-black-capped ushers were everywhere.

Gate crashers failed in their attempts. Security was tight. Policemen and firemen were all over. There was one usher for every 80 people, and a policeman or fireman for every 10 rows of seats. One said there were 3,000 policemen and 1,000 firemen. "One-Eye" Connelly, the world's most famous gate crasher, met his Waterloo. He purportedly had a ticket to a $16.50 seat but nevertheless was thrown out.

Rickard issued passes to 150 federal agents. He was forced to give space to men who would check up on ticket boxes. They wanted to make sure the government got its share of the receipts, 10% of the gate. They did not trust Tex to give an honest and accurate accounting the way others had in New Jersey and New York.

It was humid and hot. The temperature low that day was 65 degrees, with a high of 80 degrees, with an eventual .38 inches of precipitation.

Scores of white-clad dispensers of soft drinks, peanuts, and chocolate bars were present. Some folks sold field glasses, opera glasses, binoculars, and telescopes. Hot dog and peanut stands did record business. At soft-drink stands, empty bottles piled up waist-deep. Lemonade cost 25 cents a glass. Near-beer was sold as well.

Movie and still photographers were present. Word painters were there from around the world. Correspondents and telegraphers sent about 2 million words throughout the country and world. The metallic clicking of typewriters combined with the clicks of telegraph instruments. Telegraph operators were close to the ring, but sitting under the platform, waiting to take dictation.

Tex Rickard wore a blue suit, a gray felt hat, and carried a Malacca stick in one hand and a cigar in the other.

At 6:04 p.m., airplanes were flying over the Stadium, doing loops and nose dives.

Wisecracking Ring Lardner lamented how cramped the press box was, saying it was the first time he pitied the poor sardine.

Rickard said the bouts would go on, rain or moonshine. He was smiling. "No wonder. It's a sellout."

At 6:44 p.m., radio musicians were playing, "Meet Me in Old Philly Billy." Everyone was there, including Billy.

At 7 p.m., the flood lights were switched on, bringing great light. Thousands of powerful electric lamps towered above the walls. The lighting arrangements were perfect. Above the ring, hanging from a canopy of structural iron, were more than 30 reflectors, each containing a lamp of 1,000 watts. The ring could be seen clearly, as bright as day. However, the great light attracted and brought forth an annoying presence of mosquitoes.

Max Hoff was engaged in a tete-a-tete with Captain McFadden.

Shortly before 8 p.m., Dempsey arrived in Philadelphia by special car attached to the train from Atlantic City. Police accompanied him through the admiring crowd. His party included Jack O'Brien, Jerry Luvadis, Gus Wilson, Gene Normile, and Bill Tate.

Leon Britton spent $50,000 to make moving pictures of the fight. He even filmed the pre-fight scenes.

Bank presidents, uncouth truck drivers, social leaders, "riffraff from the slums," high public officials, bootleggers, and beautifully gowned young women all were there, on hard, yellow pine, wooden board seats. It was a spectacle of glamor and excitement. It was the best-behaved, most orderly, and dignified crowd ever. One estimated that at least 25,000 spectators were women, many unaccompanied by male escorts, the largest number of the "fair sex" ever to attend a fight. Women primarily wore royal blue and bright green.

Present were a dozen senators and congressmen, and several governors and mayors, including New York Mayor James J. Walker, members of U.S. President Calvin Coolidge's cabinet, and other political leaders and captains of industry. They included Secretary of War Dwight Davis, Secretary of the Navy Curtis Wilbur, and Attorney General George Woodruff. Pennsylvania Governor Gifford Pinchot was at the center of a box in the middle of the horseshoe-shaped arena. Other governors included Governor Len Small, Illinois, Ritchie, Maryland, Robinson, Delaware, Byrd, Virginia, Groesbeck, Nebraska, and Al Smith, New York.

Also present were Charles M. Schwab - chair of the Bethlehem Steel Corp., Harry Whitney, Vincent Astor, Anne Morgan - daughter of the late New York financier J. Pierpont Morgan, merchant Ellis Gimbel, and a myriad of others. Harry Greb was there, as well as Otto Floto and Barney Oldfield. Movie and theatrical celebrities included Charlie Chaplin, Eddie Foy, and Peggy Joyce.

The first preliminary bout started at 8:02 p.m.

The ring was 20-square-feet, with ropes wound with white cotton wrapping which made them gleam. It was a steel platform. It had a bit more give and spring at its center. It was a canvas floor, with an inch of felt. There was an air cushion so the canvas would not pack down hard. The corrugated bottom kept it from tying up to the floor, so there always would be air beneath it. When the canvas was strapped down, it made a smooth, fast surface, yet, when there was a knockdown, there was no danger of further shock or concussion should a boxer hit his head.

Fans all over the country jammed the streets outside various newspaper offices, waiting to hear the fight returns.

At 8:48 p.m., former President Teddy Roosevelt's sons arrived – Theodore, Jr., Archie, and Kermit.

Amongst the five preliminary bouts, 223- or 228- pound George Godfrey won a 6-round decision over colored rival 180 ½- or 186 ½-pound Bob Lawson, who held a 1926 TKO7 victory over Jack Johnson. Godfrey scored a flash knockdown in the 2nd round. Ring Lardner humorously said the bout was "marred by a lack of race prejudice." The two judges agreed that Godfrey won, so the referee's verdict was not needed. Godfrey was coming off his loss to Jack Sharkey.

Dempsey's sparring partner, 176-pound Tommy Loughran, won a clear and unanimous 6-round decision over Tunney's sparring partner, 177-pound Jimmy Delaney, winning every round and looking like a champion in giving him a boxing lesson.

By 9 p.m., there was no space left. Attendance was given out as 132,000, a complete sell-out. It was the largest gathering at any sporting event in America where admission was charged. It was the biggest crowd in the city's history. The previous record in Philadelphia was 70,000, for a college football game.

At 9:24 p.m., Tommy Reilly was announced as the referee for the title bout. Mike Bernstein and Frank Brown were announced as the judges.

Thousands of people gathered around the *Philadelphia Inquirer* offices to hear round-by-round reports of the big fight.

At 9:30 p.m., Gene Tunney approached the ring first, to great cheering and an ovation. He fulfilled the "age-old tradition of the ring – which requires that the challenger would be the first to appear."

Gene wore a navy-blue robe, with a bit of red edged about the collar and pockets, wide red cuffs, with the famous insignia of the Marine Corps in gold on the back, a gift from General Lejeune of the Marines, under whom Gene served as a Devil Dog. It was made of the same cloth which marine uniforms were manufactured. He marched down the aisle to the ring, mounted the ladder and stepped in. There was applause and cheers, but they abruptly died down. Gene nodded and sat down with a smile, but a baleful look in his blue eyes. His lip showed the training scar. He was with his friend Jimmy Bronson, manager Billy Gibson, trainer Lou Brix, and Lou Fink. Then there was a hush. A few raindrops fell.

A few minutes later, from the doorway stepped Jack Dempsey, grinning serenely and confidently. One said a cheer and pandemonium reigned, reverberating throughout the arena. He strutted down the long aisle, preceded by a dozen policemen and detectives. The crowd shouted and howled its approval. He entered the ring a minute later to wild yells and shouts that continued, on and on.

Another observer said Dempsey was not quite as well-acclaimed as was the challenger. However, there was no booing.

With Dempsey were manager Gene Normile, who wore white flannel trousers, a white cap, and a white sweater, Jerry 'the Greek' Luvadis, Gus Wilson, and chief second Philadelphia Jack O'Brien. O'Brien wore flannel trousers and a black jersey. New York detective Jack Smith and a U.S. Marshal stood guard.

Dempsey wore blue satin trunks, with a double yellow line down the seam/side, the Sesqui colors, and a red, white, and blue belt. Instead of a robe, a large Turkish white towel was around his neck, covering most of his upper torso, as shown on the films. Others said he wore a white sweatshirt or wool jersey.

Tunney wore deep purple satin trunks.

Jack shook Gene's bare hand. Both were smiling. The crowd was calm.

In the ring, both fighters wrapped yards of gauze bandages over their own hands while representatives from the other side observed. Bronson acted for Tunney, and O'Brien for Dempsey.

The weather had been fair until the main event fighters entered. A drizzle fell, and it gradually increased and thickened. The atmosphere was tense, with an ominous silence for a while. The rain drops showed spots on announcer Joe Griffo's natty tuxedo.

The vast crowd was on edge, and many called out for the fight to get started. They were concerned about the increasing rain, donning their coats. Some whistled and catcalled as Tunney slowly and carefully wrapped his hands, finishing up much later than Dempsey. Chairman Frank Wiener urged more haste. Hands were taped, and gloves donned. Jerry the Greek put on Dempsey's gloves. Both men wore "blue-ribbon gloves." At that point, there was a generous rain shower.

At 9:45 p.m., Announcer Joe Griffo introduced the officials for the heavyweight title battle, Referee Tommy Reilly of Philadelphia, and Judges

Frank Brown of Pittsburgh and Mike Bernstein of Wilkes-Barre. A couple of locals had been in charge of watching the gloves, and they were recognized. The crowd hooted. They wanted action, not words.

Griffo wisely hurried through his introduction of the two combatants. Dempsey's weight was given as 190 pounds, while Tunney weighed 185 ½ pounds. They stripped, and Referee Tommy Reilly called them to ring center. On the films, it appears that the referee wore all white, except black shoes. Dempsey's eyebrows were caked with Vaseline/cold cream. The fight started a minute later.

The vast majority picked Dempsey to win, but hoped for an upset. They wanted Tunney, and supported him throughout the fight. The odds at ringside shortened to 9 to 5, with Dempsey still the favorite.

The fight got under way and the sound of leather against flesh resounded throughout the arena.

Some said the rain began to come down in earnest. No one minded, though. The crowd was so focused on the fight that they ignored the fact that they were drenched by the eventual persistent downpour.

1st round

The films show that Dempsey came out moving forward quickly, crouching. Tunney fired a right that missed. Jack moved back, then in, and Gene clinched. Dempsey freed his left and landed a short hook. Gene clinched more firmly, Jack landed a short-arm hook to the side of the head, and the referee broke them. Dempsey bobbed, his head dipping up and down a couple times, and stepped in quickly with a right to the body and left hook to the head, landing well. As Jack fired, Tunney countered with a hook and slapping right and then clinched as Dempsey snuck in hooks to the body and head. Gene grabbed more tightly, while Jack tried to break free from Gene's clasp and punch. Referee break.

Dempsey ducked down to the right a couple times, stepped in with a couple jabs to the body and hook to the head that Tunney ducked. Gene countered with a hook and right, eluded a counter right, moved away, and peppered Dempsey with jabs as he moved. Dempsey quickly advanced, crouching. With his back to the ropes, Tunney fired away at Dempsey's head with a speedy combination of short blows, right-left-right, before clinching. Dempsey dug nonstop rights to the body and a right and left uppercut to the head, but Tunney countered with a right over the top.

Dempsey advanced as Tunney retreated. Dempsey fired at the body and Tunney immediately countered to the head before clinching. Referee break. Tunney lightly bounced back as Dempsey advanced. Tunney stepped off to the side and Dempsey kept up the pressure. Tunney fired a right and held to thwart Jack's attempted blows. Break. As Tunney moved back, Dempsey advanced into range, but again Tunney fired 1-2 over the top of a ducking Dempsey and grabbed. Break. Gene repeated the same tactic, moving back, this time landing his 1-2 and holding.

Even though he was moving back, Tunney was good at stopping and firing first just as Dempsey got into range. He also was very good at tying up and smothering. Another referee break inevitably would follow.

Dempsey again advanced, though a bit more slowly. Tunney missed a 1-2-3 and stepped off to the side. Tunney advanced with a lead right that Dempsey ducked and they clinched. Dempsey tried to get off with something, but Tunney's arms blocked him well as he held tightly. Break.

Tunney lightly bounced up and down, but remained on the ground or close to it. He was springy, able to move back subtly as Dempsey advanced, and then immediately stop and fire or step in and fire when he anticipated that Dempsey would be getting into his range.

This time though, as Tunney fired his 1-2, Dempsey stepped away off to the side, then advanced again. Tunney jabbed and grabbed. Break.

Neither man landed cleanly very often, but Tunney seemed to have more control of matters, imposing his style on the contest to that point. He was quick with his feet and hands. Dempsey was good with his head movement, eluding or riding with Gene's blows.

Back on the inside, while clinched, Tunney snuck in some short, smothered blows - a left uppercut and hook. Break. Dempsey bobbed and weaved his way in, advancing, but Tunney once again pulled the trigger first, firing jab — right - left uppercut — right, and then clinched. Tunney seemed to have better speed, timing, and command of range.

Dempsey was advancing but not really throwing. Jack tried to dig in a left body shot, and in the clinch also fired some rabbit shots with his left as Gene leaned forward and into Jack. Break. Back on the outside, Tunney jabbed and moved. Dempsey advanced and fired lead left hook - right to the body - left hook combination but missed as Tunney leaned and stepped back out of the way and then immediately countered with right - left hook - right on Dempsey and clinched. On the inside, Tunney landed a jolting right uppercut and a hook, showing that he knew how to punch up close as well, and then he clinched again. Break.

Tunney jabbed and bounced back, gliding around the ring, then firing his 1-2 before holding the advancing Dempsey, who had fired a lead right that served as a counter. Break.

Back on the outside, Gene pumped speedy, lightning-quick, snappy jabs as he moved about, but Dempsey slipped underneath them. However, seeing that Dempsey stopped moving forward, Tunney suddenly advanced and attacked the champ with a combination of alternating jab-right-jab-right, and as Jack attempted to hold, Gene kept up the attack with hook, right uppercut, and more nonstop hooks and rights as Dempsey retreated. They clinched, and Dempsey fired a left to the body and a left uppercut to the chin as Tunney leaned in and smothered and held. Break. Back on the outside, Jack eluded Gene's jab with his head movement. Bell.

Overall, Tunney had very fast hands and feet, and quick reflexes, being very alert, a master of range, moving, dancing, sidestepping, or sliding back or off to the side out of range, pumping quick, metronome jabs, and clinching well when Dempsey moved in close. Gene also moved in and fired a 1-2, or rapid flowing combinations when he saw fit. Dempsey bobbed and weaved and tried to advance with hard blows and counters, but Tunney was very elusive and countered him well, clinched, or moved. Jack worked some snappy jolting blows on the inside, particularly his left hook. He once tried to time his right over the top of Tunney's left jab. Tunney could fire and move away or fire and move in and clinch and smother. He was active with quick, relaxed, snappy, peppery blows. He was trying to prevent Dempsey from getting set for too long, and also to throw off his sense of timing and range. Dempsey moved a bit himself, either trying not to be too predictable on the way in or so he could obtain breaks between punches. Tunney was far busier with his blows, maintaining a very good pace, but also was very poised, calm, loose, and relaxed, while at the same time remaining alert.

In conclusion, Tunney was in control of the timing and range, firing more often and more quickly, as Dempsey advanced but rarely threw, not seeming to have his range or sense of distance yet, and whenever he got into range either Tunney would grab, or fire first and then grab, or he would move back out of range, or Dempsey would fire but miss and then get countered. At least Dempsey was not wasting punches, but he was not particularly working either, other than advancing and bobbing and trying to apply pressure, but it was ineffective, unless the work that he was making Tunney do eventually would wear him out. But Tunney was not necessarily overworking.

Millions of people heard the fight's details live via radio broadcast through a chain of stations hooked up with the WJZ and WEAF in New York. Major J. Andrew White (blow by blow) and Graham McNamee (additional analysis) described the championship through microphones stationed at ringside. During the round, White noted, "Jack does not show the speed he is accustomed to showing. It is not the Jack we are accustomed to at all." There was a fair amount of sparring and clinching. Tunney landed several blows with right and left. Jack backed him up to the ropes, but Tunney landed. "This is not the Jack Dempsey we were accustomed to seeing." He was taking punches, showing no defense at all, and not landing effectively.

> Tunney hit him at least six times with rights and lefts to the face and Jack gets another on the eye as the bell rings. The first round is Tunney's round by a mile. The first round has been something in the nature of what has happened a good many times when champions lay off for three years and do not do any business. Gene started off for Jack with lefts and rights and won the round without the slightest difficulty. Dempsey landed two good blows on Gene through the entire round. Tunney landed both hands, particularly during the last minute, with great effect, on the side of Dempsey's head, and Dempsey covered up.

For the *Philadelphia Inquirer*, James Isaminger noted that Dempsey focused on the body. Tunney landed a sharp right to the chin that made Jack's head wobble. Gene focused on outside boxing, utilizing his jab and right, and often clinched when close. A right sent Jack back to the ropes. A Tunney onslaught punished Dempsey about the head.

Perry Lewis said Tunney was timing Dempsey with rights, which slowed the champ's attack. Tunney was elusive throughout the round, and Dempsey was unable to get home any of his pile-driving blows. Toward the end of the round, Tunney shook him with a vicious left hook, then followed with rights and lefts to the jaw that made Dempsey bend and sag. The round was all Tunney's. Dempsey went to his corner blazing with anger. Tunney had stood him off from the start and beaten him.

Robert Edgren said Dempsey started off with his furious rushing, but Tunney had good defense, and his counter right to the chin drove Dempsey back on his heels. Tunney would evade and then suddenly leap in. Many of Dempsey's blows missed, but few of Tunney's missed. By the end of the round, Dempsey's mouth was open, and he was unable to get away from the curving right hand that was always dropping somewhere from out of the sky and hitting him on the jaw or neck below the ear. Tunney's blows hurt.

The *Philadelphia Public Ledger's* Frank McCracken said Dempsey kept rushing in but Tunney defended and hit him with counters. Occasionally Tunney took the aggressive. Tunney was good at moving around the ring, punching on the move with leads or counters and moving again or clinching. A right and left staggered the champion. It was a bad round for the champ.

Ed Pollock said it was raining hard from the start, and fans donned their raincoats. Dempsey rushed like a tiger and sank lefts and rights into the body, but Tunney retaliated with jabs that had Jack's head bobbing. The crowd roared its approval of Gene's aggressive boxing.

Philadelphia Mayor W. Freeland Kendrick said Tunney was not fooled by the champ's attempts to feint, and he beat Dempsey to the punch each time. The round clearly belonged to Tunney.

The *New York Daily News'* Paul Gallico said the crowd roared as Tunney moved, halted suddenly and landed 1-2 combinations to the head, rocking Dempsey. Gene kept hammering the champion, staggering him. Between rounds, Jack's seconds were administering him smelling salts. O'Brien held the bottle up to him. "It was a sight that was hard to believe."

Harry Newman said Tunney hurt and staggered Dempsey. In his corner, Jack appeared winded as his seconds worked furiously. Tunney seemed confident.

James Wood said already it was evident that Tunney was not going to wilt under Dempsey's attack. He backed away but kept firing.

2nd round

On the films, Tunney kept moving, punching, and clinching. Dempsey tried to get going with his offense more, firing some vicious blows, but Tunney was too quick at punching and moving away, or leaning back, rolling with blows, grabbing, and smothering. Tunney either would punch when Dempsey got in range, timing him well, or he would counter. Jack landed a glancing hard hook to the head, some solid body blows, and some short inside shots, but mostly was missing or not landing with full force. Tunney kept moving, lightly bouncing forward-and-back in subtle fashion, feinting, very calmly using his ring generalship without using excess energy. Dempsey tried to fire away with short inside blows, but mostly they were smothered, for Tunney was good at grabbing. If Dempsey stopped moving forward, Tunney would go on the attack and step forward, sometimes forcing Dempsey back and holding on a bit himself. Tunney's methods were punch, move, punch, grab, spin out, circle, punch, roll, counter, grab and smother, move and feint, fire away, move away, fire again, then dive in and prevent counters.

At one point, Tunney went on a lengthy attack with a combination of punches, 1-2-3, 1-2 - left uppercut. He even snuck in a left hook to the body. Tunney was cautious and defensive, but he knew how to fire when Dempsey got in range, or Gene suddenly would step forward on the attack and surprise Dempsey when he sensed he could do it safely, particularly when Dempsey slowed up or backed away. Tunney was very quick, active, and agile, with wonderful ring generalship.

On the radio, White/McNamee said Dempsey sped up a bit. However, "He is not the Dempsey of old; he is inaccurate, he is short on his punches, he takes a terrific jab in the face, a right. Gene follows him up, and Jack clinches." Dempsey rushed, but "Gene blocks him beautifully, covers his body up, and Jack does not land." Gene had a slight cut on one of his lips. "Tunney reaches Jack's face at will. Jack has no defense at all, he never attempts any. He does not look like the old Dempsey at all." He backed Gene up, but "Tunney's defense is perfect." Dempsey was bobbing and weaving but showing no speed. He jabbed but was met with a hard hook and then he held for an instant. Dempsey finally landed a hard hook, his first real blow. More clinching. "This is not the Jack Dempsey that we expected at all, he is a very conservative, flat-footed boxer, not indulging in his swirling rushes." Jack took several seemingly light blows to the face, backed up to the ropes, and they clinched. Dempsey "seems to have no speed tonight." He was taking punches. He landed a beautiful right on Gene's ribs. "The fight shows what happens to a fighter that doesn't fight." Tunney took well the few blows that Dempsey landed, and in the latter part of the round, "had Jack Dempsey's head bobbing all over the place."

Summarizing, the radio men said in the first two rounds, a few times Dempsey looked groggy. "He is not down by any means but he shows the effect of not fighting. Gene Tunney leads by a long margin at the end of the second round. He looks fresh as a daisy and Jack looks a little tired."

Isaminger said Dempsey landed a terrific left to Tunney's jaw, staggering him. Dempsey sent in body blows, while Tunney drove his right to the jaw. Jack landed a left to the body and followed with a left to the chin. He crowded Gene into a corner and landed a right to the head. As Dempsey was moving in, Tunney caught him with a right. In a furious mix, Tunney landed on the head and jaw. Even round.

Lewis said Dempsey rushed madly but was missing. Halfway through the round, Tunney led for the first time, stepping in with a hook to the jaw and stiff right. With a terrific right, Dempsey drew blood from Gene's battered lips. The blow appeared to worry Tunney, who was cautious as Dempsey tore after him. Towards the end, Tunney caused an uproar when he rushed Dempsey and peppered him with both hands. Dempsey was all right though.

Edgren said Dempsey rushed again, but Tunney outfought him and beat him back. Dempsey's face was expressionless, but grim. He rushed Tunney against the ropes and into corners, reaching for his body. In the middle of the round, Tunney crashed a right to the jaw, and the rain started. The ring was soaking wet. Dempsey finished the round reeling and tired, moving in with his head down, only to be driven back by blows that never missed.

McCracken said Dempsey attacked but Tunney stepped away. Tunney led and landed. Blood was coming from Gene's chin. Jack hit the body and fired away in a clinch. Tunney hit the chin. Dempsey rocked him with hard rights to the body. Tunney boxed him. Even round.

Pollock said Dempsey landed a vicious left hook that had Tunney in trouble, but he recovered. The crowd shouted, "Come on, Gene!" Tunney came on, starting an aggressive attack, wading in and landing several sharp blows. A hook at the bell knocked the champ back on his heels.

Kendrick said Tunney fought more at long range. He would pop and tap Dempsey's face. When Dempsey closed in, Tunney calmly and methodically clinched, tying him up well.

Gallico said Dempsey hit Tunney with a vicious blow under the heart, one of the most vicious the writer ever had seen. Tunney gasped and staggered. There was the old Dempsey. But, yet again, Dempsey's head began to bob, rock, and ride under the storm. The crowd caught on and started chanting Tunney's name. The Manassa murderer was not in the ring, but only a shell. He had blind fury, but his punches were landing in the air, and when he moved close, he was struck with that deadly one-two combination, sometimes the right going to the body, until again he was reeling and staggering, seemingly on the road to defeat.

Newman said Dempsey tore after Tunney, chasing him around the ring, ripping lefts and rights to the body. Tunney landed his right to the chin, but Dempsey forced him around. Both landed on the body. Dempsey was furiously chasing Tunney about. Tunney landed his left. Dempsey held him against ropes, landing rights to the body. Tunney landed his right to the head. Dempsey kept rushing and missing. In a clinch, Jack thumped his head. Dempsey paid little heed to Tunney's punches. In a clinch, Jack flailed at the body. Tunney connected two rights to the head. It was raining heavily. Dempsey drove a terrific right under the heart. A fierce scrimmage followed, with Tunney ripping both mitts to Jack's face. Tunney's round.

Wood said Tunney showed such speed that Dempsey was forced to cover. Gene went to his corner with a slightly cut mouth.

Grantland Rice said Dempsey came out with a rush, crowded Tunney to a corner and opened the gash on his lip, but Tunney came back. Dempsey was doing better infighting, while Tunney was far superior at long range. Tunney got Dempsey on the ropes, battering him.

3rd round

The films show that Dempsey was confused, because when he got close enough to punch, either Tunney would move away, or Gene would grab, or beat him to the punch and then move away or clinch. Dempsey tried to uncork his big hook as he was being held. He kept bobbing and moving in, or stepping to the side, but Tunney kept firing and moving, sometimes punching as he moved back, and sometimes on the attack.

One could tell that Dempsey never quite felt comfortable with his range, never truly being able to get set to punch when necessary. Tunney kept peppering and moving, then grabbing. Dempsey was not pulling the trigger often enough, or at the right time. It seems as if he either could not get off, or felt that if he did, he would miss and be wasting energy. When he wanted to fire, he either was getting hit, or missing, or getting held. Dempsey fired a lead right that landed, but Tunney immediately countered. Tunney occasionally attacked and went on the offense with a series of jabs and rights.

It was a masterful performance of speed, timing, footwork, defense, and control of distance. Tunney was a regular Jim Corbett and Jack O'Brien combined. He also could fire off speedy combinations in flowing fashion. He fired a rapid combination - jab – right - left uppercut – right - left uppercut, before moving away. Years later, fighters like Ray Robinson and Muhammad Ali would utilize a similar style.

Occasionally in this round, Dempsey was trying to time a right over the top of Tunney's left, but with limited success. He also dug in a couple hooks to the body, but he was landing only here and there. Often when Dempsey threw, Tunney was moving away from and riding the blows, and then countering or clinching. Dempsey simply was not moving in consistently enough or throwing at the right moments. He seemed a bit hesitant, realizing that Tunney had great speed, timing, footwork, and defense, and his punches were faster, with perhaps a bit more pop than expected. So, often Jack would hesitate as he started getting into range. Dempsey seemed puzzled and bewildered. The old Dempsey would have dipped and walked right through it all and kept firing away nonstop. Instead, increasingly Gene was attacking him and even pushing Jack back in the clinches.

White/McNamee said Dempsey seemed freshened up again. "I don't think Tunney's blows hurt him much." Dempsey was aggressive, but Tunney landed. Jack landed a left hook on the jaw. Gene jabbed him several times lightly. Jack was waiting for an opening. "Tunney is quite far the superior boxer." Gene landed a hard right hook. Dempsey was very deliberate. Tunney landed hard rights on the jaw and a left as well. "Dempsey is taking Gene's blows." They sparred and clinched. Tunney was landing his jabs and straight right. Jack only rarely clipped Gene on the jaw. The champ mostly took light blows, but some stinging ones as well. When Dempsey got close, Gene clinched very well. Most of Jack's punches were glancing.

At the gong, "Dempsey goes to his corner slowly, but he does not appear to be tired. But he has not got the pep. Tunney comes smiling to his corner." Tunney had won the first 3 rounds. "Jack is fairly aggressive. He follows Tunney all the time." Tunney was backing up continually, but stopping just long enough to jab, and every now and then follow up with a right or left-right-left-right before Jack could move. "He is outboxing the champion from start to finish. Dempsey is absolutely unable to get going. He seems to have nothing, except now and then he shoots over a left."

Isaminger said Tunney landed a left to the mouth and crossed two rights to the head, one blow knocking the plaster off of Dempsey's right eye. Tunney again feinted his left and landed a right to the jaw. Dempsey looked puzzled. Tunney's round.

Lewis said Dempsey started the round coming in with his famous crouch, apparently setting himself for a big punch. He tried to work in close, but as he came in, Tunney crashed a terrific right to the jaw followed by a left hook. Dempsey damaged Tunney's body with short lefts, but he took some severe raps to the jaw in return. Tunney fought coolly and showed defensive generalship that few thought he had.

Edgren said Dempsey took more of a beating. Jack landed some blows, and at times they hurt, but Tunney threw them off and recovered in an instant. Tunney had won the first three rounds.

McCracken said Dempsey did not tear in as he did the prior round. Tunney landed straight rights and lefts. Gene backed away but was looking for an opening. He landed a left and hard right to the chin. He eluded and stabbed with jabs. He was self-possessed and seemed to weigh his every move. Gene backed away from a rush and went into a corner. Dempsey landed a hard right cross to the chin, the hardest blow of the fight. Tunney's round.

Pollock said Tunney showed his fine boxing ability. He danced around, sending in lefts and occasional rights. He looked like a winner.

Kendrick said Dempsey began showing the marks of Tunney's blows and was irritated by his failure to land solidly on the dancing figure in front of him. Whenever they drew together for their frequent flurries, it seemed that Tunney landed first. Gene's punches were not as hard, but were disturbing, nevertheless.

Newman said Tunney stabbed several lefts to the face and two hard rights to the head. He smacked Dempsey with a right to the ear. Dempsey weaved in and drove lefts and rights to the body. Tunney staggered Dempsey with a right crack on the chin. He repeated the blow. Both pounded the body in a clinch. Tunney belted him with a straight right to the chin. Dempsey bore in, utterly fearless, while the confident Tunney snapped rights and lefts to the face. Dempsey forced him to the ropes without doing damage. They traded right smacks to the head. Dempsey plugged a right to the head. They were locked at the bell. Tunney's round.

Wood said Dempsey's low weaving style could not elude the straight punching. Jack showed signs of tiring. He sagged a bit and stopped punching entirely for the last minute.

Rice said Tunney landed and backed away. Dempsey backed him to a corner and drove in a right, but as Tunney came out, he hit Dempsey on the jaw and staggered him. He got him on the ropes, landing. When Dempsey came in, Tunney hit him on the mouth and the blood flowed. He outpointed Dempsey all the way. Dempsey's body punches seemed to be hurting the challenger. Both showed they could take the best each had.

4th round

On the films, Dempsey came out like a ferocious ball of energy, charging right in and firing a brutal hook and right, the hook landing cleanly and jerking Tunney's head. Tunney leaned back into the ropes and immediately clinched. Dempsey tried to punch himself free, but Tunney held on tightly until broken by the referee. Tunney glided back, fired and clinched as the champion charged in and kept trying to work.

Dempsey dug in a couple heavy, snappy left hooks to the body, and then a high hook to the head that staggered and buckled Tunney into the ropes. With both hands, Tunney grabbed the ropes to his right side and steadied and raised himself, and then moved away. He kept firing on the retreat, pumping jabs and rights until Dempsey got in and tried to dig inside blows as Tunney clinched.

After breaking, Tunney jabbed, but Dempsey's counter-jab rocked Gene's head back. Tunney again pegged away with jabs and a right and then clinched. Break. Dempsey bore in with head movement, ducking low as he advanced and eluded. Tunney fired, clinched and bulled forward to smother as Jack dug in some short blows. Break.

Dempsey slowed up, and Tunney went back to doing his usual punch, move, punch, grab style. While being held, Dempsey fired rabbit shots. Tunney would punch 1-2 and then grab. Dempsey was not punching like he had in the early part of the round, and even when he did, he was falling short as Gene pulled away. Most of Jack's landed blows were to the body. Tunney kept beating him to the punch and holding.

Tunney again fired off a combination, jab – right - left uppercut. Dempsey was firing only intermittently, and usually one punch at a time, either a lead right or hook to the body.

In terms of overall output, number landed blows, and ring generalship, it was Tunney's round, but in terms of who landed the cleanest, hardest, most effective blows of the round, it was Dempsey's round, as a result of the couple hard connections early in the round. Dempsey's heavy blows could snap Tunney's head and make him grab, buckling him once, but Dempsey rarely threw or landed, while Tunney kept peppering him with consistent sharp singles and occasional flowing combos, dictating matters most of the time. Even round or Dempsey. It was Dempsey's best round up to that point.

White/McNamee said Dempsey landed left and right and bent Tunney back over the ropes. Jack was beginning to rush. He landed a right. "Tunney has begun to weaken slightly on his knees, and Dempsey is now fighting."

Tunney fought back, and they clinched. Tunney's left opened the champ's right eye a little. They exchanged a bit. Jack went for the body but Gene held on. There were several clinches and misses, and both were moving slowly. It was a "typical Tunney fight, and not the Jack Dempsey we looked for at all."

Dempsey showed that he could take it. "Dempsey seems to be satisfied to take all the punches and put up no defense for his face, anything to get in on Tunney. Standing flatfooted in the centre of the ring." Dempsey took more punches in an attempt to get in. He hit the back of Gene's head with light blows. Tunney escaped, landed a right to the jaw, and five jabs to the face. Jack's nose seemed sore, and he even held a bit.

Summarizing, White/McNamee said,

> It is a very tame round, and once again Tunney shows his superiority. Tunney wins another round. Tunney has now won four rounds in succession. For a moment at the opening of that round we saw Jack Dempsey for the first time tonight for a moment. He came out and gave all he had with a right, left, right, left and jammed Tunney on the ropes, and for a moment Tunney's knees went back on him, but Tunney came to life and evidently Jack gave all he had for the moment in that first flurry for fifteen or twenty seconds long and then began again to outbox the champion and during that round he landed about three corking rights, not on the button, but awfully hard on the side of the jaw. The champion's nose looks a little battered and one eye looks very bad. Gene looks very well at this moment.

Isaminger said Dempsey rushed Tunney and sent him against the ropes with a left to the chin. He made another bull-like rush and showered Tunney with lefts to the head. Tunney dropped to one knee [sic] but was up immediately. Dempsey was after him like a cat and put a hard right to the body. Dempsey's right eye was bleeding from a cut. While they were close, Tunney belted the champ's ear. Tunney took his time and swung a hard right under Dempsey's right eye. Dempsey showed the effects of the punishment. They sparred, and Tunney landed two light lefts and a hard right. He got on top of Jack and hit him with two hard lefts and rights.

Lewis said Dempsey rushed out like a madman and sprung at Tunney like a tiger, almost carrying Gene off his feet. It was a typical Dempsey rush, but after some close infighting, Jack came out of a clinch with blood coming from his right eye. Tunney weathered the terrific storm, and with the round half over, caught Dempsey coming in with a stiff right that shook up the champ. Tunney finished this round as he did the others, crowding Dempsey and hammering his face with rights and left until he had the champ hanging on and holding.

McCracken said Dempsey landed a right and a left and Gene dropped to one knee [sic], but he was up immediately. Tunney rallied and jabbed. Jack had a smear of blood on his face. Tunney landed a right, but it did not stop Jack. Round even.

Pollock said Dempsey rushed from his corner and met him before Gene took two steps. Jack beat him back over the ropes and pounded him with devastating blows. But later Tunney opened a cut under Dempsey's right eye.

Kendrick said the champ came out with a rush, backed the challenger to the ropes several times, and shook him up with left and right punches. Tunney's eye was cut. But he continued his well-studied campaign of smash, move out of range, close in, smash, and clinch, and he seemed fresh and unwearied. Some exclaimed, "If Tunney keeps this up, Dempsey will need a knockout to win!"

Gallico said Dempsey came forth to knock out Tunney, catching him in his own corner with two murderous left and right hooks that sent him flying back over the ropes and almost out of the ring. The old Dempsey was back again. The crowd roared. But, yet again, Tunney began to punch and beat him up. Tunney threw jabs, left and right uppercuts, jabs, rights, thundering right crosses; every punch in the repertoire, and everything landed.

Newman said Dempsey nailed Tunney with a left to the head. He forced him, pounding Gene about the body with both hands. Tunney nailed him with a right to the chin, then another ripping right. A Tunney left hook opened up a cut under Dempsey's right eye, and it bled. Gene landed another hook. In a clinch, Dempsey pounded the head. Outside, Gene stabbed his left to the mouth, and landed a hard right. In a clinch, Tunney ripped an uppercut to the chin. Tunney sent two hard rights to the face. Jack landed a right to the face. Tunney staggered Dempsey with two savage rights to the chin and followed with a right uppercut to the mouth. Tunney's round.

Wood said Dempsey was furious and ripped into the midsection. He landed a right and left to the jaw, but Tunney weathered the storm and swung the tide, outfighting him enough to carry the round.

Rice said Dempsey charged, but Tunney drove him back. Dempsey was on top of him again. Jack had a cut on his cheek. He drove a right to the body and Gene held on. After breaking, Dempsey took hard smashes to the cheek bone. Jack seemed unable to complete his rushes and seemed tired after his savage assault. Both hit the body. There was a big gash on the left side of Dempsey's face, and his nose was battered. Tunney still won the round.

5th round

On the films, both men moved and circled about. Dempsey dipped to the right as usual, advanced, and Tunney moved in and held. Jack snuck a left hook to the body. Break. Jack jabbed the body. Tunney glided about, fired a 1-2 which Jack ducked, and Gene grabbed. Break. Jack jabbed at the head and body, then fired a lead right which Gene countered with his own right and they clinched. Break. Tunney pumped a jab to the face, then off another jab he dug in a left hook to the body, and a right to the head, and clinched. Jack rabbit-punched him with his left. Break.

Gene moved, threw a light 1-2 and grabbed. Jack snuck in a right and left to the body. Break. Jack fired a right over the top of Gene's left jab, but Tunney followed with a right and left that missed. Jack feinted his right. He weaved in, and Tunney rat-a-tatted his head as Jack hit the body with both hands and came over with a hard hook to the head, but Tunney rolled with it just a bit. Dempsey grazed another hook.

Tunney fired a combination, jab - jab - right - left uppercut, then clinched as Jack tried to work. Break. Gene lightly bounced about and circled, then jumped in and clinched. Dempsey fired an inside hook. Tunney countered with his own hook and then fired off his 1-2 again, and another right. He retreated, fired 1-2-2, which Jack countered with a missed left hook, and Gene leaned in and grabbed. Dempsey fired rabbit punches with his right. Break.

Tunney moved back, fired 1-2 and clinched again. Break. Tunney pumped his jab a couple times, then right - left uppercut - right. Jack badly missed a counter hook when Gene was gone already. Dempsey simply was not firing when in range, but Tunney was. Tunney moved, Dempsey advanced and dug in a left hook to the body. Tunney returned in kind and followed with a right. He moved back and jabbed.

Overall, Tunney was just too fast with his hands and feet. Dempsey tried to hit him here and there but was not relentless or active enough. By the time he threw, Tunney was gone, out of range, or inside, tying him up. When Dempsey was not throwing, Tunney was sticking and peppering him with quick blows and sliding out of range. When Dempsey threw,

Gene countered. Tunney was razor sharp, not allowing Dempsey to feel like he could work or land. Dempsey was not countering or working off of Tunney's blows soon enough. Tunney's punches were keeping Dempsey defending, and then when Jack went to punch, Tunney was gone or smothering him.

On the radio, White/McNamee said the "champion is not up to himself at all tonight." Tunney kept at a respectful distance. There was long-range sparring, followed by some clinching. "Dempsey is fighting the Tunney style of fight." Jack landed a right and they clinched. More sparring and clinching. The pace was slow. Jack had a cut under his right eye. "The champion appears to be a hollow shell." Dempsey moved in and took punches. "The champion can't stand this. He seems to be contemptuous of Tunney's punches, but he can't take them all night. … There is no whirlwind stuff at all in Jack Dempsey." He took a couple rights. He landed a left hook, but it was just glancing and had no steam. Tunney landed a hard straight right. "They both seem a trifle wary of each other." Gene was landing four or five blows for every one that the champion landed, and "they have more steam than the champion's blows with the exception of probably four blows during the entire fight, when Jack seemed to put a little of his old self behind it. That is the worst round of the five. It was Tunney's round."

Isaminger's description was of a fairly uneventful round.

Lewis noted that there was a lot of sparring around at the start. Dempsey appeared to have lost his ability to make those head-on rushes for which he was famous. He finally rushed in with a right to the jaw, but Tunney countered with the same blow and beat the champ to it. There was more fiddling around, with Tunney going back and Dempsey following slowly. At the halfway point, Tunney got Dempsey against the ropes, pounded him viciously about the face, and had the champ groggy. Jack's famed left hand seemed to have lost its power, and furthermore, he was punching wildly. Tunney, on the other hand, was shooting both hands like a sharp-shooter. The crowd, feeling that Tunney was way out in the lead, was cheering frantically for a new champion.

Edgren called it an even round. Dempsey fought carefully, pulling away from Tunney's rights. Eventually, Dempsey rushed, but Tunney backed away or held in the clinches. Some blows shook Gene. But then he rallied swiftly and smashed Dempsey to the ropes, left-right, left-right, blows that cut and jarred and kept Dempsey's head bobbing back. Tunney stopped and again became defensive.

McCracken said Dempsey crouched but did not rush. Tunney landed frequently with rights and lefts. Gene took a hard left on the chin. Dempsey spit blood. Tunney's round.

Pollock said the ring was soaking wet, and both boxers had trouble with the slippery surface. It was a rather tame round. Tunney's fine boxing, his left jab, and well-timed right were telling on the champ.

Kendrick said Dempsey lashed out, drove Tunney to the ropes, but never found the opening. Gene covered up and slipped out of the corner, then landed a surprisingly hard blow against the champ's chest. At the round's end, some cried, "Dempsey must knock him out to win!"

Gallico said it was all Tunney.

Newman said Dempsey looked worried during the minute rest before the round. He didn't rush but came out to box at long range. Both missed some blows. Dempsey landed a hard right to the head and ripping left to the stomach. Dempsey chased him around, while Tunney kept pecking with lefts to the face. Dempsey nailed him with a left to the head, then ripped a hard left to the stomach, but Tunney came back with rights and lefts to the face, staggering Dempsey momentarily. Dempsey pelted a left to the face, but Tunney retorted with hard rights to the chin. Tunney landed another right to the jaw and sent Jack reeling with another right to the head. It was Tunney's round, and all Tunney to this point, with the champ looking pretty bad by comparison.

Wood said Tunney outfought him throughout, snapping over his punches with deadly accuracy, even while moving back. He never missed, while Dempsey seldom landed cleanly.

Rice said Dempsey seemed tired, but still looking to land a heavy blow. They exchanged blows back and forth. Tunney hit and moved. Jack weaved and dodged, but even when he cornered Gene, it was Jack who got hit. Tunney drove him to the ropes and started a flow of blood. Tunney was landing three to one.

6th round

The film version shows that Dempsey attacked with a lead hook that missed, followed by a hard right to the body, and Tunney clinched. Break. On the outside, in flowing fashion, Tunney peppered with his jab, right, more jabs, right and jab again, before a clinch. Break. Tunney peppered in more jabs as he retreated and clinched. Dempsey worked the body and tried to hook on the inside, while Tunney fired a right and spun out.

Dempsey advanced with a hook that missed, Tunney countered with a right, but Dempsey followed with his own right that may have landed and a hook that missed as Tunney was retreating and leaning back on the ropes. Tunney clinched and hooked, but Dempsey fired a powerful left hook that may have landed, and Tunney held tightly. Dempsey hit the body with his right. Break.

Tunney again retreated, fired 1-2 and clinched as Dempsey hooked his head. Tunney stepped back, fired a right, and Dempsey stepped in and hooked, followed by another clinch. Tunney backed away and jabbed. Dempsey exploded with a hook to the jaw, but Tunney took it and spun away. Tunney fired a right followed by a left uppercut, but Dempsey countered with a right to the body and a powerful hook that landed on the jaw, jarring Tunney's head, and Gene clinched.

Dempsey was firing more often than before, and his blows were better timed at this point. He kept trying to dig hooks to the body and head as Tunney pushed him back and fired a right to the head.

After breaking, Tunney fired jab - right - left hook to the body, moved, and then fired another combination of jab – right - left uppercut – right - left hook to the body, and clinched. Gene sensed that he needed to get going again. Break.

Dempsey was not advancing as much, or as rapidly. Tunney fired 1-2 and clinched. Dempsey snuck in a left uppercut. Tunney launched a 1-2 and left uppercut. Clinch. Dempsey got in a rabbit shot with his left. Break. Tunney 1-2, clinch, and Gene pushed Jack back to the ropes. Break. Tunney fired a lead left hook to the body followed by a right to the body, and Dempsey countered with his own hook to the body. Tunney fired some quick blows to the head and then spun away to the side as Dempsey hit his body and missed a hook. Clinch and break. Another 1-2 from Tunney and clinch. Dempsey tried a hook to the body and snuck in an uppercut. Break. Gene jabbed. Tunney jab – right – left uppercut. Clinch. Tunney peppered with consistent jabs, then moved away. He clinched, and Dempsey hooked him to the head and jaw. Tunney jabbed and moved again.

Overall in this round, Dempsey was bobbing, weaving, and moving in rapidly, trying hard to land, but Tunney was moving away and eluding with his head movement, leaning back, blocking, and clinching. Dempsey was more active and ferocious than previously, but still found it challenging to land cleanly or often, given Tunney's speed, activity, and defensive inclinations. Jack was landing more often than before, digging in some short shots, but only here and there, not landing solidly very often, and Gene took it well even when Jack did land the occasional hard blow.

Tunney still was firing off combinations whenever Dempsey slowed down or stopped and waited, taking a break. When Dempsey wanted to work, Tunney did what he could to prevent him from throwing or landing, but when Dempsey wanted to wait and rest, or play defense, slowing his attack, Tunney punched and peppered away with consistent annoying single blows with little time in between. His cleverness offset Dempsey's desire to stand and trade. Gene mixed it on occasion though, firing, defending, then countering quickly with short, compact, flowing punches before moving or grabbing. He could flow straight punches, hooks, uppercuts, and body blows in combination. His speed and timing were excellent, as was his defense after punching. He also could time Dempsey on the way in. His footwork was brilliant, fast but controlled, doing no more than necessary.

White/McNamee said Jack tried to rush a bit but just took punches. On the inside, Gene protected himself perfectly. Jack began to fight and landed a left hook. Gene was not groggy, but knew he took a good one. Tunney landed a vicious left hook. He landed left and right, and Jack hit his body. They sparred at a respectful distance, with no speed. "You see

Dempsey crowding and pushing, but he does not show the whirling, rushing attack that has been so characteristic of his fighting, and which made him champion." While trying to find an opening, Jack was taking them, including a right uppercut. "Jack wakes up once in a while."

They said the round came close to being even, more so than any thus far. The round went to Tunney by a slight margin, although Jack woke up in the first half minute and gave Gene something to think about.

Isaminger said a terrific Tunney left to the stomach made Dempsey stagger. Another couple of lefts to the head had Dempsey groggy.

Lewis said Dempsey landed his best blow early in the round, when he backed Tunney into a corner and caught him on the jaw with a left hook. It staggered Tunney, who ran across the ring, but Dempsey caught up with him and shot over a right to the jaw. It was the best work that Dempsey did thus far. But Tunney quickly recovered and, while cautious, was as strong as ever. It was by far the best round Dempsey had in the fight, but the fact that toward the end of the round he was no longer charging in, but fiddling around, was discouraging to his followers.

Edgren said it was Dempsey's round. He rushed faster and more furiously and beat Tunney to the ropes time and again. Gene's counters seemed weak. "But the real sting wasn't in Dempsey's blows, either." Tunney weathered the punches and rallied again, landing an awful left hook into the body, bending Jack over. Dempsey took more blows and again pushed against them, but he lacked speed and his killing punch.

McCracken said Tunney backed away, but hooked lefts and rights. The champ fought hard and made Tunney back up. Tunney shot blows to the face. He jabbed cleverly. Gene had the situation well in hand, and clinched when Jack came in. Tunney's round by a shade.

Pollock said a number of bets were won and lost as Tunney came up for the start of the 6th round. Most believed the marine would not last 3 rounds. Dempsey leapt in with punches and beat the challenger about the head and body, forcing him to retreat. Late in the round, Gene came on again and made a slight rally.

Gallico said the round was even.

Newman said Dempsey missed his fierce left hook. Tunney peppered him with both hands to the face. Dempsey forced Tunney into a neutral corner, pelting hard left hooks to the head. Dempsey nailed Tunney with a left to the head. Tunney nicked Dempsey with light blows to the body in return. In a clinch, Tunney sank a hard right to the stomach. Tunney shot a left to the face and then a right to the ear. As Dempsey bore in, Tunney connected to the face with both hands. Dempsey staggered Tunney with a left to the chin, but Tunney responded, nailing Dempsey plenty with both hands to the face and body. Dempsey kept boring in, receiving many a crack to the face and body for his pains. Tunney's round.

Wood said Dempsey rushed Tunney and it was his best round. He landed the hardest blow of the battle, a left to the jaw. Yet, Tunney took his best and still was able to return with his own blows.

Rice said Dempsey drove him back but Tunney jabbed. Dempsey landed a terrific right to the jaw, staggering him. Jack was rushing wildly, but Tunney stopped and shot terrific lefts and rights to Dempsey's jaw. Jack was taking heavy punishment. Dempsey would close in but did little damage. Gene either clinched or fought back. The round was closer, but Tunney still had a slight advantage.

7th round

The footage for the 7th and 8th rounds seems to be missing/lost/not yet found/or disintegrated or damaged, so we have to rely on the written and radio accounts alone.

White/McNamee said Dempsey was bobbing and weaving and showing a little more speed. Not much work was done in the clinches. Dempsey landed a left to the jaw and right uppercut. Gene backed him to the ropes. Dempsey was not driving his blows with the dynamite that all had expected. Tunney was wrestling with him. Tunney landed rights, while Jack landed hooks, but not with full force. Tunney's right eye was showing some discoloration. He landed three jabs on the champ. Dempsey had not succeeded in breaking through Tunney's body defense. Jack kept taking blows. Tunney took one heavy blow on the jaw. Gene landed an uppercut but took a hard right. Dempsey crowded in and landed on the face. He drove one under the heart. He took a straight right. A lull followed.

> I think with a little bit of charity in our hearts we might call that round even. Gene took the first five rounds by a tremendous margin. The sixth round possibly might have been called even. The seventh round might possibly be called even. In other words, Jack Dempsey, the champion of the world, has lost at least five out of seven rounds, and possibly all seven rounds.

Tunney seemed content and happy. "He is boxing better than I ever saw him before, much better. This fight is being won with a left jab and a right cross."

Isaminger said Tunney landed first with a left to the neck. They sparred. Tunney's right eye was cut by the impact of Dempsey's fist. They clinched. Tunney fired a left to the mouth and right to the head. While close, Dempsey belted him about the head. Tunney swung two lefts to the head and made the champ hold. A rush ended in a clinch. Tunney repeated his tactics and landed with a left to the mouth and right to the jaw. Tunney's right hit the neck. Dempsey shifted and missed and Tunney landed on the jaw. Dempsey swung a left to the head. Tunney weathered the storm and came back. They struck light blows while close.

Lewis' version said Dempsey shifted like lightning, feinting with his left and driving a terrific right to the body. In a clash at close quarters in the middle of the ring, a gash was opened over Tunney's right eye, and Gene looked very worried. Nevertheless, he tore into Dempsey and sent a shower of rights and lefts to Jack's jaw. Dempsey shifted again and caught Tunney with a terrific left hook to the jaw. It was a bad round for Tunney, and Dempsey seemed to be the stronger of the two.

Edgren said Dempsey won this round too, fighting desperately and savagely. Perhaps Tunney was laying back a little and resting for the finish. He boxed carefully, backed away, and even ran. But always he caught Dempsey with his right. "Dempsey was forcing the fighting, but being badly battered."

McCracken said Dempsey's left hook opened a cut over Gene's right eye. Gene landed jabs and followed with his right to the chin. Dempsey landed a hard left hook to the chin but did not slow up the challenger. Dempsey tottered around on his heels and seemed hurt. Tunney's round.

Pollock said a left hook to Tunney's cheekbone opened a gash at the corner of his eye. He was not discouraged. Gene began another aggressive onslaught and pecked at Dempsey's face with left and right, bringing the blood again from under his right eye and raising a lump beneath his left optic.

Kendrick said Dempsey was not tearing in quite so aggressively. Tunney kept landing punches, and Dempsey retaliated only about once out of every four blows. The champ did land one short jab which caused Tunney momentary discomfort, but by then Gene clearly had demonstrated his superiority as a boxer.

Gallico said Dempsey, bleeding from a cut under his right eye and fearfully punished, cut loose on Tunney. For two rounds, the 6th and 7th, the fight was even. Dempsey, hooking his left viciously and accurately, staggered Tunney. Gene then ran, stood his ground, caught Dempsey, and again pounded, belted, and hammered his face.

During the progress of each round, all of the lights except for the ring lights were turned off. Just black with a white patch of ring, a white clad referee, the two drenched, straining bodies in the rain. But at the end of each round, in between rounds, the flood lights were lit again and suddenly the entire arena was lit up. Then the round began, and only the ring was lit. A bit of Rickard magic.

Newman said Dempsey rushed out and they locked in a clinch. Dempsey shot an inside left to the face. In another clinch, Dempsey sent a left to the head. In the clinches, Dempsey ripped both mitts to the jaw. A Dempsey left hook cut Tunney's right eye. Once more, Dempsey hooked his left to the face. Tunney staggered Dempsey with a series of lefts and rights to the face. In a clinch, Dempsey landed two hard rights to the face. Tunney struck a left to the body, and in a clinch, they both landed uppercuts. Tunney landed a right swing to the back of the ear. They exchanged lefts and rights to the face. Dempsey shook Tunney with a left to the head. Tunney sent a hard right to the face. Even round.

Wood said Tunney's right eye was cut slightly. However, between rounds, the great corner-work closed it for the rest of the fight. Tunney had taken what Dempsey had and was piling up points constantly.

Rice said both had slowed down. Tunney was jabbing left and right. Dempsey split Tunney's right eye. In the clinches, Tunney took more punches, but outboxed him at long range. Dempsey hit him with a right to the jaw but Tunney countered with a right to the head and had Dempsey clinching. Gene kept landing at long range. Dempsey hit the body. A Tunney right to the jaw sent Jack back. Tunney almost closed Dempsey's left eye. Jack was worried and worn out. Tunney had been just as aggressive as Dempsey was.

8th round

White/McNamee said it was more of the same. "[Dempsey] is not the same old fighting Dempsey, but he is trying to bore into Tunney's body." Jack took a hard one under the heart. He rushed, but Tunney backed away. The fight was getting a bit "boresome." Dempsey was showing "no defense. The only thing he has been showing is an ability to take an ungodly number of jolts on the jaw without worrying much about it. Gene is showing a nice left jab, and then a very pretty and a very fast right which catches Jack on the left side of the face. Jack must have a sore face by now."

Isaminger said Tunney met Dempsey with a left to the mouth. Gene followed with two lefts on the head. Dempsey clinched. Tunney rushed Dempsey to the ropes, landing a right to the body. Tunney shot a straight left to the head and followed with a right to the head that made Dempsey hold. Dempsey tore in but could not find the moving target. Tunney landed a left on the jaw. Dempsey landed a right to the jaw, but Tunney came back with a left to the head. Dempsey rushed Tunney to his corner but could not land cleanly. Tunney fired two lefts to the head. He danced away as Dempsey tried a left. Tunney missed a right and they clinched. Tunney landed his right to the chin. He also planted two light lefts to the chin.

Lewis said Dempsey came out with his left high and his right poised for a big punch, but Tunney was shifty and his boxing splendid. Dempsey was missing a lot as he walked around after the retreating Tunney, who halted to deliver a left jab followed by a right. Earlier in the round, twice Gene stung the champ with rights, but Jack kept on coming. A Tunney left uppercut brought Dempsey's head up at close range, making the champ's head bob. However, on the whole, it was a slow round, with both men apparently conserving energy.

Edgren said Tunney grew more aggressive, measured him, and moved in slowly. When Dempsey threw, Tunney no longer side-stepped or moved away, but instead slipped inside the punch and drove his right or left to the jaw with everything he could. It was raining heavily. Dempsey took the punches, and Tunney, wondering how he did, backed away. Dempsey ran in, only to receive a wicked left hook to the body that doubled him up. Gene fed him left jabs to the mouth. He was outboxing Dempsey and easily evading his slower blows, smashing him at will.

McCracken said Dempsey kept his left high and was not eager to rush. Tunney rushed him and drove Jack back to the ropes. Tunney tore in and snapped a straight left to the chin. Dempsey came in and shot a right to the jaw. Tunney backed away and Jack landed to the body. Gene claimed that Dempsey's punches were low. "Dempsey did not seem to have anything with which he could hurt Tunney, nor did he appear any too anxious to try too many things against the challenger. Tunney's round by a shade."

Pollock said Tunney's boxing ability was in evidence again, dancing around and driving in lefts and rights. Tunney had taken everything Dempsey had, stopping hooks, straight punches and uppercuts, but stood up under them.

Kendrick said Dempsey seemed to tire. Clinches were frequent. Tunney had a points victory in sight and continued to close in and trade.

Gallico said it was nothing but Tunney. The crowd was chanting for him. Gene was calm, with magnificent poise, fighting the greatest battle of his career. He ran and dodged Dempsey's fury, but when the attack had expended itself and Dempsey's arms grew tired, Tunney suddenly would cut loose. Time and again, Gene beat him to the punch, rocked and staggered Jack until he held. Dempsey was tired and discouraged. His left eye was half closed.

Newman said Dempsey bore in as usual, but Tunney was careful and kept sticking his left jab. Tunney landed two rights to the head, and again dropped a right chop to the chin. Tunney forced Dempsey to the ropes. Dempsey was scowling and trying to catch the elusive Tunney, who now appeared to believe he had Dempsey licked. Dempsey landed a right to the head. Tunney sent a left to the ear and right to the chin. Tunney jabbed twice with lefts to the face. The champ kept chasing, but every time Tunney stopped, he peppered Dempsey with lefts to the face. Tunney sent a straight left to the face and repeated it at the bell. Tunney's round.

Wood said that for the first time, Tunney complained to referee Tom Reilly about Dempsey's low punches. A low left was so apparent that he could not be blamed for his appeal. Dempsey was getting rougher as his title was slipping away. He roughed it in close with his elbows, threw his head around, and let his blows fall anywhere.

Rice said Tunney kept landing left and right. Dempsey could not connect. Whenever Jack did land, Gene escaped the follow-up. They clinched a bit. Tunney hit the jaw and kept away. Gene was trying for a knockout with his right. He landed repeatedly and had a big margin. Dempsey's only chance to win was with a knockout.

9th round

The films show that Dempsey circled and dipped, then fired a lead right that missed as Tunney moved away off to his right. Dempsey stepped in quickly and fired a lead left to the body that landed lightly as Tunney was moving away quickly and off to the side. Tunney fired his 1-2 and grabbed. While being held and smothered, Dempsey landed a high left hook. After breaking, Tunney pumped jabs, then 1-2 and grabbed as Dempsey dug a right to the body, solid left hook to the head, then right around the side of the head. As Tunney held, Dempsey dug a hard hook to the body. Break. Dempsey fired a powerful lead right that missed and he followed with a left and was held. Break.

Tunney missed a right as Dempsey ducked. Inside, Dempsey tried to work free with short shots to the head and body, including a hook and short right uppercut that landed, but mostly was smothered by the bulling and leaning-in Tunney. Break. Dempsey fired a lead right at the body, but Tunney came back with a 1-2 on the ducking Dempsey, grabbed and snuck in a right to the side of the head. Once again, they were clinched, and Jack snuck in a short left. Break.

Dempsey circled about and Tunney missed a jab. Dempsey dipped and Tunney stepped in with a jab and held. Break. Tunney jabbed and Dempsey fired a right, both missing. Dempsey weaved in and jabbed the body. Tunney countered with a right. Another clinch and inside scuffle, Jack working a left to the head. Break. Tunney fired his 1-2 on the downward ducking Dempsey and grabbed. Once again, Jack snuck in a right to the body, a short snappy left to the head, and also a right. Break.

Dempsey moved around a bit, weaved around, stepped to the side, but took a snappy, solid jab, which he countered with a hook that missed and right that landed around the head, which Tunney countered with a right. In the clinch, both worked the body, and Jack got in a hook to the head, which Tunney countered with his right. Tunney fired a jab and 1-2 and clinched again. Break.

Tunney bounced and pumped jabs, then stepped in with a quick straight-punch-combination and grabbed. Break. Tunney jabbed and grabbed in a couple of sequences, and each time Dempsey tried to dig in short shots to the body and head, but mostly was smothered until the referee broke them. Dempsey moved around and backwards, which cued Tunney to go on the attack with his jab and straight right and grab.

Overall, in this round, Tunney kept moving, peppering, and holding, or firing off combinations before moving or holding again. Dempsey kept advancing quickly and trying to land, but mostly unsuccessfully. At one point, Dempsey started moving off to the side, perhaps either to bait Tunney into attacking, to give him a different look, or to rest. Tunney simply did not allow him to get the right distance and timing, being too quick, crafty, and clever, fighting the perfect fight to offset a ferocious puncher. Tunney even countered Dempsey's attempts to counter, and took the initiative by attacking on occasion, never allowing Dempsey to get a read on him. Dempsey kept bobbing and weaving, and sneaking in some short shots now and then, but never could get any momentum, and his offense was not consistent enough. Tunney was far busier and more consistent. When Dempsey threw, Tunney usually would come back with more.

White/McNamee said Tunney danced about and landed a right to the jaw. Jack was trying without success to reach his body. Clinch and break. Jack missed a terrific right. "But Jack's judgment of distance was bad. He is certainly not the champion he was." Not much action. Gene jabbed away. Tunney's blows were not hard, but they were scoring points. Jack landed a left. Gene responded with a hard right to the ear. Clinch and break. Cautious sparring. The crowd was hollering for Gene. Dempsey's left eye appeared to be closed. It had been cut previously in the contest. Tunney kept landing light straight punches, and there was not much action in the clinches by either. "The Manassa mauler is not the Dempsey we expected tonight. He is fighting his in-fighting like a novice." At the bell, Gene clipped him with a right to the jaw. "The crowd is going wild. Gene has the fight sewed up unless Dempsey does something unexpected in the next round."

Isaminger said Dempsey charged after Tunney, landing a hard left at the waistline. Dempsey led a left to the head and Tunney held. Dempsey landed a left to the body and got a right to the body. The rain came down in torrents. Tunney sent Dempsey to the ropes with a hard left to the head. Dempsey peppered Tunney's face with lefts. They sparred, each seeking an opening. Tunney landed his left to the head.

Lewis said Dempsey came out ready to stake everything he had on one punch, for Tunney was in the lead. Tunney kept backing away, stalling. It was pouring rain as Dempsey swept in with a left hook to the body. The action slowed up, with Dempsey frantically looking for an opening and Tunney content to sit on the lead which he evidently felt he enjoyed. Toward the end of the round, Gene tore into Dempsey with left and right to the jaw, which slowed Dempsey down. They were engaged in a furious exchange as the round ended.

Edgren said Dempsey rushed with even greater fury, but his blows lacked speed and he missed wildly. Gene's corner told him to stay away and play it safe. Tunney ran around the ring, making Dempsey miss, then turned to crash right after right on the champ's face. Dempsey was nearly blind. His right eye was closed entirely. Still, he rushed in. He landed a right to Gene's ear, hurled him to the ropes, rushed and battered him there. Tunney was weary, hitting lightly, his blows having no sting, and it seemed that Dempsey had a chance to win. But Dempsey was growing weaker too.

McCracken said Tunney circled around as Dempsey bore in. It was raining hard. Gene led and either moved or clinched. Dempsey became cautious and backed away as Tunney took the aggressive, rushing Dempsey to the ropes. Dempsey was bleeding from the cut under his right eye. He backed away.

Pollock said before the round started, the shower developed into a downpour. Both were cautious. Tunney began another rally and forced the Manassa Mauler back into his own corner, driving in lefts and rights.

Kendrick said Tunney boxed at his best, seeming sure about his man now. Dempsey's determined rushes were less frequent. He had a target that never was still for an instant.

Gallico said Dempsey came out to take another beating, which bruised his face and cut his nose and mouth.

Newman said Dempsey rushed out like mad bull and missed a hard right. He drove a left to the stomach, while Tunney stuck two lefts to the face. Dempsey missed a right swing and the crowd roared. Dempsey missed with another and Tunney laced him with a left rip to the face. The rain fell hard. Tunney stuck two lefts to the face. The champ plunged in, missing his right, but hooked a left to the wind. Tunney dropped a right onto the chin. Dempsey landed a right to the ear, but Tunney forced Dempsey back to the ropes, pounding him at will. Again, Tunney sent lefts and rights to the face. The rain became torrential. Tunney now was forcing the issue and had the champ in the corner, flailing him at the bell. It was another Tunney round. It appeared to be all Tunney up to this point.

Wood said Tunney took it all and gave Dempsey plenty, firing left and right to the head as Dempsey weaved in.

Rice said Dempsey landed hard to the body and face. Gene fired back and they clinched. It was raining steadily, and the floor was slippery. Jack danced around and they clinched. Jack weaved and dodged and tried to land but took one in his face and spat blood. Tunney rushed him to the ropes, landing to the face. Dempsey's eyes were almost closed. He took a heavy right as the round ended. Tunney by a wide margin. The crowd cheered.

10th round

On the films, they touched gloves to start the final round. Dempsey fired a lead right that missed and Tunney countered with his own right and clinched. Break. Dempsey advanced with a lead right, while Tunney moved back, fired a 1-2 on the advancing Dempsey, and clinched. Break. Tunney fired a right to the body and clinched. Break.

Tunney moved back, firing 1-2 as Dempsey attacked the body. Tunney spun off the ropes. He jabbed, then fired 1-2 and grabbed, all of the blows missing. Dempsey hooked the head and body while being held. Break.

Dempsey attacked ferociously with left hook to the body and left and right to the head as Tunney moved away and leaned back on the ropes, threw a counter right uppercut and grabbed. Break. Tunney fired 1-2 and moved. He repeated, Dempsey leaped in with a hook to his head on the attack, and they clinched in the corner. Break.

They got back to ring center and Tunney fired off a combination to the head – 1-2-3-2, then 1-2. Tunney pumped some jabs, and Dempsey landed a right to the body and hook to the head. Tunney countered with a right and smothered and leaned in as Dempsey hooked. Final bell.

Overall, the pace had slowed. Tunney still was tapping him, moving and clinching. The dipping Dempsey still could not quite get his range and timing. Even when Dempsey got off, he could not land, but even when he did land, he got countered by the fleet-footed, quick Tunney, who clearly could take a punch. When clinched, Dempsey worked rabbit blows.

Tunney's boxing was cool, careful, and skillful. He seemed to be in control throughout, dictating the style of the fight. Dempsey simply was outboxed by a quicker, better-conditioned, sharper, masterful ring general who was superb on this night.

White/McNamee said Dempsey's left eye was closed. He could not see well. Tunney rushed him to the ropes. Gene landed rights at will. Jack's face was all red. He was cut over the eye. The rain was pouring down. Jack landed a right hook, but it had no effect. "It looks as if we are going to have a new champion. Jack is unable to rally." Dempsey was standing flat-footed. He was short with his blows. He had no speed. Jack was staying in the clinch. "He is a hollow shell of what he was. There is a new champion in the making." They were in and out of clinches. "The fight is about over, and not a sign of Dempsey trying to rally." He just took them. "There is the bell, and unquestionably we will have a new champion. There is no question but what Tunney has won this fight." The crowd was going wild, giving Tunney a great ovation. Graham McNamee said Tunney "undoubtedly" was the new champion.

Isaminger said they shook hands. They exchanged blows to the body and clinched. Tunney ducked a right. Tunney landed two lefts and a right to the chin, staggering Dempsey. Tunney hooked a right to the chin and they clinched. Dempsey's left eye was closed. Two rights landed on Dempsey's head. Tunney staggered Dempsey with a right to the head, backing him into the ropes. As the blinded Dempsey came toward him, Tunney drove right and left to the jaw.

Lewis said the crowd was roaring as they came out of their corners and shook hands. Dempsey tore in with his right and Tunney clinched. About the middle of the round, as Dempsey came in, Tunney closed his left eye. Near the end of the round, Tunney chased the champ and had him groggy. He had him bleeding badly. Dempsey's left eye was closed completely, and his knees were buckling under him. Tunney whipped blow after blow to his crimson face.

Edgren said Dempsey rushed but could not put anything into his punches. In a clinch, he hit Gene's neck, fair blows, and the crowd yelled something about rabbit punches. Dempsey showed courage, attacking the body. Tunney ripped, tore, and smashed until Dempsey's face became a matrix of blood and battered flesh. He was blind and his blows weak. At the bell, it seemed as if Dempsey knew he had lost.

McCracken said they shook hands, exchanged, and clinched. The champ's left eye was almost closed. Tunney backed away from the rushes. Gene staggered him with a right to the chin. Jack's left eye was completely closed. Tunney crossed left and right and had Dempsey's face in bad shape. It looked as if the coming of a new champion was on its way.

Pollock said a new champion appeared to be in the making. Spectators were being drenched but didn't seem to mind. Each man was determined to win. Dempsey's face was a pathetic sight. His left eye was closed and blood was flowing from under his right eye. Tunney kept jabbing and sending over straight rights with merciless precision. No one knew better than Dempsey when the bell rang that he no longer was the champion.

Kendrick said Dempsey tried but never could get set for a victorious blow. Tunney weaved in and out and showed his footwork in the slippery ring. It was obvious that there was a new champion. "I came with an open mind, I had no favorites; both men fought a clean, hard fight and both are deserving of great credit for their effort."

Gallico said Dempsey came out to fight desperately and try for a knockout, but his long swings missed by a foot. As he bore in close, crash and thud went Tunney's gloves against his face. Tunney finally elected to stand his ground and slug it out. Dempsey was licked, and in the last minute, Tunney punished him cruelly. Dempsey's left eye was closed completely and bleeding. His flesh was blue and puffed out. His knees were staggering. He was bleeding from cuts all over his face.

Newman said they shook hands. Dempsey led with a right to the head. He furiously chased Tunney, but was wild. Tunney was collected and sure of himself. Dempsey forced Tunney to the ropes, trying to nail him. Tunney staggered Dempsey with a hard right to the eye, and Dempsey reeled back. Tunney again smacked Jack's closed and bloody left eye. Dempsey seemed to be a badly beaten fighter. The rain was blinding the fighters and spectators alike, soaking everyone. Tunney hit the bad left eye. Jack was an awful sight. It was all Tunney. He did as he pleased with the old champ. Tunney's round.

Wood said Tunney battered him.

Rice said Dempsey missed and took a terrific walloping. Still, he fought furiously. His left eye was closed. He was groggy and wobbly. They slugged, and Tunney had the better of it.

Frederic Lewis (not Perry) said that when it was over, Dempsey almost reeled to his corner. His trainer Jerry the Greek flung a sponge full of water over his battered face. Tunney had triumph written in his blue eyes.

After collecting the judges' scorecards, announcer Joe Griffo whispered to the referee, held up his arms and proclaimed, "Ladies and gentlemen, I am proud to introduce the new heavyweight champion of the world, Gene Tunney." Some only heard the patter of the rain. Over the loudspeakers, Dr. Francois D'Elisen repeated what Griffo said, "Both judges agree that there is a new world champion!" A great roar went up and surged through the Stadium, smothering the name. James J. Tunney was the new heavyweight champion of the world. Referee Tommy Reilly raised Gene's right arm in the air. There was no disagreement between judges Mike Bernstein and Frank Brown, so Referee Reilly did not have to vote. No one disagreed.

Dempsey rushed over, threw his arms around Tunney, hugged and congratulated the new titleholder, and they spoke to one another. "That's sportsmanship."

The fallen champion passed almost unnoticed to his dressing room.

Those listening to matters in their homes were given an extra thrill when the winner's voice came in loud and clear on the radio. Tunney said, "I have realized all my ambition, and I will try to defend the title that I have worked so hard for six years, and I am going to try to defend it as becomes a Marine." Tunney was the first man to challenge the world by radio, or so they said.

Major Andrew White said, "Ladies and gentlemen: You have just heard James Tunney. I climbed into the ring and put the microphone up in front of the new champion and asked him to say a few words, and you heard him. ... Dempsey is gone."

McNamee said Dempsey took "terrific punishment for ten rounds. At any time during the last two rounds he might have dropped and been excused, but he didn't do it. He stayed with it, and now Jack Dempsey is probably through with the ring. He is done."

Draped in the bathrobe gifted to him by the Marines, and surrounded by 20 to 30 policemen, Tunney returned to his dressing room, receiving acclaim as he passed.

After the championship fight, Yale Okun won a 6-round decision over Martin Burke. The crowd exited quickly and in orderly fashion, without any issues.

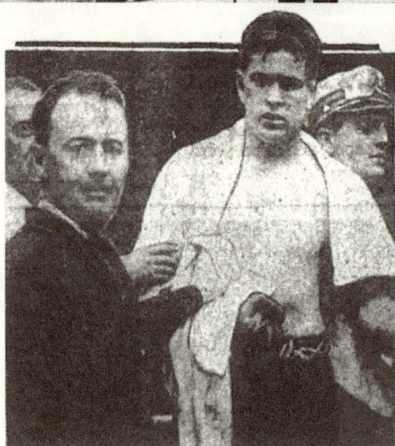

Lou Fink with Tunney

GENE TUNNEY

Tunney praised the former champion, saying, "Dempsey fought like a champion, decently and cleanly. They say what they please, but he's a man, through and through, and the hardest fighter I have ever fought."

Gene said he had achieved his ambition of the last 7 years or so. "You know a Marine is first to fight and last to leave – he's always there to the end. Well, in a sense, I have reached the end of my hopes."

The only marks of the bout on Tunney were a slightly raised bump over his left eye and a bloody lower lip. "Jack socked me two awful wallops in the Adam's apple. And believe me, they hurt. The bump over my eye does not bother me much, nor does the cut lip. ... I must admit my body is sore. You know a man always knows what's inside of him."

Regarding his own tactics, Gene said, "It does not always pay to wade in and fight, though the crowd sometimes mistakes such tactics and yells, 'Yellow!' ... It was necessary for me to stay away from Dempsey on several occasions, for there is plenty of steam left in his blows." Gene said Dempsey's rabbit punches did not bother him much.

Some claimed that Gene said he thought he could have stopped Dempsey if he had another 2 rounds. However, others quoted him as saying he was not certain.

Another reporter quoted Gene as saying,

> Jack Dempsey is a sportsman and a clean fighter all the way. He fought me fairly throughout. There was no suspicion of a foul blow, and don't let any one tell you that he can't hit. His blows were terrific. I was not hurt, because I was in perfect condition and prepared to absorb his terrible punches. I am sure that I hurt him. I have realized my life's ambition, and as the champion I will carry myself in a manner gratifying to my friends and becoming a marine and champion.

When meeting an Associated Press correspondent, Gene said, "What did I tell you? I was never in doubt, but after the first and second rounds I knew it was all over, but the shouting of my friends. He could not hurt me, and I knew I was hurting him." Gene only had a bruised lip, which was cut in training and never quite healed.

Tunney also said,

> First of all Jack Dempsey is a gentleman. The fact that he threw his arms around me after the judges gave me the decision and said, 'Gene, you are a great boy,' proves he is a genuine sport.
>
> Jack's punches had plenty of steam – more than any fighter I have ever met, but as I predicted before the fight they did not hurt me. Save for a cut over my right eye, a cut lip and an injured Adam's apple I am in as good condition as I was before the fight. ....
>
> Never once did I experience a feeling I couldn't lick Dempsey.
>
> Jack certainly had a bad eye in the tenth round. ... I had been told how Jack fights and I knew I would be able to get in my right.

Now that the fight is over and I am the winner, I'll admit I was deathly sick flying with Casey Jones in the airplane from Shawnee-on-Delaware. Even riding in the motor from the landing field made me kind of dizzy, but when I got up to the hotel it passed away and – I managed to get in a little nap.

No, I don't know whether I could have knocked out Jack in another round or two rounds. There is no way of proving that I could, but why talk of that when the title is won. I can say I was not tired at the end of the fight and that Jack's punches were not bothering me.

To win the championship, I have worked conscientiously, courageously and prudently for the last six years. It did not come to me by luck.

Another quoted Gene as saying, "I will defend my title against any man in the world. I told you before the fight that I was bound to win and I made good. Anything I might add would be just bragging. I am tired, for don't think that Dempsey didn't hurt me."

Billy Gibson said it was a cleanly fought fight. If it had been a 12- or 15-round contest, Gene would have won by knockout. "If the fight had gone a couple more rounds Dempsey would have been knocked out." Tex Rickard agreed that Tunney "had the former champion going."

A priest shook Tunney's hand, and Gene said, "Not so hard, please. I've been using those hands lately." When asked how his lip was, Gene replied, "It's all right. No bother."

Allegedly, the doctor said he just applied six stitches to Dempsey's face.

Tunney had a tough job with the horde of fans who wanted to shake hands, have him autograph something, or kiss him.

In the ring, Gene promised to give Jack a return bout. However, Gibson said he was not sure who Gene would fight next, or when. "Fight Wills? I don't know. Wills had his chance, of course, to meet Tunney and let it go by."

Rickard announced that people paid around $2 million to see the fight, eclipsing the $1.6 million record set by Dempsey-Carpentier. Tunney earned a guaranteed $200,000, but the victory was worth millions.

Ring Lardner and Hype Igoe said Dempsey earned about $850,000 ($450,000 plus 40% of the receipts over $1 million), a more than sufficient balm for his loss. That left around $950,000 for Rickard, less a myriad of other promotional expenses such as preliminaries, rent, tickets, etc.

The fight pictures began showing the very next day in Philadelphia.

In an interview with Raymond Hill, Dempsey said, "I've got no alibi. He licked me fair and square. I never had a chance." After the decision was announced, Dempsey rushed to ring center and was the first to congratulate the new champ. "Great work, Gene. I'm glad the title remains in America. I've fought all of the foreigners, and I'm proud you were the one to take me. You're a great kid and the cleanest heavyweight I ever battled." Gene replied, "Thanks, Jack." Continuing, Dempsey said, "I want another fight. How about it?" "Sure." "When?" "Well, that's up to Billy Gibson."

In his dressing room, Dempsey took two stitches to close the large gash over his left eye. "It was cut by butting Gene's head in the ninth round and the new champion's peppery right hand opened it up wide. Dempsey also was slashed deeply on the right cheek."

Dempsey took the loss in stride, exceedingly well. "Well, you can't always fight," he laughed. "Gee, isn't Gene a great kid. He'll make a fine champ, won't he? I hope he makes as much money as I did and they let him alone. If they don't hound him he will be one of the greatest and most popular champions we ever had. Say, he's simply great. … But I'd like another crack at him."

Jack said he knew he was licked after the 8th round. When it was over, he knew that he had lost. He praised Tunney.

> I couldn't seem to get going, but I have no complaint to offer. I knew I was going to get licked some time, and I am glad I lost the championship to an American. I defeated all the foreigners they could send over. I think I have given the public a run for its money every time I started. … If I had to lose I am glad that a fellow like Tunney won the championship. He is a credit to the sport, a clean, fine fellow.

Another quoted the ex-champ as saying, "I simply could not get going. … I wish Tunney all the luck in the world with the heavyweight championship."

Others quoted Dempsey as saying,

> The better man won tonight. I am sorry the old crown has gone, and yet I am glad. It meant much money, also tremendously much in trouble. Now that I've skidded from the top and I'm out of the spotlight, perhaps I'll have a little of the peace I've wanted, but which championship holding made impossible for me.

> When I entered the ring tonight I had lost some of my earlier confidence. The last 48 hours brought me many worries. One was the report that the effort had been made to murder my wife. Someone, the report said, had shot at her through the window of our home.

> When they weighed me in today I showed only 190 pounds. I didn't look so good. I was at least four pounds below my best weight, 4 pounds that I had lost in these two days without any strenuous exercising.

> I couldn't get going tonight. I couldn't get warmed up. I felt slow all the way. I could not connect with my punches. Tunney was fighting a truly wonderful battle. My hat is off to him. He whipped me fairly

and squarely. He fought a remarkable battle, met me at my own game. He slugged with me as I hoped, but in the slugging match which was my own game, he whipped me. Yes, I got over a few to his chin and some to his body, but I couldn't follow through. Once or twice when I shook him up I tried to go after him, but my legs that were so perfect in training failed me and just wouldn't respond.

Every so often during the fight I felt like myself for a while. I flashed a little of my old stuff, but it was just flashes. And all the while Tunney was methodically but skillfully sending home lefts and rights that piled up points and won the fight for him.

I wasn't afraid of his right hand. I took it 50 times with about everything that Tunney had behind it, and I didn't go down. The old jaw stood up even if the legs couldn't.

I congratulate Gene Tunney. I am sure that he will be an honor to the game and a worthy champion. He's lived clean and fine through all the years. He was working up to the pinnacle he reached and I know he'll live the same way all through his championship days.

Allegedly, when he reached his hotel, Jack broke down and cried.

At ringside for the *Philadelphia Inquirer*, Frederic Lewis said Tunney's fierce blows battered Dempsey, and by the end, Jack's eyes were almost closed. The defeated king fought bravely to the final gong of a spectacular bout, showing his true sportsmanship, hugging the man who beat him.

Lewis said Dempsey was not the Manassa Mauler, the ferocious tiger man, but just a tired businessman, a harassed litigant, and a battered, staggering, bleeding loser. His face was cut and his left eye a bleeding slit during the last two rounds, when it was clear that only a knockout would save Dempsey's title. Everyone seemed to know it. When he did come on with ferocity, the cool and relaxed Tunney usually set him back or tied him up. At the end, Tunney was confident, while Dempsey seemed worried, his face smeared with blood.

It was the greatest gate ever. Never before had 132,000 people gathered in one spot to witness any sporting event.

Writers said it was the first time in 40 years of gloved fighting that the crown changed hands on a decision. However, Jack Johnson technically won from Tommy Burns via decision, although everyone knew it was a technical knockout; and this also overlooked that Tommy Burns won the crown via 20-round decision over Marvin Hart. However, most previous champions had won or lost the crown via knockout.

Perry Lewis, who had predicted a Tunney points victory, said Dempsey fought bravely to the final gong. The vast crowd acclaimed the new titleholder despite the downpour. The former marine, confident and cool, staved off his opponent's mad rushes.

For 10 long rounds, Dempsey tried to hammer down the sharp-punching, cool, ex-marine, who was slowly but surely piling up a margin of points that was sure to bring him the championship. Dempsey tried all that he knew. He rushed with recklessness, but only found his tantalizing, quick-thinking foeman giving but not breaking before his charges. Dempsey ploughed in without regard to consequences and felt the prowess of a man who could punch faster than he could, who hit him while he was preparing to strike. Dempsey could find no openings. The faltering, puzzled champ changed plans, and moved forward slowly in a crouch. He could not see. When he got close, Tunney either tied him up or leapt forward to rain blows upon him. He cut and slashed at him.

Tunney had been ascending for three years, while the champ had been descending. Dempsey wilted under the fighting marine's clean-cut boxing and fierce attack, and was tired and weary at the end.

The rain, which started as a drizzle when they entered the ring, eventually became a downpour. Yet, no one paid attention to the elements.

Dempsey was pummeled and battered. Tunney was sure, confident, steady and heady, but also dead-game, anxious to win clearly. The challenger warily moved away, but it was an orderly retreat, and he also eventually leapt in on the attack. Dempsey surrendered ground to the onslaught. Gene's hammering right did most of the damage. Dempsey came out of one great rally with his left eye closing. Blood streamed down his face from a gash over his other eye. He was beaten, knew it, but still was courageous, trying to land a big one. Outside, he still was perfect-looking, but inside, he was gone. Yet, he fought to the final bell.

Tunney won because of his fine generalship in smothering and evading Dempsey's desperate rushes, combined with his tremendous speed and accuracy. He was younger, more vigorous, and equally as smart.

Dempsey could blame his downfall on his failure to rise above three years of idleness, and he also suffered under legal fire directed against him and the fight itself. He bore in with both hands swinging, but he couldn't drive long enough or viciously enough to bring down his foe. When he spent his force early on in each round, the cool, wise Tunney would come back to harass and torture him with lightning rights and lefts to the jaw.

Tunney piled up a big lead. It was the same story round after round. For a minute, Dempsey carried the battle to his foe, but always found Tunney to be too elusive, and even when Jack's left crashed on Gene's jaw, Tunney was too tough.

In the 5th round, after rushing Tunney to a corner, Dempsey landed his big left, but always Tunney cleverly stepped away to dance safely across the ring. As Dempsey tired, he found a charging sharpshooter upon him, showering his face with cutting and confusing, if not deadly blows. Tunney was far ahead on points at the half-way point.

Realizing he was losing; Dempsey came out like a tiger in the 6th round. He tore in, driving Gene to a corner with a terrific left hook that shook the challenger to his knees. Tunney escaped and fled across the ring, followed by the tiger seeking the kill, who caught the fleeting Gene on the other side of the ring, and again landed his famous left. Tunney's knees bent. But he recovered quickly. He stepped away and retreated with Dempsey in pursuit.

Then, in a split second, as Dempsey came charging in, Tunney stopped moving and fired back, attacking Dempsey, who was shaken up and surprised. He slowed down. Tired, weary, his strength fleeing him, he had landed his big left twice, but Tunney still was on his feet, able to absorb murderous blows and come back on the attack, which must have been a great shock to the champ, who almost was floored. That broke his morale. The sting went out of Dempsey. He had no supreme effort left.

Dempsey kept trying at the start of the rounds, but each time the effort was weaker and its duration shorter. He flashed at the start of the 7th through 9th rounds, but it merely was a flash, and after the flash had spent itself, Tunney was all over him.

Time and again, Tunney shook Dempsey until his knees bent under the storm of punches. A weaker man surely would have gone down.

In the 10th, Tunney gave definitive proof of his fitness to be champ. He drove the tottering champ to the ropes and whipped over his knifelike right to the eye. Dempsey shook his head as if to clear it, and his left eye closed. Half a minute later it was closed tight, while a lump the size of an egg was under it. Jack still came forward, but his face was a bloody smear, his left eye closed, and over his right eye was a gaping wound received earlier. Tunney met him with a relentless hammering until it seemed that he surely must go down. But Dempsey stuck to the last and still was fighting back, feebly, but trying. No one disputed the decision.

At the direction of Major General John Lejeune, the U.S. Marine Corps honored Tunney by appointing him as a first lieutenant in the Reserve. The commission was signed by U.S. President Calvin Coolidge. General Lejeune confirmed it and said, "Tell him for me that I want to convey to him my personal congratulations as well as the congratulations of the entire Corps."

The *Philadelphia Evening Bulletin* reported that 125,565 people attended the fight. Although that was a huge number, readers were reminded that this newspapers' daily circulation was 533,169. More folks would read about the fight than saw it live, and even more would see the films.

Mary Dixon Thayer said it was wonderful, extraordinary, and dramatic, but also a stupendously absurd spectacle. A huge crowd, emotional tension, the amphitheater's semi-darkness, and lurid lights over the ring made it seem grotesque, terrible, and beautiful, ludicrous, and magnificent. So many thousands came to watch a scuffle between two men who made a staggering amount of money. One wondered what the status was of a civilization that poured out gold at the feet of movie actors and prize fighters. However, as a spectacle, it was superb.

There was music that fell from giant amplifiers over the ring. The sky had been gray, but became a deep, soft azure. The great clusters of lights on the huge towers around the Stadium flooded the scene with splendor.

When the fight began, the vast crowd sat breathless, tense. An airplane circled about. The Stadium floodlights had been darkened, and only the ring was a circle of brilliant light.

Pouring rain began to fall just as the fight started, and increased in volume as time went on.

Afterwards, the new king, Tunney, had the same boyish smile. When asked how it felt to be the world champion, he replied, "Fine." Someone yelled, "Three cheers for Gene Tunney."

Robert Edgren said Dempsey never gave way, and boldly forced the fight as Tunney battered him. Dempsey staggered to his corner at the end of the 10th round. Pouring rain washed the blood from his battered face, so that it streamed down over his body and stained the canvas. Dempsey heard the decision, rose from his seat and threw both arms around Tunney's neck. "He had been a sportsman in defeat. He always said he would." Tunney quickly left the ring, as the rain fell down violently.

Tunney was a great champion. He won throughout, although he could not knock out or even drop Dempsey. At the finish, Tunney had a cut over one eye and a split lip. But Dempsey was the worst beaten. His right eye was closed and ripped. His left eye was cut, and blood streamed from his mouth. It was the same old story of the speed of youth and stamina matched against the waning powers of a once-great champion.

Still, Edgren said it wasn't entirely a one-sided fight. "Dempsey was not all gone, by any means. He was dangerous and fought with a desperate courage and determination that cared nothing for mutilation or injury. He lost the championship, but he lost like a champion."

Apparently, years ago, Billy Gibson had purchased Tunney's contract from Doc Bagley for $10,000. It had proved to be a very wise investment.

Tunney lost to Greb, his only defeat, who broke his nose "by butting him and opening a couple of nasty cuts over Gene's eyes."

Tunney tried to annex the world 175-pound crown, but Mike McTigue would not fight him, and neither would Paul Berlenbach, who took it from McTigue in 1925 but lost it to Jack Delaney in July 1926.

Edgren noted that Tunney had a great right hand, scoring several knockouts with it, including against Weinert and Spalla. He had also stopped Carpentier and Gibbons.

Lynn O'Doyle said Gene fought with all he had, while Jack fought with all he had left. Spectators cried, "Dempsey's lost his pep." That about summed it up.

Another woman reporter said, "Prize fighting isn't brutal. It's just tough."

Referee Tommy Reilly said he scored the fight 7-2-1 for Tunney. The 2nd was even. Dempsey won rounds 4 and 8. Both judges, Frank Brown of Pittsburgh and Mike Bernstein of Wilkes-Barre, scored it for Tunney, so Reilly was not called upon to give his verdict. Dempsey was a marvelous gentleman in defeat.

It was a battle of left hands. Tunney hit with remarkable precision, while Dempsey showed his long lay-off affected his work to a great extent. He hit wildly and…his plans went wrong due partly to his inability to keep Tunney in front of him.

The new champion was continually outguessing Jack.

Of course, this was made possible by the willingness of the champion to be the aggressor, showing utter disregard for Gene's counters, some of which he timed beautifully.

However, the "famous Dempsey punch was missing." He only showed his sock about four times during the entire 10 rounds. Tunney took them and refused to buckle under. Gene fought a masterful, careful fight.

Dempsey told Tunney he was glad it was an American boy who beat him, and then asked for another bout. That showed "he was not only a real fighter but a champion from the top of his head to the soles of his feet."

Reilly said both men battled cleanly. Reilly and commission chairman Wiener spoke with both about the rules in the dressing room, and both obeyed, except for a few minor infractions. There was no coaching during the rounds allowed, nor bad language. Both men fought like gentlemen.

The reopening of old wounds on Dempsey's face and fact that his left eye was nearly closed at the end might lead one to think he took a fearful beating, "while as a matter of fact he didn't." There was no time when a knockout defeat was imminent. He got staggered frequently, but his fighting instincts predominated throughout. "It is my opinion that Dempsey is anything but done." However, Dempsey needed more work. "Dempsey was a great champion when he was at the peak of his career and fighting regularly."

Benny Leonard said Dempsey landed only 50 blows in the entire fight. He threw fewer punches in 10 total rounds against Tunney than he threw in 2 rounds while training with Tommy Loughran, which was befuddling. Benny concluded that by remaining idle for so many years, Jack lost his aggressiveness. "I knew Dempsey was not the old Dempsey, but I thought he could muster three or four rounds of his old time form. By that I mean the rip-tearing aggressiveness…" He showed it in sparring. "But he came into the ring last night without one spark of the old killer aggressiveness." He did not fight even for one round the way he did in training. "He didn't even try to punch Tunney – none of the old tearing in fighting for which Dempsey is noted – which made him a champion." It seemed like a totally different fighter in there. "He stood still, moved around slowly and rarely tried to punch. Tunney was really afraid. He kept away and let Dempsey lie around and loaf and do everything but fight."

As the fight progressed, and Dempsey kept standing around, making a lead every now and then, Tunney grew more confident and began leading with a jab and right cross, and Jack was an easy mark when he stood straight up, only eluding when he bent down low. Leonard was "flabbergasted" to see Dempsey standing straight up and not dipping his head low as he should. Dempsey threw very few killer blows, only trying to land one towards the end. "Dempsey had them at Atlantic City, but he left them stretching back over a trail of idle years."

Tunney boxed cleverly, continually moving around, slipping away from Dempsey's "half-hearted charges when they came."

Only twice in the fight could Leonard recognize Dempsey the champion, tearing in with his old viciousness. "It was a pitiful sight to see a great champion hopping around and fighting a purely defensive battle without an attempt to punch at his opponent." Dempsey allowed openings to pass by without an attempt to lead or counter. If the real Dempsey, or even the Dempsey of Atlantic City, had shown himself, he could have won, "for Tunney wasn't far in front."

True, Dempsey was not himself even in training, for he was slower with his punches, and moved more slowly, but nevertheless he showed enough fight in his training to convince Leonard that if he fought like that for a few rounds, he could beat Tunney. "But even the Atlantic City Dempsey wasn't in the ring last night, let alone the old champion." Even those who thought Tunney would win expected more from Dempsey, who "was a great fighter in the days when he tore in and bored at his opponent."

Leonard gave Tunney some credit. He boxed cleverly, moving around, using a right hand to the head and body. He was cautious throughout. He tied up Dempsey in the clinches and did not allow Jack to fight on the inside, usually his best bet. The fight likely would give Tunney confidence. He possibly could have stopped Dempsey had he taken more chances.

Ring Lardner said Dempsey got soaked, for he fought badly, and everything was missing. He was a shell, and Marines are not afraid of shells. "Gene may use long words, but he won with monosyllables to the jaw and other features."

Philadelphia Jack O'Brien said Dempsey simply could not get going. O'Brien gave up hope after the 3rd round.

O'Brien said Jim Corbett was the most unpopular champion, for the public resented his victory over Sullivan. Corbett told O'Brien that the public liked him better after he lost to Fitzsimmons.

> Jack Dempsey should have been the most popular champion that ever lived. The chances are he will be yet. For I think if he ever fights Tunney again, he will beat him. This isn't an alibi, but I don't think Dempsey was himself last night. He couldn't get working. From the first round on we had a feeling the title was going, and we were sure of it after the third.

O'Brien believed Jack could come back. "Right hand punches beat Dempsey last night. He couldn't get away from them. Only one of them hurt him – it came in the ninth round – but he couldn't get away from them. I noticed when he tried his right on Tunney, he'd land." O'Brien urged Dempsey to cover his face with his left and slam away with his right. Dempsey replied, "Aw, I'm all right, Jack. I'll get going in a minute." Yet, he never did, and realized long before the fight was over that his title was gone. Next time, he would not be distracted by legal entanglements. O'Brien believed Dempsey would be champion again.

Another said Dempsey was like Jeffries against Johnson. He showed little of his true qualities, and was lethargic. Combine that with the fact that Tunney was cautious, and the bout had few thrills or spectacular moments.

Fair Play said Tunney hit Dempsey 3 blows to 1, and his winning margin was overwhelming. Tunney fought a marvelously planned and executed battle. "But no one will ever call it the battle of the century. Dempsey fought as bad a battle as Tunney fought a good one." Dempsey was a beaten man as early as the end of the 1st round. "Tunney never was in danger or distress, except for two brief moments." Dempsey never was off his feet, but at the finish, he was tired and battered.

Well ahead on points, in the last two rounds, Tunney threw caution to the winds and swapped punches, beating Dempsey in every exchange. "The point margin was overwhelming. For every punch Dempsey landed the new champion planted three and they had weight and power behind them which the blows of his opponent lacked. … Jack tried but the will was stronger than his legs and arms." Dempsey simply was not himself.

> In only one minute of the ten rounds did Dempsey show his old time form. That was at the opening of the third round when he came out of his corner like a thunderbolt and smashed blow after blow past the guard of the challenger. The flurry was short lived however. Before the round was over, Tunney was smothering the punches aimed at him. But Dempsey won the round by a good margin. That was really the only round which could be clearly credited to him. Two could be called even and Tunney took the others.

Hence, Fair Play scored it 7-1-2 for Tunney.

Dempsey never really got untracked. "His punch was gone." He did not have his former spring. Instead of short punches he swung wide and was wild. His best punch was in the 6th round, when he landed a left hook in the stomach and Gene's legs buckled from the impact.

Fair Play did not think Dempsey was through though, particularly if he fought more frequently.

Tunney had two potential fights, one with Tommy Loughran, who had recent victories over Carpentier, Risko, and Jim Delaney, and the other with Jack Sharkey of Boston. "But the real dark cloud on the sunny horizon of the new champion is Harry Wills. Men close to the new champion say Tunney has never fought a colored man and never will."

A lot of smart money was lost on Dempsey, for most had wagered on the 2 to 1 favorite.

Some noted that most heavyweight champions had won the title by knockout. Some indirectly used that as a subtle dig against Tunney, suggesting that a real champion should be able to win by knockout. However, Tunney's defenders countered that he could have won by knockout in a 15-round bout, and others had required more than 10 rounds to stop prior champions.

Jack Dempsey had reigned slightly longer than Jack Johnson. Yet, Johnson had won the title at about the same age, 30, that Dempsey was when he lost it, 31. Jeffries had reigned nearly as long. Sullivan had reigned the longest.

Tommy Gibbons said, "It was plainly evident that his three-year lay-off was too much for Jack Dempsey. He lacked all of the old fire and pep that marked him in all his previous fights." Jack gave signs in the very 1st round that the crown was about to be passed. The only time he showed his real form was during the first 30 seconds of the 2nd round, when he chased Gene all over the ring, backed him into a neutral corner, and shook him up with a fast volley of one-twos and short body blows.

Gene drew first blood in the 4th round with a left hook to Jack's right eye. That was the only round that was even. "While Jack was mauling the challenger around and rushing like a bull, Gene was calmly taking his time and landing straight rights and lefts with deadly precision. Jack started to look tired in the fifth round and showed the first sign of real worry."

In the 6th round, Tunney landed four successive one-two combinations, and he followed with a hard left hook to the liver which hurt, bringing a kink to Dempsey's knees and sickly look to his face. That round decided the battle.

During the 8th round, Dempsey lost every trace of the old weaving, crouching, aggressive fighter which used to strike terror into the hearts of his opponents. At the end of the round, his eye was beginning to close. Jack landed two slightly low blows in that round, Gene complained, and after a warning, the fight progressed.

Tunney was aggressive in the 9th, and though he retreated every time Jack showed the offensive, Gene always was right back on top of him with a volley of fast lefts and rights.

In the 10th, Tunney opened a cut over Jack's left eye and the blood poured out, spattering all over the ring. Jack's left eye seemed to close up tightly in this round.

The rain poured steadily from start to finish. Neither man slipped, though.

Gibbons concluded that Dempsey was beaten by a younger and better man who had class. "I have never seen Jack so loggy, slow on his feet and so badly off form." It was very surprising. His mind didn't even seem to be on the fight. He clearly had an off night and was dead on his feet.

Yet, Dempsey's being off did not detract from Tunney's marvelous performance. "He fought the best fight of his career and absolutely outclassed his rival. His defense and offense were perfect. His footwork was much better than anything he showed up at Stroudsburg and in every possible way he was in the pink of condition."

Gibbons concluded that Dempsey could have fought better if he had shown more defense. "He just waded right in and took Tunney's best belts in the head and body." Previously, Dempsey's offense was his best defense, and since the former was "sadly lacking last night," he needed to pay more attention to his cagey defense, and he could have made a better showing had he done so.

The *Philadelphia Public Ledger's* Frank McCracken said Tunney outpointed, outhit, and outgeneraled Dempsey, who looked to be a "total ruin in a fistic way." Jack's left eye was closed, and his right eye had a cut under it. "Dempsey did not have a chance from the start. He was not the 'Manassa Mauler' of old, and he was fighting a greater man than they have ever given Tunney credit for being." Whatever Dempsey did have to give, Tunney took.

The only round Dempsey won was the 2nd. Jack socked with what he had, but it was not enough.

The 4th was the most dangerous for Gene, and even then, he came back to hold his own. Dempsey tore in with what he had, but it was the tipoff that he did not have enough. He landed his terrific left and staggered Tunney, and with the marine on the ropes, Tunney went to the floor [actually he buckled but did not go down], partly the result of the blow and partly the rain-soaked canvas. He was up in an instant and battling back.

In the 7th, Tunney opened a cut over Dempsey's right eye and started Jack's left eye swelling.

In the 8th, Dempsey landed his terrible left again, but Gene did not seem to mind.

The bout was one-sided, as Dempsey only won 1 round. Even in the 4th, Tunney was entitled to an even break. Dempsey could not have received a more severe beating, and he likely would have been stopped if there were a few more rounds.

It was astonishing to see the challenger start the bout attacking with straight lefts and rights. Tunney stood up to the charges and blows and did not seem to mind them. He never lost his confidence or self-assurance. His attack was precise, and he attacked when warranted.

Gone was Dempsey's vaunted aggressiveness and tearing-in style. He actually backed up before Tunney's attack. From the 4th round on, Dempsey's rushes ceased. He was hurt in the 7th from a right to his eye and another to his chin, staggering him. Jack was desperate in the 9th, but blind, and could do nothing.

Throughout, Tunney landed stiff, sharp, jarring punches to the jaw. Dempsey fought hard, but he never landed his left with full force.

Tunney's straight left followed by a right cross to the chin was how he won, the old one-two. Gene was determined, self-possessed, confident. Dempsey was confused and bewildered. Tunney used all of his ring knowledge, stepping aside, retreating, or clinching now and then. It was his best fight ever.

Ed Pollock, who was ringside, said 132,000, the biggest crowd that ever assembled to see a sporting event, drenched by rain, cheered the ex-marine. A new record of $2 million was generated by the ticket sales. All prior records for receipts and attendance were shattered. Governors, mayors, merchant princes, and bankers were amongst the galaxy of notables.

As for the fight, "There was no question of Tunney's supremacy. He outfought Dempsey." He utilized left jabs and right crosses.

Not a drop of rain fell until after both boxers were in the ring. It began with a slight drizzle, but increased in intensity as the bout progressed. Raincoats and topcoats were donned. Newspapers and cardboards were pressed into service. But thousands sat without protection of any kind. Costly gowns were ruined. Yet, they sat there, unmindful of the drenching. A shower was nothing compared to the great spectacle.

Gene the Marine trounced the Manassa Mauler. With stinging lefts, he kept the champ away, and sent him back on his heels with right crosses and uppercuts. A small stream of blood came from under Dempsey's right eye. Tunney's jabs were hitting the target. The right hands began to swell Dempsey's left cheek. It spread upwards and closed his eye.

In the early rounds, the champ rushed, but later on, after Tunney's aggressive attack had smothered some of the champ's fire, less so. Dempsey was the champ of old in spirit. "He fought his fight as he had every other bout. The rushing style, which is the only one he knows, was not enough this time." Tunney stepped around and punished him severely, mercilessly, while Dempsey hoped to land one punch to turn the tide. Under the hurricane attack, the champ wilted. An uppercut snapped his head back. He was a pathetic figure at the end, his left eye closed and blood gushing from the cut under his right eye. He looked bewildered, but smiled at the end and congratulated Tunney.

Pollock believed James Joseph Tunney had popular appeal. He was born and bred in the Bohemian Greenwich Village section of New York. He was a member of the Fifth Marines during the World War. He was a gentleman. Although he had at least five pro bouts prior to enlisting, he truly began his rise in 1919, after his release from the service, but only in the last two years did he come forward as a possible heavyweight contender. Prior to 1924, he was regarded lightly, in part because of his weight, but then he got bigger and stronger and stopped Carpentier, Gibbons, and Madden, the latter of whom had gone the distance with Wills. His only blemish was to Greb, whom he beat in subsequent contests.

Philadelphia Mayor W. Freeland Kendrick, who was at ringside, said Tunney won easily, with supreme skill, but he also fought gallantly, with a whirling, slashing effort. He outboxed Dempsey, scoring blow after blow with telling effect, and he even dared to come in to close quarters and meet Dempsey at his own game of infighting. Dempsey made a vigorous, frantic attempt to center the flitting Tunney so he could set himself for one devastating punch, but he never landed that punch. True, he jarred Tunney at various times, but each time, the marine came back with determination, eager to mix it. At times, Tunney disregarded his advisers' warnings to use the ring and box him, but instead tore in with inspired effort. Tunney won 9 of the 10 rounds.

Kendrick said the fight was a credit to the city, for Philadelphia put on the contest in a way that the city could feel proud. Outstanding representatives of every industry in the country were present, as well as various federal and state government figures, capitalists, ambassadors, etc. No one appeared to mind the rain.

Major J. Andrew White's word pictures on the radio enabled 40 million people to "see" the fight. He was seconded by Graham McNamee, who discussed the fight between rounds. A greater number of people throughout the nation listened in on the fight than ever had heard any other similar event over the air. More than 30 radio stations broadcast it, including two national chains, WEAF and WJZ. The Royal Typewriter Company paid $15,000 to have the fight put on the air.

Unlike most who said Dempsey was not the same, one writer for the *Philadelphia Public Ledger*, Jay House, said Dempsey fought as he always did, no slower, and actually had been overrated. "It will be said that Dempsey wasn't as good as he was. ... But very likely, Dempsey never was." House argued that Jack beat two large, slow-moving targets in Willard and Firpo. Firpo was an "atrocious fighter" and Willard "wasn't any fighter at all." Jack "racked little Carpentier to death with the rabbit punch." Dempsey was built up as a maneater and the public accepted it without question. The experts also accepted it because they "invariably string with the man on top."

This time, some of Dempsey's old tools were absent. There was no black tape on his hands. The rabbit punch was illegal in this fight. There was no complacent referee to allow him to foul incessantly. Therefore, Dempsey looked anything but the tiger he was reputed to be.

House said Dempsey appeared to him to be as fast on his feet as ever, and his wallop carried all of its old-time sting. But, for the most part, he missed. Tunney was under or inside of the punches, and time and again beat Dempsey to the punch. Dempsey leaped out of his corner, weaving and swinging as he always had done, but unlike others, Tunney wasn't there. Tunney both outboxed and outpunched him.

Tunney was very nonchalant and serene, with nothing flashy or inspired about him. He was the least concerned fighter ever. Unlike Dempsey, he wore no scowl. Unlike Carpentier, the born showman, who played to the crowd, Tunney put on no show of any sort. He was very business-like, and his methods and plan worked.

The crowd was the least vociferous assemblage ever, polite and relatively quiet. The applause was about evenly divided.

Jim Jab said he was one of the few who picked Tunney before the fight, because he believed that Dempsey's long absence from the ring had lessened his powers, and his legal entanglements would affect his mental condition. A less agile, less accurate version of Dempsey was pitted against the most scientific rival he ever had faced as champion. He was in there with a man with speed, spunk, spirit, boxing ability, defense, and footwork. He could hit Dempsey, elude the blows, and take the few that landed. Dempsey might have won rounds 4 and 6, but that was all.

The *Daily News'* Paul Gallico said Tunney whipped Dempsey, beating his face to a ghastly pulp under a blinding rainstorm that fell from the black sky. The canvas was rain-soaked under the glare of white-hot lights. Tunney's face was fresh and unmarked. He gave the champ a frightful beating. Jack's face was a replica of what he did to Willard. Everyone knew he lost. Dempsey was outboxed, outhit, outgeneraled, and thoroughly outclassed.

As the fight started, the shower turned into a beating rain. In the closing rounds, the rain turned into a cloudburst. No one stirred, and no one left. On the water-and-blood-soaked canvas was the thrilling sight of a cleverer, younger, stronger man hammering away and beating the champion. Tunney's footwork was faultless, his counters never missed, and in the clinches, he held Dempsey helpless in his arms.

Experts all had gambled that the real Dempsey would be in the ring, but once again learned that no man can stay away from the wars for three years and come back to fight as himself. Dempsey never could get untracked. His punches were not killing blows, and when they landed, Tunney simply gasped for breath and fought back harder. Tunney fought a magnificent battle. He weathered some fierce punching and tore his man to shreds. He was a real champion. When Dempsey hit Tunney and Gene failed to go down, the fight was over. Tunney was throwing three and four blows to Dempsey's one, beating his face to a ghastly pulp. Dempsey was only a shell of his old tigerish self.

Dempsey told Jack Farrell, "I fought my best, but I just wasn't there."

Julia Harpman said she wanted Dempsey to win, because "I thought he was the more human of the two men and because he was being harassed so much that he couldn't even go bathing when the ocean was in its most inviting mood at Atlantic City, for fear of being served with some sort of legal papers." Conversely, Tunney seemed like a picture-doll, a handsome, untouched man whose picture the girls were apt to cut out. "Also, Tunney seemed very proud of his good looks and not a little conceited in his struttings about Stroudsburg."

Harry Newman said Dempsey never got started and was beaten badly. Gene punched his way to the championship over 10 smart rounds, giving

Dempsey an awful lacing, at times having him on the verge of being knocked out. In the closing moments, Dempsey was half blind, and finished looking like he had collided with a freight train. Tunney punched him silly, particularly with his left, and took the play away from him every time Jack tried to rush the priestly-looking New Yorker out of the ring. Dempsey became furious, raging against Tunney's careful but perfect attack, while he slowly but surely was yielding his crown. Dempsey scarcely won a round. His right eye was opened early on, and it practically was closed in the last round. Gene kept snapping in left pokes that sent Jack back on his heels. For a while, Dempsey paid little attention to Tunney's attack, but as Gene's shots became heavier and more accurate, Dempsey was content to box. At times he would rush like a mad bull, but the old savage was missing.

In the 6th round, Dempsey nailed him with a left hook to the head, and for a moment it looked like he might take him out, but Dempsey blew up after every spurt, and looked bad as Gene cuffed and plastered him all over the place. Tunney was too strong, snapped his punches like a marksman, timed his counters accurately, and outsmarted the old champ at every turn. Dempsey did not look like the old Dempsey, but it did not diminish Tunney's grand performance.

Tunney was game and smart and would take a licking before he would lose. He had everything that made a champion, a fine head, good punch, speed to burn, and a masterful command of ring generalship.

Dempsey was a sorry spectacle as he shuffled out of the ring. He knew the hero worshippers would desert him in defeat, so he wasn't all that disappointed. He wanted some peace.

At the end of the 1st round, Jack Kearns told New York Mayor Jimmy Walker, "He's shot to pieces – his legs are gone." Kearns had picked Tunney before the fight, and what he saw from the start only confirmed his feelings. Kearns said the champion's legs failed him.

However, Kearns did not want to gloat or rub it in. "He has had more grief and hounding in his seven years reign as champion than any titleholder in the history of the ring." Kearns simply was calling it like he saw it, and said he would sling no mud or make any personal attacks.

Kearns said it wasn't the Dempsey that crushed Willard or even Firpo. The Firpo of 1923 "would have killed Dempsey of last night." "Dempsey's legs are completely gone." He no longer was the old-time rip-tearing Dempsey. He lacked his usual aggressiveness, and his punches lacked their famous snap. Tunney won every round, though Dempsey earned a draw in the 6th. Dempsey was bleeding, blind, and befuddled. He started to rush in the 10th, but it was too late by 10 rounds.

Tunney was too young, strong, and good for a man who had been on the shelf for three years. The fight proved three things: "First, Tunney is a great fighter; second, Dempsey is game in defeat, and third, they don't come back."

Charles Murray said Tunney fooled virtually all of the boxing experts, winning decisively. Tunney possibly could have won by knockout if he had more of the animal instinct and fought more viciously. He played it safe, knowing he had the decision and the title in the palm of his hands, and did not want to gamble on a knockout.

Tunney performed surprisingly well, amazing many. "Nevertheless, Tunney didn't defeat the Dempsey of yore." Jack had gone back so far; he wasn't even a shell of his former self. There was no disputing it. He had slipped just far enough to permit a fighter of Tunney's capabilities to beat him. "The same Dempsey who crushed Willard or the same Dempsey who crucified Carpentier would have defeated Tunney."

Dempsey had lost a good deal of what made him unbeatable. His judgment of distance was poor, missing more often than usual. The killer sting in his blows had diminished. He still was powerful, but not as deadly. He landed on vital spots at times, yet only once did he have Tunney tottering or on the brink of defeat – in the 4th round. "If Dempsey had all his old punching strength, plus judgment of distance, Tunney would have gone out in the 4th." However, it was only a flash. Tunney survived the storm by clinching, and Dempsey faded. "The old dash and terrific socks vanished in a jiffy."

> Dempsey's downfall can be described in a few words. His deadly punches have faded to average heavy blows. The terrific shock has fled. His fighting eye is slightly dimmed. That accounts for his poor judgment of distance. When Dempsey was at his height he rang the bull's eye every time he let go. His muscles, after three years of inactivity in actual battle gathered a little rust and failed to work in harmony with his brain. In other words, nature had collected its toll and Dempsey's fighting days are drawing to a close.

Tunney fought wisely. He paced himself perfectly. He scored with his left and followed with a right cross to the jaw. His punch did not hurt much, except in the last two rounds. He was not a big puncher. "Dempsey went lame after eight rounds more from his own exertion than from Tunney's blows." Tunney landed at least 50 punches cleanly to the jaw, but not one stunned him. They jarred him, but only stopped him momentarily. Gene's blows helped to wear Dempsey down, though the champ's scant reserve forces were the main cause of his defeat. Dempsey could not sustain his attack, could not get the proper range, and his strength slipped away. At the end, only sheer grit saved him from a knockout. Jack was tired, weak, and stumbling.

When he returned to his dressing quarters, Dempsey's left eye was closed tight and had a deep purplish hue. Crimson came from a gash over his nose, and his lips were puffed. Tunney's jabs had done the damage. "The horse hide skin that was once Dempsey's has softened."

Regardless, Tunney took some powerful blows. "While Tunney was practically unmarked, I believe he suffered more pain than did Dempsey. Gene accepted some awful blows to the body, punches that really hurt."

But Gene could take it, and he scored the greater number of blows. He was the superior boxer and ring general. Winning the championship likely would increase his confidence and poise. "Tunney may develop into a great fighter, now that he is champion, but he played lucky in catching Dempsey on the down grade."

Murray opined that if Dempsey fought a rematch, he would need to salvage much of his old form or he would lose again. "The Dempsey I saw last night can't beat Tunney."

The fight had attracted the largest crowd in boxing's history. "The show was admirably staged. Rickard again proved he has no equal as a promoter. Only the rain marred a perfect picture."

Jimmy De Forest said Tunney licked a shell of what once was the greatest fighting machine ever. Tunney had vigor, and Dempsey was lethargic. "At that, Tunney was not impressive. Dempsey just wasn't there, that's all there is to it." Tunney was able to hurt Dempsey, but he was cautious and failed to follow up his advantages. The hollow Dempsey, with everything but his fighting spirit rusted and burned out, kept advancing pitifully. Tunney still was anxious and cautious, apparently afraid that one good blow might turn the tide.

Even when Dempsey did get in, it did not do him any good, for Tunney tied him up. And when Gene did not tie him up, Dempsey didn't have anything to shoot. Once close, instead of tearing away in his old-time manner, his blows were feeble, as if he were playing with a sparring partner.

Tunney fought a heady fight. On the few occasions when the fading champion stung him, Gene did not allow himself to be flustered. He knew how to cover and tie up. In the 4th round, Dempsey nailed his chin with a left hook, followed swiftly by a right to the body. Gene sagged, but did not drop, instead grabbing the lower rope and swaying in a sitting posture. He pulled himself up with the aid of the ropes and continued. Thereafter, Gene landed left and right to the face, many times. Dempsey emerged with a cut along the right side of his nose.

It was not a spectacular fight, but mechanical, given the way Tunney fought. Gene jabbed and followed with the right, landing.

The only rounds Dempsey won were the 6th and the 7th. Jack did his best work in those rounds, and Tunney eased up a bit. It was Dempsey's dying effort, seeing that he was losing. However, "just when it looked as if he might get somewhere, the light died down and he was again the plodding old man, flat-footed and being hurt by his opponent's punches."

In the 7th, a stiff left hook cut a small gash over Gene's right eye. But the stiff lefts did not have Dempsey's old-time force. "At no time was Dempsey able to tear through Tunney's guard with any degree of effectiveness. Time and again Tunney had Dempsey backing up." Gene actually was doing more of the real attacking, despite the fact that previously he always had been more of a defensive fighter.

Tunney never lost his confidence. His cornermen, Jimmy Bronson and Billy Gibson, were calm, barely even talking. Conversely, in Dempsey's corner, Philadelphia Jack O'Brien and Jerry the Greek were desperately busy working over him.

De Forest granted that Tunney deserved credit for winning. "But he didn't beat a live one. Dempsey is through, completely." Jack simply "wasn't there; that's all."

M. D. Tracy, United Press Staff correspondent, said when the fight started, Dempsey weaved in, and everyone expected an explosion of blows, but there was nothing. Tunney poked him in the nose with a jab. Subconsciously, folks began thinking the title was about to pass. This was not the usual Dempsey. The challenger was alert and agile. In the 4th round, Dempsey made a great assault, but it was repulsed. Tunney dominated. The skies were black and the rain fell steadily. At the end, Jerry the Greek helped a staggering, beaten, and battered ex-killer back to his seat. His 7-year reign was over.

Henry Farrell said Tunney won every round but two by a mile, and those two, the 1st and 4th, were even. Dempsey lacked his punch; although Tunney said the former champ indeed hurt him. Dempsey never really looked like himself.

Dempsey had been the 3 to 1 favorite, but the New York racetrack money was on Tunney. "Dempsey lost because he wasn't the Dempsey of old." It was no fix. He didn't have his old-time punch. Tunney could take what he had, and increasingly gained courage, round by round.

By the 5th round, Tunney began to outwrestle and outrough him in the clinches, where Dempsey usually was at his best. Jack fouled, using rabbit punches and kidney blows, barred in Pennsylvania, but Tunney never complained. Gene punched him out of the clinches and countered so vigorously that for the first time in his reign, Dempsey started holding.

Dempsey kept coming in, but found an opponent who could not be stopped with his body blows. Tunney was hurt several times, but always came back, and he was forcing Dempsey back with punches that did not knock him down, but nevertheless wore him down.

John Crews said Dempsey had been licked by a soft life, time away from the game, relaxation of stern training principles, and domesticity. After the 1st round, the wise ones knew they were seeing a new champion. Dempsey's old punch was not there. That round told the tale. Dempsey went after him, but Gene shot stiff jolts to the head and jaw, and he kept it up throughout.

James Wood said Tunney completely outboxed, outfought, and outgeneraled Dempsey in every round, with the possible exception of the 6th. The old fighting fury was gone, and the champ made a surprisingly poor showing. Dempsey had been beaten as never before, his face cut, bleeding, and swollen to the point of disfiguration. He was a sparring partner in Gene's hands.

Tunney fought a great battle, tailored for Dempsey's style. He fought him as he should be fought, and he put the experts to shame. It wasn't the same Dempsey, but Dempsey never fought anyone like Tunney either. Those who saw Tunney in his early battles never figured he could take Dempsey's blows and still outsmart and outsmash him, but he did. "He let Dempsey lead, backed away from him, and then came on to outpunch him in almost every exchange." Dempsey tired in every round and was weary all the way through. His charges were few and far between. Even when he lunged in, the effort was not worth the result. Gene backpedaled and clipped him with left jabs while sliding out of range. Dempsey spent energy, got nothing for it, and got hit. Time and again he tried to work up the old fury, but it wasn't in him. Tunney pounded his face to a pulp. Still, Dempsey kept trying, futile though it was.

Jack McAuliffe, retired lightweight champ, said the only round in which Dempsey flashed his old-time stuff was the 6th. Tunney won all of the other rounds.

Jim Tully said Dempsey was the shell that cracked. He met a great man. With his cleverness, Tunney won the exchanges and tied Jack up in knots. In the 4th round, Dempsey caught him with a hard right and left and Gene's body sagged through the ropes, but in the many exchanges thereafter, the grim Marine beat him to the punch. Dempsey was out on his feet in the 9th. He was a shell of brawn, beaten by a fast, smart, sturdy man.

Thomas Rice said Jack's old kick was missing, showing the effects of a 3-year rest. He had been out of the ring for too long. Dempsey was 31 and Tunney 28, but their paths had been much different. Tunney had gotten better with time, and Dempsey the opposite. Jack was the victim of Father Time. He lost 8 of the rounds. Some gave Tunney all 10, and few gave Dempsey more than 2. He was defeated, but not disgraced. He was thoroughly game and took a lot of stinging punishment. In the 9th round, a left jab closed Jack's left eye. He proved that he could take punishment.

The tragedy was that Dempsey could not fight even 50% as well as he and the majority thought he could. If the fight had been 15 rounds, he would have been knocked out. He had lost his punch. Several times when he landed flush, it was evident that he had lost a considerable amount of his snap. That was evident even in his training camp. "He was driving, rather than snapping."

Tunney had improved. He rarely had been convincing before. "He had always appeared cautious to the verge of timidity. His blows were seldom, if ever, delivered with a hearty and carefree abandon." Yet, in this fight, he had gone from being overcautious to fighting a cool, courageous fight against a man with a reputation as a deadly slugger. He was quick and accurate and put power into his punches. Hence, apologies and congratulations were owed. Dempsey did not hit as hard as in 1923, while Tunney hit harder than he did in 1924. Gene also tied up well, another surprise to those who thought he was not strong enough to do it.

Still, there remained a question regarding whether this improved version of Tunney could have beaten the Dempsey of 1923. "I doubt if he could, but the Dempsey of 1923 was as open to a right hook and a right uppercut as was the Dempsey of 1926, and was as susceptible to being tied up by a skillful opponent." Regardless,

> Dempsey has slipped, markedly and, to an extent, pitifully, as compared with the Dempsey of 1923, but he is no weakling or invalid. He is the most dangerous heavyweight in the country today – bar Tunney. I am not forgetting Harry Wills. Whipping Dempsey was no mean feat. It was a highly creditable achievement of brains and brawn.

Grantland Rice said Tunney gave Dempsey a beating, outpointing him in every round, hammering his face almost out of shape. Jack's left eye was closed, and there was a deep opening under his right eye pouring blood. He was bleeding from the mouth and nose like a faucet. By a twist of fate, he looked a lot like Jess Willard at Toledo, although he never was knocked off his feet.

Tunney fought the most surprising fight of his career. He met Dempsey's swings with stiff lefts and rights to the face. The punches had enough power to throw Dempsey off balance and leave him dazed and bewildered. Gene appeared extremely confident throughout.

The record crowd saw a waning, fading champion, and it was obvious from the start. Whenever Dempsey rushed, he could not keep it up, blew up quickly, and had to rest. While he was taking these rests, Tunney came on to hit him. Although Tunney fought a great fight, it was obvious that "Dempsey had blown completely up." Even when he got inside or crowded Gene into a corner, he had none of his old steam. He did no damage with the few blows he landed cleanly. He shook Tunney with a right to the body and left hook to the jaw, but each time, Tunney recovered quickly and was on top of Dempsey, jabbing him and following with his right.

The champ's rushes became slower and more futile as his face began to swell and turn orange. From the 5th round on, Dempsey became less aggressive; and he barely could see.

Tunney fought to glory with courage and straight, sharp punching. He often landed several blows with no return. Dempsey was utterly bewildered. "As Dempsey would rush, Tunney the challenger would either step cleverly away or else beat Dempsey to the punch with a left and a right delivered at either long or close range." Gene had fine generalship, mixing his offense and defense. Sometimes he would back away out of reach. Other times it would seem like he was going to back away but then would step in and nail Dempsey, who was wide open.

The *Glens Falls Post-Star* noted that back on July 18, 1925, over a year ago, Tunney had said, "I'm going to be the next heavyweight champion of the world. Dempsey will never fight Wills if he meets me first." Again, on

October 26 that year, he said Dempsey-Wills never would take place. He was right again. Tunney said when he wanted to become the logical challenger, he had sought out a fight with Wills, but was spurned. Now that he was champion, Gene would spurn him.

Hype Igoe said the fight was hard and fast, and Dempsey was punished. His end was pitiful and horrible, his face a nightmare of cruel bruises. He was a shell of the terror who once battered Willard. "Dempsey didn't have a thing, he didn't have one bit more than he showed in his training and that never was any of the old Dempsey stuff."

Dempsey tried to fight, but he was as weak as Kearns predicted he would be. He called the fight to a "T." Dempsey was hopeless after 5 rounds, a shell, just like Sullivan and Jeffries after their long layoffs. "Time takes its toll and it took it last night." One had to feel sorry for him. A great champion had passed. Even Kearns said, "The poor sucker; I can't help feeling sorry for him. You know we were good friends once."

Conversely, Tunney was better and showed even more than he did in training, in part because he was up against a man who had slipped. Whenever Dempsey got close enough to land, Tunney would hold. Even when he did land, Jack's blows had no sting to them. Tunney won with ease. "Tunney was magnificent in victory. Every act in that ring, every move, parry, counter; each bit of footwork, was done with the cool calculation that has been so apparent in everything Tunney has done in preparing for his fight – his Magnum Opus." Two years ago, Tunney had told Igoe, "Hype, I'll lick this fellow if ever we meet. I'll always lick him. I'll lick any man who checks his brains in the dressing room."

Present on behalf of the *Chicago Tribune*, Harvey Woodruff said only his fighting instinct kept Jack in the ring. The old champ looked drawn and tired. His judgment of distance was poor, and his old-time power was lacking, for his punches lacked steam. To those who had seen his great performances of the past, he was a sorry specimen. "In one respect, and one respect only, Dempsey was the Dempsey of old: that was his fighting instinct. But fighting instinct without the other qualities which made Dempsey terrifying and formidable was valueless." Tunney took his punches without flinching. Jack was beaten all the way. He kept crowding and pressing, except at those intervals when Tunney took the play away by launching a counterattack. Tunney had the better of nearly every round. The 7th was even, and the 6th as well, though some gave it to Dempsey. Tunney fought a battle far greater than most thought possible. He outpunched, outsmarted, and outfought Dempsey. He jabbed away, and whipped across his right, time and again scoring one-two, while smothering Jack's attack.

When Dempsey entered the ring, his face looked haggard, when in previous years it looked ferocious. His body showed little ridges of flesh foreign to him in years past. He hit the body, but Gene took it well. Tunney's counters were more accurate and more powerful.

Tunney's jab and right, particularly countering right, were effective in smothering Dempsey's attack. The 1st round was rather slow, but already indicated a declining champion in action.

In the 2nd round, after Dempsey's initial attack, Tunney countered and outpointed Jack all the way. At the round's end, Tunney's lip was bleeding, while a cut had been opened on Dempsey's cheek.

Dempsey appeared to be tiring early on. Tunney was stronger in the clinches. Jack had landed several body blows, but Tunney did not curl up like others had. He kept fighting right back. It was evident then that Dempsey's former power was lacking.

In the 6th round, Dempsey showed the best he had up to that time, and he got an even break in the 7th round. He showed his old body attack with whipping left hooks followed by rights to the jaw. However, Tunney did not allow them to catch him squarely on the button, and his own counterattack kept matters even.

Tunney was not loath to attack when he saw an opportunity. He slugged with Dempsey at times and did not come out second-best in those exchanges. He had Dempsey's attack solved, had a safe margin on points, and was fighting a headier battle than Dempsey. Jack was taking blows to land one, but his one had no effect. His timing and judgment of distance was off, as well as force, and he paid the toll of soft living for three years.

Dempsey might regain some lost form if he fought more often, and possibly could win a rematch, but it was doubtful, given the confidence Tunney would gain from his victory. "Tunney is a better fighter than most experts thought." He was not a big puncher, but neither man landed a blow in the fight that carried knockout force. Still, Gene was an excellent ring general with fast hands and feet.

Chicago Mayor William Dever said it was evident from the radio account that Dempsey had lost his old spirit.

James Mullen had predicted the outcome. "I have been in the boxing game too long to know that a fighter cannot lay off for three years and still retain the stuff which made him champion. Dempsey made the fatal mistake of meeting Tunney without having engaged in a few fights to get back in shape."

Dave Barry, a former fighter and boxing instructor, said, "It is a good thing for the game to have the title change hands."

The fight proved that inactivity, more than anything, was a champion-killer. To rest is to rust, particularly at the highest levels, when the best fight the best. Sullivan, out three years, lost to Corbett. Corbett, after beating Mitchell, for a three-year span only had a 4-rounder against Sharkey, and then lost to Fitzsimmons. Fitz, two years inactive, lost to Jeffries. Jeff, after six years, lost to Johnson. Willard, out three years, lost to Dempsey, and now Dempsey, three years, lost to Tunney. During those three years of inactivity, loss of sharpness, and focus, Tunney was fighting quite often, having 19 contests, improving, gaining valuable experience, and getting bigger and stronger.

That said, even a prime Dempsey might have struggled with this version of Tunney, who simply was a nightmare. Gene was lightning-fast, very active with his hands and feet, had great condition, excellent defense, and knew how to move, clinch, and smother. He had fast reactions, could sharpshoot single leads or counter well, move in or out at will, and could fire off combinations in blazing-fast fashion. He maintained a great pace. His lightly bouncing in-and-out, feinting, and overall speed and reactions would be trouble for most any champion at any time. Gene made Jack look slow by comparison, even though he was not.

But, of course, a prime Dempsey would not have fought this version, because three years earlier Tunney was smaller and not as good, even according to contemporary opinions.

It also is clear that a younger, more active Dempsey was more relentless, threw more often and consistently, and had faster feet and better head-movement. He would have gotten closer more often, been more active, and had better timing. He would have kept up the pace and not tired as rapidly. He would have been stronger and more active in the clinches and had greater snap on his blows.

Hence, the what-if of boxing will remain a timeless debate. Most believed that inactivity beat Dempsey more than anything, though they credited Tunney for a brilliant performance. Still, there were a few who said Dempsey simply met a superior technician.

Estelle Taylor was not at the fight. She learned about the result from the raucous newsboys at a train station in Indiana, but took it stoically. She telegrammed Dempsey, "Jack, boy, so sorry I can't be with you now. Cheer up and wire me where to come to you." Estelle told the press, "I want so much to be with him again and to know that he's all right. I don't care two whoops about fame, fights, or fortunes, so long as his name is Jack Dempsey and he's as crazy about me as I am about him. All I want to know is that he's all right."

On Jack's behalf, Floyd Fitzsimmons responded, "Dear Estelle: Jack is fine. Lost in a rainstorm. No disgrace. Don't worry." Jack subsequently telegrammed Estelle, "I'm all right. Only lost the decision."

Taylor arrived in Philadelphia at 3 p.m. the day after the fight, along with Mrs. Floyd Fitzsimmons, wife of "Dempsey's business adviser." She told reporters, "I'm not worrying about the title. I didn't come East after a champion. I came East after my husband."

Jack greeted Estelle with, "Hello, Ginsberg," his pet-name for her. She asked, "What did he do to your face?" "Well, honey, I forgot to duck." Taylor consoled him, and they embraced. "Oh Jack, Jack." Dempsey said,

"I lost; that's all." He held her tight and patted her shoulder. He told her not to worry, that everything would be all right. "Jack thought a lot of that title. But he was big enough to accept its loss as philosophically as any one in the world." Dempsey took the loss like a man and a true sportsman. Jack and Estelle soon would relax in Atlantic City.

Dempsey told reporters, "Gene Tunney is the best man I ever fought, but if we ever meet again, I'll beat him. ... He's a grand man and a great fighter, but I know I can stop him." Jack admitted that he felt the effects of the terrific body blows that Gene landed. He had a nasty cut over the eye, but otherwise was all right.

Some newspapers quoted Estelle as saying, "I have Jack. The championship does not mean anything to me." However, Taylor did say that like her husband, she was interested in a rematch. "Anything that interests my husband interests me just 100 per cent."

Floyd Fitzsimmons said Dempsey was okay. "The man never lived who could send Jack to a hospital." The cut was an old one, opened up by Tunney's straight jolts to the forehead. He had two stitches taken in the cut, which extended from the nose to the eyebrow.

The day after the fight, on the 24th at 6 p.m., Tunney visited Dempsey at his suite in the Adelphia Hotel. Also present were Estelle Taylor and Mr. and Mrs. Floyd Fitzsimmons. When they shook hands, Tunney said his hand was "a bit tender." Gene expressed hope that Jack was "coming along all right." Dempsey told Tunney that he was glad he had come. Gene said, "I always thought you were a great champion. And I want to say now that you are a fine, clean opponent and fought as clean and game a fight as any man who has been in a ring." Both men discussed all of the good wallops and swats they had landed, as well as missed. Gene wondered "if you felt that as much as I thought you did." They spoke for about half an hour. After he left, Gene said, "Dempsey's a fine chap, and I hope he comes around without any trouble. We had a good talk about that fight."

Floyd Fitzsimmons said,

> He's a great boy, that Tunney. Gene came into Jack's suite without any advance notice and shook his hand warmly before Jack could rise to greet him. He told Jack he had come 'just to pay my respects to a game sportsman.' I never saw Jack so affected by anything of that kind as he was by Tunney's visit this evening. You could tell it was no act – Gene meant what he said. A great boy, that Tunney.

Gene Normile said, "Tunney convinced me that he is a gentleman. If there was any doubt, he showed it by calling to pay his respects to Jack.

He will be a great champion. Jack has no alibi for his defeat and he never will have."

The *Philadelphia Inquirer* reported that Dempsey's purse allegedly would wind up being about $700,000, the largest of his career by far. That was $150,000 less than reported the day before. Tunney earned $200,000.

Another reported that Rickard announced on the 24th that the gate was $1,895,733.40, less than initially reported, but still a record. The attendance was 125,735, of which 118,736 were paid admissions, also a record, and 6,999 were passes, which included policemen, firemen, ushers, and Sesqui and Rickard employees. The fight beat out Dempsey-Carpentier by $269,153.40, which drew $1,626,580. 25,000 more people were present than for Willard-Firpo, which drew more than 100,000. (Some suggested that Dempsey would earn around $785,900, if pay was based on the gross receipts. Few knew for sure what he made.)

Rickard allegedly made a $500,000 profit. The Sesqui got $170,000. The state got $86,150, and the federal government $172,339.40. Tickets were sold at $5, $7, $10, $15, $20, and $25, plus 10% tax.

Tunney calls his mother

Tunney said he would fight whomever Gibson and Rickard selected for him to fight. However, word was that Rickard said Harry Wills never would get a chance at the title.

Gene wanted to live out of the limelight. "I never did like this posing stuff, and I'm not going to make a fool of myself now." He did not want any parades. "I wish somebody will tell Jack how much I respect him. My how that man can hit."

Pennsylvania Governor Pinchot, who saw the fight, said he thought Tunney's victory would be good for boxing:

The whole affair last night was a complete justification of the Pennsylvania law to regulate boxing ... Most of all, however, I was pleased with the superb exhibition given by Tunney, who by his superior headwork, won the championship. I was very anxious to have Tunney win. His victory will be a good thing for boxing all over the United States. I have never seen a great crowd so well handled, nor have I ever seen a great crowd that handled itself so well.

Supposedly, over 40 million people heard the fight on the radio.

James Isaminger believed that Tunney was champion simply because he happened to be the man in the ring with Dempsey on Thursday night. Dempsey was ripe for the taking by any top contender, for he "was not a flicker of the irresistible cave man that crushed down Willard, Carpentier,

Firpo, and a row of others. Gone back? Yes, so far that he ought to put on a doublet and shake the box with C. Columbus."

Dempsey wrote that his hat was off to Tunney, who whipped him fairly and squarely. "The better man won." The only positive was he earned a lot of money and now would be out of the spotlight and get some peace.

Gene Tunney analyzed the fight and his gameplan. He wrote,

> I have fought my fight and I have vindicated my theory of all things the theory of intelligent use of force as opposed to blind strength and fierce courage.

> I planned my fight the first time I ever saw Jack Dempsey in action. ... I began to study means of beating him, because I knew that some day, I would meet him and match my forces against his.

> I never doubted the issue. He tore at me in the first round and I gave ground. I had anticipated that, and I had figured my move ahead. I knew I would have to give ground until I had hurt him – until I had had a chance to sap the power of his rugged physique with a hard, perfectly timed punch.

> I knew that the first time I delivered such a punch I could safely take the aggressive. The opportunity came sooner than I expected. After I broke ground and sidestepped in that first round, Dempsey stopped his rush momentarily. That was my opportunity.

> I leaped in, shot a left to his face and then drove my right with all the power I had to his jaw. I felt his muscles tighten, then saw him sag. I knew that I was safe, that my plan had worked and that I was to be the next champion.

Gene said Dempsey's left hand was his best, and he knew that his left eye was his seeing eye for that left. By damaging his left eye, it would affect his left. So, he focused on it. Still, "At no time did I relax. There never was a moment when I could have relaxed. I knew that before the fight. I knew that to permit Dempsey to get set was to sacrifice every chance I had." He also knew that throwing caution to the winds and tearing in recklessly would be suicide. Dempsey was dangerous in every round, if Gene gave him the chance to land. "Again I say the theory of proper use of strength and force will overcome blind force." He had a plan, and followed it. "It was a plan that protected me, yet gave me my full force to use against the champion." He trained and fought exactly right.

Perry Lewis said Tunney was a master ring general, fighting a wise, elastic battle that adjusted itself to crises. No man ever fought wiser. He was efficient, cool and collected from beginning to end, and did not make one false move. Lewis granted, "Of course, Tunney wasn't facing the Dempsey who almost ripped Willard's head off" or flattened so many others. But he still was dangerous.

Jack O'Brien told Lewis, "It's the legs that fail a man." Dempsey's legs no longer were there. Jack had his punch, but he used it awkwardly and with little accuracy. "The champion's judgment of distance fled from him during these three years of idleness, fled never to return."

Regardless, Tunney met his attack with consummate skill and perfect defensive tactics. He gave ground, tied up, and worked himself out of danger in masterful style, cool as a cucumber.

For a moment in the 6th round, it seemed as if Tunney was gone. Dempsey rushed him into a corner and landed a venomous left hook. Gene's knees buckled, but he escaped and fled across the ring. Jack caught him another hook on the ropes, and Gene momentarily wilted again. But Tunney clinched, swung his foe half around, and slipped by him, getting back to ring center. His head still was clear and alert. He had just taken Dempsey's best twice, yet was all right. He suddenly halted his flight to drive his knife-like right into Dempsey's oncoming face, following it with a series of rights and lefts. At that moment, Jack was a beaten man. Thereafter, it merely was a question of keeping away from the murderous left and the title was his. Tunney had shown that he could avoid the hook nine out of ten times, and stand up under it that tenth time.

Lewis said it wasn't a great fight, and couldn't be, with Dempsey having gone as far back as he had. That was not an effort to discount Tunney's brilliant work. He fought the perfect fight. To those who scoffed at Tunney as champion, Lewis noted that he never had been off his feet, and was beaten only once, the first time he fought Greb, but had beaten him in rematches, the final time quite clearly. Tunney had not always looked good, but he fought well enough to win.[494]

The *Philadelphia Evening Bulletin* quoted Referee Tommy Reilly as saying, "It is a certainty Billy Gibson will not consider a match with Harry Wills." The Brown Panther previously had turned down an elimination bout with Tunney, which many thought was foolish. Another possibility was world light heavy champ Jack Delaney or Tommy Loughran, both of whom needed to gain weight and get stronger. A return match with Dempsey was possible, "providing the dethroned champion makes an effort to work himself back into real fighting condition and succeeds."

Tunney likely would have added confidence from his victory. The new champion was an "evasive fighting-boxer with two good hands. He jabs and hooks equally as well with his left hand while his right hand carries a damaging sock." Tunney hurt his right hand in the later rounds, so he used his left more. "Tunney's ring generalship must be commended. How he husbands his strength; makes few false motions and is fighting with something above his neck all the time." In the 4th round, when Dempsey landed his two best punches, which made Gene's knees buckle, Tunney grabbed the top ring rope, steadied himself, and fell into a clinch. He was fully composed when he broke, which also showed his ability to recover

[494] *Philadelphia Inquirer, Binghamton Press, San Francisco Examiner,* September 25, 1926.

from being hurt. Reilly was impressed. "Tunney should reign supreme at least as long as his predecessor."[495]

Dempsey snuck off to take a train to Atlantic City. Seated in the hotel lobby, unaware of his exit, were six men who wanted to serve him with summons in various lawsuits or to levy attachments upon Dempsey's share of the fight proceeds, including a suit by Kearns. Hotel attaches had refused to answer their questions or make known Dempsey's room location.

Gene Normile blamed Dempsey's loss on the rain. "The rain made the ring almost as slick as glass, and several times in crucial moments caused Dempsey to slip on the wet canvas."

Normile further explained, "The big mistake made by Dempsey was to fight his first bout after a three-year lay-off against such a good man as Tunney." After he finished training at Saratoga Springs, Dempsey was right, but he started all over again at Atlantic City and lost his keenness. "He wasn't right for that fight." Normile said Jack could win a rematch if he worked himself back into form by taking two or three fights. "Jack will fight his way back."

A very happy Rickard revealed that he had a contract with Tunney, signed some time ago, to promote his matches while he was champion. A return bout would be arranged when agreeable to both sides. Tex was pleased with how Philadelphia had treated them and the fight.

Rickard asserted that boxing had taken on an air of refinement and gentility. There were no crashers. The police did a great job. The vast sea of faces was the most inspiring scene he ever beheld in his life. "I was more interested in looking at that crowd and enjoying their enjoyment of the match than I was in looking at the fighters themselves. And what a crowd it was!" There were none of the rough and uncouth scenes from the days gone by. Prominent public, political, business, and social leaders were there. Even religious leaders.

Rickard said that although Tunney's victory was well-deserved, the lawsuits had caused worry and sleepless nights for Dempsey. Mental relaxation was as important to a fighter's preparation as physical preparation. He was harried with worry.

In another interview, Rickard said if he had anything to say about it, there would be no Wills-Tunney fight. He had Tunney under contract, so such a fight was not likely.

Motion pictures of the fight had been developed and distributed to theaters by 11 a.m. the next day, according to the Stanley Company of America. After each round had finished filming, the films were rushed immediately to the laboratories for development. The titles were quickly prepared, and the films completed for exhibition in record time.

Tunney dropped in on the home of the mother of Ray Campbell, his press representative. The new champ said he was tired and wanted a long

---

[495] *Philadelphia Evening Bulletin*, September 25, 1926.

rest. He was suffering only from a discolored eye, a sore arm, and lacerated lip. Gene said,

> Dempsey's eye was closed by a blow in the second round, but the effects of the blow did not show and his face did not begin to swell until the ninth round. That accounts for the belief that the eye was hit in the ninth round. Dempsey was at my mercy after I hit him in the eye in the second. I felt sorry for him in the later rounds as I saw his eye swelling, and knew it was hurting him terribly.[496]

The *Philadelphia Public Ledger's* Frank McCracken quoted Tunney as saying he wanted to be a fighting champion, and would fight whomever was the best. He was willing to give Dempsey another chance. Gene admitted complaining about a low punch in the 5th round, but also admitted "the blow was only a trifle below the belt line... and it did not bother me." It was unintentional. Gene said Dempsey "fought a clean battle all the way."

Tunney said the crowd was fair, for when he and Dempsey sat in opposite corners bandaging their hands, there was no more cheering for one than the other. "In fact, I think that Dempsey got the best of it in the cheering when we entered the ring. I think that Dempsey is more popular now that he has lost the title than when he was the champion. Dempsey revealed himself a real sportsman after he had heard the decision that made me the champion." He came over, threw his arm around Gene's shoulder and said, "You fought a great fight, Gene. You deserve to win."

> Yes, I will fight Dempsey again if they want me to. They say he wasn't the Dempsey of old. That he was bothered by law suits and other legal entanglements. Well, in that Stadium ring I believe I would have beaten the Dempsey of three or four years ago. I believe I would have beaten Dempsey at his best. Still, if Jack comes back and is selected as a contender for the title, he will get the same chance he gave me.

Tunney was willing to give Loughran a chance too. He said Tommy was a fine fighter but needed to gain more poundage. He had improved a great deal since Tunney defeated him (WND8) in 1922. Loughran beat a mighty good boxer in Jimmy Delaney, who helped prepare Tunney. Gene said he would fight anyone that Rickard wanted him to fight, because Tex made it possible for him to fight Dempsey.

The new champion hardly had a mark, except for a slight cut over one of his eyes, and the cold sore on his lower lip, which had opened up time and again in training and opened up in the 1st round.

Tunney promised to give the gloves he wore in the fight to the Marine Corps.

In another interview, Tunney said,

496 *Philadelphia Public Ledger*, September 25, 1926.

I thought Dempsey to be a dead game fellow and a wonderful fighter. What a hitter Jack is. He nailed me with a left hook to the head in the sixth round and I thought that I had been hit with a hammer. I have nothing but admiration for Jack Dempsey. He fought a clean fight all the way, and I want to repeat that he is the hardest hitter I have ever met.

Tunney also said he licked Dempsey in the 1st round, when he nailed him with a right.

NEW MONARCH OF PRIZE RING

GENE TUNNEY GENE TUNNEY, EX-MARINE

Billy Gibson said he would arrange a theatrical tour for Tunney. The former Benny Leonard manager said he was glad to be managing another world champion.

Ed Pollock wrote that Dempsey gained popularity and new admirers by his game battle against a superior boxer. He weakened but did not quit. He had "magnificent spirit" and heart, though his "judgment of distance was poor and the punishing power had gone from his punches." "Three years out of competition had taken much from the former champion. He lost in strength and stamina, but his will to win escaped the touch of time." He lost with his fists flying. "There were many dark spots in the career of the dethroned champion which made him unpopular, but right before the eclipse his star was shining brightly."

Dempsey and Tunney represented two extremes. Tunney provided a sharp contrast and was a new type of champion. He was an ex-Marine who fought in France, and therefore "had a wide edge on other challengers in public favor. Tunney is more colorful outside the ring than in it," with his love of books and other things unusual for a pugilist. Dempsey's "most grievous error was his failure to get in the service during the war. The public has never forgiven him, and yet it was not altogether his fault. ... His every move was dictated by Kearns, who placed the championship above patriotism and urged, yea commanded, his protégé not to join the colors."

Many were disappointed by the bout, saying it was lacking in thrills. Yet, there never was a dull moment. Dempsey tore in while Tunney shrewdly pulled him into clinches or maneuvered to get away from the flying fists. Tunney's fine boxing, clever defensive tactics, and shrewd maneuvering to hit and get away was moving, but it was a silent admiration, rather than thrilling. That was Tunney. Unlike Dempsey, Gene would not have the crowd raising the roof, cheering and yelling while he was in action. "The fan would have him stand up and fight rather than watch him race in and race out of the area where fists fly."

Paul Gallico gave Tunney much more credit. "As far as I could make out, it was Tunney who was making him look bad. They say that anybody would have licked Dempsey the way he fought. I say Dempsey would have licked anybody but Tunney." Before the fight, Gallico did not think Tunney would be able to take it. He was wrong. "He took plenty. I saw him weather punches that would have slaughtered any other man. Dempsey hit him a right under the heart that should have felled an ox. Tunney weathered it." Tunney took hooks to the jaw and stomach, and after each hard punch, he fought back harder. Gene was as vicious and ferocious as necessary, tearing in with both hands when the occasion called for it. Although primarily known as a counter fighter, Gene threw many leads and went on the attack aplenty. It was Dempsey who twice was nearly out on his feet. Gallico said everyone got their assessment of Tunney and the fight wrong.[497]

OFFICIAL—AUTHENTIC—THRILLING

DEMPSEY-TUNNEY FIGHT PICTURES

The Stanley Company of America paid a record price for these motion pictures. Perhaps you can see yourself in the crowd. Who knows? Every detail.

Greatest Fight Pictures Ever Recorded

ORGAN SOLOISTS AND ORCHESTRAL MUSIC

STAR JAY NEAR FULTON TELEPHONE, TRI 4296 — MATS. DAILY

Only 2 Theatres in Brooklyn Playing Real Traveling Burlesque Shows Exclusively. An Entirely New Big Girly Show Each Week. Not a Stock Company.

COMMENCING MONDAY MATINEE

"Parisian Flappers"
with STELLA MORRISSEY and Frank Anderson
Amateurs Tuesday Nites
Bathing Beauty Contest Thursday Nights
Sundays Continuous Vaudeville and Pictures 1 to 11 P. M.

GAYETY BWAY. AND THROOP
TELEPHONE WMSBG.0914

Burlesque's Brightest Stars
STONE & PILLARD
In Their Own Big Show
and Margie Penneti with her
Glorious Gayety Girls
Opportunity Nite Wednesdays
Big Bathing Beauty Contest
Friday Nights

MARVELOUS DEMPSEY-TUNNEY PICTURES
First Exclusive Run at Star and Gayety
ONLY TWO THEATRES SHOWING
Tex Rickard's $1,000,000 Official Dempsey-Tunney Match
TAKEN AT RINGSIDE
Now—Twice Daily—Up To & Including Sunday, Oct. 3rd. No Advance In Prices

The fight films, which had been developed quickly, almost immediately started showing throughout Pennsylvania, and soon thereafter in New York as well. Clearly, the ridiculous federal law was being ignored.

A couple days after the fight, from Atlantic City, "Jack the Giant Killer," the "Manmauler from Manassa," allegedly said that in a rematch, he would give Tunney the "Devil Dog" the worst beating of his life and knock him out. Jack said the best man won, but that was the best man on Thursday night. However, he said it was a lot of rot that he was out of condition, and as he spoke, he clenched his fists until it seemed that the blood vessels would break from the pressure. "I was in wonderful shape." When asked what then was the matter, he said, "The rain, of course. I'm just the same as a horse that can beat the world on a dry track." Tunney thrived on a muddy track. "I fight on my toes; I depend upon my speed to carry me through. ... Thursday night, the surface of the ring was a veritable soggy marsh. It was water soaked and I just couldn't get the

497 *Philadelphia Public Ledger, Daily News*, September 25, 1926.

spring with which to lurch and lunge." But, of course, Tunney had moved quite well in the same ring. Jack said Tunney was a better mud horse. When asked about the belief that his legs had gone back, Dempsey's face assumed his fighting scowl, and said it was a lot of bunk. "If my legs were in bad condition, why didn't Tunney finish me? Why didn't he knock me out?" Jack said his face only required two stitches. He would be all right in a couple of days.

Dempsey did give Tunney credit. "He is a great fighter, even greater than I had estimated him." Still, he wanted a rematch, and would fight his way to where Tunney had to fight him again.

Tunney said a terrific left hook by Dempsey in the 6th round caused him severe pain and nearly beat him. His voice was husky from a blow or several blows on the throat. One punch caught him directly on the Adam's apple in the 6th round. He finished the round in distress and had difficulty breathing in the corner. "I was in real pain for a moment, but happily for me I was able to snap out of it."

James Isaminger said the sporting world was not yet prepared to rank Tunney with former greats, because he failed to put away a "skidding Dempsey." "The remark was heard on all sides that a number of fighters would have won the championship had they been in the ring instead of Tunney."

Basically, many felt that it was a bad version of Dempsey more than great Tunney. However, perhaps it was great Tunney making Dempsey look bad. It could have been both great Tunney and bad Dempsey.

Isaminger believed Tunney likely would have stopped him if he had another 5 rounds, for Dempsey was slowing, his left eye closed tight, and right partly closed and bleeding. Tunney could have taken more chances, but that might have left him vulnerable too, so he was content to be cautious and win on points.

It was no discredit to fail to stop a champion within 10 rounds. Jim Corbett did not stop Sullivan until the 21st round. It took Fitzsimmons 14 rounds to stop Corbett. Jeffries did not stop the much smaller Fitzsimmons until the 11th round. Tommy Burns won a 20-round decision over Marvin Hart. The much smaller Burns still was on his feet in the 14th round against a great Jack Johnson. Even Johnson took 15 rounds to finish a shell of Jeffries, who was far worse physically than Dempsey was. Willard was behind on points and did not knock out a 37-year-old Johnson until the 26th round. Not everyone could be a Jack Dempsey, blasting guys out early, as he did with Willard. "Therefore it will not do to sneer at Tunney because he could not finish Dempsey inside ten rounds although his opponent was virtually helpless at the finish and could not have lasted many more rounds."

In some ways, Dempsey was receiving more accolades now that he lost than when he was champion. "For various reasons Dempsey was an unpopular champion." Folks enjoyed watching him fight, but they rooted for him to lose. A lot of it had to do with the slacker charges. Yet, many other fighters had not joined the military, nor did some of the highest salaried baseball players and other notable figures. Yet, not a word about them being slackers was heard. At least Dempsey raised a lot of money for war charities. He obtained a lot more popularity through his films, just as Corbett did on the stage.

Still, the general view was that although Tunney fought beautifully, Father Time, years of idleness, and stress of legal troubles had more to do with Dempsey losing than anything.[498]

The *Philadelphia Public Ledger* reported that Dempsey was in Atlantic City and wanted to be left alone in his suite of rooms at the Ambassador Hotel. Estelle Taylor and Mr. and Mrs. Floyd Fitzsimmons were with him. They shooed away newspapermen and curiosity seekers. Fitz answered all questions. "Jack wants to keep away from the crowd for a few days and get a good rest. Then he'll have several statements to make." So, did Dempsey make the statements claimed, or was it Fitzsimmons, or just newspaper yarns?

Regarding the fight, Fitz said Dempsey was in a bad mental state with all the continual worries about harassing lawsuits and being served. "Jack could not get started, though he did the forcing. The cut over his left eye was the result of a butt. It's coming around nicely."

Dempsey trainer Gus Wilson told Frank McCracken, "Jack hasn't any alibis to offer. He was beaten fair and square and he was beaten by a good man – better man than folks thought Tunney was." However, many said that something was wrong with Dempsey, that he was so off that he made Tunney look a whole lot better than he really was. Dempsey refused to make excuses and did not want those around him to do so either. Wilson said sometimes the best horses lose. Dempsey "would rather have died in that ring than to have quit." He went down to defeat with fists flying, trying to land a knockout blow even in the 10th round, with his eye closed. "He lost his title like a man. Why try to take credit from Tunney?"

But then Wilson did hint at something. "Jerry the Greek and I know what was wrong with Dempsey. Something happened two days before the fight. Jerry and I know, but we will never tell." Some thought it was the legal action started against him just a few days before the fight by his former manager and friend, Jack Kearns.

Wilson did say, "Jealous people made as much trouble as they could for Dempsey. He was hounded by process-servers, sheriffs, and annoyed by all sorts of legal actions directed at him right up until the day of the fight."

Tax collectors reported the collection of $172,339.40 as the 10% tax. They said admissions numbered 126,081. They claimed the management took in $1,723,394.

As Gene Tunney drove through New York, escorted by law enforcement, huge crowds of thousands lined and crowded the streets.

---

[498] *Philadelphia Inquirer*, September 26, 1926.

New York City Mayor Jimmy Walker greeted him. Marines honored him.[499]

Gene Tunney Gets Reception Befitting a Champion in New York

A proud moment. Gene Tunney, accompanied by Mayor Walker, reviews the detachment of marines sent to city hall as honor guard.

TUNNEY ACCLAIMED AT N. Y. CITY HALL

Dempsey's conqueror for the heavyweight championship is shown posing on the steps of the municipal building, with Mayor Walker (to left of Gene) after the official welcome to Tunney by the New York executive.

In subsequent days, Tunney said a short right in the 1st round helped him win the fight. In the second rush of the contest, Gene landed a short right which showed Dempsey that he could punch too.

Tunney always watched Dempsey's left, all the way to the end, for he knew it was loaded with dynamite. Anyone who thought Dempsey had lost his punch could let him hit them, and when they woke up, see if they still thought the same way.

---

[499] *Philadelphia Public Ledger, Daily News*, September 26, 1926.

Gene said that at one point in his life, he had been a stenographer and rate clerk at a $15 weekly salary. He had come a long way.

Allegedly, Dempsey changed his tune regarding the wet ring excuse, if he ever used it as an excuse in the first place. "No, the wet ring was no handicap. The only handicap I had was myself. I lost to a better man and that's all there is to it. There will be no excuses from us." He told another interviewer, "I just wasn't there." He denied being sick. At that point, he admitted that he had 4 stitches above his eye. A great deal of money, more than he ever had earned before, would serve as a balm, particularly since he did not need to split it with Jack Kearns.[500]

On October 1, Dr. Frank Russell, who now was attending to the ex-champion, claimed that an infection of poisonous matter in the blood had affected Dempsey and adversely affected his performance. Dr. Russell said Dempsey was suffering from an infection under the left arm pit, akin to boils, contracted during training. "I believe when he entered the ring he was a man intoxicated by the poisonous matter which affected his blood."

Reports were circulating in New York and Pennsylvania that the night before the fight, Dempsey was a very sick man, and a physician advised him not to enter the ring. One said he had a bacterial infection which left him weakened. Others associated with Dempsey's camp had become ill as well, just before the fight, including Captain Fred Tapscott, Captain Mabbutt, Jerry the Greek Luvadis, and one of the sparring partners, all of whom had rashes and digestive disorders. "Mabbutt knows that Dempsey became suddenly and violently ill. Tapscott also knows it. Normile has admitted the champion suffered from dysentery." Not only was Dempsey sick, but most of the other important people about the camp also "seem to have suddenly contracted a severe disorder, followed by a rash."

However, Dempsey simply said, "I lost to a better man; I have no alibies."[501]

[500] *Philadelphia Inquirer, Oakland Post-Enquirer,* September 29, 1926.
[501] *Lancaster New Era, Courier-News, Buffalo News,* October 1, 1926; *Tampa Tribune,* November 18, 1926.

CHAPTER 7

A New Shark

Harry Wills was scheduled to fight a 15-round bout against Boston's "Sailor" Jack Sharkey at Ebbets field on Columbus Day, October 12, a few weeks after Dempsey-Tunney.

The 187-pound Sharkey was coming off a very recent September 21, 1926 clear 10-round decision victory over 220-pound black George Godfrey (30-10-1) in Boston, which garnered him a great amount of prestige, credibility, and respect.

Sharkey's wins included: 1924 W10 Floyd Johnson, W10 Homer Smith, and W10 Al Roberts; 1925 W10 Jack Renault, WDQ9 (disqualification for low blows) and W10 Jim Maloney, W10 Emilio "King" Solomon, and W10 Johnny Risko; and 1926 W10 King Solomon, WDQ1 Bud Gorman (low blow), and the W10 Godfrey.

Sharkey, who had turned pro in 1924, had early losses to men like Quintin Romero Rojas (1924 LTKOby9), Charley Weinert (1924 LND12; 1925 L10), and Bud Gorman (1925 L10). He also lost a 1924 10-round decision to Jim Maloney.

In the 1925 Sharkey-Maloney rematch, Sharkey led on points for the first 6 rounds, but then Maloney came on strong, decking Sharkey five times in the 8th round. Sharkey complained of being fouled the first time he was decked. "The writer believes that Maloney's left hook for the stomach found lodgement on and just below the belt."

In the 9th round, Maloney put him down twice more, but after Maloney palpably fouled three times in rapid succession, plumb in the groin, Sharkey's corner claimed a foul, and Maloney was disqualified.[502]

The quickly-improving Sharkey had been on a nine-fight win streak over the past year, including his victories over the respected Risko, Maloney (W10 in their third contest), and Godfrey. Interestingly, Sharkey had won a few fights via disqualification, all via low blows.

Many were saying that Sharkey was a future champion in the making, and was using Wills as a stepping-stone to the title. "Sharkey is a clever boxer, besides being fast, and carries a corking wallop in either hand." The *New York Daily News* said Tunney likely would be forced to meet the winner of Sharkey-Wills.

Sharkey said, "I have been watching Wills for some time, and I feel that I can beat him. Of course, I am not silly enough to think that beating Harry Wills is a cakewalk by any means, but I honestly believe I can beat him, and so does my manager Johnny Buckley."[503]

[502] *Boston Globe*, June 6, 1925.
[503] *New York Daily News*, September 29, October 3, 1926.

Mistah Jack Sharkey of the Boston Sharkeys is all set to mass up Harry Wills's nice smile at Ebbets field. This is how he'll face the Brown Panther next Tuesday night.

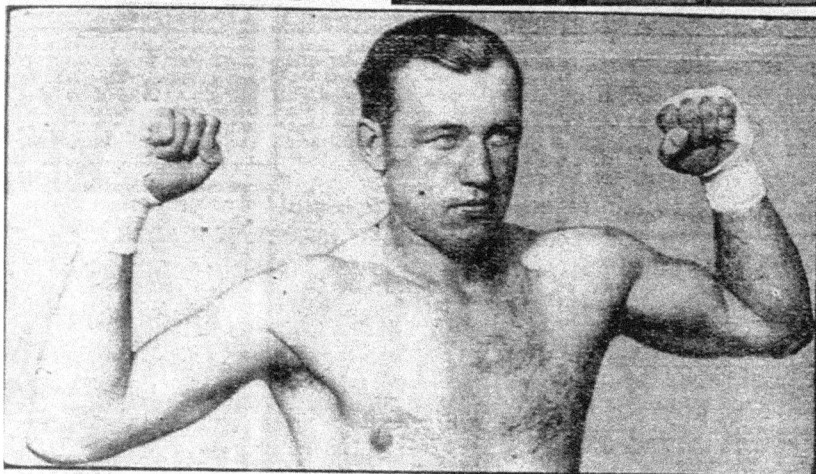

Mistah Harry Wills

Wills, Commissioner Farley, and Sharkey at the weigh in

On October 9, 1926, Tex Rickard married his second wife.

Jack Dempsey said if the public felt it necessary for him to establish his right to a return match with Tunney, he was willing to fight the winner of the upcoming Wills-Sharkey contest, whomever it was.

On October 12, 1926, at Ebbets Field in Brooklyn, New York, 40,000 fans which generated a gate of $133,514.70 saw 23-year-old 188-pound Jack Sharkey (23-6) hand 214 ½-pound 7-5 odds favorite (34-year-old – listed/claimed but 37 actual) Harry Wills (85-7-7) a terrific pasting throughout their bout, until 43 seconds into the 13th round, referee Patsy Haley disqualified Wills for hitting on the break, which Harry had done several times throughout, as well as other foul tactics, including the use of a backhand blow.

The reporters were unanimous that Sharkey beat Wills all the way, winning every round, or nearly every round but one or two potentially even ones early in the fight.

Harry Newman said Sharkey outpunched Wills all the way. He also outroughed him at his own game, and was well on his way to a clear victory at the time of the disqualification. Wills never had a chance. He was cuffed all over the place. Sharkey was dominant, inside and out, and staggered Harry several times. After the 10th round, the crowd was singing, "Bye Bye, Black Bird." Newman gave Sharkey every round but the 2nd, which he called even.

Paul Gallico said Sharkey mauled and trounced Wills.

Al Lamb said it was a one-sided fight in Sharkey's favor, and Wills was disqualified after failing to heed multiple warnings. Sharkey won every round but one, which was even (the 3rd). He cut both of Wills' eyes and lips and kept them bleeding profusely. "Wills adhered to his famed 'dirty' fighting, holding with his left and hitting with his right, hitting in the breakaway and [using] a backhand. But it gained him nothing." Sharkey was too clever and fast for him with his hands, feet, and body-shifting, so Wills could not land effectively. Sharkey staggered Wills several times, and had him confused.

Referee Patsy Haley warned Wills that one more backhand punch would cost him the fight, and yet, soon thereafter, Harry slapped another backhand blow to Jack's face, and Haley disqualified him.

Henry Farrell said Wills had joined the ranks of also-rans, having been badly and horribly beaten. Some thought he fouled to get himself out of the fight. Navy veteran Sharkey was not intimidated at all, despite being shorter by three inches and smaller by 26 pounds. He distinctly and outstandingly defeated Wills throughout. He fought a lot like Tunney did against Dempsey, jabbing away effectively, and attacking when appropriate.

Grantland Rice said the Panther merely was a shambling, shuffling old bear, and probably evaded a knockout by fouling.

The negro giant, who was labelled as a menace to the white race and the pursuer of the world's champion, looked like a novice as

Sharkey swirled on to attack round after round, pumping lefts and rights to the body and swinging heavily to the head and jaw. Sharkey's speed was amazing and he put on as fine an exhibition of boxing skill as any one would care to see.

Sharkey's speed and aggression cut Wills down. Harry had no chance at all. He was hurt, trying to survive and fight back as best he could, holding and hitting, and using backhand blows.

Afterwards, Wills said, "I laid off too long. I thought I had a few more good fights left in me, but I guess I was all wrong."

Sharkey said, "I didn't want to win that way. I had him all propped up for a knockout, and he knew it. Anyhow, I guess I gave him a pasting he won't forget in a hurry." He also said, "It was easier than I thought it would be." The sailor Sharkey wanted marine Tunney. "Now, Johnny, get me the leatherneck. A sailor can lick a Marine any day of the week."

The *Brooklyn Standard Union* said Wills was through as a contender. He lacked speed and aggressiveness, and was hit often.

The *Brooklyn Daily Eagle's* George Nobbe said Sharkey and father time combined to remove Wills as the nemesis of champions. No more would fighters run for cover when they heard the name of Wills. "For the myth of the dusky Senegambian has been exploded." Sharkey beat Wills just as conclusively as Tunney defeated Dempsey. The fact that it ended on a foul merely was incidental. Wills did not win a single round. "Wills is through now." "Old Father Time licked him just as much as did Josef Paul Cucoskey [Sharkey]."

When Harry held with his left, Sharkey was good at moving in close enough so Wills could not hurt him with his right. At the same time, he kept his own left free, working and doing damage on the inside. Nobbe said Sharkey did a workmanlike job in winning, but nothing to enthuse over. The old-timers said he was a good second rater.

> If they were sad when the colorless Tunney took the title from Dempsey, they were utterly disconsolate last night when Cucoskey-Sharkey trounced Wills. ... Sharkey is no killer. He has a well-tutored left hook. It found its way to Wills' jaw often, and on occasion landed solidly in the midsection, too. But there was no knockout force behind it.

Sharkey's hook could rock and shake up, but was not a sleep-producer.

The old-timers also had little sympathy for Sharkey's constant complaints about the Panther's ring tactics, despite the fact that Sharkey was offending against the rules almost as constantly as Wills was. The one rule that Wills violated more than Sharkey was hitting on breaks. Both held and hit and used the illegal backhand punch. Referee Patsy Haley disqualified Wills for hitting on the breakaway after warning him not to do it for the tenth time.

Sharkey afterwards said he did not want to win that way, but his constant complaints probably had something to do with it. Wills' tactics availed him nothing, and he was losing each round. Some might say Haley should have disqualified him sooner, that since he allowed it to go on for so long, he might as well have allowed the fight to finish.

Answering why he disqualified Wills, Haley said, "For pulling Sharkey's arm up as he came out of a clinch and then hitting on the breakaway. I warned him 10 different times, and I guess that ought to be enough."

Wills was not the "black menace of yore. He seemed tired and worn and old." He was slow on his feet. He waited, and Sharkey rushed right in and worked.

Thomas Rice said Wills' reactions were slow. His fists did not respond to his brain's messages, and he lost his eye for distance. "Idleness deteriorated Jack Dempsey: It obliterated Harry Wills." He did his best, but it was "dismally bad." The referee's disqualification for hitting on the breaks was perfectly correct, for Harry had been warned frequently. Wills was "thoroughly whipped." Sharkey won at least the last 12 rounds, and most gave Sharkey the 1st round as well.

Dempsey's idleness had taken a toll, but he still was a tough proposition. It took a youthful, powerful, clever Tunney, with a shockingly accurate right to beat him.

> The Harry Wills of last night would have lost to the Dempsey of Sept. 23 as surely as he lost to the Boston Lithuanian. Sharkey has no punch commensurate with his weight and boxing ability. Tunney would have knocked out Wills in 10 rounds, whereas he could not do more than disfigure and outpoint Dempsey in 10 rounds. Wills is absolutely through. Dempsey has merely gone back.

Still, Rice did not think Dempsey could beat Tunney in a rematch, "because finite man cannot repair the ravages of age and Dempsey is too old mentally to acquire sufficient boxing skill to cope with Tunney in cleverness." Rice said he noticed Wills slipping even back in June 1924, when he failed to stop Bartley Madden in 15 rounds. He was slowing then, and his coordination, speed, and power all on the wane, despite winning clearly. Tunney then became the first to stop Madden. Wills subsequently gave a dreary exhibition with Firpo in September 1924, unable to stop him, which in hindsight further confirmed Rice's suspicions.

Wills used to be the strongest man in the world at clinching, and such helped him survive against Sharkey, for his legs were quivering from lefts and rights to the jaw in the 10th round. At one time in his career, Wills could hold so well that no man could punch. But he could not prevent Sharkey from punching. Sharkey beat him to the punch, closed Harry's right eye with a left hook, and made him miss. "His ability to beat Wills to the punch and Wills' tardy reactions to mental stimuli made it difficult to tell whether Sharkey was as clever as he seemed or whether he was merely clever in comparison to the aged and decayed Wills. Sharkey is a fairly clever boxer, but lacks punch." Still, he was young and improving. Wills was a "complete bust" and "through as a championship possibility."

Plug! Right below the heart! Jack smacks over one of his wicked ones as they clinched at the end of the first round. Look at the way Barry's left is holding Jack's shoulder. This type of fighting lost the fight for him.

Harry blocks a left hook in 6th. But he couldn't find his corner at the bell!

Getting down to business in 1st! The Harlem brown panther hugs Jack in a clinch. Sharkey's blows had Harry staggering after the first bell started the gloves flying. Who'da thought it?

The *Brooklyn Daily Times* said its writer, James J. Wood, was one of the few who had picked Sharkey to win, saying, "Sharkey is the cleverest big man in the ring today. In the past year he has beaten everyone put before him." Wills had weight, experience, and strength, but Sharkey had youth and superiority in the speed and skill departments, with fast hands and feet. "[Sharkey] has got everything. And that is enough, we opine, to make him the next challenger for the world's heavyweight championship."

Wood said Wills made a sorry showing, the sorriest of his many sorry ones in the past few years. He was booed out of the ring and all the way up the aisle. Overanxiety caused Sharkey to miss more than one chance to win by knockout. But when it was over, he received cheering and applause, for he now was the "outstanding challenger for Tunney's newly-worn crown." He beat the man who "bulled" the division for ten years.

With a 26 ½-pound weight deficit, Sharkey beat Wills from gong to gong, battering his face, cutting both eyes, his nose, and mouth. He drummed his body with short rights and lefts. "He outsmarted, outboxed and outpunched the towering black man in every round. ... It was Sharkey all the way, and by a wider margin with every succeeding round." In one round, he bobbed and weaved, while in another he charged in firing away. He bewildered and dazed Wills. In the 4th round, a right flush on the chin had Harry hurt, but instead of setting up and measuring a follow-up, Jack fired off several rights and missed, overanxious. A more experienced foe, on the several occasions he hurt Harry, would have jockeyed him into position for a finishing blow. Regardless, "Sharkey was the master throughout." Wills became more discouraged, beaten long before the bout was half over.

Wood said Harry's age would prevent a successful comeback. Dempsey had a chance, but not Wills, who was "through." "His was a great advertising campaign."

Jack Kofoed for the *New York Evening Post* said Wills performed miserably, and took an ignoble way out, fouling deliberately. Sharkey had outboxed and outfought him in every round. Wills was trounced and buffeted throughout by a man 26 pounds lighter. It was an "ignominious exit" from the game. Wills showed neither spirit nor courage, but was just a tired old man. Conversely, Sharkey's speed was great, his boxing masterful, and his judgment of distance marvelous. He jolted, dazed, and cut Wills, and brought blood to his lips.

> What a waste of ballyhoo went into the effort to stage a Dempsey-Wills fight – a match that would have brought together two wornout men. Yet, Dempsey, beaten as he was before the 135,000 in the Sesqui Stadium, was incomparably a more heroic figure than the Wills who was thrashed before the 35,000 at Ebbets Field. Dempsey gave recklessly of himself. Wills gave nothing.[504]

[504] *New York Daily News, Binghamton Press, Brooklyn Citizen, Glens Falls Post-Star, Brooklyn Standard Union, Brooklyn Daily Eagle, Brooklyn Daily Times, New York Evening Post*, October 13, 1926.

Wills collected a purse of $39,406, very good money, but far less than the $150,000 he could have made for fighting Tunney, had he/Mullins agreed back when Rickard had offered them that fight.[505]

Moving pictures were taken of the contest and shown in New York, which helped make Sharkey an even more famous attraction.

ANOTHER BIG RAYMOND SCOOP!

HARRY WILLS—JACK SHARKEY FIGHT PICTURES !

Taken at Ringside—Punch for Punch.

Exclusive run—absolutely the only 2 theatres to show this sensational feature. Twice daily—up to and including Sunday Oct. 24.
No Advance in Prices.

Just like that, in the span of one month, the old guard of Dempsey and Wills had been defeated. It seemed as if there was going to be a new era.

Jack Sharkey was the new man of the hour. Born Joseph/Josef Paul Cukoschay, Zuckoschay, Sockotsky, or Juozas or Joseph Paul Zukauskas (sources widely varied), he legally changed his name to Jack Sharkey. A native of Binghamton, New York, he was born on October 26, 1902. He was the son of Lithuanian parents who came to the country and became naturalized. He attended school at St. Patrick's academy in Binghamton, but when he reached the 8th grade, he left school and began working, at age 12, at the Endicott-Johnson shoe plant in Binghamton. He earned $7 a week for a year. He quit and got work swinging a pick and shovel on a big dam under construction on the Susquehanna River, at age 13. Jack tried to enlist in the military at 14 but was told he was too young. He ran away from home at age 14 after Papa Cukoschay gave him a paddling.

Sharkey began living in Bridgeport in 1915 and did odd jobs like carrying water to elephants and currying down the zebras at the Ringling Brothers circus. Eventually, he became a coal heaver on a coal barge, a brakeman, and a ditch digger. He went back to working as a shoemaker at the Binghamton factory. Then he became a glass blower's apprentice.

At the end of the war, Sharkey finally was accepted for service in the navy, fulfilling his dream to be a sailor. It was then that he started boxing, as a 160-pound middleweight, but fought a 200-pound colored man and won the decision. He had about 50 fights in the navy, and lost only once, to Biff Crowley, heavyweight champ of the Atlantic fleet. Having always admired Tom Sharkey and Jack Dempsey, he adopted the name Jack Sharkey. He began his pro career in Boston, having many early fights there. Hence, he was listed as hailing from Boston.

[505] *New York Daily News*, October 16, 1926.

JACK SHARKEY

Sharkey was married and had two young daughters, 19 months and 5 months old. He owned a home in Boston and one in the suburbs. His hobbies included fishing and hunting, and he was an expert rifleman. He expected to fight Tunney in about a year.[506]

On October 22, 1926 at New York's Madison Square Garden, before a sold-out crowd of 18,000, Jack Dempsey and Gene Tunney were in attendance to watch Jim Maloney knock out Italian Arthur De Kuh in the 2nd round of the main bout. Before that fight, in the ring, Tunney and Dempsey both were presented with silver belts. Harry Cross wrote,

Dempsey got a bigger reception than Tunney. Strange as it may seem, they used to boo and jeer Jack Dempsey when he was champion, and now that he has been defeated they cheer him and boo Tunney, the champion. You never can tell about the fickle sport fans. Dempsey is more popular now than he ever was before in his life.[507]

Sadly, also on October 22, 1926, 32-year-old Harry Greb died unexpectedly. After a nose operation the prior night in Atlantic City, he failed to recover from the anesthetic. The operation was supposed to remove a fractured bone in his nasal area that was joined to another bony structure at the base of his skull, an injury allegedly suffered in two auto accidents one week apart from one another. The stitches from the first operation were opened by the second accident. He never came out of the ether. Others said when the bone was removed, blood rushed into the brain, resulting in a hemorrhage which caused his death. His wife had died several years ago, and he was survived by a 7-year-old daughter, Dorothy.

Harry Newman said, "There never was a time during Greb's ring career that he wasn't ready to fight any man in the world. Even as a middleweight he challenged Jack Dempsey for the heavyweight crown and really believed that Dempsey was one man he could lick." Some claimed that he had cuffed and slammed Dempsey in sparring. Greb said he could beat Dempsey, "but in his typical careless manner, he never pressed his claims for a bout in the right quarter and never secured the fight." At his best, Greb was busy and tireless, always throwing. He was a wonder, a rubber man, who

---

[506] *New York Daily News*, October 14, 15, 1926.
[507] *Buffalo Evening News*, October 23, 1926.

could fight and beat middleweights and heavyweights, including Miske, Brennan, Gibbons, and Tunney. Greb had watched Dempsey train for Tunney, and told Newman that Dempsey wasn't right and would lose.

Red Mason said, "He was the greatest fighter I ever saw, and I saw plenty of them."

Regis Welsh wrote,

> For 13 years this windmill of the ring, this defier of established ethics of offense and defense, battered his way…to the greatest honors at the command of the fight world. …
>
> Greb's record in the ring stands for itself. It is the greatest ever compiled by any fighter of his pounds; greater than any of the modern fighters. He fought more frequently; fought harder, faster and better than many who cast aspersions at his style. He fought them all, any time or place, without quibble or argument. …
>
> Greb has gone and his name goes down in fight history as one of the greatest ever to pull on a glove.

Gene Tunney called Greb one of the greatest fighters who ever lived.

Tunney was vacationing, and about to start a theatrical tour. He also was engaged in contract litigation with various parties.

Jack Dempsey sent a telegram to Greb's sister, saying, "I have lost one of my best friends and the world one of its greatest champions. In your hour of bereavement allow me to express my heartfelt sympathy."

Some said that Dempsey, despite his defeat to Tunney, "unwarranted suspicion of trickery," and the prior belief that the crowd would desert him once he lost, was "100 times more popular today. It is a phenomenon of boxing." Hence, if Dempsey was going to fight again, Tex Rickard leaned toward making a rematch with Tunney.[508]

Rickard anticipated that Tunney would defend his crown in about a year, for Tex declared that in his opinion the public did not want more than one heavyweight championship battle per year. If Dempsey was going to fight again, Tex wanted him to fight once or twice before fighting Tunney again, in order to assure himself and the public of his fighting form and condition. "He has the personality that draws people to him and a fighting style that pleases, but I doubt that he will resume fighting."[509]

Robert Edgren wrote that Harry Wills was "neither a good fighter nor a good sportsman. For two years this writer has repeatedly pointed out the fact that Wills was through as a good heavyweight, and that he was

---

[508] *Brooklyn Daily Times*, October 22, 1926; *New York Daily News, Philadelphia Inquirer, Brooklyn Citizen*, October 23, 1926; *Pittsburgh Post*, October 24, 25, 1926. Some later claimed that the real reason Greb was having nose surgery was for cosmetic purposes. He had discussed getting nose surgery as early as January 1926. *Atlantic City Daily Press*, January 2, 1926.
[509] *Brooklyn Daily Times*, October 26, 1926; *Lancaster New Era*, October 27, 1926.

being boomed for a heavyweight championship bout purely as a business proposition. ... Sharkey, a man no bigger than Tunney and not as far advanced as a fighter, beat Wills with no trouble at all." Edgren repeatedly noted in the past that Wills had gone back so far that he could not fight without holding and hitting, even against easy marks, and if the rules were enforced a referee would have to disqualify him for fouling.[510]

Jack Farrell noted that Jack Dempsey made more money in his loss to Tunney than Harry Greb had made in his entire career (300 fights), all purses combined. "Queer racket, this fight business, isn't it?"[511]

Damon Runyon said the intelligentsia always hated Dempsey because they felt he was from and of The Mob, and hence they adopted Tunney as their favorite. The Mob did not care for Tunney, who knew so much about books and could so ably deport himself in drawing rooms and in the company of intelligentsia. "I personally think Jack Dempsey was manifesting a disposition the past year or so to drift as far from The Mob as Mr. Gene Tunney himself." Nevertheless, "The Mob" regarded Dempsey as from and of The Mob, and hence he always would be popular with them. The intelligentsia also had adopted Carpentier and made him a great social and cultural figure. As a result, The Mob resented him.[512]

Robert Edgren said the average man who did not see the fight simply could not believe that Tunney could have beaten Dempsey. They wondered whether Jack had lost his punch, or what was the matter with him. Regardless of whether Dempsey had his punch, he could not land it, for Tunney made him miss, and Tunney did not. The average man could not conceive of that, feeling that Dempsey could hit any man alive, for he was too fast with his hands and feet for anyone.

Edgren believed for Dempsey to come back he had to give up all of the luxury and easy living, and to have some fights to get back to his fighting form. Yet, word was that he was busy buying race horses, which did not sound as if he had his whole mind fixed on coming back.[513]

Tex Rickard doubted that Dempsey would come back, because Jack had made a lot of money, and rich champions usually got lazy and saw no need to get hit and do all of the hard work required to train properly.

Dempsey was busy running his hotel in Los Angeles.[514]

However, in late November, Dempsey told Rickard that he was willing to fight anyone Tex chose for him in March or April 1927.

[510] *Omaha Evening World-Herald,* October 28, 1926.
[511] *New York Daily News,* October 31, 1926.
[512] *Lancaster Daily Intelligencer,* November 1, 1926.
[513] *Mount Carmel News,* November 5, 1926.
[514] *Wilkes-Barre Evening News, Buffalo Evening News,* November 16, 1926.

The public greeted that announcement with joy. "Always a great attraction, he gave 'em a run for their money. ... He was always in there willing to gamble, and when he met the tough fellow, he didn't wait on him, he went to him. That's what made Dempsey a great box office asset and a popular champion."[515]

Paul Gallico said Dempsey had been a "most unpopular champion." The only fight in which the public supported him was against Firpo, possibly because Luis was a foreigner. Now, Jack was popular as an ex-champion. Gallico said Dempsey deserved to be an unpopular champion, and did not deserve to be popular now, for against Tunney he "cheated the biggest fight audience ever assembled out of its money's worth."

> Dempsey's great reputation was made as a killer, a shock puncher who hit fast, often and with deadly accuracy. Too, whatever one may have thought of him outside the ring, he had the reputation of forcing the fighting and making a battle once the bell rang. But in the Sesquicentennial ring in Philadelphia he was a dreadful parody of himself. There were times when it appeared that he wasn't trying. Certainly he was soundly thrashed by the better man. But Dempsey was paid in the neighborhood of $700,000 for his exhibition that night, and it wasn't worth $50. In short there was no thrill and that is what people paid for. In this respect, Tunney sinned as well. He might have elected in the closing rounds to step out and knock the champion out. He didn't. He had the fight won. He played absolutely safe. He was in business for himself. He gave the public nothing for the $200,000 he got.

Gallico noted that W. O. McGeehan thought the fight was on the level, but Sid Sutherland thought it was an "out and out fake." Gallico said he did not know the truth, but,

> This I do know. When I went to Dempsey's camp I was shocked to see how poor his work was. ... He certainly looked like no world's champion as Tommy Loughran punched him around, feinted him silly and banged him to the ropes. Bad as he was, I held Tunney so cheaply, I still thought that Dempsey would lick him. But Dempsey certainly looked cooked when I saw him at Atlantic City.

Gallico granted the possibility of a fake, but if so, Rickard had nothing to do with it, for Tex would kill any one who faked a big fight on him. "Dempsey had one confessed queer one in his career, a little affair of being knocked out by Jim Flynn."[516]

Jack Kearns said Jack Sharkey would beat Tunney and knock out Dempsey if they fought. Kearns believed that Sharkey would have beaten Dempsey much more impressively than Tunney. Doc saw Sharkey beat Wills, and "consider him the best of the present crop of heavyweights."

[515] *Pittsburgh Gazette Times, Elmira Star-Gazette,* November 21, 22, 1926; *Reading Times,* November 23, 1926.
[516] *New York Daily News,* November 26, 1926.

Dempsey is all burned out and I doubt very much if he ever fights again.

Sharkey is entitled to great credit for defeating Wills. I always thought Dempsey, when at his best, could knock out the negro in a round or two. Jack did not share my belief and blocked me when I tried to make the match three years ago.

I believe the big gates in the boxing game are over. There is no puncher in sight right now and you need a fellow with a terrific sock to get the big jack in at the box office.[517]

Captain Charles J. Mabbutt alleged that Dempsey was a victim of poisoning before the Tunney fight. According to him, the Saturday before the fight, in Atlantic City, someone poisoned the cream used for Dempsey's coffee. "I offer as my firm belief the opinion that both Dempsey and I, as well as his trainer, Jerry the Greek, were victims of foul play and that a poisonous substance introduced into the cream used by our party did the work." He said Jack did no training after Saturday because he "was an ill man." Mike Trant was the only member of the party who did not get sick, and he was the only one who took his coffee black, without cream. The champion and the rest of the staff, after 7 a.m. breakfast, all suddenly became very ill. Dempsey broke out into a body rash and his digestive tract was seriously impaired. "The cream we used for our coffee was delivered to the front doorstep between 4 and 5 a.m., and was not taken into the house by the cook until around 6 a.m. ... That wasn't the real Dempsey that Tunney defeated."[518]

However, Sergeant Mike Trant, Chicago detective and Dempsey's bodyguard, denied Captain Mabbutt's story. Trant said he always took cream with his coffee. "Furthermore, I don't remember seeing Mabbutt at any meals with the Dempsey party. He ate in another part of town. Although Dempsey was not his old self he was not poisoned when he went into the ring to fight Tunney."[519]

Some writers recalled prior claims of being doped made by Fitzsimmons and Jeffries, attempting to alibi or explain away their losses. This time though, the claims were made by others, not Dempsey.

Thomas Rice said Dempsey's showing deceived nobody. He was as poor in training camp as he was in the fight. He lacked snap and judgment due to going 3 years without a fight. Combine that with Tunney being in the best form of his life, and the result was understandable.[520]

From Los Angeles, Dempsey said, "I haven't made an alibi for losing to Tunney and won't make any – it was simply a case of Tunney being better than I was that night." He added, "Capt. Mabbutt didn't eat any meals with me at my training table. If he was poisoned it was at another table. If I was poisoned it's all news to me."

[517] *Brooklyn Daily Times*, November 27, 1926.
[518] *Brooklyn Daily Eagle, Pittsburgh Press*, December 1, 1926.
[519] *Brooklyn Citizen*, December 2, 1926.
[520] *Brooklyn Daily Eagle*, December 2, 1926.

Paul Gallico noted,

> One thing is sure – Dempsey didn't go berserk in that Philly ring the way he usually does when he fights. There is a fact into which you can sink your teeth. Dempsey when hit used to go insane. He would stand up and slug until either his opponent or he himself went to the canvas. Something there was, then, that had taken that out of him the night he fought Tunney.

The cause was subject to speculation. "The surprising thing is not that he had lost what little skill he had, because his layoff would account for that, but that he lost his fury as well. ... If anything, the fact that Abe Attell and the mob were seen at the training camps would make me believe the thing was on the level. If the gamblers were going to pull something crooked the last thing they would do is make themselves conspicuous." Still, some had their suspicions.[521]

On December 3, 1926 in Chicago, 154 ½-pound former world welterweight champion Mickey Walker (76-15-2) won the world middleweight championship by winning a 10-round referee's decision (Bennie Yanger) over 159 ½-pound Tiger Flowers (120-15-5). Experts questioned the verdict, including the *New York Times'* James Dawson, who scored it 5-4-1 for Flowers, the *Chicago Tribune's* Walter Eckersall, who scored it 5-2-3 for Flowers, and Harvey Woodruff, who scored it 5-1-4 for Flowers. Jack Kearns, Walker's manager, had another championship notch in his belt. The paid attendance was 9,005, generating $77,127.[522]

From Los Angeles, Jack Dempsey said he would start doing some training to see what he could do. If satisfied that he still was there, he would try to stage a comeback.[523]

In an interesting twist, Dr. Abe Baron, examining physician for the Pennsylvania State Athletic commission, declared that Dempsey indeed showed symptoms of poisoning the *day after* his fight with Tunney. He said it could have occurred through food contamination or local infection. Yet, he also said,

> When I examined Dempsey the night of the fight there was no evidence of temperature. Still I was surprised at the condition of the champion. He was in much better shape two weeks before the battle than he was on the night of the fight, when there was no local evidence of poisoning. Accustomed to having examined hundreds of fighters before their bouts, Dempsey's condition appeared all right to me to carry him through a ten-round battle.

[521] *New York Daily News*, December 3, 1926.
[522] *Chicago Tribune*, December 4, 1926. Their weights were taken at 3 p.m. the day of the fight. Eckersall scored it: 1-E, 2-F, 3-E, 4-W, 5-F, 6-F, 7-F, 8-F, 9-W, 10-E. Flowers was badly hurt in the 9th by a Walker left hook and slipped down while trying to regain his balance from the effects of the staggering blow. Woodruff scored it: 1-E, 2-F, 3-E, 4-E (possibly W), 5-F, 6-F, 7-F, 8-F, 9-W, 10-E (possibly F).
[523] *Olean Evening Times*, December 7, 1926.

The doctor went to Dempsey's hotel the day after the fight to place stitches in the cut over his eye, not to treat him for poisoning. Yet, at that time, he noticed "maucles" and papules on the lower part of his face. "There indicated to me that there was a disturbance in Dempsey's system. I might explain Dempsey's case by saying that symptoms before the fight were those of a person who was developing a disorder that took two or three days before it made itself fully evident."

However, despite reports that Dempsey privately said he thought he was poisoned, publicly, he said, "This poisoning story is getting to be a joke. Something I said was misinterpreted. I was a little weak at the time of the fight, but it wasn't due to poisoning."

Some said it was due to mosquitos which injected their poison. Gene Normile said, "Yes, Dempsey was poisoned. Poisoned by rich lawyers and lawsuits."[524]

On December 15, 1926, in Syracuse, New York, 188 ½-pound Jack Sharkey stopped 189-pound Homer Smith in the 7th round. Sharkey had dropped Smith in the 1st round and struck him while down, though he was not disqualified. The fight generated $13,000 in ticket sales.[525]

Gene Tunney spent Christmas in the woods in Rockwood, Maine. However, he had a close call with death when he plunged through the ice on Moosehead Lake, into the water, but luckily his pals pulled him out.[526]

In early 1927, Major League Baseball Commissioner Kenesaw Mountain Landis investigated allegations that in 1917, the Chicago White Sox had purchased 4 victories from the Detroit Tigers to help them win the pennant.

Also in early January 1927, Tex Rickard said Tunney's next prospective opponent first had to beat Dempsey to justify a title shot to be held in September 1927. Rickard leaned towards Dempsey as the challenger, noting that half the population felt that Jack could reverse the loss in a return battle. Plus, he was a big box-office attraction, the biggest ever in boxing history. So, if a prospective challenger wanted to leapfrog Dempsey, he needed to beat him first. Sources reported that Rickard

[524] Buffalo Evening News, December 8, 1926.
[525] Brooklyn Citizen, December 16, 1926. In 1918, Dempsey stopped Homer Smith in the 1st round.
[526] Rochester Democrat and Chronicle, December 26, 27, 1926.

was going to pay Tunney a $500,000 guarantee for his next fight, plus 50% of everything taken in at the gate over $1,000,000, which was projected to yield him over $750,000.[527]

In early February 1927 in Los Angeles, Jack Dempsey was suffering from blood poisoning in his left hand and arm, the result of an infection from a scratch received on his middle finger, under a ring. He had six operations in 18 hours. There was pus in his elbow and upper arm, traveling downward into the wrist and hand, which were swollen to twice their normal size. Such would delay his preparations for a comeback.[528]

On March 3, 1927, at Madison Square Garden in New York, before 14,000 fans, 189 ½-pound Jack Sharkey stopped 170 ½-pound former world light heavyweight champion Mike McTigue (100-29-10) in the 12th round, the referee stopping the contest because of the worsening of a dangerous gash in the upper left side of the mouth which McTigue had suffered in the fight. A broken tooth allegedly had severed an artery. He was hemorrhaging and bleeding so profusely from his mouth that no one protested the stoppage, which many encouraged the referee to do. The contest had been competitive, with perhaps an edge to McTigue in the first eight rounds, but he tired, and Sharkey came on strong over the next four. The *Daily News* said Sharkey was ahead on points at the time of the stoppage. The fight was filmed.[529]

On May 2, 1927, in *Buck v. Bell*, 274 U.S. 200 (1927), the U.S. Supreme Court held it to be constitutional for states to require forced sterilization of those considered to be genetically, mentally, or intellectually unfit.

On Sunday May 8, 1927, at the Gables Club in Santa Monica, in the Los Angeles area, more than 8,000 fans saw Jack Dempsey enter the ring in public for the first time since losing to Tunney, putting on the mittens to spar in a charity exhibition, with the proceeds going to Mississippi flood sufferers. For the past four weeks, Jack had been training at Soper's ranch, near Wheeler's Hot Springs and Ojai, California.

Dempsey's left uppercut strikes Benny Hill

Mexican ring idol Tony Fuente lasted less than 1 round with 212-pound Dempsey, going down several times, Dempsey's right landing with deadly precision.

Benny Hill of Fresno proved to be a tough boy, repeatedly landing jarring, stiff, straight lefts to the jaw. Nevertheless, near the end of the 1st round, Dempsey dropped Hill for a short count. Hill came back strong and even landed a right cross to the jaw. In

[527] *New York Daily News*, January 8, 1927.
[528] *New York Daily News*, *Los Angeles Times*, February 7, 1927.
[529] *New York Daily News*, *Brooklyn Daily Times*, March 4, 1927. On the undercard, James J. Braddock, 167 ½ pounds, who had won 19 straight fights, won a 4-round decision over 184-pound Lew Barba.

the 2nd round, Dempsey cut loose more. After Hill landed several left jabs to the chin, the crouching Dempsey started landing some stiff jabs and crosses, and Hill stopped carrying the fight to him. Dempsey pounded on him, and Hill was oozing plenty of blood when the bell saved him.

Dempsey showed that he still had a chin and could take it, but his defense was not the same. Jerry the Greek, his trainer, tried to get him to guard his face and weave, but he seemed indifferent to the heavy blows. He was the old-time Dempsey only for about 45 seconds. They wore extra heavy gloves. Hill wore a headgear, but Dempsey did not.[530]

On May 11, Dempsey nearly lost his eyesight. He was chopping wood, and a flying splinter lodged itself into the white of his eye. Doctors removed it. Had it struck him a little higher, he might have lost sight in the eye.[531]

Here's how Jim Maloney (left) and Jack Sharkey stacked up before the battle of the stadium.

On Friday May 20, 1927, at Yankee Stadium in the Bronx, before a crowd of 30,000, 192-pound Jack Sharkey impressively knocked out 202 ½-pound Jim Maloney (27-3) in the 5th round. Maloney had several significant victories, including a recent W10 Jack Delaney (64-7-2), KO2 228-pound Tiny Jim Herman (50-14-11), TKO3 Charley Weinert (70-18-5), W10 Quintin Romero Rojas (22-6-3), and his prior good performances against Sharkey, including a win, disqualification loss in a fight Maloney was winning, and decision loss. The *New York Daily News* wrote, "Sharkey not only proved that he is Maloney's master, but that he is the outstanding challenger for Gene Tunney's heavyweight crown." Sharkey was on a 13-bout win streak, and now was 3-1 against Maloney.

The fight was filmed. Sharkey had speed, good pop, fast feet both on the attack or retreat, he could fight on the inside or outside, and he knew how to move his head. In the 5th round, a fast overhand right decked Maloney for the first time. A right - left hook - right to the jaw finished Maloney, who struggled mightily to rise, almost getting there, but then collapsed down face first, out for the count.

Tex Rickard said, "That Sharkey is one of the best boxing fighters I have ever seen. I have him signed up to meet Dempsey in the next number of eliminations, and I know it will be a great fight."[532]

[530] *Los Angeles Times*, May 8, 9, 1927.
[531] *Los Angeles Times*, May 12, 1927.
[532] *New York Daily News, Binghamton Press*, May 21, 1927. Undercard: James J. Braddock, 165, D6 George La Rocco, 178.

In June, word was that a Dempsey-Sharkey fight likely would be set for July 21 at Yankee Stadium, with the winner to meet Tunney in September.

However, Rickard said Dempsey needed to sign for a Tunney fight in September before he would make a fight for him with Sharkey.

Rickard offered Dempsey and Sharkey a 50% split of the gate, 25% each, with the other 50% going to Tex. Negotiations were ongoing.[533]

On June 23, Rickard, Dempsey, and Sharkey agreed to terms for a 15-round bout at Yankee Stadium, to be held on July 21, one month away. Dempsey likely would earn 30% of the gate, and Sharkey 20 or 25%. Others said Dempsey would earn a $250,000 guarantee, with an option of 25% of the gate if receipts exceeded $1 million. Sharkey accepted 25% without a guarantee. Another said Dempsey would earn 27

---

[533] *Yonkers Herald*, June 13, 1927; *New York Daily News*, June 17, 21, 1927; *Brooklyn Daily Times*, June 21, 1927. It was anticipated that each fighter would earn around $200,000 to $250,000. Rickard believed the fight could draw around $1,225,000.

½% and Sharkey 22 ½%. Both men agreed that if victorious, they would fight Tunney in September.

YEP! IT'S ALL FIXED NOW!—Jack Dempsey, the great ex-king of Fistiana, put his name on the dotted line yesterday for a fifteen-round go with Jack Sharkey at the Yankee stadium July 21. Above you see (standing) Arthur Driscoll (left), and Jim Buckley; (seated) Dempsey, Tex Rickard and Sharkey, who seems to be trying hard to give Dempsey the piercing and devastating eye.—*Story on page 15.*

Sharkey said, "I'll win by a knockout in less than 10 rounds."

Dempsey said, "They tell me Sharkey is a tough fighter. … I'm going to keep on fighting until I know I'm through. I never have believed I was finished. Just because I made one bad fight - and Lord knows it was a bad one – is no sign I can't fight any more. Everyone has a bad fight once in a while."

Dempsey said he weighed 212 pounds when he started training at his mountain camp in Ojai, California, and now was down to 204 pounds. He expected to lose another 6 to 8 pounds in training.[534]

On June 24, 1927, Jack Dempsey celebrated his 32nd birthday at his training camp at White Sulphur Springs, New York, having arrived there that day. It was the same location where he trained for Firpo.

John C. Righeimer, chairman of the Illinois Athletic Commission, wanted Rickard to stage a Tunney-Dempsey fight there, and said they would place no obstacles in his path if he selected Chicago as the battleground.[535]

On June 27, Dempsey sparred for the first time at his White Sulphur Springs, New York camp, working under the watchful eye of new manager Leo Flynn. He boxed 190-pound coffee-colored black Carl Carter, middleweight Eddie McMullen, and colored middleweight Joe Gans, 1 round each.

[534] *Yonkers Herald, Brooklyn Daily Times, Elmira Star-Gazette, Brooklyn Citizen, New York Daily News,* June 23, 1927.
[535] *New York Daily News,* June 25, 1927.

Jack Farrell said Dempsey still packed a mean punch. The so-called hollow shell was loaded with dynamite. The popular notion that he was a physical wreck and past the stage of physical redemption was not entirely accurate. True, his judgment of distance and timing were off, he no longer had the same spring in his legs, his girth was larger, and the zip of his attack was not the same. Yet, time had not robbed him of his greatest asset – his punch. "Don't let anybody tell you Dempsey is a physical wreck. And by the same token don't let anybody tell you he is the same old Jack."

On June 28, Dempsey sparred 1 round each with Carl Carter, Martin Burke, Allentown Joe Gans, and Eddie McMullen, the latter two being middleweights. They landed at will and outboxed him with ease, smacking him with everything.

Here's the Manassa Mauler looking over his training paraphernalia which he starts using today in training for Sharkey go.

As of the 29th, Dempsey was dealing out a bit more punishment. He had power, but was slower than he once was, and still was taking blows. He again sparred 1 round each with Carter, Burke, Gans, and McMullen.[536]

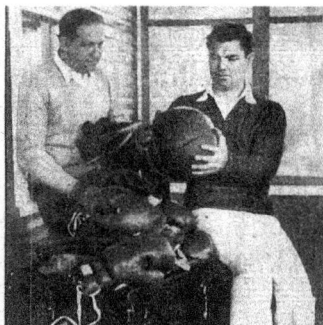

Dempsey belts McMullen

Carl Carter

On June 30, Dempsey was his murderous old self, showing astonishing improvement in speed. He was peppier, faster, and shiftier than he had been since he started his work. He sparred with welter Johnny Saxon, Carl Carter, Marty Burke, and Joe Gans, showing improvement in his defense. However, he still was open to left jabs. He was bobbing and weaving more, but had slowed down, having lost the knack of it the way he once did, being hit more often than in his heyday.

Dempsey's catchers for his training licks are turning out to be pitchers and they are making the ex-champ step lively in preparation for his comeback go with Jack Sharkey. The camp retinue above left to right, includes; Carl Carter, Joe Gans, Jack Dempsey, Leo P. Flynn (manager), Jerry the Greek (trainer), Gus Wilson (trainer), Marty Burke, Eddie McMullen.

Jack Farrell said Dempsey was an enigma. One day he looked great, and the next he appeared slovenly, slow, and without pep.

Dempsey said, "I have been fighting close to ten years, but shucks, I'm not old nor decrepit by any means." Actually, he had been fighting since 1914, so it was more than 10 years. Jack said his hands were good, and he was not punch-drunk. He had plenty of money and did not need to fight, but he wanted to regain the title. "I think I can lick Sharkey and Tunney. I wasn't right, either physically or mentally, for that Philadelphia fight. Things will be different this time."[537]

On or about July 2, 1927, at 847 Emmet Street, Schenectady, New York, Jack Dempsey's brother John Dempsey (allegedly 38; actually 34) shot and killed his 21-year-old wife, Edna Carlow Dempsey, in their apartment, and then shot and killed himself. Jack raced by auto with his business adviser Leo P. Flynn to Schenectady, where he identified the bodies. As tears ran down his face, Jack said, "It's terrible, but that's life, isn't it?" Jack confirmed that at intervals, John had suffered from mental depression.

---

[537] *New York Daily News*, July 1-3, 1927.

John Dempsey had married Edna Carlow in Saratoga three years prior. He had met his wife in 1923, when his brother was training for the Firpo fight. They had a 2-year-old son, Bruce (likely named after Dempsey's deceased brother, who was murdered). Several months ago, Mrs. Dempsey had separated from her husband, whom she said had threatened her life.

The landlady said John appeared to have been drinking heavily. He shot Mrs. Dempsey in both the side and the head, and himself through the right temple. She still was alive when police arrived, but died before medical aid could be summoned.

Edna previously had John arrested in August 1925 on suspicion of insanity and addiction to drugs. On March 17, 1927, she had shown up to a hospital with a deep knife wound in her breast, and there was discussion regarding whether it was a suicide attempt, an accident, or whether John had inflicted the wound, but she would not say. Nevertheless, after that incident, she had left her husband.

Elsie Carlow, Edna's sister, said, "My sister had been afraid of John when they were living in California before they came here. He stabbed her with a knife and he threatened at other times to kill her."

Johnny Dempsey had entered a Salt Lake City hospital for treatment of a narcotic habit on May 16 and was discharged on June 4. Apparently, he wanted a reunification with Edna, but she refused.

Brothers Joe Dempsey, who managed the Barbara Hotel (owned by Jack), and Bernard Dempsey, who ran a gym owned by the champ (and had taken over from Johnny), declined to comment.

Jack's mother Cecelia/Cecilia Dempsey (maiden name Mary Pricilla Smoot) said Johnny would be buried in Mt. Olivet cemetery in Salt Lake City beside Bruce Dempsey, who had been murdered at age 18 on June 26, 1917. Remaining members of the family included Hiram/Hyrum Dempsey, Mrs. Florence Timmons, Mrs. Effie Clark, and Miss Elsie Dempsey, all of Salt Lake. Jack's mother lived at 974 East South Temple street in Salt Lake City.[538]

Although there was some initial concern that the incident might derail Dempsey-Sharkey, Dempsey did not cancel the upcoming fight.

Paul Gallico predicted that Dempsey would beat Sharkey, but then lose again to Tunney.[539]

Jack Farrell said the Dempsey he saw on July 4 was greatly improved over the slow-moving, wild-swinging, pepless Dempsey he saw the previous week. "But the bobbing, weaving, rip-tearing Dempsey of old has been transformed into a boxer, which to my mind is a grave error." He boxed 1 round each with 7 different sparring partners, most of the time blocking and countering. He worked with welter/middle Johnny Saxon, middleweight Dave Shade (106-18-53)(who in 1925 had lost a controversial split 15-round decision to Mickey Walker for the world

[538] *Brooklyn Daily Eagle, Salt Lake Tribune,* July 3, 1927; *Deseret News,* July 2, 1927.
[539] *New York Daily News,* July 4, 1927.

welterweight championship), 190+-pound Pietro Corri, middleweight Allentown Joe Gans (88-23-19), Eddie McMullen, Young Bill Beatty, and light heavy Martin Burke (47-25-7).

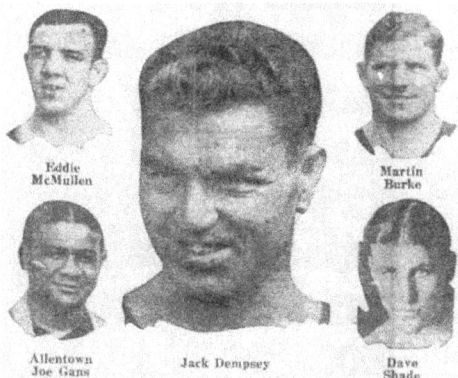

Eddie McMullen

Martin Burke

Allentown Joe Gans

Jack Dempsey

Dave Shade

On the 5th, Dempsey reverted back to his original style, and scored the first knockout of this training camp, knocking out Eddie McMullen with a murderous left hook to the mouth.

Former champ Jim Corbett said, "Gosh, this fellow Dempsey isn't anything at all like the broken-down decrepit gladiator I expected to see. That boy still has a lot of fighting left in him. He may have lost some of his speed, he may have lost a lot of other things, but he still retains his almighty wallop."

Jack also decked the speedy Joe Gans with a right hook. Gans said, "That man seems to be hitting harder every time I go in there with him." Even the elusive Dave Shade was on the receiving end all the way. Dempsey's timing and hitting were better on this day, moving in close to land short blows.

Dempsey sends McMullen through the ropes

On July 6, Dempsey knocked down light heavy Jack Hildebrand twice within 2 minutes with vicious shots under the heart, and then knocked him out flat on his back with a short left hook to the jaw. Pietro Corri went down on one knee under a withering barrage of body smashes. Johnny Saxon survived, and so did Dave Shade, though his knees sagged from some body blows. Joe Gans took several rib crushers. Martin Burke had a tough time as well, absorbing a terrific slugging. Jack's blocking was not very effective, but he was beginning to beat his man to the punch.[540]

In his workouts in Boston, 193 ¾-pound Jack Sharkey was pummeling his sparring partners, looking fast and strong. He already was very sharp, coming off the late May victory over Maloney.

On July 8, Dempsey boxed Johnny Saxon, Tillie Kid Herman, Pietro Corri, Martin Burke, Dave Shade, and Joe Gans. Dempsey floored Herman twice with short left hooks, and twice decked and knocked out cold Corri with the same devastating punch. Dave Shade landed many solid blows, one right even rocking Dempsey, but Jack eventually countered with some pile-driving body smashes.

---

[540] *New York Daily News,* July 5-7, 1927.

Jack Delaney observed the sparring, and said of Dempsey, "He is a little slow, but he is punching hard." Jack was being hit a fair amount.

Jack Farrell said Dempsey looked slow and soggy, but still punched hard.[541]

Martin Burke hits Dempsey   Dempsey jabs Dave Shade

Sharkey was very confident, training as if it were just another fight for him. Some even called him cocky. He was lighter and more jovial in his mood than Dempsey, who was more serious and business-like.

Paul Gallico said Sharkey would win if he could assimilate Dempsey's murderous left hooks to the body. If not, he would lose.[542]

World light heavyweight champion Jack Delaney, who had watched both Dempsey and Sharkey work out, said Dempsey was slow but not sluggish, and he still had a heavy punch. He had a knack for moving in close and hitting with short punches. However, his only defense was his offense. "His left hook is the most wicked weapon I have ever seen wielded by a fighter." Dempsey also liked to fire right counters to the head. He was more than a hollow shell. A man with dynamite in his fists always had a chance, even against a clever fellow like Sharkey. The one criticism of his camp was that there were too many little fellows. He needed bigger men to absorb his blows, rugged fellows who could stand the gaff, whom he could hit as hard as he wanted without having to stop work to pick them up off the floor. Jack was a sucker for a straight left, but it would require many fast, sharp lefts to stave off his bull-like rushes. "If Dempsey can weave under and away from Sharkey's left hand he is bound to make things hot for the Boston fighter at close range."

[541] New York Daily News, July 9, 10, 1927.
[542] New York Daily News, July 11, 1927.

On July 11, Marshall Hunt saw Dempsey spar 2 rounds each with Johnny Saxon, Marty Gallagher, and David Shade, part of a round with Chief Metoquah, a round with Italian Jack Herman, and 1 round with 190-pound black Larry Gaines (33-8-2). Dempsey was a sucker for lefts, both jabs and hooks. He was very hittable, but still could hit hard.

Jack Farrell said Sharkey would have to show more speed and aggressiveness before the writer would subscribe to contemporary opinion that the Shark would win with ease over Dempsey. Farrell noticed that Sharkey was paying little attention to infighting, specializing in long-range boxing, which was good if he could hold Dempsey off, but even the very clever Gibbons, who had one of the best lefts, could not keep the Manassa Mauler away. Sharkey was sure to take plenty of body punishment, and he had better be prepared to take it at close quarters. His greatest fault was he backed out of clinches with his hands down and his chin up, and he had better not do that with Dempsey. Still, Sharkey's wind was excellent, and he was as strong as a young heifer.[543]

Veterans, including Mike McTigue (who lost to Sharkey), Jack Britton, Tom Sharkey, and Philadelphia Jack O'Brien, all were predicting that Sharkey would beat Dempsey with relative ease. Dan Morgan said Sharkey was younger and faster than Dempsey. He could take a punch and had heart. He had beaten George Godfrey, "who is about the toughest heavyweight in the class," as well as Wills, McTigue, and Maloney. Benny Leonard said he leaned toward Sharkey because Dempsey was not himself.[544]

Jack Delaney said Dempsey used the rabbit punch and backhand punch on his sparring partners too frequently, for such punches were barred in New York. Dempsey's body movements and shifts were perfect, but his timing was off. He was wide open for any kind of left, but "I am not so sure that a flatfooted fighter like Sharkey can land often enough to offset his vicious counter attacks." Dempsey led with his right, which Delaney thought would leave him open to Sharkey's counters. "But they tell me Dempsey always led with his right so he must have some good reason for doing it."

Delaney said Sharkey was one of the cagiest and most resourceful heavyweights he ever saw. He had mixed results early in his career, but had developed into a very good fighter. It would take a mighty good man

---

[543] *New York Daily News*, July 12, 1927.
[544] *Brooklyn Citizen*, July 14, 1927.

to beat him now. He proved it by licking Maloney, Wills, McTigue, and Godfrey, "three exceptionally clever men." He had genuine nerve and grit. Sharkey wasn't the best gym performer, but he looked great in his biggest and toughest fights. His left was not as good as Dempsey's, and he was just as open for a punch as the ex-champ. Sharkey was working on his left hook, but Delaney felt that he should be jabbing more instead, for that punch landed on Dempsey quite often.

Dempsey decks Chief Metoquah

Paul Gallico said Dempsey looked twice as good as he did before the Tunney fight. On July 13, he knocked out 207-pound Chief Metoquah in 1 round. The Chief had hit Dempsey with three rights to the chin that would have felled most anyone, but it only spurred Dempsey on, and he began rushing with both fists flying to the chin and body. He battered the Chief dizzy until he collapsed. It was the only time that day that Jack really let himself go.

The Chief had 10- and 12-round newspaper decision victories over Chuck Wiggins and had gone the distance with Johnny Risko, so it made Dempsey's feat more impressive. "He may not be able to lick Tunney, but he's the second best heavyweight in the world. There'll be no boxing match at the stadium the night of the 21st. Dempsey wants to fight. Sharkey will hit him with everything he has, but he'll never hold him off."

Dempsey sparred with Gans and Larry Gaines as well. Jack Renault said of Dempsey, "He's the greatest looking wreck I ever looked at."

Most experts shook their heads at how wide open and hittable this version of Dempsey was. He got hit with everything. His sparring partners plastered him with punches, but they couldn't keep him off. "And when he gets in, he murders them. Dempsey takes anywhere from two to six punches to get in close, but when he lets them go, they mean something. The Dempsey I saw today is a well conditioned athlete who can punch like fury." He was just a slugger now, and that was his only game, but unlike before the Tunney fight, his condition was good.

Henry Farrell noted that because Tunney had failed to knock out Dempsey, he had not been accepted with the recognition that should be granted to a champion. Sharkey could exceed his prestige if he knocked out Dempsey. Sharkey was fast, with a left jab that was a "work of art." He had strong and sturdy legs, but did not move much, rolling and weaving for defense. He had better be careful, for although Dempsey was far from the Dempsey of old, he still had his punch. Some were concerned that Sharkey might slug with Dempsey, which could be a mistake.[545]

[545] *New York Daily News*, July 13, 14, 1927; *Brooklyn Daily Times*, July 14, 1927.

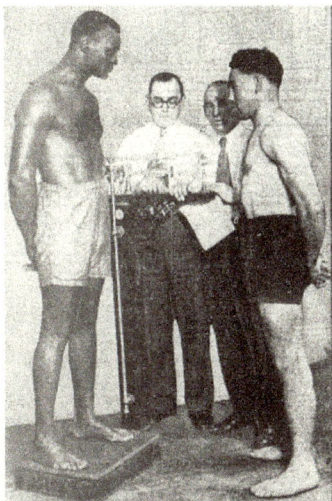

On July 13, 1927, in Brooklyn, before a crowd of 12,000 (or 15,000), 195-pound Paulino Uzcudun of Spain (28-2-1) knocked out 214 ½-pound Harry Wills in the 4th round. A right decked him the first time in the round, and a right and left hook sent him down for the count. The fight was filmed. The gate was $41,719.70. Most said Wills' career was over.[546]

Jimmy De Forest was picking Dempsey to beat Sharkey. Although Dempsey had gone far back, he still had enough to beat Sharkey. Jack Renault agreed, saying Sharkey was not so good at fighting backing up, and Dempsey would make him retreat.

Jack Delaney said Sharkey was not a good inside fighter, and he was very hittable, particularly up close. His wind was excellent though, breathing normally even after 10 rounds of work.

Sharkey and Delaney

Sharkey on the right, sparring

On the 14th, Dempsey pummeled his partners but did not try to knock them out. Yet, he still took solid, hard blows to the jaw. Jack Herman nailed him with a terrific right that made Jack's knees sag, but Herman paid for it. The Chief nailed Dempsey with a right too, but Jack hit him with a barrage of short body blows, a right under the heart doubling him up.

The New York Commission decided that Dempsey should wear purple and blue trunks, and Sharkey should wear red and black, so the fans could tell them apart more easily.

[546] *New York Daily News, Yonkers Herald, Brooklyn Daily Times,* July 14, 15, 1927. Uzcudun's record included: 1925 KO6 Phil Scott and KO3 Marcel Niles; 1926 D10 Franz Diener and W12 Erminio Spalla; and 1927 TKO7 Homer Smith and W10 Tom Heeney.

Leo Flynn requested that the commission mark their waistlines, so there could be no claim of a low blow in the tummy. "I ask this, due to Sharkey's claims of fouls in most of his fights."

Dempsey believed he could come back. At age 32, he wasn't old. He never had been knocked out, was strong, had good wind, a strong pair of hands, sturdy legs, and he had the punch. "I've never really been knocked out in my life. I never will." (Which suggests that he threw the first Flynn fight.) He was better mentally now that Leo Flynn was taking care of things and he didn't have sheriffs to dodge, jails waiting for him, or court suits to worry about. He was more motivated. He wasn't just in good physical condition, but in good *fighting* condition. "The old sock is back. I can tell when I whip my rights over on my sparring partners. I can feel the big ones curl up under the steam of my left hook. That gives a man all the confidence in the world." He never lost his strength, but his speed had been missing, and he felt that he was getting it back. Also, his ring sense had returned. He knew when to duck, bob, weave, counter, and block. "My ring sense is back because my head is cleared of all worries, financial and otherwise." He believed he could beat Sharkey and Tunney.

George Currie said when you met Dempsey and shook his hand, he had a heart-warming smile and a he-man grip. He was eager to say, "How do you do?" He might slap you on the back.

When one met Tunney, you got a handclasp from a book of etiquette, a society-talk-greeting with the formality of an exclusive politeness that was unmistakably Broadway.

When you met Jack Sharkey, you received a glare from a pair of hard, glinting gray eyes that looked like they were sizing you up and deciding where to strike, a wide smile with teeth made to bite nails, and a grip from a calloused palm that hurt. You quickly realized you were in the presence of one who thought like and wanted to be a very tough guy. He had a confidence about him.

Grantland Rice said even if Dempsey was 25% better than the version that met Tunney, he still would take a terrific mauling from Sharkey. "It will take a Dempsey close to his best days to win." It wasn't impossible. Jim Corbett put up a better fight against Jeffries at 34 than he put up against Fitzsimmons several years earlier. Sharkey was a first-class fighter, and no has-been was going to beat him. He had speed, skill, weight, courage, aggressiveness, youth, power, condition, and confidence. "Sharkey is a much better man than Carpentier or Firpo. He is a more dangerous party than Tom Gibbons, for he is more aggressive, faster, younger, and stronger." Sharkey was sharp, and had beaten several very good fighters over the past year in Wills, Godfrey, McTigue, and Maloney. Men like Wills and Godfrey regularly weighed 215 and 225 pounds. Sharkey proved that he could handle big, strong men. It would be some feat for Dempsey to beat him.[547]

[547] *New York Daily News, Brooklyn Daily Times, Elmira Star-Gazette, Brooklyn Daily Eagle, Glens Falls Post-Star*, July 15, 1927.

Jack Delaney said Sharkey needed to box Dempsey, for to fight him would be foolish. The ex-champ hit too hard to take a chance with him at close quarters. Dempsey had beaten every man who ever came to him. If Sharkey jabbed and moved and circled, it would be to his advantage.

The New York Commission ordered Sharkey to wear baby blue trunks, trimmed with bands of royal purple, and Dempsey to wear black trunks trimmed with red, which was a reversal of what the fighters originally had been told. The commission was living up to its reputation as being impetuous, fickle, and controlling.

Jack Sharkey meets Tom Sharkey

Dempsey's final sparring was on July 15. He pounded on Martin Burke, Tillie Kid Herman, Dave Shade, Jonny Saxon, and Marty Gallagher.

Paul Gallico said that mentally and physically, Dempsey was much better than before his last fight. "Sharkey may batter him down over a long stretch of rounds" but "that one punch on the chin won't stop Dempsey the way Wills was stopped."

One writer said Dempsey was the same as the one who lost to Tunney, differing only in that he went at his tasks with more enthusiasm and determination. He still was the mere remnant of the real Dempsey. The question would be whether this version could beat world-class top fighters like Sharkey and Tunney.[548]

When asked to compare Sharkey at age 24 with Dempsey at age 24, Tex Rickard said,

> Sharkey is faster than Dempsey was then, a better boxer and a more confident one. Dempsey was the harder hitter. Dempsey could hit harder with both hands than any man I ever saw. He was the most aggressive challenger I ever saw, but Sharkey isn't so far behind. ... Sharkey is aggressive, but he also knows how to defend himself. He mixes up attack and defense with about as good generalship as I ever saw. I won't say that the Sharkey of today could have whipped the Dempsey of Toledo. I won't even say that the Sharkey of today can whip the Dempsey of today, for any man who can hit as hard as Dempsey can hit is always dangerous and may win with a punch. But I will say that Dempsey must catch his man pretty quickly or he will run into a lot of trouble after the first few rounds.

548 New York Daily News, Rochester Democrat and Chronicle, July 16, 1927.

Rickard said Sharkey had extreme confidence. "When you talk to Sharkey he makes you believe he can whip anybody." Dempsey was a confident man, but never said much about it. Sharkey had a way of making you believe he could not be beaten. He really seemed to believe what he was saying. He begged to fight Dempsey. He told Tex that he wanted to beat both Dempsey and Tunney.

Rickard said he could not prognosticate the upcoming fight. Dempsey looked and seemed better physically and mentally than the previous year. His manager Flynn believed that Dempsey hit too hard for anyone, and Sharkey could not hit hard enough to keep him away. And yet, "I think Sharkey is one of the best fighters I ever saw." Rickard called Sharkey "one of the fastest big men I have ever seen, and he knows how to use his speed." The longer it went, the better Sharkey's chances would be. It was speed, youth, confidence, and skill against aggressiveness and the punch. Everyone anticipated a great fight, for the rush for tickets had beaten anything Tex ever saw, particularly for a non-title fight.[549]

Jack Delaney was predicting a 5th round knockout for Dempsey, but a decision for Sharkey if it went the 15-round limit. "I don't think Sharkey can hit hard enough to knock out a rugged fellow like Dempsey." Delaney did not think Sharkey could hit quite as hard as Tunney, so if Gene could not stop Dempsey, then Sharkey could not either. Dempsey's gameness was unquestioned. Sharkey was younger and faster, strong and courageous, with supreme confidence, regarding his foes with contempt, but Dempsey had the knockout punch to deck anyone he hit, particularly with his left. Both were hittable. "I expect Sharkey to outpunch Dempsey three to one, but if the former champion wings the ex-gob with one of those short left hooks in the first five rounds before it loses its effect, choose your nearest exit. Sharkey is lost in a clinch. That's where Dempsey will get in his best work." But Dempsey first would have to get past Sharkey's left to get inside. If Sharkey could weather the storm, and defend himself well enough, he had a chance to earn a decision. If Sharkey tried to slug it out, he'd likely get knocked out.

Jack Farrell said Sharkey had 32 fights, 10 victories by knockout, and had been stopped only once, three years ago at the start of his career. Dempsey had 68 fights, 48 wins by knockout, and he too had been stopped only once, by Jim Flynn. "That fight, as has since been proved beyond any question of doubt, was a phony one, Dempsey taking a dive…" When the fight was made, Sharkey was the 9 to 5 favorite, but the odds had grown tighter as a result of the reports of Dempsey's good/improved form in training.[550]

Dempsey said he was 100% better than he was against Tunney, and he did not think Sharkey was half as good as Tunney, though Jack admitted that he never had seen Sharkey fight. He heard that Sharkey was pretty cocksure of himself, which wasn't a bad trait for a fighter to have.

[549] *Binghamton Press*, July 16, 1927.
[550] *New York Daily News*, July 17, 1927.

Dempsey noted that his critics claimed he was easy to hit and could not box a lick. In response, Jack said he had a punch and the ability to take it, and that would be enough.[551]

The fans were picking Dempsey, but most experts were picking Sharkey.

Sharkey said, "I'll fight Dempsey any way that fellow wants to fight! And another thing, you can tell everybody that I'll knock that Dempsey flat!" He never felt better in his life. In beating 215- and 220-pounders in Wills and Godfrey, Sharkey had beaten men much bigger than Dempsey. He wasn't at all worried about his strength.[552]

Paul Gallico picked Dempsey. He might not be the old Dempsey, but he wasn't a hollow shell either. Most figured that Sharkey was the improving, hungry, young fighter who was coming into his own and going to use Dempsey as a stepping stone to a championship fight with Tunney, but likely it was Dempsey who would use Sharkey, the man who beat Wills, to get a rematch with Tunney. When Dempsey hit, it hurt. He connected no more than three solid blows against Tunney, and each time, he had Gene on the brink of ruin. "Sharkey is no Tunney in defense."

Jack Farrell believed Dempsey would win by knockout. "There isn't a human being in the world who can stand up under Dempsey's sledge-hammer body blows when he is right." Farrell was convinced that Dempsey was right for this fight. True, he was not as fast as he once was, but he still had a death-dealing punch and indomitable courage. His mental attitude was remarkable for one who was undertaking to disprove the adage, "they never come back." Sharkey was a good boxer, but could not punch hard enough to stop the granite-jawed warrior. He wasn't fast enough to keep Dempsey away. He might land three to one, but Dempsey's one would do far more damage. If Dempsey did not stop Sharkey, then Sharkey likely would win a decision.[553]

[551] *New York Daily News,* July 18, 1927.
[552] *New York Daily News,* July 19, 1927.
[553] *New York Daily News,* July 21, 1927.

CHAPTER 8

Past Meets Present to Determine Future

As of the day of the big fight, July 21, 1927, Jack Sharkey was the betting favorite to beat Jack Dempsey, allegedly at 5 to 7 odds. Marshall Hunt predicted that Sharkey would win within 6 rounds, for he was young and strong, his wind was good, and he hit hard. Grant Powers picked Dempsey in 8 rounds. Walter Ryan picked Sharkey inside of 10 rounds. He said Sharkey was the old-man-killer. Harry Schumacher picked Sharkey by decision. Al Copland said Sharkey would win in 5 rounds.[554]

The *Yonkers Statesman* said most New York papers were picking Sharkey to win, including John Kieran for the *Times*, Igoe for the *Morning World*, Frayne for the *American*, Jennings for the *Graphic*, Conway for the *Mirror*, Van Every for the *Evening World*, and Corum for the *Journal*.

Davis Walsh said it was a question of whether a man who floundered against Tunney was any better with another year tacked onto his life. Dempsey was as much as a 2 to 1 underdog. He had fought just 11 and a fraction total rounds since late 1923, while Sharkey had fought around 30 rounds in just the last 9 months. Sharkey was fresh, with only three years of wear, while Dempsey had been in the ring for 12 years.[555]

George Palmer predicted Sharkey would stop Dempsey in 10 rounds with his youth, cleverness, and punch.

Other experts picking Sharkey included: Tommy Loughran's manager Joe Smith, former Tunney manager Doc Bagley, Jimmy Maloney's manager Dan Carroll, Paulino Uzcudun, bantam Tony Canzoneri, bantam champ Bud Taylor, former lightweight champ Benny Leonard, lightweight Sid Terris, Jack Kearns, Tex O'Rourke, Eddie McMahon, Lou Brix, Philadelphia Jack O'Brien, Jack Curley, and writers - Frank Getty, United Press, Joe Williams and George Underwood, *New York Telegram*, Jack Conway, *New York Mirror*, W. O. McGeehan, *New York Herald-Tribune*, Hype Igoe, *New York Evening World*, and Tad, *New York Journal*.

Those picking Dempsey included: Tom O'Rourke, former Greb manager George Engel, light heavyweight champ Jack Delaney, lightweight Ruby Goldstein, former bantam champ Abe Goldstein, lightweight champ Sammy Mandell, Jack Renault, famous trainer Jimmy De Forest, former Dempsey manager Gene Normile, Tim Mara, Kid Herman, Mike McTigue, and Luis Firpo, and the writers - *Self Defense Magazine* editor Dale Gardner, Henry Farrell, United Press, Jimmy Wood, Damon Runyon, *New York American*, Paul Gallico and Jack Farrell, *New York Daily News*, and Sid Mercer, *New York Journal*.

[554] *New York Daily News*, July 21, 1927.
[555] *Yonkers Statesman*, July 21, 1927. Dempsey likely would earn a $250,000 guarantee.

Sharkey's manager Johnny Buckley said the Shark would knock out Dempsey within 10 rounds.

Sharkey said, "I'm going into this fight to knock out Jack Dempsey. But I'm not making the mistake of underrating Dempsey. There's nobody who has more respect for his punch than I have. Anyone who thinks he is gone is fooling himself."

Dempsey said, "In this fight game there are no easy marks. Sharkey is no sucker. I'm prepared to take anything and everything he has to offer. It's either he or I and I'm out to get him. I'm better mentally and physically now than I have been for several years and I'm confident of the outcome."

Gene Tunney said, "I don't care. I think I can beat either one of them."

Henry Farrell said Sharkey was the 9 to 5 favorite. There was a chance that Dempsey would knock him out because Sharkey was so cocky that he likely would swap punches and try to knock out Dempsey, and anyone who tried to outfight Dempsey was due to lose. He had to be outgeneraled.

Some said Dempsey's left arm was injured, but Farrell said such stories were exaggerated terribly. "There is nothing wrong with Dempsey's left arm, his heart or his legs."

In another interview, an extremely confident Sharkey said Dempsey was overrated and not the invincible man that he had made himself out to be in the eyes of his admirers. Dempsey was at his best against Willard 8 years ago, when Sharkey was only 16 years old. Over the years, Sharkey had come to realize that although Dempsey was a great fighter, he was not as great as most imagined.

To Sharkey, Dempsey's championship career had not proved much. Miske had a fatal illness, and Sharkey heard that Dempsey merely gave Billy a chance to get a fair purse. It took Dempsey 12 rounds to beat Brennan, a fair second rater, and Jack did not look too good. "The alibi in this case was that Dempsey had been none too careful of his living at that time and that his laxity had almost proven a costly lesson. A man who neglects his condition is not a great champion in my estimation." Most now admitted that Dempsey's fight with Carpentier was not a contest.

Sharkey actually defended Dempsey's performance against Gibbons. Dempsey's admirers had to do a lot of explaining for his failure to stop Tom, but "I do not find so much fault with Dempsey as some. Gibbons apparently fought not to win over Dempsey, but to stay the fifteen rounds. If a man is going to fight you that kind of a fight it is pretty hard to get him."

The Firpo fight was a thriller, yet Sharkey said it showed Dempsey to be lucky. He faced a big, heavy-footed fellow, one made to order for him. "And yet, Jack was lucky that he wasn't knocked out, and was also lucky he did not lose on a foul." Sharkey said if Firpo had been more experienced, and had more intelligent seconds, he possibly could have finished Dempsey.

Jack Sharkey and Leading Fighters He Has Met

Dempsey put up a poor exhibition with Tunney. "Although Tunney proved himself to be a better fighter that night than I had thought, still I have no profound respect for the present champion's abilities."

In summation, Sharkey said Dempsey was no superman. "Within less than a year I have defeated George Godfrey, Harry Wills, Mike McTigue, and Jimmy Maloney, and I think this more than measures up to what Dempsey has done in all the years that he held the title." Even if Dempsey recaptured his youth, "I still think my speed and skill will give me the edge over the Dempsey punch." Sharkey believed himself to be the best fighter Dempsey ever had met.

Grantland Rice said that based on form, Dempsey was sure to be outboxed. He was up against a much younger foe who in the years that Dempsey was idle and ruining himself, Sharkey obtained 33 fights. Sharkey had speed, an annoying left hand, youth, condition, stamina, skill, ring work under fire, the upward urge, and confidence. Dempsey's advantages were the superior wallop and possibly a tougher chin and greater ring spirit. Dempsey had proven more than once that he had a chin of granite. If Dempsey had enough fire and flame left to keep his charge going and keep crowding in as he slammed away, Sharkey's advantages might be melted under the flame of assault.

BIG GATES		
Dempsey vs.:		
Tunney	......	$2,000,000
Carpentier	....	$1,626,580
Firpo	....	$1,082,590
Sharkey	.....	$1,000,000?

PAST RECORDS		
DEMPSEY		SHARKEY
MATCHES		
78	ENGAGED IN	33
47	KNOCKOUTS	9
2	NO DECISIONS	2
4	DRAWS	0
11	WON DECISION	14
3	LOST DECISION	4
1	LOST BY K. O.	1
10	EXHIBITIONS	0
0	WON ON FOUL	3

BIG CROWDS		
Dempsey-Tunney	..	125,732
Dempsey-Carpentier		90,000
Dempsey-Firpo	...	85,500
Dempsey-Sharkey		,80,000?

HERE'S HOW THEY COMPARE!

DEMPSEY		SHARKEY
32	Age	24
194	Weight	191
6 ft. 1½ in.	Height	6 ft.
75 in	Reach	74 in.
17	Neck	17
14	Biceps	13½
12½	Chest (Normal)	41
45½	Chest (Exp.)	45
13½	Forearm	12
9	Wrist	7¾
35	Waist	34½
22	Thigh	22¾
15	Calf	13½
8½	Ankle	9

DEMPSEY will wear red trunks with black border.

SHARKEY will wear purple trunks with blue border.

"I'LL LICK THAT SHARKEY IN 2 PUNCHES!"—That's how confident Jack Dempsey is of the outcome of the battle. If he loses there'll be no alibis, no second comeback, he said, and will quit the game he loves forever. But right after that he set his fighting jaw and added: "But, put this down on the book. I'll lick Sharkey in just two punches."

WHAT IT'S ALL ABOUT
THE TIME—10 o'clock tonight.
THE PLACE—Yankee stadium, River ave. and 161st st.
THE BOYS—Jack Dempsey, Los Angeles, Cal., vs. Jack Sharkey, Boston, Mass.
THE DISTANCE—Fifteen rounds to a decision.
THE REST OF THE FARE—Five bouts of six rounds each.

"EVERYTHING JAKE WITH THIS JACK!"—And that's how Jack Sharkey voices his confidence. He goes farther, in fact, with the remark: "Staying away from my kids is a lot harder than stopping Dempsey will be."
—Stories, pp. 2, 15, 35, 57; other pic. p. 1.

The *Brooklyn Daily Times'* Jimmy Wood predicted Dempsey by knockout. Yes, some of his speed was gone, some of his snap and power was lacking, and the legs were not as limber or strong as they once were. Years of idleness had taken its toll. His coordination was coated with rust. Yet, he seemed to be better than he was for Tunney, and he still was an all-time great fighter.

Sharkey had a splendid chance, for everything was in his favor except punching power. He had youth, speed, skill, competitive fitness, all-around ability, and the mental edge. He beat Wills with youth and speed. "He is big and fast and clever. He has generalship and is ringwise. He is game. And he likes to fight." The flame and desire of ambition was burning brighter in Sharkey than the aging Dempsey.

Yet, Wood said Dempsey held the trump card – the knockout punch.

The *Brooklyn Daily Times* reported that its poll of 28 experts had it 14 for Dempsey and 14 for Sharkey.

Alan Gould said odds ranged from 8 to 5 to as high as 2 to 1, with Sharkey the favorite. Sharkey was backed strongly by a majority of newspaper critics and gamblers. Dempsey was the fans' choice.

The fight would be broadcast via radio stations WEAF and WJZ. Ticket prices were $27.50, $22, $16.50, $11, $7.70, $5.50, and $3.30. Ticket speculators/brokers made huge money, getting as much as $125 or even $200 for ringside seats which had a $27.50 face value.

Sharkey's mother, 55-year-old Agnes Zuckoschay of Binghamton, New York, and his father Benjamin, did not attend their son's fights or even listen on the radio. But their son always telegrammed them the result afterwards.

Sharkey's mother said there had been a misunderstanding about the correct spelling of their name. Sharkey himself gave the spelling as Cushoscakay. A family bank account was held in the name of Cuckosekay. The Binghamton city directory gave it as Cushosicky. Sharkey's mother declared it to be Zuckoschay.[556]

On Thursday July 21, 1927, at Yankee Stadium in the Bronx, River Ave. and 160th/161st streets, New York, 32-year-old 194 ½-pound Jack Dempsey fought 24-year-old 196-pound Jack Sharkey, their weights as taken by the commission at 1 p.m. on the day of the fight (instead of the previously scheduled 2 p.m., to avoid mobs). Dempsey weighed in first at the New Garden, in the Rangers' Hockey club locker-room, and then left. When Sharkey arrived, he asked, "Where's that mug? Has he arrived yet?" He was informed that Jack had arrived and departed.[557]

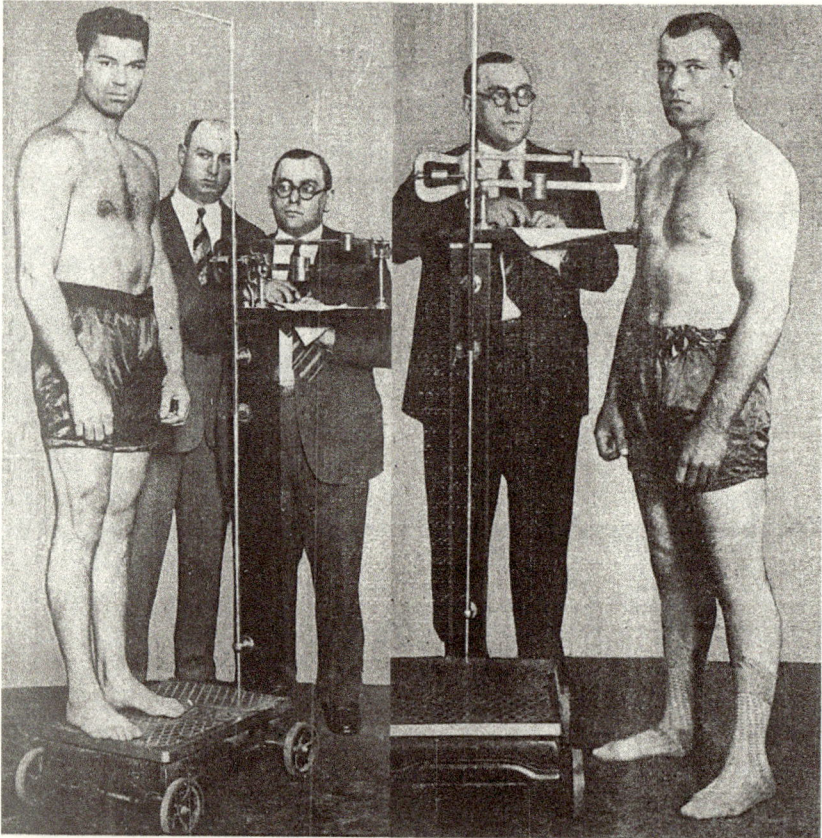

[556] Brooklyn Standard Union, Glens Falls Post-Star, Brooklyn Daily Times, Binghamton Press, July 21, 1927.
[557] The following fight description and analysis is taken not only from the films, but also the New York Daily News, Brooklyn Standard Union, Brooklyn Daily Eagle, New York Times, New York Sun, New York Evening Post, Binghamton Press, Yonkers Statesman, Glens falls Post-Star, Brooklyn Daily Times, Brooklyn Citizen, Allentown Morning Call, Yonkers Herald Elmira Star-Gazette, Yonkers Statesman, Binghamton Press, all July 22, 1927.

Empty Yankee Stadium with the ring at center

Supposedly, 80,000 to 83,000 people flocked to the big sold-out arena, generating an estimated $1.1 million gate. Rickard said he had 83,000 tickets printed.

The temperature that day was a low of 65 degrees and a high of 80 degrees.

Damon Runyon said almost the entire infield was filled-in with pine benches. Thousands of spectators brought binoculars and field glasses. All of Rickard's well-known millionaires were there. More interest was taken in the fight than any pugilistic attraction in the history of non-championship fights. "It is doubtful if Mr. Gene Tunney, the champion, could have drawn as much against Sharkey with the title at stake."

Mayors and judges held ringside seats. Millionaires rubbed elbows with ordinary folks. Huge incandescent lights illuminated the platform. Actors, actresses, opera stars, captains of industry, kings of finance, and leaders of the social world; all were there. Jack Kearns was present, as well as Hiram Bloomingdale, Irving Berlin, William Brady, Anthony Drexel Biddle, Bernard Gimbel, Benny Leonard, Mike McTigue, Franklin D. Roosevelt, Charles M. Schwab, W. L. Stribling, Gene Tunney, John Ringling, Tom Sharkey, New York Attorney General Albert Ottinger, Flo Ziegfeld, Tom Mix, and William Muldoon.

In one of the preliminary bouts, which started at about 8:15 p.m., James J. Braddock, 165 ½ pounds, in purple trunks, won a 6-round decision over George La Rocco, 179, having La Rocco down twice in the fight, in the 2nd and 4th rounds.

The big fight was narrated and broadcasted live via radio, which went to an estimated audience of 50 million, the largest radio audience on record up to that point, via a nationwide hook-up set up by the National Broadcasting Company and allied stations. The radio story was announced by the *New York Evening Telegram* and 25 other Scripps-Howard newspapers. It was recorded by the *New York Times'* shorthand writers of the State Law Reporting Company as the narrative came from the lips of Graham McNamee and Phillips Carlin at ringside.

At 9:31 p.m., Dempsey entered first, wearing a white wool sweater over his shoulders. Upon his entry into the ring, the crowd gave him as great an ovation as any man ever received. Radio: "Jack Dempsey looks more like Jack Dempsey than I have seen him in the past four years." He danced lightly in his corner, looking ready to go.

Robert Edgren and several papers said Dempsey wore red trunks with a black trim and belt, though the radio broadcast said Dempsey wore black trunks with red trim. Paul Gallico insisted that Dempsey's trunks were black with red trim, and subsequently questioned the eyesight of those who claimed otherwise. William Morris said Dempsey was attired in black with a red waistband. The commission had ordered him to wear black with red trim.

Sharkey entered wearing a robe to protect him from the wind, receiving a tremendous ovation as well. He raised his hand in the air to acknowledge the crowd.

Sharkey wore purple trunks with dark blue bands at the top and bottom (Edgren, Morris, and radio), though some said he wore blue trunks with purple trim.

Dempsey came over and shook his hand. Sharkey tried to give the ex-champ the glaring eye, but Jack simply turned around and returned to his corner.

Dempsey's seconds were Leo Flynn, Jerry 'the Greek' Luvadis, Billy Duffy, and Gus Wilson.

Sharkey had manager Johnny Buckley, Harry Kelly, and trainer Tony Palazola//Palazolo/Polozolo (sometimes spelled with two "zz"s).

Dempsey had his back turned away from ring center, talking to some friends, keeping up his little dance on his tip toes, warming up.

Both men seemed cool and collected.

They fought with 6-ounce gloves made by Jack "Everlast" Golomb, manufacturer of the mitts. They were made of special elk-skin leather, oak colored (some said red), filled with curled rabbit hair. It was a more pliable glove than the regulation horse-hide glove. The cords/laces were made of a special brand of gut, and had no metal ends.

Introduced from the ring were fighters Paulino Uzcudun, Tom Heeney, and Mickey Walker, world's middleweight champ. Walker entered the ring in a blue suit and a red, green, and white tie. He shook hands with Dempsey, and they smiled at one another.

Joe Humphries introduced world's champion Gene Tunney to the roars of the crowd, and he entered the ring and shook both fighters' hands in their respective corners. He had offered no opinion as to who would win. Tunney was announced as the man who would meet the winner.

Sharkey was quiet, with his eyes on Dempsey, whereas Dempsey hardly had glanced at Sharkey, seeming uninterested. Last year, Dempsey had looked at Tunney in a "rather odd sort of a way all the time."

The judges were Charles Mathison and Tom Flynn. Jack O'Sullivan refereed.

Joe Humphries introduced Dempsey first, and then Sharkey. Dempsey received the greater reception, being cheered lustily. Sharkey joined the applause for the ex-champ.

They went to ring center, posed for the still cameramen, shook hands, and received final instructions from Referee O'Sullivan. As they headed back to their corners, Sharkey's bathrobe was removed.

Dempsey was sunburned to a dark brown, while Sharkey was white skinned.

At 9:40 or 9:44 p.m., the fight started.

1st round

The films show that they immediately went to the inside and fought up close, clinching and roughing it. Clearly, Sharkey wanted to show his gameness right away, and perhaps take away Dempsey's momentum. Dempsey was far more active and aggressive, digging short body blows, ferociously keeping up the attack, consistently hitting the body with uppercuts. Sharkey was firing more intermittently, with a quick shot and then clinching and leaning in. He seemed to be looking to land a right uppercut. Dempsey was good at dipping to the side and ducking down low, crouching and weaving. Sharkey occasionally lashed out with the faster punches, of all kinds, primarily to the head, but Dempsey's defense held up fairly well.

The aggressive Dempsey just walked or slid right on in, dipping, and kept working and plugging away, primarily to the body, in consistent nonstop fashion, trying to wear him down, bulling in on Sharkey. He clearly was an excellent inside fighter. Sharkey didn't make much of an effort to get away, but when he did move, Dempsey quickly walked right to him, giving him no respite. The pace was quite torrid. Both fought hard, but Dempsey was calmly relentless.

Eventually though, Sharkey timed and nailed the advancing Dempsey with a brutal lead left uppercut. He followed up with a clean, jarring left hook, and then, sensing that he may have stunned Dempsey, followed with a fast jab - right - left uppercut combination, then right – left – right – left – right - left in constant succession on the attack, all landing and backing up a stunned Dempsey to the ropes.

Despite being momentarily staggered, Dempsey ducked down, went right back to the inside, fired a short right, clinched, and got close. After breaking, Dempsey advanced and fired a right uppercut to the body and kept working away with short inside blows. The iron-chinned Dempsey once again had shown his ability to recover quickly from big blows.

Sharkey fired a quick lead hook to the body. He also fired a fast lead right to the head that missed as Dempsey rolled away from it, and again they were in close, with Dempsey firing a grazing left hook to the head. Bell.

Overall, Sharkey came out aggressively, showed strength, and made little to no attempt to move away, and even when he did, Dempsey was right back on top of him again. Dempsey was very content and comfortable on the inside, crowding in, consistently digging nonstop, single, short body blows. Sharkey did better when he had a bit more punching room. Although Dempsey mostly outworked him, late in the round, Sharkey landed explosive, fast, clean left uppercuts/hooks, then followed up with combinations, jolting Dempsey and sending him back to the ropes, staggered and stunned. Dempsey quickly regained his balance and stepped inside to crowd Sharkey again. After the break, Dempsey seemed fine, going back on the attack.

The round was somewhat even and hard to score, depending on one's criteria. Sharkey landed the most significant, damaging succession of blows in an explosive rally, briefly hurting Dempsey, but the vast bulk of the work and landed blows were from Dempsey's consistent, workmanlike body attack. So, the round could be Dempsey's on volume and long-term investment-value of his work, but more Sharkey's on explosive, eye-catching, damaging rally.

Graham McNamee/Phillips Carlin, on the live radio broadcast, said they immediately rushed in and mixed it up. Dempsey drove in body blows. Sharkey hit the body and face. Dempsey ducked down low. They worked hard, shoulder to shoulder, close up. McNamee said, "So far the infighting has been in favor of Dempsey." Sharkey landed a right to the back of the head and again to the side of the head. Dempsey kept coming in and pounding the midsection. Sharkey landed a nice right to the jaw. Dempsey shook his head but came in and pounded the midsection. Sharkey was trying to work away so he could do a little outside, long-range fighting. Dempsey followed in, and, with his head laying right on Sharkey, pounded his middle. He pounded hard at the body and landed a right uppercut that sent Sharkey's head back. Sharkey ducked in close. After the referee separated them, Sharkey hit the body and they tied up. After breaking, Dempsey landed a hard left to the jaw.

Sharkey landed two lefts and two rights and had Dempsey "going." "It looked as though Dempsey were being knocked out. Sharkey puts over a left, a right, another left, another right. Dempsey is groggy for the moment and falls against the ropes, but he is back again."

A hard Dempsey left sent Sharkey back. Sharkey came back with a left and right to the jaw. "Dempsey is a little better at the infighting and Sharkey is better at boxing." Bell.

Phillips Carlin said,

Dempsey was quite groggy. It did not last long, but he took three hard lefts and three hard rights, and they did not do him a bit of good. ... Dempsey seems to go in with just one idea, to get in and rip those hard lefts and rights to Sharkey's body, and he already has Sharkey's midsection quite red from the effect of those ripping left and right hand blows. ... Dempsey looks great, but he is just a bit slow on the boxing.

Jack Farrell said Dempsey bore in and kept up a two-handed body attack even when Sharkey held. They exchanged vicious short punches. Dempsey kept hammering the body, even pinning Sharkey on the ropes. The confident Sharkey snapped his head back with a left. The Shark landed three left hooks to the jaw, and Dempsey was floundering around in a groggy condition. He held on for dear life. Dempsey's courage carried him through to the bell, but he was wobbly as he went to his corner. His cornermen, manager Leo Flynn, Jerry the Greek, Gus Wilson, and Billy Duffy, worked feverishly over Dempsey during the minute rest. It looked as if he would not last another round. Round even.

Paul Gallico said Dempsey plunged in, head down, and began to murder Sharkey in close. He piled in, leaning well in, firing murderous short hooks to the pit of the stomach. It looked as if the midsection attack would tear Sharkey in half, but suddenly the sailor unleashed a two-fisted swinging attack to the head that in a second had Dempsey reeling, groggy, and dizzy, bleeding from the eye. It looked like it might be all over and Dempsey soon would be knocked out. Sharkey evened the round by the spurt, and it looked as if Dempsey really was a tired old man.

Thomas Rice said Dempsey hammered Sharkey all around for two minutes. In the last minute, Sharkey came to life and hooked and uppercut Dempsey to such extent that some gave Sharkey the round or called it even.

Robert Edgren said the 1st round was even and full of action. Sharkey rushed him. Dempsey took the aggressive and soon Sharkey was holding and wrestling. Dempsey shook him with a fierce left hook on the jaw. Sharkey ran at Dempsey, landing left and right several times, forcing him back to the ropes. Dempsey seemed shaken, and the crowd groaned. It looked as if Dempsey's finish was in sight. But he came off the ropes fighting, and never stopped fighting.

Damon Runyon said Dempsey pumped both hands hard to Sharkey's body. They kept close together throughout the round. Dempsey was bulling in, hitting the body and occasionally trying to chuck him under the chin with an uppercut. Sharkey once pushed his own stomach out, unprotected, as if to say to Dempsey that he could not hurt him, but Dempsey kept doggedly pounding away. Suddenly Sharkey opened up with a fierce attack, rights and lefts, dazing the Mauler.

Wilbur Wood scored the round for Sharkey.

Joe Vila said that from the start, Dempsey's plan was apparent, which was a persistent drive for the body. Sharkey either blocked or clinched with fine skill. Suddenly, Sharkey turned loose with effective smashes, rendering Dempsey groggy, with a cut lip.

Despite the battering, Dempsey kept boring in, hitting the stomach and forcing the issue by sticking close. "Sharkey's blows were cleaner, and in fact many of them were harder. Yet, none of them had force enough to knock Dempsey off his feet. But he cut Dempsey's eye open and drew more blood from his mouth."

William Morris noted that Sharkey staggered Dempsey, pushing him across the ring. "Sharkey looked like a winner as he sat in his corner. Dempsey lacked his usual pep as he shuffled to his chair."

The official scoring for the 1st round was – Referee Jack O'Sullivan: Even; Judge Tom Flynn: Even; Judge Charles Mathison: Sharkey.

2nd round

The film version shows Sharkey starting with an attacking series of blows that sent Dempsey back, bouncing off the ropes, but no significant damage was done. Dempsey dug body shots with his left hook, then a left uppercut to the head. He came in with some rights to the body. Dempsey kept digging rights to the body, and left hooks to the body and head. When Sharkey backed away, Dempsey rapidly advanced, walking right in and firing a lead hook at the head and right to body to get inside. Dempsey snapped a short right uppercut to the jaw. Sharkey fired a quick, short left uppercut/hook and a right over the top, as well as a right to the body.

Sharkey would lash out intermittently with fast, hard blows, but took breaks in between. Dempsey was more consistent at getting in and plugging away with shorter but not as fast or flashy blows, but heavy and effective nevertheless; sometimes even snappy.

Sharkey snuck in a left hook to the body and a couple quick, short hooks to the head. Sharkey advanced with a series of blows as Dempsey dipped and stepped back, mostly making the blows miss or land in glancing fashion.

Back on the inside, Dempsey hooked away at the head and then dug short body blows. Dempsey advanced and dipped as Sharkey fired jabs and they clinched. They scuffled on the inside, with Dempsey landing his short body blows. Dempsey advanced, ducked under a left, and fired a right to the body and left hook to the head.

Dempsey kept working, until Sharkey lashed out in another furious attack, lefts and rights in rapid succession as Dempsey tried to duck and crowd in. Dempsey kept plugging away with his single snappy blows, body shots and hooks to the head. He kept forcing.

Sharkey appeared to be firing back more to try to keep him off or to get some respect. Dempsey seemed more relaxed and consistent, whereas Sharkey appeared to be intermittently lashing out with furious, speedy, explosive energy, followed by breaks or single shots.

Sharkey pumped in some jabs, but Dempsey bulled in again. Sharkey fired a snappy hook to the body. Dempsey dug his right uppercut to the body. Sharkey again hooked the body.

Overall, in this round, Dempsey landed solid inside body shots, hooks, and uppercuts, and clearly was the superior inside fighter. However, when the gritty Sharkey had some punching room, he was able to land on Dempsey, stepping in with quick straight combinations that sent the ex-champ back momentarily. Sharkey occasionally fired a quick solid blow or series of blows. However, overall, Dempsey was controlling and dictating, forcing his way in, working on the inside consistently with body blows, and Sharkey really did not make much of an effort either to move or clinch that tightly. Some said Sharkey cut open a gash over Dempsey's right eye in this round. Dempsey's round.

On the radio, McNamee/Carlin said Sharkey jabbed and rushed Dempsey across the ring. Dempsey hit the body and kidneys. Dempsey chased him across the ring and hit the body. Clinch and break. As they broke, Dempsey landed a short right to the face. Sharkey landed a terrifically hard right on the side of Dempsey's head. Dempsey got in close and drove lefts to the body. Dempsey came in with head down and ripped a right to the side of Sharkey's head. "Dempsey has been a bit more aggressive than Sharkey so far." In and out of a clinch. Sharkey landed a hard left and two short rights to side of the face. Dempsey landed two good short left hooks to the face. A Sharkey left sent Dempsey's head back. Sharkey's jabs had a "lot of stuff behind them, whereas Dempsey's left hooks are terrific."

They again were laying on each other's shoulders, pummeling at the body. Sharkey bounded back against the ropes and took a hard blow. Sharkey pounded Dempsey's head with three rights and three lefts. Dempsey came back with a left jab and left hook. They were up and at each other again. Dempsey pushed Sharkey across the ring and landed a right uppercut. Dempsey landed a left to the side of the jaw, and another left. Sharkey came back with two lefts. Dempsey danced and moved in.

After the round, Carlin said, "I have been to quite a few prizefights in my life, but this one has got us all sitting on the edge of our chair. The seconds are rubbing the two fighters and fixing their noses, giving them a little ammonia or something of that kind."

Jack Farrell said Sharkey rushed Dempsey across the ring, landing right and left. Dempsey pinned Sharkey on the ropes with lefts to the body. Sharkey complained that Dempsey was hitting low. Sharkey again jarred Dempsey with a left hook to the head. They clinched. Dempsey was not his old weaving self, and tried to box with Sharkey. Sharkey again unleashed a two-handed attack and Jack wobbled under the punches. Sharkey played a steady tattoo of lefts on Dempsey's face without a comeback. Dempsey socked a left to Sharkey's midriff and started a glorious rally. Sharkey appeared to be hurt and he clinched. Dempsey socked a left to the jaw and right to the body but Sharkey straightened him up with lefts to the head. Blood was coming from Sharkey's mouth, and Dempsey had a small cut below his right eye.

Dempsey's round by a narrow margin, having recovered quickly from the prior round's barrage he endured. Dempsey had his right eye cut during a brisk exchange at close quarters, but it meant nothing. He never stopped fighting.

Gallico said the Dempsey that came out was a ripping, tearing Dempsey who got his left hook working, rocked Sharkey to his heels, and made him break ground. Dempsey followed him to the ropes, where he hurled in body blows. Sharkey had to fight back. He cut loose with his two-fisted attack to the head, driving Dempsey back again. But he simply could not keep him off. The ex-champ won the round, although he came to his corner bleeding from the mouth and with a slight cut under the right eye.

Rice said Dempsey had all the best of the round except for two flashes in which Sharkey landed lefts and rights to the head.

Edgren said Dempsey took the round. There was sting in his blows. One fast overhand left caused Sharkey to grit his teeth and back away. He held more, and Dempsey worked on his body. When the blows came too fast at close quarters, Sharkey crossed his arms just above the belt and pushed the blows down a few inches. There were cries of foul, but nothing deterred the fury of the fight. Dempsey was rushing him against the ropes and into corners, trying to beat him down by the constant attrition of an endless body pounding. Sharkey was feeling those blows. His confident smile was gone.

Runyon said Sharkey came bounding out on the attack, opening a slight cut under Dempsey's right eye with a left jab, and following with a volley of rights and lefts to the chin. Dempsey closed in, driving for the body. One punch seemed to double up Sharkey up a bit, but he quickly recovered and immediately smacked away at Dempsey, seeming to have no fear of his punches.

Wood scored the round even.

Vila said Dempsey was flatfooted and floundered around awkwardly, in striking comparison with his magnificent form of earlier years.

Morris noted that Sharkey cut Dempsey under the left eye and battered his head with rights in close. Dempsey landed a hard left, the noise of which was heard far from the ring, but it hit the glove. "Dempsey was fighting, but his efforts were taking the toll on his rusty physique. Wilson was rubbing the ex-champ's legs in his corner."

Official scores were – O'Sullivan: Even; Flynn: Sharkey; Mathison: Dempsey.

3rd round

On the films, Dempsey kept dipping and eluding, and sliding back on occasion. Sharkey wasn't throwing much. Dempsey fired his usual right uppercut to the body and left hook to the head. Sharkey stepped away and jabbed. Dempsey advanced, and on the inside, fired a lead left hook. He kept digging rights to the body. Dempsey ducked a right. He dipped and jabbed his way in, then threw a wide right to the body. Sharkey jabbed and dug a right to the body of his own. Dempsey advanced with a right to the body and left hook to the head in rapid succession.

Sharkey landed a lead right and a couple left uppercuts, then a lead hook to the body, a right uppercut to the jaw, and a subsequent left uppercut to the jaw.

Dempsey went back to hooking the body. Sharkey mostly missed the few jabs he threw. Sharkey landed a hook and Dempsey came back with a hook of his own. They mauled a bit in the clinches, each firing away.

Finally, Sharkey really got going with another powerful spurt, which included a fusillade of right uppercuts and left hooks, to the body and head, and a powerful right which snapped Dempsey's head.

However, Dempsey went right back to the inside again and kept digging body blows and a sharp hook to the head. Sharkey countered with some light head blows, and Dempsey kept plugging away at the body, nailing him with a right and left hook to the body.

Sharkey either was crouching over from the force of the body blows or he was ducking, and his foot slipped a bit from the moisture in the corner as he stepped back, and he went down to the canvas in the corner. Dempsey may have slightly put his weight on top of Sharkey's head. The impact of the blows may have had something to do with it, but it seemed to be more of a slip than anything. The referee immediately got between them, wiped Sharkey's gloves when he rose, and the bell rang. No count was given.

The round was similar to the first two in that Dempsey controlled the style and tempo. He was doing the better work on the inside with body shots and hooks, working more consistently. He would move his head and step in on Sharkey, undeterred by outside punches. However, Sharkey occasionally lashed out and landed, keeping it competitive and entertaining.

Late in the round, Sharkey got going with some right uppercuts, a hook, and a right that badly snapped Dempsey's head. However, the ex-champion was not hurt, and kept bulling in on Sharkey. Sharkey was landing some flashy, eye-catching punches, but overall, Dempsey was in control. Sharkey appeared to be more of a burst fighter, waiting for moments of opportunity, testing Dempsey with flashes of explosive offense, and then he would reload, defend, clinch, and smother as Dempsey tried to plug away. Sharkey's punches were snappier, more obvious, and cleaner, but Dempsey's punches were more subtle, compact, closer in, and consistent. Fairly even round. Take what you like.

McNamee/Carlin said they dashed out, danced around, and Dempsey drove a left to the midsection. They sparred, Sharkey landed a left to the body and left-right. Sharkey landed another left to the face, and then Dempsey landed a 1-2 to the body. Dempsey drove a left to the face. He landed a right to the body and left to the jaw. He also landed a left to the jaw, and a terrific left that drove Sharkey halfway around. Sharkey came back with a right to the midsection. He also landed a left. Dempsey landed another left jab and Sharkey landed right and left to the body.

Dempsey came in fast. Sharkey caught him with a left on the nose. Clinch. Sharkey landed a hard left to the side of the head, and while clinched, a hard left uppercut that knocked the ex-champ's head back. After another clinch and break, Sharkey landed a right and left to the sides of Dempsey's face. Dempsey came in and drove both hands to the body, and then right to the face. Dempsey constantly was trying to weave in more closely, to get in tight.

Sharkey landed two long lefts and a right, and also pummeled Dempsey's body with his left. Dempsey seemed tired, but kept weaving in, driving his right to the body and another to the side of the face. The round was a little bit slower.

Sharkey drove in body blows, and then right and left to the face, straightening up Dempsey. "We thought he was going down for a moment, but he came back and drove his left into a lot of gloves and elbows." Sharkey was improving his guard, blocking many of Dempsey's body hooks.

Sharkey's foot slipped out of the ring and he went down partially, but it was not a knockdown, though just before he slipped Dempsey landed a couple lefts and two rights. Dempsey grabbed him and helped him to rise (just as he often did with his sparring partners). Neither one looked in any way particularly ruffled.

Farrell said Sharkey came out confidently. He drove a left to the stomach and nailed Dempsey with a left hook to the head. Sharkey took the offensive with right and left to the head, making Dempsey cover. Dempsey hooked his left to the jaw twice and they clinched. Dempsey tore in and hooked Sharkey's body with right and left. Dempsey blocked down a left lead and then sent a right to the body. They mauled and hauled in a clinch. Dempsey was shuffling and appeared a trifle unsteady on his pins. Dempsey kept reaching with his left but Sharkey kept backing away. Dempsey pinned Sharkey on the ropes and pelted him with rights to the head and lefts to the body. Dempsey threw another left and right, but Sharkey walked in with left and right to the head, which straightened up the ex-champ. Sharkey slipped in his own corner and Dempsey nailed him with a left to the body that sank in deep as he slipped down to one knee just at the bell, but apparently from the slippery, water-soaked surface and not from the force of the punch. Round even.

Gallico said Dempsey again piled in close, always working short jolts to the body. Sharkey had his usual one flurry of fighting in which he rocked Dempsey, but each time, the tired old man piled back in again. Just before the end of the round, Dempsey sank his left wrist deep into the pit of Sharkey's stomach, and Sharkey went down on one knee in his corner. It clearly was Dempsey's round.

Rice said it was all close work, and just at the bell Sharkey went down on one knee in his corner, partly from a body punch and partly from slipping.

Edgren said at the round's conclusion, Dempsey rushed, Sharkey slipped to his knees, and just then the bell rang. Dempsey's round.

Runyon said Sharkey began taking his time, waiting on Dempsey's rushes to smother him in the clinches, then punch him with short, sharp jolts. Dempsey tried to bob and weave in his old style, but got caught with many a smack, while there seemed to be little behind his own punches. Just before the bell, Sharkey slipped and fell.

Wood said Dempsey landed low quite often, but Sharkey made no complaint.

Vila said Sharkey outwitted and outboxed him, though Dempsey kept going after his breadbasket with hammerlike wallops. Many were blocked or pushed down, or avoided with footwork. At long range, Sharkey was the master, pouring in lightning lefts to the face. Dempsey looked clumsy, yet maintained his strength. In view of what he took, Dempsey's endurance was surprising.

Morris said Dempsey sent Sharkey's head back with a short left hook. Sharkey smothered a lot of his punches. The Shark ripped left uppercuts to Dempsey's jaw. Dempsey hit the stomach, and Sharkey apparently made no effort to defend himself. The Shark endeavored to keep him off with left jabs, but Dempsey refused to keep away. Yet, his punches seemed to have no sting. Dempsey missed a vicious left, and excitement was in the air as Sharkey went down in his own corner, going over the edge of the ring. A second later, he got his foot back in and the bell rang.

Official scoring – O'Sullivan: Dempsey; Flynn: Sharkey; Mathison: Dempsey.

Daily News: **Sharkey partially slips, partially knocked down in the 3rd. Dempsey helps him up.**

4th round

The films show that Dempsey circled, dipped, and played defense as Sharkey threw some blows. Sharkey started off the round being pretty active. Dempsey hit the body with rights, and he also landed a right uppercut to the jaw. He kept plugging away with close-in blows. Sharkey fired at the head, but Dempsey countered to the body. They were mixing it up more, back and forth, Sharkey mostly trying to hit the head, and

Dempsey mostly attacking the body. Sharkey was punching, moving a bit, then punching again. Dempsey kept boring in.

Sharkey was content to work and fire on the inside as well. They were going at it at a very good pace, both men hitting the body and head. Sharkey was working more consistently than he had in prior rounds. Both were landing some good blows. At one point, when he saw Sharkey trying to time him on the way in, Dempsey turned and stepped to the side.

Dempsey maintained his poise. He had a calmer quality about him in the heat of battle. He seemed to pick and place his punches just a bit better. He also seemed more comfortable with the nonstop grinding style and action of the fight. Sharkey appeared to be forcing himself to get going more. The round featured lots of back-and-forth exchanging.

Overall, Sharkey was more active in this round, realizing that he needed to be more consistent with his punches, and also that he needed more punching room. He moved his feet just enough to gain the bit of space he required to get off. Yet, he also was perfectly content to work on the inside as well. However, Sharkey did not land solidly all that often, for Dempsey moved his head well, and even when Sharkey did land, Dempsey did not appear to be bothered, continually moving forward and applying pressure, employing the same type of consistent, nearly nonstop attack that he had been utilizing, particularly to the body. There was more overall action and exchanging on both of their parts, but fewer of the eye-catching, explosive moments, which was somewhat ironic given that Sharkey was so much busier in this round than he had been. Even, or slight Dempsey round.

McNamee/Carlin said both came out fast. Sharkey landed jabs, and a right. Dempsey landed five lefts to the body and a right to the face. He then pounded the midsection with both hands. Sharkey landed a right and left to the jaw. Dempsey came in and drove a left to the face, and Sharkey retaliated with left and right to the face.

Dempsey was working almost constantly to the body, while Sharkey paid attention to the head. Sharkey drove in rights and lefts to the face, short but hard blows. Dempsey drove a hard left to the ear. Sharkey came back with a right, and then a left. Dempsey landed a beautiful right that twisted the Shark's head around, and Sharkey covered up. Dempsey landed rights to the body. Dempsey constantly was working to get in under Sharkey and play for the body. Sharkey drove a right to the jaw. Dempsey scored a hard right to the jaw, then left at close quarters, and another. Sharkey landed a right. Dempsey landed a couple short lefts to the head. He was in close. Both worked the body, landing many blows. They were close all the time. Dempsey was landing hard blows to the jaw when he came up out of the clinches. It was a nice round.

Summarizing, Carlin said that in the 1st round, Dempsey landed to the midsection time and again without difficulty. In the 2nd, Sharkey learned how to keep away from some of the lefts. In the 3rd round, he got even better, but Dempsey came back (in the 4th?) and pummeled him pretty hard with short, vicious left hooks.

Farrell said Sharkey remained confident. Dempsey closed in and battered Sharkey's stomach with rights and lefts. Sharkey backed away under the attack. Dempsey kept crowding, but Sharkey wiggled out of it. Dempsey came out of a clinch with his right eye cut. Sharkey kept jolting Dempsey with lefts and rights to the head, but the ex-champ fought back gamely. Sharkey kept mauling Dempsey. Dempsey crowded Sharkey into neutral corner, a vicious right to the heart forcing the Shark to cover up. Sharkey missed right and left and was trying to box as Dempsey clipped him with a right to the jaw. Sharkey tried to hold while Dempsey sent in a murderous body attack. Dempsey was fighting furiously at the bell. Dempsey's round.

Farrell also said that Sharkey was missing, while Dempsey again confined his attack to the body and gave Sharkey a terrible two-handed pasting. Sharkey held on at every opportunity, and it was apparent that he was slowing up from his relentless foeman's withering bombardment. Nevertheless, Sharkey played a steady tattoo of lefts on Dempsey's bad eye, and Jack's face was a gory smear.

Gallico said Dempsey gave Sharkey fits with his body attack, and he cut loose with a left hook that could have been heard clear to the subway tracks. It rocked and staggered Sharkey and sent him reeling back to hold on for dear life. But Sharkey was by no means through. He was fighting a backpedaling fight, but at the same time was craftily cutting away at Dempsey's head. Dempsey won the round but went back to his corner with a badly cut right eye. He was breathing heavily.

Rice said Sharkey was a punching bag, because he made no effort to keep himself in the clear. He did exactly what Dempsey wanted. Sharkey showed his state of mind when he started an uppercut but held it back, fearful of a Dempsey comeback.

Edgren said Sharkey held him even. Near the end of the round, which was a mixing melee from start to finish, Sharkey was trying to stand up to Dempsey's rushes. He crossed his arms to guard, and pushed against Dempsey as hard as he could, but every time he was forced back.

Runyon said Dempsey came out lumbering; Sharkey coolly, like a man biding his time. Dempsey walked into him, chugging both hands to the body. Sharkey held, but the moment Dempsey raised his bowed head, Sharkey banged him hard on the chin. Blood flowed freely from the cut under Dempsey's eye, and soon his face was masked with red. Dempsey kept hitting the midsection, but the sailor did not seem to be bothered much. The crowd screeched, "Come on, Jack," but one could not tell which Jack they meant. A hard left to the chin jolted Dempsey's head back. They bulled together, fighting desperately in the clinches. Just before the bell, Dempsey landed a sharp left hook to the chin. Dempsey's round.

Wood said the round was Dempsey's by a shade, but he was tired and wobbly.

Vila said Dempsey had a palpable advantage, the result of persistent assaults, mostly to the body.

Morris said Sharkey was attempting to box. Dempsey kept going in and would not be sent back, no matter what blow hit him. "He was not doing much damage with punches to the stomach, but his left hook drives to Sharkey's head seem to have had plenty of snap to them. Dempsey took his chair with blood flowing from his cut eye."

Official scoring – O'Sullivan: Dempsey; Flynn: Sharkey; Mathison: Even.

5th round

The films showed Sharkey to be very active with his jab, moving about more, trying to time and pepper Dempsey on the way in and then clinch when he got close. He spun away to get to long range again. The Shark attacked, but also backed away, trying not to remain on the inside as often or as long as he had before.

Dempsey kept pressuring, putting in body blows when he could, firing the occasional hook to the head, dipping and rolling his head. Sharkey fired a couple jabs, moved away, threw a lead left uppercut on the dipping Dempsey, then spun away again. Sharkey was jabbing more in this round, firing, clinching or smothering, and then getting back out again. Dempsey was the same methodical pressuring man, though perhaps with a bit less activity and pressure, possibly owing to Sharkey's alteration in style, or, perhaps Dempsey's slowing his attack allowed Sharkey to move a bit more.

Sharkey kept jabbing away, smothering, then moving off to the side again. He was trying to utilize more of a Tunney style. He snuck in a right uppercut. Dempsey just kept plugging away at the body, determined to wear him down over time. Sharkey's sliding back, pushing off, and maintaining more room and distance appeared to be helping him. Sharkey landed another lead right uppercut, but Dempsey instantly plugged away at the body and fired a right uppercut of his own. Sharkey pushed him away. Sharkey fired and moved, or fired, clinched and smothered, then pushed off.

Both did good work early in the round, but the second half of the round was owned by Sharkey, who threw and landed more from the outside, and was more effective at smothering Dempsey's inside attack than previously had been the case. Dempsey still was doing his thing, but Sharkey's adjustments and generalship made the round more to his liking. He was more in control, but Dempsey clearly was not fighting to win any particular round, but to wear down Sharkey gradually with pressure and body punching, no matter what Sharkey did in the way of points. Dempsey was concerned with long-term effectiveness. It was Sharkey's round though.

On the radio, McNamee said both came out fast again. Dempsey barely caught him with a right. Sharkey landed some rights, drove in his left twice, and then his right a couple more times. Dempsey landed a short left to the face. Sharkey landed two short lefts to the face. Dempsey was working at the midsection again, landing half of his blows. Dempsey really was the aggressor thus far. He landed a right to the body, and he kept following Sharkey. Sharkey landed a hard left, and again his jab. He had an awfully mean left jab, and Dempsey had an awfully mean left hook. Both were tired, locked in the middle of the ring.

Dempsey was bobbing and weaving, trying to get in. Sharkey was trying to keep him off with his left. Close together, Dempsey slid over his back and pummeled his body with short blows. Sharkey again landed his left. The infighting was considerably slower than previously. Both were tired. Sharkey landed a hard left and hard right to the head. Dempsey still came in though, boring in all the time, driving hard lefts to the body. He never stopped for a moment. He was right after him all the time. Generally, the man who backed up was Sharkey. Dempsey caught a hard left on the way in but sent one back in return, both to the face. Dempsey landed a beautiful short left hook to the jaw, and another, and a right hook, all of them short blows in close. Sharkey jabbed him twice. End of round.

Carlin said they were boxing hard, and it was a pretty good bout. "This is nothing like Philadelphia."

Farrell said Sharkey clearly outboxed Dempsey to win the round, and staggered him once again with lefts to the head and short snappy right uppercuts. Dempsey tried to weave out of the way of these blows, but Sharkey never stopped firing in his bold attempt to bring him down.

Gallico said Sharkey started to look like Tunney. He waited for Dempsey to come to him, and began picking at his head as he moved in. Sharkey used short blows, and again the boys began to kiss Dempsey good-bye. He still crowded in but came out of the round a gory sight. It was Sharkey's round by a good margin.

Rice said Sharkey did more boxing, the most since the 3rd, but was lacking in consistency. He would hit over Dempsey's guard smartly and effectively with either hand, but then would allow Dempsey to crowd and hammer him.

Edgren said Dempsey looked as if he was taking all the punishment. His face was cut. Still, he forced the fighting and would not be denied. Sometimes he was slow or tired for a moment, but then he would recover and pick up speed again. Sharkey did not look tired at all, and was unmarked, but he was worried, and Dempsey was not.

Runyon said Dempsey came out with his curious little circle, then took a Sharkey left hook to the chin as he walked in trying a right. Sharkey fired his own body hook. Dempsey seemed tired as he walked into clinches, but ducked a right and swung like a real boxer.

Wood said it was Sharkey's round. Dempsey was a wreck of a once-great fighter. O'Sullivan finally cautioned Dempsey to keep his punches up.

Vila said Dempsey was slow, flatfooted, and puzzled. Sharkey let him force the fighting, but continually jabbed him in the face until the former champ's right eye was swollen and bleeding. Sharkey seemed to have the endurance to fight all night. Dempsey appeared to be losing strength and vitality. He took so many punches to the face that spectators expected him to drop at any moment. Yet, he took his medicine with remarkable gameness.

Morris said Sharkey sent Dempsey's head back with a short left uppercut. Dempsey kept weaving and boring in, but doing no damage, though neither was Sharkey. Dempsey walked in and worked the body. Sharkey jolted his head back with short left and right hooks. Dempsey walked in again, and Sharkey met him with jabs and right uppercuts. Dempsey unleashed a hard left hook to the head. "At the bell Sharkey took his corner fresh and at ease while Dempsey's face was covered with blood around both eyes."

The judges' scores were – O'Sullivan: Sharkey; Flynn: Dempsey; Mathison: Sharkey.

6th round

On the films, Sharkey was firing away, but finding it difficult to land often or cleanly, for Dempsey moved his head well. However, Sharkey was being active, while Dempsey mostly was playing defense early in the round. Dempsey still was pressuring, but in a milder way, not as rapidly or consistently. He was not throwing as much or as often, and was stepping away or angling off to the side more before stepping in, as if he was taking somewhat of a break, letting Sharkey work. When Dempsey got close, he would work, but he wasn't getting in tight quite as much.

Sharkey nailed him with a good right uppercut, and repeated the blow, as well as a sharp hook, jab, and right. Whenever he did land a clean shot, Sharkey was good at following up with a succession of blows. In the clinch, Dempsey launched a heavy hook. He peppered the body again, but Sharkey was clinching and smothering better than he did earlier.

Dempsey got in again and ripped a couple right uppercuts to the body. Sharkey hooked, but Dempsey kept plugging away at the body, followed by a left hook to the head. Dempsey was picking up his offense, as Sharkey tried to fire, smother, and deter his momentum. Sharkey landed a sharp, clean left jab. Dempsey simply went back to plugging away at the body. Just after the bell, Dempsey snuck in a right hook and Sharkey responded in kind.

In summary, in this round, Dempsey kept applying pressure, mostly throwing body shots, but it was clear at this point that his pace had fallen off a bit, and he was less relentless, both with his moving in and his throwing, perhaps taking a break. Sharkey seemed more comfortable, landed the cleaner shots, and his offensive consistency had improved. Still, Dempsey was making him work at a fairly fast clip. Each exchanged light rights to the chin after the bell. Sharkey's round, or even.

McNamee/Carlin's version said they circled one another. Dempsey landed a long left. Sharkey landed a couple light lefts. Sharkey straightened him up with a short right uppercut. Clinch and break. Sharkey was missing rights. Dempsey was trying to come in. He finally got in and drove a couple body blows with both hands. Sharkey landed a left and right to the face. Sharkey landed a hard right uppercut to the jaw. Sharkey was pretty good at coming in under Dempsey. They were shoulder to shoulder, but not much was going on. Sharkey landed a light left, right, and left.

The action had slowed, and they were wandering around the ring. They went into a half clinch, and Dempsey landed a hard left on the top of the head. He constantly was boring in. Sharkey landed the hardest blow of the fight, shaking Dempsey very badly with a left uppercut to the jaw. Yet, Dempsey came back and landed a number of body blows at close quarters. He was leaning his head up against Sharkey's chest as he strove to beat up the body.

Sharkey certainly had been taking a fair amount of body punishment. Dempsey kept pounding the midsection. After a break, Sharkey landed a short left to the face, but Dempsey constantly bore in, trying for a knockout. Both swung rights and lefts, both landing. Dempsey landed a long left that was a "pippin," and Sharkey retaliated with a right to the face. Sharkey appeared to be in better shape than Dempsey.

After the bell rang, Dempsey struck Sharkey once, and Sharkey hit Dempsey twice, to show that he did not care to be hit after the bell. The crowd booed.

Farrell's version said both missed several blows. Dempsey crowded Sharkey into his own corner and hooked both hands to the body. In a clinch, Dempsey hooked the kidneys. Dempsey weaved and followed Sharkey as the latter retreated around the ring.

Sharkey shook up Dempsey with a right uppercut. Dempsey appeared to be hurt, clinching. However, Dempsey punished Sharkey severely with rights to the stomach in close. Dempsey backed Sharkey all over the ring, bobbing and weaving under his left leads and stepping away from the right uppercuts. Dempsey shook up Sharkey with a left hook and spun him around with a right to the jaw.

After the bell, Dempsey kept sending in lefts to the jaw, and Sharkey turned and repaid the compliment. The crowd booed. Dempsey's round.

Gallico said Sharkey went out to win and stop Dempsey, and had the better of the opening, staggering Dempsey again with his looping right to the ear. But Dempsey quit his puffing, threw off his years, and with the speed that they said he no longer had, and the legs they said would fail him, moved in, weaving and swaying, and cut loose a two-handed attack to the head and body that made Sharkey break ground and eventually return to his corner dizzy, breathing hard, with a slightly swollen eye. "I think that round took the heart out of Sharkey." Dempsey was no shell, but a ripping, dangerous man, still able to hit and go the route. It began to look as though Dempsey was going to hammer out a win, possibly by decision.

Rice said Sharkey in one flash smashed Dempsey with two lefts and two rights to the head, and the punches certainly bothered Dempsey, but it always was the same, with Sharkey abandoning the system that would save him, and returning to Dempsey's style, at which he had no chance.

Edgren said Sharkey turned on more speed, shaking Dempsey with a hard right on the chin. Dempsey reeled back, but kept fighting. His heart and courage had no limit. He looked battered on the surface, but inside he must have been all right, for as he reeled back, he hooked a vicious left at the jaw and Sharkey barely ducked and was holding again.

Sharkey had a neat trick. He held for a moment, leaped back, then leaped in again with a sudden blow that landed. He outboxed Dempsey. He was faster and stronger. But then Dempsey clipped him on the ear and Sharkey staggered. Dempsey was after him like a bulldog. They were mixing at the bell. Dempsey landed a hook, dropped his hands and turned, but Sharkey swayed back and hit him on the chin, glaring at him defiantly. Both had landed a blow after the bell.

Runyon said Dempsey kept up his battering attack to the stomach.

Wood said it was Sharkey's round, but nothing to brag about. A fraction of a second after the bell, Dempsey tapped Sharkey with a left to the face, a harmless punch, but Sharkey returned it with interest. The crowd booed.

Vila said Dempsey was revived and had enough strength in his punches to stagger Sharkey momentarily. But Sharkey held his advantage on points, boxing confidently and cleverly in such a manner that it seemed impossible for him to lose. From the start, Sharkey had been confident and cool-headed, making few mistakes.

Morris said Dempsey was bobbing and jabbing, keeping in close. The Shark shook up Dempsey with a hard right to the forehead. Sharkey later jarred Dempsey from head to heels with a sharp right uppercut. Dempsey kept pounding away at the body. Dempsey forced him back with short rights, and the crowd was in an uproar. Sharkey was backing up as the bell rang, with Dempsey letting a punch go after the bell. Sharkey purposely returned the compliment, for which he was booed.

Official scores – O'Sullivan: Even; Flynn: Sharkey; Mathison: Dempsey.

7th round

Dempsey returned to bulling in aggressively, being more active, and hitting the body nonstop. After several body blows, he snuck in a hook to the head, right to the body, and right uppercut to the jaw. Sharkey lashed out in response with a counter right and left hook.

Still on the inside, Dempsey kept plugging away, digging in a couple left hooks to the body, followed by three rights to the body. Dempsey's right arm was on the other side of the camera, with Dempsey's back to the viewer, so it is not clear exactly where the punches landed, but they likely either were borderline, flirting with going low, or slightly low, but seemed to be more off to the side, in the hip/leg area, not in the central, delicate/dangerous area. It isn't certain, and no definitive objective opinion can be rendered based on the films.

What is clear though is that after the third right to the body, Sharkey immediately cringed with a look of pain, turned and looked over at the referee, who stepped in and reached out to put his hands on the two men, either to give a caution and/or to break them. As the referee approached and arrived, a cringing Sharkey stepped back slightly, with his right arm down low by his stomach (not private area), on the opposite side from where Dempsey had struck. Dempsey immediately fired a snappy/explosive left hook that nailed him flush on the jaw. Sharkey went down on both knees, and then face-forward, down with a thud.

After 3 to 4 seconds had elapsed and Dempsey had walked off to a corner, having lingered momentarily, the referee started the count. Sharkey struggled to rise, slowly pushing up on his hands and knees, but could get no further, despite his apparent efforts, and he was counted out.

Dempsey and various cornermen picked up and carried the Shark to his corner. Jack Dempsey had knocked out Jack Sharkey, conqueror of Harry Wills and George Godfrey, at 45 seconds of the 7th round.

Jack Sharkey had violated the first rule of professional boxing – protect yourself at all times. He had failed to protect himself against a devastating inside fighter, got hit on the jaw, and knocked out.

The fight's big debate was about whether the body blow or blows, prior to the knockout hook to the jaw, were low. Even amongst those who claimed there was a low blow, very few said it was to the delicate area. Hence, many believed that Sharkey was putting on an act at being hurt. It was his own fault for not protecting himself by tying up Dempsey, or getting far enough away with his guard up before complaining. The referee disallowed Sharkey's complaint. Several noted that Sharkey's trunks were a bit high.

One thing no one noted or complained about, but which was shown on the films, was that at the time Dempsey threw the hook, the referee appeared to be in the process of breaking them, his arms on the fighters' arms (Sharkey's left and Dempsey's right) on one side while Dempsey fired his left hook from the other side. It is unclear whether the fighters were supposed to break clean, or whether any command had been given. It is unclear whether the referee was moving in to break them, or to issue a caution for a low blow. Why move in and touch them?

The radio broadcasters did not notice any low blows whatsoever. Describing the round, McNamee/Carlin said Dempsey landed a left to the jaw. Sharkey retaliated with a left to the body. Dempsey landed a left to the body as well. Close in together, there were three or four body punches, and Sharkey seemed to be a little arm-weary. Dempsey drove another short left to the body, and another, and a right. He brought his right up to the jaw, and Sharkey caught him with a right to the jaw.

> Sharkey is down from a left to the side of the body. Sharkey is down! Dempsey has returned to his corner. They are counting over Sharkey, and he is out. Sharkey, knocked cold by Jack Dempsey, is carried to his corner by Dempsey and the referee. Sharkey is knocked cold! … That was one of those terrific left hooks to the jaw. …. It was a left hook to the jaw. … Time, 45 seconds. Joe Humphries just told me – a left hook to the jaw. … In just a few moments we hope to have Dempsey over here to say a word to his admirers. Dempsey tonight seems to be the most popular pugilist that ever walked. Jack, Jack, Jack! Just say 'Hello,' Jack. …

> [Dempsey]: "Hello, everybody! I am tickled to death to be here. Thank you very much."

> McNamee: At the time of the knockout, it did not seem that there would be a knockout, but all of a sudden this far-famed left hook of Dempsey came over with terrific force and Sharkey fell forward. … Sharkey has just recovered from the effect of his terrific knockout and is now retiring from the ring.

Joe Humphries announced, "Time of round, 45 seconds, 7th round, the winner, Dempsey by a knockout."

Farrell said Dempsey got his second wind and appeared refreshed. He looked stronger and fought with more confidence than in the earlier rounds. He went right after Sharkey's stomach, and the ex-gob held on for dear life at every opportunity until separated by the referee. Dempsey took a lot of punishment to get inside, but when he reached his goal, he lost no time in execution. He ripped lefts and rights to the stomach with everything he had. The fans encouraged him.

Dempsey got inside and ripped his right to the waistline. Sharkey doubled up in pain, raised one protesting hand to Referee O'Sullivan, and the other to his groin [sic]. Dempsey, ever on the alert, let his left glove fly with a left hook/uppercut motion, struck the defenseless Sharkey flush on the chin, and he fell flat on his face to be counted out. He did not move at all until Referee O'Sullivan had reached eight. He tried to get up but fell back down and remained until the referee completed the count. Dempsey picked him up, aided by the referee and Sharkey's seconds, and carried him to his corner. The fans were wild with excitement, throwing their hats in the air. There were cheers and jeers.

Farrell also said Sharkey proved that he could not take it. Dempsey hooked Sharkey with a right to the belly and left to the jaw and knocked him out.

Gallico said Dempsey came out strong and began to double up Sharkey with short body rips. Sharkey gave ground again and again, until suddenly at ring center he made his stand, cutting loose for Dempsey's head with both hands. As he did so, Dempsey threw a short right into Sharkey's stomach that landed on the waistband of his trunks. Sharkey buckled. His knees caved. His mouth opened in a gasp. He looked at Referee Jack O'Sullivan and hollered foul. Dempsey stepped back for a moment, and Sharkey dropped his hands too low. O'Sullivan was shaking his head and denying the claim, and at the same moment Dempsey's left glove came whizzing up to crash dreadfully against Sharkey's jaw, dropping him on his face.

As the crowd was going wild with excitement, O'Sullivan counted out the inert Sharkey, who seemed to be getting a long count, but only because the referee had not picked up the count from the timer. After it was over, there was cheering. Dempsey shook hands with several people.

Rice said Dempsey crowded the willing Sharkey, and after three blows which undoubtedly were below the belt, Sharkey bent over. Then came the hooking left to the jaw that dropped Sharkey for the count. He was groggy for several minutes thereafter.

Edgren said Dempsey forced and rushed Sharkey to the ropes. He hammered his stomach. Sharkey began crumpling a little more, until the left hook knocked him out.

Runyon said Dempsey seemed to have recovered his spring, belting away at the midsection. That was his plan, and it never deviated, even though he took many smacks throughout. Though Sharkey seemed stronger, he didn't have enough of a punch to keep Dempsey off of him. Once close, Dempsey's hands never were still for an instant. Sharkey never seemed to be in distress, until his face crinkled and turned towards O'Sullivan appealingly. And then the knockout blow landed.

Vila said that at the round's start, the crowd had no idea that a Dempsey triumph was near. Dempsey kept trying to punch the body. "Sharkey received a blow that looked as though it was well below the belt." It was a right hander, and Sharkey quickly appealed to the referee, but O'Sullivan paid no attention, and the fight went on. A moment later another right "looked as if it had rested in the region of the groin." Sharkey dropped his hands, and a left clip on the jaw dropped him.

Morris said Dempsey was attacking the body, holding with one hand while punching with the other. "Quicker than a flash, Dempsey brought his left glove in a hook that started at his waist line, knocking Sharkey flat on his face." Before that final blow, Sharkey had gestured that he was fouled, which gave Dempsey the chance to bring over the deciding punch. As the fans realized that Dempsey had won via knockout, bedlam broke loose and the fans threw straw hats into the air and in the ring. "Referee O'Sullivan said that Dempsey's punches were fair and right on the line."

Dempsey, Sharkey   Sharkey fires left

Dempsey ducks blows

As of the end of the 6th round, two of the three officials had Dempsey slightly ahead by one round, while one judge had Sharkey in the clear lead:

Referee O'Sullivan: 1-E, 2-E, 3-D, 4-D, 5-S, 6-E. (2-1-3 for Dempsey)

Judge Mathison: 1-S, 2-D, 3-D, 4-E, 5-S, 6-D. (3-2-1 for Dempsey)

Judge Flynn: 1-E, 2-S, 3-S, 4-S, 5-D, 6-S. (4-1-1 for Sharkey)

The two judges differed sharply with the referee and each other in the scoring of each round. The judges did not agree with one another on a single round, while Referee O'Sullivan agreed with Mathison only twice, and Flynn only once. Indeed, it was a close and difficult fight to score, and all three perspectives were justifiable. If one were to score each round based on what a majority of the officials scored for that round, it would be 1-E, 2-E, 3-D, 4-E, 5-S, 6-E, or 1-1-4, for an even fight through 6 rounds. It certainly was a close, competitive, entertaining contest, with both men doing effective work.

In a walk-out bout after the main event, 178 ½-pound Martin Burke outpointed 198-pound Ray Neuman/Newman over 6 rounds.

The gross revenue figure Tex Rickard gave out was $1,083,529.70, the fourth million-dollar fight in ring history. Dempsey had been a principal in all of them. The government would receive 10% and the state 5%. 27.5% of the net would go to Dempsey (about $253,275), and 22.5% to Sharkey. Even though this was a non-title bout, both men would be paid quite well, more than what most champions had earned for title defenses.

Some claimed that Dempsey's share was $345,375.09, and Sharkey's share was $207,225.06. Another said Dempsey earned $352,759 and Sharkey $206,803.

Rickard said 83,000 people were present. The rest heard it over the radio. The crowd was handled beautifully. Rickard knew how to hire good ushers who could "ush."

Brian Bell, Associated Press sportswriter, said 82,000 paid $1,100,000 to see the fight at Yankee Stadium. The weather was kind; no rain.

Others reported a gate of $1,075,000. Federal tax: $107,500, state tax: $53,750.

The Bureau of Internal Revenue/Treasury Department announced that 77,283 paid $985,027 (or $988,027) to see the fight. Dempsey earned 27 ½%, or $270,882. The federal tax was 10% of that amount. Another said Dempsey would earn $252,759, and Sharkey would earn $221,631. They would have to pay federal and state taxes out of those amounts. $454,188 went to Rickard, who managed never to be knocked out. Some said these were the amounts after the taxes were deducted.

Walter Ryan quoted Dempsey as saying, "That old title is coming back to its rightful owner." Sharkey was "one tough boy." The Shark could punch really well, "but there was never a time that I was in real danger." Jack gave Leo Flynn credit for the job he did training him. Speaking of the knockout, Jack said, "I hit him with a right to the stomach, and then poked him with my left." Both of Dempsey's eyes were cut. He had a small gash over his right eye, and a similar cut under the left eye.

According to the *Brooklyn Daily Times*, Dempsey said of Sharkey,

> He is a tough, rugged young fellow who can hit, and hit hard, but he never had me badly hurt or seriously shaken. Always my head was clear and always I had plenty left. ... [H]e is very quick and it is hard for me to land fairly, but when finally I did get a shot at his chin you know the answer.

Jack also said, "Sharkey is a good hard puncher. He shook me up several times and he is liable to hurt anybody. He's rugged and got a world of strength, yet he is not as good as Gene Tunney, and I doubt if he ever will equal the present heavyweight champion."

Dempsey said Sharkey gave him a tough time of it in the first two rounds, but he always was certain that he would win. Sharkey was not the same after those initial rounds. "My plan was to sock him in the body round after round and when I had slowed him down and made him a bit wobbly to let fly with the old left hook the first chance I got. The plan worked."

Regarding the alleged low blow, the *Brooklyn Daily Eagle* quoted Dempsey as saying, "I never struck a fairer blow in my life. I could feel my right bury into Sharkey's body just under his ribs and I knew he was gone. He just slumped, and a left hook to the jaw finished him."

Another quoted Dempsey:

> I slammed him with a right on the ribs and he winced. I brought another one over and he gasped. He said, 'Oh.' Jack O'Sullivan, the referee, said, 'Be careful and keep your punches up, Dempsey.' Then he said immediately, 'Go on and fight.' When the referee said that, I walloped Sharkey with a left hook on the jaw, and he went down on his face.

Dempsey said the fight turned in the 3rd round, when he clouted Sharkey with a left on the jaw.

Another newspaper quoted the former champion the next day as saying,

> The right hand punch I landed on Jack Sharkey's body at the start of the 7th round last night was a fair one, as I recall it. It started fair and I thought it landed fair. Sharkey made a complaint to the referee. I could have hit him then, and not been unethical, but I didn't. I waited for a ruling to be made on the punch. The referee said, 'Go on, fight,' which meant that he was deciding against Sharkey. So I got busy, hooked a short left into the liver and then hooked it for Sharkey's chin. He went down and out.

Dempsey also said,

> I didn't foul him. I hit him with hard rights at the belt line and as his guard dropped I brought over a heavy left which turned the trick. I'm happy to be back in the running and I hope to get another chance at the championship. It was quite a stunt, beating a rough, tough fighter like Sharkey and I wasn't in serious trouble at any time. I must give pretty much all the credit to Leo Flynn. Leo gave me invaluable advice during my training and also while the fight was on.

Concluding, Dempsey said, "I'm sorry there was any question over the finish. I thought I knocked him out with a left to the stomach and a blow on the chin. I'm ready to go on and meet Tunney in September."

Another writer said that while in the dressing room after the fight, Dempsey said, "I knew I'd win – and I won. My heart and soul were in it." When asked if he got hurt, he said, "Well, there's my right eye. But it's nothing. It's all right."

Dempsey's trainers, Leo Flynn, Bill Duffy, Gus Wilson, and Jerry the Greek all said, "We told you so. He can't take it in the body."

Sharkey complained, "Four times during the bout I felt Dempsey hit me low. I thought the referee was going to award the bout to me on a foul, but he didn't." He also said not to count him out of the heavyweight championship title picture just yet. "Why, he hit me on the chin several times, and didn't even hurt me. He can't break an egg with that so-called deadly left hand! He never hurt me once, and that's on the level." Of course, he overlooked the fact that a left to the jaw had knocked him out. Sharkey insisted that none of Dempsey's legal punches hurt him. It was the low blow that paralyzed him. "I was playing it safe until I had Dempsey primed for a finish."

Another paper quoted Sharkey as saying,

> Dempsey knew I had his number from the start, and he was hitting low, all right. He deliberately hit me in the groin four times just before he clipped me. I was falling from the pain when the last blow brushed my chin. I was not knocked out. I simply doubled up from the pain and could not rise. … Say, that guy couldn't break an egg. His punch is gone, if he ever had a punch. I had him licked, and he knew it, and that's why he fouled me. Dempsey was drunk and groggy a dozen times, while he never was able to feaze me.

In another interview, Sharkey said Dempsey hit him low six or seven times throughout the contest.

> I didn't raise a yell about them, but when he nailed me in the 7th way below the waist, well I put in a kick to the referee. And while I was doing that Dempsey hit me on the chin – and dropped me. But it was the low punch that weakened me and really sent me down. I heard them counting me out all right. But when I got up I supposed they would disqualify Dempsey and give me the fight.

Sharkey said Dempsey deliberately fouled in order to save himself.

> I know I had him in pretty bad shape and that his blows didn't mean a thing to me until he had me weakened by a lifting right to the groin. But the pain from this blow was so fierce that I doubled up and turned to the referee thinking he would step in and disqualify Dempsey. Jack stepped in and swung a left to my jaw with everything he had left. It was not his shot to the jaw that kept

me down, however, but the pain of the right blow below the belt line that had me so weakened my legs wouldn't straighten out.

Sharkey said Dempsey fouled him throughout. His legal blows did not hurt.

> Dempsey's blows didn't mean a thing to me at any time. ... Of course, there will be many who'll claim that I fought a foolish fight and that I battled Dempsey too much in the clinches. To tell the truth, Buckley and Kelly, my seconds, kept telling me to do more boxing, but Dempsey was so bad after the first round that I thought it advisable to let Dempsey wear himself out in the clinches. His drives to the body which he kept pumping in at close quarters didn't mean a thing to me, and I had him marked up and bleeding from the eyes and mouth early in the fight.

Sharkey said folks might say he was too reckless and should have stabbed Dempsey off with more frequent use of his left. Sharkey admitted that Dempsey kept plunging in and insisted on mauling close. So, it wasn't entirely his choice. Sharkey still insisted that "none of Dempsey's blows hurt me, or at least had me in trouble at any time."

Several low blows hurt, but he made no appeal. "What I cannot understand is why the referee never even gave Dempsey one warning for his foul work." Once the pain of the final foul blow wore off, he could have continued fighting. "I'm sure I gave him a punching that will stay with him for many days."

Sharkey claimed that Dempsey worked an old trick, getting him in a position where the referee was behind and unable to see the blow, then hitting him low. (Actually, the referee had the best view of matters.) When informed that Charles Mathison, one of the judges, intended to file a report saying that the blow was low, Sharkey responded, "Oh, what the hell. It's all over now. They can't change it."

Sharkey told Homer Thorne, "I wasn't fouled once or twice but twelve times. And when I appealed to the referee he just laughed. Laughed in my face. ... Dempsey didn't have a thing. I took all he had until he slipped one over on my groin, and when I put down my hands in bitter pain he clipped me on the jaw with the blow which knocked me out."

Johnny Buckley, Sharkey's manager, protested vigorously that the *left hook* to the stomach that started Sharkey on his slumber trip was foul, but the referee paid no attention. (Yet, it appears that Sharkey did not complain after a left landed, but rather a right.)

The mayor's brother, Dr. William H. Walker, who was the official New York state athletic commission physician/doctor, examined Sharkey in the dressing room and said there was no outward evidence of a foul, though it was possible to be fouled and show no signs of it.

One doctor said, "When a man is really fouled, his legs give way completely." However, Sharkey did not go down until after he was hit on the jaw.

A Boston doctor, John Connor, representing the Massachusetts commission (Sharkey's home base), also examined Sharkey and declared that he had been fouled in the left groin. Sharkey was unmarked, except for a slight swelling under his left eye.

Judge for the fight, Charles Mathison, said, "Jack Sharkey was hit below the waistline immediately before the knockout punch and Dempsey should have been disqualified. Dempsey was also guilty of hitting low in several other rounds." Mathison said Dempsey hit Sharkey low with a right.

Referee Jack O'Sullivan saw the punch and denied it was foul. He said,

> The blow which preceded the knockout punch, a left to the jaw, was a fairly delivered one. It was a right uppercut that landed on the waistline, but not below. It is true that Dempsey landed several times below the waistline in previous rounds, but in no case were the punches injurious or deliberate, nor was there any protest made by Sharkey previous to the final round.

Another quoted Referee O'Sullivan as saying,

> The punch that Sharkey claimed was a low blow in the seventh round was not low, as I viewed it. The punch was fair, and when Sharkey made the protest, I naturally overruled him. Then I ordered the men to go on with the fight. After I made the ruling Dempsey got into fighting action first and hooked his left to Sharkey's chin, the blow that dropped Sharkey and ended the fight.

Yet, O'Sullivan also was quoted as saying,

> During the fight Dempsey landed three or four punches that were low, but they were not vital. They were light blows. Sharkey also landed a couple of low ones. I cautioned both of them.

> As to the episode where each landed a punch after the bell, it is my judgment that Dempsey's blow, the first delivered, was in the nature of a good-natured slap as they parted to go to their corners. Sharkey's return was a real punch, with some sting on it.

> I would like to call attention to the fact that Dempsey did not use his rabbit punch at any time.

> I was right on top of the boxers preceding the knockout. Dempsey brought up a sweeping right for the body. It was a low punch, but it was not a damaging blow. It landed on Sharkey's left thigh and swept on up. I took a step nearer to them and said, "Watch your punches, Jack." Then I realized that they both were named Jack, and added, "I mean you, Dempsey." Quick as a flash Dempsey sent his left to the pit of the stomach. Sharkey grunted, "Oh!" as though in pain and bent his head forward, pulling his stomach back. Then Dempsey sent another left to the jaw and Sharkey went down. I

bent over Sharkey and said, "You had better get up. I am counting on you." He made no reply. He did not claim a foul.

Tex Rickard, who was sitting at ringside, said, "I would have seen a foul blow if one had been struck in the seventh round. No, Dempsey hit Sharkey in the pit of the stomach – right in the pit of the stomach. ... A man would have dropped quicker than that if he had been hit low. He didn't act like a man who had been hit low."

Rickard sat in the first row, so he had a good view.

> I faced the fighters, Dempsey and Sharkey, in the front row. I saw no foul blow struck. The punch that Dempsey gave Sharkey and which was one of the deciding factors in the fight, was a blow to the pit of the stomach. This blow, which I saw very clearly, caused Sharkey to drop his guard. Sharkey's hands dropped and the punch to the jaw that followed knocked Sharkey out. ... Sharkey dropped to his knees and didn't buckle like a man hit low. I know this is correct. Sharkey has made no complaint to me; neither has his manager, Buckley.

> I am particularly interested in the opinions of the expert newspaper writers on the fight. Take the ones who picked Sharkey to win. They all say a foul blow was struck. Take the ones who picked Dempsey to win. They all say there was no foul blow struck.

Rickard further said, "It was the old Dempsey – he took all Sharkey had to give and won. It was a great fight."

Chairman James Farley said, "I have nothing to say other than that the referee who was assigned to that bout rendered the decision as he saw it. This commission never has reversed a decision of its officials. Referee O'Sullivan has always been considered by newspaper men who write boxing as being one of our most efficient and capable referees."

Men at ringside differed. Some said there was no question that the blow or blows were legal, others thought the punch was just on the belt line, while others insisted it was low. There even was a question of which body blow or blows were low, if at all, since Dempsey threw so many in a row into the body with both hands. Some said the blows were low, but not in a dangerous area, and Sharkey foolishly dropped his hands, causing his own demise. Others said the low blow or blows set up the knockout punch.

Foul:

Bill Corum, *New York Journal*
Benny Leonard, *New York World*
James Dawson, *New York Times*: "Dempsey had his right hand loose while Sharkey locked his left. The former champion dug his right repeatedly into Sharkey, trying for the body, but there were unmistakably low punches, four of them, though concededly unintentional."
Bill Cunningham, *Boston Post*

Mark Kelly, *Los Angeles Examiner*
Tommy Laird, *San Francisco News*
S. M. Bell, *Cleveland Press*
Joe Williams, *New York Telegram*
George Underwood, *New York Telegram*
James Burchard, *New York Telegram*
William Granger, *Brooklyn Citizen*
Harry Cross, *New York Herald Tribune*
W. O. McGeehan, *New York Herald Tribune:* "Dempsey landed low on the purple trunks of Sharkey. The Lithuanian protested to Referee O'Sullivan and, as he protested, Dempsey drove in another right, even lower."
Grantland Rice, *New York Herald Tribune:* "Dempsey struck Sharkey two foul blows early in the seventh round and as Sharkey apparently doubled up in pain Dempsey followed with a left hook to the jaw."
Thomas Rice, *Brooklyn Daily Eagle*
James Jennings, *New York Evening Graphic:* "The writer will always hold that Dempsey should have been disqualified for fouling his opponent."
Fred Keats, *New York Mirror*
Ed Van Every, *New York Evening World:* "It is hard to cast any shadow on his victory, but that Dempsey should have been disqualified for hitting low with a right well below the belt, which was followed by the ex-champion's left hook flush to the chin, is something that doubtless was pretty plain to most of those at the ringside."
Sam Taub, *New York Morning Telegraph:* "Dempsey after delivering four foul right hand punches sent Sharkey writhing to the canvas."
Al Lamb, *Binghamton Press:* "The last right hand blow looked low. Perhaps there is something to the claim that Sharkey had his trunks pulled up higher than they should have been. But it was up to the referee to see that they were where they belonged."
Alfred Dayton, *New York Sun*
Joe Vila, *New York Sun*
Wilbur Wood, *New York Sun*
Paul White, United Press: Two body blows in the 7th were foul. White did not see any low blows prior to that.
Charles Mathison, judge for the fight

Fair/No Foul:

Sid Mercer, *New York Evening Journal*
Frank O'Neill, *New York Evening Journal*
Robert Edgren, *New York Evening World*
Jimmy De Forest, *New York Evening World*
Walter St. Denis, *Newark Star-Eagle/New York Globe*
Jim Corbett, *New York American*
Gene Tunney, *New York American*
Ed Sullivan, *New York Evening Graphic*

Paul Gallico, *New York Daily News*, "Dempsey threw a short right in Sharkey's stomach that landed on the waist band of his tights. To me the punch looked right on the dead line."

Jack Farrell, *New York Daily News*: "Dempsey ripped a short right hook into Sharkey's mid-section just above the danger zone."

Henry Farrell, United Press editor. "The blow was legal."

Frank Getty, United Press: It was "on the belt line."

Hype Igoe, *New York World*: "It did seem a bit close to the belt line, but I defy any man to say it was below the belt."

Sid Mercer, *New York Journal*: "I saw no evidence of foul."

Alan Gould, Associated Press

William Spring, *Yonkers Statesman*

George Currie, *Brooklyn Daily Eagle*

George Palmer, *Brooklyn Standard Union*

Tim Byrne, *New York Evening Post*

Westbrook Pegler, *Chicago Tribune*

Graham McMamee/Phillips Carlin: radio broadcasters for the fight

Tex Rickard

Tommy Loughran

New York Mayor James Walker: Sharkey wore his tights higher than ordinarily is done, giving the false impression that the blow was low. "I don't think there was a foul. The blows looked low because Sharkey wore his tights so high. It isn't good sportsmanship to make alibis."

George Brower, one of the state athletic commissioners: "I was sitting pretty close and I didn't see any foul."

Referee Jack O'Sullivan

Damon Runyon, *New York American*, was on the fence about matters, saying, "Some of the punches Dempsey let go at Sharkey in that final mix-up seemed low. But as I understand it, even when a low punch is struck in the ring the referee frequently uses his judgment and discretion as to whether it damaged the recipient before awarding a decision on foul."

> Sharkey went down under a rat-a-tat of glove smacks to his middle, some of which I thought were dropping a little low, Dempsey was always a little careless when he lets his body punches fly. Sharkey's face crinkled with pain, and he muttered something to Jack O'Sullivan, the referee, evidently complaining of the punches. But, O'Sullivan seemed to think they were falling in fair territory. Then Sharkey started to crumple from the body punches. As he crumpled Dempsey swung his left hook to the chin, and Sharkey fell face forward, as men nearly always fall when they are hit solidly on the chin, and Kid McPartland, the old-time lightweight, rose from his chair at the ringside and began counting, punctuating the seconds with swings of his left hand. He counted to eight, and Sharkey attempted to arise, but toppled over again, unconscious. Sharkey was knocked out.

Runyon also noted, "Sharkey's record shows that he has won three fights on fouls. It has always been the contention of the Bostonians who do not like the ex-gob that he 'can't take it' around the body, yet up to the moment his body began getting soggy under Dempsey's belting he had 'taken' plenty there."

Runyon said although at times Dempsey's punches appeared weak and slow, they began to carry some snap and zing, and he actually began out-boxing a very good boxer, getting away from the swings as nimbly as a lightweight. His footwork previously had been heavy, and though he tried to bob and weave, he couldn't seem to get his body or legs to respond.

Jack Farrell said Dempsey was old and just a mere shadow of himself, but matched his indomitable fighting spirit and his punch against his youthful and overconfident opponent. It was a sensational finish. Dempsey, after being all but knocked out in the 1st round, in the 7th round ripped a short right hook to the midsection, just above the danger zone. When Sharkey tried to claim a foul, Dempsey nailed him with a left hook and Sharkey went down face first, where he remained until Referee Jack O'Sullivan counted ten.

Paul Gallico said Sharkey was young, strong, confident, and well trained, but Dempsey knocked him out with a smash that turned him into jelly. Sharkey claimed a foul, dropping his guard for a fraction of a second, and in that split-second, Dempsey whizzed his left over in a half-hook half-uppercut that crashed on his jaw, and Sharkey fell flat on his face with a thud, totally out. It was absolute pandemonium as 83,000 fans were on their feet, excited by the sudden drama.

Referee O'Sullivan had started to shake his head, indicating that he did not recognize any foul, and he picked up the count from the knockdown timer who was beating on the ring with his mallet. Dempsey retired to his own corner at the referee's order. O'Sullivan counted Sharkey out, but he was insensible. Dempsey helped lift him up and carry him to his corner. Sharkey left the ring to a storm of boos and catcalls.

Sharkey's claim of foul made him unpopular with the crowd, and brought about his immediate knockout. "But the way Dempsey was going at the time, it would have come sooner or later in that round. Sharkey simply succumbed to stomach punishment." People were calling Sharkey "yellow" for claiming a foul when there was none. They believed he simply was breaking physically and psychologically under relentless pressure and power, sought a ruse, and foolishly failed to protect himself.

Gallico believed that Dempsey was winning up to the end. There were moments in which he was in dire trouble, but then, with his head shaken and reeling from Sharkey's furious one-two-hook attack, he looked like his old self as he bent forward and piled in.

Gallico scored it 1 – Even, 2 – Dempsey, 3 – Dempsey, 4 – Dempsey, 5 - Sharkey, 6 – Even or Dempsey by a shade, making it 3-1-2 for Dempsey before the fateful 7th. Sharkey's face was unmarked, while

Dempsey was cut up badly and bleeding from his right eye and nose. His lip was cut as well.

Dempsey's boxing was a surprise. He made Sharkey miss many swings, danced away from uppercuts, and often was blocking lefts with his right glove in pretty fashion. His defense was much better than expected. Even when hit and hurt, he recovered quickly and well.

All that said, Dempsey was not what he once was. "I still feel that on what Jack showed he will never defeat Tunney in a return bout. He was good enough to beat Sharkey, who played into his hands by not keeping away from him in the early part of the fight, until he found that later on Dempsey was gaining in speed so that he couldn't keep away from him." Sharkey's body had been punished badly. "To me the punch looked right on the dead line, and the protective cup was undented." The punch did not land in the delicate area.

The Dempsey of the past was no more. But this version still was good enough to whip a dangerous youngster, one who beat Godfrey, Wills, and other good men. "You cannot take that away from him." If Sharkey dogged it in the end, it was because Dempsey's body punishment made him dog it.

The films would be shown the following week to help settle the matter. They only could be shown legally in New York, for the Interstate Commerce Commission forbade their shipment to other states, pursuant to federal law. That is, if the law was followed. One writer pointed out that the films might not settle the matter, for the camera angle was not the best to determine what happened.

The *Brooklyn Standard Union* noted that Dempsey, who was bleeding from cuts beneath his eye, on his nose, and on his mouth, had been striking body blows. "Jack O'Sullivan, the referee, started to say something, hesitated a moment, and Jack Dempsey caught Jack Sharkey with another terrific blow squarely on the chin. Sharkey dropped like a bag of grain tossed ashore by a stevedore. Those who could see, knew it was all over." Sharkey did not cry foul at that time. "It is worth noting that Sharkey wore his belt a good two inches higher than did Dempsey."

Another article said Sharkey's attempt to win the fight on a foul cost him a chance at the title.

George Palmer said Dempsey won cleanly and decisively. "He drove in a hard right to the body and as Sharkey's knees sagged and his hands dropped, Jack whipped home the left to the point of the jaw. Quick as light went that finishing punch and it found its mark."

Palmer also said, "Above any fighter of the present era, Dempsey has symbolized to the crowd the spirit of the fight game. A fighter first, last and all the time – dead game and possessing a love and a lust for fighting that has no counterpart in all the annals of the sport." He was a man-killer, and the "fight game is his." He stood alone as the producer of thrills. "His entire career has been a succession of sensational episodes – each one of them leaving a lasting imprint on the minds of the enthralled hosts which saw it." The crowd wanted to see Dempsey win, and it was gratified.

The *Brooklyn Daily Eagle* said half of the sporting writers polled claimed foul, and the other half said it was fair. A special showing of the films that evening in Manhattan failed to settle the controversy, some thinking it was fair and some foul. The angle was not the best to settle matters. A slow motion showing revealed that Dempsey struck three hard rights to the stomach area before he delivered the final knockout left to the jaw. "The picture showed that Sharkey was wearing his trunks pulled up higher than Dempsey was wearing his." That was said to contribute to the confusion among witnesses.

Some said Sharkey fought Dempsey's fight, while others said Dempsey forced him to fight his fight. Others said Sharkey lacked consistency. Sometimes he boxed and moved, sometimes he attacked and fought, and sometimes he clinched. Dempsey primarily forced and hit the body, constantly pressing except when hurt.

Although the victory was impressive, most said Tunney still would beat Dempsey. The ex-champion remained far from the Dempsey of old. He was slower, more hittable, and did not have the same snap and ferocity that he once had. He hit hard, but not as hard as he once did.

Paul White said slow motion pictures did not settle the foul dispute. The pictures failed to show the blows clearly, in part due to the angle. Some thought they showed a foul, some insisted they did not, and others were not sure.

Thomas Rice said Sharkey played into Dempsey's hands by continuing his unwise rushes. It was a popular victory, but gave no indication that Dempsey could beat Tunney in a return match. Tunney had been vastly underrated prior to their first contest. Sharkey had been overrated.

Rice believed Sharkey had been hit low, but deserved defeat. He fought a foolish fight, just to Dempsey's liking. When he stood off and sparred, he hit Dempsey. But most of the time he rushed into clinches, where he was outfought and outgeneraled, being weakened persistently, even though Dempsey's assaults were feeble compared to what he once could do seven years ago. Some thought Sharkey was trying to allow Dempsey to wear himself out, and then would box him cleverly, but the longer the fight went, the more it became evident he had no such plan.

The man who "exploded the Wills myth" and proved his ring sense against Maloney perhaps tried to send his stock soaring by stopping Dempsey, but after a few rounds, must have realized that Dempsey was stronger than expected. It would have been wiser to use Tunney's tactics of boxing at long range, using his jab and straight right, and utilizing footwork. Sharkey instead threw away his cleverness and fought inside, up close. Either he was hurt, or tight, or perhaps just believed in the wrong tactics. It seemed that he could have changed tactics had he so desired. In every round he flashed his ability to keep away and box, but he soon wearied and resumed the style that suited Dempsey.

Except for the Bostonians, who were for Sharkey, the crowd was for Dempsey, even the ones who thought he would lose. Hence the victory was quite popular. "He had more genuine well wishers last night than he had in any previous bout in his career." Still, enthusiasm for him "could not blind those who had seen him in his previous championship bouts to the fact that he was far, far from the Dempsey of old."

The victory was as much due to Sharkey's astounding reversal of form in cleverness as to Dempsey's own efforts. The Gene Tunney of 1926 would have whipped last night's version of Dempsey just as thoroughly. Dempsey's punches seemed more forceful simply because Sharkey's style allowed him to reach him and land almost at will, but the old snap still was not there and likely never would be again. He landed blows in several rounds that in the old days had decked men like Fulton, Willard, Firpo, and others. If he had been the Dempsey of old, "he would have beaten Sharkey last night in two rounds, or possibly even in one." The old deadly snappy jolt was gone. He had heavy wallops, but nothing more. He hurt Sharkey with a hook in the 6th, but did not drop him.

Rice opined that Dempsey possibly could beat Uzcudun, because Paulino was a rusher and a swinger, which would suit Jack. It was possible that Tom Heeney, the New Zealand heavyweight champ, who lost a thrilling 10-round points verdict to Uzcudun, might be able to stand off Dempsey. "Heeney is a boxer with a light punch, but his punch is fast and accurate." Rice saw nothing about the current version of Dempsey which made him think that Jack could beat Tunney in a return match.

Gene Tunney said, "The blows that were questioned were not in the groin. As I saw them they were fair."

Tunney said Dempsey always was dangerous, and his opinion had not changed. "Dempsey can still hit." "I never saw him fight better. ... Yes, Dempsey can hit. He has always been able to hit and I suppose he always will, as long as he stays in there." Tunney said Dempsey fought better than he did against him, landing a lot of hard blows to the body and head. "Yes, I think Jack was better than he was against me in Philadelphia. Surely we should have a great return bout." "No one can accuse me of holding Dempsey lightly. ... He is always dangerous."

Tunney said of Sharkey, "He's just starting. He will win many bouts before he is through."

For the *New York Sun*, Joe Vila said 82,000 spectators looked on in amazement as Sharkey was counted out. "In the opinion of many ringside observers, including the writer, Sharkey was hit below the belt at least twice before a short left hook to the neck or jaw dropped him to the floor for the count of ten." Up to that point, Sharkey had outboxed Dempsey by a wide margin and looked like a sure winner. Sharkey had won 5 of the first 6 rounds on scientific fighting. His defense to the body attacks was invulnerable, and he took Dempsey's head swings without wincing, except in the 5th round, when a flying wallop staggered him for a second or two. Dempsey was completely outboxed and outgeneraled.

The ex-champion was an awful-looking winner. He was bruised and tired. "But for the punch that ended the fight so suddenly Dempsey might not have lasted much longer."

After the fight, Dempsey's face was quite badly bruised, and he had to take several stitches in cuts over his eyes. Dr. Frank Russell said three stitches were taken in a cut in the right eyelid and one stitch in a cut over the left eye.

Vila said Dempsey showed no improvement from the version that fought Tunney, except that he had strength enough to stick close and take punishment with remarkable pluck. The Dempsey who stopped Firpo would have stopped Sharkey much sooner, for Sharkey took desperate chances and received many blows which lacked the old-time sleep potion.

Though Sharkey was the betting favorite for the past two weeks, two hours before the fight, there was a rush of money on Dempsey, causing the odds to shift to 11 to 10 in Dempsey's favor. "In conclusion, THE SUN repeats: Don't Bet on Fights."

It now was a sure thing that Tex Rickard would promote Dempsey vs. Tunney II, it would be limited to 10 rounds, and held in Chicago.

Wilbur Wood said a shell of a once great Dempsey was beaten, battered, bruised, and weary. "Dempsey was only a shell, but a shell loaded with poison gas. He was slow, clumsy, just a shadow of the old Dempsey. But he won – and that seemed to be what the public wanted."

At the end, Dempsey landed three blows below the waist. Sharkey dropped his arms, turned to protest, Dempsey landed his left to the jaw, and Sharkey went down and was counted out. "Sharkey was struck by perhaps twenty low punches in all." The knockout was set up by a foul blow. Sharkey was younger, stronger, more skillful, and faster.

The Dempsey camp believed Sharkey could not take it to the body, and that is where Dempsey focused. Yet, his old steam was not present. Sharkey took the blows, fair or foul, without complaint, throughout, until the end. Dempsey committed a half dozen fouls against Firpo, too, but was permitted to get away with it, and he did so once again.

Wood opined that Sharkey should have kept at a greater distance from Dempsey, retreated and jabbed. Instead, he allowed Dempsey to get to close quarters constantly. He did this perhaps because he was satisfied that he could handle Dempsey's power. But that allowed Dempsey to make the fight his own way. Dempsey was slow, but getting in close was smart, because speed meant less there. "Gene Tunney, boxing in the form he showed at Philadelphia last September, would have had a cinch with either Sharkey or Dempsey."

Dempsey had courage, while Sharkey had foolish courage. "Why he failed to give ground and jab Dempsey silly as the former champion made his clumsy rushes is another of the many mysteries of fistiana." Either Dempsey's relentless attack made him fight, and Sharkey did not want to wear himself out moving, or Sharkey thought he could handle Dempsey's inside attack, and possibly wanted to and thought he could knock him out.

Wood said Dempsey played steadily for the body at close quarters, "but showed none of his one-time punching power." Sharkey drove him across the ring with a series of staggering lefts and rights to the head. Dempsey was groggy. "He was just the same old hollow shell that rattled around in the ring at Philadelphia last September. But Sharkey would not or could not do what Tunney had done." Dempsey showed superb courage in the face of what seemed to be a hopeless task, and he kept banging away at the body. He was cut on the cheek under the right eye, bleeding from the mouth and nose. Through 6 rounds, Wood had it scored 3-2-1 for Sharkey.

The *Sun* claimed the motion pictures revealed two low blows, and they put out Sharkey, not the hook to the jaw. Only two blows were visible on the films. One was delivered with Dempsey's back to the camera in a clinch. "But as the men shifted their positions, still at close quarters, Dempsey was seen to drive a right into the folds of Sharkey's tights below the belt. This was followed by a similar punch with the right hand to the same spot in Sharkey's left groin."

H. I. Phillips said the punch looked low. Further, "Dempsey at no time looked anything like the Toledo man killer. … Dempsey was not exactly a hollow shell, but he was no blazing Big Bertha, either." He was bleeding most of the time, and up to the finish, it seemed that Sharkey was fighting a cool, crafty battle that would send Dempsey out.

James Dawson for the *New York Times* said a vast crowd of 80,000 paid over a million dollars to witness a Homeric struggle. Many believed Dempsey should have been disqualified. Jack O'Sullivan hesitated, started to bend over Sharkey, hesitated again, then picked up the count from timekeeper Billy 'Kid' McPartland. Joe Humphries raised Dempsey's hand aloft in a victory that was popular, even though its legality was questioned.

Those who occupied seats on the third base and left field sides of the field were in the best position to see what occurred, and it seemed that this section of the crowd raised the greatest hullabaloo. Dawson was in a good seat, and his verdict was,

> Sharkey was hit low four times with a right. It was not deliberately or intentionally, for Dempsey is not that kind of a fighter. But Dempsey was fighting a desperate, savage battle last night, a losing last-stand encounter, in which he was rocked and shaken and groggy under the blows of his rival and the pace of the bout, and his attack probably became erratic under the circumstances.

Sharkey had "boxed rings round Dempsey for six rounds," trading blows when he might just have easily stood off and peppered him. Sharkey stood up to Dempsey's left hook to the jaw and vicious digs to the body without cringing.

In the 7th, as usual, Dempsey plunged into the body, and four punches were low. Sharkey stood up to three of them, but sank under the fourth, protesting. Dempsey's face was smeared with blood which oozed from his mouth, nose, and cuts under and above his right eye. While Sharkey was down, cries of "foul" were mixed with cries of "quitter."

Dawson said public demand likely would lead to Dempsey-Tunney II, but Dempsey was "revealed as a shell of his former self, a man whose fighting spirit and effectiveness has left him." He had the will, but "the flesh is weak."

One of the greatest and most distinguished gatherings enjoyed every second of the fight. Dempsey carried the sentiment and hopes of the crowd. Conversely, Sharkey was subject to scorn and abuse.

Dempsey fought a losing, uphill battle, but "gloriously, inspiringly, savagely, courageously, with a fighting heart that only a Dempsey can possess." He fought gallantly even in the face of defeat. Dawson thought Sharkey was going to stop him. Regardless of the result, "Dempsey is passe as a fighter. He has absolutely no chance against even the Tunney of today, with a year of soft living as champion behind him."

Dempsey could not contend with the ex-marine's skill, accurate, precise attack, and smart fighting head. Tunney was superior to Sharkey in speed, skill, and strength. Dempsey was a "hollow shell," "slow and awkward, cumbersome, stiff and has not a remnant of his former fighting speed and agility left." Years ago, he had coordination of mind and muscle, but no longer. He even had lost his punch, which had not a semblance of its once destructive force. "Dempsey hit Sharkey repeatedly and squarely with the left on the chin and Sharkey never faltered." His left used to contain dynamite and had been a tool of destruction.

Sharkey did not show anything indicating that he threatened Tunney's reign. "If Dempsey was poor, Sharkey was just a little better, just a few degrees. Sharkey's plan should have been to step around Dempsey, box him, cut him and tire him. Instead, he elected to fight Dempsey…" Even fighting Dempsey's fight, Sharkey cut, bruised, tired, and rocked him, though he could not bring down the shell of Dempsey. "On the strength of this Sharkey is no world beater. At best he qualifies simply as the man who revealed Dempsey as a remnant of a once great fighter."

Ed Hughes said Dempsey was a miracle-man by proving that he wasn't just a hollow shell. He was the fight-game's biggest drawing card. He was the goose that laid the golden eggs. Neither Sharkey nor Tunney were the draws that he was. Fandom liked the underdog, so as the underdog, for the first time in his life, the ex-champion knew what it was like to be popular with the crowd.

Dempsey was full of pep and refused to be intimidated. He was the aggressor from start to finish. He was more flatfooted and less lightning-like than he once was, but he crowded in without letup, boring in with a half-bent position. He forced the close fighting, working the body with piston-like regularity in ramming home heavy blows.

Sharkey was disconcerted, but landed several blows that hurt and wobbled Dempsey, particularly in the 1st round. In his corner, Gus Wilson rubbed Jack's legs, while Leo Flynn applied smelling salts to his nostrils.

In the 2nd round, Sharkey jabbed him off balance repeatedly and cut his right eye with those jabs. Dempsey kept forcing close fighting and managed to land repeatedly with short right body jolts, now and then whipping up to the face. His blows did not have the deadening sting of yore. Sharkey paid practically no attention to them, and did not seem to be affected. In some instances, he did not even try to block, and even laughed.

Sharkey peppered Jack with jabs, now and then hooking smart blows to the chin that stood Dempsey back on his heels. Dempsey worked in close, landing frequently enough, but seemed to be lacking power. Conversely, Dempsey seemed more shocked by Sharkey's blows.

The battle had been fairly even up to the 5th, but at the end of that round, Sharkey seemed to have the situation in hand, outboxing the former champ and scoring more often and heavier. Dempsey's right eye was crimson, and left eye blackening. Though aggressive, ceaselessly the pacemaker, the old champ's prospects did not look too bright. He missed a lot, and what blows he did land would have been sufficient to drop a man like Sharkey in the old days. Dempsey seemed weary at the end of the 6th.

The finish was unexpected. Many of Dempsey's body wallops previously landed below the belt, though no protests were made. In close, he rammed another right somewhere in the region of Sharkey's belt line. Sharkey turned, as if to complain to the referee. Dempsey promptly struck a left hook to the jaw, and Sharkey crumpled to his stomach, groaning about foul blows. O'Sullivan refused to recognize the claim and counted him out, while Sharkey made several efforts to push himself up to his knees. Dempsey helped drag him to his corner. "Whether or not the low blows inflicted by Dempsey previous to the finishing left hook defeated Sharkey is not certain." Perhaps the nonstop body attack finally did it. Nevertheless, "Sharkey suddenly turned turtle when the battle seemed to be well in hand."

Doctors said there was no physical evidence of a low blow.

George Currie said it dawned on Dempsey in the 6th round that he had his man. He seemed to sense that the furious pace was beginning to tell on Sharkey. A red glove hit Sharkey on the jaw and rocked his head. Another smashing right followed. Sharkey clinched, and the confidence left.

Between rounds, the Manassa Mauler seemed like a predator who knew he had his prey. Gene Normile said, "Just look at him. He's got him."

During the 7th round, Normile said of Sharkey, "Look, he's gone, his eyes are just like pale china blue marbles. The fight's gone out of him. Nobody in the world could stand the lambasting he's had on his stomach." Agony was shown as Sharkey took a crushing right on the stomach. The red-leathered left fist found his jaw and he dropped to the floor to be counted out. Dempsey's bleeding forehead gave him an appearance of a knightly hero, receiving roaring crowd's adulation.

Robert Edgren said the ex-champion's ability to take it and courageously come back with harder punches won it for him. Sharkey had taken a terrific body pounding through six rounds. He was holding, jumping away and trying to land as Dempsey plunged after him. He guarded his body with both arms crossed at the belt, and several times pushed Dempsey's glove down. Dempsey hit him on the jaw, and Sharkey went down to his elbow and his knee with forehead on the floor. He was in agony from the blow in the pit of the stomach.

Superior courage won the fight. Dempsey came after him and never stopped plugging away. He took plenty of heavy rights and left hooks but refused to be driven back.

As the fight progressed, Dempsey's face became swollen. His right eye was cut and bleeding. Sharkey was not marked. But it was Sharkey who backed away, who held desperately, wrestled, and broke ground first, time after time, when he started mixing and found that Dempsey would not and could not be kept away.

"Dempsey outgamed Sharkey. That was the whole story of the fight." Even when he was shaken by blows two or three times, Dempsey kept coming back, plunging in to fight all the time. Round after round, he pounced at Sharkey's body and whipped left hooks at his jaw. Sharkey was stronger than Dempsey at the start, but after a few rounds, Sharkey began weakening under the constant hammering, driven to the ropes again and again. Sharkey was faster than Dempsey, but whenever the ex-champ was hit hard, he came back with renewed fury and hit harder and faster, and always it was Sharkey who backed away. Unable to hold him off with blows, Sharkey began meeting him by jumping in with his shoulder like a football player.

Dempsey won with sheer gameness and endurance. He had the superior fighting heart. "But he is not the old Jack Dempsey." Everyone knew that.

Dempsey never again would be the absolutely irresistible force, the socking terror who finished nearly all of them in the 1st round. He had the endurance to continue fighting when hurt, to weather heavy blows and keep plunging in, and he had a hard punch, but he had to set himself to deliver it. And even at its present best, it wasn't the killing punch of his championship days.

Davis Walsh said the painfully confident Sharkey failed to keep away, and a knockout was the result. A left to the body and jaw and Sharkey was no more. Hitting Dempsey meant nothing to him. He still had the punch and the chin. As long as he breathed and stood up, he was dangerous.

Dempsey kept charging in with the old aggressiveness and hit the body as viciously as of yore. Except for his painful lack of speed and stamina,

he fought his typical fight. It merely was unfortunate that Sharkey did not get around to doing the same for himself.

Sharkey lost as much as Dempsey won. He was like a pitcher who had two strikes on Babe Ruth, but like a fool threw one down the middle of the plate and it was hit over the fence for a home run. Tunney sensibly declined to meet Dempsey body to body, and moved rapidly about in circles, only making a stand long enough to land quick blows and then move away. Sharkey was no Tunney. He had superior speed, but refused to use it, being too vain to back away. It didn't matter that Dempsey's legs were gone. Sharkey was too arrogant.

Walsh said Dempsey's left to the body landed at or under the belt, but not over it. "But the writer is not particularly concerned with the punch in question. You can't foul a man with a punch on the jaw, and it was such a punch that finished Sharkey." Sharkey's own corner made no claim of foul at the time. Regardless, when a ball was hit over the fence and the umpire said it was fair, it was a home run. The general impression was that the potentially low blows were not damaging or in a harmful area, and the knockout was due to the left hook to the jaw.

Dempsey-Tunney II would be huge, because "Dempsey is the greatest man before the public today." He was the darling of the galleries again. No ballyhoo for the fight would be needed. Walsh admitted that he had picked Sharkey to stop Dempsey in 10 rounds.

Grantland Rice said two left blows were at least eight inches below the belt and were palpably foul. As Sharkey turned to claim a foul, Dempsey in a flash struck him on the point of the jaw with a short left hook.

The fight was about even up to the 7th. They had fought savagely and bitterly. Sharkey had greater speed and skill, hitting the face, drawing streams and pools of blood. Dempsey surged in with endless rushes, concentrating his attack on the body, which he hammered, round after round, forcing the battle at almost every stage. Dempsey took everything, including hooks to the jaw with full force, and right crosses to the chin that snapped his head back but never brought him down. Time and again they rushed together and slugged. Dempsey's right eye was half closed and bleeding, and his crimson-smeared nose took all of Sharkey's salvos in order to thump booming thuds into the body. Dempsey landed a left hook on the jaw in the 5th, but Sharkey took it well.

In the 7th, they were battling upon fairly even terms, with Dempsey possibly in the lead through his greater aggressiveness. Dempsey had been hitting low all night. He drove a left hook at least eight inches below the belt line. He followed with a left jab ten inches below the belt. Sharkey half backed away to claim foul. As he turned his head slightly, in a flash, Dempsey struck a short left hook to the point of the jaw and the Sailor fell on his face. He lay there and quivered as Dempsey was sent to a neutral corner. He rested on his face, taking the full count.

Thousands in the crowd roared and cheered, throwing their hats in the air. But others were silent, wondering why the fouls were overlooked.

"Whether the blows hurt Sharkey or not is another matter. In any event he was claiming a foul as Dempsey nailed him with a hook to the jaw." That punch would send him into a fight with Tunney.

Rice granted that this was an improved Dempsey. "The Dempsey who rushed and tore into Sharkey tonight was an entirely different Dempsey from the man who lost practically every round to Tunney a year ago. On this occasion he was full of fury and fight every moment of the battle." This time he had no cool Tunney to face, but he also had no thought of easing up and backing away when struck or punished.

Dempsey struck low five or six times prior to the 7th round. But there was no questioning the fact that Dempsey did most of the rushing and leading. If he was a hollow shell, he was a shell filled with T.N.T. He took a savage pelting to the jaw, head, and face without weakening. Sharkey could snap his head with blows that had everything on them, but he could not keep Dempsey away.

At times, Sharkey tried to keep away, but he could not, for Dempsey was like a surf amidst a storm. Sharkey tried to box, but Dempsey kept moving in close no matter what, thumping away with both hands. "This body punishment was doing Sharkey no great good." He was being hurt, and lacked the punch to keep him away. He could cut, bruise, and jolt Dempsey, but could not punch hard enough to keep him off. There was no letup in the Dempsey attack. He allowed Sharkey no rest. He had more fight in him than Sharkey and was more aggressive in every round.

> He proved again his remarkable ability to take crushing punishment without going down, without giving up his endless pursuit of the younger and faster man. Dempsey found himself out classed at long range, where he took most of his punishment, but he more than made up by the ceaseless fury and power of this body attack, an attack Sharkey could not elude.

Hence, it was regrettable that the fight ended the way it did.

Many claimed that the low blows were not struck with enough force to hurt Sharkey, "but that doesn't alter the fact that Sharkey had a claim to make and that he was knocked out while in the act of starting his appeal."

James J. Wood said the legality of the ex-champion's body punch would long be debated. Wood said he was behind Sharkey and not in a position to judge the blows. Regardless, Dempsey found his fistic fountain of youth.

> This I am going to say. Jack Dempsey made the fight. The old Manassa Mauler was the gent who made the battle as good as it was, if not great. He may have been tiring. He may have been slipping round by round. But he was the aggressor all the way through and in my humble opinion the winner at the time the bout ended with Sharkey on the floor, groveling in the ring resin, his hands pressed to the pit of his abdomen.

Referee Jack O'Sullivan was one of the fairest and most competent referees in the ring, and he thought the blows were fair. He warned Dempsey perhaps two or three times for low punching. Wood said,

> The blows weren't foul to the extent of hurting Sharkey. The Bostonian himself never complained until the final smashes which put him down and out – officially at least. Then he protested, and I thought rather weakly, to Referee O'Sullivan as both his hands went down in pain and he turned as Dempsey delivered a terrific left hook to the jaw that settled the million-dollar dispute.

Regardless, Dempsey was not anywhere near the form necessary to beat Tunney. "I don't think he'll ever see that peak of perfection again or any height like that." Wood hoped Dempsey would not fight Tunney again. He could not defeat immutable laws. "He can't come back that far. His day is past. He is a has-been – a great one, of course, but still a has-been." Regardless, Dempsey won, and was good enough to beat Sharkey.

> [Dempsey] was winning when the end came to give him complete victory, whether deserved or not. I gave Dempsey almost every round after the opener. In that Sharkey outboxed him and outfought him and my co-worker Mr. Frank Kearns thought Sharkey had a shade in the fifth although I called it even. But Dempsey forced the fighting all the way. He made the battle. He kept boring in, plugging away with both hands to the body – always trying – always coming in. Time and again Sharkey had to break ground. Time and again Youth had to back away from dogged, persistent Age. Time and again Sharkey gave way to the old Manassa Mauler and time and again Dempsey actually outboxed him.

Yet, Wood doubted that Tunney, who was sitting in a front-row chair, had any concerns. "He must have figured that either of the Jacks would have been perfect for him." Sharkey's speed, skill, and cockiness disappeared as Dempsey moved into him, digging hooks and smashes into his midsection. The "Dempsey of 24 years was a better fighter than Sharkey ever will be at any time."

> [This version of Dempsey] was flat-footed, slow and far different from even the Dempsey of the Firpo days of 1923. Then we had a rushing, speedy, gambling Dempsey. Now he is old, slow and conservative. He is trying to make the best of a punch that has lost a great deal of its power, that is nothing compared to the old wallop...

> I doubt very much that the Dempsey of the Stadium was better in any way than the Dempsey of Philadelphia, if he was as good. I've always held that Dempsey wasn't so bad against Tunney as Tunney was good against him. And I think the same today. I still believe

that Tunney is his master at the sunset of the smartest career ever known to heavyweight history.

Tunney could beat this version of Dempsey. But Sharkey never could beat Dempsey, not even this version.

Wood was told that Sharkey didn't like body punching, but always got up. But he didn't get up against Dempsey. "He wasn't hit that low. Even though the punches were below the danger line at least I could see from where I sat that they were not so low as to cause terrific pain or injury that would have prevented his getting up. And he was able to walk out of the ring under his own steam. ..."

Afterwards, when Sharkey's handlers were calling Dempsey several uncomplimentary names and being loud in their squawks about the decision, Sharkey exclaimed, "Ah, shut up! It's all in the racket. Wot-the-hell!" And that was all he would say.

William Granger of the *Brooklyn Citizen* said Dempsey looked beaten, but a low right started Sharkey on the road to defeat. The former champ's face was puffed badly and his legs were weak at the finish. Sharkey emitted a cry of pain from the low right, his hands dropped, and Dempsey swung a hook to the jaw. The referee did not start counting until the timekeeper reached eight.

Alan Gould, Associated Press sporting editor, said the hollow shell was loaded after all, for it exploded and blew the tar out of Sharkey's title shot. The dynamite in Dempsey's mauling fists was too much for Sharkey, who crumpled under the awful body punching. It was a sensational comeback and a stunning knockout victory. It was a vicious right to the midsection followed by a short left hook flush to the chin.

It was a hard-won triumph, a slashing, mauling battle that saw Dempsey rally from impending defeat in the 1st round. He proved that he still could take it, for he was tottering and groggy from solid hooks to the head, and bleeding from his mouth. Yet, he battered his young rival with a relentless, terrific body attack that finally brought him down. He had summoned back much if not all of his punching power, and all of his old gameness and stamina. He might not be what he was in 1919 or even 1923, but he had come back a long way from his dreary, floundering performance against Tunney in late 1926. "Dempsey's once lightninglike speed of foot has vanished, although his shiftiness remains. His punches carry again terrific power," and he could take it and come back to win.

Those who claimed his punches were low could not even agree on whether it was a right or a left that was low. It was a right to the body, on the waist line, and after Sharkey turned his head toward the referee to complain, a left hook to the jaw decked him. After hesitating for a second or two, the referee decided it was fair, picked up the count, and counted to ten.

According to Gould, to the majority of ringside critics, Dempsey seemed to have a distinct advantage on points. Sharkey's offensive wilted or was held back after the slashing 1st round. He gave ground steadily under Dempsey's persistent body hammering. Occasionally the sailor countered with hooks to the jaw that jarred Dempsey, notably in the 3rd and 6th rounds, as well as the 1st. He cut Dempsey's right eye, mouth, and nose, and remained virtually unmarked himself. But for the most part, Sharkey's attack was wild. His usually accurate jab failed to stop Dempsey's rushes. Dempsey often blocked or ducked the sailor's vaunted right cross.

Sharkey's confidence seemed to ebb as he found his best blows either missing or failing to bring down his foe, while Dempsey beat a steady drum-fire on his ribs. Sharkey's youth and speed were not sufficient to stand off Dempsey's aggressive bulldog onslaught. Sharkey found something far more explosive, consistent, and relentless than what he had encountered with Godfrey, Wills, McTigue, and others.

The fight set a radio record, having been heard by listeners from coast to coast via over 51 stations.

Word was that Dempsey–Tunney II likely would be in mid- to late-September, in 2 months, at Soldier's Field in Chicago, given its massive seating capacity.

Jimmy De Forest said Dempsey made a flashing comeback as the Boston Sailor fizzled. It was a right to the body and left to the jaw. Sharkey tried to rise at nine but then fell flat on his face, knocked out. The Manassa Mauler stalled Sharkey's attempts to make it a boxing match.

Before the fight, Dempsey seemed jaunty, smiling, and full of spirit. Sharkey seemed more serious. In the 1st round, Dempsey led the attack with body blows. Sharkey stung him with his left to the body and right to the jaw. Sharkey's counterattack slowed Dempsey's onslaught. In the 2nd round, Sharkey mixed furiously, but found Dempsey willing, and there was a moment when Sharkey was near slumberland. In a mix-up against the ropes, Dempsey landed a right hook to the jaw that turned Sharkey's eyes glassy. In the 3rd, they went at it with savagery, with little defense. Dempsey hit the body, while Sharkey hit the head. Both landed freely. In the 4th and 5th rounds, Dempsey showed that his strength had come back to him, and he was running the fight like a champion once more. He was pounding the stomach and landing several straight lefts. He made Sharkey back up and run out of the mix-ups.

Sharkey began displaying respect by trying to make a boxing match of it. However, the former champ would not have it. He closed in repeatedly and forced Sharkey to mix it up. The way Dempsey's strength held out throughout the mauling showed him to be in far better condition than he was for the Tunney fight. In the 7th round, a right to the body and left hook to the jaw knocked him out.

Sharkey tried to protest and claim a foul when he was hit by the right to the body, but then the hook knocked him out. Screams of foul were heard, but referee Jack Sullivan did not recognize a foul.

Dempsey-Tunney would be next. Dempsey had shown his ability to take punishment. He took a considerable amount of it from Sharkey and came back strong, which gave him the right to fight Tunney again. Gene had jabbed his head off in their fight. It was splendid work to prepare Dempsey for the rematch. "And Tunney had best look out, for last night's fight showed that Jack's eye is with him again. He missed very few. Most of the prophets had thought Dempsey would blow to pieces. But it was Sharkey, the meteor, who fizzled away like a damp Fourth of July skyrocket."

William Spring said Dempsey was back. Three right hooks to the stomach and a left hook to the jaw did it. Jack still could sock as hard as ever. "Foul? By no means! They were fair to everyone but Sharkey, and it seemed cruel that such a promising fighter should be the victim of these crushing blows."

They had whaled away at one another at a maddening pace up until the end, to the delight of the 90,000 who received their money's worth. Sharkey's roundhouses and uppercuts had plenty of sweep and were more colorful and eye-catching, but Dempsey all the while continually was ripping and digging in short six-inch body blows that the average spectator could not see, but nevertheless were effective.

To the average fan, Dempsey was a hero and real champion. He put up entertaining battles. They came in droves to see him.

> The reason for the Dempsey charm is apparent. He can unleash a knockout blow on a moment's notice – as he did last night – and that's what makes him popular. He can take punching and return with a wallop more deadly than the man who's hitting him. Jack Dempsey, the hardest-hitting heavyweight in years, may not be champion in the sense that Tunney is. But, to millions throughout the nation he is still champion – in popularity and ring ability as well.

Many, while recognizing Tunney as champion, often noted that he had won the championship by decision, and had not knocked out Dempsey, which caused some to be begrudging in their praise and recognition. The reality is that fight fans always have admired and been excited to see the aggressive puncher more than the careful boxer. Men like Sullivan and Dempsey always were going to be more popular than Corbett, Johnson, and Tunney.

Jim Brodie said Dempsey's steady two-handed body attack to the midsection wore down Sharkey and won him the fight. It was a great fight, and Dempsey looked 100% better than he did against Tunney in Philadelphia. "Sharkey couldn't stand off and box Jack because the latter kept boring in and his punches were too heavy for Sharkey to block." This version of Dempsey would have a chance to knock out Tunney.

An elated Estelle Taylor, from Hollywood, California, said, "I was certain that Jack would win. Now I want him to whip Tunney and then retire. I have wanted him to leave the ring for some time."

From Salt Lake City, Dempsey's mom said, "I thought he would win, but then I was awful nervous." She knew it was a hard test and believed that Sharkey was better than Tunney, though her son was in better shape than in his last fight.

Henry Farrell said a scowling, head-down ex-champion kept tearing into the cocky Sharkey and refused to be outsmarted. Dempsey had forced the fighting all the way and seemed to have at least an edge in every round, and in some a wide margin. There was not a second in which Dempsey was not plugging in and forcing Sharkey back. In the 7th, Dempsey shot a right into the body, perfectly fair, and Sharkey dropped his guard and writhed in pain, trying to protest that the blow was foul. Dempsey closed in with a solid left to the chin and the fight was over.

Rickard already had signed both and got them to agree that the winner would meet Tunney in mid-September.

When Sharkey entered the ring, he attempted to stare Dempsey down, but Jack refused to look at him, and refused to be annoyed as Sharkey constantly tried to direct his gaze toward him.

Up to the 7th, Dempsey had won every round, although for a moment in the 1st he looked bad, and often tired. Sharkey rarely stepped forward, for Dempsey attacked all the time. When Dempsey was pouring vicious left hooks into his body, Sharkey kept looking at the referee, Jack O'Sullivan, who waved him back and said, "Come on and fight."

Several times it looked as if Dempsey was in trouble and about to go. His left eye was cut slightly. But he kept on courageously. Dempsey took Sharkey's best punches and kept tearing lefts and rights into the body that had Sharkey "almost crying."

Dempsey almost scored a knockout in the 3rd, when he clipped Sharkey with a left hook to the chin and right to the body, and Sharkey sank to the floor. The referee waived Dempsey back and Sharkey got to his feet just as the bell sounded. (Most said this was a slip.)

The fight ended dramatically in the 7th round, when Dempsey caught Sharkey with a right under the heart and a terrific left to the jaw. Sharkey dropped to his knees, hands on the floor, then rolled over on his side, lifting his hands to his stomach, and kept rolling. Dempsey walked to a neutral corner and watched the referee count.

Unpopular as he was supposed to have been in previous fights, Dempsey was the hero from start to finish.

Many thought that Dempsey would weaken after the 4th round and slow down, but they were wrong.

Dempsey said to Farrell, "Well, I'm still here. I got that little bit of a cut under the eye, but what is that?"

Dempsey's eyes were puffy, and several stitches had been taken. Yet, he was up early the next morning and played 18 holes of golf with his manager, finishing the course in "about 100 strokes."

Tim Byrne, sports editor for the *New York Evening Post*, said Dempsey's speed was gone, so he had to rely on his ring experience. He won because he had a better mind. He plodded forward flat-footed now, whereas in previous years he dashed in with killing force. Now he needed to fire ten blows to do the work that one punch used to do. "That does not mean Dempsey cannot hit hard any more. They are the same short jolts, but it takes more of them." Four years ago, those same blows put Firpo on the floor, down and out in 2 rounds. It took 6 rounds of steady body punching to wear down the strong, young Sharkey to the finishing point.

Ultimately, courage and determination won it for him, for he was nothing like the Dempsey that beat Willard. He no longer was the rip-roaring boy of age 24. His style had not changed, but rather was modified. He "carried a great burden of punishment with a spirit that did not weaken." Dempsey took it, especially to his face, but he gave in return body blows which were not as sensational but had their long-term effect.

Dempsey often looked clumsy and awkward. In the 1st round, it seemed as if he would be knocked out. His legs wavered. Folks said, "I told you so; he's all through." His legs, weakened by age and luxurious living since the Firpo fight, stayed under him, and lugged around a courageous fighting heart that Sharkey could not break.

> In the end it was Sharkey's heart that weakened under the accumulation of punishment to the body.

> Wilting slowly from this relentless attack, which was concentrated at the belt line, Sharkey led himself to believe he had been fouled and, dropping his hand, opened his chin to that short left hook that knocked him out.

> Dempsey was not trying to foul Sharkey. In carrying out a plan to whale away at the midsection, the man from Manassa often played right on the danger line. The punches were low on the legitimate area, but they were not foul. The three quick blows, right, left, right, which struck Sharkey just before the knockout did not land in the groin. But they must have hurt terribly. Sharkey gasped, his face was distorted as in pain and he dropped his right hand. Dempsey nailed him.

However, Dempsey's courage most likely would not be enough to beat Tunney. Gene was more cautious and defensive. Sharkey fought more, which gave Dempsey the opportunity to fight.

> Notwithstanding all this, he fought a magnificent fight last night and earned a victory that was hailed as glorious by the more than 80,000 cheering men and women who packed the Yankee Stadium. For what age had taken from him in agility and punching power, age had given back to him in experience and ring intelligence. He won because he had a better mind than Sharkey and greater courage.

Walter Trumbull said most expected Dempsey to wilt over time, but, "The fact is that Dempsey's worst round was the first, and that from that time he grew better and Sharkey worse." Sharkey's supporters claimed he was fouled. "Dempsey hit him with a right and left to the body before the final punch to the jaw…" Referee O'Sullivan, "one of the best referees in the game," was close to the fighters and considered the punches to be fair. "From where we sat, it looked as if the right punch was perhaps an inch below the top of Sharkey's trunks. But Sharkey did not fall from that punch. He went down from the left to the jaw." Trumbull believed that Sharkey fought poorly, making little use of his boxing ability or speed, allowing Dempsey to take the play away from him and make him fight as he wished.

Early on, Dempsey seemed old, a once great fighter with nothing left except courage. It seemed as if he might be stopped within the first two rounds. In the 2nd, Dempsey landed a left hook to the jaw and Sharkey's knees bent. Dempsey still could punch. Dempsey kept absorbing blows, getting staggered again in the 3rd, but his heart was strong, and he kept shuffling in doggedly, always for the body. His punches seemed ineffective, but instead of weakening, he grew stronger. In the 4th, his eye and nose were bleeding, but he bore in with body blows that seemed to have more of the old snap. Sharkey began to box, and landed some stiff wallops, but he was not as fast as he had been. Sharkey sped up again in the 5th. In the 6th, despite being hit with powerful blows, Dempsey kept driving forward, hitting the body, and even landing a jab. Both men hit after the bell. "This was the first round which was clearly Dempsey's." In the 7th, "Sharkey plunged face forward to the floor from the two body blows and the hook to the jaw." O'Sullivan counted him out.

The crowd roared for the victor and shouted themselves hoarse. Again Dempsey had proved George L. Rickard a prophet when he said, "That feller is the greatest drawing card in this here world."

Courtenay Terrett said the crowd was delirious with joy when the unshaven Dempsey sent the man in purple tights crumpling to the floor. "They had wanted Jack Dempsey, once champion and an unpopular one, to win. They had wanted him to beat down and shame this braggart young man from Boston."

DEMPSEY and SHARKEY

OFFICIAL FIGHT FILMS
ONLY AT
PARK HILL & ORPHEUM THEATRES
Today, Tomorrow, Sunday, Monday
AFTERNOON and NIGHT
NO ADVANCE IN PRICES

Frank Wallace wrote, "There will be those who say that the blow was foul. Others that Sharkey quit. But to my mind the rise of our old champion from the ashes where he had been consigned quite overshadows all of that." Regardless, Dempsey "isn't the fighter he used to be" and "would be easy game for the champion." And yet, he still was the biggest gate draw in boxing, and would be yet again against Tunney.

The *Brooklyn Citizen* said even the moving pictures failed to settle the foul question. Neither of the radio broadcasters noticed any low blow. They believed the blows that ended the fight were fair.

Referee O'Sullivan said Dempsey did throw a low blow in the 7th round, but it glanced off the leg and did no damage. "I do not regard the blow Sharkey received on the leg as sufficient cause for disqualification." The punches that knocked out Sharkey were a legal body blow and a left to the jaw.

The *Daily News* quoted Referee O'Sullivan as saying that after he cautioned Dempsey for hitting the leg, to keep his punches up,

> Dempsey nodded his head and then let his right fly for the belly. He caught Sharkey right in the pit of the stomach. Sharkey started protesting and dropped his hands, and when I refused to allow it, Dempsey let fly with a left to the jaw and there was nothing left for me to do but count Sharkey out.

Before the fight, Leo Flynn had noted Sharkey's penchant for making foul claims, and Leo asked for an indelible mark to be made on the waist to prevent a false foul claim. The request was denied, with the statement that the competent officials provided would be able to handle any situation that may arise. Flynn had said the day before the fight that he was going to ask the referee to watch not only for fouls, but to "watch just as particularly blows that are not fouls so that there will be no chance for Mr. Sharkey to get away with anything."

Jack Farrell said 40 out of 50 experts agreed that the movies showed no foul.[558]

Paul Gallico insisted the blows were fair, in the pit of the stomach. He believed that Dempsey's relentless attack was breaking Sharkey down, the body attack had him softened up, and he was ready to go. Dempsey ripped his heart out.

When Dempsey was hurt, he recovered and fought back hard. Dizzy and groggy, he always moved in. He made Sharkey fight the way he wanted, and grew stronger every minute. He broke him mentally and physically. When Sharkey was hurt, he tried to cry foul.

> Will the gentlemen who claim foul kindly consider these facts: Sharkey's tights were pulled high at the start of each round; Sharkey

[558] *Brooklyn Citizen, Binghamton Press, New York Daily News,* July 23, 1927.

is a notorious foul screamer and has won three fights on fouls; Dempsey has never lost a fight on a low body punch; Sharkey was starting for the floor the way a man does who has been hit in the stomach and not low; Sharkey's protective cup was untouched; Sharkey was able to leave the ring, lifting his leg easily OVER the bottom strand of rope. ... Sharkey fouled Dempsey in the sixth when he deliberately hit him with a right after the bell. The pictures show this.

Thomas Rice said Sharkey showed up better in the pictures than he did in real life. The movies established nothing about the allegedly low punches. The deceptive angle made it impossible to see exactly what occurred. Further, despite Sharkey's brilliant rallies and the heavy punishment he inflicted, Dempsey was winning all of the rounds after the 1st, which was about even, and although Sharkey did well in the 6th, he was nailed by a left hook to the jaw from which he had not recovered when the bell rang to start the next round.

Some writers said Sharkey had it on Dempsey all the way. Others agreed that Dempsey had the better of the milling by a wide margin up to the finish. (And others said it was close or even. It simply was a matter of perspective.)

Rice's answer was that Sharkey, when he did box openly and cleverly, landed neatly and cleanly, so the punches could be seen by all, for his blows were spectacular and easily recognized. Hence, his flashes carried undue weight with observers, who overlooked the incessant piling up of points by Dempsey at effective infighting which was more subtle and less noticeable and flashy, but quite effective.

Still, Rice thought the blows before the knockout were low. He said probably about 20 writers, including himself, would take an oath that Dempsey hit low. He saw three land low. And yet, the victory was fair, for "A man on his feet must protect himself at all times." Sharkey made the huge mistake of looking at the referee and dropping his hands, which was foolish and unnecessary.[559]

Gene Tunney agreed to meet Dempsey in two months, on September 15 or 22. He said,

Dempsey won fairly from Sharkey. I saw every punch that was delivered by Dempsey during the seventh round, and I watched the fight very closely, and I failed to detect any low punch. I think Dempsey was absolutely within his rights when he landed that final left hook, because a man is supposed to protect himself at all times. Sharkey's pride and negligence in a crisis brought about his defeat.[560]

[559] *Brooklyn Daily Eagle*, July 23, 1927.
[560] *New York Daily News*, July 24, 1927.

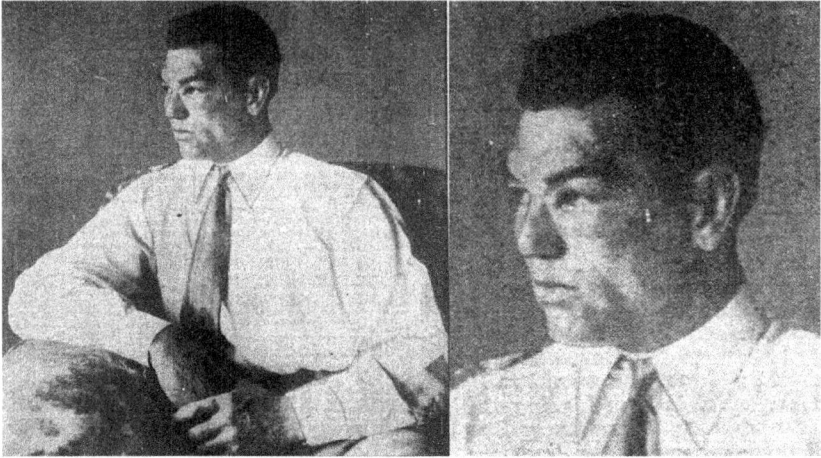
Dempsey's puffy face the day after the fight

Ed Hughes said Dempsey's ring engagements always bristled with extraordinary incidents, giving folks food for endless argument. He was unfailing in giving fans something to watch, talk, and read about, "and after all that is the type of fighter most beloved in ringdom." It helped his amazing popularity, despite the fact that he once was one of the "most anathematized" fighters. "Picturesqueness, ability, mystery, glamor, drama and even hints of scandal – these are a few of the essentials of 'color.' Jack Dempsey can lay claim to all of them."

Dempsey-Willard had the controversy of the weak bell, whether Willard was knocked out or saved by the bell at the end of the 1st round, whether Dempsey's leaving the ring (not having heard the bell and thinking he had won) should cause him to lose, and the speculation regarding whether his fearful hitting was aided in some way by plaster of Paris in his bandages. Dempsey's prior and subsequent knockouts proved that he did not need anything extra, particularly since his hands and gloves had been inspected prior to the fight, as well as in subsequent bouts.

The Brennan fight had the question of whether rabbit punches had helped dispose of Brennan. "Under any kind of rules then existing this was legitimate enough. However, by some mysterious code of reasoning the raps appeared unethical to discriminating ringsiders." Thereafter, the rabbit punch became a blacklisted illegal swipe, but not prior to that fight.

The worst some said about the Carpentier fight was that Dempsey possibly carried him for the motion pictures, when he could have stopped him in the 1st round had he so chosen.

Hughes said the rulebook should have been destroyed for the Firpo fight. "Dempsey, maker of thrills extraordinary and controversies white heat, was again on the job in the memorable Firpo encounter." The wild, untamed, longshoremanlike action was more than enough, but there was more to discuss. Some said Firpo was on the canvas for 14 seconds before rising the first time. Also, "Dempsey with the Argentine on the floor refused, or forgot, to retire to a neutral corner. He bent over the form of the South American and smote him, practically as 'Dead Pan' Luis was arising." Several times, Firpo appeared to drop without being hit, which could have caused his disqualification. When Dempsey was catapulted through the ropes, he was "given a slow count, to say the least. Actually Dempsey must have been out of the ring some 18 seconds. However, it was a caveman's battle from the start; the rule book might as well never have existed." (Jack hit after the bell as well.) Several of these claims were not true. Ultimately, the better man won. Regardless, folks always had something to discuss after a Dempsey fight.

> Nevertheless, it was a typical Dempsey fistic production, ornamented with magnificent, Homeric slugging, odd, spectacular happenings and followed by the usual wrangles, squabblings, bickerings and controversies.
>
> Dempsey never fails the fans. He furnishes them a whirlwind spectacle in the ring and a bagful of choice morsels for debate afterward.

Folks wondered what was wrong with Dempsey against Tunney. Now they would debate whether he fouled Sharkey. He seldom failed to provide arguments. "What will it be after the next Tunney fight? Something. Like the Lord, Dempsey never fails to provide."[561]

Both judges for the fight saw low blows. Charles Mathison said he saw three low blows, which set up the knockout. Tom Flynn, the other judge, said he saw two low blows, but in his opinion neither did much damage nor gave ground for disqualifying Dempsey. He supported the referee.

According to Dr. Spellman in Newton, Massachusetts, Sharkey had suffered from internal bleeding since the fight. The body punishment had taken its toll.

The controversy and the fight's competitiveness fueled the film showings in New York, so a bundle of money was made that way too.[562]

Referee Jack O'Sullivan told Thomas Rice,

> Sharkey did not say a word to me in the 7th round. He merely started to look in my direction, then Dempsey clipped him on the chin with a left and he went down.
>
> He was never unconscious and he did not fall as a man falls when he has been fouled by being struck below the belt.
>
> What made Sharkey ready for the knockout was a short right hand drive to the solar plexus that traveled about eight inches and was so quickly delivered that nobody who was not on top of the men, as we say, could see it.
>
> Dempsey did hit Sharkey below the waist line in that flurry, but it was a glancing blow, upward, and along the leg, not the groin. None

[561] *Brooklyn Daily Eagle*, July 25, 1927.
[562] *Brooklyn Daily Eagle*, July 26, 1927.

of the blows in that flurry landed in the groin and he showed no signs of having been fouled when examined in the dressing room after the bout.

I had warned Dempsey twice earlier in the contest about a tendency to swing too low.

What everybody has overlooked is that I also warned Sharkey twice about the same thing.

Sharkey several times held Dempsey with one hand and hit with the other, which was against the rules, but the violations were not flagrant enough to warrant calling a foul. Dempsey never holds and hits. His style is entirely the opposite. He wants both hands free in order to keep pounding away at the body.

Rice agreed that the low blows he saw did not injure Sharkey. "Public opinion seems to be veering around to accepting the insistence of the referee and of the official physician that Sharkey was not hit in the groin." No one saw any sideswipe that could have hit the groin area, as Sharkey claimed. Given that he was wearing a foul protector, and any low blow was more off to the side, there was no reason for him to leave himself totally open to the left hook. He was foolish to have done so.

In another interview, Referee O'Sullivan said the right hand was hammering the body, and one scraped along the leg and hip, but did no harm. The referee approached them and said, "Keep your hands up, Jack – I mean you, Dempsey." He replied, "All right." And then he drove a right to the abdomen above the belt, then one to the solar plexus. "Sharkey's face registered pain and he drew back, at the same time starting to turn his head toward me, but he did not speak. Almost quicker than the eye could see, Dempsey clipped him on the chin with a left and Sharkey sank down, forward." The injuries came from clean punches to the body and jaw, not any low blow. "What caused my seeming hesitation in taking up the count was the necessity for seeing that Dempsey not only stepped clear of his fallen opponent but complied with the New York Boxing Commission's rules by going to a distant corner. After that I took up the count at four from Bill McPartland, the official knockout timekeeper, who was hammering out the seconds on the canvas with a wooden mallet alongside the bell." Sharkey never got up, despite the referee telling him to get up, that he was counting him out.[563]

Paul Gallico insisted that Dempsey's trunks were black, with a red stripe down the side. Yet, three papers reported that his trunks were red – the *Times, Telegraph,* and *Evening Telegram.* Those same papers were the ones which howled foul the loudest. Yet, they couldn't even get the trunk colors correct. Gallico believed the blows landed in the stomach.[564]

Jack Kearns had sued Dempsey for payment on a contract dated August 3, 1923, saying he was owed 33 1/3% of Dempsey's earnings

[563] *Brooklyn Daily Eagle,* July 27, 1927.
[564] *New York Daily News,* July 28, 1927.

while the contract was in force. Dempsey answered Kearns' $519,999 lawsuit with a counterclaim for $279,926.

Dempsey alleged that Kearns forged his name on the contract, and he did not know of the forgery until Kearns informed him after the commission had discovered it. Kearns then begged him to sign the paper in order to save him from possible prosecution for forgery, and Dempsey did so with the understanding that the contract was not enforceable. They had an oral understanding that Kearns would continue as his manager and receive 50%, but it could be terminated whenever Dempsey so desired. The counterclaim alleged that he was owed $144,750 for his fight with Gibbons alone, as well as money from other contests. Dempsey also alleged that Kearns, whose prior name was McKernan, had plead guilty to a criminal charge of forgery in Washington state in 1914 and served time in a jail/penitentiary for a part of one year.[565]

Former trainer Teddy Hayes also had filed (in late 1926) a lawsuit against Dempsey, claiming he was owed $62,500 in salary for his services as a secretary and personal business agent for Dempsey from December 1, 1919 to February 23, 1925, and as trainer during 1920 and 1921. Hayes had Dempsey's purse from the Sharkey fight attached for that amount. It all was based on alleged oral contracts. He and Dempsey had split when Dempsey broke away from Kearns. Hayes was a secretary, agent, fixer, adviser, confidant, friend, and Dempsey trainer for the Miske, Brennan, Carpentier, and other fights. In his filing, Hayes set forth alleged sordid details of Dempsey's private affairs. He described Dempsey as pettish (childishly bad-tempered and petulant), and said he had to be nursed. It mostly was scandalous mud-slinging and not a proper bill of particulars regarding the lawsuit.

Dempsey was portrayed in the bill as becoming involved in difficulties because of a 16-year-old girl in a hotel in Butte, Montana, and being in jeopardy on the slacker charges. Hayes alleged that he had to sit up night after night with the champ when he could not sleep, owing to worry about the slacker charges. In January 1920, Dempsey was anxious to get back the letters he wrote to Maxine Dempsey, so Teddy brought her in for an "interview." Hayes dug up witnesses for Dempsey. "I got many witnesses and the case was fixed up." Hayes went to Salt Lake City and took charge of brother John Dempsey, who was ill, and took him to the hospital. The elder Dempseys were on the outs with each other, and Teddy got them to make up so they could be relied upon for affidavits for the slacker trial.

For the Brennan fight, Hayes secured an apartment at the corner of 97th street and Broadway. He got up at 6 a.m. and ran with the champ around the Central Park Reservoir.

Hayes again went to Salt Lake City when the family was in another uproar. Jack's father and sister had left home, and brother Johnny was ill again.

---

[565] *Brooklyn Daily Eagle*, July 26, 1927.

When Kearns had to go to New York to arrange the Carpentier fight, Hayes would go on stage during the theatrical tour and impersonate Kearns, introducing the champ at each performance.

During the Carpentier camp, Hayes censored the mail so Dempsey would not be annoyed. After Kearns divided the $300,000 purse with Dempsey, he gave the champion an extra $10,000 as a birthday present.

Hayes was prevailed upon to take the Carpentier fight pictures to Boston. He got jailed and fined $1,500.

When Dempsey had a nose operation, Hayes waited on him and was his chauffeur.

Hayes then became Estelle Taylor's servant. It was after a conference with Miss Taylor that Dempsey announced, "I am through with Doc."

Hayes also alleged that he once had to placate a vengeful husband whose wife had been the object of Dempsey's admiration. The husband had beaten his wife. Teddy "squared that, too."

Dempsey's answer insisted that Jack Kearns inspired the Hayes suit simply as a way to annoy, harass, and embarrass him, and it was without merit. Hayes had been paid in full, and furthermore, never was employed by Dempsey, but by Kearns. Dempsey's attorney also asserted that at least part of the claim was barred by the 6-year statute of limitations.[566]

In other news, emblamatic of the rapid growth of the Ku Klux Klan throughout the 1920s, in both the North and the South, in late August 1927, thousands of Klansfolk attended the first annual KKK celebration held in Freeport, Long Island, New York. The *New York Daily News* even printed a photo of the flaming 100-foot cross which was erected, surrounded by 5,000 Klansfolk, and noted that the "affair was voted a huge success, only one fight being recorded."

FLAMING CROSS illuminating the countryside for miles around marked the close of K. K. K. first annual celebration at Freeport, L. I. Five thousand Klansfolk gathered around as 100-foot cross blazed. The affair was voted a huge success, only one fight being recorded.

New York Daily News, August 22, 1927

566 *Brooklyn Daily Eagle, Brooklyn Daily Times, Brooklyn Standard Union*, July 31, 1927. Theodore F. Hayes' real name was Theodore Weinstein. *Omaha World Herald*, February 6, 1929. Court documents.

CHAPTER 9

The Road to Redemption

Tex Rickard secured permission to host the Dempsey vs. Tunney rematch in Chicago, at Soldier Field, on September 22, 1927. He would pay $100,000 to rent the stadium. Unlike New York and other cities, Illinois would not limit the ticket prices, which would range from $40 or even $50 ringside, down to $5 for the cheapest seats. New York had refused to allow anything over $27.50. The local South Park board voted 4 to 1 to allow Rickard to hold the bout. A record crowd of 150,000 was expected, which would make it the richest fight in history, with over $2 million in ticket sales. Chicago wanted the fight. Money talks.[567]

Some folks protested the fight being held in Chicago, or even at Soldier Field, owing to Dempsey's failure to enlist in the war. They even attempted to secure a court injunction. These efforts, although annoying, ultimately were unsuccessful.[568]

On August 14, while en route to Chicago, Dempsey stopped in Salt Lake City to visit his mother. More than 1,500 admirers met him at the train station, cheering him and his wife.

Dempsey was so popular; large crowds turned out to see him at every railroad stop. He arrived in Chicago on August 18.

Jack promised to be ready this time. "I simply didn't know how much I had slipped when I lost the title until I got in there. I won't be guessing this shot." The good battle he had with Sharkey had helped to prepare him.[569]

Tunney did his early training in Speculator, New York. He expected to come to Chicago around September 1. On August 21, 5,000 watched Gene spar with Paul Cavalier and Billy Vidabeck, 3 rounds each.[570]

On August 22, one month after the Sharkey contest, Dempsey opened his training camp at the Lincoln Fields

---

[567] *New York Daily News, Brooklyn Daily Times*, August 2, 1927.
[568] *Chicago Tribune*, August 13, 1927.
[569] *Chicago Tribune*, August 16, 18, 1927.
[570] *Chicago Tribune*, August 22, 1927. Gene ran 6 miles in the morning.

417

racetrack, south of Chicago. He weighed about 202 pounds, according to trainer Gus Wilson, who expected him to be about 195 for the fight.[571]

On August 27, Leo Flynn opened Dempsey's camp to the public but charged $1.10 admission. Still, 500 paid to watch him spar 1 round each with K.O. Christner (around 190-195), Pete Wistort (about 195), and light heavy Benny Krueger (or Kruger). Jack tore loose with right uppercuts to the body and mixed his punches nicely, both to the body and head. His straight right to the body and left hook to the jaw landed repeatedly, and his blocking was much improved. He occasionally blocked and then shot either hand in counterpunches. He was boxing more flatfooted though.

Dempsey does road work at Crete, IL.

Dempsey belted Christner relentlessly and had him all but out. Christner nearly had been flattened on the 25th and 26th as well. Wistort gamely took a battering and was tired and weary at the bell. German light heavy Benny Krueger did not land as effectively as he had previously and took a body lacing. Jack nailed him early with a left hook, and after that, the German was not so eager to get in close.[572]

Dempsey spars Pete Wistort   Dempsey pounds on Benny Krueger

On August 30, in Speculator, Tunney sparred 4 rounds, 2 each with Chuck Wiggins (86-43-22)(coming off a DND10 Young Stribling), whom Gene had decisioned twice, and Billy Vidabeck (50-11-5).[573]

Tunney opened as the 8 to 5 favorite to win. On the 31st, Gene buffeted Wiggins for 3 rounds and Vidabeck for 2 or 3 more.

---

[571] *Chicago Tribune*, August 23, 1927. Jack would work out primarily in private, though on occasion he would train for the public.
[572] *Chicago Tribune*, August 28, 1927. Before the sparring, Dempsey worked the pulley weights, punched the bag, and wrestled with Erickson, a 228-pound wrestler. Flynn said Christner would be dropped from the camp, for he could not give Jack any real work.
[573] *Chicago Tribune*, August 31, 1927.

At Dempsey's camp on August 31, 3,500 jammed the Lincoln Fields lawn to watch Dempsey spar 4 rounds, 1 round each with Dutch Meisner, whom Jack floored with his left hook and drew blood from his mouth and nose, Jack McCann, Benny Krueger, and Osk Till, who was in Tunney's camp the previous year and had a left similar to Tunney's, landing it frequently. Dempsey then pushed and pulled with wrestler Marty Cutler for a round.

The *Chicago Tribune* said Dempsey was getting more accurate and hitting faster. His sparring partners could last only a round each, given his punching power, even though they hit him often and sometimes outpointed him.

Sam Hall said Dempsey was working on right-hand counters. Hall said you could not judge a fighter's ring performance by his training. Dempsey looked bad in training for Sharkey, and Tunney looked worse in training for Dempsey last year, but both won. "When they pull on the small gloves and the light shoes and step out in front of the thousands everything looks differently." Dempsey sometimes allowed sparring partners to outpoint him, but if it was a real fight, he could ruin them.

Eddie Egan, national amateur light heavy champ, was one of Tunney's sparring partners.

The *Chicago Herald and Examiner* declared that no matter what they said about Tunney's "high hat," he was fast and could fight.[574]

Johnny Buckley, Sharkey's manager, advised Dempsey to retire after the Tunney fight, regardless of result, fearing that he was liable to become "punch-drunk." Dempsey responded that he was a long way from being punch-drunk. "A fellow gets that way only by being punched aplenty. I think my record shows that I have not been on the

Jack with manager Leo Flynn and wife Estelle Taylor

receiving end very often." Jack said he had fought about 70 fights and won quite a few in the 1st round, without taking more than a tap or two. Another dozen or more foes were taken out in 2 to 4 rounds, so he had not taken a lot of punishment. "I went 15 rounds with Gibbons, but barring a half dozen fairly solid shots, Tommy never even made a dent in me." Bill Brennan "spanked me around quite a bit," but most of it was done with "left jabs that kept throwing me off balance and stopping me from going in at him rather than damaging me in any noticeable way." The worst pounding that he ever received was from Tunney. "I guess he

[574] *Chicago Tribune, Chicago Daily News, Chicago Herald and Examiner*, September 1, 2, 1927. Dempsey also did 4 miles of roadwork. Tunney departed from his Speculator training camp on September 1 to head to Chicago.

hit me more punches that really had a sting in them than any dozen fighters in my list." Yet, as often and as hard as Tunney hit, Jack never was floored. Sharkey did some jabbing, and shook him up in the 1st round, but "beyond that he never did much." Dempsey believed he gave the Shark more than he took, and the aftermath was worse for Sharkey. Jack's injuries were external, while Sharkey's were internal. Dempsey said his 70 fights, about 280 rounds, had not averaged above 4 rounds each, spread out over about 14 years. Hence, he had not been punished. By way of contrast, Sharkey had fought 33 fights, and his rounds total was 280, which meant his fights averaged around 9 rounds. "Sharkey already has taken as many punches as I've taken. He's taken his battering in a concentrated three years, while mine has been spread over 14 years. And it's the concentrated pounding that counts against a man."

Dempsey runs with Leo Flynn and Jerry Luvadis

In another interview, Dempsey said, "There's no secret about what I am going to do. This other guy's the champion and it will be up to me to make the fight. I'll make it all right."

At Lincoln Fields on September 1, at just after 3 p.m., a crowd of 2,000 watched Dempsey spar 7 rounds total with middleweight Oskar Till (47-16-10)(a former Tunney sparring partner), St. Paul's Jack McCann, and welterweight Andrew "My" Sullivan (21-4-1). Dempsey mostly played defense, rolling his head and body better than usual. Leo Flynn said he had Jack hold back and work on defense because he did not want him to murder his sparring partners. He wanted him to get used to dealing with fast jabs and to counter.

Jack also wrestled with Marty Cutler, in addition to his usual other exercises, bag punching, pulley weights, shadow boxing, calisthenics, and roadwork.

Sam Hall said Dempsey's "sickening" left hook was looking quite good. It would be more challenging to land his right, a.k.a. his Iron Mike, on a man like Tunney, because it had further to travel. Jack was good on defense, but of course he was not boxing Tunney, "who is a better fighter than many people seem to think."

Tex Rickard denied charging more than face value for "choice" tickets.[575]

Tunney arrived in Chicago on September 2, receiving a mighty welcome. The streets were lined with a cheering mass of humanity. He went from the train station to City Hall. He would train near Lake Villa.

---

[575] *Chicago Herald and Examiner, Chicago Daily News, Chicago Evening Post,* September 1, 1927.

Tunney arrives in Chicago with Rickard and disabled marine veteran/friend Jack Miller

Tunney with wealthy businessman and co-promoter George Getz

Gene Tunney Welcomed at City Hall Reception. Left to Right
—Edward F. Moore, Deputy Commissioner of Public Works; Ald.
John Toman, John C. Righeimer, Chairman of the Illinois Boxing
Commission; George F. Getz, Chairman of the Mayor's Committee;
Tex Rickard (Rear), Fight Manager, Tunney and John W. Gibson.

The blonde Tunney told reporter June Provines that he had no plans to marry. "I'm engaged to fight, that's all. I'm never going to marry. I'm not the marrying kind. Why? Oh – My manager won't let me."

When asked if he thought Dempsey was in better condition now than a year ago, Tunney replied, "He ought to be." When asked if he thought Dempsey was sick back then, Gene replied, "He didn't punch like a sick man."

Tunney said he was there for a boxing match, not a prizefight. "If there is to be a fight, I know nothing of it. I don't know anything about a fight. I am opposed to prize fighting. I don't like fighting, but I do like boxing, and as far as I know, this is going to be a boxing contest." Warren Brown said their prior fight was "more of a boxing lesson than a contest."

With Gene were amateur light heavy champ Eddie Egan, trainer Lou Fink, trainer/rubdown man Joe Malone, sparring partners Chuck Wiggins, Frank Muskie, and Billy Vidabeck, and advisers/secretaries Billy McCabe and Jimmy Mehaney. Manager Billy Gibson had everything ready at the Cedar Crest County clubhouse at Fox Lake, Illinois.

L to r: Sgt. Bill Smith, Eddie Egan, trainer Lou Fink, Tunney, Tom Grady Jr., Bill McCabe, trainer Joe Malone, sparring partners Frank Muskie and Billy Vidabeck, manager Billy Gibson

Warren Brown said thus far, Dempsey had monopolized customers' attention, and it was quite possible that even with Tunney in town, Dempsey still would hold the bulk of the public's interest. "Tunney is the sort of a fighter who is either taken as a matter of course or disregarded entirely."

Yet, Tunney's reception upon his arrival proved that he was popular. Throngs of thousands hailed him, jamming the streets.

On September 2, the pestiferous B. E. Clements and the Chicago Coliseum Club filed for an injunction to stop the Tunney-Dempsey fight set to be held on September 22. The plaintiffs claimed to have a Dempsey-Wills contract, pleading losses for the alleged failure of Dempsey to honor that contract. Cited in the complaint was an injunction secured in Indianapolis restraining Dempsey from fighting until he honored that contract. Both Tunney and Dempsey had evaded service of the complaint in Philadelphia before their prior fight.

The complaint in part alleged that Dempsey had demanded $300,000 in advance money, which sum later was posted for him in Chicago. Dempsey refused to accept the money, but instead announced that he had no valid agreement.

The Defendants named in the complaint included George Getz, co-promoter of the upcoming bout, George L. (Tex) Rickard, Floyd Fitzsimmons, Dempsey, and Chicago's south park commission and its members - Paul Prehn, Sam Luzzo, and John Righeimer.

Illinois Governor Len Small and screen star Will Rogers visited Dempsey at the Lincoln Fields racetrack in Crete, Illinois.

Experts noted that no prior heavyweight champion ever had regained the title after losing it in the ring. Yet, Dempsey noted that the only ones to try, Fitzsimmons and Corbett, had to fight Jeffries, "and Tunney is no Jeffries." Fitz and Corbett were older than Dempsey, and going up against a champion whom many called the greatest heavyweight ever, who was unhurtable and could take more punishment than any man ever, had amazing strength, limitless endurance, and a terrific punch in either hand.

Dempsey reasoned that Tunney was only three years younger, and not the murderous puncher that Jeffries was. Tunney was a good puncher, but "that's all." "I have an idea that Tunney can be hurt – and Tunney can be dropped if hit right." Dempsey anticipated a knockout victory.[576]

On September 3, a crowd of 2,000 watched Dempsey spar with Ben Krueger, Jack McCann, My Sullivan, and Allentown Joe Gans.[577]

Tunney said he already was fit to fight. "I wish the fight were tomorrow." He had been training for the past few months at Speculator. He weighed about 191 pounds and planned to fight at around 188.

Jack spars Allentown Joe Gans

> I am satisfied I am a better fighter than when I met Dempsey a year ago. I feel stronger and I know I am hitting harder with my right hand. I am not underrating Dempsey. He can hit and I must respect his punches. His fight with Jack Sharkey has helped him a lot and I know I have a fight on my hands. But I will be ready and perhaps I may do better than I did a year ago.

[576] Chicago Daily News, September 2, 1927; Chicago Herald and Examiner, September 3, 1927; Colorado District Court complaint – Chicago Coliseum Club v. Jack Dempsey, July 30, 1926.
[577] Chicago Tribune, Daily News, September 4, 1927. Dempsey ran 5 miles in the morning.

Billy Gibson believed that Tunney would stop Dempsey this time, but was confident that Gene would win the decision if it went the limit. Gibson said if the fight drew more than $3 million, Tunney's end would be more than $1 million. The champ was set to earn 50% of the first million dollars, 37 ½% of the second million, and 25% of the third million. He undoubtedly would earn more for one fight than any champion ever had.

Gibson would charge $1.10 admission to watch Tunney train.

Dempsey said there always was an argument after his fights, so he wasn't surprised when Sharkey made a claim of foul. "It's gotten so that I always know there's going to be some flare-up after the show is over." Dempsey insisted that it was the left hook to the chin that sent Sharkey down, after a right to the body. It clearly was the hook that dropped him, not the body blow. A man who was hit low would have gone down immediately as if shot, but Sharkey did not drop until after the hook landed a few seconds later. "They do not usually stand up and make complaint to the referee when they are hit a blow that crippled them." Sharkey did not drop, but stood up and complained, but the referee told them to fight on. "And then I hit Sharkey with a left on the chin." Sharkey crumpled completely. When he went down, he went down on his face. "So far as I could see, he did not double up his body, as men usually do who are hit foul blows." Men hit with foul blows curl up rather than flatten out. Dempsey noted that newspaper opinion was divided. He believed that those who picked him to win said it was fair, and those who picked Sharkey said it was foul. Dempsey insisted it was a fair punch.[578]

On Sunday September 4, about 4,000 - 6,000 paid $1.10 each to watch Jack Dempsey, the greatest drawing card ever, train at the racetrack. He sparred 5 rounds, 1 round with each man. He worked easily with 140-pound Norman Link. 215-pound Sergeant Lorenz got decked with a left and lasted about two minutes, for Dempsey slaughtered him. Jack then worked with his regular sparring partners. Against 180-pound Benny Krueger, Jack

Dempsey hits Sailor Lorenz with a right

tried to work on evading jabs, not really trying to hit Kruger, or hit him hard. Welter My Sullivan jabbed him and whipped over right crosses to the jaw, jerking Jack's head. Dempsey once again held back his offense. Negro middleweight Allentown Joe Gans jabbed him on the nose with even more accuracy and enthusiasm. Reporter Westbrook Pegler noted that it was not all that hard to hit Dempsey, whose specialty clearly was not defense. He got such a dabbing on his nose that one might have thought *he* was the sparring partner.

When asked to explain Tunney's lack of popularity, Estelle Taylor replied, "I met Gene Tunney twice, and he's really a very nice fellow, good looking, well mannered and worthy of being well liked by any one. But the thing that's the matter with him is as clear as daylight to me, since his nature is very much like my own. I hate crowds. ... Gene Tunney is just that way."

Dempsey was different. "On the other hand, my Jack enjoys meeting crowds." He had a natural tendency to smile when anyone hailed him. "A champion fighter really belongs to the public in more ways than the public generally will ever know. In a way, it's as hard as the work in the ring. It doesn't bother Jack a bit, though. It never did." Conversely, "Gene Tunney hates it and I know why. He can't do it well. Neither can I." They simply did not do well with large groups or people they didn't know.

Jack and Estelle Dempsey.

---

[578] *Chicago Tribune, Chicago Herald and Examiner,* September 4, 1927.

Dempsey noted that some writers quoted Tunney as saying he would knock him out this time. Jack hoped that was true, because if he tried to do it, it meant Gene would mix it with him, and that would give Jack the chance to knock out Tunney. "I'll concede that Gene is better than I am so far as boxing and keeping away is concerned. But I don't think that the day will ever come when he can slug it with me and win the fight." In their prior fight, Tunney was careful and cautious, keeping away, and "I wasn't fast enough that night to rush him and force a slugging exhibition." Jack would be faster this time. Previously, he had to furnish the aggressiveness, but could not do it because he wasn't right. This time, he would crowd Gene from start to finish. "If he's a real champion, he won't make too much use of his legs for backpedaling purposes. He will stand up and fight. ... I may not be all that I was when I was 21 or 24 or 27, but I haven't lost the punch."

At Lake Villa, Tunney said, "I never felt better in my life. I really would be most happy if the battle were tomorrow."[579]

Folks confident that Dempsey would regain the title were wagering on him, narrowing the odds, such that Jack was only the slight 3 to 2 underdog. Those from the Middle West and Pacific Coast liked Dempsey, while those in the East liked Tunney.

Tunney, avid golfer   Tunney and Billy Gibson

On September 5, at Cedar Crest, in Lake Villa, Illinois, Tunney showed a crowd of 2,000 why he was the ring's best at present. Walter Eckersall for the *Chicago Tribune* said Tunney boxed 6 rounds with three sparring partners, 2 rounds each, outsmarting all of them with clever execution and defense. He moved around with the speed of a welterweight. He feinted his foes into leads and then stabbed them with jabs, frequently shooting across straight rights to the body and head. In close he also did considerable execution, and tied up his opponents' arms so they could not do any damage. He had quality sparring partners who were good and strong, too. Chuck Wiggins was aggressive like Dempsey. He landed one left swing, but Gene gave him plenty in return. Billy Vidabeck charged in and kept coming. Gene feinted him and nailed

[579] *Chicago Tribune, Chicago Herald and Examiner*, September 5, 1927.

him with left hooks and right crosses. 178-pound light heavy Frank Muskie charged in, but Gene stung him several times, sidestepping and catching him with flush counters. Unlike most, Tunney did not wear a headgear, or head harness as it was called.[580]

Frank Muskie spars Tunney

When Dempsey visited the Soldier Field Stadium on the 5th for a Labor Day celebration, the 40,000 in attendance greeted him with an ovation, cheering and throwing seat cushions.

Sam Hall said that on September 5 at Lincoln Fields in Crete, Illinois, 5,000 watched Dempsey train for the last time in public. He boxed 4 rounds, 1 each with Allentown Joe Gans, Jim McCann, Osk Till, and Benny Krueger. Hall said Dempsey was pretty good on defense and was hitting wickedly. McCann and Krueger were well-pummeled and bleeding. Half the crowd argued that Dempsey had slowed down too much to win back the crown, while others said he was getting back into his old form and would ruin Tunney.

Joe Burman, former bantam star, was a bit doubtful about the change in Dempsey's style, as he saw it. "I would like to see him up on his toes the way he used to fight. I don't think a flat-footed stance is the best against a boxer like Tunney, it will make it easier for Gene to jab him with that knife-like left."

Leo Flynn announced that Dempsey would not spar again for a few days, and only would work out privately except for newsmen. Jack did not like the crowds, and he had taken in enough money the last couple days to pay all of his training expenses.

In his column for the *Chicago Herald and Examiner*, Dempsey admitted that his early boxing in this camp looked bad, but that was because he was practicing keeping away from right-hand punches. No one was much enthused over his work during his first ten days of training, and many had grown alarmed, saying he looked bad. Some thought he should look better than he did, given that it was only a few weeks since the Sharkey fight, but he disagreed. He did not want to overtrain and peak too early,

---

[580] *Chicago Tribune*, September 6, 1927.

lest he might go stale. He already was in good shape from the Sharkey camp and fight, so he was not letting loose as much. He started boxing earlier than he might have done, in part because he wanted to work on not getting hit with Tunney's rights so often.

On September 6, 1,000 fans saw Tunney receive his first training injury, when in the 3rd round of their sparring, Chuck Wiggins accidentally butted him on the right eye, opening a cut nearly an inch long, but it was not deep. No stitches were necessary, but it needed time to heal. Wiggins had charged in, they clinched, and the top of his head hit Tunney. Nevertheless, Gene finished the round. After Lou Fink stopped the flow of blood, Tunney still boxed 3 more rounds with Billy Vidabeck, who only threw to the body.

Gene showed his speed and fast footwork, slipping punches, countering, and taking well the ones that did land on him. Afterwards, he noted, "Accidents are bound to happen. Wiggins did not mean it. It is not a deep cut and will be well in a day or two."

Harry MacNamara said in the 2nd round, Wiggins landed a left hook that cut Tunney over the right eye. Blood spouted and trickled down. Wiggins apologized, but Gene motioned for him to continue. Trainer Lou Fink called time, administered first aid, patched it up, and Gene kept boxing. Gibson announced it was a butt that did it. However, MacNamara insisted it was a left hook.[581]

Harry Hochstadter said Tunney could punch, make the other fellow miss, and keep punching with rapid lefts and counter rights. He had strong powers of anticipation. Gene declared, "I am much better today physically than I was a year ago."

Chuck Wiggins opens up cut on Tunney with accidental head butt

Don Maxwell noted that Tunney was not like a prizefighter. His training camp had neither the appearance nor atmosphere of a fight camp. Located 52 miles Northwest of Chicago, it was called the Cedar Crest Country Club. It was a splendid country residence. They all were living as if they were wealthy men vacationing at an expensive, richly-adorned summer home. There was a golf course and swimming pool. Tunney lived a quiet and unassuming life. He liked to mix with the upper classes, and clearly had social ambitions.

---

[581] *Chicago Daily News, Chicago Evening Post, Chicago Herald and Examiner, Chicago Tribune*, September 6, 7, 1927. Gene ran 4 miles, too.

Address Jack Dempsey and he would answer, "Hello, kid." Talk loudly and he would answer in a matching tone. Jack was boisterous, more likely to slap your back or feint at your midriff than to shake hands. It was "Hi there," and "How's the gang?" His response when a reporter hailed him was: "Howdy. Well, how's the gang smoking the big fight up?" And most of the fellows who knew Dempsey liked him for it.

Gene was as different as black is from white. He spoke in a low voice, looked you in the eye, and said, "How do you do. I'm very glad to meet you, sir." Tunney spoke easily, his voice carefully modulated, his manner restrained. "I don't know whether you get it or not, but Tunney is a strange fellow to be the heavyweight champion. He's different because he acts like a gentleman."[582]

WGN, the *Chicago Tribune's* radio station, would broadcast the big fight, along with several other Chicago newspaper-owned stations. A chain broadcast would be made available by

Tunney and Eddie Egan on the road

the National Broadcasting corporation, a New York concern.

Dempsey said Gene would meet a better fighter than he whipped previously, and he would have to be better than he was in their first fight to win this time. Jack said he was not right, physically or mentally, for the first Tunney fight. He now weighed around 200 pounds.

Floyd Fitzsimmons, his close friend, offered various excuses for Dempsey's prior performance against Tunney, including that Jack's stomach was out of order, he was poisoned, his mind was troubled by the evil machinations of the sinister Jack Kearns, he missed the companionship of his wife, who remained in California, and he had been out of competition for so long that he had lost his touch, the latter likely being the real reason, combined with the fact that Tunney was pretty darn good and underestimated. Jack was even older now, but at least he had been more active and had the Sharkey bout to sharpen him up a bit. He was showing his old sprightliness, but Tunney remained the 7 to 5 favorite in Chicago.

Dempsey said the experts simply would not quit picking on his legs, saying they were "gone." They said the same thing before the Sharkey fight, too. They wrote about him as an object of pity. All the while they spoke of Sharkey's great legs and speed, and how he would make Dempsey look like a lame truck horse, hobbled and anchored down with anvils.

---

[582] *Chicago Tribune*, September 7, 1927.

If Sharkey outstepped me at any time in that fight I can't remember when it was. I carried that fight to him. Whenever he tried to back away, as fast as he was supposed to be and as slow as some of the experts claimed I was, I stepped forward a little faster than he stepped backward. I was on top of the so-called 'whirlwind' Sharkey all through that fight. He never outspeeded me at any time. When it came to legs mine held me up through all his punching, but his began to falter in the fifth and failed him completely in the seventh.

Dempsey said his legs clearly still were reasonably good. Yet, many experts insisted that his legs were gone, or far from what they once were, and such would be their opinion even if he won by knockout.[583]

[TRIBUNE Photo.]
CIRCUIT COURT TO PASS UPON DEMPSEY-TUNNEY FIGHT ON MONDAY.
Judge Otto Kerner (left foreground) watching Jack Dempsey (center foreground) being sworn in as witness in injunction proceedings involving world's championship battle.

On September 9, 1927, Jack Dempsey was in court for a hearing regarding the injunction applied for by B. E. Clements/Chicago Coliseum Club to stop the fight, perhaps the latter's method of trying to apply pressure to get Dempsey to settle and pay damages Clements claimed were owed on a breach of contract. It was a two-year-old contract calling for a fight between Dempsey and Wills, which supposedly was transferred to Clements by Floyd Fitzsimmons after a $35,000 check tendered by clients of the latter had bounced.

Ralph Rosen, attorney for B. E. Clements, president of the Coliseum Athletic Club, owner of the purported Dempsey-Wills contract, cited many instances in which celebrated persons had been enjoined, including Lillian Russell, Napoleon Lajoie, and Luisa Tetrazzini, "a Russian dancer." Actually, Tetrazzini was an Italian singer. Mr. Rosen said, "I made a mistake in calling Tetrazzini a Russian dancer." Arthur Driscoll,

[583] *Chicago Herald and Examiner*, September 7, 9, 1927; *Chicago Tribune*, September 9, 1927.

Dempsey's lawyer, responded, "That's all right. You made another error in calling Wills a fighter, didn't you?" Dempsey and the crowd joined in laughter.

Mr. Driscoll argued that the Dempsey-Wills contract was invalid, for Clements never paid a cent of the $350,000 called for in the contract. Also, Driscoll claimed the contract transfer was executed after the date of the proposed September 1926 Dempsey-Wills fight.

Driscoll argued that Clements' only potential remedy, even if arguendo a remedy hypothetically was warranted, was a suit for damages, not an injunction. In the agreement, Dempsey was described as "the world champion," which he currently was not, and Wills as "the leading contender," which he no longer was. Dempsey could not carry out the contract even if he wanted to, because the Illinois commission would not grant him a license to fight a "decrepit old man." Clements' attorney interrupted with the comment that the reason Dempsey didn't fight Wills was because he was afraid of him. At that point, Jack and several others engaged in loud and boisterous laughter/guffaws, until the bailiffs restored order. The judge took the matter under consideration.[584]

Dempsey said all talk of Tunney's alleged plan to wade in and slug it out so he could secure a knockout was bunk, and everyone knew it.

> Never in his life did Tunney carry the fight to any man. It's a dangerous procedure – and Tunney is a safety fighter. He always has been – always will be. And for this fight, when he is protecting the championship, he will be more so than ever. Tunney figures I will carry the fight to him and thus let him counter – which is his only way of fighting. Maybe I will – and maybe I won't. If I don't – if I wait to counter his leads and he's waiting, as he always does, to do his countering – what a terrible, terrible fight it will be!

Jack said if he had stayed away from Tunney as Gene did with him, the crowd would have hooted them out of the ring. Jack had to force the fight all the way, and that allowed Tunney to punch him. Dempsey hinted that this time he might be more patient, wait, or even step back and force Tunney to engage in leading, rather than wade in and take punches the way he did last time. Dempsey challenged Tunney to prove that he was a real champion by coming to him and fighting.[585]

Westbrook Pegler said the prospective referee for Tunney-Dempsey could make or mar the title fight. "The refereeing in heavyweight championship bouts has not been very good in recent years." Dempsey sometimes had been allowed to slug his foes from behind, or stand right over them after knockdowns, "instead of retiring to the furthest corner, as the rules require." He did this against both Willard and Firpo. Tommy Riley did a good job in their first contest, but there wasn't much to do. "He never had to pick up the count for a knockdown."[586]

[584] *Chicago Tribune*, September 10, 13, 1927; *Chicago Herald and Examiner*, September 10, 1927.
[585] *Chicago Herald and Examiner*, September 10, 1927.
[586] *Chicago Tribune*, September 10, 1927.

After four days off from sparring, Tunney resumed sparring on September 10, showing good speed and power. He decked Jackie Williams with a lightning-fast 1-2. He landed his jab repeatedly, shot his right to the head and body, and danced away from most returns. A right cross shook Vidabeck, who also took jabs. Each time that Gene hurt his foes, he backed off or clinched, allowing them to recover.

Tunney said he was in great shape and ready. Harry MacNamara said, "The champion has looked very good indeed in the two days of boxing he has engaged in since his arrival."

A devout Catholic, Tunney would attend mass the following morning.

Dempsey claimed to have Cherokee blood in his veins. Representatives of the Blackfeet tribe from the Glacier Park reservation, after presenting him with a feathered headpiece and an eagle-claw necklace, danced fervently around the ex-champ. They dubbed him the Thunder Chief, saying he was a powerful bird who flew high.

In his training on the 10th, Dempsey sparred with amateur middleweight Rocky Russell - who was knocked out in one minute, as well as Allentown Joe Gans, Charles Scherer, Benny Krueger, and Osk Till. Most of the time, Jack worked on countering jabs. One observer said Dempsey's punches were short and well-timed, and he had little trouble weaving and bobbing away from the practiced left hands of Gans and Till.

Yet, Sam Hall said, "Dempsey has not been impressive in his boxing or in his hand and foot speed so far." Jack said he didn't want to leave his fight in the gym. In their first fight, in the 4th round, when Dempsey had Tunney hurt on the ropes, he did not follow up, and seemed too weak to do so. "The truth was, Dempsey says, he was so weak he could hardly stand himself, let alone land a knockout punch at that time."[587]

Wurlitzer was using the upcoming fight to advertise its radios, which sold for $119 each.

[587] *Chicago Tribune, Chicago Herald and Examiner*, September 11, 1927.

GENE TUNNEY, THE MARINE   **JACK DEMPSEY, THE SHIPYARDS WORKER**

AND NOW FOR THE SHOWDOWN!—Do you remember 'way back when Gene Tunney was over in France with the marine corps and Jack Dempsey, resplendent in a glistening pair of patent leather shoes, a blacksmith's apron protecting his spotless overalls, played his own anvil chorus and operated a rivet hammer in one of the shipyards? Above you can see what they looked like then. These two are scheduled on Thursday, September 22, to renew in Chicago their own private war, at which time the former shipyards worker will try mightily to wrest from Tunney the crown the ex-marine won in Philadelphia.

The *Daily News* simply could not let go the contrast in their military records

The Dempseys and the Rickards. Jack is holding baby Maxine Rickard

Estelle Taylor said she had seen only one ring battle, shortly after they were married, and didn't like it. "As for watching Jack in the ring – I just wouldn't. I prefer not to see that side of him. Besides, every blow he took would hurt me, almost physically, and I wouldn't care to watch him hurt anyone else." Neither of them interfered with the other's career. He did not get involved in her film career, and she stayed away from his training camps and fights. They saw each other on weekends.

On September 11 at the Cedarcrest Country Club, Lake Villa, Tunney worked out before 4,000 spectators who paid $1.10 each, including women and children. In addition to punching the light and heavy bags for 4 rounds, he sparred 2 rounds with Chicago light heavy/heavy Jackie Williams, then 3 with Billy Vidabeck. He had a patch over his right eye, and his sparring partners were asked to direct their punches to places other than his eye.

Harry MacNamara, for the *Chicago Herald and Examiner,* said, "There is no denying the fact that [Tunney] is in perfect physical condition, but it will take more than that to beat Dempsey."

Tex Rickard, who was present with his wife and 3-month-old daughter Maxine Texas, said of Tunney's form, "That fellow looks awfully good. I don't know who will win, but I think it will be the greatest fight in the history of the game." Jim Jeffries and Jimmy De Forest also were there, but declined to be interviewed.

Robert Edgren, who watched him spar that day, said Tunney was more "assured and confident" of his every move than he was a year ago. "He is faster, more the boxer. He moves more lightly and with greater precision." "His foot work is cleaner and neater, and you don't see him off balance or out of position even for an instant." He reminded Edgren of Jim Corbett back when Jim was "smooth as oil and slippery as an eel." Gene could retreat swiftly and come back just as suddenly. He circled around, having no objection to using the back step and side step. Unlike Dempsey, he did not plunge in relentlessly, refusing to be stopped or driven back.

Jack Johnson had been there prior to the sparring, smiling, and told bystanders that "he'd love to put the gloves on with the new champion." Johnson said, "You'd be surprised. I can box as well as ever." No invitation was forthcoming. "It was whispered around that Tunney regarded Johnson's presence as not in the best interests of boxing." Tunney did not come out to box until Johnson left.

Tunney explained why he would be doing more secret training in the future. "I do not want any one to know the style of attack I am going to use against Dempsey. I made a study of Jack when he defeated Sharkey and I intend to fight him according to the deductions I made after that fight."

Don Maxwell noted, "Gene Tunney's personality has been the subject of comment. Some of the folks who know him say he is a diffident, modest fellow, who speaks grammatically and likes the association of cultured people. Some of Tunney's critics find him upstage." Dempsey was said to be much more accommodating to newsmen and photographers.

John Keys for the *Chicago Daily News* reported that Tunney would be paid $1 million and Dempsey $425,000. Rickard posted the amounts, for state law required fight purses to be put up before the contestants entered the ring. Such purses set a new record, surpassing by $300,000 total the purses earned by the same two men the prior year.

Judge Otto Kerner denied the B. Clements/Chicago Coliseum Club petition for an injunction to prevent the fight. The judge held that the Indiana court was without jurisdiction. Dempsey testified under oath denying that any such contract existed (given that the contract had been breached by failure to pay him any required money). Furthermore, the Club was not in a position to produce Wills in the ring, nor was Wills of such standing at present as to be able to demand a Dempsey bout. The Court also pointed out that Wills had violated the contract when he fought Sharkey.

Robert Edgren said Dempsey was looking good, and very serious in his training, with grim determination.

Sam Hall said Dempsey was looking vicious, strong, and formidable, his left better than his right. He might be old as a fighter, and might get trounced again, but Tunney might be surprised.

Some suspected that Dempsey was doing some secret sparring, either in the late evening or early morning. Dave Shade had a marked-up left eye, so the suspicion was that he was sparring with Dempsey on the sly.

Dempsey noted that Tunney said he was there to box, not fight, preparing for a contest, not a battle. "Tunney's ideas and mine are very different." Jack was there for a fight, and he intended to make a fight of it. "That's what I feel the folks are paying a couple of million dollars to see and I'd hate to disappoint them." People didn't pay big cash to see "two men stand off, make motions at each other and do some fancy stepping." They wanted to see slugging and a knockout. Their first fight was a disappointment. There was no wild or cyclonic action. "I was a terrible flop that night as a puncher. I couldn't land. And Tunney, although he landed a hundred times or more, never flattened me. So the thing became one of those 'boxing contest' things such as Tunney talks about." The fans wanted to see Tunney knock him out or for Jack to knock out Tunney, to establish supremacy clearly. That's what they paid to see.

Dempsey's manager, Leo P. Flynn, said Dempsey would surprise everyone. His stamina and legs were better than they were in his last two fights, showing wonderful progress. He had improved 25% over the Sharkey battle and 125% over the prior Tunney fight. Of course, Tunney claimed to have improved 40%.[588]

Dempsey was working out at night in private, under the lights, to get used to them. Leo Flynn reported that on Sunday evening the 11th, Jack had decked Allentown Joe Gans. "Mr. Dempsey has a tendency to knock them prostrate when he is practicing his lessons." He then boxed with Oskar Till, Roy Williams, Whitey Allen, and Charlie Scherer, one after another, and dropped all of them as well. Flynn said Jack would do the same with Tunney. They were aware that Tunney liked playing a game of tag and run, with Dempsey chasing.

Jimmy Bronson, who handled Tunney's corner for the first fight, and would do so again, said,

> Tunney is at least 25% better than he was at Philadelphia a year ago. … I am convinced he is punching more accurately and harder than he did last year. Gene is a straight puncher and I believe he will beat Dempsey, who is more of a hook artist, to the punch most of the time. Tunney's left hand is his best asset. He will jab out Jack's eyes unless Dempsey shows a better defense than he did against Sharkey. The thing that makes the greatest impression upon me is Tunney's feinting. He draws an opponent's leads by feinting with his head, shoulders, hips or arms. When an opponent turns loose a punch, Tunney is ready for the counter. Gene's defense also has improved. We realize that Dempsey will show best at close quarters, and we have been working on a defense for his body punches. Gene has tied his sparring partners' arms so they were helpless when they were in close. Dempsey, of course, will be harder to handle, but I am sure he will not pump many hard

[588] *Chicago Tribune, Chicago Daily News, Chicago Herald and Examiner,* September 12, 1927; *Chicago Daily News,* September 13, 1927.

punches into Gene's midsection. Considering every angle of the game, I cannot see anything but a Tunney victory.[589]

Jimmy De Forest said Dempsey lacked both speed and the endurance to maintain a killing pace until he finished the job as he once did. He would fight in spurts, and then take a while to recover. Dempsey had been training sporadically, working for a time and then backing off, and he sparred the same way. That said, even when at his zenith, he used to back off a bit after carrying on for any length of time. He never did set the relentless nonstop pace of a Battling Nelson, Ad Wolgast, Dick Hyland, or Willie Ritchie. However, those fellows, although they could keep going for a long time, "never traveled at any lightning pace, as Dempsey did. Jack was more like a firecracker, a high explosive in action, than a slow fuse." Still, Dempsey was not the same. "What Dempsey has lost is his old-time effectiveness, his marvelous speed, his deadly accuracy and his powers of swift recuperation." Yet, his punch remained. However, he was easy to hit, particularly with the right, Tunney's best punch. Tunney had a good left jab, which was improving, and it would set up his right hand.[590]

Separate lawsuits had been brought against Gene Tunney by Max "Boo Boo" Hoff, who demanded $250,000, and Tim Mara, asking for $125,000. A lesser suit for $15,000 for breach of contract also had been filed by Thomas McHale, who claimed he was Gene's social secretary.

Hoff, a Philadelphia fight manager and promoter, claimed that before the Dempsey-Tunney bout, he entered into a contract with Tunney and Gibson, in which Hoff was to receive 20% of Tunney's earnings. Hoff claimed to have paid $20,000 as consideration. Abe Attell's name cropped up in connection with the transaction. Attell was known or strongly suspected to have had something to do with fixing the 1919 World Series.

Tim Mara, a prominent sportsman/bookmaker/gambler and owner of the New York Giants football team, was seeking 10% of Tunney's earnings, which he claimed was owed pursuant to an agreement with Tunney to pay said amount if Mara succeeded in getting him a fight with Dempsey at a time when Wills was regarded as the logical contender. Tunney responded that the agreement with Mara was for a fight in New York, and when the New York license committee refused to sanction Dempsey-Tunney, the agreement with Mara was nullified.

Jack Kearns still was seeking 50% of Dempsey's earnings from the last Tunney fight. Although the fight took place after his contract ended, he claimed that the match was made while the contract still was valid. He was asking for half of Dempsey's alleged $800,000 purse.

Dempsey said he did not believe in the old idea that a fighter's wife had no place in training camp. His wife was a help and inspiration, not a hindrance. Tom Gibbons had his wife and family with him when he trained to fight Dempsey. Jack Sharkey's wife was with him in most of his camps. Dempsey was lonely without her and enjoyed her companionship.

[589] *Chicago Tribune*, September 13, 1927.
[590] *Chicago Daily News*, September 13, 1927.

Estelle was staying at a hotel in Chicago, 25 miles away from his camp, so they were able to visit one another.[591]

189-pound Tunney was holding as the 7 to 5 favorite. One brokerage house was willing to lay 2 ½ to 1 that Tunney did not knock out Dempsey.

On September 13, according to Fred Hayner, Dempsey was impressive in boxing 5 rounds, 1 round each with Whitey Allen, Big Boy Peterson, Dave Shade (109-18-53), who was one of the world's best middleweights, Roy Russell, and Joe Gans. Jack crouched and appeared unhittable, and even when his foes did land, they could not do so with damaging power. Jack moved in, crowded, and worked fast all the time.

Robert Edgren said Dempsey was wrecking his sparring mates in secret nighttime sparring sessions under the bright lights in the ring at the racetrack. This felt more like the old-time Dempsey. He wore his scowl again, and it fit him better. His speed and footwork had improved. "He knows that Tunney will not stand flat-footed to swap punches or come bulling in the way Sharkey did. Dempsey must have speed and a versatile attack to offset Tunney's elusiveness and circling attack."

In their prior fight, Dempsey did not seem like himself, for he was so slow that Tunney had no trouble hitting him or eluding his attack. Jack was much different in that fight than his pre-three-year-layoff version. From 1918 to 1923, "Jack Dempsey was the greatest fighting machine in the world when he fought in his own natural style."

Herbert Corey wrote that Dempsey gradually was ceasing to be fun-loving, and his fighting temper was beginning to show through the mask of good nature. When himself, Dempsey was "as pleasant as a salesman for a new car. He roughs his friends, but gently." As the fight drew near, he held back less in training and hurt his sparring mates more. The old savagery was coming back.

Jimmy De Forest called it a soft era in which toughness had passed out of the game. Tunney's living quarters were sumptuous and soft. Champions like Sullivan and Fitzsimmons never would be found in such palatial quarters. Tunney and Dempsey were training and sparring less than 10 rounds, light compared to what the old timers did. Jack and Gene

[591] *Chicago Herald and Examiner*, September 13, 1927.

only had to fight 10 rounds, also much less than what the old timers had to do. Yet, they were earning more. "Soft? I'll say it is!" Dempsey had an excuse for laying off, for he was old for a fighter. "When Jack Dempsey passes it looks as if the fight game would lose the last of the romantic, blood-tingling type of battlers." "Tunney is doing just as he announced he would do – he's training to outbox and outpoint Dempsey, and if fortune smiles, strive for a knockout when and if the wide-open opportunity presents itself. It is the safe and sane policy of the ring today."

Warren Brown reported that the contracts were filed with the commission. Tunney was to receive $1 million and Dempsey $437,500, with an additional $12,500 if the gate exceeded $3 million.

The promoters were required to make every endeavor to prevent tickets from falling into the hands of scalpers.

Sam Hall said Dempsey had a dual nature. While boxing, he was a scowling, savage caveman, abysmal brute, with a killer instinct, game, merciless, relentless, cruel, deadly and cold, a true warrior, a man who never yelled 'foul' in his life. He asked for no quarter and gave none. Outside the ropes, he was a loving, kind husband, a pal, good friend, dandy company, a gentleman, charitable, and a game loser. He was the greatest box-office attraction in boxing history.

Dempsey said the toughest time for him was the 24 hours wait preceding a fight. "I'd rather fight 200 rounds against the toughest battlers in the world than live through the 24 hours that precede a battle in which I'm going to figure. The day of the fight seems to be a million years long, with nerves tensed all the time, with the mind full of worries and with nothing seeming to help do any of this cheering up stuff." All through his career it was that way. He never worried during training, but the wait during the last day was agony.[592]

Dempsey told Fred Hayner, "I had to chase Tunney to make it a fight then. If I hadn't we both might have been chased from the ring." Hayner said Dempsey could kill a stationary target but had much greater difficulty with a moving one.

Commissioner Paul Prehn said the referee would not be selected until fight night, and would be picked from a group of six men.

On September 15, the official Illinois boxing commission physician examined Tunney, and reported a 68 pulse and blood pressure of 128/80.

Tex Rickard said he never thought he'd witness an eclipse of the gate and attendance record of Dempsey-Carpentier, but Dempsey-Tunney I had done it, with a $2 million gate, and this fight would eclipse that, with a $3 million gate. Tunney would be paid a flat $1 million. Dempsey would earn $450,000. Tex did not see how there ever could be a bigger gate. "I can't believe there'll ever be anything bigger than this." 169,000 spectators would be present.

The 6-ounce gloves, made by Sol Levinson of San Francisco, were in the Illinois State athletic commission's safe.

592 *Chicago Daily News, Chicago Tribune, Chicago Herald and Examiner,* September 14, 1927.

Jimmy De Forest said, "Dempsey doesn't look so good in training here. He looked better two weeks ago." A lot of folks said Dempsey never looked showy in training. However, De Forest remembered how effective Jack was in training back when he was working with him for the Willard fight. "When he socked sparring partners – men with whom none of his present sparring mates could have lasted a round – they stayed socked. They went down and out. Then it was news if Dempsey didn't drop his man. Now it's news if he does." Furthermore, Jack was hit a lot now, so much that his face appeared swollen. "That's not like Dempsey."[593]

Dempsey admitted that Tunney's left jab was the best he ever had encountered. Tunney "jabs with the force and power that most men can generate only in hooks or straight right hand drives." Jack had met a lot of jabbers, but none of them ever had the same "crushing" force of Tunney's jab. Every time Gene landed his jab it either knocked his head back, shook his head, rattled his teeth, or cut his face. It had to be respected, for it was a dangerous punch. Jack understood why Tunney had been able to defeat so many good fighters just by jabbing them.[594]

Billy Gibson said he would insist on Dempsey taping his hands inside the ring, under observation. He said Dempsey would not be allowed to load his hands heavily with many layers of tire tape, which Billy claimed Jack did for the Firpo fight. Firpo's second watched, but hardly objected. Gibson also suggested that Dempsey did the same for another fight (some speculating Willard).

One writer for the *Chicago Tribune* explained why Tunney never would be as popular as Dempsey, and it had to do with his style. The paying public liked aggressive, hard-punching knockout artists like Dempsey. Jim Corbett never was going to be as popular as John L. Sullivan for the same reason. The hit-and-run win-on-points style never was quite as popular.

> Those who saw the moving pictures of the Tunney-Dempsey fight a year ago saw Dempsey continually going forward and Tunney continually running away. Tunney can never knock Dempsey out, because to do so he will be compelled to stop backing up long enough to impart the necessary power to his punch, and to slug with Dempsey for only a minute would likely prove fatal – and Tunney knows it. So the fight will prove to be just another Philadelphia affair, Tunney jabbing and running away and Dempsey ever going forward. If Tunney wins on points, he will be more unpopular than ever. If Tunney elects to meet Dempsey in the middle of the ring and fight like a real champion should fight (and like the fight fans expect a champion to fight), the battle will be of short duration, but Tunney would emerge from defeat more popular than if he defeats Dempsey on points alone.[595]

[593] *Chicago Daily News*, September 15, 1927.
[594] *Chicago Herald and Examiner*, September 15, 1927.
[595] *Chicago Tribune*, September 15, 1927.

Sparring Big Boy Peterson

On the evening of September 15 at Lincoln Fields, in the lit outdoor ring, Dempsey showed his old-time power, pounding on his sparring partners. Jack boxed 5 rounds with six men, including Dave Shade; 190-pound Big Boy Peterson; Whitey Allen - who was knocked out in less than a minute; after which Allentown Joe Gans finished the round for him; "dusky" Roy Williams; and Benny Kruger.

Many said Jack's legs looked great. Others said he was slow. Some said they were worried because of the way Big Boy Peterson slapped him.

Robert Edgren said Dempsey's blows were hard and faster than the prior year. Jack looked good, even though he was hit often.

Jim Jeffries was on hand, and said, "He looks like a big bear." "While Dempsey seemed easy to hit at times, he tossed back faster and harder punches and seemed to have more in reserve." His speed was improving and he was moving swiftly.

That same day, the 15th, in their 1st of 2 rounds, Tunney dropped Chicago light heavy Jackie Williams with a left hook. 180-pound Chuck Wiggins rushed in like Dempsey, but despite connecting a few times, he received stiff jolts in return. Billy Vidabeck boxed 2 rounds as well, and Tunney's left hook landed often.

Gene was putting his body weight behind his wallops, which he could fire to the body or head. He landed his snappy blows 90% of the time. His blocking was clever, and the way he tied up his foe's arms when in close brought favorable comment.[596]

John Murphy of the *Chicago Daily News* said even if Dempsey was a much better man than he was the prior year, "Jack is going to have one tough evening out-clouting the champion. If Gene is as good Thursday as he is now, the Manassa Mauler will have to be 60 per cent better than he was last September, if he regains the crown."

Likewise, Jimmy De Forest said, "Tunney may be only a boxer, but I have a suspicion that if he has to, Gene can fight and mix it with the best of them." Tunney had been focusing on speed, accuracy, and footwork. "Gene will need plenty of footwork against Dempsey. He will have to move around." Remaining stationary against Dempsey, or moving in straight lines back and forth, would doom anyone. Tunney circled around in order to prevent a straight rushing attack from being effective. "Tunney is fast. He is accurate. He boxes well." However, Gene's one bad habit was he dropped his left, which left him open for Dempsey's right.

[596] *Chicago Tribune*, September 16, 1927.

Herbert Corey said Tunney's hitting power unquestionably was greater than ever before. "He has perfected a short right chop that bursts like a bomb." Although Tunney was a boxer, Corey believed that he would try to win by knockout.

Tunney said, "I shall win, cleanly and surely." The weather had been warm, around 90 degrees, so he had not trained quite as much. He ate vegetables, fruit, eggs, and meat, and drank milk. He said he weighed 193 pounds.

Warren Brown said the local referees who could handle the fight and do a good job were Dave Miller, Dave Barry, Joe Choynski, Jimmy Gardner, and Emil Thiery. Barry and Gardner were official referees locally for a long time, even before the fight game came into Chicago, and "neither is likely to have stage-fright, or stadium fright, as the case may be."

Dempsey said he wanted the title back. Otherwise, he would not have taken the chance that he did against Sharkey. "Sharkey might have won from me. I'll admit he had me in a bad way in that first round. If he hadn't got a bit excited in the second and thrown too many wild punches, or if my jaw had been a bit frailer than it is, he might have sent me down in the second or third."[597]

Rickard was certain that the gate would eclipse the $3 million mark. The police were investigating ticket counterfeiters. Tickets would be scrutinized carefully.

John Keys said if Dempsey tried to box with Tunney, he would make it easier for Gene to whip him. He needed to apply relentless pressure and hit the body.

The fight's anticipated radio audience in the U.S., Canada, and Mexico would be about 50 million. It would be the most extensive broadcast and greatest hookup of stations in the history of radio. 400 working newsmen and 150 telegraph operators would be in the press seats. There even would be reporters from London, Paris, Tokyo, and Havana.

De Forest said Dempsey was in at least as good a shape as he was for the Sharkey fight. "In nearly all his sparring, Dempsey has been rather sad-looking until he let loose one or two of his heavy socks on his sparring partners – socks that hurt them and made them curl up or slow up."

Previously, De Forest had asked Dempsey why he allowed his sparring partners to hit him so much. Jack never allowed that back when Jimmy was training him. He also didn't hold back so much in those days. He needed to let loose to get into winning condition. Since that talk, Dempsey had been less lenient with his sparring partners.

Jimmy also noticed that the sparring partners who circled like Tunney gave Jack plenty of trouble, landing on him freely and getting away from his counters and leads. However, they quit circling once he caught them. Jimmy thought perhaps Dempsey realized he never would be a boxer, and

---

[597] *Chicago Daily News, Chicago Herald and Examiner,* September 16, 1927. Others said Tunney was weighing 188-192 pounds.

had to rely on his hitting ability and capacity to take punishment. Overall, though, De Forest thought the training of both Dempsey and Tunney was a bit lackadaisical.

On September 16, Dempsey boxed 1 round each with colored Chicago middleweights Roy Williams and Allentown Joe Gans, and also white Dave Shade. That day, Jack was working on defense and speed, with very little offense.

Sam Hall said he had a hunch that Dempsey would fight Tunney at least half the time straight up, without crouching, and utilize straight punches rather than bobbing and weaving into close quarters.

Dempsey believed he still was good enough to flatten Tunney. But if he was whipped, he would retire and run his hotel.

Forecasted weather for the fight was between 60- and 70-degrees Fahrenheit.

Sharkey and manager John Buckley watch Tunney train on the 16th

On September 16, before 1,000 spectators, including Jack Sharkey, Tunney sparred 6 rounds total with Chicago light heavy Jackie Williams, Chuck Wiggins, and Billy Vidabeck. Gene was wearing a plaster over his right eyebrow. Some said Williams' left thumb accidentally gouged into Tunney's right eyeball or the cut over his right eye,

Wiggins on left spars Tunney

and inflamed it. Doctors said the injury should heal rapidly, but cautioned

Gene to avoid blows, or it might be reopened. One writer said Gene did not look as good as he did the previous day. He was a bit sluggish.

Jack Sharkey said, "I didn't realize Tunney was such a large man. He is taller than I am. His showing impressed me very much. I liked the way he pumped his right and left hands at short range. He is clever defensively. At long range his right hand appeared effective."

Tunney was a 7 ½ to 5 odds favorite.[598]

Dempsey said his training had been criticized because he didn't go through stiff intensive training every day. Jack explained that he already was in good shape from the Sharkey fight, which put him on edge. He did not want to overtrain and become stale. He worked privately at night quite often, and practiced some things he hoped would help him beat Tunney.

Experts said Tunney was confident, but too wise, cagey, and careful a fighter to get overconfident.

George Strickler said Tunney was in perfect health and ready, with the only doubtful point being the condition of his eye, opened by Wiggins. It had healed, though the question was whether a Dempsey thrust would reopen it.

Don Maxwell said the fight was so big that practically every newspaper in the country was printing columns about it. 200 reporters already were on scene. Dempsey had a meteoric rise, winning the title in 1919 and holding it for 7 years. He was only three years older than Tunney, but they had different career trajectories. Dempsey essentially was burned out on boxing by 1923, whereas Tunney still was on the rise, which was more gradual and longer. Dempsey had the better knockout record and had fought the superior opponents, who were younger than they were when Tunney took on some of the same men. In their first fight, Dempsey fought like a hollow shell and appeared through as a fighter. He looked better against Sharkey, but still, if he was no better than he was in that fight, Tunney likely would repeat his former victory.[599]

Although Rickard was the actual promoter, George Getz was the official promoter, because the laws required a Chicago resident to be the promoter.

LATEST PORTRAIT SHOWS CHAMPION AS HIGH BROW. Gene Tunney as he appears in photograph what gives no intimation of his line of endeavor.

CHALLENGER ALSO POSES IN NATTY ATTIRE. Jack Dempsey was once a movie actor, so this picture may give some hint of one of his occupations.

[598] Chicago Daily News, Chicago Tribune, Chicago Herald and Examiner, September 17, 1927.
[599] Chicago Herald and Examiner, September 18, 1927.

Speaking about the rules, the *Chicago Tribune* noted that 10 rounds was the maximum allowed under Illinois law.

Regarding knockdowns, the rules stated, "When a contestant is down his opponent shall retire to the farthest corner and remain there until the count is completed. Should he fail to do so, the referee shall cease counting until he has retired." The rabbit punch was barred. Six-ounce gloves were to be used.

A California film owner, Orville A. Eddy, appeared before a U.S. Commissioner in Omaha, Nebraska, and pleaded guilty to violating the federal law prohibiting the transport of fight films from one state to another, namely the Dempsey-Sharkey fight films.

On September 17, Tunney ran 5 miles. His right eye was slightly discolored.

Gene then visited the nearby estate of well-known sportsman Otto Lehmann. He saw Lehman's many horses and rode in a 100-year-old coach.[600]

(By Pacific & Atlantic)
Tunney (stepping on coach) looking over ancient road coach
HOBNOBBING WITH SOCIETY!—To break monotony of his training camp, the literary champion, Gene Tunney, takes part in festivities of Chicago elite, quite unperturbed by echo of rumblings at Dempsey camp. Above, he's shown on Fox Lake estate of Otto Lehman of Chicago's Four Hundred. —*Stories on pps. 34, 36 and 37.*

l to r: Otto Lehmann, Eddie Eagan, Tunney. Behind the coachman are Cassie and Jeanne Lehmann. Far right is Mrs. Otto Lehmann.

In quite a surprise, given how civil they had been towards one another previously, Dempsey and/or his manager charged that there had been an attempt to fix the 1926 title bout. Jack had been informed that he needed to win by knockout if he was going to win at all.

---

[600] *Chicago Tribune*, September 18, 1927.

Some thought Dempsey's making such a claim was a way of giving the impression that the fight was a grudge match, to stimulate ticket sales, or to rattle Tunney and get him to fight him more instead of just box.

Still, there was some evidence that the day before their first title fight, Tunney and Gibson had contracted to give a sizable 20% share of the purse, plus the same percentage on any future earnings for the life of the contract that Tunney had with Gibson, to a "shady bootlegger" named Max "Boo Boo" Hoff, in consideration of payment of only $1 (plus a purported $20,000 loan), the contract being valid only if Tunney won the championship. Folks were wondering why Tunney/Gibson would do that, given that the payment made was far smaller than the tremendous present and future value of the Tunney/Gibson contract.

In an open letter, Dempsey challenged Tunney to tell the truth about the Hoff business. Jack linked the contract with a gambling plot to fix their first fight. Jack wanted Gene to explain to the public and him about all the angles involved with Max "Boo Boo" Hoff and his lawsuit. He wanted to know why gamblers, steered by Abe Attell, a Hoff associate, who allegedly had something to do with the fixing of the 1919 World Series, made a huge betting plunge on Tunney to win AFTER Tunney, Hoff, and Gibson had a conference. "You owe the truth to the public."

Dempsey believed that Jimmy Bronson, Tunney's chief second for the Philly fight, who again would be his second in the upcoming contest, was the one who inspired the "draft dodger" charges hurled at him. Bronson was the man who picked him out of 20 million American men who were exempted from war duty "and tried to wreck and ruin me in public opinion" so he could get his fighter Bob Martin a shot at Carpentier. Perhaps Bronson would speak up. "Or, if you and Gibson and Bronson need an official spokesman, why not let your little chum, Attell, the tool for a gigantic gambling clique in and around New York, speak in your behalf?"

Dempsey claimed that before he arrived in Philadelphia, he was tipped off that there was something phony about the fight. He had been told that a deal had been made whereby somebody was going to steal his title for Tunney, "that when I went into the ring I didn't have a chance to win unless I knocked you out...and that I might get disqualified even then." He also was told that the judges would be there to assist Tunney.

After the secret meetings with Attell and Hoff, there had been thousands of dollars bet on Tunney, but suddenly, the evening of the fight, the backing ceased. The reason was that the boxing commission had switched referees to Tommy Reilly, known to be honest and not on anybody's payroll.

Dempsey acknowledged, "You whipped me fairly and squarely that night. The ring experts say that you easily took eight of the ten rounds. I agree with them. I'll give you credit for giving me the worst beating anybody ever handed me in my lifetime."

But Jack wondered what would have happened if he decisively outpointed Gene, or if it was close, and the first referee had been working the fight. "What was the meaning of the secret conference you had with Attell…[and] what was the meaning in the secret conference you and Gibson had with Hoff on the evening of fight day, after which gamblers passed out the word: 'Sink the ship on Tunney; he can't lose.'"

Dempsey said he understood Hoff to be a political power in Philadelphia, and a mighty figure in boxing affairs. There was a saying that "whatever 'Boo Boo' wants – well that's what 'Boo Boo' gets."

The contract that Hoff, Gibson, and Tunney signed struck Dempsey as strange, and it puzzled him and the public. "And it is one that I think should be explained." The contract said that Gibson borrowed $20,000 from Hoff, and he agreed merely to pay it back if Tunney did not win the fight, but if Tunney won, Gibson was to pay it back and Hoff would get 20% of Tunney's future earnings as champion. Hoff paid $1 for that privilege. That was odd, given that if Tunney won, the title would be worth over a million dollars. Why would they pay Hoff a likely $200,000 bonus on a $20,000 loan? "What could Hoff do to help you on to victory that would be worth $200,000?"

It also seemed strange that Gibson would need to borrow money right before a fight that he and Tunney were to be paid $200,000, a whole lot more than $20,000. They easily could have borrowed that amount from Rickard without any bonus arrangement, or obtained an advance payment. Even if they were given a $20,000 loan, as Hoff claimed, such a relatively paltry amount would not make any sense given the huge money that Tunney was making on the fight, and the much greater amount above and beyond $20,000 that the 20% share on future earnings represented.

The whole thing seemed very fishy. It also seemed odd that Attell and gamblers were lukewarm in their support, but after the agreement was signed, gamblers made a terrific plunge on Tunney to win. Dempsey challenged Tunney to explain it all to the public.

Tunney merely responded, "My Dear Dempsey: Your so-called open letter to me was brought to my attention. While my reaction is to ignore it and its evident trash completely, yet I cannot resist saying that I consider it a very cheap appeal for public sympathy. Do you think this sportsmanlike? Gene Tunney. P.S. – I might add that I wrote this letter myself." The actual letter in Tunney's handwriting was reproduced in the *Chicago Herald and Examiner*.

Indeed, Hoff and Attell had shady reputations. The press said Dempsey wanted to know "what sinister influence that pair might have had on the fact that Mr. Dempsey was so rotten in the Philadelphia fight and Mr. Tunney won with such astounding ease. He hints rather openfacedly that Hoff and Attell had everything fixed privately so that Tunney could not have possibly lost the bout unless he dropped dead."

Tunney admitted that Gibson brought Attell to the training camp at Stroudsburg. Attell said Hoff wanted to purchase a 20% interest, provided that Tunney won the title. The purchase was to be made from and taken out of Gibson's share. They presumed Gibson had a 33 1/3% share. However, Tunney said his contract with Gibson had expired shortly before, and had not been renewed. Therefore, Attell and Hoff paid $1 for something that Gibson did not have. Tunney did not say anything at that time, because he feared they might do something to prevent him from winning had they known the truth.

However, the day before the fight, Hoff, Tunney, and Gibson signed a contract. So, Tunney himself assented to it and admitted that he signed the contract. Yet, Tunney said he signed as Eugene Joseph Tunney, which was not his name, and not how he usually signed contracts; his way of trying to make the contract invalid, null and void, for his real name was James Joseph Tunney. He was subtly suggesting that it was a matter of extortion.

Of course, it didn't really matter all that much, because everyone agreed that Dempsey had lost to Tunney, fair and square. Still, there was some real suspicion regarding why they would sign such a contract at all.

Tunney said he signed because he feared that harm might come to him if he did not sign, having heard of Hoff's "evil ways." "It wasn't that I wanted Hoff to fix the fight so that I couldn't lose. I just didn't want him to be sore at me and doing his utmost to help Dempsey win." It did not occur to him at all that Hoff might fix the fight against Dempsey.

However, some thought that Gibson/Tunney had given Hoff an interest as a result of his promise to, or their hope that he would, as an insurance policy, fix the judges or referee. Others wondered whether Hoff had Dempsey doped, which would explain his poor performance.

Rickard was distressed by the controversy. Tex said the fight films proved the fight was on the level. He said making such claims was not good for the sport. Dempsey might have been sick, but Tunney had nothing to do with it.

Others said Rickard enjoyed the publicity because it only stimulated greater interest and more ticket sales.[601]

Robert Edgren said he was picking Dempsey to win, and it would not surprise him if he did so

[601] Chicago Herald and Examiner, Chicago Daily News, Chicago Tribune, September 19, 1927.

within 8 rounds. Tunney's best chance was to win a decision, but this time he was fighting a much more dangerous man. The chance to land a knockout was all Dempsey's, though his aggressiveness might win him a decision even though Tunney was a more skillful boxer. The age difference, Dempsey 32, and Tunney 29, was slight. Tunney was faster and his legs looked better than one year ago. But he was not hitting harder, and his sparring partners hit him too often. Tunney was preparing to land body blows, particularly his left hook to the liver, but he could not trade blows with Dempsey on even terms. "Nobody can."

Tunney had been out of the ring a year, enjoying social popularity and "rather looking down on boxing as a profession." Dempsey had been working grimly to come back. Luxury as champion had sapped some of Dempsey's fighting energy, but his training grind had restored a lot of it. Tunney had been living rather softly the past year, thinking of a lot of things other than fighting. He cared for the championship because of what it could get him, saying he would retire as soon as he made his fortune or began to slip. "Gene feels superior to his profession. Dempsey doesn't. He only wants to be known as king of the fighting game. Dempsey loves fighting. Tunney tolerates it as a useful round in the ladder he hopes to climb."

Both men were in good shape. Dempsey had worked harder, though he had further to go. "Dempsey ranks as one of the greatest fighting champions in history." Billy Miske once told Edgren that Dempsey could knock out anyone in half a round if he wanted. Tunney's ring record was good, but was not to be compared with Dempsey's. "Both at their best, Dempsey would easily outclass Tunney. Naturally Dempsey is not in his Toledo form, but he's pretty good." He was better than the version who floundered though 10 rounds with Tunney in Philadelphia. That version of Dempsey was very slow, too slow to land or evade blows.

Edgren believed there was dirty work afoot in that first fight.

> To avoid going into too much detail I'll say this: Dempsey was drugged or poisoned in his training quarters at Atlantic City. It was done undoubtedly, by agents of the gamblers who plunged in the betting on Tunney – Tunney knew nothing about it. ... Dempsey had two violent all-night attacks of nausea, and vomiting in his camp during the week before the fight. He collapsed on the way to Philadelphia, with another violent attack of nausea, and was laid in a berth while restorative measures were used. Dempsey has denied this – he absolutely will not alibi a defeat – but I know from reliable sources that it is true – it was too late to postpone the fight.[602]

Edgren's claim was very interesting in light of the revelations that Boo Boo Hoff via Abe Attell had purchased an interest in Tunney for $1 and a loan before their fight. Of course, Edgren had a history of enjoying stirring up and fostering controversy. It made good copy. But was it true?

---

[602] *Chicago Daily News*, September 19, 1927.

TUNNEY.		DEMPSEY.
29	Age	32
191	Weight	195
6 ft. 1½ in.	Height	6 ft. 1½ in.
76½ in.	Reach	76
17 in.	Neck	17
41 in.	Chest (Normal)	41 in.
44½ in.	Chest (Expanded)	45½ in.
35 in.	Waist	34 in.
14¼ in.	Biceps	14¼ in.
13¾ in.	Forearm	13½ in.
8½ in.	Wrist	9 in.
23 in.	Thigh	22 in.
15 in.	Calf	15 in.
9 in.	Ankle	8½ in.

Jimmy De Forest said he measured both men. They both stood 6'1½", though Tunney appeared to be slightly taller, for Dempsey was stretching a bit when he was measured. Tunney weighed 191 to Dempsey's 195.

James J. Jeffries did not believe Tunney had done enough hard work, only half as much as *he* would have done. (Of course, Jeff might have been overlooking the fact that he trained for 25-round fights, and this was only 10 rounds.) Jeffries believed that Tunney was open to being hit by straight punches. "Tunney is not as great a boxer as I expected to see. … It is my opinion that Tunney lacks the snap he should have for such an important battle." His timing was fair, but judgment of distance nothing to brag about. Gene had not worked hard or lived cleanly. He had attended three formal dinners the past two weeks, retiring well after midnight. "If he can retain the championship by training on formal dinners, then I kick myself all over for being such a sap to work like I did when I was in the game." Jeff acknowledged though that Gene was supremely confident. "A more confident champion never trained for a bout."[603]

Jack Sharkey said Tunney looked great and was in top-notch condition. He looked bigger, stronger, and better in every way than when he won the title. The champ seemed calm and happy, not one bit worried.

Sharkey said that in sparring against Jack Williams, Chuck Wiggins, and Billy Vidabeck, Tunney had a powerful straight right. He had short but powerful blows. He always did have a killing left jab, but his right seemed more powerful than before. Tunney's timing and accuracy, both in delivering and blocking blows, was impressive. He had a mighty keen circular backaway, though Sharkey said there was such a thing as too much backing, for a fighter could back himself right out of a decision. Sharkey noted that Tunney didn't really get his fighting pep up very much until he was stung. Some believed Gene didn't have much fighting spirit, but he showed it whenever he received a good wallop. "But even then he never lets his anger blind him. He keeps cool and watches his chances." He was one to save his fight for the fight. The champion was motivated to prove that his victory in Philadelphia was no fluke and that he was a great fighter. "I believe Tunney today is a better man than he was then."

On September 18, Dempsey looked good to observers of his training. His speed, punch, and aim were better than against Sharkey. He boxed 4 rounds total, one each with Joe Gans, Rocky Russell, Dave Shade, and Osk Till, battering them. Dempsey showed speed in jabbing, ducking, and weaving. He still had a bruise under his right eye, but no one was sure when or how he had received it.

Jack Sharkey said he was surprised by the speed Dempsey showed.

---

[603] *Chicago Daily News*, September 19, 1927.

Jack Johnson, who was there, said Dempsey showed a lot of boxing skill that he never knew he possessed.

Dempsey was confident that he could win by decision even if his plan to win by knockout failed. He said in the West, aggressiveness was favored. "I'll force the fighting and I'm confident aggressiveness will outbalance any retreating taps that might go for points in an eastern ring."

Dempsey told Franklin Grant, "This time I'll be right. This time I won't be shaky and wobbly and without pep."

Leo P. Flynn gave three reasons for Dempsey's prior loss. 1. He received no assistance from his corner between rounds. 2. Mental disturbances brought on by lawsuits and other annoyances, and 3. "The surreptitious administration of an emetic that weakened him." The third allegation was that he had been poisoned by a drug that causes vomiting. Had mobsters/gamblers done this to him so they could win bets on Tunney? Or was this the usual ex post facto alibi that fighters and/or their managers came up with after losing?

On September 18 at Lake Villa, before a crowd of 4,000 - 4,500 spectators, according to George Strickler, Tunney appeared faster and timed his punches better in 5 rounds of sparring, 3 against Billy Vidabeck and 2 against Jackie Williams, than he had for the past two weeks. His right wreaked havoc. Tunney was more willing to mix; he hit the body, feinted with both hands, and landed with "murderous precision." He looked 20% better than the prior year.

Another writer said Tunney exhibited a real punch and finished as fresh as he started. His punches were so fast that some spectators could not follow them. He hit with so much steam that Williams and Vidabeck fell into clinches and held after being hit.

Tunney said he never felt better, was pleased with his timing and power, and perfectly satisfied with his condition, which was even better than last year. His eye was not bothering him in the least. Gene said he would box on the 19th in private only.

Others said Tunney sparred carefully, fearing the cut would reopen.

Billy Gibson said Dempsey's published letter was just a desperate attempt to try to fluster Tunney, but it would not work, for Gene had a fine, evenly balanced mind.

Jimmy Bronson said Dempsey must want to win the fight mighty bad to stoop so low. "It is well known that Dempsey cannot bob or weave or stoop so well inside the ropes any more, but outside of them he can duck, bob, stoop and crawl, even if he has to get a bit dirty doing so. This is a pretty late date for Dempsey to prove that he was back in the shipyards during the war."

Gibson said he would demand that any hand

bandaging be done in the ring. He did not care how much gauze bandages were used, but he wanted a limit on the amount of heavy tape – only that which was necessary to settle the gauze in place and hold it there.

Odds had shifted slightly to 3 to 2, with Tunney remaining the favorite.

Rickard was hoping for a $3 million gate. $2.3 million in tickets already had been sold. The arena could seat 163,000 ticket holders. The federal government would take 10% of the total gate. The state government would get 10% of the remaining admission total.[604]

| Estelle and Jack | Leo P. Flynn | Billy Gibson |

Rickard was concerned that radio broadcasts might hurt the gate.

Tunney allegedly was fighting on percentage, but Dempsey was guaranteed a flat $450,000. Tunney likely would earn very well, for their fight the previous year generated $1.895 million, and this fight likely would approach the $2.5 million mark. Most thought Tunney would earn at least 1 million dollars. Both fighters had earned plenty more from their sparring exhibitions.

On the 19th, three days before the fight, Tunney boxed for the final time, 2 rounds with Williams and 3 with Vidabeck. He gave another clever exhibition, blocking all punches sent his way. His blows were harder than at any time in his training. He landed jabs and right crosses at will, and at close quarters tied up his foe's arms so they were unable to inflict any punishment. When he hit the heavy bag held by Lou Fink, it sent Lou back one or two feet every time. George Strickler said Tunney was quick, accurate, and showed no fatigue.

Benny Leonard and old-timer Tom Sharkey were impressed. Sharkey said it would be a great fight, and he could not make up his mind about

[604] *Chicago Herald and Examiner, Chicago Tribune,* September 19, 1927.

who would win. "Tunney is fast and clever. Dempsey is a puncher and must be given a chance." Another quoted Sharkey as saying of Tunney, "That fellow looks like the best in the world."

Tunney hits bag held by Lou Fink.

Gene said his eye was all right, and it had not been hit. He would forget all about it when the bell rang for the fight. He was weighing about 189 pounds and expected to enter the ring about a pound lighter.

Gene Fowler believed Tunney's careful points boxing would tire out Dempsey until he was ripe for the pile-driver finish in the 8th round. However, Fowler also said that only if Gene got the Manassa mauler so cut up and fatigued that he could put over a pile-driver would Tunney run the risk of catching one of the ever-dangerous Dempsey "Iron Mike rights or safe blower left hooks." Tunney had a great mental attitude, and was unperturbed by anything, including lawsuits, eye injuries, or Dempsey's letter.[605]

Dempsey said, "I know I am in the best of condition. I feel it. When I fought Tunney a year ago I did not have a fight in three years. It took that bout and the one I had with Sharkey to bring me back. I'll regain the title. I feel sure of it."

Leo Flynn said he and Jack wanted to know what Boo Boo Hoff did for Tunney that Gene was willing to allow him to become a shareholder, when Hoff was a known bootlegger and undesirable character.

Rickard was not happy about the sordidness and wanted them to keep quiet and not continue to pursue the matter. He thought it was bad for business if the public thought it was possible to corrupt the officials. He said Tunney had whipped Dempsey fairly.

Some speculated that Dempsey was trying to anger Tunney, to make him fight, engage harder, and more often.[606]

Robert Edgren said the charges alleged to have been made by Dempsey most likely were not actually written by him. Dempsey never knocked anyone before. It was entirely unlike him to do so, regardless of whether the charges were true. Normally, he was quite diplomatic. "It certainly was not written by Dempsey, for it doesn't sound like his wording." Perhaps his backers were convinced that dirt slinging might unnerve Tunney. Edgren took it as an indication that those behind Dempsey were not all that confident if they thought they needed to utilize such methods.

---

[605] *San Francisco Examiner, Chicago Herald and Examiner,* September 20, 1927.
[606] *Chicago Tribune,* September 20, 1927.

Edgren said Tunney was a natural fighter like Dempsey but did not have Jack's terrific hitting power. Little known was the fact that Gene had about 10 bouts before he joined the marines and won military tournaments, outpointing Bob Martin. Back then, he was young, light, and undeveloped.[607]

Gamblers such as Tim Mara, Arnold Rothstein, Jim Coffroth, and Maxey Boo Boo Hoff had invested heavily in Tunney, keeping him the odds favorite at 7 to 5.[608]

Fred Hayner believed Dempsey was 25% better than he was just before the Sharkey bout. They said he was about 203 pounds, but since he did not get on the scales publicly, it could not be verified. He had worked on his boxing and was faster of foot and hand. He was blocking more, and using more straight punches than ever before. Still, he had aged and slowed down from his early championship days. He never again would equal his Toledo form. "His punch is not the punch he had then, in my judgment." His coordination was not the same, either.

Commissioner John Righeimer said the rules limited the length of hand bandages, which would be inspected prior to the bout.

John Murphy said Tunney preferred cooler weather, while Dempsey preferred the heat. The temperature had been dropping lately, and at night it was even cooler, which Tunney liked. Dempsey had been training at night to get used to the cooler air. At 189 pounds, Tunney was like a ballet dancer. He could dodge and sidestep like a fly. He could feint and counter beautifully.

John Keys said the recent verbiage between Dempsey and Tunney made it seem like more of a grudge match than simply a business affair, which would swell the gate receipts. Fans wanted to see a real fight.

After seeing Jack in his final workout, Jimmy De Forest was convinced that Dempsey was in fine condition, ready to put up his best fight since Firpo. His only training damage was a slightly cut mouth and a black right eye. He was much better physically than he had been in a couple years. He had been working on his accuracy more than power, and practicing his footwork. "He is pretty fast – faster than he has been on his feet for several years." He was a much better boxer than he used to be as well. He was hitting harder than he did against Sharkey. His wind was good. The Sharkey fight had done him a world of good.

Jim Jeffries said Dempsey's speed was better than expected, but his timing and distance was not what it should be or needed to be to beat Tunney. He was hit with too many jabs as well. Still, he was a vicious puncher, with plenty of speed and snap on his blows. He was working hard, with pep, and was better physically and mentally than a year ago. Jack was not underestimating Tunney, realizing fully well that Tunney was a good fighter and a hard man to catch.

[607] *Chicago Daily News*, September 20, 1927. Edgren said the Soldier Field's seating capacity was 170,950 at the extreme.
[608] *New York Daily News*, September 21, 1927. Report from Jack Farrell on the 20th in Chicago.

Joe Williams (sporting editor for the *New York Telegram*) said Dempsey's biggest mistake last year was taking on Tunney without having any tune-ups, for no fighter could stay away from active ringwork for three years and expect to come back as a first-class foeman. His last two fights had helped prepare him, and if he had a chance to hurt and finish Tunney like he did in the 4th round of their prior fight, he might knock him out this time. Then again, if Tunney was good enough to win in a landslide the prior year, he might do so again. "And it may be that Tunney could whip Dempsey the best day he ever saw." But, of course, he did not whip Dempsey at his best; far from it. Yet, that did not detract from his remarkable performance.

This time, Dempsey would be better, but how much was a matter of conjecture. He looked mediocre against Sharkey. Still, he had an outside chance to land a killing punch at any time. Yet, Tunney ought to win. He was cautious, fast, accurate, and had stamina. He was a splendid body puncher with a hard right hand, and his prior victory gave him even more confidence.[609]

The *Chicago Herald and Examiner* said more than $2 million would be wagered on the contest, and Dempsey might even enter the ring as the favorite.

Warren Brown said Tunney was not nervous at all. Gene said of Dempsey, "I happened to see him box Sharkey. He had not improved in that bout. In fact, he showed me that he had gone back, even from the form he had against me. Consequently I am certain that I can defeat him, and will do so." Tunney said Dempsey was hard to hit in the body because of his crouch, but nevertheless, he hit and hurt Jack there last time, and would do so again. Furthermore, "I do not agree entirely with those who hold that Dempsey's jaw is invulnerable. Perhaps it was once. But that time has gone. It is no great task to hit Dempsey on the jaw."

Jack Sharkey said Tunney was punching fast and furious, and was in top shape. Dempsey had his old-time steam, vigor, dash, pep, and punch. He was in better shape than when he and Sharkey fought, and seemed determined to win back his crown by knockout. He was aggressive and had improved his defense. Sharkey predicted a great fight.

> Dempsey is putting his faith in his smashing power, and he certainly has it. Gene is a boxing machine. Dempsey is a fighting machine. And I believe even the cool Gene Tunney is going to be a little confused when Dempsey wades in slugging ferociously. It seems that Tunney is going to have to fight back, which is just what Jack wants.

Dempsey said, "They tried to put the other fight in the bag and I know it. I want to get a fair deal Thursday night and think a little true publicity will help to that end." Regarding Tunney's reply to his letter, Jack said,

---

[609] *Chicago Daily News, Chicago Evening Post*, September 20, 1927.

Tunney's answer was not an answer. It was evasive. He did not answer a single one of my questions but ducked the issue completely. ... My gloves will talk for me Thursday night. ... I am not seeking public sympathy. I don't need any. But the public has a right to know what happened at Philadelphia. I surely wish Gene would tell.

Yet, Dempsey denied that he was poisoned in the prior fight.

Leo Flynn said, "Dempsey will knock out Tunney in 3 rounds if Gene stands up and fights. If Gene runs away Dempsey will stop him in 7 rounds."

Dempsey wrote that he had a better attack and defense, 100% improved over Philadelphia, and 50% better than against Sharkey. No matter what happened, he would have no excuses. He was fit and ready. "I have trained for speed, for durability and to get the zip back into the old punch." He also had worked on ring patience, something Tunney had but he did not. In the past, Jack just blindly rushed and tore in and swung without waiting for a real opportunity. He also had perfected a defense for Tunney's blows, and would use more jabs as well. "I will guarantee that Tunney isn't going to slap and cuff me around with the same ease that he did in Philadelphia."

Department store magnate Bernard Gimbel complimented Tunney for his clean living and being an example for the youth. Dempsey had been regarded as unbeatable until he met Tunney. Sharkey had defeated the strongest field of contenders, but Dempsey knocked him out and reestablished himself as one of the greatest heavyweights of all time. Gimbel believed Tunney would win again, with his will to win and great boxing ability.

Pennsylvania boxing commissioner Havey Boyle (yes, Havey) said if Dempsey (or his representatives) claimed that an 11th hour change was made to the choice of referees for Dempsey-Tunney I, he was telling a lie. Until 30 minutes before the bout, Tom Reilly did not know he would work the contest, though the commission decided upon him a week before. No change was made. Dempsey's performance was so inferior to Tunney's that his own brother as referee could not have helped him. Under Pennsylvania law, the referee had no vote in the decision unless the two judges disagreed, which in this case they did not. No one disagreed. The judges were selected via the same careful, secret method, and not assigned until a few moments before the fight started.[610]

The Illinois commission would select the referee at ringside, so there could not be any attempts to fix him. Six referees would be summoned. Just before the main bout, one of them would be named. The judges' names would not be given out until the fight was about to start.

The commission said a 20-foot ring would be used.

[610] *Chicago Herald and Examiner*, September 20, 1927.

Dempsey said he was willing to bandage his hands in the ring if it was a warm evening, but if it was cold, he did not want to sit in his corner and freeze while they were put on. "I'll fight without bandages, if Tunney will. Or I'll put them on in the same room with Tunney and let him have twenty men in there. They can hold my hands while they're taped, if they like."

The commission likely would supply the bandages to both men. The rules called for 10 yards of two-inch gauze and one layer of adhesive tape.

DEMPSEY FAMILY RALLIES ROUND FORMER CHAMPION ON EVE OF FIGHT.
Left to right: Roy Stannard, cousin; Dick Dempsey, uncle; Hiram Dempsey, father; Jack Dempsey, the pride of the family; Lew Dempsey, uncle; Hiram Dempsey Jr., cousin.

For the
WORLD'S
HEAVY WEIGHT
CHAMPIONSHIP

THE LONG AWAITED REMATCH!

10 ROUNDS

JACK DEMPSEY
CHALLENGER

GENE TUNNEY
CHAMPION

SOLDIERS' FIELD
Sept. 22, 1927
Chicago, Ill.

Tickets: $5, $10, $20 & $50

Billy Gibson suggested that Dempsey's purse should be forfeited to charity if he fouled Gene. Leo Flynn answered that Tunney should agree to forfeit his purse if he was thrown out of the ring for stalling.

Tunney responded to charges that he was temperamental. "No, I am not temperamental. When I am asked to do something I do not want to do, like posing for some ridiculous feature photograph, and I refuse, I am called temperamental and sometimes upstage. It really is just my view of what is fitting and proper."

Tunney said he was stronger, hitting harder, and satisfied that his defense was better as well. He had a world of confidence. Trainer Lou Fink predicted a knockout victory.

Dempsey weighed 196 pounds after his workout on the 20th, but it was a harder, firmer 196 than last time.[611]

The lights over the ring would have the power of 1,000 watts and make the ring as bright as day on Thursday night.

[611] *Chicago Tribune*, September 21, 1927.

Robert Edgren said the odds were 6 to 5, with Tunney the favorite. Jimmy De Forest said the odds were even.

De Forest said Tunney did very little ducking, relying more on blocking and sidestepping. He also pulled his head away out of range with a jerk, making punches barely miss. The recent cooling of the weather was favorable to him, for he did not like the heat. His eye seemed to be bothering him more than he admitted. He was stronger than he was a year ago, but not faster.

Former champ James J. Jeffries predicted that Dempsey would win by knockout. He had seen both men in training. Jack was a far better hitter and more vicious. He hit all the time, rather than the 1-2 and pause. Tunney was "absolutely a defensive boxer. Now and then he will mix it for ten seconds or so, and if he is getting the best of it will continue to mix it. But let him get a little the worst of it and he backs away quickly." Gene backed away quite often. He had a good right cross and straight left. "I don't believe he is rugged enough to withstand Dempsey's rushes and snappy hitting. However, if it were to be a boxing match I would pick Tunney to win." The fight reminded him of Corbett vs. Fitzsimmons. "Tunney, I believe, does not compare favorably with Corbett as a boxer. However, Dempsey rivals Fitz as a hitter." Dempsey had nothing to lose and everything to gain.

Jeff did not believe Tunney would take the lead, but rather content himself with jabbing, side-stepping and backing away, and that would make him hard to catch, but Dempsey was capable of doing it. If Dempsey boxed too, it would be a poor bout to watch. The two ways Dempsey could win was to go at him quickly in slashing fashion, or the way he beat Sharkey, with continuous, monotonous body punching. When he got Sharkey in just the right condition, he "sent a left to the chin and the fight was over."[612]

Alan Gould, Associated Press Sports Writer, said although a majority of writers favored Tunney, the drift in opinion by them toward Dempsey had been as pronounced as the shift in the betting, with some wagers having Dempsey the favorite. Just as many believed Tunney could not lose as believed Dempsey would knock him kicking.

A radio hook-up of record-breaking proportions would be present, involving 56 stations, in one national chain, and 6 others operating independently, carrying the fight blow-by-blow perhaps to 50 million listeners in the U.S.A. and other countries. Millions more would get the story from newspapers via nearly 200 telegraph wires located at or near ringside. A record 130,000 saw Tunney defeat Dempsey, and even more would see this fight.

Chicago police guarded both men like visiting royalty or presidents, under strict orders to prevent the slightest annoyance to either fighter. Thousands of fight fans had arrived in the city from across the country. Hotels were packed.

[612] *Chicago Daily News*, September 21, 1927.

In a poll of 72 boxing writers, 38 picked Tunney and 24 picked Dempsey. 10 refused to go on record one way or the other.

One noted that Tunney would earn a guaranteed $1 million, or $33,333.33 a minute if it went the limit, far greater than the $1 a day he earned as a soldier during 19 months of military service.

Dempsey said he hardly used his right hand a year ago, but this time would be different.[613]

Dempsey hoped Tunney would not make a runaway fight, but prove he was a real champion and meet him halfway, for fans paid to see slugging until one man or the other was knocked out. He would do his part. "I hope it is all true about Tunney having those fearful punches and also about his having a wild desire to knock me out. All he needs to do is step right in and do it – if he can. He certainly will find me ready to let him try it."

The *Chicago Herald and Examiner* noted that former heavyweight champions Corbett, Fitzsimmons, Jeffries, and Willard all had failed to regain their lost laurels, and wondered whether Dempsey could succeed where others had failed.

Sam Hall picked Dempsey to win by knockout within 8 rounds, even though Tunney unquestionably was an experienced fighter, the best counter hitter, a cool, brainy boxer, with an expert left and good right, who would hit and hurt Dempsey some, and box a game battle, even if he lacked Dempsey's superb gameness. This version of Dempsey would punch Tunney into submission, for Jack no longer was mentally worried, physically unfit, and 3 years out of fights. This version carried too much dynamite. Dempsey had registered 21 knockdowns in 7 championship battles. Firpo was the only man to put him off his feet in title scraps. Tunney had failed to put him down even when Jack was a shell.

Hall called Dempsey's right his Iron Mike, and his left his Man o' War (though others called his left a "safe-blower").

The forecast was for cool and fair weather.

Federal court Judge George A. Carpenter removed another legal obstacle when he denied Reverend Elmer Williams' petition for an injunction against the match. Williams said the use of Soldier Field, dedicated to American war dead, would desecrate it. The judge said to Williams' attorney, "If you had said things about me as you do in this bill against Dempsey and Rickard, I'd invite you out in the alley and adjust things that way." Judge Carpenter disagreed with the contention that the fight would serve no public purpose. "I see by the newspapers 150,000 persons want to see the match. Isn't that of some benefit?" The judge ultimately ruled that the matter was for the state courts, not federal courts.

George Strickler said Tunney was gentlemanly, quiet, cultured, reserved, gentle, and considerate. He was not a killer. It was hard to imagine him knocking out Dempsey, and if he did, it would be because he played the game better, not because of his savagery.

---

[613] *Chicago Evening Post*, September 21, 1927.

Jack's father Hiram Dempsey was there with Jack's nephew Lloyd Stannard, Hiram's brother Lew Dempsey of West Virginia, and cousin Hiram. Salt Lake City's mayor was there too. Jack's father said, "My boy in condition is the best fighter in the world. I know he was in bad shape last year when he fought Tunney. I only needed one peek at him today to know that he is ready. He should win by a knockout in seven rounds."

Jack Sharkey believed Dempsey would pay more attention to boxing principles than ever before, rather than swing wildly. He would await his chances, but when he saw an opening, he would seize upon it. "In the old days, Jack could afford to waste a few, but now he must make every blow count." Also, he was not anxious to get hit too much. He knew the weakening effect of Tunney's blows. Furthermore, "In spite of his fine showing when I saw him, Jack hasn't got the power behind his punch that he had in his best days, and I think he knows it." Dempsey had developed a pretty good feint which would fool Tunney on occasion. Jack knew how to duck and come up in a flash. Unfortunately, Dempsey was a rusher by nature, and Tunney did his best work when he was being rushed. If Dempsey could coax Tunney into trading, he would have the advantage, for Tunney got socked plenty when he traded blows.

Franklin Grant said Tunney money was scarce. It seemed that many folks were disregarding the Philly fight. In his workouts, Tunney boxed well one day, but not so well another, hitting well at times, missing a lot at others, and his sparring partners seemed to have no real difficulty in hitting him.

Tex Rickard refused to referee the fight, saying, "Not for $100,000." He did so only for the Johnson-Jeffries fight because he was the only one the two could agree upon, even though he had no refereeing experience.[614]

Gene's mother Mary Tunney never had seen her son fight, nor had his three sisters. His father was dead. They would listen to the bout on the radio.[615]

Dempsey said he was eager to make history by becoming the first former heavyweight champ to regain the title. He wanted to explode the belief that champions who lost their title could not come back. He said the Tunney who beat him last year would get beat by him now. He was on to Gene's tactics, and Tunney could not backpedal fast enough to keep out of his way again. If the champion "will stand up and fight I'll win by a knockout."

Tunney said he had done more road work and a lot of bag punching. He was an improved boxer and a harder hitter than before. "I respect Dempsey's punching ability. I know he can hit with his left hand and there is sting in his right crosses, but I do not think he will

[614] *Chicago Herald and Examiner*, September 21, 1927.
[615] *Chicago Daily News*, September 22, 1927.

reach me with a solid wallop." Gene had planned his attack and defense from watching the Sharkey contest.

The commission said each fighter could wind their hands with 10 yards (30 feet) of 2.5-inch surgeon's gauze bandages, covered by 6-feet of 1.5-inch adhesive tape. The gauze and tape would be put on by the boxers in their quarters while a commission inspector and two representatives of the opponent watched. Each fighter could have three seconds and his manager in his corner. The fighters would weigh in at different locations, not open or announced to the public. The ring would be 20-feet square.

The *Chicago Tribune's* Westbrook Pegler said there had been so much talk of burglary or attempted burglary in boxing that it never was clear whether a fight was square or not. He predicted a Tunney victory.

The night before the fight, wagers were being placed at even money. The majority of fight critics, about 400 in town, were picking Tunney. The majority of fight fans were picking Dempsey.[616]

Former Ohio Governor James Cox said Tunney was the cleanest and finest man, misunderstood by a public which considered him to be aloof. Tunney should win on form, though Dempsey was dangerous.

Former lightweight champ Willie Ritchie said, "A slugger never can beat a strong and clever boxer, and Tunney's clever."

The first preliminary would start at 8:15 p.m., with the main event at 10 p.m. No rain was expected, but overcoats and heavy clothing probably would be needed. The forecast for fight time was 52 degrees Fahrenheit.

Dempsey told Louella Parsons, Universal Service Motion Picture Editor, that Tunney would have to fight to win. "People aren't paying $3 million to see a pleasant little boxing match."

Making his prediction, Dempsey said, "I will win by a knockout in 7 rounds. I think I am good enough to finish Tunney inside of 7 rounds, but if he happens to last the limit, I am sure I will be far out in front and entitled to the decision." He was ready.

Dempsey said he went into the ring to fight, not tape his hands. Tunney could have as many folks as he wanted watch him tape his hands in his dressing room, but he was going to do it there, pursuant to Illinois rules, not in the ring, where he would get cold as a result of the delay.

Parsons said Estelle was no mere pretty gal, but a woman of brains, and Dempsey did not make a move without consulting her. Estelle did not like to watch boxing, so she would stay in her hotel room, but she was certain that Jack would win.

In other interviews, Dempsey said any talk of Tunney trying to knock him out was disproven by his insistence on a 20-foot ring, which would be swell for "sprinting purposes." "If Gene were not going to get on a bicycle, why did he not urge a 16-foot ring, a size in which I would love to fight him?" Dempsey said he would carry the fight to Tunney, and no man living could stop him. He was ready to fight, and hoped Tunney would do the same.

---

[616] *Chicago Tribune,* September 22, 1927.

In his hotel suite at the Morrison in Chicago, Dempsey said he was not himself in their prior fight and could not get going. The three years had been too much. "My aim was horrible and I got a good licking. Tunney will find me entirely different now. I am boxing in good form."

Jack said he had a dual personality in the ring. Either he got off to a whirlwind start, like he did against Willard, Morris, Pelkey, Fulton, and Firpo, or he could not get untracked for a while, as shown against Brennan, Gibbons, and Tunney.

At Lake Villa, in northeast Illinois, the confident Tunney said, "I am in the peak of condition and will be victorious. I am even more certain I will win than I was when I first engaged Dempsey. ... I have improved considerably and will win without any great difficulty." Another quoted him as saying, "I expect to win without any great difficulty, this time by a knockout."

According to the *Chicago Herald and Examiner*, Dempsey had figured in the four largest gates in boxing history, and the upcoming fight likely would surpass them all.: 4. Dempsey-Firpo, $1,082,590, 3. Dempsey-Sharkey, $1,083,529, 2. Dempsey-Carpentier, $1,626,580, and 1. Dempsey-Tunney I, $2,000,000. Dempsey had participated in the only million-dollar gate fights.

The next closest heavyweight gate was Firpo-Wills at $462,830. Dempsey-Willard was $452,522. Other large notable gates included: Firpo-Willard, $434,260; Wills-Weinert, $339,000; Johnson-Jeffries, $270,755, the record at that time; Sharkey-Maloney, $232,199; Dempsey-Brennan, $200,000; Willard-Moran, $151,521; Tunney-Gibbons, $142,989; Tunney-Carpentier, $136,400; Sharkey-Wills, $133,514; Sharkey-McTigue, $133,147; Johnson-Burns, $131,000; Dempsey-Gibbons, $130,000; and Carpentier-Levinsky, $120,000.

Benny Leonard had featured in several large gates, the biggest being $452,640, against Lou Tendler in New York.[617]

Those picking Tunney included Ed Dickerson, *Grand Rapids Herald*, Sec Taylor, *Des Moines Register*, Ed Hughes, *Brooklyn Eagle*, Ned Brown, *New York World*, Harry Cross, *New York Herald Tribune*, Ray Campbell, *Cleveland News*, Harry Hochstadter, *Chicago Evening Post*, James Gould, *St. Louis Star*, James Harrison, *New York Times*, W. O. McGeehan, *New York Herald Tribune*, Harry Smith, *San Francisco Chronicle*, Ed Cochrane, *Kansas City Journal-Post*; as well as Otto Floto; Jim Mullen, Chicago - "I can't see where Tunney can be beaten."; Willie Ritchie, Abe Pollock, Denver - "Tunney should walk in."; James Dougherty, Philadelphia; Harry Smith, San Francisco - "Tunney fight, decision."; Arnold Rothstein, Max "Boo Boo" Hoff, Abe Attell, Johnny Kilbane, Benny Leonard, Billy McCarney, and Battling Nelson.

Those picking Tunney generally said on form he ought to be a huge favorite to win decisively, for he was younger, faster, and had been

---

[617] *Chicago Herald and Examiner*, September 22, 1927. Other large gates included Delaney-Berlenbach, $469,000; Berlanbach-Stribling, $221,261; and Maloney-Delaney, $201,613.

improving, while Dempsey was too old and far removed from his best days.

Those picking Dempsey included Jim Doyle, *Cleveland Plain Dealer*, Bob Edgren, *New York Evening World*, Harry Bullion, *Detroit Free Press*, Hype Igoe, *New York World*, and Jack Farrell, *New York Daily News*, as well as James J. Jeffries; Tom Sharkey; Johnny Dundee - "Dempsey will knock out Tunney."; and Packey McFarland – "I believe Dempsey will win with the wallop."

The Dempsey prognosticators said he had improved his form greatly over the past year, and had the power to win, even at less than his best.

On the eve of the battle, Dry prohibition agents were engaging in raids, seizing alcoholic spirits.

Jimmy De Forest picked Dempsey to win a 10-round decision. He had improved 100%, while Tunney was the same. Dempsey was the harder hitter, had improved his stamina, improved as a boxer, and was determined to win. Still, De Forest said Dempsey would have to get lucky to win by knockout. He anticipated that Dempsey would be a bit more careful, studying out his moves and striving for accuracy, being a bit more patient, maneuvering to get in close so he could pump heavy artillery into the body. Dempsey would be aggressive but more defensive than last year, gradually increasing his pace. His footwork had improved. The fight likely would be so close that Dempsey would win on his aggressiveness. Dempsey believed he could withstand more punishment than Tunney, could hit harder, and would bring the fight to him. Tunney's hope would be to escape or weather the attack until Jack tired from his own exertions. Tunney would make a runaway fight of it, retreat and remain defensive, which would count in Dempsey's favor in the scoring.

Dempsey's punch had lost some steam and had slowed up, but still was harder than Tunney's blows. "I would rate Dempsey about 60% of what he was in Toledo, making up in increased boxing ability what he has lost in speed, endurance, and ability to hit fast and hard." If Dempsey hurt Tunney like he did in the 4th round of their first fight, he would be able to follow up his advantage and do more than he did then. But he would have to be lucky more than once to score a knockout. Tunney was fast and knew how to protect himself. Yet, "I believe Dempsey will be lucky."

The day of the big fight, Harry Hochstadter picked Tunney to retain the title because of his boxing ability. Dempsey had a harder task on his hands than many realized. A mere 10 rounds was too short a time to get to a man like Tunney, who could stall, clinch, and run.

Damon Runyon said at least $5 million would be wagered on the fight, and the gate would be well over $2 million. Prize fighting was big business.

The press, which usually liked Jack, was not happy that Dempsey mostly had closed his training. Conversely, Gene had been less "high-hatty." "Tunney is a bit of an ass in may ways, with a lot of pose that ill becomes him, but he is a good fighter. He is a serene, dignified sort of boxer, plodding and colorless, but he works with a smoothness that is superb." Dempsey's best chance to win was if Tunney's "insufferable ego" caused him to take unnecessary chances. Sharkey should have boxed, but instead fought Dempsey, "and the man hasn't yet been born who can swap smacks with the old Manassa Man Mauler."

Tunney beat Dempsey with ease in their first contest, for he was on the upgrade, while Dempsey, once mighty and great, no longer was. Although Gene was not a knockout artist, he hit hard enough that Dempsey had to respect his blows.

Jack Sharkey picked Dempsey to win by knockout but believed it would not be easy. Tunney looked 75% better than the year before, but Dempsey looked 200% better. He was in shape and had the old ferocious fighting spirit back. He had one of the fiercest fighting hearts ever. Tunney had courage, could take plenty and come back for more, and could battle right through when things look bad, but he did not have Dempsey's fire and snap. "I think Jack can hit the hardest blow, even if he has lost some of his punching power." Sharkey did not believe Tunney could knock out Dempsey. Yet, Jack would find it quite difficult to hit and knock out Tunney, who had a way of staying on his feet that was disconcerting. "Gene has never been knocked down, much less out." He was tough. Yet, he never had developed a killing punch. Dempsey could win a decision, for aggression counted a lot, and he always waded in. Tunney could not trade punches to advantage, and he would retreat. Gene would not be able to tie him up as well this time, for Dempsey was stronger now. Gene was cool and collected, while Jack was restless, raring around, itching to fight. Both were ready.

The reason why Sharkey thought Dempsey would win was that he had a chance to knock out anyone, and even if he did not, his aggression and superior power would count a lot in any decision, particularly in Chicago. That might make Tunney fight more, which would leave him more vulnerable to getting hit by damaging blows.

George Strickler picked Tunney to win by decision due to his fine boxing. Tunney's defense simply was too superb.

James Wood predicted that Tunney would win by knockout, utilizing his left jab and piston right. Dempsey still had his punch, heart, and courage, but his legs no longer were there, and the snap was gone from his work. Tunney would fight more intelligently than Sharkey did. No one could outsmart Tunney, and the elder version of Dempsey was very hittable. Gene could take it, too. Even if he got hit, he was tough enough to ride out a storm. He had improved boxing form, added strength and size, and general confidence.

Davis Walsh said although Dempsey's legs no longer were there, and he wasn't the offensive juggernaut he once was, he still could give a licking and take one, so he had an even chance. James Joseph "Gene" Tunney was younger and faster, and hit cleanly, with persistent, pestiferous, pecking punches. He had the confidence of his prior victory, and seemed to be bigger and stronger than a year ago, despite not having fought in a year.

The stadium capacity was 170,950, with total seat value at $3.2 million. Tunney was guaranteed $1 million and Dempsey $450,000. The weather was clear and cool, with a chance of rain. Dempsey had a ½" reach advantage at 77".

Alan Gould said Dempsey's hopes for victory were built on a rushing, give-and-take fury of attack, hoping to weather Tunney's punishing fire with sufficient stamina to finally break through the former marine's shifty defense. Tunney would rely on footwork, effective counterattack, resourcefulness, and stamina. He had youth and speed, while Dempsey had hitting and aggressiveness. Tunney's right eye had been cut and injured twice in training, though it had healed rapidly and seemingly completely.

Robert Edgren said the general mob of fans were for Dempsey, who was "more popular than he ever was before in his life." Fans liked his style and wanted to see him recover his lost laurels, becoming the first heavyweight champion to do it. If Tunney won another decision, he would go back to playing golf and the conversation would go flat. "No color in Tunney as champion, cautious self-playing Tunney, who relies on boxing. Dempsey, the Manassa man-mauler, the 'killer,' is different. Color there, blazing and glittering color – plenty of it." The fans did not appreciate Tunney's circling, blocking, and holding, hitting forcefully only now and then, when he could do so safely. He did not bring them thrills the way Dempsey did. Dempsey possibly could win a decision. "Every judge and referee likes aggressiveness." He lost at Philly because although he was aggressive, he was missing, and at the same time was being hit. Dempsey had more of his scowling rage this time. Last year, his "lack of animosity was almost pathetic."

The day of the fight, Edgren said the "colorless" champion and the "broken down" challenger would draw the world's biggest gate ever, between 2 and 3 million. Even Rickard never thought the Carpentier gate would be surpassed, but Dempsey-Tunney I had done it, and this fight would exceed that.

Dempsey showed nothing but heart in their first fight. He was slow, clumsy, and missed his punches by far. Whenever Tunney, the dancing marine, stopped to fight, he plastered Dempsey as easily as if the champ's hands had been tied behind his back and his feet hobbled. Dempsey fought as if he had been drugged. Yet, Tunney showed very little aggressiveness. He had a lot of skill but no punch, against a Dempsey who looked like a dazed, helpless caricature of the real Dempsey.

Dempsey was the big attraction, the sport's greatest draw ever. He had drawn all of the million-dollar gates. The world expected thrills when it came to his fights, for there always had been something sensational with Dempsey. The Firpo fight was the greatest thriller ever. Dempsey was a polarizing character. His friends were violently for him, and his enemies violently against him. He was well-liked by those who met him. But many went to his fights hoping to see him beaten.

After the Tunney loss, everyone expected Dempsey to come out with an alibi, that he was sick, drugged, tricked by his seconds, etc. Instead, he said, "Nothing to it. I was all right. I was beaten by a better man." That earned him admiration. By working hard and then fighting and beating the favored Sharkey, the man who beat Harry Wills, he achieved popularity he never had as champion. Now he was the underdog, and underdogs got plenty of sympathy.

Alibi or not, Dempsey was not in fighting shape in Philadelphia. Since then, he had come back a long way, proving it against Sharkey, when he took a fierce hammering, survived, and beat down Sharkey with a terrific body battering. "He won fairly, too." He was in better shape now, and more confident.

Tunney, whom Jack called a "nice boy," was fast and clever, and Dempsey knew it. Jack said he would prefer a 20-round fight against a man so hard to reach, but was satisfied with his punch this time. "In the old days, when Dempsey was undoubtedly one of the greatest heavyweight fighters of the century, it made little difference to him whether men were fast or slow, clumsy or clever. He could drive a knockout punch fast enough to catch any of them." Battling Levinsky fought a lot like Tunney, but in 1918 it did not matter, for back then, Dempsey had fast enough hands and feet, and was relentless enough that he could catch up with anyone.

Tunney never had been in finer physical condition. He had trained for two months in Speculator, New York before coming to Illinois.

> Tunney is essentially a defensive boxer. He takes his time, and even when he had Dempsey blinded in the last two rounds at Philadelphia he boxed with exceeding care, risking nothing. He did jump in when he had safe openings, and he threw his punches hard, but jumped out again when Dempsey refused to be driven back. He is a skillful boxer without a real knockout punch. A tearing, bruising punch Tunney has, but not the shock-punch that drops a man and dazes him enough to make him stay down. He has knocked out a lot of poor boxers, but has not stopped many who had real class. But he outpoints most of the men who meet him in the ring. Tunney's hope tonight is undoubtedly to win again on points.

Win or lose, Dempsey had come a long way in life. He once earned $2 a day as a coal miner. Records of a Gay, West Virginia coal mine, the Gay Coal and Coke Co., revealed that during the last half of December 1913, 18-year-old Harry Dempsey earned $17.16 over the course of two weeks for labor in the Gay mines. The sheets showed he loaded 132 tons, working 8 days out of a 15-day span, earning 13 cents for each ton of coal loaded. A Charles Dempsey also was on the payroll. Harry earned less than most of his co-workers, having worked less. He came back there occasionally. Last summer, he laughingly asked if he could have his old job back.

Dempsey once had been matched to fight Pat Canepa at Charleston, West Virginia, but the match fell through when Dempsey could not scrape together enough money for a forfeit.

Johnny Kilbane said Dempsey was a sucker for the straight punches that Tunney had. He never was a defensive specialist, but his defense was worse now in part because his offense was not what it once was. Dempsey could punch, but lacked his old dynamite. He used to pulverize his sparring partners, but now he was tender with them. Tunney was stronger now and his defense better, and history showed that Gene improved in rematches. He knew Dempsey better now. "But if Jack breaks through – just once – anything may happen."

Ed Hughes picked Tunney. Dempsey would put forth an effort to batter him down and do better than their first meeting. However, although he had improved over the prior year, he still was not the Dempsey of old, and was too far past his peak. If Dempsey did not score an early knockout, as the fight progressed, Tunney likely would outbox and punish him. Gene was as good or better than he was the prior year, and with increased confidence, he likely would have the fight well in hand by the 5th round, and it would not be surprising to see Dempsey stopped in the second half of the contest. Yet, many Dempsey fans had a hunch, belief, or hope that he would find a way to win, and they practically had wagered the fight to near even odds.

Fair Play favored Tunney to win another points decision. Tunney said he had no nerves, and he acted that way. He knew the public had been slow to accept him as a real champion. The recent deluge of words by Dempsey and Flynn had not helped matters. Tunney wanted to win convincingly and prove his right to hold the crown.

> In science, ring generalship and versatility, Tunney has an edge on Dempsey. This will count in his favor in a ten round bout. Jack has lost some of the snap to his punches. But still he hits hard enough to bring down any man he really connects with. A hitter always has a chance and it is here that Dempsey may shine to upset the dope.

The fight was so important that couples had postponed weddings until after the fight-returns came in.

Grantland Rice said it would be better for the sport from a financial perspective if Dempsey won. He was the greatest drawing card in sport. He had drawn crowds beyond the drawing power of any other human. His fights had drawn millions – Carpentier: $1.6 million, Tunney I: $2 million, Sharkey: nearly $1 million, and it would be nearly $3 million for Tunney II.

This fight would "cast a great white light on the Philadelphia affair. If that was strictly on the up and up, Tunney should win about eight of the ten rounds. ... If Tunney wins again most of the shadow around the Philadelphia jamboree will be dispelled. Tunney realizes this. He also realizes the sinister buzz that will follow if he is beaten." Meaning, if Dempsey won, it might cause more folks to believe he was doped in Philadelphia.

Local Judge Harry Fisher denied the Chicago Coliseum Club's further attempt to obtain an injunction to stop the bout. Clements had lost again. "The entire action in this proceeding is based on the decree of a court in Marion County, Indiana. This decree on its face expired with the date of the alleged contract, and thus can be considered as having expired."[618]

IN SUSPENSE

[618] *Chicago Daily News, Chicago Herald and Examiner, Chicago Tribune, Chicago Evening Post, New York Daily News, Cincinnati Post, Wilmington Every Evening, Glens Falls Post-Star, Richmond Times Dispatch, Allentown Morning Call, Pittsburgh Sun-Telegraph, Pittsburgh Press, Yonkers Herald, Yonkers Statesman, Binghamton Press, Brooklyn Daily Eagle, Brooklyn Daily Times, Brooklyn Citizen, Ithaca Journal, Elmira Star-Gazette, New York Evening Post,* September 22, 23, 1927.

CHAPTER 10

A Legendary Rematch

On Thursday, September 22, 1927, at Soldier Field in Chicago, Illinois, 29-year-old Gene Tunney defended his world heavyweight championship for the first time, against 32-year-old former champion Jack Dempsey.[619]

Warren Brown said one New York broker brought $110,000 to wager on Tunney. The odds were even. Plenty of Dempsey money was in town, with few takers. The *Chicago Herald and Examiner* also said bets were being taken at even odds. The *Chicago Evening Post* said that on the afternoon of the fight, the odds shifted to make Dempsey the favorite at 6 to 5.

Normally, fighters weighed in at 3 p.m. on the day of a fight. However, since heavyweights did not need to make a certain weight, they were allowed some leeway regarding their weigh-in times that day.

At around 1:30 p.m., at the Illinois Athletic Club, Jack Dempsey officially tipped the beam at 192 ½ pounds. The commission physician examined him and cleared Jack to fight. Dempsey said, "I have nothing to worry about. I will win." Another quoted him as saying, "My admirers will see a different Dempsey in the ring tonight than they did a year ago when I lost the crown to Tunney. I will win by a knockout, and it will be before eight rounds."

Jack was fortunate enough to arrive and depart before the crowd assembled. He returned to the Morrison hotel, where he would stay until ready to be escorted to the stadium.

When Dempsey weighed in, the boys puffed away at cigars, but Jack did not object. However, before Tunney appeared, word was sent that smoking must cease, for the king did not like it, so they obeyed.

Tunney arrived at 2:20 p.m. By that time, 3,000 people were outside to see the champion pull up in his car, even though the weigh-in had not been made public. It required a dozen police to restrain the crowd that waited outside, pressing in on the champ as he walked through a narrow alley of cheering admirers, both from and later back to his automobile.

Gene said, "This weighing in is all foolishness. It does not make any difference to me whether Dempsey weighs a ton and I'm sure he feels the same way about it." Yet, when Gene stepped on the scales at 2:30 p.m., and initially commissioner Paul Prehn announced 190 pounds, Gene reached over and moved the bar one notch and said with a smile, "I think 189 ½ is more like it, commissioner." Prehn replied, "You're right about that. Thank you, sir." Tunney officially weighed in at 189 ½ pounds.

---

[619] The following fight descriptions and post-fight analysis primarily are derived from: *Chicago Daily News, Chicago Herald and Examiner, Chicago Tribune, Chicago Evening Post, New York Daily News, Cincinnati Post, Wilmington Every Evening, Glens Falls Post-Star, Richmond Times Dispatch, Allentown Morning Call, Pittsburgh Sun-Telegraph, Pittsburgh Press, Yonkers Herald, Yonkers Statesman, Binghamton Press, Brooklyn Daily Eagle, Brooklyn Daily Times, Brooklyn Citizen, Ithaca Journal, Elmira Star-Gazette, New York Evening Post,* September 22, 23, 1927.

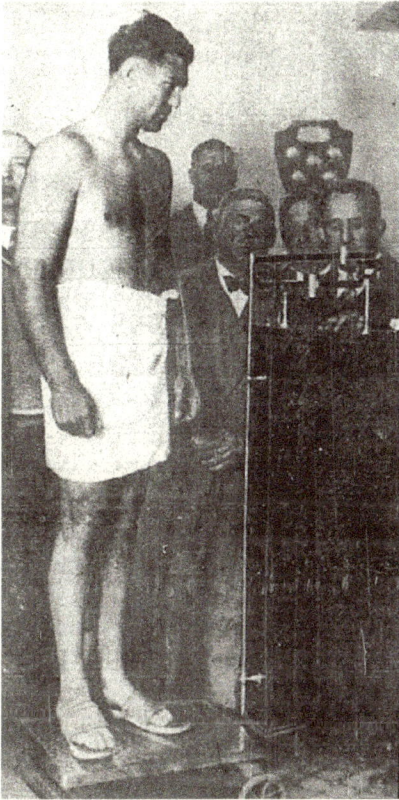

Upon seeing a sign that said, "If Dempsey does not win, we all walk back to Pittsburgh," Tunney laughingly replied, "It's a shame to have to make those fellows walk back."

Tunney said, "No matter what are Dempsey's plans for tonight, I am going to win. If he chooses to stand back and wait, then I will carry the fight to him. I expect to be busy every minute and will seek an early knockout. Dempsey will not be able to travel the pace I intend to set for the battle. I feel stronger than I did in Philadelphia and I am confident that I will retain the title." Gene would stay at the Hotel Sherman.

A few hours before the fight, as a surprise, Estelle Taylor visited her husband. She said, "Jack is in great shape. ... I'm going home now to await the news of his victory." She returned to her apartment to listen to the fight news on the radio.

Estelle and Jack in "good-by" kiss.

Chicago radio dealers had noted a 300-400% increase in sales.

By 7:30 p.m., the stadium was well-filled, with people still pouring in. Rickard was joyous.

The temperature low that day was 43 degrees, and the high only 60 degrees, so it was chilly.

The 6-round preliminaries, which began at 8 p.m. sharp, included: 174 ½-pound Billy Vidabeck (a Tunney sparring partner) W6 187 ½-pound Jack McCann (a Dempsey sparring partner); George Manley, 169 ¾, W6 Yale Okun, 169 ¼; Chuck Wiggins (Tunney spar mate), 187 ¾, W6 Jim Byrne, 186 ¾; and Big Boy Peterson (a Dempsey sparring partner), 190 ¾ (or 194 or 196), W6 Johnny Grosso, 190 (or 188 or 193)(sparred Tunney). The bell was so weak that when the show started, someone yelled, "Another Toledo bell!" As the show progressed, the bell was rung more loudly. Harvey Woodruff called the preliminaries four "wearisome" bouts.

Without much breeze, the air was foggy with the lingering smoke from photographers' flashlights, with the hint of rain. There was a light sprinkle from the cloudy sky at about 8:20 p.m., near the end of the first bout, but it did not last long. Many came prepared with umbrellas and slickers. A third of the crowd carried binoculars. The scoreboard was used to show what round it was.

By 9 p.m., both Tunney and Dempsey were in their arena quarters.

Scores of politicians, dignitaries of city and state, governors, mayors, Congressmen - representatives and senators, were on hand. Chicago's mayor, William Hale Thompson, in his cowboy hat, and Illinois Governor Len Small, were present. The scene stood in stark contrast to the days of John L. Sullivan, Jim Corbett, and Bob Fitzsimmons in years past, who were chased out of towns by legal authorities and often had to fear arrest and incarceration for fighting. Now, officials applauded, supported, attended, and protected the sport.

Other politicians included Michigan Governor Fred Green, Senator Jim Watson, former Ohio Governor Cox, and various mayors from all over the country. Every state in the Union was represented, as well as many foreign countries.

Millionaires, movie stars, bankers, stage darlings, and front-page notables all slid into their seats practically unnoticed. Hundreds of celebrities sat on the backless $40 ringside seats.

Boxing folks in attendance included Jack Sharkey, Spain's heavyweight Paulino Uzcudun, James J. Jeffries, who sat with Tom Sharkey in the fourth press row, Jim Corbett, Battling Nelson, New York commission chairman James Farley, Willie Ritchie, Johnny Kilbane, Billy McCarney, Mike Jacobs, Benny Leonard, Otto Floto, and Jimmy De Forest.

Also present were New York Yankees owner Col. Jacob Ruppert, Chicago Cubs owner William Wrigley, Jr., who never was without chewing gum, baseball commissioner Kennesaw Mountain Landis, Ty Cobb, department store owner Bernard Gimbel (a Tunney friend), John Hertz, who discovered that taxis wore yellow best, David Sarnoff, president of the Radio Corporation of America, Vincent Astor, the duke and duchess of Marlborough, Gloria Swanson, Marshall Field III, General Electric president Gerald Swope, motion picture producers Adolph Zukor and Joseph Schenck, steel magnate Charles Schwab, motor car company manufacturers Walter Chrysler and Horace E. Dodge, General Motors' president Alfred Sloan, circus entrepreneur John Ringling, businessmen Percy Rockefeller, Harold Vanderbilt, and the presidents of Carnegie Steel, Standard Oil, and Cadillac.

Movie and entertainment stars at ringside included Charlie Chaplin, Will Rogers, Douglas Fairbanks, Tom Mix, Buster Keaton, Norma Talmadge, John Barrymore, Al Jolson, George M. Cohan, Harold Lloyd, and race-car driver Barney Oldfield. The movie stars mostly were there to see Dempsey.

Some said Jack Kearns was there, while others said he was not. Thousands of women were present. Chicago society made this more of a social event than any fistic function in history. Thousands of ushers, police, and firemen were scattered about.

Caroyln Bishop

A rumored Tunney girlfriend, Carolyn Bishop, was there. She said she bet every cent on Tunney to win.

Rickard initially had barred "dry agents" from the stadium. He did not want prohibition agents bothering or spying on the fans. A compromise was reached to allow them to take up posts by the refreshment stands in the entrances leading to the field.

Over the ring, on a high steel platform, suspended from rafters of gas piping, was a cluster of at least 44 huge metal-hooded lamps which lit the ring with a blazing white or golden glare that made the ring as bright as daylight. Frank Bartley, the ring builder, said the ring was better lit than any ring in history. The ring was covered with smooth white canvas with padding beneath.

26 huge American flags floated over the ramparts of the stadium, even though they were supposed to be lowered at sundown.

One said a chilling wind whipped out of the northwest to cause some shivers, but the packed humanity created warmth. Another said that by the time the big fight began, a cool breeze had come floating in off the lake. There was a hint/threat of rain, but it held off.

The motion picture cameramen had three crow's nests on stilts, all on one side of the ring – the north, from which they looked down.

Each camp sent their inspectors, along with the Illinois commission inspectors, to oversee the hand bandaging in the dressing rooms. Dempsey kidded with Jerry the Greek, while Tunney was very serious. Gene's only smile came when told that the late betting had taken him from even money to a 5 to 7 favorite to retain the game's most precious crown.

Some said that at ringside, Tunney was the slight 5 to 6 favorite, while others said the odds were even. Odds were 1 to 6 that Tunney knocked out Dempsey, 1 to 3 that Dempsey floored Tunney, 2 to 5 that Jack won in 5 rounds, 5 to 7 that Jack won in 8, and 5 to 6 that it was a draw. At least $1.2 million had been wagered.

By fight time, the last seats were filled, except those in the distant corners of the north end. It was announced officially that Chicago had rung up a new world's record for attendance at a sporting event. It was a "breath-taking picture." At least 145,000 were in attendance. Some said 150,000. Either way, it was a record. Telegraph keys were clicking, and radio announcers shouting.

At 9:55 p.m., Dempsey, wearing a spotless, long, white or cream flannel robe, with his initials "JD" in big black letters on the front, entered first. The crowd roared, giving him a cordial greeting, and he briefly took a short bow with a nod. Overall, though, the crowd was rather reserved. Under Jack's robe was a thick white wool sweater. He began dancing on his toes, his head bent and lowered, skipping around to keep from getting cold. One writer said he looked savage, with several days of facial hair growth. Another writer said he looked grim, thin, and old – older than his 32 years. He talked briefly with the mayor, still hopping. He shook hands with several writers and spoke a word or two over the radio. He shook hands with Gene Normile, his manager the prior year. Jack tugged the ropes in his corner.

With Dempsey were manager Leo P. Flynn, in a white sweater jersey and cap, and Jerry 'the Greek' Luvadis, who wore spectacles and a white sweater, with both of their sweaters having "Jack Dempsey" printed in black on the back. Also with them were New Orleans sportsman Remy Dorr, Bill Duffy, and Gus Wilson. Some said Joe Benjamin was part of his crew as well.

Waiting for Tunney and watching guard over the Dempsey corner were Tunney attendants Lou Brix, in golf trousers, and Jimmy Bronson. Tunney's entourage had a country club atmosphere.

Promoters Tex Rickard and George Getz climbed into the ring and received cheers. Rickard wished Jack good luck.

Gene made Jack wait for quite a while, about 5 ½ minutes. Some thought he was trying to make Jack get cold.

When old Jim Jeffries, wearing cap and golf trousers, entered the ring and was introduced, he raised more enthusiasm than anyone. The mere mention of Jim Corbett's name raised a storm of cheering. Jack Sharkey also was introduced. Both Jeff and the Shark shook Dempsey's hand.

When Gene Tunney finally appeared, he received a hearty reception and rousing ovation. The handsome Gene smiled and bowed his head. Tunney's robe was made of the colors of the marines – dark blue, with red/scarlet, and the Marine anchor/insignia in gold on his back, the same robe the Marines gave him to wear in Philadelphia. With him were Jimmy Bronson, Billy Gibson, who wore a pink sweater and check cap, Lou Fink, and Lou Brix. Some said Joe Malone was with the crew as well.

Dempsey immediately crossed the ring and shook Tunney's hand as he entered the ring. They might have murmured some words.

Tunney's skin was pink. Dempsey's was brown, like an "Indian."

The weather was comfortable, though fans had come equipped for the cold.

The photographers were all on the north side of the ring.

Paulino Uzcudun was introduced to the crowd.

The fighters' bandages were inspected.

The gloves were dark red or reddish brown, with baby blue laces. Both camps examined the gloves.

Dempsey removed his robe. He was wearing the same black trunks trimmed with red edgings/stripes that he wore against Sharkey.

DAVE BARRY.

The commission selected Chicago's Dave Barry, a former Chicago lightweight boxer back in his day, to referee, and he entered the ring. Assigned as judges were local businessman George Lytton and Commodore Sheldon Clark, chair of the Chicago Athletic association's athletic committee. The knockdown timekeeper was Paul Beeler, and the regular timekeeper was Marty Lavin.

Al Smith was the announcer. He had announced most of the big Illinois shows. When Smith presented "the challenger, Jack Dempsey," Jack received a tremendous cheer. "The champion – Gene Tunney, the Fighting Marine." He too got a big hand, with a few boos mixed in. The crowd was about evenly divided in its sympathy. Weights were announced as Dempsey, 192 ½ pounds, Tunney, 189 ½.

Tunney wore pure white trunks, contrasting him with Jack's black.

They gathered at ring center for final instructions from Referee Barry.

The championship fight started at 10:07 p.m.

On the films, Dempsey immediately advanced quickly and launched a sharp jab that Tunney eluded by leaning his head back, clinching, and both spun around. Break. Jack quickly fired another jab and stepped in fast, while Gene clinched. Jack dug in hooks to the body, then a couple lefts to the side or back of the head as Gene kept grabbing. Break. Tunney lightly bounced around on the outside. Jack fired a jab at the body. Tunney stepped in with a quick 1-2 and clinched. While being held, Jack snuck in a hook to the head. Referee Dave Barry was busy continually breaking them from clinches.

Dempsey settled down, and they circled one another, each moving to the right. Gene feinted, and both men backpedaled and moved around. Gene jabbed and clinched. Break. Dempsey kept circling and dipping to his right in anticipation of a potential fast Tunney punch. Jack shot a quick jab into the body. Tunney fired a 1-2 as Dempsey dipped and they clinched. Break.

Dempsey circled, advanced and dipped warily, trying to get a feel for when to attack without running into something. Tunney looked very alert, as if wanting to counter or time him on the way in. He lightly bounced, then stepped in with a flurry, but Dempsey backed away. They went into another clinch. Break. Tunney threw a lightning-fast jab and right to the head of the ducking Dempsey, then clinched. Dempsey could not break free from Tunney's grasp. Break.

Tunney lightly bounced and backed away as Dempsey jabbed at his body. Tunney advanced to attack but Dempsey stepped back and off to the side. The men were jousting and feeling out one another, trying to get a read for their correct timing and distance. Dempsey advanced, but then backed away as Tunney attacked with a hook, right, left uppercut in combination before both clinched. Dempsey snuck in a left to the body and a left rabbit punch. Break.

Dempsey slid to his right. Tunney advanced with a 1-2 that Dempsey ducked and they clinched. It seemed as if Dempsey's retreating or waiting turned Tunney tiger. Break. Tunney led with a quick 1-2 and clinch. Round over.

It was a fairly even, feel-out round. Dempsey started quickly and aggressively, with Tunney being very defensive. As the round progressed, Dempsey slowed his advance, became more cautious, and even retreated a bit or slid to the side, and Tunney took the aggressive. Neither landed much, and the round primarily was jousting, in and out with quick advances by either one followed by immediate clinching.

Paul Gallico called it a slow, uninteresting, even round.

Chicago sportswriter Walter Eckersall said the fight opened cautiously, with neither leading much. Gene led with his left and Jack shot a couple jabs to the body. There was a lot of clinching, but Gene had the edge.

Chicago's Sam Hall called it an even round.

Damon Runyon said Dempsey kept walking around Tunney, trying to make Gene lead. Tunney watched warily, and occasionally led. Both were cautious. The round was fairly even.

In the corner, Flynn did the talking to Dempsey. Duffy smoothed his hair back. Jerry the Greek stood silent. Gibson spoke to Tunney.

Grantland Rice said Tunney won the round by a wide margin, landing four blows to one, all clean.

Robert Edgren called it even.

On the radio, after the round was over, Graham McNamee, who gave a blow-by-blow account of each round, said, "We will call the round just a little party between two boys feeling themselves out before the fight begins."

2ⁿᵈ round

They circled one another. Dempsey attacked with jabs to the body. Tunney fired a 1-2 that Dempsey ducked and they clinched. Jack tried to free himself and fire in some short rights to the body, but Gene was really good at holding and smothering. Break. It usually required the referee to break them from each clinch. Dempsey jabbed the body again.

Dempsey often dipped several times as he approached Tunney, but if Jack was too cautious or stepped back, that would embolden Tunney to attack. Tunney feinted a right and Dempsey backed away. Tunney stepped in on the attack with his 1-2, 1 2 3 (jab, right, hook) as Jack backed up to the ropes and held. Dempsey had dipped and rolled to diminish the force of the right, but it landed. Break.

They sparred, waited, and moved. Tunney missed a 1-2 as Dempsey backed away and dipped along the ropes. Jack was trying not to allow Tunney to time him on the way in, perhaps to get Tunney to be more aggressive and lead, though Dempsey was not firing when Gene attacked. With Dempsey on the ropes, Tunney followed with a flurry and they clinched. Dempsey fired a left to the body and a left uppercut to the chin. Tunney pushed Jack back to the ropes and leaned in to smother further blows. Break.

Tunney circled to the right, then fired his 1-2 that was missing over the top of the dipping Dempsey, followed by the usual tight clinch. Break. Dempsey advanced slowly, Tunney fired 1-2 but Jack backed away. Another 1-2 by Tunney over the top and clinch. Dempsey was trying to work inside, unsuccessfully, because Gene held so well. Break.

Tunney moved, jabbed, lightly bounced, fired 1-2 and clinched. Gene snuck in a hook to the head in the clinch. Break. Dempsey circled to the right, and then eluded a Tunney jab. Jack approached cautiously, dipping, and Gene clinched. Dempsey snuck in lefts to the body. Tunney got in a left uppercut. Break. Jack jabbed the body and Gene missed a hook off the jab. Bell.

Primarily the round was another cautious feel-out, with jousting and sparring, each trying to get a read on the other. Dempsey was moving in, dipping, and Tunney was feinting, lightly bouncing and moving, trying to time Dempsey on the way in, but Dempsey was good at dipping to the right or sliding back as he saw Tunney about to throw. Tunney felt comfortable attacking when Dempsey backed away, for Jack usually did not throw after retreating. Mostly though, it was a lot of missing and clinching by both. Neither was landing effectively or often. Even round, or slight shade for Tunney.

Although not much effective work was being done by either, to that point it was more of a Tunney type fight. Dempsey was not able to get going with any real offense. Tunney was doing most of the firing, but generally was missing or only partially landing. Although Dempsey was not throwing much, he was fairly efficient, and his defense was holding up well, dipping and/or sliding away, not allowing Tunney to do much effective work. Still, Dempsey was not getting much going, which was contrary to his style. It seemed as if he felt that if he threw, it would be wasted energy, for Tunney was good at jumping away or tying up. Perhaps Jack feared the fast counter and did not want to leave himself vulnerable at the wrong range. Tunney seemed content to spar cautiously. Dempsey likely was happy that he was not missing, wasting energy, or getting countered or hit by leads like he did in their first fight. Thus far it was more of a chess match, both showing a lot of respect.

Gallico said the aggressive Dempsey gave Tunney a terrific body beating, forcing him to hold. Tunney kept hitting and moving, and tying up in close. Tunney's round, but it was slow and uninteresting.

Eckersall said Tunney had a slight shade, content to outbox him.

Hall scored the round for Dempsey.

Runyon said Dempsey bobbed. Tunney hit him with a right. In a mixup, Dempsey slugged the body. "There was so little the fight would have been booed had it been a preliminary." Dempsey by a shade.

Rice said Tunney landed the cleaner blows and showed more boxing skill. He was tying up Dempsey at close quarters, where Jack normally was at his best.

Edgren said that over the course of the fairly even first two rounds, Tunney missed a lot, and there was a fair amount of clinching and holding. Inside, Dempsey pecked away at his ear with short hooks. Dempsey had scored more often and was more aggressive, though overall the first two rounds were pretty even.

3rd round

The films show that the round featured lots of approaching, backing, feinting, sliding, and dipping, the cautious jousting/sparring pattern of the two prior rounds. Each time either man fired, Tunney would clinch tightly to neutralize Dempsey.

Dempsey fired a right over the top. Tunney pumped some jabs as he moved in and out. He fired a 1-2 over the top while Dempsey worked the body before the clinch. Dempsey fired rights to the body and several rabbit shots in frustration at Gene's incessant clinching. Break.

Tunney went on the attack with 1-2 1-2, with the last right landing as Dempsey moved away to the ropes, ducking, and they clinched. This time, Dempsey fired rabbit shots with his left on the clinching Tunney, who pushed and leaned in on him on the ropes. After breaking, Dempsey attacked the body and Tunney grabbed. Break.

Dempsey moved around and dipped to the right. Tunney was looking very alert, lightly bouncing, ready to strike. He fired his right over the top, while Dempsey dug lefts to the body, and then a left hook to the head as Tunney clinched harder. Break. Dempsey advanced and Tunney fired an overhand right to the head of the dipping Dempsey and then left uppercut before clinching, which Gene usually did after firing to prevent Dempsey from punching back. In the clinch, Tunney snuck in a left to the body. Dempsey fired a right to the body and then right rabbit shots and blows to the side of Gene's neck while being held. As the referee broke them, Tunney snuck in a short left uppercut.

Dempsey moved to the side and missed a jab for the body. Tunney, lightly bouncing, pumped a couple jabs and a right as Dempsey attacked the body, neither man landing effectively. Tunney jabbed, and again Dempsey fired at the body. Tunney jabbed again. Tunney 1-2. Tunney was moving, bouncing, looking to fire a jab and then move, or 1-2 and grab. Dempsey again fired in the clinch, rights to the side and back of the head. Tunney fired a right to the head as he moved back.

The round once again was mostly even or slightly Tunney. It was fairly uneventful from an action standpoint, though the pace picked up slightly. Neither really was getting going with much offense, and what was thrown mostly missed. Tunney probably landed a bit more, in part because he was throwing more. A lot of in and out, moving, feinting, dipping, firing and grabbing. Lots of holding. Dempsey was getting rougher and more frustrated with the holding, firing rabbit shots quite often. Jack was trying to hit the body and work on the inside a bit more, but Tunney was very good at clinching and smothering, leaning in. Tunney was more active in this round in terms of trying to time Dempsey's approach.

Thus far, Tunney was using his ring generalship and defense, movement and clinching, with occasional fast blows, trying to outbox Dempsey by small margins. Dempsey seemed like an old fighter compared to what he once was, without his usual nonstop aggression. He did not throw many punches, in part due to Tunney's style, and also in part owing to his own cautiousness. However, Dempsey was not being hit as often as in their first fight. Neither man was effective with their blows. It had been tactical and careful up to that point.

Tunney bounced lightly on his feet, with his hands down, but he was too quick for Dempsey. Gene either would beat him to the punch, step away just as Jack got in range, or effectively tie him up. Dempsey was unable to get off his usual short inside shots because Tunney was a master at neutralizing opponents on the inside with his clinching. Certainly, against Sharkey, Dempsey had been able to be much busier. Tunney clinched better and moved more than Sharkey. Tunney was more active with his punches than Dempsey. That said, Tunney was not exactly throwing a great deal of punches either, and he held a lot. Yet, he essentially dictated the terms of the fight, giving the impression that he was in control. Still, the first few rounds were close and difficult to score.

Gallico said it was Dempsey's round, but not a good fight thus far. Dempsey hit the body several times. Tunney hit from long range and grabbed in close. Jack landed a punch on the back of Tunney's head. Gene staggered Jack with a right. Dempsey again hit the back of the head. Between rounds, Tunney complained to the referee about Dempsey's punches (likely rabbit blows), but the referee paid no attention.

Eckersall said Tunney had the best of the exchanges. Dempsey used the rabbit punch a lot and Tunney's seconds protested.

Hall said it was Dempsey's round.

Runyon said Dempsey walked in and Gene danced away, but popped Jack's head with both hands. They danced about, Dempsey half bobbing forward and Tunney retreating. Dempsey focused on the body; Tunney the head. In a clinch, Jack used the rabbit punch. The pace was picking up. Dempsey clipped him on the chin with a right. Dempsey's round.

Between rounds, Bronson called Barry's attention to Dempsey's fouling.

Rice said the round was about even, as Jack got in a number of punches at close quarters. He still apparently was baffled by Tunney's defense.

Edgren said Dempsey won the round by a good margin. He wasn't rushing in headlong, but boxing, holding his own. It seemed odd to see Dempsey now and then step back and make Tunney miss.

On the radio, McNamee said they were not shooting nearly as many blows as they did in their prior contest. "Gene seems to be taking it easier." "I rather think that they should give the round to Dempsey."

4ᵗʰ round

Tunney circled, eluded a jab to the body, and retreated. He then advanced with a 1-2-3, then moved to his right again. Dempsey jabbed the body a couple times as Tunney jabbed and moved, poking in quick lefts and circling away. Gene again fired 1-2 over the top and grabbed as Dempsey hit the body with his right. Break. Tunney again jabbed. Dempsey advanced with a jab to the body, and in the close-up clinching scuffle, Tunney left hooked his head, Dempsey dug his left into the body and left uppercut to the head, Tunney bulled in, they clinched more, and Jack fired his right to the body and side of Gene's head. The referee struggled to break them as Jack kept trying to work the body.

Tunney fired a 1-2 over the dipping Dempsey, who dug a left hook into the body. Tunney fired a left hook to the body and moved away. Jack jabbed his body, Gene missed a counter hook, followed by more tight clinching, bulling, and leaning in by Tunney. Break. Dempsey jabbed the body a couple times and Tunney countered with a three-punch flurry that missed. Tunney again fired several blows at the advancing, dipping Dempsey, a right partially landing. Gene then moved again. His 1-2 missed and he grabbed. Tunney was good at pushing Dempsey back while grabbing him. Break.

Tunney was firing jabs and his right on the ducking Dempsey, who was advancing on the moving Tunney. Jack's head-movement was eluding the blows, but he could not counter the fast-retreating champion. Gene fired jab - right - left uppercut in combination, the final punch seeming to land, and he grabbed, then dug a left hook into Dempsey's body. Jack rabbit-punched with his right. Break.

The action was picking up in this round. Tunney was not grabbing quite as often, but rather moving instead and punching more. Dempsey was advancing with more determination, but still finding it difficult to get his timing and distance, for Tunney was so fleet of foot and fast-handed, or good at grabbing when the first two options did not work to throw off Dempsey.

Tunney let his hands go 1-2, the jab landing solidly, Dempsey countered with his right but missed, and Tunney countered the counter with his own right that landed and sent Jack back for a moment. In blazing-fast combination, Tunney fired 1-2 and jolting left uppercut, repeated the uppercut, then followed with a right and jab. Tunney was letting his hands go more often and in greater bunches in this round.

Tunney moved back, feinted, Dempsey dipped and stepped off to the right, and Tunney advanced with a 1-2 and clinched. Tunney pushed him off, as opposed to waiting for the referee to break them. Tunney landed a left jab and hook. He advanced with a powerful 1-2 that grazed as Jack moved back and off to the right.

In combination, Tunney fired a powerful overhand right, practically in Firpo fashion, immediately followed by a left uppercut which landed solidly and sent Dempsey back to the ropes. They clinched, and Dempsey immediately fired lefts to the body. The referee broke them.

Dempsey moved off to the left, then moved to his right, away from Gene's right, and dipped/rolled right, but Tunney stepped in with a lightning-fast overhand right that landed over the top and sent Dempsey careening into the corner, off balance, apparently shaken, his legs buckling, reminiscent of the Sharkey fight. Likely if not for the ropes/corner post, Dempsey would have gone down from that initial overhand right. Tunney quickly followed with a left hook that landed as well, but he missed a right as Jack ducked to the left and grabbed. Gene pushed off and stepped back.

Tunney fired a right over the top and they clinched. Break. Tunney again attacked and Dempsey rolled and eluded a right as he leaned against the ropes, but Gene snuck in a follow-up right hook in close. Clinch, Jack snuck in a right hook, and bell.

This was a clear Tunney round, the first really clear round of the fight, Gene's best to that point, for he was more offensive and aggressive, firing more and landing often, putting his punches together in rapid combination, even staggering Dempsey back and stunning him momentarily, landing the most powerful and significant punch of the fight thus far, an overhand right. Dempsey still was not firing very often, and could not get a read on Tunney. Jack seemed puzzled about how to get going. He tried to open up a bit early on in the round, but it did not last. He seemed to be a slow-motion, less active, less diligent version of what he once was, unable to pull the trigger, or unsure about when to do so.

Gallico said it was all Tunney's round. Dempsey landed three low punches with his right. Tunney got him on the ropes with a furious exchange and had the better of it. Dempsey held on. Tunney staggered him with a wicked left uppercut. Jack hit the body, while Tunney hit the head. Tunney hit him with everything he had. He staggered Jack with a terrific right to the chin. Jack was groggy. Gene staggered him at the bell. Jack returned to his corner and informed Flynn that he was all right. Still, they gave Dempsey smelling salts in the corner.

Eckersall said it looked bad for Dempsey. Tunney smothered him with straight lefts and right crosses. He kept up the relentless attack after forcing Jack to the ropes. Dempsey was wobbly as he went to his corner.

Hall said it was Tunney by a big margin, landing a volley of rights and lefts to the jaw, pinning Dempsey on the ropes.

Runyon said Tunney backed away but suddenly halted and banged Dempsey with a 1-2. Dempsey landed a hard left to the stomach. Dempsey eluded rights. Not many solid punches were landing.

However, in an exchange, Tunney let fly with both hands and staggered Dempsey with a right to the chin. He followed up, pounding away with both hands, driving Jack into a corner and belting him. Dempsey seemed to be in a bad way at the bell. Big Tunney round.

Jack's seconds worked hard over him. They put something on him that caused Gibson and Bronson to yell to Referee Barry, "Take it off." Another said Gibson and Tunney's seconds claimed something was being put on Dempsey's gloves. Others claimed that Tunney's corner complained that giving Dempsey stimulants was unfair.

Rice said Tunney's solid blows had Dempsey a bit groggy.

Edgren said they fought furiously. Tunney landed hard rights to the head, but didn't shake Dempsey, who chased him. Gene jabbed lightly. Dempsey hooked a right to the ear, and Tunney was shaken to his knees. The ex-champ went tearing after him, driving him around the ring. Jack plunged in but Tunney crossed a right that stopped him in his tracks. Dempsey was forced back to the ropes. But he was fighting all the time. Tunney reached the jaw with his overcurving right, his best punch, one of which crashed on the chin and had Jack looking groggy. He slammed back and tried to dodge, but was slow. Tunney grazed another right to the jaw. Tunney's round.

McNamee said, "Gene seems to be beginning to box. ... Gene is seemingly beginning to wake up. ... Dempsey is groggy, unquestionably. Dempsey is in bad shape and is going down in a neutral corner. No, he is not down! No, he is not down, but he took three hard lefts to the face and bounded around on the ropes. Finally he came out as only Dempsey can. ... Tunney's round by a terrific margin."

5th round

Tunney advanced with a 1-2 and they clinched. Break. Tunney fired a quick jab and Dempsey responded with a counter 1-2 to the body. Dempsey missed a left hook. Tunney shot 1-2 over the top and clinched. Dempsey tried to sneak in a left to the body but Tunney moved away and circled. Dempsey jabbed the body while Tunney jabbed the head and lightly hooked off of it. Dempsey stepped in with a quick, powerful hook to the body, and repeated it as Gene clinched and then broke away.

As Jack retreated off to the right, Tunney stepped in with his usual 1-2 and Dempsey as usual ducked underneath it and they clinched. Dempsey fired some rabbit punches with his right. Break. Tunney peppered with jabs as Dempsey moved back and away. Dempsey was not good at giving the impression that he could step back and fire, which usually caused Tunney to continue to advance and attack whenever Jack moved back. Gene fired a flurry as Jack backed and rolled away along the ropes. They clinched, and Jack dug lefts into the body. Break.

Tunney jabbed, stepped back, then stepped in with a 1-2-3, only the hook landing, and he clinched and bulled in. Break. Tunney held his ground a bit, exchanged lefts, then a right, and Dempsey countered with a hook to the head that landed. Tunney clinched tightly, then fired a left hook to the body followed by a right uppercut to the body, and clinched some more. Break. Outside, Tunney pumped his left jab several times as Jack moved his head. Dempsey finally countered with a heavy jab to the body. Tunney landed a hard right, then moved.

Dempsey advanced with a hard jab that snapped Tunney's head back. Gene missed a counter left, Jack missed a follow-up hook, and Gene clinched tightly. Dempsey snuck in a right hook to the head. Break. Tunney grazed a 1-2-3 as Jack dipped down. Gene clinched and Jack dug rights into the body. Gene pushed him away.

Tunney fired his 1-2-3 and clinched. Dempsey tried to get his right to the body going, but Tunney pushed him away.

Tunney again launched a quick 1-2-left uppercut combination, then followed up with left and right as Jack snuck in a left hook to the body, and Gene landed another right as Dempsey advanced and fired but missed his hook as the champ stepped away. Tunney landed his 1-2-left uppercut combination solidly, doubling up the left uppercut, then leaned in and clinched. Tunney's punches were lightning-fast and powerful. Dempsey was advancing but running into the blows, despite his head movement. In the clinch, Dempsey rabbit punched with his right. Break.

Tunney jabbed him, though Jack moved away. They missed a couple jabs. Tunney shot his 1-2 and grabbed as Jack dipped under the blows. Tunney snuck in a left hook to the body, then smothered and pushed, while Jack hit the back of his head with a right, until the referee broke them. Tunney missed a 1-2 and Dempsey countered underneath with a body hook. Tunney circled, then fired left-right-left, grabbed, then snuck in a hook and left uppercut, and Dempsey responded with a right rabbit shot. Tunney's round.

Gallico's version said Dempsey hit the body and again punched low. Tunney was trying for a knockout, but Jack was strong again. Gene had Jack on the ropes and they clinched. They slugged in close. Gene jabbed. Jack staggered him with a left hook. Gene nailed him with a right to the chin. Gene had Dempsey groggy again from a two-handed attack to the head. Jack tied up. Tunney's round.

Between rounds, Dempsey again took smelling salts, and his handlers worried over him. In Tunney's corner, Gene was sitting calmly, with a towel around his shoulders.

Eckersall said the champ had a wide margin of points. Jack landed a couple left hooks, but not solidly enough to jar the champ.

Hall said it was a Tunney round. Dempsey's mouth was open, and he looked tired.

Runyon said Tunney came out banging away, wading in. Dempsey went on the defensive. Jack hit the midsection and held. He eluded a lot of punches, but Tunney still picked him off with his left. Dempsey came to life and shook Gene with a right to the jaw. Tunney let fly for the chin with both hands, punishing Dempsey's head. Tunney said something to Barry (some claiming he was complaining about low blows, or perhaps rabbit punches). A Tunney right to the chin made Jack hang on. Tunney's round. "It was not the old Dempsey by seven lengths, but it was a different Tunney... I never before saw Gene so aggressive. They gave Dempsey smelling salts in his corner..."

Rice also said it was another Tunney round by a wide margin, for he was landing at will. There was a big black spot under Dempsey's eye, where he caught a hard right swing.

Edgren said Tunney appeared to be master of the fight. He was poised, calm, confident, and smiling. He began forcing, and Dempsey was retreating slowly. Jack was trying to use his skill and defense. Dempsey took up rushing again and forced Gene to run and clinch. At the end, Tunney landed a perfect one-two, the right cracking heavily on the jaw, shaking Dempsey and driving him back.

On the radio, McNamee said Tunney "for the moment seems to be out-Dempseying Dempsey. … Jack leaps in with a hard left to the side of Tunney's face, and Tunney seemed almost wabbled for a moment. I am not sure. … Tunney said something to the referee. I don't know what it was."

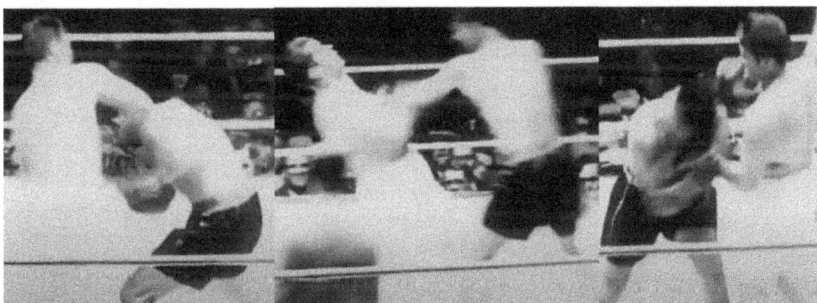

6th round

Tunney fired a right to the head and Dempsey threw a right to the body. Tunney launched his usual 1-2 and Dempsey tried a left hook to the body. A Tunney 1-2 while Dempsey hooked at the same time, they clinched, and Dempsey landed a jolting left hook to the head. Tunney pushed off and stepped back.

Tunney jabbed and jumped away from a Dempsey counter jab to the chest. Tunney circled right, fired 1-2 and smothered, but Dempsey countered with a right uppercut to the body and left hook to the head that landed, which Tunney countered with his own left hook to the head.

Thus far in the round, Dempsey seemed friskier and more combative than previously in the fight, with better timing. He finally was opening up and getting going.

Tunney circled. Jack jabbed the body but Gene landed a counter right to the jaw that backed up Dempsey momentarily, though Jack then advanced with another jab to the body. Tunney circled left, missed 1-2, which Dempsey countered to the body underneath with both hands. Then, as Tunney leaned in, Dempsey rabbit punched with his left. Break.

On the outside, Tunney attacked with 1-2-3, the hook landing, and grabbed. Both dug in left hooks to the body. Break. Tunney missed 1-2 and grabbed. Jack rabbit punched with his right. Break. Both missed their jabs, but Gene followed with 1-2-left hook to the body, landing. Gene lightly bounced to the left.

Dempsey landed his jab to the head solidly, but Tunney immediately countered with but missed hook-right-left uppercut-right, while at same time, Dempsey powerfully counter hooked the head but just missed or grazed. Tunney moved away and circled. Dempsey moved into range and Tunney landed a right to the head and clinched. Dempsey left hooked his head with some ferocity and Gene grabbed more tightly as Jack bulled in. Break. Tunney moved. Dempsey jabbed the body and Tunney countered with a right to the top of his head. A Tunney 1-2 missed, which Dempsey countered with a hard right to the body. Gene circled to his left.

As Tunney advanced with a jab, Dempsey beautifully timed his right at the same time over the top of the jab onto Tunney's chin, jolting his head back. Tunney immediately responded with his right followed by a left uppercut that missed and Dempsey countered by nailing him with a well-timed hard left hook, following with right and hard left to the body as Gene missed another left uppercut. Jack got the better of the exchange, landing really hard blows in succession for the first time in the fight, showing a better sense of timing than heretofore.

Tunney backed away, then advanced as Jack waited and did not follow up his advantage as a younger version would have done. Dempsey stepped back as Tunney attacked with 1-2-3, landing the final hook as Dempsey went into the ropes. Dempsey snuck in a left uppercut to the jaw. Gene broke away. A Tunney 1-2 missed over the top and Dempsey countered to the body with both hands. Gene snuck in a little right uppercut and pushed off. Dempsey fired a jab at the chest and advanced.

Tunney jabbed and Dempsey fired a near simultaneous counter right over the top that landed. Tunney immediately fired a counter right and left uppercut, but Jack followed with a left hook that landed at the same time as Gene's uppercut was en route, with Dempsey's punches landing harder and more solidly, but Tunney took it well and kept punching, though Jack raised his guard to block the blows. Gene stepped away. Dempsey advanced and fired a ferocious combination, right-hook-right, the first punch missing, the second blocked, and the final right landing.

Tunney stepped off, landed a jab and a 1-2, and Dempsey dug a right uppercut into the body. Tunney glided away, fired his 1-2, landing high, and clinched. Jack leaned in with his head. Break. Tunney fired a lead left hook or uppercut, stepping in with it, then smothered as Jack snuck in lefts to the body. Gene stepped back with a lead hook and right, and the bell rang.

The pace really picked up in this round. The combat was at its heaviest and most ferocious, particularly since Dempsey was starting to feel more comfortable with his timing and distance, letting his hands go more and at better moments. Jack landed his best punches of the fight thus far. Tunney kept a very good pace himself, both with hands and feet. It was a fast-paced round for heavyweights, although the younger Dempsey would have followed-up more after landing.

The round was fairly even, or slightly Dempsey's. Tunney probably punched and landed more, but Dempsey landed the hardest and a few of the cleanest, well-placed, and best-timed blows of the round. Tunney's punches were flashier overall from a distance, but Dempsey's were solid, subtle, and effective. Dempsey's punches were more head-jarring, but Tunney proved that he took a really good punch, usually countering instantly. One could not argue too hard with someone giving the round to Tunney, but there is a valid argument that Dempsey's heavy punches, inside work, and ability to ride with blows kept it even or gave him an edge. Jack seemed to sense that his counter right over the top of Tunney's jab was a good move, and by firing at or nearly the same time as Tunney, he could nail him.

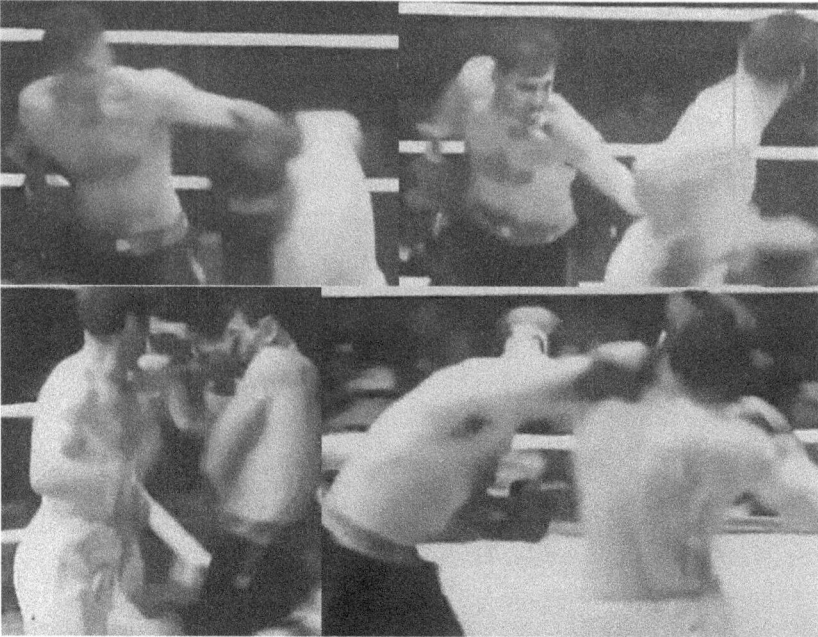

Gallico said it was Tunney's round. Jack mauled in close. Gene landed both hands to the head. He had the better of a terrific exchange. Jack staggered him with a right and left to the chest. Gene was missing. Jack pounded the body. Jack had bruises over his left eye. He was fighting hard. Gene landed a right to the head.

Between rounds, they paid more attention to Tunney, and held his trunks open so he could get air. Jack merely was being rubbed.

Eckersall said Dempsey showed a remarkable recovery. He planted some hard lefts on the jaw and at times forced the champ to go into close quarters and hold on to avoid punishment. Jack won the round and showed more of his old-time fighting ability, more than at any prior time in the fight.

Hall said it was Dempsey's round. Tunney's left eye was cut slightly.

Runyon said Dempsey took some hard punches to the face and body. His face was quite red where he was taking the champ's lefts. Jack jabbed Gene's head back. In one of his old-time flares of fighting, Dempsey nailed him on the chin with a staggering right and punched him hard to the body. But Tunney never backed up, taking Dempsey's smashes well. He kept fighting. Regardless, "It was Dempsey's round, in my opinion." Between rounds, Duffy told Jack, "Get your chin down."

Rice said the round was about even, but Dempsey's best showing thus far, hurting Gene with rights to the head, staggering him once. Dempsey showed vast improvement over his prior work in the fight.

Edgren said Dempsey began leading, driving after Tunney, making him clinch, pounding rights to the head and neck whenever he could escape Gene's grasp. Tunney's seconds protested the rabbit punches. Barry said something to Dempsey. Jack pasted his stomach, and Gene hung on desperately. Tunney was a master at the holding tricks. He held with one hand, let go with one and hooked his free hand onto the side of Dempsey's head. The referee made Tunney let go. Gene landed a right to the jaw, and Jack rushed. Jack still would circle right, off towards Tunney's left, causing Gene to miss. Near the end, they mixed, and Dempsey landed lefts to the body and clipped his ears with hooks. Dempsey actually was outboxing him, winning the round.

McNamee said, "They have been giving Dempsey smelling salts in his corner, but Tunney hasn't taken any relief whatever." Tunney's midsection had become very red. Dempsey's skin retained the same brown.

7th round

Dempsey circled and dipped to the right, but he was not attacking. Tunney sensed this and stepped in with a three-punch combination – a 1-2 that missed and a final left possibly landing as Dempsey was backing away. Clinch. Tunney broke away. Tunney missed a 1-2 over the top of a ducking Dempsey. Gene stepped away. He peppered with jabs as Dempsey moved his head, but then Tunney landed a 1-2 as Dempsey dipped down, the jab landing solidly and the right being slightly diminished by landing high as Jack was dipping. Gene pushed off to get back to the outside again.

Tunney fired a lead left jab which Dempsey eluded by ever so slightly dipping his head to the left and immediately simultaneously landed an overhand right counter over the top of Tunney's jab, as he had done in the prior round. It was very well timed and landed solidly, jolting Gene back a step. Sensing that he may have affected Tunney, the advancing Dempsey stepped forward and slightly twisted/dropped down to the left, then leapt in quickly, landing an explosive long left hook to the jaw and solid right to the jaw that put Gene into the ropes. Tunney instinctively fired a counter right that missed as he was moving backwards and leaning back into the ropes, his legs unsteady. Dempsey immediately followed with a brutal hook-right-hook-right fast combination, landing all of the punches solidly on the chin or face as Tunney's legs awkwardly gave out and he sagged down into the ropes and down to the canvas throughout the combination.

Gene was laying backward, parallel with the ropes, grabbing the middle rope with his left hand, his right leg bent back awkwardly, in an unnatural position. It was the first time in Gene Tunney's career that he had been knocked down. Jack stepped back. Still holding the rope with his left, Gene gradually brought his right leg out from underneath him, but he seemed dazed.

After Tunney went down, Referee Dave Barry initially raised his right hand high with his index finger outstretched as if to indicate a knockdown and the start of a count, but then dropped it down horizontally towards the right and at the same time outstretched his left arm as he rushed in and put his left hand on Dempsey's chest to push him back slightly, saying something to him, and then pointing to the left with his left hand, indicating to him that he wanted him to go to the furthest corner. However, Dempsey was looking down intently at Gene while heading to his left, in the other direction, towards the nearest corner, behind Tunney, where Jack went and leaned back against the corner post.

It looked as if Dempsey initially did not realize that the referee wanted him to go to a particular corner. He simply thought he needed to go to *a* corner. Barry kept pointing to the left, across the ring, to the furthest neutral corner. Dempsey finally got it and started walking to his right towards the other corner. Only once Dempsey was well on his way toward the other side of the ring did Barry turn and start counting.

However, Barry did not pick up the count from the timekeeper, but rather had suspended his count as a result of Dempsey's failure to retire to the furthest corner. Barry re-started counting at one from that point. Tunney had been down for about 5 seconds already.

At Barry's count of three, while still on the canvas with his left hand on the middle rope, Tunney turned and looked up at him counting. Seeming cogent, Tunney intently watched the referee's hand moving up and down with each count as Barry moved in closer to him. When the referee put his hand down for the count of nine, Tunney immediately rose, pushing off the canvas with his right hand, using his left glove on the rope for assistance.

At the time that Tunney was in the process of rising at nine, with his right hand still on the canvas, Dempsey stepped away from the furthest neutral corner and started moving quickly towards him. By the time Tunney's right hand left the canvas and he was in the process of standing erect, Dempsey already was nearly halfway across the ring in rapid pursuit of his prey, in a fast walk, practically running forward. Once Tunney rose, the referee did not wipe his gloves, as he could have done, nor did he send Dempsey back, as he also could have done, but rather he saw Dempsey advancing, and Referee Barry stepped back out of the way.

Dempsey rapidly approached and launched a powerful lead left hook that landed on the side of the head/neck as Tunney was moving away and off to his left. Tunney was able to move away rapidly with excellent footwork, initially circling left, but then changing directions on the charging bull who fired and missed a hook as Tunney leaned away from it and now was moving to the right. Jack missed another left. Tunney stopped and landed a 1-2, stopping just for an instant to fire and then clinch. Dempsey landed a heavy left hook to the head as Gene tried to hold.

Tunney lightly jabbed as he voluntarily stepped back and moved away rapidly, back and then off to the right, where, off of an outstretched measuring left he stopped and landed a right on the advancing Dempsey and then clinched while Jack snuck in a left hook to the body. Dempsey landed a short hook as he broke away from being held. He then moved forward. Tunney quickly jabbed his face and kept moving away, circling to the left very well, like a dancing, sidestepping master. Dempsey jabbed his body. Tunney circled rapidly as Dempsey advanced. As Jack got into range and jabbed, Tunney fired a hook and right and then clinched and smothered. Dempsey fired a left hook into the body. Tunney pushed off and moved away again. Tunney jabbed, pushed Jack back, and then moved back and to the right.

When the stalking Dempsey got into range, Tunney landed a lead right and held while leaning back against the ropes. A leaning-in Dempsey dug in body shots with both hands, and a short head-jolting left hook. Tunney jabbed and moved, escaping off to the right again. He stopped his side-to-side movement to miss a right over the top and smother, as Dempsey fired his left to the body. Tunney pushed off and moved away again, moving back and then circling rapidly to the right. He stopped to fire a 1-2 that missed, followed by a left hook to the body, then grabbed. Dempsey got his left free and hit Gene's head with a hard left hook.

Tunney pushed off with a couple touch punches and moved back. Dempsey ducked a jab and advanced. Tunney was moving too quickly for him, stepping back and side-stepping, circling around to his right. Dempsey followed and eluded as Tunney peppered some light jabs while on the move. Tunney was sidestepping quickly in a counterclockwise circle as Dempsey followed him around but failed to cut off the ring.

Frustrated, Dempsey momentarily waived his hand towards himself as if to stay, "Come here and fight." But Tunney kept circling to the right while Dempsey with a slight grin kept walking towards him.

Dempsey finally took a very quick step towards Tunney and fired off an explosive left hook as Gene was moving to the right, towards it, landing high on the head, immediately following in combination with a powerful right-left-right-left in rapid succession. A couple of these follow-up blows, particularly the rights, may have partially landed, but Tunney was moving away at the time, so the force was diminished.

Tunney kept moving, hitting the ropes briefly, but continuing to move to his right. He momentarily stopped to fire a 1-2 at the advancing and ducking Dempsey, clinching after missing, then stepping back as Jack missed a left uppercut. Gene jabbed and bounced away, circling right again, then launched a 1-2 over the top, pushed and stepped away, jabbed, stepped back, landed a right off a lead left hand, then clinched as Jack snuck in a hard left hook to the head. Tunney clinched tightly until the referee broke them.

Gene stepped left, missed a left hook and grabbed. He pushed and stepped away as Jack tried to get in a left to the body. Gene moved right, fired a 1-2 and held. Dempsey dug left hooks to the body. Bell.

Although he had hurt and decked Tunney, having him on the verge of a knockout, clearly winning the round, Dempsey could not finish him or land many blows after Tunney rose. Gene's fast footwork, ability to stop and punch instantly, then clinch or move away again, showing superior sense of distance and timing, was a great obstacle for Dempsey, who did not advance fast enough, or get off enough punches once he got into range. Gene took well whatever punches that did land.

Mostly, Tunney was on the move for the rest of the round, but still stopped to fire and land when he could, and still clinching fairly well. For the most part, Dempsey could not catch up with him. He tried, and did land some good shots, but it was clear that Gene was okay and that his movement was too much and too fast for Dempsey to overcome. Tunney recovered very well. His great legs certainly did not betray him once he rose.

Gallico said Tunney went down for nine-count, but it appeared to be a long count. Dempsey chased him all over. Gene staggered away but Jack could not knock him out. Gene held on. Jack kept chasing him all around the ring. Tunney was recovering. Jack hit the body. Gene kept running but landed a right. While Tunney was running, Dempsey asked him to come in. Jack cut loose. Tunney was in bad shape. He kept running away as Jack chased him. Clear Dempsey round. Through the 7th round, Gallico had it 4-2-1 for Tunney.

Eckersall said Tunney was winning the round early. Jack finally got him to the ropes, nailed him with several blows, and Tunney went down. He rose before the count of ten and managed to weather the round by running away, holding, and firing left jabs. To that point, Eckersall had it 5-2 for Tunney.

Hall said it was Dempsey by a mile, flooring Tunney for a 9-count. Hall had it 4-2-1 for *Dempsey* in rounds to that point.

Runyon said Jack's mouth hung half open as he bobbed into Tunney, who was missing his right. Suddenly Jack nailed him with a right and long left hook that drove Tunney falling back into the ropes. Dempsey piled on top of him, banging away with both hands to the chin, and Tunney went down in a heap. The crowd was up, roaring.

When Gene rose, Dempsey rushed him. A dazed Tunney backed up, fairly running away. The crowd booed Gene for running. Some bawled, "What a champion – stand up and fight." But Tunney kept retreating, and Dempsey could not catch up with him. In the corner, Bronson and Gibson worked hard over him. Like Hall, Runyon had the fight 4-2-1 for Dempsey thus far.

Rice said a right and left to the jaw decked Tunney, but he rose at nine, groggy and badly hurt. Gene backed and ran away. Dempsey's round by a mile. Rice had the fight 4-1-2 for Tunney.

Edgren said Dempsey rushed and leaped at him. A terrific hook to the jaw and Tunney was half twisted around. He tried to grab, but Dempsey landed a right and Tunney fell heavily on his back, his left arm flung across the rope, right in front of Edgren, within 2 feet. Edgren, sitting in the front row of the press section, had a watch, and started it. "I always carry a split second watch to time knockdowns, for in the old days a favorite trick was to give a fighter a long count to save him from a knockout especially if he was a favorite in the betting." Tunney was on the floor for 14 seconds, and "evidently needed plenty of time." "In most places and under the usual run of prize-ring circumstances a man is out when he is knocked down and fails to rise within ten seconds. But apparently not under Chicago rules. Tunney was knocked out, but they let him go on fighting." Tunney rose at the referee's count of 9, ran around the ring backward, and Dempsey could not catch him. "I'll say for Gene Tunney that he is not out until he's counted out by a referee."

Edgren noted that initially, the referee turned around toward Dempsey, who had turned uncertainly toward his own corner. Tunney fell only a couple of steps away. Time went by, and there was no count. Then the referee bent over Tunney, and after looking around toward the timekeeper, began to count slowly.

Edgren had Dempsey winning the fight through the 7th round, 3-2-2.

On the radio, McNamee said that "neither boy is cut or marked, as yet. They both look as if they mean business and plenty, but they don't seem to get [to] each other quite vitally." Eventually, though,

> Tunney, is down! Tunney is down from a barrage of lefts and rights to the face. The count is going on. Tunney is down. Dempsey is on the other side. Eight. Nine – but Tunney is up, and now they are at it again. Tunney is backing away, but Dempsey is following Tunney. … He is following Tunney all around the ring. Then Tunney lands a right and a left and Dempsey keeps on following, but can't quite get him. Tunney is now out and gets Jack on the jaw. It seems that the shock is gone. Gene is still backing away. Oh, a left hook and a right and then – now Tunney drives his left and his right to Jack's face; he seems to be in pretty good condition again, but Jack is still following him. … Jack isn't even trying to protect himself. He is trying to get in where he can hit. … Dempsey is still following Tunney, motioning Tunney to come in and fight. Dempsey is standing in the middle of the ring. Now with one leap he is on Tunney and he drove his right and left to Tunney's face and head three times and Tunney's face looks bad, and Dempsey weaves in. … Then as Dempsey comes in Tunney does land with his right to Dempsey's face, and Dempsey laughs at Tunney and motions for him to come on and fight instead of backing away. … [I]t was almost a new champion. Almost but not quite. … If I am not mistaken, this is the first time that Gene Tunney has ever been off his feet since he has been in the prize ring.

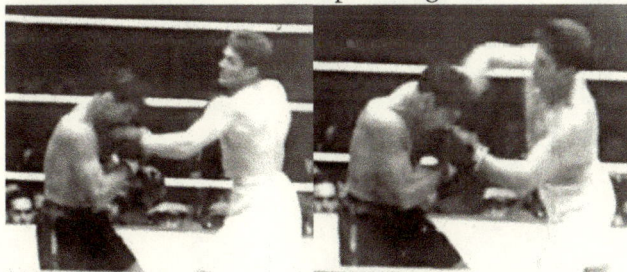

8th round

Dempsey started cautiously, dipping. Tunney was moving slightly, looking alert and ready to punch. Tunney missed a fast 1-2 and clinched. Dempsey dug a left hook into the body, and missed a left uppercut as Gene broke away. Dempsey advanced, while Tunney moved. Both jabbed and missed, Dempsey to the body and Tunney towards the head, Gene following with a missed left hook. Dempsey jabbed the head, but Tunney countered with a solid right and head-jolting left uppercut, then clinched. Dempsey fired a left hook to the head, and left hooks to the body in the clinch, and then a couple hooks to the side/back of the head as Tunney leaned in close. Break.

Dempsey missed a lead left hook as Tunney leaned back away from it, countered with a hook of his own, and clinched. Dempsey sent hooks into his body. Break. A Tunney 1-2 which Jack ducked as usual, and Gene clinched. Tunney broke and stepped back, but his snappy jab jolted Jack's head back as he did so, and he repeated it. Tunney slid back cautiously but appeared ready to fire. Dempsey advanced slowly. Tunney missed a lead right as Dempsey fired a hook. Dempsey followed up and countered with a short right to the body and a big hook that glanced high on Gene's head. In the clinch, Dempsey hit him with a short, snappy hook to the head, but Gene mostly smothered by tightly clinching. Break.

Dempsey dipped, Tunney fired a lead right over the top, Dempsey countered with a hook to the body, and then tried to get in little hooks to the head as Tunney smothered and held. Break. Dempsey stepped in with a lead right to the body and followed with a left that missed. Tunney grabbed, partially spun, then countered with a left that missed as Dempsey fell past him off balance. Dempsey turned, stepped in, and as Tunney fired a right, Dempsey landed a powerful hook to the head and heavy right to the body that sent Gene back.

Tunney moved about, side to side to the right in a circle, sensing that he needed to get away from the power. Jack missed a jab. Dempsey stepped in with a very ferocious quick combination, landing both hands to the body, left-right-left-right, then hook that missed the head, and Tunney got away from the ropes off to his left side, bounced off the other set of ropes and landed a left hook on Dempsey, who was advancing with a right into Gene's body. Clinch. Jack snuck in a left to the body, and then the referee broke them. Dempsey advanced, Tunney fired a lead right over the top and left hook to the body. Dempsey dug in his own snappy hook to the body. Tunney pushed away. To that point, Dempsey might have been winning the round with the much harder, more effective blows.

However, as Dempsey was advancing, Tunney landed a jab followed by a right that landed over the top of Dempsey's attempted but missed left hook as Jack was dipping and twisting to the right from the punch's momentum, which enabled the Tunney right to land, and Jack's right leg went out from underneath him and he collapsed to the canvas, his right knee and right hand on the ground. The knockdown was a flash, in part because of the momentum of Dempsey's missed left hook. Gene missed a follow-up left hook as Jack was going down.

Referee Barry immediately raised his hand in the air just as he did initially for the Tunney knockdown, but instead of pointing Tunney to a neutral corner as he did Dempsey, Barry ran in and dropped his hand down to count one immediately as he rushed over to them, before Tunney went anywhere. However, as Barry was advancing and dropping his hand to count one, Dempsey immediately rose, so by the time Barry stepped in, Jack already was up. Barry did not point Tunney to the neutral corner, possibly because Dempsey got up so quickly. Regardless, it is clear that after the knockdown, Tunney just stood there and made no attempt to go towards any corner, let alone a neutral corner, and Barry did not suspend the count or direct him there. Yet, he likely saw no need for it given that Dempsey rose immediately, and since there was no mandatory count, the fight was to resume immediately as soon as a downed fighter rose. Barry was about to step between them, but then backed away and allowed the action to resume (without wiping Dempsey's gloves). Still, some later used this as an argument of bias. Some felt that it appeared to be an inconsistent application of the neutral corner rule. At least Dempsey had gone to *a* corner, whereas Tunney had not gone to one at all. Barry likely would argue that the difference was how quickly Dempsey rose. (He had not wiped off Tunney's gloves either.)

With Dempsey right there in front of him after he rose at one, as soon as the referee backed away, Tunney fired a 1-2, the jab landing and the right missing as Jack ducked down. Clinch. Tunney stepped away. Dempsey backed away. Tunney advanced and fired a 1-2-3, the final blow partially landing/partially blocked as Jack backed away into the ropes and held. Tunney got free from the clinch and fired 1-2-left uppercut, the jab landing but Dempsey ducking the right. They clinched, and Dempsey worked in a couple body blows. Break.

Tunney leaned back from Dempsey's jab to diminish its power, and then countered with a hook, right uppercut, and hook, the final hook landing. Dempsey ducked down, Tunney fired two left uppercuts, the second landing, a grazing right high on the head, and then moved away, sidestepping to the right. Dempsey advanced, but again Tunney fired left and right and tied him up. Break. Both posed and waited until the bell.

Some called this an even round because Dempsey was aggressive, landing several solid body blows and some hooks and rights to the head. However, Tunney's generalship held him in good stead, moving and firing fairly often with leads and counters, and he landed the most significant blow of the round, decking Dempsey for a one-count with his right, though some perceived this as a slip or more of Jack being off balance from the momentum of missing. It was just a flash, for he rose immediately. Still, it was the first time that Tunney had decked Dempsey, and he did it the very next round after being down himself.

Tunney seemed to be fully recovered at the start of the round. However, Dempsey appeared reinvigorated. He pulled the trigger more, threw faster, in combination, and was more aggressive. Still, he was nowhere near as relentless, active, or consistent as he had been in his heyday. Tunney took a few, but took them well, often countering even when hit. He still utilized footwork, quick flowing punches, and clinching. Certainly, it was impressive that one round after being decked, Tunney was back to boxing well and was able to drop Dempsey. Hence, most gave Tunney the round.

Gallico said it was Dempsey's round. Gene still was running. Tunney shook Dempsey with a right. He seemed to have recovered his strength. Jack hit the body and landed a right on the chin. Gene was moving all the time. Jack staggered him with a right to the body. Gene was running away and Jack was nailing him. Gene was groggy again. Down went Dempsey for a one-count from a right to the head. Jack was blocking. Gene staggered him with both hands.

Eckersall said Tunney recovered remarkably and crossed a right to the jaw. It was a short overhand cross which put Jack to the mat. He was up at one. He was tired. Blood flowed from his left eye, and Gene tried to finish him, but Jack's great fighting instinct permitted him to pull through.

Hall said it was Tunney's round. Gene floored Dempsey, who hopped up immediately.

Runyon said Tunney seemed determined, standing Jack off with his left stab. Dempsey bore in and battered the body. Yet, Tunney dropped Dempsey with a left hook [sic], but Dempsey was up at once without a count. Gene banged away with both hands, winning the round. There was a slight cut over Dempsey's right eye as he went to his corner.

Rice said Tunney cut Dempsey's right eye with a hard smash. Tunney knocked Jack down with a right to the jaw, but Jack was up in a flash and there was no count. A left hook staggered Dempsey. His face was cut. Although Gene was backing away and taking some punishment, nevertheless, he won the round with his knockdown.

Edgren said Tunney ran, but his strength was coming back fast. Dempsey hit the stomach and Gene held. Jack hit his ear, forced him back, and hit him with several blows, but he could not catch him squarely again. The blows lost their force against a fleeting target.

Then, Tunney began to hit. A sharp left slashed Dempsey's right eyebrow. Blood ran down his face in streams. Dempsey came after him, not paying attention to defense. Like a flash, Tunney whipped a curving right to the chin, with Dempsey leaning forward in pursuit, and he went down to his knees. He did not wait for a count but leaped up instantly. He went after Gene again, only to run into lefts and rights to his blood-smeared face. Tunney's round.

On the radio, McNamee noted,

> Now Dempsey's eye is cut, just a bit. Dempsey lands a terrific left, followed by a hard right to Tunney's jaw, and then Dempsey comes in like a wild man, driving left and right and Tunney has all he can do to guard and try to keep on his feet. Again Tunney looked as if he might go down...and so far it is again Dempsey's round.

> Ha, Dempsey is down from a hard left to the jaw, and is up. He didn't wait for a count. He only went down to his knees. ... Tunney is now developing into just a bit the aggressor... And now again Jack looks as if he didn't particularly like the going for a moment. ... Jack hasn't landed a blow, now, in the last 15 seconds. Jack's eye seems to be cut just above the eye, just a little bit. ... Yes, Jack has a pretty good cut on his forehead.

Dempsey fired a lead hook, but Tunney eluded it by blocking with his right glove lifted up high and moving away. Dempsey jabbed the body. Tunney snuck in a short counter left uppercut to the forehead and clinched. Dempsey fired a right hook to the head in close, which he followed with some rabbit blows as Gene turned and leaned in. Break. Tunney moved, then fired a lead right over top of a dipping Dempsey and clinched. Dempsey dug a right to the body, and Gene clinched more tightly and bulled in. Break. Dempsey's left eye appeared to be puffy.

Tunney moved, landed a 1-2 and clinched. Dempsey dug rights to the body and then right hooks to the side of the head, and Gene clinched more tightly. Break. Tunney fired some quick jabs at the moving, dipping, elusive Dempsey, only one landing as Jack pulled his head back away. Dempsey missed a hard lead right, which Tunney countered with a right uppercut, clinched, and snuck in a short left uppercut. Dempsey rabbit punched once with his right, but could not get his left free, and Gene held more tightly. Break.

Jack backed away. Tunney fired 1-2-3-3, only the jab and final hook landing, as Dempsey ducked and fired a right to the body. Another Tunney 1-2-3 as Dempsey moved his head to take some of the sting off the blows, but the right and hook appeared to land. Tunney missed a 1-2 and grabbed, then stepped back. Gene landed a solid jab and Jack stepped away. Another 1-2 landed high on the head of the dipping Dempsey, who fired a right uppercut to the body and they clinched. Jack snuck in his little right hook to the head. Break.

Tunney fired off a combination 1-2-3-2, but Dempsey ducked to elude, snuck in a right to the body, and then stepped away. Tunney launched 1-1-2, then short hook, but Dempsey again was elusive with his head movement and blocking. In the clinch, both dug in little body hooks. Dempsey also cuff-hooked the side/back of Gene's head with his left a couple of times. Break.

Tunney lightly bounced. Both cautiously posed and feinted. Tunney jabbed the head while Dempsey jabbed the body at the same time. Tunney countered with 1-2 and 1-2, the rights landing. Clinch. Each dug in several short shots to the body and head on the inside. Tunney broke away. He saw Dempsey about to start (or feint) a right so he moved away. Tunney's 1-2 was short as Dempsey moved back, but Tunney followed with a left hook to the body and right to the body as he advanced and moved in close, with Dempsey leaning up against ropes. Dempsey was not good at moving back and stopping and firing, or giving the impression that he would, which allowed Tunney to feel confident to go on the attack whenever Dempsey stepped straight back.

Tunney stepped back a little from the clinch to create room, and immediately attacked with a combination, 2-3-2-3, mostly landing, and then backpedaled away. Dempsey stalked forward. Tunney fired a right, followed by a left uppercut that landed as Jack ducked and dug a right and left hook to the body. Gene side-stepped away to the right. Tunney shot a 1-2 on the ducking Dempsey, partially landing high, sneaking in a short hook and then clinching. Jack tried a couple smothered inside lefts, body and head. Break. Tunney 1-2, to which Dempsey dipped and countered with a right uppercut to the body. Tunney stepped away. Bell.

It was a clear Tunney round on superior activity and number of landed blows. He wasn't necessarily landing at a very high percentage, given that Dempsey moved his head pretty well, but Dempsey barely was throwing at all. His punch output was paltry. His advance was slower. Tunney landed jabs, some rights, and a few hooks here and there. He was much more consistent than Dempsey, who rarely threw, one at a time when he did, mostly to the body, and without any sudden combinations or ferocity as he had been doing in the last couple rounds. The old days of his nonstop attack were long gone. Tunney was outworking and outhustling him. Dempsey was moving forward more slowly now, with less consistency, and also either standing still or backing up. The energy level simply no longer was there. Tunney had superior conditioning. Plus, Gene's movement, fast reactions, hand speed, and clinching prevented Dempsey from getting off very often. Gene was alert and his reflexes keen. He could counter or attack.

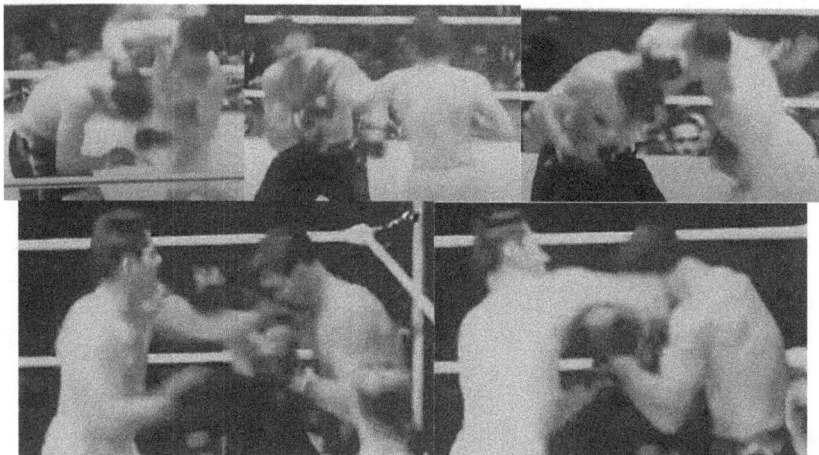

Gallico said it was a Tunney round. Inside, Jack pounded his head. Tunney was running. Jack nailed his body. Jack landed rights to the neck. Tunney landed his jab to the nose and a right uppercut. Jack had a bad cut on his nose. His face was cut, but he landed a terrific right to the stomach. Gene tried for a knockout. Jack was weaving and bobbing. Gene landed a hard right. Jack pounded in close. Gene landed five punches without return. Jack chased him. Dempsey had three bad cuts on his face. In his corner, they worked on him furiously.

Eckersall said Tunney kept outboxing Dempsey.

Hall said Jack's face was covered with blood, and he looked leg weary. Tunney round.

Runyon said Dempsey tore in, bobbing and working in close, but Tunney tied him up in the clinches. Jack banged the back of his head, and

Gene complained to the referee. Dempsey's face was covered with blood. Tunney's body was red. Tunney fought desperately, smashing with both hands. Jack's lips were bleeding. Tunney jabbed and landed a terrific right to the chin. Dempsey was a sorry sight, but never stopped pushing forward. "It was Tunney's round by a wide margin."

Rice said both of Dempsey's eyes were cut and bleeding. He was taking terrific punishment, but boring in nevertheless. It was all Tunney. Dempsey was in a bad way.

Edgren said Tunney took the round, for Dempsey seemed spent. Tunney was fresher by far. They fought doggedly. Tunney landed most of the blows, and only now and then did Dempsey shake him with heavy smacks. Jack tried hard but was weary. Tunney's blows were harder. Nevertheless, Jack hooked a left to the stomach and Tunney ran away.

On the radio, McNamee said,

> Tunney tries his old one-two, but Dempsey had learned to protect and duck for it and is getting away. … Lands this time, but doesn't seem to bother the Manassa Mauler very much. Dempsey forgot his weave for three or four rounds and now is beginning again weaving and ducking. … Tunney drove another right to the side of the head, then the left jab gets that bad eye of Jack's and the eye getting marked up as to color. Jack's eye looks bad. Again the left and then the right. Jack almost went down. … Jack's head is down low on his chest to keep from catching that right on the jaw. … Both of Jack's eyes are in very, very bad shape now. …

> This is Tunney's round so far. Unquestionably. It begins to look as if the superior condition… Dempsey's eyes are getting worse. … Tunney's round.

10th round

They touched gloves to start the final round. Dempsey started a hook but held it back, kept stepping in, and then followed with a very powerful short hook that clipped Tunney's jaw. Gene immediately held with both hands, but the force of Dempsey's forward momentum combined with Gene's left leg oddly moving to the right caused Gene to lose his balance, and he fell backward to the canvas. The punch possibly had something to do with it, some considering it a knockdown, but it looked more like a slip or part punch/part push. Dempsey stepped back just a bit but did not go to a neutral corner. Tunney rose immediately. Referee Barry did not raise his arm or count, but as Jack was advancing again, Barry stepped between them, wiped off Tunney's gloves on his shirt, and then stepped away. Barry had not wiped off the gloves of either Tunney or Dempsey after they had been down previously.

Tunney lightly bounced, missed a 1-2 as Dempsey advanced with a left hook that went around the back of his head. Gene clinched. Dempsey tried to work free, sneaking in a short body hook, until Tunney pushed off to the outside.

Tunney landed a lead right to the jaw followed by a left uppercut in combination while Dempsey dug a counter right to the body followed by a hook to the head. Gene moved back, both fired lead rights, but Jack's landed, and Tunney held the ex-champ's head down with his right which had missed over the top as Jack dipped to the left from the momentum of his own right. Dempsey fired a hook to the body and head, and Tunney snuck in his own hook to the body. Dempsey countered with a hook to the head and rights to the side/back of Gene's head. They scuffled on the inside as Gene kept holding, Jack landing a very short hook to the head.

Tunney broke away and moved back. As Dempsey advanced and seemed to be about to start a right, Tunney immediately fired his own right, landing on the forehead. Gene clinched and pushed Dempsey back while holding his arms. Gene pushed off to break away. Tunney fired a jab and clinched the ducking Dempsey. Break.

Tunney moved about as Dempsey tried to fire but was at the wrong range, and he missed his hook. In response, Tunney fired 1-2-left to the body (the lefts landing), pushed Dempsey back, landed a jab, then 1-1-2-3-2, landing fairly well, then clinched after Jack missed a counter hook. Jack dug in a left to the body. Break.

Tunney jabbed at long range a couple times, missing, then exploded with a ferocious, fast combination, 1-1-2-3-2, a couple blows landing solidly, then clinching. Break. They each missed jabs. Dempsey fired a lead right that was partially blocked by Tunney's simultaneous left jab arm, and Gene followed with a counter right uppercut, while Dempsey landed a hook to the head, and Tunney grabbed. Break.

Tunney fired jabs and a right, missing, then smothered, clinched, and leaned in, while Jack worked his right to the body and right hook/rabbit shot. Break. With several blows, Tunney fired away at Dempsey's moving, weaving, ducking head, tapping him a bit, but mostly missing. Dempsey jabbed the body, and Tunney counter-attacked with a lead hook, right, and left uppercut. They scuffled and fired in close. Gene clinched until the referee broke them as usual. Jack's left eye clearly was puffy and bloody, evident even on the old black and white films.

Tunney launched a fast five-punch combination with both hands on the weaving Dempsey, who countered, landing a solid left hook to the head, but Tunney countered with his own hook, then kept pumping his left jab, followed by a right on the ducking Dempsey, and then he moved away. Jack missed a jab. Tunney missed a 1-2 and grabbed. Dempsey dug in several rights to the body, and then a right hook to the head as Tunney held, leaned in, and pushed Dempsey back to the corner. Break.

Tunney lightly bounced and waited. Dempsey missed a lead right and Tunney countered quickly with a combination - right, left uppercut, right, left hook, and then stepped to the left. Jack mostly ducked the blows, though the left uppercut and possibly a right landed solidly.

Tunney stepped in with a nonstop nine-punch combination of rights and lefts in fast succession, alternating his right with left hooks and left uppercuts, while Dempsey ducked, but some got through solidly, particularly one right and a left uppercut. Tunney stepped back and nailed him with a jab. Bell and end of the round and fight.

It was Tunney's round. He had outworked and outlanded Dempsey. Still, Jack was not as hurt as some of the writers said. He simply was tired and outboxed. He was not staggering or seeming to be on the verge of going out, as some claimed. But the energy simply was not there.

Tunney clearly outhustled Dempsey in the 9th and 10th rounds with jabs, 1-2s, and combinations. Dempsey seemed befuddled and uncertain about when to throw. Perhaps he feared that if he led, he would miss and get countered. He seemed to want Gene to lead so he could counter, but when Gene threw, either Dempsey did not counter, or he often missed, or Gene would clinch and prevent counters. Jack landed solidly here and there, particularly to the body, but not enough to overcome Tunney's superior volume of work. Dempsey hit harder, but Gene landed many more clean blows.

Gallico said Dempsey knocked Tunney down with a left hook for a count of one. Tunney landed a right to the head and Jack a right to the eye. Jack was murdering him in close. Gene was running away, but had the better of a swift exchange in close. Gene landed left and right. Jack landed a hook and right cross. Dempsey pounded the body in counter blows. Jack's left eye was a bad sight. Tunney was aggressive and hammered away at Jack, who seemed tired. Gene staggered Jack with left-right-left. Dempsey kept after him.

Gallico scored the fight 6-3-1 for Tunney. 1-E, 2-T, 3-D, 4-T, 5-T, 6-T, 7-D, 8-D, 9-T, 10-T. Yet, he had it close, 4-3-1 after 8 rounds.

Eckersall said it was another Tunney round. 8-2 for Tunney.

Hall said Dempsey wrestled him to the floor. Tunney hooked lefts and rights to the head and had Jack staggering at the bell. Tunney round.

Hall scored it 5-4-1 for Tunney, close, making a comeback in the final three rounds after being behind. Dempsey won rounds 2, 3, 6, 7, while Tunney won rounds 4, 5, 8, 9, 10, with the 1st being even.

Runyon said, "Dempsey knocked Tunney down with a long left to the stomach [sic] almost as soon as the round opened, but Tunney came up at once without a count. It was a half slip." Tunney reopened Dempsey's wounds. Gene shot both hands hard into Jack's face. He hammered Jack all around the ring. Dempsey was very tired. "It looked as if he was on the verge of a knockout. His face fairly dripped with blood as the bell rang."

Runyon's score was the same as Hall's: 5-4-1 Tunney, who came back from being behind after 7 rounds. 1–E, 2–D, 3–D, 4–T, 5-T, 6–D, 7–D, 8-T, 9-T, 10-T.

Rice said a Dempsey rush crowded Tunney to the floor. Jack was trying to rally with everything he had. Tunney landed often, and clinched in close. Tunney was far in the lead at the bell, which neither man heard. 7-1-2 for Tunney. 1-T, 2-T, 3-E, 4-T, 5-T, 6-E, 7-D, 8-T, 9-T, 10-T.

Edgren said Dempsey tried desperately. A left hook took Tunney off his feet. Dempsey smashed his jaw, and Gene grabbed and hung on. Dempsey tried, but his speed was leaving him. Tunney was hitting harder, landing his right to the jaw several times.

Edgren did not state a score for the final round, but presuming he scored it even, it would be 4-3-3 for Tunney. 1–E, 2–E, 3–D, 4–T, 5–T, 6-D, 7-D, 8-T, 9-T, 10-E.

On the radio, McNamee said,

> Tunney is down from a hard left and half a push. Now Tunney looks mad. Tunney went down, and they are together, body to body and blow to blow, fist to fist, one after the other. ... Gene is protecting himself for the moment, more than fighting. ... And

now this round is getting toward the end. Fairly close and trying to measure each other. ... Jack is fairly well cut up, but they are both fighting hard. ... Tunney has a little the better of the argument...and Dempsey is very, very tired. I don't mean on the verge of a knockout, but very tired. And now a right staggers Dempsey, and another right and a left and a right. A left and a right and Dempsey is almost down, and the fight is over.

It is all over and Dempsey is practically out on his feet, and I think there is no question now who is the champion. Yes, Tunney, I feel sure, retains his championship, because at the last moment Dempsey was practically out on his feet.

Ladies and gentlemen, I assure you there were no fouls in this fight. ... There was nothing questionable that I saw.

The judges and referee were unanimous: Gene Tunney had won another 10-round decision over Jack Dempsey.

Gene briefly spoke on the radio, saying a few words into the microphone, saying hello to some friends. "I made a real contest all the way through."

One woman was determined to shake Tunney's hand after the fight, and tried to climb up into the ring, but she was held back. She stuck out her hand as Gene was leaving, and he smiled at her but kept on moving.

There were two walkout bouts after the main engagement was over, though more than half of the huge throng had left. Armand Emanuel, 175 ¾, won a 6-round decision over George LaRocco, 185 ½. Martin Burke, 172 ½, won a 6-round decision over Benny Krueger, 171 ¾, a Dempsey sparring partner. Burke belted the daylights out of Krueger.

Most reported that the gate was $2,658,660, according to the treasury department, a record in pugilism. There were at least 145,000 spectators, also a record, at least 135,000 paying.

Tunney earned $900,000; Dempsey $450,000.

One said the federal tax was $280,000, state tax either $241,659.43 or $252,000, stadium rental $100,000, additional expenses $100,000, and Rickard's profit, $576,660 or $551,134.57. Another said there were about $750,000 total taxes owed, including a 10% amusement tax of $265,866.

The gate was $763,660 more than their previous bout, $1,032,000 more than Dempsey-Carpentier, and $1,376,670 more than Dempsey-Firpo.

Tunney would owe $241,133 in taxes and Dempsey $103,558.

Dempsey would pay/reward his various entourage members, including $25,000 to trainer Jerry Luvadis, $7,500 to business manager Gus Wilson, and $5,000 to his secretary, Leonard Sachs.

Lou Fink, Tunney's trainer, would receive $20,000.

Tex Rickard praised Illinois Governor Len Small, Chicago Mayor William Thompson, the state athletic commission, the South Park Board, and George Getz, his associate in the venture. "I received wonderful treatment in Chicago." The police and fire protection were excellent. There was no hitch, everything was handled perfectly, and the show was a success. Rickard noted that he doubled the greatest gate he ever had drawn in New York, a gentle reminder to the New Yorkers that promoters had other options.

At ringside, Dempsey told the AP,

> There's not much for me to say except that I was beaten again tonight by a man who demonstrated beyond all question of doubt that he is the better man. I felt in the 7th that the championship had come back to me, that I had shattered that old stuff alone, they can't come back; but the gameness of Tunney, his recuperative powers and his generalship saved him then, won him the fight and perpetrates him as the champion of the world. I take my hat off to him. He's a real champion, worthy of the name and title.

Leo P. Flynn argued that Dempsey was robbed and the decision should be reversed, given that Tunney was down for 15 seconds in the 7th round, according to dozens of stop watches. "Even if Tunney could have got to his feet at the end of an up and up count, Jack would have floored him again. He needed those extra five seconds mighty bad. I'll file a formal protest as soon as possible."

Flynn said Dempsey won 6 rounds, Tunney won 3 rounds, and 1 was even. In the dressing room, Flynn, Billy Duffy, and Jerry Luvadis were highly incensed. Luvadis said, "He's still the champ to me."

Dempsey was quoted as saying, "It appeared they gave Tunney a generous count in the seventh, just enough extra time to let him get his bearings and climb back on his bicycle. Gus Wilson's watch ticked off 15 seconds while Tunney was on the floor... I'll go back to California immediately, but beyond that my plans are up in the air."

However, Dempsey also said, "Oh, it's all in the game. What's the use of squawking?" Jack said it was one of the breaks of the game, and Tunney "got the breaks – that was all." Jack said he never had been a squawker and would not squawk about the result or decision.

After the fight, Dempsey's eyes were cut and bleeding from the incessant shower of mittens tossed at him. The next day, though, the only sign of the wounds was a cut above the left eye, hidden under a bit of court plaster. Dempsey's spirits were good and he was light hearted. Jack said, "I'm not through. I'll fight whenever the public wants to see me. ... I still think I'd have an even break with Tunney in the ring."

Tunney said, "I fought exactly the kind of a battle I had planned and which I knew would defeat the challenger. I was not hurt when I took a count in the seventh round, but considered it just as well to take my time about arising. Dempsey offered no surprises, although his showing was somewhat better than at our first meeting."

Tunney also was quoted as saying that Dempsey was very much better than a year ago.

Tunney blamed carelessness for the near knockout. Gene said he had been working towards Dempsey's right side to avoid the left hook. He wobbled Jack and attacked, but grew careless, and

> [T]he first thing I knew I was on the floor. My first thoughts were, 'What is this? How did I get here? I ought to be ashamed of myself. That smash stunned me but I could have gotten up all right at the count of five. But instead I looked across to my corner and there was Jimmy waving to me to stay down. So I did until the count of nine. Then I made very certain that I would be hit with no more punches like that, at least until my head cleared.
>
> Dempsey said, 'Come on and fight.' He could have said, 'Come on and get hit and knocked down again.' My lips never moved but my mind said to Dempsey, 'So long Jack. I'll see you next round when I'm feeling better.' Then I went to dancing and when I felt better I came back and won the fight.

Jimmy Bronson said Gene came back to the corner after the 7th round badly hurt. Jimmy asked him how he felt. Gene replied, "Don't worry about me. I'm all right." Nevertheless, Bronson gave him smelling salts. He again asked him how he felt, and Gene gave him the exact same response, insisting that he was all right, not to worry. Bronson said, "I gave him a little hell, some more smelling salts, and some more hell and sent him out there to answer the bell for the eighth. I really made him mad enough to chase Dempsey around but I didn't know it." Tunney indeed felt better, and he went on to win the fight. Gene said Bronson's advice to attack, and the application of smelling salts, helped pull him through.

Afterwards, Tunney did not have a mark on his face, but his hands hurt. Speaking of Dempsey, Gene said, "I'm afraid he's through now. ... I doubt if he ever will fight again. He has been a grand warrior, one of the greatest in the history of the ring, and the gamest foeman I ever faced."

Tunney also said,

> I don't think there should be any doubt in the people's mind after tonight who is the better man. I won my title in Philadelphia by boxing Dempsey. I retained it tonight by fighting him. I never felt that I was in danger even in the 7th round. It was then that all my

months of training and careful year-around-conditioning came out. My head cleared rapidly and I was ready for anything.

Dempsey fought gamely, I'll say that for him. But I have no hesitation in saying that if we fought a dozen times the outcome would be the same.

In an interview with June Provines the next morning, Tunney said, "I feel great; perfectly great. The only thing that is bothering me at all is my hands."

Fred Hayner reported that the next morning, Tunney said,

In that round when I was down I could have come up at the count of two. I went down and the first thing I heard was the count of one. I said to myself, 'I am entitled to a nine count and I am going to take it.' I planned when I got up to wheel and face Dempsey, if the referee left him still behind me. Later in the round I had just one idea and that was to knock him down and out in a sensational comeback manner. I was backing away and I stopped suddenly and shot a punch at him, which pretty nearly did the trick.

Dempsey fought a very foul fight this time … Jack tried to break my arms. He butted me continually under the chin, on the temple and on the side of the face. My neck is sore, not from punches, but from butting. … I have a lump on the back of my head from those rabbit punches he gave me. I didn't say anything to the referee. …

I had Dempsey almost out in the fourth round. I gave him an awful belting with my right hand.

Tunney's right hand was sore and bruised from landing on Dempsey's cheek so often. He did not care to shake hands with anyone, it hurt so much. "I did not get many shots at his chin. Most all my punches hit him on the cheek bone."

When asked about a third fight, Tunney replied, "I have beaten him twice; why fight again? What interest would there be?"

Tunney admitted that Jack still was a terrific, heavy hitter. "He has a big kick in those gloves and you don't know where he is going to hit you."

When asked how he was dropped, Tunney said, "I was against the ropes and did not pull far enough away from them. He hit me with the left, then with the right and the left again."

Timekeeper Paul Beeler said, "As soon as Tunney fell in the seventh round, I began counting. I had counted four before Dempsey reached a neutral corner. Barry then began to count and I dropped my count and resumed it with him. Tunney got up on the count of nine."

Dave Barry said both fighters were instructed as to the rule requiring a boxer to retire to the farthest neutral corner in case of a knockdown, and both fighters declared to him that they understood the rule.

The *New York Daily News'* Jack Farrell said Tunney was down for 15 seconds in the 7th, getting a slow count. Barry did not pick up the count from the knockdown timekeeper, who belted the floor of the ring with his wooden gadget. Precious seconds sped by as Barry busied himself chasing Dempsey from his own corner, which was the nearest parking place to the spot where Tunney went down, to another, more neutral corner. He was up officially at 9, but it had been about 14 or 15 seconds when he rose.

Dempsey tried to finish him, but Gene ran backwards at such a gait that Jack was not able to catch him with a solid punch. His golden opportunity slipped away right then and there.

Dempsey took a fearful scourging in the remaining rounds, and was a pathetic, gore-smeared, staggering spectacle when the final bell rang.

The record crowd of 150,000 paid a record $2,800,000, to see a bitterly-fought contest, and were not disappointed. They saw Tunney on the floor twice and Dempsey once. Gene took his second trip to the canvas in the 10th round, when Dempsey hooked him with a left to the head and gave him a healthy push as he retreated and went down. Gene got a one-count before coming up.

Dempsey was down in the 8th for a one-count, a legitimate knockdown.

Dempsey fought as courageously as he could, but his gameness was marred by his foul work. He hit Tunney low about five times, and used the rabbit punch in chops to the back of the neck, yet the referee only gave him polite warnings. Tunney offered no complaints. His manner of repaying him was to rip him to shreds in the last two rounds. His seconds complained bitterly though. On several occasions, his handlers complained that they were smearing Jack's face with a greasy substance, and one time the referee walked over and wiped it off with a towel.

Tunney took to running in the 7th round to survive, and he used his fine legs to good advantage. But he was the undisputed master both before and after the 7th round. He boxed rings around Dempsey, hit him with everything, had him out on his feet at the end of the 4th round, and well on his way to being out when the final bell rang. There were times when Gene hit him with four or five left jabs without a return. With a steady, relentless one-two attack, he ripped a cut over Jack's right eye early on, and in the 8th round, brought the claret oozing from his left eye in copious quantities. After suffering a brief knockdown in the 10th, Tunney pasted him around at will. Nevertheless, Dempsey was trying with whatever he had left to land a knockout blow, and Tunney's fight was not perfect. He missed many rights.

The referee, though slow with his count, was fair and impartial. The judges were correct with their verdict, honest and accurate.

Jack Farrell's scoring was 6-3-1 for Tunney. 1–T, 2–T, 3–D, 4–T, 5–T, 6–D, 7–D, 8–E, 9–T, 10–T. It was 4-3-1 after 8 rounds, though.

Paul Gallico explicitly said Tunney retained the title after being knocked out. All that saved Tunney would henceforth be known as the "Chicago count." Tunney was given 15 seconds to recover. He went down and out from a sudden vicious flurry. He sat on the ground with his left hand clutched at the lower strand of the ropes. "He was out. No question about it. His legs refused to function. His mind was gone." Dempsey went to the nearest corner, which happened to be his own. The referee motioned him to go to another corner. Dempsey did not understand. The referee moved over to Dempsey, took him by the arm, and motioned him to another corner. Dempsey finally ran to the southeast corner, and the referee then turned to observe Tunney. He had not been counting, but the timekeeper had. The referee started to count at two and then up to nine, when Tunney rose.

Gallico also said that with the exception of the round in which he should have been counted out, Tunney won the fight. He had Dempsey on the verge of a knockout in the 4th round, and at the end of the fight Dempsey's face was a gory mess, the same as in Philadelphia. Tunney was the same unperturbed boxer and punishing hitter, outboxing and outhitting Dempsey, who fought foul throughout, including hitting low on Gene's white silk trunks, though Gene never once complained.

After the knockdown, Tunney rose and ran from Dempsey, all but turning his back. Jack chased him for a while, but then stopped and laughed, dropping his hands. He motioned Tunney to come in and fight. He sneered and talked to him, but Jack was too tired to chase. He simply could not lure Tunney into standing still. Dempsey unleashed one more killer flurry, and again it looked like it might be over, but the bell rang before Jack could finish the job.

Both got gifts in a way. "If Tunney should have been counted out, as I believe he would have been if the count had started, then Dempsey should have been thrown out of the ring for his dirty fighting before that seventh round ever happened." Dempsey hit Tunney with enough foul punches below the belt to have been disqualified. Barry failed to see Dempsey's fouling.

Gallico scored three knockdowns. Tunney went down in the 7th for a nine-count, Dempsey in the 8th for a one-count from a right to the head, and a one-count for Tunney in the final round from a left hook to the chin and a half slip, half push.

The first three rounds were dull, drab, and colorless, with endless circling and jabbing. It was "pit-a-pat" and run-around.

In the 4th round, Tunney suddenly opened up and began throwing long rights to the chin, one of which broke up Dempsey on the ropes. He crumpled and sagged and just stayed on his feet. Tunney went after him with both fists flying, all caution to the winds, but the bell saved Dempsey.

In the next 2 rounds, Dempsey hit enough foul punches to disqualify six fighters. Many looked deliberately low. Tunney's white silk trunks formed a perfect background against which to see the dark red of Dempsey's left fist thudding a good two and three inches below the waistline. Tunney said nothing, but his seconds, Bronson, Gibson, Brix, and Fink, hollered murder. They also accused Dempsey's corner, Flynn, Wilson, and Jerry the Greek, of greasing Dempsey between rounds. The referee wiped some Vaseline from Dempsey's face and chest.

In the 7th round, over 150,000 men and women rose to their feet, screaming with excitement as Dempsey smashed rights and lefts in rapid succession on Tunney's chin. The dramatic knockdown came, followed by the champion's utterly brilliant recovery. Tunney was on the floor for at least 15 seconds. Gene ran and ran throughout the round until he recovered and grew stronger.

Tunney was so clever and recovered so well that in the very next round, the 8th, he smashed Dempsey to his knees with a straight right to the jaw.

In the 9th round, Tunney slugged Dempsey hard, trying to put him out, and had him cut, both over and under the left eye, and on the left side of the nose and on his mouth, with blood dripping from all of the wounds.

Gene reopened the wounds in the 10th, again punching away at him. Dempsey soaked up every punch. When the bell rang, Tunney unquestionably was the winner.

Tunney was in splendid physical condition, but he missed many rights. Dempsey's boxing was almost a miracle, but his body could not hold out. The champion was the better and cleaner fighter.

For the *New York Daily News*, Grant Powers said quick thinking and a creeping count won for Tunney. "The big marine should personally thank the referee for acting as an usher to Dempsey." After a storm of rights and lefts had sent him down along the ropes, the referee took his time in starting the count. Still, Dempsey threw several low blows throughout.

The *Chicago Tribune's* Harvey Woodruff said the two judges, Sheldon Clark and George Lytton, and referee Dave Barry, all awarded the fight to Tunney. The majority accepted the verdict as sound, but a great cry arose from the Dempsey camp that Jack had been robbed by a slow count in the 7th round, when Tunney went down for the first time in his career. After a furious fusillade of right crosses and left hooks sent him down, Tunney had a surprised and dazed look on his face and a glassy stare in his eyes. Referee Dave Barry motioned Dempsey to a neutral corner.

The Dempsey party claimed that the referee delayed picking up the count from official timekeeper Paul Beeler. The count had reached five before the referee began tolling off the count. Many said Tunney was down from 12 to 15 seconds. "Possibly Dempsey's failure to go to a neutral corner, as ring rules dictate, proved costly to him." In the meantime, Gene coolly awaited the count of nine before rising.

Dempsey tore in, and Tunney retreated, but his strength returned rapidly, demonstrating his superb condition. As the round progressed, Gene began firing and exchanging a bit.

Whether the count was long or correct, Tunney could have stepped to his feet before he did. He was awaiting 'nine' to get up. Each second of rest, however, was doing him a world of good. There will be those who think Dempsey was entitled to the fight. There will be those who think Dempsey lost his own opportunity by failing to retreat from his prostrate foe.

Some said Dempsey should have torn at him more, in an attempt to finish, but either he was too tired, or he tried but could not keep pace with the speedy Tunney. Dempsey instead stopped chasing, smiled in derision and called on him to come forward and fight. But Gene did not deviate from his tactics until he was himself again, keeping Jack away with his left and clinching when the challenger came in. That 7th round, and the 6th, in which Jack had a shade, were the only two of ten accredited to the challenger.

Tunney slipped in the 10th. He partially slipped and partially was wrestled down as he emerged from a clinch. He at once jumped to his feet.

Dempsey was down in the 8th when Tunney caught him flush on the chin with a right cross. He didn't even take a count and was up at once.

Ultimately, there was no question of Tunney's superiority. He fought a greater fight than the first time, in part because he was forced to fight a greater fight. Dempsey was 50% better than he was in their first fight. He was at all times dangerous, his timing was better, and his judgment of distance better. He was not the Dempsey of the Willard fight, but dangerous enough that he caused argument in the corner between Tunney and his manager and chief second Jimmy Bronson. They kept telling Gene, "Don't take chances, Gene; you're winning by a mile on points. Don't slug with him. You'll tire yourself out." However, there were times when Tunney tried hard to knock out the old warrior to silence the charge that he was a boxer and not a fighter. He took more chances than he did in their first fight. He always was a superb boxer, a ring stylist, but he also showed championship spirit.

The former champ had worn off some ring rustiness, and because Tunney was seeking to prove his championship caliber, Dempsey landed more often than in their first bout. In the 4th, Tunney was aggressive and battered Dempsey around until it looked as if he was through. Combining that moment with the excitement of the 7th and 8th rounds, the fight was full of thrills.

At the finish, Tunney practically was unmarked, except for red spots on his body. Some of Dempsey's blood was on him, from the cut opened over his left eye in the 7th round. Jack also had suffered a lump under his left eye and a cut over his right eye in the 8th. He was a gory sight, but not as badly battered as in their first fight. Tunney seemed fresher at the end.

Dempsey's retainers said, "That was an awful decision. Tunney was out for fourteen seconds, but the referee didn't start counting until the sixth second. Ask any of the newspaper men who had stop watches. Five of them told us Tunney was down fourteen seconds."

One of the judges, George Lytton, said Dempsey, with his several days growth of beard, showed no fear as he toiled after Tunney. "It was only by a fraction that he missed connecting when Tunney in a marvelous way evaded the blow. Dempsey put up a courageous fight against a man he realized was too clever for him."

Lytton declared that if Dempsey had gone to a neutral corner three seconds sooner after flooring his foe in the 7th round, he would have won the fight. "He beat himself by being slow in getting back to his corner. There have been many remarks to the effect that Tunney could have risen sooner. I don't think so. In my opinion Tunney would have been counted out if the ex-champion had moved away faster." Lytton added that Dempsey himself had insisted on the rule that the man who scored a knockdown should move to neutral territory before the referee could begin counting. "That has been Dempsey's contention ever since the Firpo fight."

Lytton believed that referee Barry had been fair throughout, but his one mistake was failing to penalize Dempsey for the use of the rabbit punch, which he used at least 25 times.

In another interview, Lytton opined that Barry could have disqualified Dempsey for all of his low blows and rabbit punches, so any accusations that he was not fair to Dempsey were unfair.

> [Dempsey] knows that important fights are not stopped except for very serious violations of the rules and took advantage of that situation to strike low blows and club Tunney at the back of the neck. He has been guilty of that style of battling in most of his big fights. …
>
> Dempsey knew the rules perfectly and had no excuse for delaying the count. He was entirely to blame because he guessed wrong in thinking he could get away with another infraction of the rules.

Paul Prehn, a member of the boxing commission, explained,

> [A] count over a boxer who has been floored cannot begin until his opponent has gone to the farthest corner from the place in the ring where the knockdown has occurred. Any delay in starting the count would be attributed to Dempsey's delay in stepping back to the farthest neutral corner. … Dave Barry, the referee…warned Dempsey to go to a corner and withheld his count when Jack hesitated. The count was begun as soon as Dempsey complied with the state boxing rule covering this point.

The actual text of the rule read,

When a knockdown occurs the timekeeper shall immediately arise and announce the seconds audibly as they elapse. The referee shall first see that the opponent retires to the farthest corner and then, turning to the timekeeper, shall pick up the count in unison with the timekeeper, announcing the seconds to the boxer on the floor. Should the boxer on his feet fail to stay in the corner, the referee and timekeeper shall cease counting until he has so retired.

The Leo Flynn argument was that the referee should have picked up the count from the timekeeper rather than suspend the count altogether. Flynn argued that nowhere did it say in the rule that the count initially would be suspended, but only that it was suspended if the boxer refused to *stay* in the corner. The referee was supposed to send the boxer to the neutral corner and then *pick up* the count as it was in progress in unison with the timekeeper who was counting already, not that the referee should start all over again. Hence, the argument was that Barry should have picked up the count at about 4, once Dempsey had gone to the furthest corner.

Ultimately, the commission rejected that argument. The logic and rationale for suspending the count if a boxer failed to stay in the corner was the same as when the boxer failed to retire to the corner in the first instance. The potential penalty for substantially delaying retreat to the farthest corner was suspension of the count.

James O'Donnell Bennett said the fight had terrific ebb and flow. Tunney held up against Dempsey's ferocious assaults. The moment of high drama came in the 7th round, at 10:34 p.m. After being knocked down, Tunney lay almost flat. His eyes were open but his face was expressionless. At the count of nine, he propelled his body upward. Screams of delight from 145,000 could be heard. Gene had perfect composure as he eluded the follow-up attacks. "In one minute Tunney had done more to endear himself to the American people" than he had done in his entire career up to that point. He recovered with composure.

Tunney fought throughout as a gentleman. He took nasty rabbit punches and never squawked. His people did though, and rightly so. It began in the 4th round, when Dempsey landed three rabbit punches to the base of Tunney's skull. "Rabbit punches, Dave! Stop 'em," came from Tunney's corner. But Barry said nothing. In that same 4th round, Tunney made Dempsey pay, punishing him with several hard wallops.

In round 5 came the Vaseline scandal. They caught Dempsey's people smearing his face with Vaseline and roared, "Take that off! Take that off!" Jack's men wiped it away.

Through several rounds, Dempsey was tired and without steam. Tunney was suave, intent, unperturbed. At no time was Gene stained with any blood, except Dempsey's. Gene's cut never reopened. Dempsey was gory. He fought a lumbering, inexpert fight.

In the 9th round, Dempsey's face was a crimson mask. Tunney's white tights were splashed with Dempsey's blood. Occasionally, Gene's seconds called out, "Steady yourself now, Gene, steady yourself."

Between rounds, Tunney took water guardedly. He did not speak. He was serene. He delivered smacking blows to Dempsey's face.

Walter Eckersall said Tunney's ringcraft, superior generalship, and endurance enabled him to save his crown and retain his title, weathering the 7th round knockdown. When hurt, he hung on, moved, and kept Dempsey at long range by stabbing with left leads. When the 8th round began, he was himself again. Tunney sent Dempsey to the mat with an overhand right cross. Dempsey was up as timekeeper Paul Beeler tolled off the count of one. Tunney's endurance enabled him to out-finish Dempsey in the closing rounds. It would have been suicide to trade punches. He did what any smart fighter would have done. Most of the time, Tunney kept out of harm's way by boxing. When Dempsey started punches, Tunney either stepped inside of them or pulled away.

There were only two knockdowns, but the one scored by Dempsey was by far the most damaging. Tunney had sense enough to take the full count, and he made no effort to get up until the count of eight. He clearly was on his feet at the count of ten.

Eckersall gave Dempsey the 6th and 7th rounds, but all the rest to Tunney. Hence, Tunney, 8-2.

It simply was the boxer against the fighter, and in a short fight, the former usually was the victor. The champion was too smart. He feinted Dempsey so that he could be nailed with left leads followed by right crosses to the jaw. Gene threw few body punches. Jack went for the body early, but shifted to the head as the battle wore on.

Eckersall said it was a clean fight, contrary to expectations. Still, Jack was guilty of using the rabbit punch, an illegal blow, in practically every round. Dempsey made a dying man's effort to win. He had trained faithfully, and gave it all that he had, but his best was not quite enough. The once-great fighter could not come back. He had the desire, but his muscles would not answer the call. The old reserve was not there. This was shown conclusively at the end of the 7th round when he could not muster the attack and ferocious power which had spelled defeat for so many others.

Tunney's plans had been laid carefully. He knew he could outbox the challenger, and realized he had to stay away from the wicked swings. He succeeded until the 7th round. All fighters, no matter how clever, can be nailed.

Tunney's countering was much superior to Dempsey's. He feinted Jack into leading and then countered well. Jack did little feinting. He tore in after taking a punch and then tried to land with either hand. Gene either was well inside or too far away. He carried no marks. Jack's left eye bled and his face was a little puffed. His right eye was swollen.

It simply was a boxer who was much faster winning a decision over a fighter who always commands respect because of his punching power.

Westbrook Pegler said the knockdown in the 10th round wasn't really a knockdown. True, Dempsey hit him with a left hook, but then Gene grabbed, and then was bunted over by a collision as Dempsey rushed him. It was not a genuine knockdown.

Irving Vaughan saw the fight from a cheap seat, where many used binoculars or opera glasses. Many believed Dempsey had won, figuring that his knockdown outweighed all of Tunney's jabs.

Vaughan said Tunney won the 1st with ease. He outpointed and outdanced Dempsey in 3 of the next 4 rounds. The 6th was even or a slight shade for Dempsey. Dempsey unquestionably won the 7th. After that, it was a hit and run fight. The 8th appeared to be Dempsey's by a slim margin (despite the knockdown), the 9th even, and the 10th Tunney's. Hence, even this version, which was generous towards Dempsey, had it 5-4-1 in rounds for Tunney.

Don Maxwell (who also reported for the *Chicago Tribune*) said Dempsey came within one second of success. That one second was all that separated both men from victory and defeat. That was what thousands would remember about the fight.

Regardless, Tunney showed himself to be a master boxer, ring general, and strategist. He also proved his gameness, outsmarting Jack en route to a clear victory. Dempsey fought, but Tunney boxed, dancing away, feinting, teasing, and dodging. He boxed smartly and did the same things that earned him victory the first time. He had one careless moment that almost cost him. No one could censure Tunney for fighting in the manner that he did. Caution was smart. Conversely, Dempsey was no hollow shell. He was not humbled. He came out fighting and chased Tunney around the ring. He kept trying throughout. Sure, he wasn't the Dempsey of old, but he tried hard.

Up to the start of the 7th round, Maxwell thought Tunney had won 3 rounds, Dempsey 2 rounds, and 1 was even. After the 7th round, the fight was even in rounds, with Dempsey having an edge based on nearly knocking out Gene. It was amazing for Dempsey to come back and fight so well. But it also was a credit to Tunney to come back from the brink of defeat to win the fight.

When Tunney was down in the 7th, his eyes were glassy. He looked dazed and surprised, as if someone had snuck up on him from behind and hit him with a mallet. The referee motioned Jack to a neutral corner. Dempsey hesitated, and the referee almost led him away. Then he began the count. At the count of five, Tunney's head cleared. He looked up at the referee. At nine, Gene got up, using his left hand on the rope to leverage himself up. One second more and it would have been over.

Tunney kept dancing away, and Jack could not find him. Dempsey beckoned him, "Come on and fight." Gene kept boxing, and Dempsey kept trying in futile attempts. Tunney was too smart, too agile, too brainy.

The *Chicago Daily News* said Flynn protested the decision, but the officials would not accept his petition. Flynn vowed to file an appeal, despite Dempsey telling him to let it go. The commission said the articles of agreement that were filed never named Flynn as Dempsey's manager, so any protest would have to be signed by the fighter himself. Flynn's protest stated that Tunney was knocked out, and through a lack of proper co-ordination between the referee and the counting timekeeper, Tunney was on the floor from 3 to 6 seconds more than the time allowed.

The statement that Dempsey would abide by the decision was made by his personal attorney, Arthur Driscoll of New York.

For the *Chicago Daily News*, John Keys said Dempsey almost upset tradition in one fleeting dramatic moment, but the old axiom that "they never come back" still remained true. When Tunney went down, 145,000 screamed themselves into a frenzy, but fate snatched the prize from Dempsey's grasp, "and it was gone – all, perhaps, because of an odd rule." Tunney was down, with a "crazy, glassy look in his blue eyes." Terrific blows streaking out of nowhere and landing with the swiftness and power of a trip hammer had crashed on his jaw. While he lay there, "all but senseless and seemingly gone, the odd rule of boxing in Illinois came forward to render valuable first aid." The referee and timekeeper's counting arms were stayed for several seconds while Dempsey was being herded into a far corner. "And because of that delay that allowed him time to recover, Gene Tunney still is heavyweight champion of the world today."

> No human being could have stood on his feet after those three mulelike kicks that came from Dempsey's fists. Tunney bounced backward against the ropes and, helpless, his legs collapsed under him, slid like a drunken man to the floor. There was a foolish expression in his eyes and a dazed look on his face. His right leg was bent beneath him and he clutched feebly and frantically at one of the ropes.

He was "all but gone." The crowd was swept to its feet like a mighty wave; a deafening roar went toward the heavens. The championship seemed to be on the verge of changing hands. But destiny intervened.

The knockdown came within a few feet of Dempsey's corner. When Gene toppled to the floor, Jack stepped back to the ropes near that corner. Referee Dave Barry motioned for him to get to the other side of the ring so the count could begin. Jack seemed confused and excited. He moved around and then made his way to the opposite corner. "Then, and not until then, did the count over Tunney start." Those extra seconds were "priceless" to Tunney, for

> [F]our or five seconds are of the utmost value when one has just been clipped three times on the jaw and has a heavyweight title to hang on to. By the time the count was under way Gene's head was beginning to clear and before it had progressed half way he had

managed to raise himself to a sitting position ready to get up when the count of nine was reached.

> He did get up, and he began to run backward with the deftness and fleetness of a deer. It must have pained any marine in the audience grievously to see Gene Tunney, marine, running away from a foe. But there was nothing else for Gene Tunney to do at that particular moment if he wanted to retain his heavyweight crown.

Dempsey came after him with loaded dynamite, but Tunney had no desire to allow him to crash those fists against his jaw again. Dempsey followed him around and even motioned to him to fight. After a half-dozen laps of the ring, Jack finally caught up to him, landing a left and right, and Gene's knees bent, but he fell into a clinch and held until the bell. The thrills were over.

A somewhat battered Dempsey saw Tunney's hand raised.

> Dempsey wasn't the Dempsey of old, not by a considerable distance. He was better than the Dempsey of Philadelphia, but so was Gene better than the Tunney of Philadelphia. Tunney fought like a champion. He rallied after the seventh to floor Jack with a chopping right in the following round and win that session and the last two from him.

At the end, Tunney was unmarked, while Dempsey's face for the last three rounds dripped with crimson that spurted from a cut beneath his right eye and another over the left. "In the writer's opinion Dempsey won only three of the ten rounds, the third, sixth, and seventh. The second was close enough to be called even. The other six went to the champion." Hence, Keys scored it 6-3-1 for Tunney. Yet, he had it even in rounds after the 7th. Still, "Jack took a trouncing in the six rounds he lost."

Tunney often rained lightning-like blows on his jaw, until Jack tottered and was near collapse. Many times, it seemed like he was ready to go, but Tunney was cautious, willing to win on points, and didn't always press his advantage, for fear of running into a chance wallop.

In another article, Keys said the record books would say Tunney was the winner, but many who saw him lie on his back for 12 or 14 seconds "may want to dispute the fact." The question was whether Dempsey scored a legitimate knockout but was robbed of it.

> It is pretty well agreed that fully twelve or fifteen seconds elapsed between the time he hit the canvas and the time he got up. ... The delay...was because Dempsey, apparently confused over what was required of him, didn't get into the most distant corner so the count could start. The four or five seconds leeway that Tunney thus received in recovering his senses may have done him a world of good. Had the count started when he first went down he may have been considerably more dazed when he got up and might have been easy prey for a finishing wallop. That always will be a question.

Anyway, it was a tough break for Jack and a fortunate one for Gene.

It really was a world championship contest, because the whole world listened in. The radio broadcast of the fight was heard by millions around the world, even in foreign countries. Capt. Gene Morgan, via special radio, *Chicago Daily News* Foreign Service, from Paris, France, said veterans went wild at news of Tunney's victory. They stayed up late to hear the returns. Even the French were happy, for Tunney was a Legion comrade.

From Berlin, Germany, German fans listened to the radio broadcast of the event between 2:30 a.m. and 5:15 a.m., German time. The German correspondent from Stuttgart telephoned asking, "Please tell us the result of the fight. We were able to follow it from the beginning to the end, but could not hear the referee's announcement because the yelling of the crowd drowned it out."

Dempsey's defeat was a blow to his admirers in Italy.

In Manila, Philippines, the fight news was the biggest event in the annals of the city's history. Extras were on the streets before noon, carrying the flash, "Tunney wins." The contest was received by radio round-by-round, the 1st round reaching Manila at 11 a.m. Friday morning. It was a Dempsey town.

Radio officials estimated that at least 50 million people in America, including Canada and South America, listened in on radio sets.

Many listened on the radio in the United Kingdom as well.

Robert Edgren said Dempsey scored a clean knockout in the 7th round but did not get it. Tunney was on the floor for 14 seconds, but not counted out. It was the most mixed-up mess ever. It was a magnificent battle, but Dempsey got a raw deal.

Up to then, Dempsey did not bore in, but crouched a little and circled to the right, Tunney's left, which made Gene miss constantly. Whenever Tunney missed, he rushed in and grabbed Dempsey's arms, holding. Gene was poised and moved swiftly enough to escape most blows.

Edgren said Tunney scored a knockdown in the 8th with a right and Dempsey in the 10th with a left hook.

In the 7th round, the referee's count did not start until timekeeper Paul Beeler's count already had reached four. According to Chicago rules, the referee waits to count until the fighter who has delivered a knockdown reaches the farthest corner of the ring. "But according to all the rules of boxing in the world there is no excuse for giving a knocked out fighter fourteen seconds in which to regain his feet. Tunney deserved credit for a wonderful fight after being knocked out, but many who looked on believe that Dempsey won."

Jimmy De Forest said Tunney got a long count, and looked like a beaten man, but came back to win the decision. He rose from the knockdown and used all the skill he had to keep bicycling away until the bell came to his rescue.

In the early rounds, Tunney landed hard rights and stiff lefts, but Dempsey kept sliding with the punches so nicely that they did not do any damage. In the 7th, Dempsey landed his blows true and clean, Tunney went to the ropes, kept getting battered, and went down.

> It looked as if he were out. He finally got himself into a half-sitting, half-reclining position, and, with his left arm resting over the lower rope, listened in a dazed sort of way to the count. The count seemed a bit long, but Tunney got up and before Dempsey, who had been shoved toward a neutral corner, could get back to him Tunney was on guard and he began to take it on the run. The round ended and Tunney was saved.

De Forest believed Tunney was down for about 12 seconds, "but I will say in all fairness that I believe Tunney could and would have gotten up a second or so sooner if he had been called upon to do so, but in that case there is a question whether Tunney could have gotten away as well as he did if he had been forced to drag himself up earlier." The referee waited to count until after he turned and motioned Dempsey to his corner.

In the next round, Tunney kept away for a while, boxed, stalled, and grabbed, until halfway through, he suddenly came to himself and fought again. "I think Dempsey lost the fight in the last round. He tired after he had Tunney on the floor, from his own efforts of chasing Tunney, and he finally stood and said, 'Come on and fight.' He tossed away his advantage in the ninth round and the last one told the tale."

Jim Jeffries said it was the greatest crowd that ever watched a prize fight. He too discussed the 7th round controversy.

> Jack Dempsey failed to regain the heavyweight championship from Gene Tunney because he did not go to a neutral corner when he had the champion on the floor. It was fully four seconds before the referee and his handlers could make Dempsey get out of his own corner.

> If Jack had not been a little groggy himself, he most certainly would have stepped to a neutral corner. Had he done this he most certainly would have accomplished the thing that no other heavyweight has ever done, regain the championship after once losing it.

Dempsey had decked Tunney with punches that carried plenty of steam, and the champion, "while not out cold – was in such a condition that if the referee could have started counting at once, the fight would have been over."

Regardless, Jeffries scored the fight for Tunney: 7-2-1.

> Dempsey only flashed his old self twice during the fight. On these two occasions he looked great, the rest of the time he looked bad. Tunney was never in distress with the exception of the seventh

round. He was in superb condition and had the fight been for fifteen rounds it looked as if he would have won by a knockout, as he had both of Jack's eyes just about closed.

However, Tunney demonstrated that he hasn't a knockout punch because, if he had, he would have knocked out Dempsey in the early rounds. He hit Dempsey several times flush on the chin, but Jack did not seem to let them worry him. Nevertheless, Tunney gave Jack a good boxing lesson and was easily the best boxer.

Experts said Tunney was a real champion, a master boxer, with generalship and resourcefulness. He had remarkable recuperative powers after being knocked down. Various members of the press offered their thoughts:

Joe Vila, *New York Sun*: "Gene Tunney again proved himself a real world champion by outclassing Jack Dempsey. I doubt if any other heavyweight champion would have exercised the remarkable judgment which saved Tunney after he was knocked down in the seventh. His quick thinking and remarkable defensive tactics saved him."

William Ratner, *Newark News*: "Tunney...replaces Jim Corbett as the master boxer. In what other way could he have proved his class than in the eighth round when he outboxed Dempsey, scored a knockdown, after being floored himself in the seventh? Then he proceeded to win by a mile."

Edward Cochrane, *Kansas City Journal-Post*: "Gene Tunney defeated Jack Dempsey because he is a better boxer and because he could stand the strain of the hardest punch Dempsey ever had in his right hand. He won seven of ten rounds, two were even and the seventh round...went to Dempsey. Dempsey's only chance was for a knockout and he failed. Tunney won fairly and made a splendid battle."

R. A. French, *Toledo Blade*: "Tunney's coolness, his generalship and his gameness in the seventh round saved the day for him. Dempsey was as game as ever and showed he still can hit. Jack's body punches didn't do much harm, but his left to the head was a powerful weapon."

Fred Digby, *New Orleans Item-Tribune*: "Tunney won because he had the youth, the speed, the skill, the courage and the punch of a champion. He will reign long and add luster to the crown. Dempsey had his chance...but Tunney got up and by a wonderful exhibition of generalship weathered the round and then came on to win."

Frank Ward, *Youngstown Vindicator*: "Gene Tunney deserved the decision, but he is the most unimpressive heavyweight champion during the last quarter century. Dempsey's failure to finish Gene in that eventful seventh marks him as ready for retirement on the brink of oblivion as a sports idol."

Louis McNeely, *Louisville Times*: "Tunney...clearly carried seven rounds. By keeping away from Dempsey's supreme effort after the knockdown he displayed real generalship. Dempsey was fortunate the Illinois law does not permit twelve round exhibitions. Jack is through."

Wilbur Wood, *New York Sun*: "[Dempsey's] failure to make the most of his chances [in the 7th round] caused him to fail. Tunney's coolness saved the day for him."

L. S. McKenna, *St. Paul Dispatch* and *Pioneer Press*: "The champion's comeback after a nine count in the seventh round convinced the skeptics that he is as game as they make them. It is our opinion that he would have stopped Dempsey within a few more rounds, as the challenger was in a bad way at the close of the fight."

Sid Keener, *St. Louis Times*: "The boxer completely outclassed the knuckle fighter and relegated him to the long list of has-beens."

Hy Baggerly, *San Francisco Bulletin*: "Our Jack was every bit as determined and pugnacious and stuck by his guns until the last gong sounded. The overpowering element in this instance was youth."

H. G. Salsinger, *Detroit News*: "Tunney was vastly improved over the form of a year ago. He won eight of the ten rounds, with the third and seventh Dempsey's. Tunney had more poise, more aggressiveness, punched better and was just as effective on defense as a year ago."

M. Carl Finke, *Dayton Daily News*: "The world has had a great heavyweight champion for one year, but not until last night was that fact realized by the followers of the ring game. Gene showed that he can punch and he has nerve."

Ed Bang, *Cleveland News*: "Mind triumphed over matter when Tunney's ring generalship saved him..."

Otto Floto, *Denver Post*: "I predicted the fight would go the limit with Tunney the victor and wasn't surprised at the outcome."

Chester Youll, *Buffalo News*: "Dempsey came back to do or die, and even though he made a mighty bid for victory, the speed, skill and resourcefulness of the world's champion triumphed in the end."

Charles Dunkley, Associated Press Sports Editor, reported that Tunney was down from 12 to 15 seconds, but the athletic commissioners explained that Illinois rules compelled the fighter scoring a knockdown to go to a neutral corner before the count started. Dempsey forgot to observe the neutral corner rule, and it cost him the title. Dempsey went to his own corner, but Barry would not start the count until he went to the furthest corner.

Ring observers pointed out that Dempsey himself inspired the ring regulation which had he remembered it in time might have restored him to the world's heavyweight championship. The rule requiring a boxer scoring a knockdown to retire to the furthest corner of the ring was made a ring regulation when after his match with Luis Firpo there was complaint because Dempsey hit the Argentine after Firpo was struggling to his feet after a knockdown.

In order to eliminate all future possibility of question on the point in a similar situation Dempsey proposed the very rule which had such an important bearing on last night, but...instead of going to the farthest corner Dempsey stood over the fallen Tunney then suddenly heeded a warning to go into his own corner. He stood there waiting for Tunney to rise when Referee Dave Barry ordered him to the furthest corner before starting the count.

Tunney took the count while groggy and in bad shape. "Had the count started sooner, he probably would have been able to regain his feet, but he might have been wobblier and an easier target." The additional rest allowed him to collect his faculties and ward off Dempsey's attack.

Others said the neutral corner rule was in effect in the East as well, but simply not enforced. Regardless, many believed that Dempsey's own delay cost him the championship.

The critics were unanimous that Dempsey, while improved over the versions that fought Tunney the first time and Sharkey, no longer was the amazing fighting machine that he was when he fought Firpo. He lacked coordination and speed in his legs. This version of Dempsey was too slow to catch the retreating Tunney. No one could escape the version of Dempsey that existed in 1923 and earlier. At his height, he never would have allowed Tunney to escape. He no longer could keep up his attack, and only fought in short spurts.

The day after the fight, Dempsey only had two wounds over his left eye. The biggest one was a diamond-shaped gash at the edge of the eyebrow, while the second was a gash an inch long at the end of the eyebrow. Both were old scars caused previously, which reopened.

Allegedly, eight or nine fans who heard the fight's radio descriptions got so excited that they collapsed and died of heart attacks. One was only 33 years old. Several occurred during the 7th round. A James Dempsey died while arguing over the defeat of his namesake.

Dunkley said Dempsey accepted the decision, and soon would retire from the ring. Having failed in his quest, his friends believed the ring's lure no longer appealed to him. In two fights in the past two months, he had earned nearly $800,000. He earned $317,000 for Sharkey and $450,000 for Tunney, or $767,000. Financially, it was the best year of his career.

Alan Gould, Associated Press Staff Correspondent, said boxing ability and courage brought Tunney the victory. He pulled himself from the brink of a knockout after being floored, dazed and shaken, one second away from defeat, and subsequently outfought, outboxed, and outgeneraled Jack.

If not for an interpretation of the Illinois boxing rules, Tunney might have been counted out. The rule compelled a halt in the count until Dempsey had gone to the furthest corner. Instead of the count starting and continuing uninterrupted as in the old days, it was delayed while the referee waved him to a distant corner. "The time elapsing during Dempsey's backing off to a corner accounted for the late start of the count, boxing commissioners explained." Tunney rose at the official count of nine, and then circled about in full retreat until his faculties cleared. But he already had the benefit of 3 to 5 extra seconds to pull himself together. Many debated the rules and their interpretation. Regardless of the close call, other than the knockdown, Tunney had been Dempsey's master, both before and after.

At the finish, there was a mighty ovation for the ex-champion's gameness and unquestionable spirit. He was one of the greatest battlers of all time. Yet, there also was a great tribute to the blond-haired, blue-eyed man who got up and came back to slash and cut his foe into semi-helplessness at the end.

In the 7th, the downed Tunney was dazed badly at first, but relatively quickly seemed to recover his senses sufficiently to watch the referee's count intently and then climb up to his feet at nine. He rose and circled very quickly around the ring. Dempsey could not catch him, and seemed annoyed by Tunney's tactics, even stopping, dropping his hands, and beckoning, "Come on and fight!" Tunney intelligently and cautiously dodged and clinched. Dempsey's spurts were ineffective and too late. Tunney had weathered the storm.

In the 8th round, Tunney once again was the clear-headed, confident boxer. He took the play away from Dempsey. In the 9th, Dempsey's left eye was cut severely, and blood streamed down both sides of his face. He was a gory figure. Tunney actually was the aggressor in the final few rounds, except for a moment in the 10th when he was wrestled to the floor in a clinch. Tunney's right jolts repeatedly staggered the challenger. His hooks opened cuts, drawing blood. Dempsey sagged under the punishing barrage. Only Dempsey's heart kept him up. He was a warrior to the finish, even if a beaten one. "Victory unquestionably went to the better man, the craftier boxer, the faster and stronger fighter, but was his only after the closest call he ever has had."

For the *Chicago Evening Post*, Harry Hochstadter said the commission upset the rumored plot to fix the fight for Dempsey, selecting upstanding officials, judges George Lytton and Sheldon Clark, and referee Dave Barry, all at the last moment. Hochstadter had predicted Tunney by decision, feeling that Dempsey was at the end of his rope, and he was proven correct.

Tunney did to Dempsey what Corbett did to Sullivan. And like Sullivan, who called on Corbett to step in and fight, Dempsey called on Tunney to fight, but Gene danced circles around him, hitting, moving, and clinching. "Ring strategy and skill is a great thing and that is the reason that Gene today is greater than ever in the eyes of the public."

Dempsey made a great fight of it by boring in constantly, but Tunney was on the alert, his left hand a big stumbling block to Dempsey's efforts. Dempsey was outboxed, but never outgamed. He simply could not connect with the fatal wallop. After being on the receiving end for 6 rounds, Dempsey came within a hair's breadth of making good. Tunney went down, but rose and footed all over the ring. "This is where Tunney showed himself a ring master."

Dempsey was exhausted from his own efforts in the 7th round. His legs were weary and he could not get within whacking distance. Conversely, the one-minute rest worked wonders for Tunney. He was all right again in the 8th, and he landed his left with precision. Jack even went down to the canvas, and whether it was a slip or knockdown, Tunney was rallying and showing the fighting spirit and coolness of a great warrior.

To start the fight, Dempsey was anxious, but not sure, fiddling in and out and trying to find a way to land. For the first 6 rounds, Tunney always was the master, stabbing lefts to the face and mouth without any great returns. Gene was cool, collected, and confident, while Dempsey was missing. However, when in close, Dempsey would use savage methods, including his old rabbit punch. He bore in, using his head as a buffer until the referee cautioned him. Dempsey was hoping to land a knockout, while Tunney the master boxer was content to wear him down with stinging wallops.

In the 4th round, Tunney had Dempsey groggy from a series of right crosses. Dempsey's legs were a bit shaky. Tunney outslugged and outboxed him. When Jack returned to his corner, his handlers gave him smelling salts.

In the 5th and 6th, Dempsey kept rushing in, but each time, Tunney repulsed him with left hands and right crosses. Nevertheless, Dempsey at all times was dangerous.

Dempsey made his great rally in the 7th. The 8th saw Tunney's recovery.

The 9th and 10th rounds saw Gene keep giving Jack a great boxing lesson. Dempsey showed heart, tearing in with both eyebrows ripped open and blood flowing from the wounds.

Hochstadter complimented Dave Barry. "He proved himself a great and capable referee, handling the situation in a capable and masterful manner." He also said the Dempsey betters were looking for an out. However, "Dempsey lost his own fight when he refused to take a neutral corner while Dave Barry counted." Those who subsequently saw the films saw Barry waving Dempsey to the neutral corner, and in view of the fact that the fighters understood that either was to retire to a neutral corner in the event of a knockdown, Barry was justified in stopping the count and starting over.

Paul Gilbert said the contest was a superb demonstration of stamina and skill. Few protested the decision.

Musical critic Karleton Hackett said Gene was too clever for the hard-hitting Dempsey. "And that seventh round was the best demonstration of brains and legs that I ever saw."

Joe Williams said Dempsey just missed doing what all others had failed to do. For a breathless second, he was on the verge of a fistic miracle. The count had reached four before Dempsey's handlers could get him to move from where he stood, a foot or so from the dazed Tunney, to a corner on the far side of the ring. Once there, the official count was started. The champ rose at nine. Dempsey plunged in, but Tunney proved his remarkable ring generalship, which made him a great champion. He "climbed on a bicycle as the boys say." He circled around the ring, and Dempsey could not catch him. Jack dropped his hands at his side, laughed, and said, "Come on and fight. This isn't a foot race." By that point, Tunney had recovered his wits. He had gone through hell, survived, and was himself again.

According to Damon Runyon, who was ringside, immediately after the fight, Manager Leo Flynn said he would appeal, for three stop watches showed that Tunney was down for 14 seconds in the 7th round, decked by Dempsey's rain of smashes.

Tunney went down on his back, then sat up, his pallid features pinched with a strange expression of bewilderment, on the floor for the first time in his career. The count seemed long. Once he rose, he began running, with Dempsey pursuing.

After that round, Tunney proceeded to slice and cut up Dempsey with his spearing left. "It was a fairly even fight as I saw it going into the tenth, with the knockdown weighing strongly in Dempsey's favor. But all through the tenth, Tunney battered Dempsey until the old ex-champion's face streamed blood from wounds over his eyes, and from bruised lips."

Many would debate whether the count was the difference between Dempsey's recovering the title or not. But Runyon doubted it would produce another match, for Tunney demonstrated that, barring an unexpected punch, he was Dempsey's master at the boxing game.

> Under the rules that prevail in Chicago when a man goes down, the official timekeeper at the ringside starts counting and the referee is supposed to pick up the count immediately. But a member of the boxing commission says that its rule is that the count does not start until the boxer who has knocked the other down is in the corner furthest from the fallen man. Dempsey first went to his own corner, within a few feet of Tunney…then moved along the ropes over to a neutral corner as the referee, Barry, pointed it out to him.

For the first three rounds, both were cautious. Dempsey was trying to make Tunney do the leading. Gene, thought to be strictly a counter puncher, frequently took the aggressive. Dempsey finally abandoned his waiting policy and began bobbing and crowding Tunney. Oddly enough, he even at times outboxed the master. Tunney kept missing his right, though he rarely missed his left. Tunney never was a great puncher. He was a stiff puncher but did not have the "kill" to his blows. "Dempsey dropped once tonight as Tunney landed a blow, but it seemed more of a slip than a real knockdown, and the same thing happened later to Tunney."

Some booed the decision, some cheered faintly. Jack and Gene shook hands in a perfunctory manner, not at all friendly.

Tunney truly stood out in his defense. He could hit and not be hit. "He wears a man down gradually, stabbing, stabbing, stabbing, patiently, methodically. Tonight he was a boxer at his best, meeting a once great fighter slowed down to a walk, but still very dangerous."

Official timekeeper Paul Beeler said the count had gone to 4 before it was discovered that Dempsey was not in a neutral corner, and then the count was started all over again. Beeler admitted that he counted 13 over Tunney. "In other words, Tunney really had the benefit of a thirteen-second count, because Dempsey failed to observe the rule of the local commission, an error that may have cost him dear. I would say that for at least nine seconds Tunney was thoroughly befogged as he knelt on the floor. ... He was not unconscious, but he was certainly dizzy." Dempsey cost himself precious seconds. "Perhaps Tunney could have gotten up just the same if the count had continued on from the four at which it was discontinued to the nine. That is not for me to say. Then again, the added four seconds may have been just the time he required to thoroughly clear his befogged bean. Who can tell?"

It was Dempsey's third fight without his former mentor, Jack Kearns. Dempsey was 1-2 without Kearns, though he kept a much greater portion of the proceeds without him.

James J. Corbett said Tunney won fair and square, and if there was a long count, it was Jack's own fault for failing to go to a neutral corner as soon as Tunney went down. Instead, he went to his own corner until Referee Barry ordered him to go to a neutral corner. Only once Dempsey went towards the neutral corner did the count start. The "referee acted in strict accordance with the rules."

Jim said the fight once again demonstrated the superiority of the boxer over a slugger. Dempsey nearly won the title back, but Tunney's skill, generalship, and keen brain thwarted the slugger. Everyone thought Tunney's left would win him the fight, but it was his right hand that won it. The right drove Dempsey around the ring, staggered him frequently, and rolled up points for Tunney. But when Gene did use his left, his execution was perfect, and it was this hand that ripped and tore Jack's face into a bleeding mass. "Tunney has now cleaned up the heavyweight field and there now is no man on the field who looms up as a conqueror."

Davis Walsh said age defeated Dempsey. The Manassa Mauler of five years ago would have finished Tunney in the 7th, but this version could not. Tunney deserved admiration for getting up and winning. Many were saying that without a long count, Dempsey would have won. Once again, a Dempsey fight got folks talking. "We know why so many observers thought Dempsey unbeatable before 1923."

Tunney carried the uneventful early few rounds. In the 4th round, a series of rights had Dempsey rubber-legged and all but out. Yet, Dempsey was able to get through the 5th, and revived to win the 6th with a series of exchanges. He nearly ended Tunney in the 7th round. Even after being on the floor in the 7th, Tunney had Dempsey on the floor for a one-count in the 8th. Some noted that in the 8th, Barry started to out-count his own timekeeper over the fallen Dempsey. For the remainder of the fight, Tunney cut him up and won every exchange. He tried for a knockout that never came.

During the fight, someone in the crowd yelled, "Kill the dirty slacker." Hiram Dempsey, Jack's father, replied, "You stop that; the war's over now." Hiram said the worst his son should have received was a draw.

Jack Sharkey said age had caused Dempsey's downfall, while gameness alone carried him through. In the later rounds, his eye was in bad shape, and he was fighting blind. His friends were certain that the Manassa Mauler would hang up the gloves. Tunney was clean, keen, courageous, clever, and as cool as a cucumber. Youth won over age, "for regardless of his actual years, Jack is old now. His fire is gone. I realize now that his fight against me in New York two months ago was his last flash." The flame finally had burned down, for he lacked his old steam and spirit.

Dempsey boxed cautiously and only rushed in flashes. "Right then I knew that the old Jack Dempsey had faded." Tunney attacked more than expected, and like a machine, kept up a cool, deliberate assault. Dempsey's brain seemed to give orders to his muscles that they no longer could carry out. He needed to pep up and go after Gene, but he couldn't, and "it was so pitiful to see Old Jack Dempsey without the steam that made him a great fighter." He no longer was as strong in the clinches either. Gene handled him well there, and Jack's inside body attack never materialized. What few inside head shots he landed had no effect on the tough Tunney.

Regarding the 7th round knockdown, Sharkey said, "I could see that he wasn't going to take the count." When Tunney got up, he ran all around the ring, backpedaling to keep away and recover his strength. Tunney soon recovered and came back strong.

Sharkey believed that had it been a 15-round contest, Tunney would have knocked out Dempsey.

Still, Dempsey fought bravely, and gave it what he could. "His spirit was willing, but his body is burned out for the ring game."

Henry Farrell said Tunney won decisively on points, displaying power and stamina many doubted he possessed. But the fight left Dempsey's backers with a great big "if" to salve their wounds. Dempsey drove Tunney to the canvas in the 7th for longer than the 10 seconds which normally constitutes a knockout.

But under the rules of boxing exhibitions in Chicago the referee cannot begin to count over a fighter who is down until the opponent has withdrawn to a neutral corner. For two or three seconds or more after Tunney went down Dempsey failed to go to a neutral corner and the referee failed to count. On the other hand Tunney seemed deliberately to have waited for the count to get the benefit of a moment's rest, and had Dempsey gone immediately to the corner, the champion might still have been able to get to his feet before the fatal 10.

Tunney saved himself by dancing around the ring. "But, even then, if Dempsey had been the old Dempsey of Toledo he would have crashed through for another finishing blow." Overall, Dempsey had "failed miserably to show his old-time form."

Farrell believed that Dempsey would have been knocked out in another round or two. Tunney had the superior condition and was as strong at the end of the fight as he was at the start of it, while Dempsey was in bad shape at the fight's conclusion.

Tunney had a clear majority of the rounds, while Dempsey scored a moral victory with his knockdown in the 7th.

In Gene's dressing room after the battle were Bernard Gimbel, a New York department store magnate, and Lord Clydesdale, both pals and admirers of the champ. Also with the champ was a fellow marine who lost his arm in the war, and a police officer friend from New York.

Tunney did not like being known as a prizefighter. He was proud of being known as an efficient *boxer.* He relished society but abhorred being called a social climber. He was flattered by being called an intellectual, but was pained when called a bookworm. Tunney was not girl shy, but simply was "not interested in the sort of girl who would be interested in a prize fighter."

Outside the bungalow on the Hotel Sherman roof. l to r: Lou Fink, Tunney, Joe Malone, Billy Smith, Bill McCabe.

Ed Hughes said four seconds of thoughtlessness cost Dempsey the title and millions of dollars. In the 7th round, Dempsey seemed tired, but suddenly, with the swiftness of a venomous rattlesnake, he darted in with an unexpected furious onslaught, catching the champ by surprise, and his once majestic "iron mike" right and his left hook reached the chin, badly stinging Tunney. Right and left followed, and Tunney crumpled to the floor on the ropes near Dempsey's corner. Tunney was badly dazed.

> It looked like a certain knockout, and it would have been had Dempsey's tigerish fighting spirit not rooted him on a convenient spot to resume killing had Tunney arisen.

> The rules here provide as in New York that fighters who score knockdowns must retire to a neutral corner. Dempsey had ignored this sacred provision in the Firpo fight under similar circumstances and had got away with it. But the Polo Grounds are as far removed in mileage from Soldiers Field as the strict interpretation of the rules.

So, unlike others who said the neutral corner rule was new, Hughes said it always was in effect, even for the Firpo fight, but referees often ignored it.

Dempsey stood a few feet away, "suicidally violating the knockdown rule until Referee Barry motioned him to retire to a neutral corner. Dempsey saw the referee's motions to him, but the commands fell upon a dumb brain. Not until Barry touched him forcibly on the arm, directing him toward the neutral angle, did Dempsey understand."

It was Dempsey's colossal blunder, for those extra four seconds saved Tunney, who was spread in bewildered wonderment on the floor. He was down for at least 14 seconds. "Referee Barry rightly started his count after his attentions to the erring Dempsey." At the count of nine, Tunney used his left hand as leverage on the second rope and hoisted himself up. It was the first knockdown of his career, and he did not suffer another one.

Tunney circled the ring rapidly. "The tiger spirit in Dempsey…has become a mysterious, uncertain and undependable element where once it was efficiency personified. When needed it was missing, when uncalled for it flamed uncontrolled." Meaning, he should have been more controlled and calmer in retiring to the neutral corner right away, but also should have been more consistently furious in trying to finish Tunney. He did not advance faster than Tunney's retreat, which allowed Gene to survive and recover. Dempsey's killer instinct seemed to have left him.

> Dempsey is not one-half the fighting man that conquered in such kingly fashion Jess Willard, Georges Carpentier and Luis Firpo. The Dempsey of each of those combats would never have permitted Tunney to survive the seventh round. … Yet the defeat is tinctured with some solace for Dempsey and those who regard him, at his best, as the greatest heavyweight that ever drew on a glove.

The 7th round "vindicates the impression that the Tunney of today would have been a mark for the Dempsey of championship days." Even Dempsey at 50%, a shell of his former self, "actually though not technically" knocked out Tunney. Despite the fact that Tunney's margin of victory was large, and Dempsey only won the 3rd and 7th, possibly the 6th, Dempsey made a real fight of it in all the others. Even in defeat he was a revelation.

James Wood said Tunney proved his greatness in outboxing Dempsey. The decision was undisputed, despite the knockdown. Tunney could have risen from the knockdown sooner than he did. Gene was clever, strong, and courageous. He disproved all rumors of scandal in his title-winning effort in Philadelphia. The fight was a piece of fistic drama that carried all the thrills and excitement any ring ever held. Tunney came through to turn the tide in his favor. He was a great ringman.

> They say he got a long count on that knock-down, but disregard that. It may have been long; it may have been correct. It was the official count. It was tolled right into Tunney's ear, and he waited for at least five seconds to get the full benefit of the respite. It wasn't as if he could not have got up. Perhaps the count was long, but then again perhaps the punches that Dempsey shot into Jack Sharkey's stomach were low.

Dempsey deserved credit too. He was game and courageous. He did most of the forcing in both fights. He was stronger this time, even better than against Sharkey. Tunney "beat a real two-fisted slugger, who was dangerous right down to the final bell. Tunney outboxed and outsmarted Dempsey and at times he even outpunched him." Hence, Tunney proved his greatness. "It was a great Tunney who fought a great Dempsey. And both deserve a world of credit." It was the age's greatest boxing spectacle.

Wood gave Tunney 7 rounds, although Gene may have had only a shade the better of some of them. Dempsey won the 3rd, 6th, and 7th, though he might have been even in the 9th. Dempsey could not get by Tunney's left jab, which prevented him from getting to Gene's body.

Grantland Rice said Tunney won 8 out of 10 rounds before the greatest crowd that ever saw a contest of any kind, but he came close to losing. Dempsey took terrific punishment. His face was a horrible smear and his body weary at the end. Tunney won unanimously.

In the 7th round, the game and rushing Dempsey, after taking terrific punishment, finally broke through the champion's skillful guard. Tunney fell heavily, catching the bottom rope with his left hand as he lay on his back, staring up into the blazing white arc lights. At nine, he rose, and only his amazing condition and stamina saved him. He had come closer to losing than any prior champion. He had come within a half second of being counted out.

Upon rising, Tunney had enough ring sense left to start a running fight, as Dempsey chased him fruitlessly, until he stopped dead in his tracks and called out, "Come on and fight." Tunney showed wisdom in utilizing a rapid retreat. He was cool and cunning.

In the 8th round, Tunney came back fresh and strong, showing his marvelous condition and stamina, knocking Dempsey down with a right cross to the jaw. Jack rose without a count, and Gene was upon him and cut his face to ribbons. He slashed a deep gash above his right eye. There was a protruding knob above his temple. Dempsey's face was a series of red streams, but he never backed away. Tunney had been jeered for running in the 7th, but he proved his gameness in subsequent rounds. Discretion had been the better part of valor.

In the final rounds, Tunney outpointed Dempsey. "Only Dempsey's amazing gameness and courage and his great durability kept him on his feet." He took a beating, but nothing could keep him from advancing. He kept crowding and fighting, but Tunney tied him up at close quarters, and landed effectively against every Dempsey charge.

It was evident that Dempsey's "old coordination was gone. His judgment of distance was poor. The heart was there but not the tiger-like speed and power of the old days." Plus, he was up against a master boxer. Round after round, Gene's jolting left and jarring right landed and broke up his rushes. Even when Dempsey got inside, Tunney tied him up and blocked his punches.

Tunney tried to stop Dempsey in the 8th and 9th but could not. Dempsey had shot his bolt and was like an unarmed man who had little to no ammunition left, but, showing his great championship heart, walked right into his foe, who had a knife and a club. Tunney easily parried, ducked, and returned fire.

Overall, Dempsey had courage and a punch, but his judgment of distance was poor, he was uncertain of his leads, and could rush but found no openings. He was up against a cool, crafty, heady boxer who was not afraid to meet his rushes, who was in marvelous condition, and at close range knew how to tie him up. Tunney knew when to back away and when to step in and counter, utilizing the finest possible judgment. Even when hurt, he knew how to move and survive. He showed courage by pummeling Dempsey in subsequent rounds.

Dempsey's failure to go to the neutral corner caused Barry to stop counting, which cost Dempsey at least four seconds. The delay was Dempsey's own fault. "If he had stepped away at once he might have been heavy-weight champion of the world again. But Tunney, although dazed, was watching the counting judge, and he could have gotten up sooner…and his speed of foot when he got to his feet would probably have saved him." Ultimately,

> Tunney won because he was the better boxer, because he was in better condition through longer, harder training dating back through seven years. He won because his timing was better; because his coordination, which means team play between mind and muscle, was in better working order. But he had to beat a great fighter; a fighter with the heart of a lion, to win. He had to use his head and his heart as well as his fists. He had the closest call any champion

ever faced. If he had lost his head for one half second there would be a new champion tonight and his name would be Jack Dempsey.

The record crowd never would forget Dempsey's 7th round charge. It took something special to absorb from Tunney what Dempsey had for 6 rounds and to come back with that fusillade. It was one of the greatest assaults ever, for it came from sure defeat. It was in that last charge that one could understand Dempsey's drawing power. A great fighter had passed, but he failed only by a breath. He gave what he had, but it was not enough, for too many lefts and rights fell heavily upon his face and head and took away his strength. He was much better than the Dempsey of Philadelphia but had not come back quite far enough. He was off by a single step. One more swift sure step might have meant a different story.

William Granger said Tunney proved that his title-winning effort the prior year was won on the merits. Previously, "A great majority of the fans, and even some of the experts, too, always believed Tunney's win over Dempsey last year was not strictly on the up-and-up. But Gene proved last night in Chicago that he is Dempsey's master beyond the question of a doubt."

Many Dempsey fans were raising quite a fuss over the 7th round count given to Tunney. However, the claims were baseless. "Dempsey himself delayed the start of the count by failing to go to a neutral corner…which is called for in the rules. It is a rule that is in force here in New York as well as in Chicago." Dempsey had violated the rule against Firpo. But this time it was enforced, and the count did not start until Dempsey went to a neutral corner. "At that Tunney could have arisen sooner than he did but wisely took advantage of a nine second count."

During the fight, one of the contest's official judges, George Lytton, a wealthy department store owner, at a time when Dempsey was hitting low, rose from his seat and called, "Foul 2." It may have been that action that put an end to Dempsey's low body attack.

To Tunney's credit, he never once complained when hit low or butted, and the manner he came back after being floored proved his gameness and toughness, which would make him even more popular. It also proved that it would take a 1919 Dempsey to keep him on the floor.

Tunney's clean-cut victory also proved false the rumors that it was fixed for Dempsey to win so Rickard could make a bundle with a Dempsey-Sharkey championship rematch.

The aggressive Dempsey put up a far better performance than the prior year, but Tunney's careful boxing at times made him look bad. Gene landed numerous jabs, and Jack's face was a bloody sight at the end. Both eyes were cut and he also bled from his nose and mouth.

For the *New York Evening Post*, Jack Kofoed said it was his opinion that Tunney could have beaten the count.

Tunney did not seem so vitally distressed that he could not have arisen had Barry begun the instant Gene hit the floor. He simply took advantage of the situation to clear his head. … The count was long, but the ruling of the commission says that the referee should get the man on his feet into a neutral corner before beginning the count. The possibility exists, of course, that Gene might not have got up, but my impression was that he could have done so. Beyond that one flash the night was all Tunney.

Gene was a master boxer, cool and smooth, proving his courage. Dempsey always would have danger in his fists. "Jack Dempsey is still the second best heavyweight in the world."

In today's era, not only do we have the neutral corner rule, and occasional slow/long counts and suspended counts, but some referees are extending the time even further by having fighters walk back and forth across the ring after knockdowns, giving them even more recovery time. In Dempsey's era, such a thing practically would have caused a riot and been considered biased favoritism in assistance of the downed fighter.

The day after the fight, Dempsey allegedly said,

> When Tunney fell I did go into a corner. Not a human being in Soldiers' field had even a faint suspicion that I would hit Tunney when he was down. No one in that crowd had an idea that I would try to strike him as he was rising. I repeat that I did go into a corner. I was behind Tunney as the pictures will show. In spite of these things the referee made me go into still another corner. All this took time. Seconds were years right then. And those seconds used up in making me perform useless acts gave Tunney the time to recover. That cost me a championship and I think I have a right to protest.

Dempsey had a point. Why did it matter the corner to which he went? The purpose of the rule simply was to ensure that the downed fighter was not struck before he rose fully. Even the original Queensberry rules stated that the fighter scoring a knockdown was to retire to his own corner. Dempsey did that. The Dempsey folks thought the referee was being hyper-technical when it was completely unnecessary.

However, the boxing board commended the referee's performance, so Dempsey realized that there was little hope of a remedy.

Dempsey acknowledged that Tunney was a great boxer, and there was none better in the division. "But I still think I can whip him." He did not think the public would be too satisfied with a champion who got knocked down for 13 to 16 seconds and then danced around the ring trying to keep out of the way.

Dempsey had an abrasion over his left eye and one on his forehead. There was a lump under his left eye. But he said he felt all right.

> I wasn't groggy at any time in the battle. I see that the experts thought that I was about all-in during the 4th round and again in the

10th. I wasn't. I saw after three rounds that Tunney wasn't going to fight with me, and in that 4th round I decided to pull the old trick of pretending to be all in. I figured that Tunney might grow careless, and he did in that 7th round. That's when I caught him. When he began running away from me I realized that the only way to win was to catch Gene napping. So in the 10th round I looked bad in order to get a chance for a knockout blow.

Still, Dempsey admitted, "I'm not complaining about the fact that Tunney outpointed me, or that I didn't make as good a showing as my friends thought I would." His only complaint was that Tunney got 14 seconds on the canvas when he should have gotten only 10 seconds.[620]

Referee Dave Barry said,

> One of my most emphatic instructions was in regard to knockdowns. I told both fighters that the man who scored a knockdown must retire to the furthest corner before I would start the count. Dempsey did not obey this instruction. When he finally did get into the proper corner the timekeeper had tolled off four seconds. I think I started the count at one and he took it up with me. Dempsey knew the rule and has only himself to blame for the long count which Tunney got.

Most agreed that the referee had followed the rules. Some might feel, however, that given that Dempsey indeed did go to a corner and did not stand over Tunney, and eventually went to another corner as directed, that Barry simply should have *picked up* the count at 4 and continued from there, as opposed to starting over from 1. However, the general feeling was that the referee was within his rights to suspend the count totally until Dempsey followed his directives.

Dempsey did raise a valid point though. What possible adverse impact would it have had for him to remain in any corner, as long as he was not standing directly over Tunney? This wasn't the situation of the Willard or Firpo fights, where he stood directly over his foes and hit them as they were in the process of rising, just as soon as their knees and/or hands left the canvas. Still, some considered it karmic justice that the rule finally was enforced, after he had violated it so many times in his career.

Some of Dempsey's friends cited the procedure that Barry used in the 8th round as evidence of bias. When Gene floored Jack for a one-count, Tunney did not go anywhere near a corner. Yet, Barry rushed in with his right arm raised to start a count. The claim was that he did not enforce the neutral corner rule in that instance. However, he simply allowed the fight to resume given that Dempsey had risen immediately.

When Gene went to the canvas in the 10th round, Barry got between them and wiped off Gene's gloves. However, he did not wipe Gene's or Jack's gloves after either of their knockdowns in the 7th or 8th rounds.

[620] *Chicago Tribune*, September 24, 1927.

In fairness to Barry, he raised his arm to indicate a knockdown when Tunney was down too, and the difference in the 8th round was that Dempsey rose immediately, so there was no need to direct Tunney to a corner, for the rule was that the fight resumed as soon as the fighter arose (there was no mandatory count). Barry raised his arm with both fighters, only he suspended the count in one instance, but did not need to suspend it in the other because Dempsey rose immediately. Still, some might say he should have pointed Tunney away, but never did, despite counting one on Dempsey. Yet, also in Barry's defense, he could have given Tunney extra recovery time by wiping his gloves off in the 7th round, prior to allowing the action to resume, but did not do so.

Tunney said,

> I won the fight cleanly and decisively. Dempsey fought hard, but I don't think he fought fairly. My head aches today from the rabbit punches he used in the early rounds. I was not marked by the fight. And all that argument about the long count is useless as I could have arisen several seconds sooner than I did. Some folks are saying that I should fight Dempsey again. I don't agree with them. I have beaten him twice and I see no reason why the public should want to see us matched again.

Tunney told Walter Eckersall that Dempsey hit him with the rabbit punch in practically every round. Jack landed at least a dozen low blows. Dempsey also had oil and Vaseline rubbed on his body and face.

> In regard to the knockdown in the seventh round, I could have gotten up at the four count had it been necessary. I listened carefully to the referee's count and made sure to get my bearings before I got to my feet. I knew Dempsey would try to end the fight as soon as I regained my feet, but I was ready for him. I stayed away from him and near the close of the round he was in no better shape than I. I won the fight by a decisive margin and that is what I went in the ring to accomplish.

Tunney's purse from the fight exceeded the total life earnings of former champions. Tunney sent $900,000 to his New York bank. Dempsey earned $450,000. In contrast, Babe Ruth, the world's highest paid baseball player, received about $450 per appearance during the 1927 regular season ($70,000 for 154 games).[621]

Tex Rickard said Tunney was the luckiest guy in the world, for he got the longest count he ever had seen. Regardless, Tex predicted that Dempsey would not fight again.

The feeling was that it was not good for Rickard for Dempsey to lose, for he had been the biggest draw in boxing's history. Tunney's hit, move, and clinch style was not likely to draw anywhere near the same.

---

[621] *Chicago Tribune*, September 24, 1927.

Gene Fowler said many were bemoaning the fact that Tunney had 14 to 15 seconds to recover and rise, while others said it was Dempsey's own fault for not retiring to the furthest corner.

Some criticized Tunney for failing to knock out Dempsey in two fights. Gene said although Jack might have lasted another round, he would not have survived 12 rounds with him.

Still and motion picture records were being broken by the photos and movies of the fight, showing immediately and generating huge revenue.

Sam Hall said the moving pictures were shown in local theaters the very next day after the fight. Even slow-motion views were provided. Tunney remained seated on the ground all the way up to nine, and did not get to one knee and foot the way most fighters did when taking counts on purpose, leading some to believe he was not as good as he claimed.

The pictures proved that Dempsey was decked in the 8th. Hall believed Barry raised his hand to begin counting over Dempsey immediately, which he did not do for Tunney. The films disproved the claims of rabbit punches, though Dempsey did club his head in the clinches, but not that far around. The decision was correct. Despite missing a lot, Tunney fought well and outscored Dempsey in the majority of rounds. His brilliant finish was impressive.

Dempsey believed that Tunney could not have climbed up in 10 seconds, because he was in a sitting position longer than that. Jack was glad to hear his friends tell him he won, but he was not squawking. His manager was, though. Still, Dempsey knew that any protest would fail. "Dempsey concedes that he knew about the corner rule, but insists that he did not bother Tunney while he was down and is certain he would have won in any other state in the union."

Dempsey was not sure whether he would fight again.

Jack was proud of the way he made Gene miss so many rights and lefts, when Gene could not miss him the year prior. Jack was the only heavyweight champ attempting a comeback who decked his foe for 13 or 14 seconds and then was forced to continue and drop a decision.

From Logan, West Virginia, where she was visiting relatives, Jack's mother said, "Tunney was the better man. If he had not been better than my son, he could not have won. When Jack retires from the ring, the public won't claim his time to such a great extent and I will have a chance to be with him more."

British experts Trevor Wignall and Fred Dartnell declared that Dempsey threw away his victory.

The *Chicago Herald and Examiner* reported that the majority said the 7th round verdict was fair.

Estelle Taylor said Jack won, for Tunney was on the floor for 14 seconds. Many wanted Jack to protest the verdict, but he said, "A good loser is as important in the prize fight game as a good winner."

On September 24, John C. Righeimer, chairman of the Illinois Athletic commission, officially put to rest the long-count issue. He said the rules governing the count on a knockdown had been in existence for a long time, ever since the commission was organized. "The same rules prevail in a majority if not all of the states in which boxing is regulated by a commission. Every one seems to be satisfied, and there is no doubt whatever but that the ruling of the referee and the judges was right." He announced that there was nothing in the conduct of the fight or actions of Referee Dave Barry, timekeeper Paul Beeler, or the two judges, George Lytton and Sheldon Clark, which gave any ground for a protest. "The contest between Dempsey and Tunney was conducted according to the laws of the State of Illinois and the rules of this commission." Nothing happened which was not in accord with the instructions given to the officials and fighters, which were understood perfectly before the fight began. "Consequently we will not enter into any further discussion of the matter."

Given that Leo Flynn had no formal contract with Dempsey, when he appeared at the commission office to present a protest, he was told that the commission could not recognize him as Dempsey's representative, and any complaint or protest would need to be signed by Dempsey before it could be considered. However, it seemed pointless, given that the Illinois commission was on record with its position.

Flynn said they would protest to the national body if necessary, the National Board of Boxing Commissions, but most questioned whether that board would have jurisdiction.[622]

Debate about the fight continued in the days that followed. Warren Brown said Dempsey was a victim of his own bad judgment. Both boxers understood prior to the contest that the man scoring a knockdown must retire to the corner farthest from the fallen foe before the count would start. That was the Illinois boxing code. Hence, the count had to be stopped until he did so. Instead, he merely stepped back a pace or two and remained in his own corner, directly behind Tunney. Dempsey took his time in leaving and heading to the proper corner. That was his own fault. His seconds did not exactly help either, for they should have shouted at him to go to the other corner.

Regardless, "I do not agree entirely with those who hold that had the count begun the instant Tunney hit the floor he would have been counted out." Brown believed that Tunney was not in such bad shape, but rather took advantage of the full count. "Make no question of the fact that Tunney would have arisen before ten was reached." Gene also was cagey enough to keep away from Dempsey for the remainder of the round.

Tunney initially claimed he could have arisen at 1, but the films showed otherwise, although perhaps he meant at the referee's second count of one. Either way, he turned and looked up at the referee at the referee's count of 3, still within the actual 10 seconds. Tunney said both boxers knew they had to retire to the furthest corner after scoring a knockdown. He neglected to mention that he did not attempt to do so

[622] *Chicago Herald and Examiner*, September 24, 1927.

when he decked Dempsey, although he had a valid excuse given Jack's rapid rise. Tunney told Brown,

> We had our instructions about retiring to the corner farthest away from the man who was knocked down. It was perfectly clear to me, and I assume it was to Dempsey. I can say that I could have arisen after one second had I wanted to. But I was entitled to remain down until the count of nine, and did so. It was not for me to figure elapsed time. I had my eyes on the timekeeper, though I'll admit that if they hadn't chased Dempsey out of the corner behind me I'd certainly have kept my eyes on him. After all, he was the man to watch, as far as I was concerned.

Billy Gibson complained that Dempsey's seconds tried to grease him after each of the first 3 rounds. Gibson also said Dempsey hit low repeatedly and used the rabbit punch throughout. "As far as that count thing goes, Tunney stayed down because I waved for him to do so. He wasn't in distress at any time."

Tunney admitted that Dempsey's recuperative powers were surprising, but Gene felt certain that the ex-champ could not have remained on his feet for another 2 rounds. Gene said Dempsey was the one who had the "breaks" in both fights, because they were only 10 rounders (the most the jurisdictions' laws would allow), and Dempsey would have been knocked out in both contests had they been longer.

Gene said he could tell that Jack was annoyed after knocking him down, because he could not catch him again. "I had lashed out a right hand during that retreat and it stung him. I could see that he was puzzled at my tactics, and the sensible thing for me to do was to keep him that way." Gibson replied, "Yes, and I understand that Flynn is still puzzled, and the thing for me to do is to keep him that way."

Tunney said Dempsey's low punches did not distress him. He was inclined to dismiss the rabbit punches as unimportant, though Gibson pointed out a bump on the back of Gene's neck. Gene said, "I guess he must have landed 40 or 50 of those kind of punches, but what's the use of worrying about them now?"

Government agents said if the fight films were shown in New York, they would take action under the law prohibiting the interstate transport of fight films and subpoena the fighters, the film distributors, and the managers of the showhouses exhibiting them. The government was aware of the fact that the Dempsey-Sharkey films had been exhibited in some states after fines for their transport had been imposed. "The fate of the new films appeared to turn largely on the attitude of individual prosecutors and judges."

Word was that the films already were in New York and were shown there the day after the fight. The films had been taken by Metro-Goldwyn-Mayer newsreel cameramen, developed immediately, and rushed to a waiting airplane.

The government seized five sets of the films and one set of negatives the day after the fight, arresting Henry Sonenshine, president of Goodart Pictures, Inc. just as soon as he was about to take off in an airplane in Chicago. The government charged that he was going to deliver the films to Michigan, Indiana, and Ohio, in violation of federal law.

Sonenshine denied that he had any such intent. He said he was taking the films to Canada, and such was not a violation of the law.[623]

The *Chicago Daily News'* Fred Hayner said Dempsey had practiced the trick punch that led to the knockdown. Hayner saw him working on it in training. It was a left hook that appeared to "come from nowhere."

Tunney said he was willing to fight Dempsey any time, for he knew how it would turn out. "Tomorrow if he wants it. After beating him twice what do you think would happen at a third fight. Look at his face." "Observe the difference between Dempsey's face and mine."

Tunney subsequently said Dempsey was the only man ever to floor him. Some said Risko did it, but Tunney said Risko wrestled him down.

Rickard allegedly said if Dempsey wanted to fight Tunney again, he needed to prove himself with another interim match in order to justify it. Others reported that Rickard said he needed to think about it.[624]

Walter George said that the day before the fight, the referees and timekeepers all were called to the commission offices and told that in the event of a knockdown, the man scoring it had to retire to a neutral corner or the count would be stopped. "Managers of both Tunney and Dempsey and their seconds were told the same thing so that the rules were well defined in advance. ... These instructions were given to the managers and contestants in the ring before the bout started by the referee."

Al Auerbach paid $3,000 in lost wagers. He said he still would allow sentiment to get the better of him and bet on Dempsey, but he doubted that Jack ever would fight again. "Dempsey told me that he had all the money he ever needed and saw no further necessity to get back into fighting harness. But you can't tell how those boys feel when they are offered $500,000 to come back."[625]

Harry MacNamara said the long count argument likely would end in ballyhoo for another battle between the two. Tunney's bitter verbal attack against Dempsey, charging him with foul tactics, would be additional material for putting on a grudge match. No one realized better than Rickard that Dempsey was the greatest box office attraction in the history of sports. Dempsey said he was retired, but some thought he might change or be convinced to change his mind. Tunney said he would fight him again, and would knock him out this time.

MacNamara said Dave Barry was slow to count when Tunney was down, but Barry fairly leapt across the ring to begin counting when

[623] *Chicago Herald and Examiner*, September 24, 1927.
[624] *Chicago Daily News*, September 24, 1927.
[625] *Chicago Evening Post*, September 24, 1927.

Dempsey went down. That added to the controversy, for many thought that Barry was biased against Dempsey.

Gene Tunney, heavyweight champion of the world, dines with the civic committee which brought the title bout to Chicago. At the luncheon yesterday at the Chicago Athletic club Gene received the city's official congratulations. Left to right: William Wrigley, John Hertz, Sheldon Clark, George Getz, Everett Brown, Gene Tunney, Eddie Eagan, Mayor Thompson, Elmer Stevens, Tex Rickard, George Lytton, and George M. Reynolds.   [TRIBUNE Photo.]

Gene Tunney, Chicago Mayor William Thompson, and Tex Rickard at a banquet honoring the champion

George Strickler said Tunney was more displeased with Dempsey's open letter prior to the fight than Dempsey's tactics in the ring.[626]

For future contests, Chicago Mayor William Thompson said he would ask the governor to task the legislature with authorizing a 15-round contest when a championship was involved.

Joe Benjamin blamed Leo Flynn for the loss, saying Jack was overtrained by a week. Furthermore, Dempsey was the type of fighter who had to be sent out to fight in the early rounds, but Flynn never turned him loose. When he had the championship in his grasp in the 7th round, his handlers should have motioned him to the neutral corner.[627]

Sam Hall said it would be a long time before a puncher like Dempsey came along again. Tunney was not a hitter, and not aggressive.[628]

[626] Chicago Herald and Examiner, September 25, 1927.
[627] Chicago Evening Post, September 25, 1927.
[628] Chicago Herald and Examiner, September 26, 1927.

A week after the fight, Rickard announced that $1 million was paid to Tunney, $447,000 to Dempsey, $470,000 in state and federal taxes, $150,000 in miscellaneous expenditures, and rent of the field $100,000, totaling $2,167,00, leaving a profit of $491,660. That amount did not include the proceeds from radio rights and motion pictures, which would increase Rickard's profit considerably.

The internal revenue service said Tunney earned $990,000. Rickard may have given Gene a $10,000 bonus to make it an even million. They said Dempsey earned $437,500.

The state athletic commissioner said any protest merely was a way to ballyhoo a third fight between the two, for the commission already was on record that there was nothing wrong with the contest as it was conducted.[629]

Dempsey disputed Barry's version of events. "I received no warning or instructions about retreating to a neutral corner in the event of a knockdown. ... I knocked Tunney out and I can do it again." Still, Dempsey admitted, "Gene is a much better fighter than he is given credit for being. He's a better fighter than Jack Sharkey because he hits straighter and is more clever."[630]

Tunney said he knew that eventually Dempsey might knock him down. One could avoid a big puncher for only so long. Odds were that he was going to get caught with a big one sometime. But he also knew that he would get up and win anyway.

> I was master of the situation from the time I arose. The best proof of that is that I made Jack chase me. Dempsey has had trouble hitting a man going away from him, so I used my legs. They say I ran away from Dempsey. You don't realize that I could have traveled twice as fast as I did. Instead I put on steam only when I thought it necessary, and slowed down enough to let Jack catch up with me whenever I thought he would come close enough for a stiff counter wallop. Those counters slowed up Dempsey and made him easy prey for the attack I launched in the closing rounds.

Regarding his popularity, or lack thereof, Tunney said, "I'm not unpopular except with the professional fight crowd. They don't understand me, and never will. Which may be all for the best."[631]

In San Francisco on September 28, a theater manager and his employees were arrested and charged with violating the federal law against the interstate transportation of fight films by showing the Dempsey-Tunney II fight films. Tex Rickard was named in the action, and a telegraphic warrant for his arrest was sent to New York. The theater owner denied violating the law, which he said did not prohibit the exhibition of the films, but only their transport.

[629] *Chicago Evening Post, Daily News*, September 27, 1927; *Chicago Herald and Examiner, Chicago Tribune*, September 28, 1927.
[630] *Chicago Tribune*, September 28, 1927.
[631] *New York Daily News*, September 28, 1927.

Tex Rickard was not concerned. "I had absolutely nothing to do with the production or distribution of the fight film. I am to receive a percentage of the profits when the films are exhibited, that is all."[632]

Some government agents were looking to bring prosecutions for conspiracy to violate the federal law. The Dempsey-Tunney II films had been exhibited as far as the Pacific Coast, including California and Washington state. The government would have to prove who transported the films across state lines.[633]

Spokane, Washington ad   Richmond, Indiana advertisement

Chicago, Illinois ad

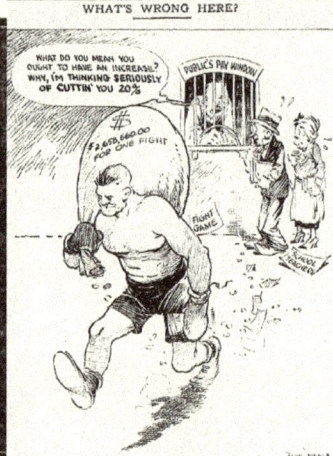

The fact is that the films were copied and quickly disseminated for exhibition all over the country. There simply was too much money to be made to cause worry about the ridiculous federal law, which had been violated with impunity when it came to most of Dempsey's fights since the Carpentier contest.

The *New York Age* wrote,

[632] *Chicago Tribune*, September 29, 1927.
[633] *Chicago Herald and Examiner*, September 30, 1927.

The recent Dempsey-Tunney fight...again brings to public attention the absurdity of special class legislation passed to discriminate against a particular group of citizens. One of the most absurd of these laws is the federal statute which forbids the transportation of motion pictures of a prize fight from one state to another. This law, sponsored by a group of southerners in Congress who objected to seeing a Negro prize fighter beating a white one, was passed to stop the showing of the Johnson-Jeffries pictures, and other fights in which Jack Johnson engaged while he was champion. ... Most sane persons realize this law should be repealed but it is doubtful whether, because of the remote possibility that a Negro may again become the heavyweight champion, the Nordic congressmen will admit their mistake by repealing it.[634]

Rickard and others seemed content to violate the law, exhibit the pictures, make boatloads of money, and pay fines if prosecuted by the government. Federal judges were loath to issue sentences of incarceration for transporting Dempsey's fight films. Fights that were not mixed race were not likely to cause public disorder. Hence, most of Dempsey's bouts had been exhibited all over the country and made a lot of money, and this fight was no exception.

The *New York Daily News* called the anti-fight-film law "idiotic." It too noted the law's origins as Jeffries-Johnson. Boxing was legal in Illinois, where the fight was held, and New York, where the films were exhibited, so it did not make sense to prohibit folks from seeing the fight films.[635]

Some who saw the films believed that Dempsey won, regardless of the long count. They simply did not like or appreciate Tunney's style. Fans and the general public liked aggressive punchers. *Godwin's Weekly* wrote,

Dempsey took the fight to Tunney at all times. Tunney skipped about and in every way avoided a toe-to-toe fight, Jack chasing the champion around the ring for several miles. Go and see the pictures at the American theatre. Forget who the contestants are and after you see the fight decide upon whom you would place your money. Dempsey did all the heavy work in that fight. ... Had Dempsey played the same tactics as Tunney, it would have been a very rotten contest. ... In fact Dempsey so far outshone the champion that he is still considered the best drawing card in the ring and a majority of the fans believe that he is a better man than Tunney.[636]

Many mourned that Dempsey had lost. They could not appreciate Tunney's personality or style. They preferred the aggressive hard puncher who had his man on the floor, nearly knocked out, to the one who cautiously and carefully won rounds on points, sticking, moving, and holding. In a loss, Dempsey actually obtained greater appreciation, which

[634] *New York Age*, October 1, 1927.
[635] *New York Daily News*, October 13, 1927.
[636] *Godwin's Weekly*, October 1, 1927.

only increased in the wake of his subsequent retirement. Many believed the rematch only proved that the 1919 - 1923 version of Dempsey would have stopped Tunney.

Further debate ensued regarding whether Tunney could have risen on time, and whether Dempsey could have finished him if Gene had not had the extra recovery period. However, the films reveal that Tunney looked up at the referee at the count of 3, after he had been on the canvas for 8 seconds. He quite possibly could have risen on time, as he did after the actual count of 9. Also, even if Tunney rose and did not have the benefit of the extra time, it is unlikely that Dempsey could have finished him, because Tunney's lightning footwork, as well as holding would have and did make it too difficult for Dempsey to follow up on his advantage. After the knockdown, for the rest of the round, Dempsey barely laid a glove on him, and even when he did, Tunney took it well. Even before the round ended, Tunney was landing punches while continuing to avoid them. Some argued though that the extra seconds of recovery are what enabled Tunney to rise on time and/or recover so well, feeling that he would have been finished off even if he had arisen on time with a true ten-count. They also noted that Tunney did not get to one foot and knee, remaining on his rear end until the count of 9 was reached.

One thing most have overlooked is that Dempsey failed to remain in the neutral corner, actually leaving it early, prior to Tunney's hand leaving the canvas. Dempsey was well on his way across the ring before Tunney had risen fully, but Referee Barry did not force him to go back to the neutral corner, and did not suspend the count at that point, even though he technically could have done so under the rules. Also, as noted, Barry did not give Gene any extra recovery time to wipe off his gloves, for he did not wipe them at all, which also could have taken some time. So, it seems that one way or the other, Jack Dempsey probably was destined to give Tunney some extra recovery time, either on the front end or the back end of the count.

Tunney made a good argument that as a fighter, he was not required to go into the ring with a stopwatch. He only had to rely on the referee's count. Tunney claimed that referee Barry told both fighters at ring center that he would not begin a knockdown count until the standing fighter went to a neutral corner, and that both fighters nodded to his instructions.

Regardless, much of the general public felt that Dempsey had been wronged, and it actually helped Jack become more popular. He likely knew that he had lost his best opportunity to recover the title, and probably was not going to improve as he continued to age.

The bottom line is those three years off had a big impact on Dempsey. He still was a very good, powerful fighter, with knowledge about the subtleties of the game, but he simply was not anywhere near the same as he had been in 1923 and before. He threw less, attacked less diligently, consistently, and ferociously, and even though he still had a heavy punch, he did not have the same speed or snap. His defense no longer was as good either, probably in part because without the same aggressive fast pace and explosive, ferocious, nonstop, two-fisted attack, it allowed his foes to feel more comfortable setting up their own attacks, and they did not have to deal with as much incoming all the time. Some also said that Dempsey did not move his head as much as he once did. His footwork clearly was slower, less pronounced, and much less relentless as well.

Even against fine, experienced boxers like Levinsky, Carpentier, and Gibbons, men with speed and skill, the latter two having solid power as well, who could move and clinch, Dempsey's relentless attack just walked them down and overwhelmed them. Those who fought back and fought to win like Willard, Miske, Brennan, Carpentier, and Firpo, all got knocked out. Dempsey forced Gibbons to go into survival mode, covering and clinching, rarely throwing or exposing himself, while Dempsey kept working. He walked through Carpentier's speedy, snappy blows and kept on top of him. So, although Tunney's speed, footwork, and clinching abilities probably would give even a prime Dempsey stylistic challenges, the younger version of Dempsey, who would have been more relentless and active, with faster feet and hands, with better head movement, likely would have forced Tunney to hold more and throw less, and probably lose a decision as did Gibbons. Or, if Tunney tried to fight back more, as he would be forced to do if he fought to win and not just survive, then he likely would have opened himself up to getting knocked down and finished off. But, of course, reasonable minds can differ.

It was and is the same debate as was the case with Corbett and Sullivan. Some folks believed that the John L. Sullivan who was not idle for three years, particularly the version that existed in the early 1880s, would have been able to overcome the quick boxer, while others said Corbett was such a fast and masterful boxer, he could have neutralized a younger Sullivan. Some might say the same about Tunney and Dempsey. We will never know for sure.

Tunney and Jim Corbett

On September 30, 1927, Babe Ruth hit his 60th home run of the season, breaking his own record of 59 set in 1921. The record would stand until October 1, 1961, when Roger Maris hit 61.[637]

In his denial of Teddy Hayes' breach of contract lawsuit, Dempsey called Hayes "another hanger-on" whom he called a trainer "simply to make him feel good." Dempsey said he met Hayes when Teddy was working in a motion picture studio earning $12 a week. Hayes appealed to him for work and Jack made him his chauffeur. There was no agreement as to salary, but Jack gave him from $25 to $200 a week. He never was employed regularly. Hayes admitted to having received $10,000. Jack denied writing any article in which he called Hayes his trainer. He said the articles were not written by him, but a ghostwriter, and he read very few of them.[638]

---

[637] "Sixty! Let's see some son of a bitch try to top that one," Ruth allegedly exulted after the game. In subsequent years, it would require either a lengthier season, or performance enhancing drugs, to break the record. Of course, some may argue that Ruth never faced black pitchers, so every record, and its eclipse, has its contours.
[638] *New York Times, Buffalo Courier-Express*, September 30, 1927.

CHAPTER 11

The End of an Era

On September 8, 1927 before a crowd of 14,000 at Madison Square Garden (MSG), in New York, in a great rematch, New Zealand's 193-pound Tom Heeney (29-8-3) fought 195 ½ or ¾-pound Paulino Uzcudun (29-3-1) to a 15-round draw. Uzcudun had won a prior 10-round decision.

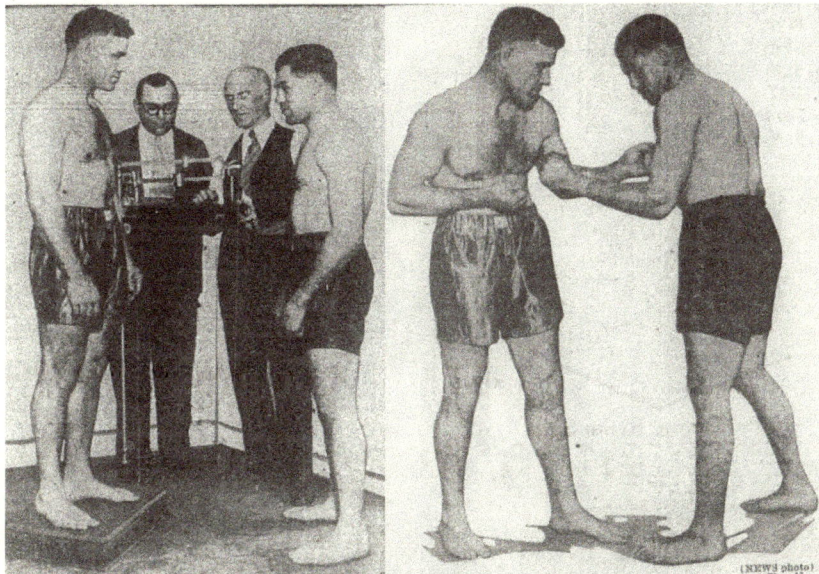

Heeney on left, Uzcudun on right, both photos

James Wood said Heeney would have to be reckoned with, for he took all the body punishment handed out and came back stronger than ever, finishing like a ball of fire, hot and heavy.

Walter Ryan said the powerful Uzcudun piled up a lead but tired and allowed Heeney to come back. "The decision was eminently fair, although there were many who thought that Paolino had a slight edge. However, Tom's great finish wiped out entirely whatever advantage Uzcudun had."

Ed Hughes said Heeney usually won his fights, but somehow or other could not get the decision. He thought Heeney had won both bouts with Uzcudun. "To say that it was a rancid decision is couching it mildly."[639]

Back in 1923, in Auckland, New Zealand, Tom Heeney had scored a 15th round technical knockout over Cyril Whittaker, who shortly after the fight collapsed and fell unconscious, requiring emergency brain surgery, but died the next day.

---

[639] *Brooklyn Daily Times, New York Daily News, Brooklyn Daily Eagle,* September 9, 1927.

On September 30, 1927, also at MSG, New York, before a crowd of 12,000, 198-pound Tom Heeney scored a 1st round knockout over 205-pound Jim Maloney (29-5), landing a right to the jaw. Jack Dempsey was present, and he received a roaring, red-hot, ear-splitting reception.[640]

On October 26, 1927, in Detroit, Michigan, 196 ½-pound Tom Heeney won a very close 10-round referee's decision over 187-pound Johnny Risko (42-19-7), who was coming off a 10-round decision victory over the respected Jack Delaney. Referee Elmer McClelland scored it 5-4-1 for Heeney. The net gate was about $60,000.[641]

On November 25, 1927 at MSG, before a crowd of 15,344, 192-pound Johnny Risko won a 10-round decision over 198-pound Paulino Uzcudun.

On December 7, 1927, in Cleveland, Ohio, before a crowd of 10,000 or 12,000, Johnny Risko won a clear 10-round decision (6-3-1) over Phil Scott (58-9-4), decking him in the 1st and 7th rounds.[642]

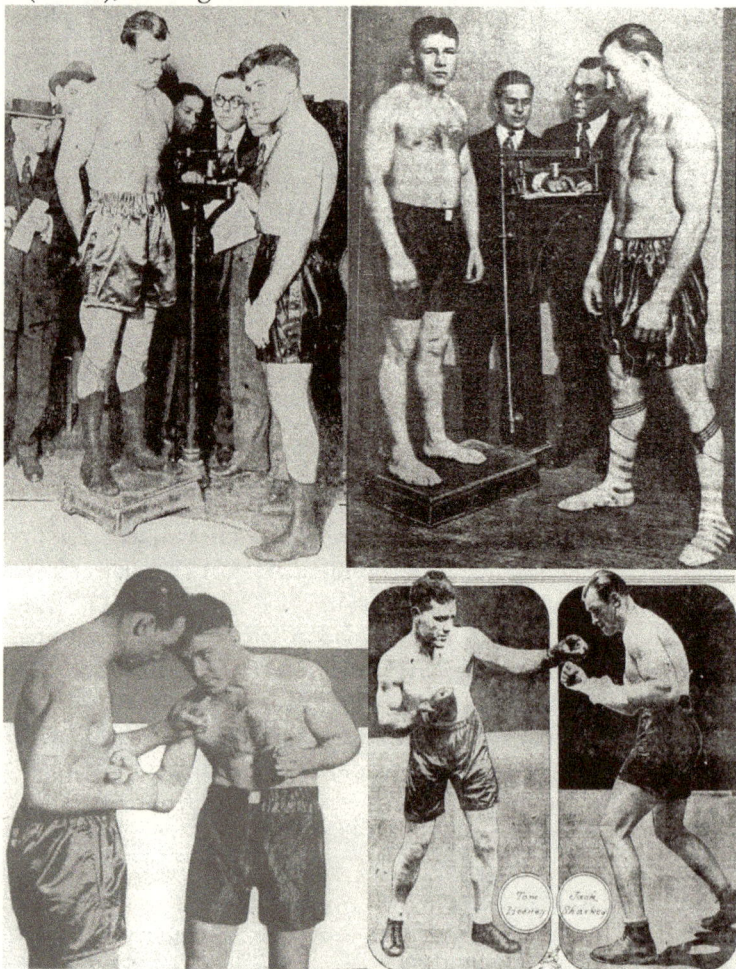

Jack Sharkey and Tom Heeney facing off

[640] *Brooklyn Daily Times*, October 1, 1927.
[641] *Detroit Free Press*, October 27, 1927.
[642] *East Liverpool Review-Tribune*, December 8, 1927.

Sharkey		Heeney
26	age	28
194	weight	193
5 ft. 11 1-2 in	height	5 ft. 10 1-4 in
76	reach	72
16 1-2	neck	17
42	chest (normal)	43
45	chest (expanded)	47
32	waist	34
14	biceps	15 1-2
14	forearm	13
22	thigh	25
15	calf	15 1-2
8 1-2	ankle	9 1-2

On January 13, 1928 at MSG, 193-pound Tom Heeney fought 194-pound Jack Sharkey to a 12-round draw. Sharkey was more of the boxer and Heeney more of the attacker. Based on the films, on the outside, Sharkey was better, landing the cleaner, more obvious blows. However, Heeney seemed to impose his will on the bout, getting to the inside often and outworking Sharkey, keeping the contest mostly on the inside, which was to his liking. His punches did not land as obviously though, or with as much power. The judges split, George Patrick voting for Heeney and George Kelly for Sharkey, while Referee Jack Denning voted for a draw.

George Kirksey for the United Press said the stout-hearted New Zealander outfought Sharkey most of the way, causing many to boo Sharkey when he left the ring. Sharkey "failed, utterly and dismally, to establish himself as the leading active contender for Gene Tunney's title last night in Madison Square Garden."

Benny Leonard said Sharkey's failure to box cost him the win. Leonard gave Sharkey the slight edge but also said one could not call the decision a bad one. Heeney played for the body and kept ripping away, and Sharkey played right into his hands by slugging with him. "Sharkey is a boxer. He ought to box, not fight these hard, aggressive fighters, but that is just what he did, and as I said before, this cost him the decision." Tommy Loughran also thought Sharkey won.

Paul Gallico said the bout left the top contendership up in the air. Yet, he scored it 7-2-3 for Sharkey.

Jack Farrell scored it 6-4-2 for Sharkey.

Alan Gould, Associated Press Sports Editor, said Sharkey rallied at the end and saved himself from defeat. The 16,948 fans in attendance booed the decision, appreciating Heeney's bulldog aggressiveness, but ringside experts either agreed that a draw was appropriate or felt that Sharkey won. The gate was $161,031.

Some wondered whether the layoff affected Sharkey, or whether Dempsey had taken something out of him.

Ed Hughes wrote, "Sharkey, on the form he delivered last night, would not draw a corporal's guard to see him combat Tunney, let alone a gate of a couple of million."

Damon Runyon said the crowd was equally divided, which indicated that a draw was about right. However, "I thought Sharkey won going away, as they say at the race course." Yet, others told him they thought Heeney won by a mile.

William Granger said Heeney's game, aggressive finish earned him a draw. The "decision was a good one." Granger agreed that it was 6 rounds apiece.[643]

In February 1928, it was reported that Jack Dempsey had retired. He had been having eye troubles, particularly his left eye, with impaired vision and twitching of his cheek and eyelid muscles, and he would not be able to fight again any time soon, either against Tunney or in an elimination contest. Initially it was Rickard who made the announcement. Later, it was said that Dempsey did not want to get to the point where he would be punched goofy. He had made plenty of money. Still, he kept open the possibility of a comeback.

For Dempsey, the controversial 7th round against Tunney made him a lot of fans, particularly those who thought he had been robbed of victory, but also those who were convinced that the 1919-1923 version would have finished the job. Hence, in retirement, Dempsey found even more followers and supporters than he did when he was champion. As time passed, folks found themselves missing and increasingly appreciating Dempsey's talented dominance and ferocity. He was their idea of a champion, a man who came forward throwing powerful blows, trying to knock out his foe. Tunney, the dancing master who won decisions over him, was not as well-beloved, in part because of his style.

Jimmy Wood said he never would concede Tunney to be a better champion than Dempsey was in his prime. He shuddered to think what might have happened to Tunney had he encountered the Dempsey of 1919-1923. Dempsey was a "great champion" who, although never overworking himself, once in the ring certainly gave everyone a run for their money. "And it wasn't the kind of run Mr. Tunney gave him in Chicago." Dempsey's style made a great hit with the public, for he was a gambler who thrust himself into the fray, giving the customers what they wanted. Tunney was one to gallop when danger threatened. "And for this reason alone I believe Mr. Dempsey's reign will be regaled in high praise long after Mr. Tunney's regime is merely mentioned in passing in the days to come when groceries will be delivered by parachute."[644]

[643] *Brooklyn Citizen, Binghamton Press, New York Daily News, Glens Falls Post-Star, Brooklyn Daily Eagle, Buffalo Courier-Express*, January 14, 1928.
[644] *Daily Bartlesville Enterprise, Minneapolis Morning Tribune*, February 1, 1928; *Brooklyn Daily Times*, February 2, 1928; *Buffalo Times*, February 3, 1928; *Yonkers Herald*, February 9, 1928.

Dempsey subsequently would do things like manage fighters, promote fights, and referee, in addition to his various business ventures. Dempsey wound up refereeing at least 393 contests from 1916 to 1963.

On March 1, 1928, at Madison Square Garden, New York, 198-pound Tom Heeney won a 15-round decision over 178 ¼-pound Jack Delaney (70-9-2), who held a victory over Uzcudun. Heeney's ruggedness and power were too much for Delaney. Australia's Heeney was called iron-jawed and rock-ribbed. The gate was $174,444, with 18,009 paid admissions.[645]

On March 12, 1928 at MSG, New York, before a crowd of 10,943, in a rematch, a 193 ½-pound Johnny Risko won a 15-round split decision over 191-pound Jack Sharkey. Judge Stuart Douglas had it 6-4 Risko, Judge George Kelly 8-7 Sharkey, and referee Billy Kid McPartland, with the tiebreaker, had

Risko and Sharkey

it 9-4 Risko. The receipts were $100,901. Sharkey held a prior 1925 10-round decision win over Risko.

Paul Gallico wrote, "The Cleveland tough boy outsmarted, outboxed and outslugged Sharkey. He won cleanly by his vicious left hooks to Sharkey's stomach." Gallico had it 7-5-3 for Risko.

Frank Getty, United News Sports Editor, wrote,

What Johnny lacked in boxing skill and clean hitting, he made up in aggressiveness and persistence. …

As it was, Risko won on points by a slim margin, and Sharkey was eliminated beyond recall. But Risko already has been whipped by Tunney and would certainly be no great drawing card as a challenger for the heavyweight title.

Ed Hughes scored it 7-4-4 for Risko. "Risko's aggressiveness and superior slugging qualities earned him the verdict." Sharkey failed to open up.

Alan Gould had it 9-6 for Risko.

Al Palma said the shot at Tunney's title was further away from Sharkey than ever. Sharkey was 0-2-1 in his last three fights.

Sid Mercer had it 6-4-5 for Sharkey.

Damon Runyon had it 8-4-3 for Risko.

[645] *Yonkers Herald, New York Daily News*, March 2, 1928.

James Wood said Rickard was up against it to select a title-challenger who meant something in terms of box office value. Sharkey was lethargic, and neither Heeney nor Risko generated great enthusiasm. "What is Mr. Rickard going to do? For one thing Risko doesn't measure up to a championship bout. Heeney would be a much better attraction. And Sharkey can't be used after what has happened." Wood said the heavyweight situation was in a bad way. No one had a real punch, which made folks miss Jack Dempsey even more.

Edward Neil agreed that the real loser was Tex Rickard, who had a contract to pay Tunney a lot of money for his next title defense, but it was unlikely that either Risko or Heeney would generate that type of revenue against Tunney.[646]

Johnny Risko

Risko's victory over Sharkey made Heeney's victory over Risko even more impressive, given that Risko had beaten both Uzcudun and Sharkey. Tunney already had won a 12-round decision over Risko in 1925.

In entertaining contests, Heeney had fought evenly with the two men (Uzcudun and Sharkey) who had defeated Harry Wills, and he had beaten Risko, who beat Sharkey and Uzcudun. Plus, the fans liked his style.[647]

On March 31, 1928, Tex Rickard announced that he was matching Gene Tunney with New Zealand's Tom Heeney. Rickard said Heeney was the strongest man to meet the champion.[648]

TOM HEENEY, CHALLENGER

---

[646] New York Daily News, Buffalo Evening News, Brooklyn Daily Eagle, Glens Falls Post-Star, Brooklyn Standard Union, Brooklyn Daily Times, Yonkers Herald, Mount Vernon Daily Argus, Cincinnati Enquirer, March 13, 1928.
[647] Also, in late February 1928, Paulino Uzcudun lost a 10-round decision to George Godfrey, whom Uzcudun previously had defeated via 10-round decision in 1926.
[648] Buffalo Courie-Express, Brooklyn Standard Union, April 1, 1928; Buffalo Evening News, April 2, 1928.

TUNNEY	HEENEY
AGE	
30	29
WEIGHT	
194	196
HEIGHT	
6 ft. 1½ in.	5 feet 10½ in.
REACH	
76½ inches	72 inches
WRIST	
5½ inches	8 inches
FOREARM	
13½ inches	13 inches
BICEPS	
14 inches	15½ inches
CHEST (NORMAL)	
41 inches	43 inches
CHEST (EXPANDED)	
44 inches	47 inches
WAIST	
34½ inches	37 inches
NECK	
17 inches	17 inches
CALF	
16 inches	15½ inches
ANKLE	
9 inches	9½ inches

Jack Kearns in Court Against Jack Dempsey

Here is Jack Kearns, right, with Teddy Hayes, his faithful retainer, left, looking over some of the dope which Jack will shoot at the legal talent of Jack Dempsey during the suit for over $700,000, which is now being heard in New York.—International Newsreel.

In the meantime, on or about April 19, 1928, the Jack Kearns vs. Jack Dempsey breach of contract trial began in federal district court in New York. Kearns' suit had been pending since September 18, 1926.

In court with Kearns was Teddy Hayes, Kearns' secretary and former Dempsey trainer. Hayes, who also had sued Dempsey, still was training fighters for Kearns.

Dempsey's lawyer, Arthur Driscoll, did not challenge any of the proposed jurors.

The judge dismissed one cause of the complaint dealing with Dempsey's alleged failure to perform on a Kearns-Rickard contract for a Dempsey vs. Harry Wills fight, because Kearns could not show that Rickard could produce Wills for a fight.

Dempsey testified that the contract he signed with Kearns was a phony. The only reason for the contract was that the New York State Athletic Commission required a manager and fighter post with them a contract binding their relations. No written contract ever had been needed previously between them. Without Dempsey's prior knowledge or consent, in early August 1923, before the Firpo fight, Kearns signed both of their names to a contract and filed it with the commission.

In late August 1923, Doc approached Dempsey and induced him to trace his name over the signature Kearns already placed upon the document. One of the commissioners had noticed that the two signatures were in the same handwriting, suspecting that Kearns was attempting to deceive them and Dempsey. Kearns told Dempsey, "I signed your name to a contract and they're on to it, and might take my license away. If anything comes up you say you signed it." Jack replied, "Why, certainly, Doc, if it'll help you out." Dempsey signed over it only to obviate a forgery charge against Kearns, who originally had signed Dempsey's name. He did it to save his manager, spare him embarrassment, and "keep Kearns out of trouble." Dempsey traced over the forged signature and acknowledged it as his own before a notary. Dempsey said he actually signed the document on August 22, not August 3, the date listed on the document.

Dempsey argued that the contract never was lived up to, never was intended as a real contract, and didn't mean a thing. The contract was for Kearns to receive 1/3 of Dempsey's earnings for a 3-year period ending on August 3, 1926. Dempsey said Kearns never complied with a provision to pay him a lump sum of $1,560 in advance, and even after the signing, Kearns still divided their earnings 50-50, as he had done before.

Kearns never mentioned the contract again until they split in July or August 1925. Whenever requested for an accounting of Dempsey's earnings, Kearns kept stalling. When Dempsey eventually told Kearns that he no longer was his manager due to poor handling of money and business details, the contract subject popped up. A property split was agreed upon, giving Kearns the Wilshire Apartments and Dempsey the Hotel Barbara, both in Los Angeles. Dempsey believed that they had agreed to part ways at that point.

Dempsey denied that his marriage to Estelle Taylor in February 1925 had precipitated their split, although the decision was reached following his honeymoon trip to Europe. Dempsey said that newspaper stories claiming otherwise, written under his name and signature, were ghost-written by a syndicate, for Kearns had sold his name for 6 years. He didn't see the stories until after they were printed.

Dempsey said for his share, he received $238,000 for the Firpo fight and another $200,000 more from Kearns for his share of the Gibbons fight, motion pictures, and a loan of $50,000 to Kearns. Dempsey's attorney Arthur Driscoll submitted Kearns' 1923 and 1924 tax records, showing that Kearns received ½ of Dempsey's earnings.

Promoter Tex Rickard showed the Madison Square Garden books, demonstrating that Dempsey had received $718,000 after the first Tunney fight. Jack claimed he gave $368,000 to Gene Normile, whom he then recognized as his manager, for taxes, expenses, and compensation.

A. C. Weisberg, South Bend, Indiana hotel owner and member of the ill-fated syndicate that sought to promote Dempsey-Wills, admitted that Dempsey's contract never went into effect because the $100,000 binder provided for him was not paid. He claimed that Mullins had been paid a $50,000 binder for Wills.

On the evening of April 25, 1928, after 4.5 hours of deliberation, a federal court jury ruled that Jack Dempsey did not owe Jack Kearns anything. The jury determined that Dempsey and Kearns had signed a valid contract at Saratoga Springs in August 1923, but also agreed that it was terminated by mutual consent of the parties in July 1925 when they split their hotel holdings. Dempsey had scored another knockout.

Dempsey said, "Kearns beat himself out of the money he thought I owed him. I would have paid him one-third of my earnings until the contract expired if he had stayed away from me and not tried to keep on managing me after we agreed to part." When asked if he planned to fight again, Dempsey replied, "No, I'll never box again."[649]

On April 30, 1928 at MSG, 192-pound Jack Sharkey knocked out 178-pound Jack Delaney in the 1st round.

On June 27, 1928 in Brooklyn, New York, 190 ½-pound Johnny Risko won a 10-round decision over 235-pound George Godfrey (52-11-1).

On June 29, 1928, the Indiana Court of Appeals dismissed Dempsey's appeal of the injunction granted to the Chicago Coliseum Club. It did not rule on the merits of the case, but rather held that the case was moot, since the injunction expired, by its own limitation, with the passing of the month of September 1926, and since that time, it had been without legal force and effect. Hence, to the Court, at that point, whether the lower court should or should not have granted the injunction was irrelevant.[650]

On Thursday July 26, 1928 in New York, before a crowd of 50,000 paying customers at Yankee Stadium, 31-year-old 192-pound Gene Tunney (79-1-3) defended his world heavyweight championship for the second time, against New Zealand's 30-year-old 203 ½-pound Tom Heeney (32-8-5).

[649] *Buffalo Courier-Express, Yonkers Herald, New York Times*, April 24, 1928; *Brooklyn Daily Times, Imperial Valley Press*, April 26, 1928.
[650] Dempsey v. Chicago Coliseum Club, 162 N.E. 237, 88 Ind. App. 251 (1928).

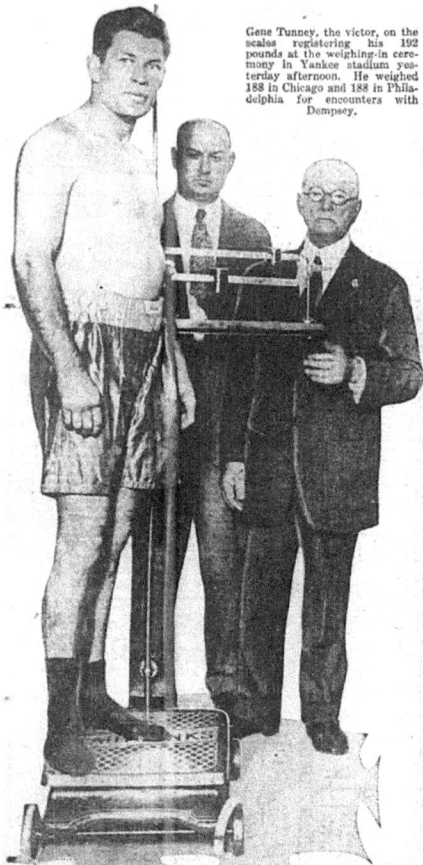

Gene Tunney, the victor, on the scales registering his 192 pounds at the weighing-in ceremony in Yankee stadium yesterday afternoon. He weighed 188 in Chicago and 188 in Philadelphia for encounters with Dempsey.

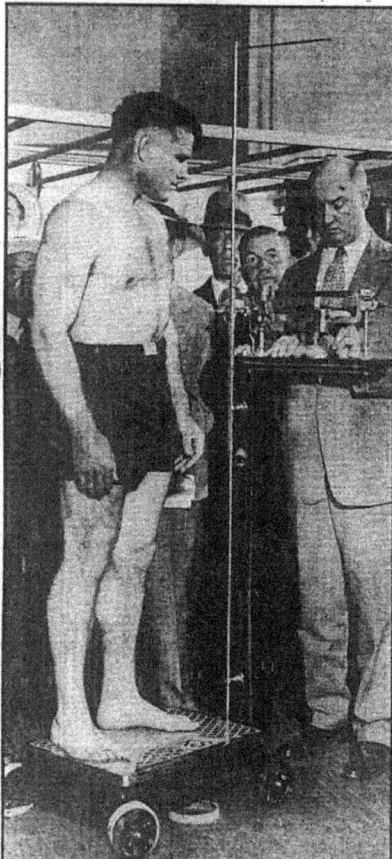

The fight was filmed. Heeney was tough, but Tunney's superior boxing skills were too much, launching quick one-twos, cutting Heeney, and gradually breaking him down. Tunney demonstrated his beautiful footwork and timing. He was a spatial master. He knew how to step back when his opponent tried to step forward with offense. He knew how to punch on the move, stepping off to the side after his punches, or he could quickly step in with forward momentum after initially having retreated. Gene was good at switching directions, pivoting and dancing off to the left or sidestepping and gliding to the right, keeping Heeney from guessing which direction he was going. His forward-and-back bouncing and feinting also prevented him from being timed. Tunney was good at clinching and neutralizing Heeney on the inside, just as he had done with Dempsey.

At first, Heeney tried to initiate combinations, or punch at the same time that Tunney did, or quickly counter. Tunney's punching at the same time raised his arms and caused them to block Heeney's punches. He also would go in to grab, or pull away and move, snapping jabs. Tunney wasn't big on dipping much or using head movement.

Heeney eventually slowed down, and Tunney imposed his style, taking his time to wear him down. As the bout progressed, Gene did not slow down, having paced himself well, moving, punching, and clinching in a well-balanced, relaxed approach to the fight.

The two clinched a great deal in the 10th round, but eventually Tunney moved more and found some punching room, landing a number of shots. Gene even threw short shots on the inside, as a fatigued Heeney was trying to hold. Tom went back, ducking down to the right, but went between the ropes. Tunney did not follow up, in sportsmanlike fashion allowing Heeney to pull back from between the ropes.

Shortly thereafter, after Heeney stepped back from a clinch, Tunney threw a lead right, then stepped in off a double jab and dropped Heeney with a slightly overhand right. Heeney went down hard but was saved by the bell. His handlers helped him up and to his corner.

In the 11th round, Tunney pounded on Heeney, snapping his head with every jab. Gene sent Heeney back to the ropes with a left uppercut and right, then followed up with a jab and right uppercut. At that point, the referee halted the action and awarded Tunney the contest via technical knockout.

Referee Eddie Forbes said, "Heeney was in a helpless condition when I stopped the fight. There was no need to submit him to further punishment, for he could hardly swing his arms and was an easy target for the punches of the champion."

Tunney said, "I am positive my right hand punches to the body are what won the fight for me. ... Heeney put up a wonderful fight. He was a worthy challenger."

Tunney believed it was one of his best performances. Indeed, his performance was impressive, outboxing and stopping a rugged challenger.

James Wood said Tunney was a real champion who could reign for some time to come. "For it took a great champion to batter down Thomas Heeney. None of the contenders could do it. In fact none of the contenders could even beat him, much less shake him with their punches." That included Uzcudun, Sharkey, Delaney, and Risko. "True, Gene was going away most of the time, backing up under the Heeney charges, but he was firing as he retreated and his hitting was cleaner and heavier than Heeney's was." Tunney was a "revelation," even more accurate than he was against Dempsey, going up against a fighter who had been very active during the past year. Heeney was game and waded in, but Tunney was too clever. "All Tunney battles are examples of methodical, efficient pugilistic warfare." Tunney was conservative, not reckless or a gambling type, but a sharpshooter who pegged away at a foe until he collapsed. Gene took no more punishment than necessary, always careful. Hence, his battles were not very thrilling unless his foe contributed to the excitement, as Dempsey did. But it was exciting enough to watch a master stop Heeney.

Frank Kearns said Tunney punched harder and more accurately than he did against Dempsey.

Regis Welsh said Tunney likely could hold the title until he had grandchildren or grew a beard. He had administered a systematic beating. "Even Jack Dempsey, whom many still rate as the world champion, sitting at the ringside, saw enough to convince him that he need make no apology for having bowed twice to this really remarkable champion."

However, Tex Rickard said he would lose about $225,000 on the promotion. The fight drew about 60,000 people and $700,000, very good money, but his expenses, including purses, were about $925,000. Tunney was paid a guaranteed $525,000. Hence, some called it the "Bloomer of the Century or the "Fistic Fizzle of the Age."

Max Buckingham noted that Jack Dempsey, even as a spectator, still was the greatest drawing card in the business. Such was evident when he was introduced at the fight. Joe Humphries announced him as, "The greatest and most colorful champion of all times, whose name will live forever." The crowd cheered, "Dempsey, Dempsey, Dempsey!"[651]

[651] New York Daily News, Brooklyn Daily Times, Brooklyn Standard Union, July 27, 28, 1928.

Despite the impressive performance, a few days later, on July 31, Gene Tunney announced his retirement, at the peak of his prowess, retiring a rich man. "I have fought my last bout as a professional boxer." It is unfortunate that he retired so early in his reign, at the age of 31. He likely could have reigned for much longer, because he had developed into a superior fighter. Perhaps he foresaw no big fight on the horizon, particularly after Rickard took a loss on the Heeney promotion. Gene said, "There is no contender at the present time who appears capable of attracting real public interest. If there were, I might delay my retirement long enough to face him in the ring, but it looks as if it might be two or three years before a dangerous opponent is developed. That is too long to stand and wait."[652]

Perhaps Tunney had another reason for retiring as well. A couple months later, on October 3, 1928, in Rome, Italy, in a Roman Catholic wedding, 31-year-old Gene Tunney married 21-year-old Mary Josephine Lauder, a.k.a. Polly Lauder, a philanthropist, socialite, and heiress to the U.S. steel fortune through her billionaire grandfather George Lauder and great-uncle Andrew Carnegie. Apparently, Tunney had promised Lauder that he would retire from boxing following the Heeney fight.

[652] *Binghamton Press*, July 31, 1928.

Many years later, one the champion's four children, John Tunney, became a U.S. Representative and U.S. Senator from California, serving from 1965 to 1977.

Although his boxing style never truly captivated the public the way Dempsey's did, Tunney was one of the finest boxers ever. He had a beautiful, fluid style, with footwork that wouldn't be seen again in the heavyweight division until almost 30 years later in Cassius Clay, later known as Muhammad Ali. Ali later would say of Tunney that he was the best of all the old-time boxers. Perhaps he recognized much of himself in Tunney. Both Ali and Tunney utilized quick footwork, sharp, quick blows, rapid combinations, leaning or pulling back, clinching, and good reflexes and timing to outbox and gradually wear down their opponents. Tunney wasn't a ferocious aggressor like Dempsey, but he was a busy boxer, throwing consistently, and had enough power to enable him to move no more than necessary, timing his opponents' rhythms and dictating the action. He appeared to have gotten stronger with age. Perhaps a longer reign would have garnered him even more admiration and appreciation.

On December 28, 1928, in Boston, 192 ½-pound Ernie Schaaf won a 10-round decision over 192-pound Johnny Risko.

In a surprise, on January 6, 1929, in Miami Beach, Florida, at 59 years of age, Tex Rickard, boxing's greatest promoter, died. Five days before, after suffering appendicitis, Rickard had his appendix removed. He suffered further infection, inflammation, and a 103-degree fever, leading to his death. One of his last calls was with friend Jack Dempsey.

Mrs. Tex Rickard and her baby, Maxine (left), and the famous promoter, who yesterday was waging the greatest of his battles—against death. Mrs. Rickard has been almost constantly at his side.

After Rickard's passing, Dempsey said, "I am terribly grieved. I have lost the best pal I ever had. ... He was a great man and the most loyal friend a man could have. His word was better than a gold bond. He never went back on it. ... He said what he meant and meant what he said." All of boxing mourned his death, saying he was an honest businessman, always paid in full, and a credit to the sport, having brought boxing to a higher plane. He had promoted some of boxing's greatest fights and all of its biggest revenue generators.[653]

10,000 people attended Rickard's funeral on January 9 at Madison Square Garden, including Dempsey, Tunney, and Sharkey.

Rickard's Million Dollar Gates.
1921 — Dempsey-Carpentier, $1,-626,580.
1923—Dempsey-Firpo, $1,838,S22.
1926—Dempsey-Tunney, $1,892,733.
1927—Dempsey-Sharkey, $1,083,-529.
1927—Dempsey-Tunney, $2,658,660.

On February 1, 1929, at MSG, 185-pound Max Schmeling stopped 190-pound Johnny Risko in the 9th round.

On February 20, 1929, in Palm Beach, Florida, for charity, Jack Dempsey exhibited for 2 rounds with Babe Ruth, mostly taking it easy and playing with the Babe, who could not land.[654]

On February 27, 1929, in Miami Beach, Florida, in a title elimination contest, 192-pound Jack Sharkey won a 10-round decision over 182-pound Young Stribling (214-10-17). It was the power-punching Stribling's first loss since a 1927 10-round decision loss to Tommy Loughran.

On March 5, 1929, in Nassau County, New York, a judge dismissed Teddy Hayes' lawsuit against Jack Dempsey, when Hayes failed to appear for trial to press his charges. The judge's order (perhaps filed on the 7th), stated, "The cause having been called for trial in its order on the Calendar, and Plaintiff failing to appear, and on reading and filing proof of due service of notice of trial on Plaintiff's Attorney and on motion of Defendant's Attorney, it is ordered that the Plaintiff's Complaint be and the same is hereby dismissed with costs." Hayes now *owed Dempsey* $98 in court costs.

Dempsey, via his lawyer Arther Driscoll, claimed that the case against him was meritless, brought simply to annoy, harass, and embarrass the ex-champion, Hayes was acting as a tool of Jack Kearns, and the two had been acting in concert with one another. The Hayes case had been filed about nine days after the Kearns case was filed.

On March 26, Hayes requested a reconsideration of the matter, to open the default and vacate the judgment entered on behalf of Dempsey, and to restore the case to the calendar for a trial in December.

In opposition, on April 3, Dempsey's attorney Arthur Driscoll asserted that Dempsey had at all times contended, and still contended, that Hayes

---

[653] *Brooklyn Citizen, Chattanooga Times,* January 7, 1929. On November 30, 1925, Rickard's first wife died. He was remarried on October 9, 1926.
[654] *New York Daily News,* February 21, 1929.

never intended to try the case, and it was begun only as part of a scheme to harass and annoy Dempsey. The same lawyer who represented Kearns was the mastermind behind the institution of the action on behalf of Hayes, Kearns' pal, in 1926, and they continually delayed trial in the hope of obtaining a settlement which never occurred. They utilized the same strategy with Kearns, until finally forced to try the case, and Kearns lost. Dempsey and his witnesses showed up to court on March 5 ready to testify, and Plaintiff Hayes failed to show up. Furthermore, "Defendant contends that plaintiff would not have moved to vacate the default herein except for the fact that a judgment for costs was entered against plaintiff and a demand for payment was made upon the surety company that furnished a bond for plaintiff as a non-resident."

On April 8, 1929, the judge ruled that Teddy Hayes would be entitled to his day in court against Dempsey and the default judgment would be vacated *if* Hayes first paid Dempsey the $98 in costs, and upon doing so, trial in the matter would be reset for December 2, 1929.

The Hayes vs. Dempsey case never was tried, and one has to presume that Hayes never paid Dempsey that $98.[655]

On June 27, 1929, at Yankee Stadium, 187-pound Max Schmeling won a 15-round decision over 192 ½-pound Paulino Uzcudun.

MRS. KEARNS PURSUES DEMPSEY EX-TRAINER

(NEWS photo)
Mrs. Jack Kearns and her attorney yesterday in West Side court where she obtained summonses for Teddy Hayes and Two Gun Murphy in raid row.

On July 23, 1929, Lagana Angell Kearns, the estranged wife of Jack Kearns, charged Teddy Hayes with assault, disorderly conduct, and trespass. She alleged that Hayes and three others broke into her apartment at 40 West 77th St. in New York at 2:30 a.m. and searched her entire apartment, searching for evidence that Kearns could use in divorce proceedings. She claimed that they pushed, mauled, and shoved her around. Had they done so at Jack Kearns' behest? Mrs. Kearns, formerly of the Ziegfeld Follies, who several years ago had won a separation from Jack Kearns, thought so, saying, "I guess Kearns just wants to quit paying alimony."[656]

In mid-August, Jack Kearns fired Teddy Hayes, ending their 14-year relationship. The trouble arose from Mickey Walker's family issues, which

[655] *Brooklyn Standard Union*, April 8, 1929; *Montana Free Press*, April 12, 1929.
[656] *New York Daily News*, July 24, 25, 1929.

led Mickey to break training. Kearns blamed Hayes for allowing things to go so far. However, Kearns and Hayes eventually would work together again.[657]

On September 26, 1929, at Yankee Stadium, 196-pound Jack Sharkey stopped 186 ½-pound Tommy Loughran (92-15-7) in the 3rd round, a very impressive feat. World light heavyweight champion Loughran had not lost a contest since 1925, and his victories included: 1926 W10 Georges Carpentier, W10 Johnny Risko, and W6 Jimmy Delaney; 1927 W10 Risko, W10 Young Stribling[658], W15 Mike McTigue, and W15 Jimmy Slattery; 1928 W15 Leo Lomski, W15 Pete Latzo, and W10 Armand Emanuel, and 1929 W10 Mickey Walker, W10 Ernie Schaaf, and W15 Jim Braddock.

From October 24 through October 29, 1929, the U.S. stock market crashed, signaling the start of the Great Depression. The Roaring 20s, a time of great wealth and excess, essentially was over. It was the end of an era for boxing as well. The days of Rickard and Dempsey's million-dollar gates were gone, but there still was very good money to be made in boxing.

On December 18, 1929, a judge ordered Jack Kearns and Teddy Hayes to pay $10,800 total for damages and injuries suffered by two young men in a 1925 auto accident. They had alleged that Hayes/Kearns, driving Kearns' vehicle, drove too fast and recklessly close to them, causing them to go off the road to avert disaster, but nevertheless striking a tree.[659]

---

[657] *St. Petersburg Times*, August 16, 1929; *Philadelphia Inquirer*, August 17, 1929.
[658] On May 3, 1927, at Ebbets Field, Brooklyn, New York, 174 ½-pound Tommy Loughran (74-15-7) won a 10-round unanimous decision over 173-pound Young Stribling (159-9-16).
[659] *Los Angeles Record*, December 18, 1929; *Los Angeles Evening Express*, May 5, 1930.

Life After

On February 27, 1930, in Miami, 197-pound Jack Sharkey stopped 205-pound Phil Scott (64-10-4) in the 3rd round.

On June 12, 1930 at Yankee Stadium, Germany's 24-year-old 188-pound Max Schmeling (42-4-3) won the vacant world heavyweight title, when 27-year-old 197-pound Jack Sharkey (34-8-1) was disqualified in the 4th round for a clearly low blow to the delicate area. The blow potentially landed low in part because Schmeling's left arm missed a punch and went on top of Sharkey's dipping head and neck as Jack was firing his left. The estimated gate receipts were about $750,000, generated by a crowd of around 70,000. It had been two years since Gene Tunney retired.

On November 5, 1930, during the Tim Mara vs. Gene Tunney breach of contract trial, Gene testified that at age 16, he left parochial school and took a $5 per week job in a steamship office. After four years, in 1918, when he was a freight clerk earning $16.50 per week, he left to join the marines. He had boxed for fun every night, but did not take the sport seriously until he won the light-heavyweight championship of the A.E.F.

Tunney told of a conversation he had with Tex Rickard in July 1925, in which Rickard said, "Jack Dempsey will fight for no one but me." Jack had one experience with an outside promoter, but had not been paid yet, which convinced him not to fight for anyone but Rickard. "Gene, I can make you champion if you'll string along with me." Gene agreed and signed up with Rickard. He said it was Rickard who got him the Dempsey fight, not Mara. Back then, Gene also signed to fight Wills for Rickard for $200,000. Wills turned down the bout, but Gene fought Dempsey for that amount instead.

Lawyers put into evidence telegrams and testimony proving that Tex Rickard, not Dempsey, thwarted the Wills-Dempsey contest and convinced Dempsey to fight Tunney. In 1926, Rickard advised Dempsey to fight Tunney instead of Wills. Initially, Dempsey refused to sign a Tunney contract, saying that western promoters were making a "big affair" for him to meet Wills. Jack asked for offers from Rickard for a Wills fight, but Rickard advised him that the "Wills show" would be "awfully hard to pull off." Furthermore, "You should know that any one who attempts to promote a Dempsey-Wills match will kill boxing. You are taking less chances with Tunney and there will be less trouble in promoting it."

Negotiations between Dempsey and Rickard were identified in telegrams from January 7, 1926, when the first offer was made, to March 31, 1926, when the final agreement was reached. Rickard offered Dempsey $475,000 for a Tunney match in New York, plus $25,000 for training expenses, with a privilege of 50% of the gate if more, with the promoter having final say as to the bout's location, which Jack accepted. Initially, Dempsey had wanted the fight in New Jersey, where only no decision contests were allowed, not feeling comfortable with the treatment he had (and would receive) in New York, but Rickard offered him more money for a New York fight, assured him of full protection in New York, and even the ability to choose (or approve of) the judges and referee, and Dempsey accepted.

Conversely, Rickard assured Tunney that Dempsey was a sick man, afflicted with boils, greatly aged, and sure to lose his crown to him.

Tunney argued that Mara had nothing to do with the making of Tunney vs. Dempsey.

The only reason Tunney contracted with bookmaker Mara (who also was the owner of the New York Giants football team) to give him 25% was because Mara promised to get New York to allow the Dempsey fight to be held there, which did not happen. Gene alleged that the Dempsey fight already was made by Rickard. Gene was willing to contract with Mara to make the fight happen in New York, because Chicago or Philadelphia were risky undertakings, given that up to that time, there never was a fight in those cities which drew more than $50,000 or $60,000 respectively.

Mara alleged that their verbal contract created in April/May 1926 was to pay him 10% of Tunney's share of the first Dempsey fight and 25% of his earnings thereafter for assistance in making Dempsey vs. Tunney and bringing it off, regardless of locale. Mara produced a letter from Tunney on June 6, 1926 which said, "Of this you can be sure, you will receive 25 per cent of all moneys earned by the exploitation of Gene Tunney after he wins the championship from Jack Dempsey on September 16, 1926." However, Mara wasn't exactly able to say what he did to make the fight, which eventually had to be moved out of New York, to a different date.

A stenographer, Rose Salzberg, testified that the original written contract stipulated that the Dempsey-Tunney match, then barred in New York, had to take place in New York. That stipulation was removed when Mara insisted, "We'd better leave New York out of this. If the boxing commission or the license commission or the newspapers get hold of it there'd be trouble. You and I are good friends, Billy, we understand each other." Tunney signed that contract but did not sign two others which would have given Mara 25% of his earnings.

Tunney earned $200,000 for the first Dempsey bout. Tunney's biggest year was 1927, when he made $1,090,465.79, of which $990,445.54 was his share of Dempsey-Tunney II. He also made $63,000 from theatrical engagements. In 1928, he made $525,000 from the Heeney bout, but his income from other sources was only about $50,000. Mara was suing for $435,570.51, or 25% of Tunney's total earnings of $1,742,282.04 since Gene won the championship, plus 10% of the $200,000 first Dempsey purse, or $20,000. Billy Gibson's cut as manager was 1/3, or $580,760.68.

Ultimately, on November 11, 1930, after just 8 minutes of deliberation, a jury found Tunney not liable for any money whatsoever. Mara intended to appeal the verdict.[660]

R.A. Cronin noted that just like Mara, Jack Kearns and Teddy Hayes had learned that it did not pay to take a champ into court. "Neither was able to collect a dime. And there were costs of the suits to consider."[661]

Max Hoff, a.k.a. Boo Boo, called the king of Philadelphia bootleggers, also had filed a breach of contract lawsuit against Tunney, which had been pending for years. In 1926, Hoff had given as gifts over $250,000 to the New York Police Bureau. The government considered him to be a gangster who had bribed the police, and it noted that Hoff had an arsenal of machine guns and bullet proof vests. Yet, he had not been indicted for any crime. Hoff eventually became known as one of the richest mobsters in the U.S.

For whatever reason, on January 13, 1931, Hoff decided to dismiss his suit against Tunney voluntarily, without any settlement.[662]

In late March 1931 in Chicago, Illinois, trial finally was held on the Clements/Chicago Coliseum Club lawsuit against Jack Dempsey for breach of contract. On the witness stand on March 26, Dempsey testified that he should have been paid $125,000 up front in cash under the contract upon which the Coliseum was suing. He said he still was willing to fight Wills, provided someone paid him the $125,000 cash advance to bind the agreement. "I'll fight Wills, anytime, any place, anywhere." He said his refusal to fight under the contract was due to their refusal to pay him the cash advance. He wanted to see the money, not promissory notes. "I'm ready to fight Wills any time they get the money."

Dempsey's attorney Arthur Driscoll successfully objected to evidence of damages based on money spent before the contract allegedly was made,

[660] *Olean Evening Times*, November 1, 1930; *Buffalo Courier-Express, New York Daily News*, November 6, 8, 1930; *Brooklyn Daily Eagle*, November 4, 7, 11, 1930; *Baltimore Afro-American*, November 15, 1930.
[661] *Los Angeles Daily News*, November 12, 1930.
[662] *Brooklyn Daily Eagle*, September 6, 13, 1928; *New York Daily News*, January 14, 1931.

as well speculative profits. "It was also brought out that Dempsey's signature was not on the contract, but that it was typed in."[663]

Dempsey with his attorneys, W. J. Corboy (left) and Arthur F. Driscoll (right)

On March 27, 1931, Illinois Circuit Court Judge H. Sterling Pomeroy directed the jury to return a verdict of dismissal in Dempsey's favor in the lawsuit brought against him by the Chicago Coliseum Club (William E. Clements, President) for breach of contract. The judge told the jurors, "I find no competent evidence of damages having been suffered by the complainant." Clements vowed to appeal.

R. A. Cronin noted that Dempsey had a habit of winning his court battles, having defeated Jack Kearns, Teddy Hayes, and now the Chicago Coliseum Club/Clements. "If Dempsey could fight before a referee as well as he can before a judge, he still would be the champion."[664]

Also in late March 1931, and continuing through mid-April, word was that Dempsey's marriage with Estelle Taylor was on the rocks, and eventually they separated. He was refereeing around the country, and she was acting, and they were apart quite often. She also was not interested in having children. He still loved her, but wanted a home, family, and family life. She had refused to quit the movie-making life.[665]

On July 3, 1931, in Cleveland, Ohio, 189-pound world heavyweight champion Max Schmeling stopped 186 ½-pound Young Stribling (238-13-17) in the 15th round.

On July 17, 1931, Mrs. Ellen Dorothy Hayes, the wife of Teddy Hayes, sued Jack Kearns for $150,000 for breach-of-promise. She asserted that Kearns promised to marry her on July 18, 1928, but subsequently, upon learning that he had impregnated her, broke his promise, then "conspired" with Hayes to make the latter her husband instead, and persuaded her to marry Hayes in order to legitimize the expected child. Apparently, Hayes later abandoned her.

[663] *Vincennes Sun-Commercial,* March 26, 1931; *Chicago Tribune,* March 27, 1931; *Indianapolis Times,* March 27, 1931.
[664] *Chicago Tribune, Streator Daily Times-Press, New York Daily News, Illustrated Daily News,* March 28, 1931.
[665] *New York Daily News,* March 29, 1931; *Reading Times,* April 14, 1931; *San Francisco Examiner,* April 18, 1931; *Livingston Enterprise,* April 19, 1931; *St. Louis Star,* April 29, 1931.

Kearns was pursuing an annulment suit against Angel Leganna Kearns, whose existence Mrs. Hayes knew nothing about.

Mrs. Hayes' attorney had prepared court papers in February 1930, but had not been able to serve Kearns until June 1931. Kearns and Hayes had been palling around together at Mickey Walker's camp.[666]

On July 22, 1931, at Ebbets Field, Brooklyn, New York, 198 ½-pound Jack Sharkey fought 169 ½-pound world middleweight champion Mickey Walker (111-17-2) to a 15-round draw.

Although retired, after four more years of ring inactivity following the 1927 Tunney rematch, from August 1931 to late March 1932, and again in August 1932, 36-year-old Jack Dempsey made money by participating in several short 1- to 4-round boxing exhibitions in a barnstorming tour, including with solid contenders, like black 212-pound Ed "Bearcat" Wright (64-19-18) (4 rounds, November 11, 1931, Omaha), Jack Roper (2, 1, and 2), Charley Retzlaff (1, 1), Art Lasky (2), KO3 202-pound K.O. Christner (42-25-2) (February 11, 1932, Cleveland), and King Levinsky (41-16-4) (4 rounds, February 18, 1932, Chicago, filmed). Jack often knocked out lesser-known locals who took him on.

In the meantime, on September 21, 1931, after 6 years and 8 months of marriage, Jack Dempsey and Estelle Taylor were divorced. Jack alleged mental cruelty and was granted a divorce in Reno by default.[667]

On October 12, 1931, at Ebbets Field, 202-pound Jack Sharkey won a 15-round decision over 261-pound Primo Carnera (48-3), scoring a knockdown in the 4th round with a left hook to the jaw. The fight was filmed. Both men appear to be capable battlers in a competitive contest. Jimmy Wood wrote, "Sharkey needed all his skill and experience plus his full punching strength to batter his way to victory over Primo. And he didn't win by such a wide margin at that ... Carnera, believe us, is a tough fellow. He'll beat any number of those around today."[668]

Nearly a year after the case had been dismissed, on March 16, 1932, on appeal, the Illinois Appellate Court ruled that judgment should have been for the plaintiff Chicago Coliseum Club, for there was a contract and Jack Dempsey breached it. On March 13, 1926, Dempsey signed/executed a contract (with a March 6 date) with the Chicago Coliseum Club for $10, the receipt of which was acknowledged, to fight Harry Wills either in Chicago or some other suitable place, in September 1926, with Dempsey to be paid $300,000 on August 5, 1926, another $500,000 in cash at least 10 days before the date fixed for the contest, plus 50% of the net profits of the gate receipts over $2,000,000, and 50% of the net revenue from the moving picture concessions or royalties. Dempsey agreed not to engage in any other boxing match until the date of the contest. He also was required to have his life and health insured in favor of the Club in a manner and at a place designated by the Club. The contract declared void the prior Floyd

[666] *New York Daily News*, Nevada State Journal, *Wilkes-Barre Evening News*, July 18, 1931.
[667] *New York Daily News*, September 22, 1931.
[668] *Brooklyn Daily Times*, October 13, 1931.

Fitzsimmons contract. The Club had entered into a contract with Wills on March 6, agreeing to pay him $50,000 no later than 10 days before the date of the contest.

When B. E. Clements, club president, wired Dempsey at Colorado Springs, asking him to be examined for insurance purposes as required by the contract, Dempsey telegrammed his response on July 10, 1926, declining to do so, and repudiating the contract, saying, "Entirely too busy training for my coming Tunney match to waste time on insurance representatives stop as you have no contract suggest you stop kidding yourself and me also Jack Dempsey."

The Court held, "We are unable to conceive upon what theory the defendant could contend that there was no contract, as it appears to be admitted in the proceeding here and bears his signature and the amounts involved are sufficiently large to have created a rather lasting impression on the mind of anyone signing such an agreement."

The Court reversed and remanded for a new trial on the issue of damages.

However, in an interesting twist, the Court severely limited the damages the plaintiff could seek, holding that lost prospective profits were too speculative, and furthermore, attorney's fees were not part of the contract, and therefore could not be sought. The $50,000 that was to be paid to Wills never was paid. Only expenses incurred from March 13, 1926 to the breach date of July 10, 1926 could be recovered. Nothing before or after those dates were legally cognizable damages.

The incidental damages which the Court allowed to be proven in a re-trial likely would have been less than the unrecoverable attorney's fees for another trial, and certainly nominal in relation to the total amount spent in pursuing injunctions and lawsuits against Dempsey for years. Hence, Dempsey lost the battle but de facto won the war. The original trial judge had dismissed the case, ruling that the Club had failed to prove cognizable damages, which would remain a hurdle for the Club in a retrial after the appellate ruling. Ultimately, Clements let it go and did not seek a retrial.[669]

In late May 1932, it was reported that Jack Dempsey was in a romantic relationship with screen and theatrical actress Lina Basquette, who was the widow of Sam Warner, co-founder of the Warner Bros. film studio. However, in an interesting twist, the way the relationship was revealed was because Teddy Hayes claimed that Dempsey had "stolen" his girl Lina from him. Dempsey denied it. "I wouldn't take anything from Hayes, last of all a girl." Dempsey also declared, "My next wife's career is going to be that of Mrs. Jack Dempsey." Hayes said, "She's too good for him he's just a mug that thinks he's a big shot." Joe Benjamin took Hayes' side, saying, "I know all about this thing. Teddy was going with Lina for a long time and Dempsey knew it." Apparently, Dempsey hosted a banquet/party at his Barbara Hotel on West Sixth Street in Los Angeles.

[669] Chicago Coliseum Club v. Dempsey, 265 Ill. App. 542 (Ill. App. Ct. 1932).

Teddy said, "I took Lina down there and Dempsey started muscling in right away." Hayes claimed that Dempsey paid her marked attention and seduced her away from him.[670]

Lina Basquette   Lina Basquette,   LINA BASQUETTE.

Basquette publicly denied romantic involvement with either man, claiming that Hayes simply was her manager, and Dempsey had appeared with her for business purposes in vaudeville.

Unbeknownst to the general public, Hayes had married Basquette in October 1931 in Newark. However, when asked about it, both denied it. In her autobiography, she wrote that after discovering that Hayes was a bigamist, still married to another woman (likely Ellen Dorothy Hayes, and possibly another woman as well), Basquette separated from him. She then initiated an affair with Jack Dempsey, in part as revenge against Hayes.

JACK DEMPSEY

SAM WARNER   TEDDY HAYES.   LINA BASQUETTE.   As WIFE of PEVERELL MARLEY.

[670] Los Angeles Times, New York Daily News, May 26, 1932; Los Angeles Record, May 27, 1932.

Lina Basquette and Teddy Hayes

Dempsey ended the affair in July 1932, after which, on July 28 in Los Angeles, Basquette attempted suicide by poison. Her suicide note, obviously to Dempsey, read, "Jack, I love you – only you. I couldn't help it. I couldn't go on without you."

Oddly enough, her suicide attempt came only a few hours after she had announced her *engagement* to *Teddy Hayes*. Earlier that day, she said, "Teddy and I have patched everything up. We are engaged again and he is handling my business matters for me once more." At that time, when asked, "What about Dempsey?" she replied, "There's nothing about Dempsey; there never was, and that's that." She telephoned both men before taking the poison. After receiving treatment, she said, "Tell the world I'm nuts."[671]

On September 10, 1932, Lina Basquette filed for and was granted a quick uncontested Mexican divorce from Teddy Hayes, which revealed that they indeed had been married, despite their denials of such. Basquette alleged desertion for more than 6 months and cruelty. (Hayes also was a bigamist; but eventually got divorced from his prior wife or wives.) "Thus comes to an end one of Hollywood's strangest romances." The writer spoke too soon.[672]

In an interesting twist, Basquette and Hayes eventually reconciled and remarried three months later, on or about December 27, 1932, in Washington, D.C. Teddy said, "And say, this is the first time I've ever really considered myself married. Those other two Mrs. Hayes didn't count."

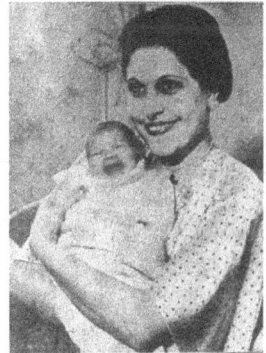

Lina and Teddy had a son, Edward Alvin Hayes, born in Los Angeles on April 8, 1934. However, on December 19, 1935, Lina was granted another uncontested divorce from Teddy, on the grounds of extreme mental cruelty.[673]

---

[671] *Los Angeles Times, Minneapolis Star, Border Cities Star*, July 29, 1932; Basquette, Lina, *Lina: Demille's Godless Girl* (Denlingers Pub Ltd, 1990).
[672] *Los Angeles Times*, September 10, 11, 23, 1932; *Idaho Statesman*, September 11, 1932.
[673] *New York Daily News*, December 27, 1932; *Evening Star, Charlotte Observer*, December 28, 1932; *Los Angeles Times*, December 20, 1935.

In her autobiography, Lina Basquette claimed that Teddy Hayes was controlling and violent, struck her, pointed a gun at her and also fired a shot, associated and worked with mobsters, had an Al Capone hitman lean on her on his behalf (but she later had a brief fling with that same hitman), suggested he might put out a hit on Dempsey, and later on threatened to take their child away from her. She and Teddy had a hot and cold, passionate relationship.

Hayes spoke about Dempsey to Basquette, saying, "If he'd stayed with Doc [Kearns] and me he'd still be champion of the world." Also, "Teddy had told me that he had loaded Dempsey's gloves with plaster-of-Paris at Toledo when Jack won the championship from a bewildered and battered Jess Willard. Of course, Teddy could be a liar. That's for sure!"

When speaking about Hayes to Lina, Dempsey said, "Teddy Hayes is no good. Never was. He's been married so many times he can't even remember all the names. He'd doublecross his own grandmother!"

Basquette once saw Dempsey in action in sparring. She said that Dempsey was exciting to watch, "a virtual symphony of rippling muscles, every movement a poem dedicated to attack and defense. Those long symmetrical legs surely would have delighted Da Vinci. His reach was phenomenal, flicking out like a striking serpent, relentlessly subduing a reeling target." The only thing odd was Dempsey's voice was higher than one might expect from one with such a "massive physique."

Lina painted a much nicer, kinder, more loving picture of Dempsey than Hayes. She and Dempsey discussed marriage, but eventually the love triangle with the more determined Hayes caused Jack to walk away. She still remembered Dempsey fondly, and she seemed hurt and disappointed that he only spoke about her briefly in his autobiography. "Anyhow, in my memories of you, Jack, you're still CHAMPION."

Dempsey purportedly also had relationships of some sort at various times with Miss Universe Dorothy Dell, show girl Agnes O'Laughlin, Bee Palmer, and actress June Gale.

Title Fight Score Of Officials

Here's how Referee Gunboat Smith and Judges Charles Mathison and George Kelly scored the Schemling - Sharkey fight.

Round	Mathison	Kelly	Smith
1	Jack	Jack	Even
2	Max	Jack	Jack
3	Max	Jack	Jack
4	Max	Jack	Even
5	Jack	Jack	Jack
6	Jack	Jack	Jack
7	Jack	Jack	Jack
8	Max	Max	Max
9	Max	Max	Even
10	Jack	Max	Max
11	Max	Max	Even
12	Max	Max	Max
13	Max	Max	Jack
14	Max	Max	Even
15	Max	Jack	Jack

On June 21, 1932 at Madison Square Garden Bowl, Long Island City, Queens, New York, in a rematch against champion 188-pound Max Schmeling (44-4-3), 29-year-old 205-pound Jack Sharkey (35-9-2) won a close and controversial 15-round split decision to win the world heavyweight championship. Judge Charles Mathison had it 10-5 for Schmeling, but judge George Kelly had it 8-7 for Sharkey, and referee Ed Smith 7-3-5 for Sharkey. The gate generated by 70,000 fans was $537,320.

If one were to score each round based on the majority of the judges, it would be 7 Sharkey, 7 Schmeling, 1 Even, for a draw: 1-Jack, 2-Jack, 3-Jack, 4-Even, 5-Jack, 6-Jack, 7-Jack, 8-Max, 9-Max, 10-Max, 11-Max, 12-Max, 13-Max, 14-Max, 15-Jack. Apparently, Sharkey controlled the first half of the contest, while Schmeling came on strong in the second half.[674]

It had been 5 years since Sharkey had been knocked out by Dempsey. The fact that Jack Dempsey once had knocked out the now reigning world heavyweight champion further improved fans' estimation of him.

On July 1, 1932, the Appellate Division of the Supreme Court of New York reversed the verdict in Gene Tunney's favor in the Mara v. Tunney suit and remanded for a new trial, holding in a 2-1 split decision that the trial judge improperly allowed in prejudicial evidence.[675]

On January 14, 1933, Gene Tunney settled with Tim Mara for $30,000. Mara believed the settlement gave him vindication. Tunney believed the amount was small compared to the many hundreds of thousands that Mara had sought, stating that it would cost him more than $30,000 to continue the legal action with Mara and try the case again.[676]

The retired Jack Dempsey had become a promoter, signing up Max Schmeling to fight Max Baer.

Regarding the failure of Dempsey-Wills to take place, in January 1933 a 43-year-old Harry Wills said,

> I know that Mr. Rickard didn't want us to fight, because he was afraid of what might follow. But that's all past now. … Somewhere there must be a promoter who would put us into the ring together. Maybe Jack could promote it himself. That would suit me. Jack is a great fellow. A great fighter, too. I always liked him a lot and I think he liked me, too.[677]

In 1933, 37-year-old (one month from 38) Dempsey boxed 1-round filmed exhibitions with ex-champion Max Schmeling (May 27, Lake Swannanoa, NJ) and future champion Max Baer (May 28, Atlantic City).

On June 8, 1933, at Yankee Stadium, in a contest promoted by Jack Dempsey, 203-pound Max Baer (38-7) stopped 189-pound former champion Max Schmeling (45-5-3) in the 10th round.

On July 14, 1933, at McCullough's arena in Salt Lake City, Dempsey refereed Max Baer's 2-round exhibitions with Billy Murdock and Ed Sheppard, and then boxed 1 round with Baer as well.

Jack's mother Cecilia Dempsey, Jack's fiancé Hannah Williams, and Jack's sister Elsie watch Dempsey referee Max Baer's exhibitions and then spar 1 round with him.

---

[674] For more on Jack Sharkey's life and career, check out *Jack Sharkey: A Heavyweight Champion's Untold Story*, by James Curl.
[675] Mara v. Tunney, 236 App. Div. 82 (N.Y. App. Div. 1932), 258 N.Y.S. 191.
[676] *Buffalo Courier-Express, Rochester Democrat and Chronicle*, January 15, 1933; *New York Daily News*, January 22, 1933.
[677] *Evening Star* (Washington, D.C.), January 17, 1933.

On July 18, 1933, in Elko, Nevada, 38-year-old Jack Dempsey married 22-year-old Hannah Williams, a former Broadway musical comedy stage star. It was the third marriage for both. Jack and Hannah had two daughters, Joan (b. August 4, 1934), and Barbara (b. August 28, 1936).[678]

Eventually, after 10 years of marriage, on July 7, 1943, Jack was granted a divorce. Dempsey alleged that Williams had committed adultery. Williams alleged that Dempsey slapped her, threw her around a bit, and threatened her life. The New York judicial referee agreed that Dempsey had proven beyond a doubt that she had committed adultery with Benny Woodall, ex-fight promoter, on November 22, 1942. There were allegations of adultery with former lightweight champion Lew Jenkins as well. The judicial referee granted Jack custody of their two children, Joan, 8, and Barbara, 6, with Hannah being granted reasonable visitation rights.[679]

Hannah Williams Dempsey

In 1936, Jack opened the famous Jack Dempsey's restaurant in New York City, which would remain open for 38 years, until 1974.

In the *Brooklyn Daily Eagle* on May 23, 1936, Ed Hughes reported that Harry Wills did not blame Dempsey for his

"The Meeting Place of the World"
Jack Dempsey's Broadway Restaurant

inability to obtain a title shot, though in former days he did. Harry said, "Yes, I know, now, that Dempsey wanted to fight me. But the politics of the game were against it. Powerful politicians said that a black man shouldn't fight Dempsey for the title – and that ended it."

[678] *Hartford Daily Courant, New York Daily News*, July 19, 1933.
[679] *Troy Record*, June 11, 1943; *Sydney Daily Mirror*, June 12, 1943; *New York Democrat and Chronicle*, July 16, 1943; *New York Daily News*, July 8, 17, 1943. Hannah alleged that Jack had a relationship with Yvette Colbert but was unable to produce her at trial.

For most of the 20th century, Jack Dempsey absorbed only very limited criticism for not fighting Harry Wills.

In 1937 in Chicago, Joe Louis would be the first black man to fight for the heavyweight championship since Jack Johnson lost his title in 1915, 22 years prior. Louis was the first black man ever to challenge for and win the world heavyweight championship in the U.S.A. Johnson had won his crown in 1908 in Australia.

Major League Baseball would not allow any black participants whatsoever until ten years later, in 1947, after World War II.

Proof positive that he never did entirely lose his punching power is demonstrated by a filmed, scheduled 10-round pro fight with 6-ounce gloves that Jack Dempsey had on July 1, 1940 in Atlanta, Georgia, his last, against wrestler Clarence "Cowboy" Luttrell. Close to 10,000 attended.

The fight was a mixture of charity to raise money for the Red Cross and vengeance. Dempsey had refereed some of Luttrell's wrestling contests, and Luttrell was not pleased with the job that Jack did. Wrestler Luttrell had thrown punches at Dempsey and said Jack was not able to fight now or ever, garnering publicity and momentum for a match.[680]

Even at age 45, 205-pound Dempsey remained quite powerful, knocking out 224-pound Luttrell in the 2nd round with brutal power punches. The films are a real treat to watch, and show that even at an advanced age, Dempsey still was ferocious, attacking and blasting away nonstop with hooks, body shots, and uppercuts. Dempsey pulverized and brutalized Luttrell, who fought back as best he could, even landing some blows, but he often was frozen and defenseless, and went down at least four times, including the last time through the ropes and out of the ring, unconscious, the result of Dempsey's famous left hook. Nat Fleischer, editor of the *Ring*, refereed the contest, and probably allowed it to go on longer than most referees today would. It was an official 10-round bout, so it should be listed on Dempsey's record.

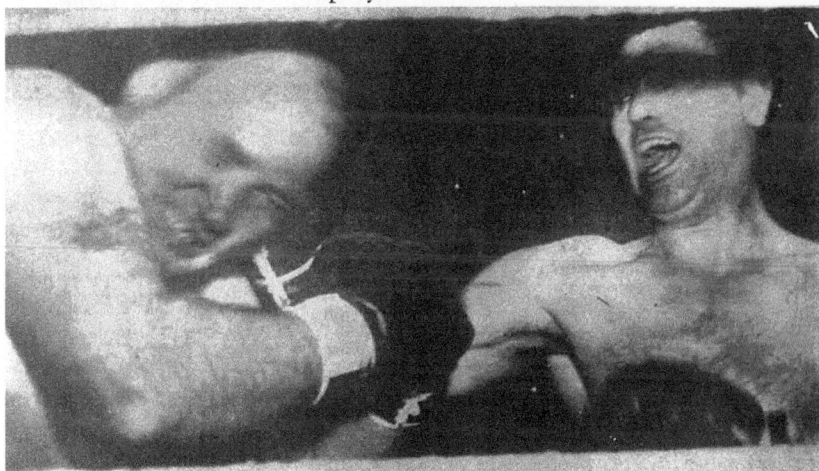

[680] *Columbus Enquirer*, July 1, 1940; *Atlanta Constitution, New York Daily News*, July 2, 1940; *New York Daily News*, June 9, 1940.

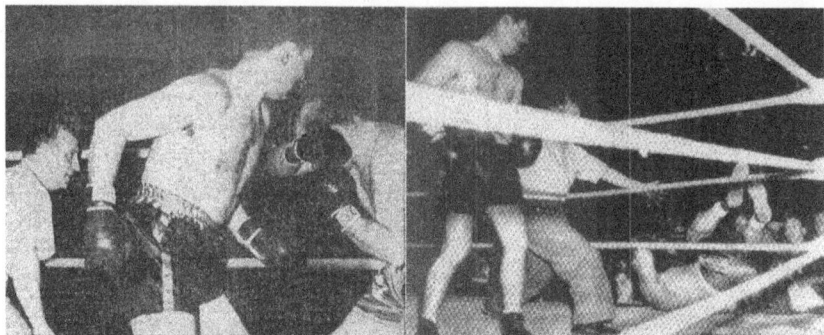

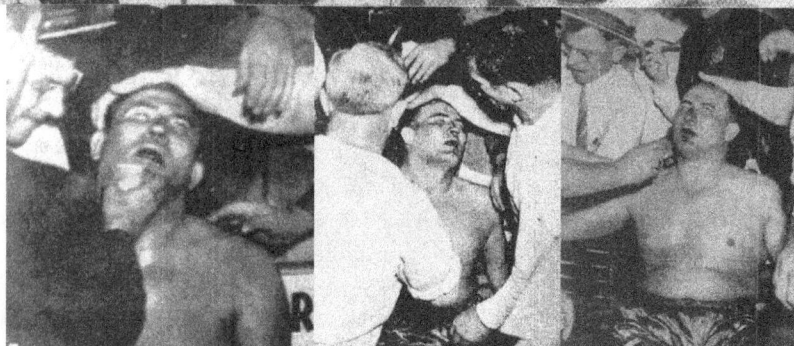

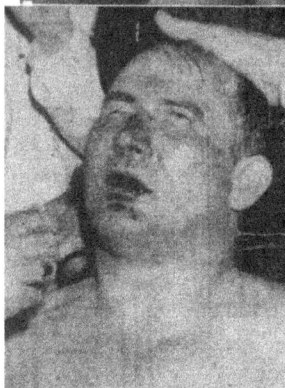

During World War II, as his way of serving his country, perhaps in part to eradicate any ghosts of World War I, despite being 46 years old, Dempsey enlisted. On his 1941-42 military registration card, Jack listed his residence as 25 Central Park West, New York. His business address was 1619 Broadway, in New York, the address of his restaurant.

Dempsey initially joined the New York State Guard, commissioned as a lieutenant. He subsequently accepted a U.S. Coast Guard Reserve commission.

Dempsey reported for active duty on June 12, 1942, at the Coast Guard Training Station in Manhattan Beach in Brooklyn, NY. He was assigned as the Director of Physical Education. Once again, he took publicity photographs for the military. To boost morale, he also made personal appearances at fights, military camps, hospitals, and War Bond drives. In December 1942, he was promoted to lieutenant commander.

In March 1944, Dempsey was promoted to commander and assigned to the transport USS Wakefield.

In 1945, he served on board the attack transport USS Arthur Middleton for the invasion of Okinawa. He also spent time on the USS General Willliam Mitchell. In July 1945, Dempsey was assigned as Commander, 11th Naval District for assignment to Military Morale Duty. He was released from active duty in September 1945, at age 50. Dempsey was honorably discharged from the Coast Guard Reserve in 1952.

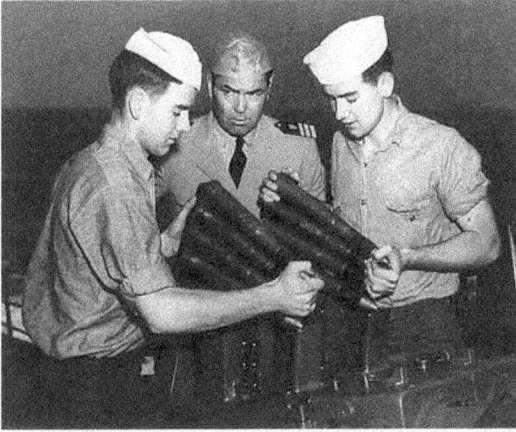

Over the years, Dempsey allegedly dated women, such as Mamie Van Doren, Doris Lilly, Maria Elena "Lina" Romay, and many others.

Dempsey said he got married for the fourth and final time in 1958 to Deanna Piatelli, who had a daughter, Barbara, from a prior marriage. No newspaper mentioned it. The first time that newspapers at all alluded to Dempsey seeing Deanna was in 1959. In 1960, 65-year-old Dempsey claimed that he had been secretly married for 1.5 years to a 38-year-old who operated a New York jewelry store. "I don't want any publicity out of it." At that time, Deanna's daughter Barbara was 11 years old. However, New York marriage license records indicate that Jack and Deanna were legally married in 1964.[681]

Regardless of the exact date, Jack and Deanna remained married until his death on May 31, 1983, in New York City, at age 87. Gene Tunney had died on November 7, 1978, in Greenwich, Connecticut, at age 81.

On Friday December 26, 1969, Jack O'Brian of the *Paterson News* reported that two criminals attempted to mug a 74 year-old Jack Dempsey, and he flattened both of them. A puncher always is a puncher.

In mid-1970, Jack briefly spoke about the incident, saying, "A couple of guys tried to mug me on Third Avenue a few months ago. They tried to rob me but I flattened them."[682]

---

[681] *Pittsburgh Post-Gazette*, August 13, 1960.
[682] *Glens Falls Times*, June 24, 1970.

A couple years later, when Dempsey was asked when was the last time he used his fists in anger, he referenced the incident, which took place near his home in New York. Milton Richman wrote,

> It looked like a perfect set-up. All the ingredients were there for nice clean mugging. The elderly gentleman was walking home late at night by himself, nobody else was in sight on the block and there wasn't any place to go for help. Two young muggers, each about 20, jumped on the old gent from behind and grabbed his arms. He struggled free somehow and began moving on but his attackers came right after him again. Their intended victim, Jack Dempsey, finally did what came naturally. Two left-handed bone-smashers plus a couple of rights to the belly...clearly demonstrated the old master hadn't lost his touch. Both youths lay stretched out flat on the sidewalk. "I just let 'em lie there and walked away," says Jack Dempsey, who, at 76, still singularly symbolizes prize fighting more than any other figure past or present and whom many still consider the foremost fighter who ever lived.[683]

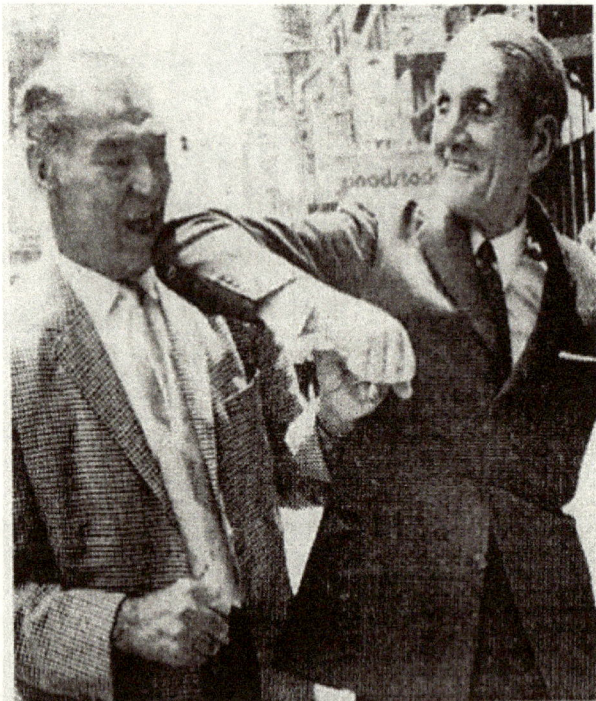

Jack Dempsey takes a friendly elbow from France's Georges Carpentier as they spar playfully in New York while reminiscing about their memorable bout in 1921 for the world heavyweight championship. Dempsey retained his title with a knockout. Carpentier came to celebrate Dempsey's 75th birthday. Their fight 49 years ago drew boxing first $1 million gate. (Associated Press Photo)

[683] *Rockland County Journal-News*, July 23, 1971.

Joe Frazier, Jack Dempsey, Jack Sharkey, Georges Carpentier, and Gene Tunney all celebrate
Jack Dempsey's 75th birthday at Madison Square Garden in 1970

'Mauler' has a birthday party

Friends of Jack Dempsey help him celebrate his 75th birthday with a party in the Jack Dempsey Restaurant in New York last night. From left are Mrs. Barbara Piatelli, stepdaughter of Dempsey; Sen. George Murphy of California,

Mrs. Deanna Dempsey, Jack's wife; Dempsey, Joan O'Flaherty, Dempsey's daughter, and Jack Amiel, Jack's business partner and friend for 20 years.

IN THE COLORFUL *Room of Champions* at *Eddie Arcaro's* new restaurant, *Jack Dempsey poses beside his portrait with his daughter Barbara McMillan. His portrait was the first of stellar list to be painted by renowned artist Nicholas Volpe.*
See Joan Winchell's column

Dempsey, Harry Houdini, Benny Leonard
Houdini died on October 21, 1926.

Dempsey and Taylor at home in Laughlin Park, Hollywood, California

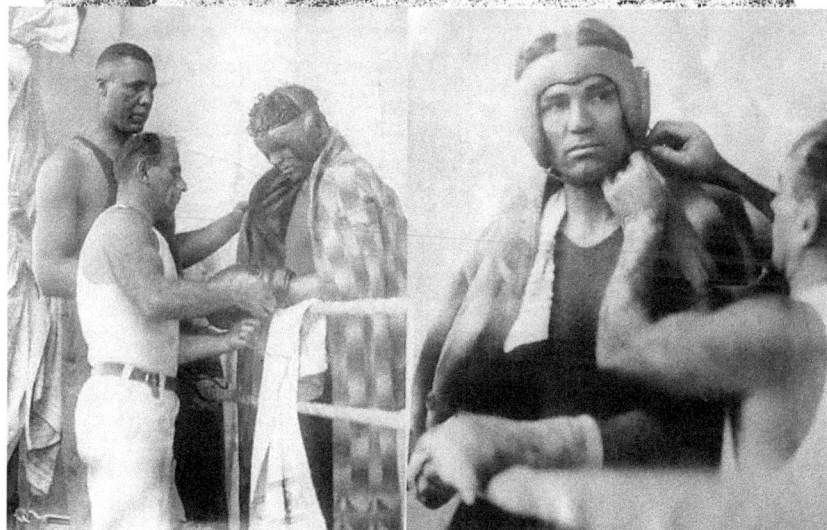

Acknowledgments

Thank you to all who have helped me in some way with this book, be it research, photographs, promotion, or general support:

Gregory Speciale

Mike DeLisa

Bob Yalen

Kurt Noltimier

Barry Deskins

John Ochs

Clay Moyle

Kevin Smith

Vincent Ciaramella

Evan Grant

Thomas Hauser

Matt McGrain

Stephen Quinn Lee

S. J. Wickett

Lisa Sanchez, Cleveland Public Library

Deborah Bryant, Marion County Records Division

Cheryl A. Max, Nassau County Deputy Clerk of Court

University of Iowa / Interlibrary Loan

Boxrec.com

BoxingForum24.com

Cyberboxingzone.com

Trufanboxing.com

Index

244, 247, 248, 249, 293, 298, 302, 303,
   318, 322, 328, 386, 387, 389, 391, 410,
   412, 460, 472, 518, 547, 559, 577
Lehmann, Otto, 445
Lejeune, General John A., 221, 258, 294
Lenglen, Suzanne, 250
Leonard, Benny, 35, 71, 167, 221, 228,
   231, 232, 234, 236, 238, 241, 242, 244,
   296, 319, 349, 356, 361, 389, 452, 463,
   473, 553, 585
Levinsky, Battling, 4, 37, 46, 157, 210,
   215, 463, 467, 549, 572
Levinsky, King, 572
Levinson, Sol, 242, 439
Lewis, Frederic, 283, 292
Lewis, Mary, 95
Lewis, Perry, 85, 224, 229, 249, 253, 262,
   292, 316
Lewis, Willie, 89
Lincoln, President Abraham, 169, 417,
   419, 420, 423, 427, 441
Link, Norman, 425
Lodge, Farmer, 41, 168, 176, 180, 181,
   210
Lodge, Walter 'Farmer', 41, 168, 176, 180,
   181, 210, 217
Loew, Marcus, 85
Londos, Jim, 181, 221
Long, James, 19
Lorenz, Sergeant, 425
Loughran, Tommy, 8, 18, 33, 44, 60, 85,
   90, 186, 198, 210, 223, 224, 227, 228,
   230, 232-234, 237, 239, 247, 257, 296,
   298, 316, 318, 336, 356, 391, 553, 565,
   567
Louis, Joe, 579
Luttrell, Clarence, 579
Luttrell, Clarence 'Cowboy', 579
Luvadis, Jerry 'the Greek', 100, 164, 187,
   195, 221, 224, 244, 256, 258, 283, 307,
   322, 324, 337, 341, 362, 365, 386, 474,
   477, 509, 514
Lynch, Joe, 70
Lyons, Dan, 28
Mabbutt, Captain Charles, 221, 244, 324,
   337
MacKay, Gordon, 222
MacNamara, Harry, 428, 432, 434, 543
Madden, Bartley, 34, 37, 46, 49, 55, 126,
   128, 140, 144, 155, 166, 182, 206, 329
Malone, Jack/Jock, 17, 422, 475, 532
Malone, Joe, 422, 475, 532
Maloney, Jim, 100, 325, 333, 341, 347,
   349, 350, 352, 356, 358, 394, 463, 552
Mandell, Sammy, 356
Manley, George, 472
Mara, Tim, 207, 356, 437, 454, 568, 577
Marbutt, Captain, 244
Marriage, 50, 51, 95, 103, 113, 145, 164,
   217, 558, 571, 572, 576, 578, 581

Martin, Bob, 203, 446, 454
Mason, James, 19
Mason, Red, 19, 79, 106, 334
Masterson, Bat, 94
Mathison, Charles, 20, 22, 27, 166, 203,
   362, 366, 368, 371, 374, 376, 378, 383,
   387, 388, 390, 413, 576
Maxwell, Don, 428, 435, 444, 519
Mays, Harold, 213, 215, 219, 220, 222,
   229, 239
McAuliffe, Jack, 233, 248, 308
McCabe, Billy, 422, 532
McCann, Jack, 419, 420, 423, 472
McCarney, Billy, 237, 463, 473
McCracken, Frank, 85, 211, 212, 222, 250,
   251, 262, 264, 266, 269, 271, 274, 276,
   278, 280, 282, 300, 318, 322
McGann, Sparrow, 88, 147, 156, 157
McGeehan, W. O., 21, 63, 203, 336, 356,
   390, 463
McGinnity, James J., 42
McGoorty, Eddie, 37, 89, 90
McGowan, Frankie, 198
McKenna, L. S., 525
McKetrick, Dan, 221
McMahon Brothers, 356
McMullen, Eddie, 343, 344, 347
McNamee, Graham, 261, 263, 266, 268,
   271, 273, 275, 277, 280, 282, 284, 302,
   361, 364, 367, 369, 372, 375, 377, 381,
   477, 480, 483, 485, 489, 493, 499, 503,
   506
McPartland, William 'Kid', 391, 397, 414,
   555
McTigue, Mike, 27, 89, 295, 340, 349, 350,
   352, 356, 358, 361, 405, 463, 567
Meehan, Willie, 34, 44
Meeks, Curtis "Tex"', 132, 140
Mehaney, Jimmy, 422
Meisner, Dutch, 419
Menke, Frank, 5, 166
Mercer, Sid, 356, 390, 391, 555
Metoquah, Chief, 37, 349, 350
Miller, Dave, 442
Miske, Billy, 3, 4, 7, 15, 17, 34, 56, 165,
   334, 357, 415, 449, 549
Mix, Tom, 361, 473
Mixed-race, 27, 115, 126, 127, 153, 167,
   171, 175, 547
Monahan, Walter, 37
Montana, Bull, 52, 112
Moore, Jack, 52
Moore, Lee, 112
Moore, Mark, 105
Moore, Ted, 60, 155, 157, 199
Moran, Frank, 115
Morgan, Dan, 349
Morgan, Tod, 100
Morris, Edward, 241, 362, 366, 368, 371,
   374, 376, 378, 383, 463

Adam J. Pollack is a professional boxing referee and judge, attorney, publisher, author of the *In the Ring With* series, and member of the Boxing Writers Association of America.

To learn about more boxing books published by Win By KO Publications, go to winbykopublications.com.

www.ingramcontent.com/pod-product-compliance
Lightning Source LLC
Chambersburg PA
CBHW020409100426
42812CB00001B/253